# Forensic Science

# Forensic Science

Second Edition

## Volume 1

A - D

**Edited by**

Ayn Embar-Seddon O'Reilly
*Capella University*

Allan D. Pass
*National Behavioral Science Consultants*

SALEM PRESS
A Division of EBSCO Information Services
Ipswich, Massachusetts

**GREY HOUSE PUBLISHING**

**Library of Congress Cataloging-in-Publication Data**

Forensic science / editors, Ayn O'Reilly, PhD, Allan D. Pass, MD. — Second edition.
  3 volumes : illustrations ;  cm
  Includes bibliographical references and index.
  Contents: v.1. Accelerants-DNA database controversies — v.2. DNA extraction from hair, bodily fluids, and tissues-Mycotoxins — v.3. Napoleon's death-Y chromosome analysis.
  ISBN: 978-1-61925-729-0 (set)
  1. Forensic sciences.  I. Embar-Seddon, Ayn.  II. Pass, Allan D.

HV8073 .F5776 2015
363.25

2008030674

# Publisher's Note

This is the second edition of *Forensic Science*, a three-volume reference work that addresses the growing academic and public interest in the application of the sciences to criminal investigations. The extent of this interest can be measured by the expansion of academic courses on forensics and criminal justice in schools and colleges and by the proliferation of popular television programs, both dramatic and documentary, on crime scene investigations. Although articles in *Forensic Science* cover many topics that figure prominently in the media, the set's basic approach to forensic science is factual, and it lays great stress on offering up-to-date material on hard topics in this rapidly advancing field.

Often called simply "forensics" within the legal world, forensic science is essentially the application of the natural sciences to the analyzing and interpreting of legal evidence, particularly in criminal cases. Since the beginning of the twenty-first century—and especially since the terrorist attacks on the United States on September 11, 2001—there has been an explosion of both public and academic interest in the use of forensic techniques to investigate criminal acts. American television audiences have developed a seemingly insatiable appetite for shows such as *CSI: Crime Scene Investigation* that go into the minutiae of forensic techniques. However, while shows such as this tend to emphasize crimes of violence, particularly murder, the real-world applications of forensic science are far broader.

Indeed, while the forensic sciences play a major role in investigations of murder and other violent crimes, they play equally important roles in investigations into many other types of criminal and civil cases, ranging from arson fires and contract disputes to forgery, paternity suits, and war crimes. Forensic techniques are also often central to efforts to identify victims of major accidents and natural disasters. All these subjects are covered in detail within these volumes.

## Scope

*Forensic Science* contains 500 articles arranged in alphabetical order that range in length from 500 to 3,000 words. The set includes several different perspectives of the forensic sciences, from its many specialties to how forensics is handled in the media. NEW topics include Arson Dogs, Athlete Drug Testing, Backspatter, Inconsistent Eyewitness Testimony, Legality of Electronic Documents, Liquid Dead Array Technology, Plant Toxins, and Under Policing Certain Populations and Geographies.

The primary focus of this work is **investigators and specialties of forensic science.** The diverse subspecialties that make up the forensic sciences can be seen by glancing at the Table of Contents: accounting, anthropology, archaeology, botany, entomology, geoscience, nursing, odontology, palynology, pathology, photography, psychiatry, psychology, sculpture, and toxicology are among those forensics specialties that are covered in detailed. In addition, you will find articles on Ballistics, Computer forensics, Cryptology and number theory, Living forensics, Parasitology, Physiology, Serology, Structural analysis, Taphonomy, Thanatology, Viral biology, and Wildlife forensics.

Attention is also given to the many professional organizations in forensic science fields, such as the American Academy of Forensic Sciences, the American Society of Crime Laboratory Directors, and the International Association of Forensic Toxicologists. In addition to the core articles on subspecialties and allied fields, this set has articles on dozens of specific types of investigations, ranging from Alcohol-related offenses, Arson, and Art forgery to Ritual killing, Sports memorabilia fraud, and Suicide.

More than 100 articles focus on investigative techniques and procedures. These include overviews of general subjects such as accident investigation and reconstruction, crime scene investigation, and quantitative and qualitative analysis of chemicals, along with more specialized techniques and procedures, such as autopsies, chromatography, crime scene photography, fingerprint analysis, and polygraph analysis. Many articles examine specialized equipment, such as biodetectors and other detection devices, protective gear, and chemical reagents.

**Scene of the Crime** is a second broad perspective in *Forensic Science*. Particularly important within this category are articles on types of evidence, such as fire debris, fibers and filaments, glass, soil, and bloodstains. Other articles cover both general and specific aspects of chemical and biological agents, such as biotoxins, carbon monoxide, illicit drugs, and a variety of poisons. At the center of crime scenes are the participants—the offenders, victims, and witnesses. More than 40 articles cover diverse diseases, medical conditions, and injuries, including various kinds of wounds.

A third focus in *Forensic Science* is the role of the forensic sciences in the **American legal system.** The set includes brief articles on some of the most important federal laws applying to controlled substances, such as the Harrison Narcotic Drug Act of 1914, the Controlled Substances Act of 1970, and the Anabolic Steroid Control Act of 2004, as well as such international agreements as the Chemical Weapons Convention of 1993. Articles on selected U.S. Supreme Court decisions, including *Miranda v. Arizona*, and a variety of important legal principles, such as habeas corpus and *mens rea*, also help to illuminate the legal dimensions of the forensic sciences. Law-enforcement bodies and government investigative units covered in the set include the U.S. Drug Enforcement Administration, the Federal Bureau of Investigation, and the U.S. Secret Service as well as the Environmental Measurements Laboratory and the National Transportation Safety Board.

**Specific historical subjects** is a fourth perspective of *Forensic Science*. These range from overviews of ancient criminal cases and crime mysteries and ancient science to examinations of such high-profile modern criminal cases as the O. J. Simpson murder trial, the Unabomber case, and criminal cases involving celebrities. The set also includes articles on such subjects as the Lindbergh baby kidnapping case, the exhumations of the remains of U.S. presidents Zachary Taylor and Abraham Lincoln, and mysteries sur-

rounding the deaths of the French emperor Napoleon I and composer Ludwig van Beethoven. These historical topics serve as fascinating case studies in the practical application of forensic science.

Finally, *Forensic Science* makes a special effort to address depictions of **forensics in the media.** Long overview articles examine misconceptions fostered by the media and the treatment of forensic science in television, literature, and journalism. Briefer articles cover such iconic individual television programs as *CSI*, *Cold Case*, and *Forensic Files*. A special appendix offers brief descriptions of many other television programs.

### Organization and Format

The set's alphabetical arrangement make topics easy to find. See and See also terms are included in abundance (such as "Lie detectors. *See* Polygraph analysis"). As in Salem's other encyclopedic reference works, articles in *Forensic Science* contain helpful top matter that defines the topics and offers compact summaries of their relevance to forensic science. Every article also contains a "Further Reading" section, followed by a generous list of cross-references to related topics within the set. Articles are also supplemented by photographs, maps, charts, graphs, and illustrative sidebars.

Following the articles are six valuable appendixes:

- Guide to Internet Resources – More than 60 listings organized into four categories: General; Forensic Subspecialties; Indexes to Periodical Publications; and Professional Organizations and Government Agencies
- Television Programs – Nearly 30 shows, many still on the air, in which forensic science figures prominently
- Key Figures in Forensic Science – Biographical sketches of 33 key figures in forensic science, mostly from the nineteenth and twentieth centuries, with a few from earlier periods
- Time Line – Starting in 1194, marking the establishment of the Office of the Coroner by King Richard I and ending in 2015, with the successful identification of twin

DNA, the nearly 200 listings include court cases, legislation, inventions, famous books and people, and significant firsts in the field of forensic science

- Bibliography – Each work included is not only thoughtfully annotated, but listed under one or more specialized areas of forensic science, from Ballistics to Trace Evidence
- Glossary – More than 300 terms used by the forensic science community, from accelerant and acquittal to whorl fingerprint and witness interviewing

Additionally two indexes – by Category (23) and by Subject — complete the set.

## Acknowledgments

Salem Press would like to thank the many contributors of this set. Their names and affiliations are listed in the pages that follow here. This publication is especially indebted to its editors, Dr. Ayn Embar-Seddon O'Reilly of Capella University and Dr. Allan D. Pass of National Behavioral Science Consultants.

# Contributors

Richard Adler
*University of Michigan, Dearborn*

Timothy C. Antinick
*Michigan State University*

Alyssa J. Badgley
*Michigan State University*

Catherine G. Bailey
*Stetson University College of Law*

Thomas E. Baker
*University of Scranton*

Jane Piland-Baker
*Former Instructor Marywood University*

Carl L. Bankston III
*Tulane University*

Amy L. Barber
*Michigan State University*

Charlene F. Barroga
*University of California, San Diego*

Eric J. Bartelink
*California State University, Chico*

Kevin M. Beaver
*Florida State University*

Raymond D. Benge, Jr.
*Tarrant County College*

Alvin K. Benson
*Utah Valley State University*

R. L. Bernstein
*New Mexico State University*

Vivian Bodey
*Southwestern Law School*

Megan N. Bottegal
*Florida International University*

Cliff Boyd
*Radford University*

Donna C. Boyd
*Radford University*

Jocelyn M. Brineman
*University of North Carolina at Charlotte*

Michael P. Brown
*Ball State University*

Kevin G. Buckler
*University of Texas at Brownsville and Texas Southmost College*

Amy Webb Bull
*Tennessee State University*

Michael A. Buratovich
*Spring Arbor University*

Mary Car-Blanchard
*iHealthSpot.com*

Russell N. Carney
*Missouri State University*

Dennis W. Cheek
*Ewing Marion Kauffman Foundation*

Michael W. Cheek
*American University*

Jennifer L. Christian
*Indiana University*

Armand R. Cingolani III
*Pennsylvania Association of Criminal Defense Lawyers*

Douglas Clouatre
*Mid-Plains Community College*

Helen Colby
*Portland, Oregon*

Robert Colby
*Portland, Oregon*

Susan Coleman
*West Texas A&M University*

Sally A. Coulson
*Institute of Environmental Science and Research*

Anne Coxon
*Institute of Environmental Science and Research*

Martiscia Davidson
*Fremont, California*

Jennifer Davis
*University of Dayton*

Seth G. Dewey
*Canisius College*

Thomas E. DeWolfe
*Hampden-Sydney College*

Shawkat Dhanani
*Veterans Administration Greater Los Angeles Healthcare System*

Jackie Dial
*American Medical Writers Association*

Joseph Di Rienzi
*College of Notre Dame of Maryland*

Kimberly D. Dodson
*Lincoln Memorial University*

Douglas Elliot
*Institute of Environmental Science and Research*

Stephanie K. Ellis
*Marymount University*

Ayn Embar-Seddon
*Capella University*

Patricia E. Erickson
*Canisius College*

Elisabeth Faase
*Athens Regional Medical Center*

Erin J. Farley
*University of North Carolina at Wilmington*

Ronald P. Fisher
*Florida International University*

Dale L. Flesher
*University of Mississippi*

David R. Foran
*Michigan State University*

Carl Franklin
*Southern Utah University*

Dante B. Gatmaytan
*University of the Philippines*

Gilbert Geis
*University of California, Irvine*

Kaitlyn J. Germain
*Michigan State University*

James S. Godde
*Monmouth College*

Timothy L. Hall
*University of Mississippi*

David T. Hardy
*Tucson, Arizona*

Elizabeth K. Hayden
*Northeastern University*

Peter B. Heller
*Manhattan College*

Taiping Ho
*Ball State University*

Jerry W. Hollingsworth
*McMurry University*

Kimberley M. Holloway
*King College*

Mary Hurd
*East Tennessee State University*

Domingo Jariel
*Louisiana State University at Eunice*

Edward Johnson
*University of New Orleans*

Helen Jones
*Manchester Metropolitan University*

Phill Jones
*Spokane, Washington*

Susan J. Karcher
*Purdue University*

Ryan Kelly
*Monmouth University*

Kelvin Keraga
*New York State Energy Research and Development Authority*

M. A. Q. Khan
*University of Illinois at Chicago*

S. F. Khan
*University of Illinois at Chicago*

Brianne M. Kiley
*Michigan State University*

Paul M. Klenowski
*Thiel College*

Robert Klose
*University College of Bangor*

David B. Kopel
*Independence Institute*

Steven A. Kuhl
*V and R Consulting*

David J. Ladouceur
*University of Notre Dame*

Lisa LaGoo
*Michigan State University*

Kristin E. Landfield
*Emory University*

Abraham D. Lavender
*Florida International University*

Justyna Lenik
*Loyola University Chicago*

Erin J. Lenz
*Michigan State University*

Thomas T. Lewis
*St. Cloud State University*

Contributors

Scott O. Lilienfeld
*Emory University*

Keith G. Logan
*Kutztown University*

Arthur J. Lurigio
*Loyola University Chicago*

Richard D. McAnulty
*University of North Carolina at Charlotte*

Kimberley A. McClure
*Western Illinois University*

Richard L. McWhorter
*Prairie View A&M University*

Eric Madfis
*Northeastern University*

Marianne M. Madsen
*ARUP Laboratories, University of Utah*

Sergei A. Markov
*Austin Peay State University*

Lucas J. Marshall
*Michigan State University*

Kimberley A. McClure
*Western Illinois University*

Eric Metchik
*Salem State College*

Ralph R. Meyer
*University of Cincinnati*

Randall L. Milstein
*Oregon State University*

Damon Mitchell
*Central Connecticut State University*

Peter Molinaro
*Florida International University*

Robin Kamienny Montvilo
*Rhode Island College*

Mario Morelli
*Western Illinois University*

Lilliana I. Moreno
*Florida International University*

R. K. Morgan-Smith
*Institute of Environmental Science and Research*

Alexandra E. Mosser
*Florida International University*

Turhon A. Murad
*California State University, Chico*

Michael J. Mutolo
*Michigan State University*

Edward C. Nwanegbo
*Siouxland Medical Education Foundation*

Douglas A. Orr
*Spokane, Washington*

Robert J. Paradowski
*Rochester Institute of Technology*

Allan D. Pass
*National Behavioral Science Consultants*

Cheryl Pawlowski
*University of Northern Colorado*

John R. Phillips
*Purdue University Calumet*

Nickie D. Phillips
*St. Francis College*

Nancy A. Piotrowski
*University of California, Berkeley*

Daniel Pontzer
*University of North Florida*

Judy L. Porter
*Rochester Institute of Technology*

Frank J. Prerost
*Midwestern University*

Maureen Puffer-Rothenberg
*Valdosta State University*

Cynthia Racer
*American Chemical Society*

Robert J. Ramsey
*Indiana University East*

Lillian M. Range
*Our Lady of Holy Cross College*

Shamir Ratansi
*Central Connecticut State University*

Rebecca L. Ray
*Michigan State University*

Margaret C. Reardon
*Florida International University*

Betty Richardson
*Southern Illinois University at Edwardsville*

Alice C. Richer
*Spaulding Rehabilitation Center*

xi

Gina M. Robertiello
*Felician College*

James C. Roberts
*University of Scranton*

James L. Robinson
*University of Illinois at
Urbana-Champaign*

Charles W. Rogers
*Southwestern Oklahoma
State University*

Stephen F. Rohde
*Rohde & Victoroff*

Carol A. Rolf
*Rivier College*

Kelly Rothenberg
*Valdosta, Georgia*

David A. Rusak
*University of Scranton*

Lawrence M. Salinger
*Arkansas State University*

Neva E. J. Sanders-Dewey
*Canisius College*

Lisa M. Sardinia
*Pacific University*

Geri E. Satin
*Florida International
University*

Elizabeth D. Schafer
*Loachapoka, Alabama*

Heidi V. Schumacher
*University of Colorado at
Boulder*

Jason J. Schwartz
*Los Angeles, California*

Miriam E. Schwartz
*University of California,
Los Angeles*

Julia E. Selman-Ayetey
*King's College London*

Brion Sever
*Monmouth University*

Manoj Sharma
*University of Cincinnati*

Elizabeth Algren Shaw
*Ziegler, Metzger & Miller*

Taylor Shaw
*ADVANCE Education and
Development Center*

Martha Sherwood
*University of Oregon*

Lisa J. Shientag
*New York University School
of Medicine*

David Shrager, Esq.

R. Baird Shuman
*University of Illinois at
Urbana-Champaign*

Dwight G. Smith
*Southern Connecticut State
University*

Ruth Waddell Smith
*Michigan State University*

Richard S. Spira
*American Veterinary Medical
Association*

Steven Stack
*Wayne State University*

Sharon W. Stark
*Monmouth University*

Rick M. Steinmann
*Clarion University-Venango
Campus*

Joan C. Stevenson
*Western Washington
University*

Russell S. Strasser
*George Washington
University*

David R. Struckhoff
*Loyola University Chicago*

Patrick Sylvers
*Emory University*

Rena Christina Tabata
*University of British
Columbia*

Lawrence C. Trostle
*University of Alaska
Anchorage*

Dwight Tshudy
*Gordon College*

Ruth N. Udey
*Michigan State University*

Oluseyi A. Vanderpuye
*Albany State University*

Alana Van Gundy-Yoder
*Miami University Hamilton*

Sheryl L. Van Horne
*Pennsylvania State
University*

Linda Volonino
*Canisius College*

C. J. Walsh
*Mote Marine Laboratory*

Donald A. Watt
*Dakota Wesleyan University*

Contributors

James Watterson
*Laurentian University*

Marcia J. Weiss
*Point Park University*

George M. Whitson III
*University of Texas at Tyler*

LaVerne McQuiller Williams
*Rochester Institute of Technology*

Bradley R. A. Wilson
*University of Cincinnati*

Richard L. Wilson
*University of Tennessee at Chattanooga*

Michael Windelspecht
*Ricochet Creative Productions*

Ming Y. Zheng
*Gordon College*

# Complete List of Contents

## Volume 1

# Volume 2

# Volume 3

# Forensic Science

# *A*

## Accelerants

**Definition**: Any substances, most commonly ignitable liquids, used intentionally to increase the rate and spread of fires.

**Significance:** In a fire investigation, the primary goal is to identify whether the fire was accidental or intentional. The presence of an accelerant at a fire scene is often indicative of an intentional fire, or arson. Accelerants can be identified from fire debris through conventional forensic analysis.

Accelerants are commonly used in arson fires because they provide additional fuel in areas where the items present may not burn easily. Arsonists often pour accelerants over the areas they want to burn to ensure that their fires spread as much as possible to maximize damage and destruction. Common accelerants are commercially available ignitable liquids—such as gasoline, lighter fluid, and kerosene—that are readily accessible to the arsonist. The identification of an accelerant is significant evidence in a fire investigation because it suggests that the fire was set intentionally.

### Identification at the Fire Scene

The identification of accelerants at fire scenes is often a challenge for investigators. Examination of the fire debris by various techniques can be useful in identifying the origin of a fire and any areas of potential accelerant use. After the preliminary identification of a potential accelerant source, samples can be collected and taken back to the forensics laboratory for further analysis.

The types of fire debris most likely to contain sufficient accelerant residue for analysis are porous materials, such as wood and carpet, which can trap residual liquid. Accelerant residue can also pool in the cracks in floors, where it is somewhat protected from the fire. Investigators should collect and store any debris suspected to contain accelerant residue in airtight containers, preferably metal paint cans with friction lids, to eliminate the possibility of the loss of the volatile components within the samples.

### Extraction Techniques

Gas chromatography coupled with mass spectrometry is the most common technique used for the analysis of accelerants from fire debris. Before fire debris evidence can be analyzed using the dual instrument known as the gas chromatograph-mass spectrometer (GC-MS), however, the accelerant residue must first be extracted from the debris that was collected. Several techniques can be used to perform this extraction, and each has its own advantages and disadvantages.

In a solvent extraction, the fire debris is washed with a solvent that will dissolve the accelerant residue but not the debris, such as carbon disulfide. The extract can then be injected directly into the GC-MS. A drawback of solvent extraction is that large amounts of potentially hazardous solvents are required to perform an efficient extraction; in addition, this method does not concentrate the accelerant residue effectively. Although solvent extraction was at one time a popular method, it has generally been replaced by quicker, more efficient preconcentration techniques.

In passive headspace extraction, the metal paint can used to collect the debris is heated so that any accelerant present is vaporized and becomes saturated within the area above the debris in the can, which is known as the headspace. A small hole is made in the top of the can and a gastight syringe is used to draw up a sample of the vapor in the headspace, which can then be injected into the GC-MS. Passive headspace extraction is biased toward the more volatile components, but it minimizes the capacity for cross-contamination of the evidence because the accelerant residue is extracted from the same container in which the debris was collected.

A variation of the passive headspace extraction technique is adsorption/elution, in which the debris is heated in the can with a strip of activated charcoal suspended in the headspace. The accelerant vapor is trapped on the strip, from which it is dissolved by a solvent for injection into the GC-MS. Adsorption/elution is affected by the same volatility bias as the passive headspace method, but because the vapor is concentrated onto the charcoal strip, adsorption/elution greatly decreases the potential loss of low-volatility compounds.

The solid-phase microextraction (SPME) technique employs a coated fiber that is housed in a retractable apparatus. The can containing the debris is heated, and this fiber is subjected to the headspace of the can, where the accelerant vapor adsorbs onto the fiber. One advantage of SPME is that the fiber apparatus can be placed directly into the injection port of the GC-MS. The heat of the injection port causes the accelerant trapped on the fiber to desorb from the fiber so that it can be carried into the instrument for analysis. Another advantage of SPME is its potential use for on-site accelerant collection. An investigator can use the SPME fiber apparatus to adsorb accelerant vapor at the fire scene; with the fiber retracted into the apparatus, it is protected from the environment and can be transported directly to the laboratory for analysis.

### Instrumental Analysis

Although many techniques have proven useful in accelerant identification, gas chromatography (GC) is by far the most commonly used technique in the forensics laboratory for fire debris analysis. GC is a separation technique that is capable of isolating the numerous individual compounds present in typically complex accelerants. The result of a GC analysis is a chromatogram, which is essentially a chart in which all the components are represented as individual peaks. The pattern of these peaks does not change for a substance and thus is characteristic of that substance. Therefore, when an accelerant residue is examined by GC, its peak pattern can be matched to the peak pattern of a known sample of the same accelerant analyzed for comparison.

When GC is coupled with mass spectrometry (MS), the chemical composition of a sample can be identified conclusively. The pairing of GC and MS allows the identification of individual peaks within the peak pattern and thus is the standard convention for accelerant identification. It should be noted that accelerant identification is considered class evidence because it cannot be individualized to one source. For example, if an accelerant is identified to be gasoline, the pump or even the service station from which it was purchased cannot be determined because of the inherent variation in the process of refining crude oil.

The American Society for Testing and Materials (ASTM), an organization that generates and maintains standards for procedures and materials in a wide array of fields, has developed standard accelerant classes for the identification of accelerants in court. The ASTM classification system for ignitable liquids provides a standardized method of accelerant description for forensic scientists. In this system, nine classes of ignitable liquids are subdivided into three boiling point ranges (light, medium, and heavy). The nine classes—gasoline, petroleum distillates, isoparaffinic products, aromatic products, naphthenic-paraffinic products, normal alkane products, dearomatized distillates, oxygenated solvents, and a final miscellaneous grouping—and their subdivisions provide standard guidelines for the identification of ignitable liquids based on chemical composition.

### Difficulties in Identification

Although chromatographic pattern matching is the convention for the identification of accelerants in a forensics laboratory, some factors can alter chromatographic patterns and make it difficult for investigators to identify conclusively any accelerant that may be present. Most common accelerants contain refined petroleum products, which are mixtures of hydrocarbons, and several of these hydrocarbons are found in everyday household products. For example, basic carpeting such as that found in many homes contains compounds similar to those found in common accelerants. This overlap presents a problem for a scientist attempting to identify an accelerant that soaked into a carpet before it was burned.

An efficient extraction technique, such as adsorption/elution or SPME, can separate an accelerant from the fire debris itself. Investigators can also use a data-processing technique called extracted ion chromatography (EIC)—in which specific characteristic peaks can be isolated from other peaks—to understand the data more fully. Because of the potential problem of interference, fire investigators should collect several debris samples, including samples in which no accelerant is expected to be found, in order to understand which chromatographic peaks correspond to the debris and which peaks correspond to an actual accelerant.

*Lucas J. Marshall*

### Further Reading

Almirall, José R., and Kenneth G. Furton, eds. *Analysis and Interpretation of Fire Scene Evidence*. Boca Raton, Fla.: CRC Press, 2004. Presents comprehensive information about fire scene investigation and the chemical analysis of fire debris.

DeHaan, John D. *Kirk's Fire Investigation*. 6th ed. Upper Saddle River, N.J.: Pearson Prentice Hall, 2007. Detailed volume covers the physical nature and chemistry of fire and also discusses the various types of fires.

Nic Daéid, Niamh, ed. *Fire Investigation*. Boca Raton, Fla.: CRC Press, 2004. Compilation provides material on the basics of fire investigation with emphasis on laboratory reconstruction and analytical techniques.

Redsicker, David R., and John J. O'Connor. *Practical Fire and Arson Investigation*. 2d ed. Boca Raton, Fla.: CRC Press, 1997. Presents extensive information on the various undertakings of the fire investigator, from scene investigation to courtroom testimony.

Saferstein, Richard. *Criminalistics: An Introduction to Forensic Science*. 9th ed. Upper Saddle River, N.J.: Pearson Prentice Hall, 2007. Textbook discusses the different forensic science fields, including arson investigation.

Tilstone, William J., Kathleen A. Savage, and Leigh A. Clark. *Forensic Science: An Encyclopedia of History, Methods, and Techniques*. Santa Barbara, Calif.: ABC-CLIO, 2006. General reference work covers a broad range of topics in forensic science.

**See also:** Arson; Bureau of Alcohol, Tobacco, Firearms and Explosives; Burn pattern analysis; Column chromatography; Fire debris; Gas chromatography; Mass spectrometry; National Church Arson Task Force.

## Accident investigation and reconstruction

**Definition:** Collection and analysis of evidence at the scenes of transportation accidents to create models explaining what happened.

**Significance:** In determining responsibility for motor vehicle and other kinds of transportation accidents, forensic scientists attempt to reconstruct what happened during these events by analyzing the available evidence. The testimony of accident investigators often plays a role in criminal and civil proceedings that stem from accidents.

In the United States, transportation accident investigation and reconstruction are usually carried out by police departments. Some accident investigations, however, fall under federal jurisdiction. The National Transportation Safety Board (NTSB), formed in 1967 as part of the U.S. Department of Transportation, replaced the Civil Aeronautics Board and expanded the role of the federal government in accident investigation and reconstruction. The NTSB became an independent agency in 1975; its duties include the investigation of all civil aviation accidents in the United States as well as all major railroad, highway, marine, and pipeline accidents and any transportation accidents that involve the release of hazardous materials. Private companies also offer accident investigation and reconstruction services.

## Accident Investigators

When transportation accidents occur, law-enforcement agencies, insurance companies, manufacturers of the vehicles involved, and the persons involved, including those injured, all have interests in understanding the causes of the accidents and in assigning responsibility. Police officers normally are the first individuals to investigate traffic accidents. Typically, when a serious accident has taken place, the police deal first with any injured people and any hazardous situations created by the accident; they then record information that will allow them to assess how the accident occurred. Most police officers in the United States receive at least brief training in accident investigation; some receive additional specialist training. The accuracy and completeness of the evidence collected by the police at an accident scene affects the degree of accuracy of the accident reconstruction.

In accidents that fall under the jurisdiction of the NTSB, the NTSB becomes the lead investigative agency. In such a case, the role of the local police department initially is to handle any casualties and hazards caused by the accident and then to preserve the scene to the greatest degree possible. NTSB specialists are experienced investigators with strong academic backgrounds in forensic science, physics, structural engineering, aeronautical engineering, and similar fields. NTSB investigators are qualified to serve as expert witnesses in court.

Insurance companies often have their own accident investigators. These investigators, as well as independent investigators hired by attorneys and other interested parties, often enter the accident and reconstruction process after much of the debris from the accident has been cleared away. They may have the opportunity to examine the damaged vehicles, but in attempting to reconstruct the accident they usually must depend on other evidence collected by the police at the accident scene.

Some disagreement exists among experts in accident reconstruction concerning the degree of training and education necessary to qualify an individual as an accident and reconstruction specialist and as an expert witness. Since 1991, the Accreditation Commission for Traffic Accident Reconstruction (ACTAR) has promoted voluntary standards for traffic accident investigators in order to encourage accuracy, consistency, and professionalism in accident investigation and reconstruction. These standards have not been universally adopted, however.

At the highest level, accident reconstruction specialists hold university degrees in engineering, mathematics, physics, or similar fields and have years of experience related to crash analysis and reconstruction. In the United States, the National Academy of Forensic Engineers is empowered by the Council of Engineering and Scientific Specialty Boards to certify accident investigation and reconstruction specialists as "diplomate forensic engineers." This is the highest level of certification, the engineering equivalent of being a board-certified medical specialist. The International Institute of Forensic Engineering Sciences also awards diplomate status to qualified forensic engineers and forensic science professionals.

At the other end of the spectrum, individuals who do not even have high school diplomas can enroll in vocational training programs that focus on accident investigation and reconstruction. These programs call their graduates "certified accident reconstructionists," although many lack the background to do necessary mathematical analyses of accident scenes. Some courts in the United States have begun to reject certified accident reconstructionists as expert witnesses, requiring those who provide expert testimony on accidents to have higher levels of education and expertise.

## The Investigation Phase

After immediate needs involving injuries and hazards have been attended to at the scene of an accident, the investigation phase begins. In collecting evidence at an accident scene, the investigators perform some or all of the following tasks: taking witness statements, photographing damage to vehicles and property, measuring and recording tire (skid) marks, recording paint and gouge marks, recording the postcrash locations of all vehicles involved, and recording the positions of all pieces of debris from the accident with photographs and measurements. Using this information, the investigators create a grid map of the crash scene that shows, with measurements, where each skid mark, vehicle, and piece of collision debris and damaged property is located in relation to all others.

Primary accident investigators also use a Haddon matrix to record situational evidence relative to the accident. This tool, developed around 1970 by Dr. William Haddon, the first head of what later became the National Highway Traffic Safety Administration, is a grid on which investigators record information about various conditions before, during, and after the accident at the accident scene. The most common Haddon matrix used for traffic accidents has three rows and three columns, creating nine cells. The rows represent events occurring before the crash, during the crash, and after the crash, respectively, and the columns identify the following factors that could have affected the accident in each time period: human factors (for example, impaired vision, precrash alcohol consumption, speeding, failure to wear a seat belt), vehicle and equipment factors (for example, failed brakes, nonfunctioning lights, malfunctioning air bags, poorly designed fuel tanks that leaked or exploded), and physical, social, and economic factors (for example, missing road signs, nonfunctioning traffic signals, absence of or poorly designed guardrails, cultural attitudes toward alcohol consumption or speeding, interference with or delayed emergency services response).

### The Reconstruction Phase

During the reconstruction phase, accident investigators apply their knowledge of the laws of physics to the evidence to determine such elements as the speeds of the vehicles involved, the angle of initial impact, the occurrence of second-

> ## Electronic Evidence Improves Precision and Confidence
>
> Many new automobiles are equipped with crash data recorders (CDRs) or event data recorders (EDRs). These recorders store data about cars' speed and handling that can provide crucial evidence in accident cases. In November, 2004, Danny Hopkins was convicted of second-degree manslaughter for causing the death of Lindsay Kyle in a car acci- dent. The event data recorder in Hopkins's car had shown that the vehicle was traveling at 106 miles per hour just four seconds before it crashed into the back of Kyle's car, which was stopped at a red light. If Hopkins's car had not been equipped with an event data re- corder, a forensic investigation of the physical evidence, such as skid marks and crash damage, could have been used to estimate the speed of the car. The recorder's data evidence, however, provided better precision, increasing the investigators' confidence that the driver's speed was 106 miles per hour at the time of impact.
>
> *Linda Volonino*

ary impacts, mechanical failures that may have caused the accident, and environmental factors that may affect responsibility for the accident. Damage-based reconstruction is one of the oldest and simplest forms of accident reconstruction. In this approach, the reconstructionist looks at the damage done by and to vehicles and property.

By using information from vehicle manufacturers and applying knowledge of the laws of physics and structural analysis, the reconstructionist is able to determine the approximate rates of speed of the vehicles and their angle of impact. Damage-based reconstruction requires many assumptions and simplifications. For example, car manufacturers provide the results of crash tests for reconstruction engineers, but in using such results, a reconstructionist must assume that the vehicle involved in the accident had the same structural properties as a new vehicle of the same model that was used in the crash tests.

Ideally, damage-based reconstruction should be done in conjunction with trajectory-based reconstruction, which is based on the principle that momentum (speed multiplied by mass) is conserved in a crash. Starting with where the vehicles and debris ended up after a crash, reconstructionists work backward to determine the speed of each vehicle at impact. This method must also take into account forces such as friction of tires on the road, which reduces momentum, and whether the road was wet or dry. The mathematics required to perform trajectory-based reconstruction can be complex, and software programs are available to help with these calculations.

Ultimately, the reconstruction of an accident is only as good as the original information provided by those who measured and recorded the accident scene. All reconstructions involve assumptions, simplifications, and interpretations. Good reconstruction engineers are able to explain their analyses and provide scientific justifications for their conclusions that will stand up to expert examination in a court of law.

*Martiscia Davidson*

**Further Reading**

Accreditation Commission for Traffic Accident Reconstruction (ACTAR). An agency that offers voluntary accreditation to traffic accident investigators who meet NTSB training standards. < http://www.actar.org/>

Andrews, Dennis R. "Accident Reconstruction from the Outside in." *Claims* 54 (June, 2006): 18-22. Presents a nontechnical explanation of the information that can be gained from traffic accident reconstruction.

Brach, Raymond and Matthew Brach. *Vehicular Accident and Reconstruction Analysis.* 2nd ed. Warrendale, PA: SAE International, 2011. Updated information for experienced accident investigators

Daily, John, Nathan Shigemura, Jeremy Daily. *Fundamentals of Traffic Accident Reconstruction.* Jacksonville, FL: Institute of Police Technology and Management, University of North Florida, 2006. Textbook uses both a mathematical and practical approach to traffic accident reconstruction.

Hermance, Richard. *Snowmobile and ATV Accident Investigation and Reconstruction.* 2d ed. Tucson, Ariz.: Lawyers & Judges Publishing, 2006. Focuses on the investigation of accidents involving off-road vehicles.

Palmer, Scott. "Fighting Fraud with Forensic Intelligence." *Claims* 55 (September, 2007): 54-59. Explains how accident reconstruction can be useful in the investigation of insurance claims.

Rivers, R. W. *Evidence in Traffic Crash Investigation and Reconstruction: Identification, Interpretation, and Analysis of Evidence, and the Traffic Crash Investigation and Reconstruction Process.* Springfield, Ill.: Charles C Thomas, 2006. Comprehensive volume addresses all aspects of the investigation of traffic accidents, including preservation of evidence and accident reconstruction.

Rivers, R. W. *Traffic Crash Investigators' Manual: A Levels 1 and 2 Reference, Training and Investigation manual.* 3rd ed. Springfield, IL: Charles C. Thomas, 2011. Outlines the requirements for proper investigation of traffic crashes and specific evidence appropriate to various types of crashes

Wheat, Arnold G. *Accident Investigation Training Manual.* Clifton Park, N.Y.: Thomson/Delmar Learning, 2005. Provides an extensive introduction to accident investigation, including reconstruction techniques.

**See also:** Crime scene measurement; Crime scene reconstruction and staging; Cross-contamination of evidence; Direct versus circumstantial evidence; Flight data recorders; Hit-and-run vehicle offenses; ValuJet Flight 592 crash investigation.

## Acid-base indicators

**Definition**: Substances that show the acidity or alkalinity of solutions within a narrow range.

**Significance:** Among the tools forensic scientists use to identify unknown substances are acid-base indicators, also known as pH indicators. Such indicators can also enable scientists to detect the presence of contaminating chemicals in solutions, and their use in the analysis of human tissues can provide clues to cause of death.

The acidity or alkalinity of a substance is indicated by its pH, which is a measure of the concentration of hydrogen ions ($H^+$) in a solution. The pH scale is logarithmic and ranges from 0 to 14. The lower the pH, the more acidic the solution, and the higher the pH, the more alkaline, or basic, the solution; pH 7.0 is neutral and is the pH of pure water.

Acid-base indicators are organic dyes that change color depending on the concentration of hydrogen ions present in a solution. The change does not become visible at a precise point; rather, it happens within a fairly narrow pH range. Many different acid-base indicators are available, and they change colors within different pH ranges. For example, phenolphthalein is colorless at a pH of 8.2 but turns red at a pH of 10. Methyl orange is red at a pH of 3.2 but turns yellow at a pH of 4.4.

The most common acid-base indicator is litmus paper. It comes in two forms, red and blue. When dipped into a solution, blue litmus paper turns red if the pH of the solution is 4.5 or below, indicating the solution is acidic. If the pH of the solution is 8.2 or above, blue litmus paper remains its original blue color. Conversely, red litmus paper remains red when dipped into an acidic solution but turns blue when dipped into a basic solution.

Most often, acid-base indicators are used with a technique called titration. Titration allows analytical chemists to make quantitative determinations of how much acid or alkaline material is in a solution. In the titration of an acid solution, a known quantity of base is added until the correct acid-base indicator changes color. The chemist then measures how much base was used and can calculate how much acid is in the solution. The procedure is reversed with a basic solution.

When investigating an unknown substance such as a confiscated drug, a forensic technician may dissolve a small amount of the substance in water and then test its pH. Conversely, if the substance has been identified and the pH of that substance in pure form is known, the technician may dissolve a small amount of the substance in water to see if the pH varies from the known pH. If it does, this suggests that the substance is contaminated with another chemical.

Acid-base indicators are useful but crude analytical tools. To complete most chemical analyses, forensic scientists usually need to employ more precise analytical tools.

*Martiscia Davidson*

**Further Reading**

Blei, Ira. and George Odian. *General, Organic, and Biochemistry: Connecting Chemistry to Your Life.* 2d ed. New York: W. H. Freeman, 2006.

James, Stuart H., and Jon J. Nordby, eds. *Forensic Science: An Introduction to Scientific and Investigative Techniques.* 2d ed. Boca Raton, Fla.: CRC Press, 2005.

James, Stuart H., and Jon J. Nordby, eds. *Forensic Science: An Introduction to Scientific and Investigative Techniques.* 4th ed. Boca Raton, FL: CRC Press, 2011.

Malone, Leo J. and Theodore O. Dolter. *Basic Concepts of Chemistry.* 9th ed. Hoboken, NJ: John Wiley & Sons, 2013.

Oxlade, Chris. *Acids and Bases.* Chicago: Heinemann Library, 2007.

Willis, Laura. *Fluids & electrolytes made incredibly easy!.* 6th ed. Philadelphia, PA: Wolters Kluwer, 2015.

**See also:** Crime scene screening tests; Quantitative and qualitative analysis of chemicals; Reagents.

# Actuarial risk assessment

**Definition:** Formation of judgments and predictions regarding dangerous behavior through the application of formulas to particular variables and statistics in preparation for the adoption of necessary preventive measures.

**Significance:** Forensic psychologists use numerous factors to evaluate the likelihood that particular persons will be involved in violent and dangerous behavior. Predictions based on actuarial risk assessment influence many decisions made in the criminal justice system.

Actuarial risk assessment is one of the many tools that forensic psychologists use to evaluate the likelihood of future violent and dangerous behavior on the part of certain persons. Other methods include clinical predictions, which are based on evidence derived from counseling and experience, and anamnestic predictions, in which psychologists analyze the behavior of specific persons in the past in similar situations. The scientific community has demanded greater reliability in predictions than either clinical or anamnestic methods can provide, and an outcome of this demand has been the use of mathematical formulas to make predictions of risk. Actuarial risk assessment thus employs many of the tools of statistical analysis.

## Uses of Risk Assessment

Many people and organizations rely on forensic psychologists and similar experts to make predictions of human behavior. For example, officials in the U.S. criminal justice system rely on risk assessment in making decisions concerning sentencing—for example, in deciding whether to impose probation as a sentence instead of incarceration or whether to sentence a violent offender to death rather than life in prison. A psychologist's prediction concerning a given individual's risk of violent or inappropriate behavior could support the issuance of a restraining order in a domestic dispute or abuse case. Risk assessment may also be used in child-custody decision making and in decisions concerning whether child visitation by a parent should be supervised. Some companies use risk assessment to evaluate the potential for violent behavior in the workplace by terminated employees, and some educational institutions use risk assessment to predict the likelihood of school violence.

Experts also use actuarial risk assessment to predict the potential for recidivism in determining whether to parole prisoners from correctional facilities and in considering the release of offenders who have been confined to mental health facilities. One area of risk assessment that has seen substantial growth concerns the prediction of sexual offending. Predictions in this area may influence whether particular released prisoners must register as sex offenders

with their local communities.

Forensic psychologists may also be called upon to predict the likelihood that certain persons will attempt suicide. In addition, psychologists may have a legal obligation to warn others of any potential danger of harm from any persons they are treating. In some cases, the goal of risk assessment is to determine whether to commit persons to mental health facilities involuntarily because of the likelihood that they may cause serious harm to themselves or others. Risk assessment is also used to decide whether persons who have been involuntarily confined to mental health facilities have become stable enough in their behavior that they are no longer dangerous and can be released.

## Risk Assessment Factors

Actuarial risk assessment involves looking at statistical relationships between variables to make judgments and predictions about future behavior. Risk assessment involves a delicate balance between protecting society from physical harm and ensuring that the rights and liberties of the persons subjected to risk assessment are not unduly restricted. Forensic psychologists look at various behavioral characteristics and other factors to increase the accuracy of their scientific approaches to risk assessment. These factors are derived from research involving large groups of people who have exhibited risky or violent behavior in the past and from data gathered by professional clinicians. Some of the factors or variables considered in risk assessment are specifically associated with one behavior, whereas others are predictive across the entire array of potentially risky or dangerous behaviors.

One of the most significant factors considered in risk assessment is the presence or absence of a history of violent behavior. Other risk factors include static predictors such as psychological and physiological characteristics of the person and the person's personal and family history.

Higher risk is associated with relationship and employment instability, education maladjustment, a history of drug and alcohol abuse, and being young. Dynamic characteristics—that is, characteristics that change over

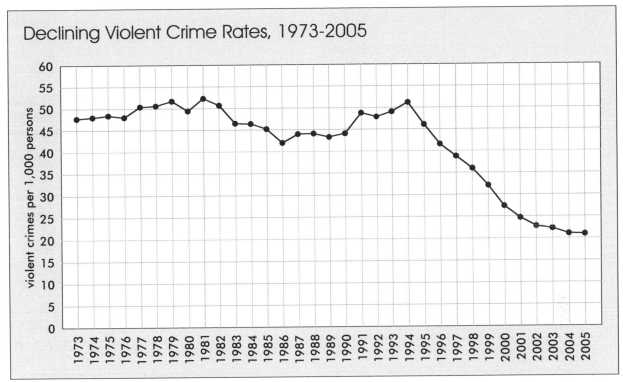

Declining Violent Crime Rates, 1973-2005

*Source:* U.S. Bureau of Justice Statistics, 2008. Data represent aggregate violent victimization rates for murder, rape, robbery, and assault.

time—that are associated with higher risk include a lack of insight about personal behavior, the inability to control hostile and impulsive behavior, negative emotions in response to treatment, and ongoing psychotic symptoms such as hallucinations.

Finally, in assessing risk, the person's potential living environments and social networks must be considered, as well as the person's ability to harm others in the future.

Research has found that actuarial risk assessment is more accurate than clinical assessment. Jurors, however, tend to believe the testimony of clinicians over that of actuarial experts, as jurors perceive that clinicians have stronger relationships with and thus more knowledge of the persons being assessed. Despite the scientific basis of actuarial risk assessment by forensic scientists, the prediction of human behavior is very difficult, and significant criticism has been directed toward actuarial risk assessment.

Research has shown that a person's behavior changes over time and that actuarial prediction has an accuracy rate of little more than 50 percent.

Actuarial risk assessment continues to gain acceptance among members of the scientific and legal communities, however, and as risk factors and formulas are enhanced through research, the accuracy rates of this technique should also improve in the future.

*Carol A. Rolf*

**Further Reading**

Freeman, Naomi J. "Predictors of Rearrest for Rapists and Child Molesters on Probation." *Criminal Justice and Behavior* 34, no. 6 (2007): 752-768. Compares the recidivism rates of former prisoners who were convicted of rape with those of former prisoners who were convicted of child molestation.

Gran, Martin, and Niklas Langstrom. "Actuarial Assessment of Violence Risk: To Weigh or Not to Weigh?" *Criminal Justice and Behavior* 34, no. 1 (2007): 22-36. Addresses the validity of using risk factors in actuarial formulas for the purpose of predicting violent criminal behavior.

Prins, Her. *Will They Do it Again? Risk Assessment and Management in Criminal Justice and Psychiatry*. New York: Routledge, 1999. Using statistics and discussion of real cases, compares and contrasts the low risk of public harm posed by the mentally ill with society's perception of a high risk of harm. Provides recommendations for managing risky behavior on the part of mentally ill persons.

Webster, Christopher D., and Stephen J. Hucker. *Violence Risk: Assessment and Management*. Hoboken, N.J.: John Wiley & Sons, 2007. Focuses on violent offenders and provides suggestions for protecting the rights of these offenders when they are released from mental health facilities and prisons while also protecting the public from harm. Includes a list of variables that should be considered in the process of risk assessment.

**See also:** Alcohol-related offenses; Child abduction and kidnapping; Child abuse; *Daubert v. Merrell Dow Pharmaceuticals*; Forensic psychology; Psychological autopsy; Sexual predation characteristics; Suicide; *Tarasoff* rule.

## Adipocere

**Definition**: Naturally occurring substance produced by dead bodies under certain conditions from the hydrolysis of body fat and a sufficient amount of water or moisture.

**Significance**: Also called grave wax, corpse wax, and mortuary wax, adipocere is commonly formed by the bodies of human beings or animals with sufficient body fat when they lie under wet or moist conditions. The presence of this substance on a human body may help or hinder forensic scientists in estimating the postmortem interval.

The production of adipocere by a body generally requires an anaerobic surrounding (that is, one without free oxygen), a sufficient quantity of body fat (that is, adipose containing connective tissue with lipids present), and any of a variety of bacteria that take oxygen away from other compounds and thus assist in the hydrolysis of the fats. The material was first recognized and described in the seventeenth century, when Sir Thomas Browne wrote in *Hydriotaphia, Urne Buriall* (1658) of encountering the substance while relocating previously buried individuals from an English cemetery. The process of adipocere formation is called saponification, which literally means "soap making" (in times past, soap was made with a combination of animal fat, water, and lye, which produced a grayish-white material that was similar to adipocere in appearance and texture). Because adipose, or body fat, can be either white or brown, adipocere may appear grayish-white or tan in color. It was not until the use of microscopes became widespread during the seventeenth century that scientists began to understand the chemical process of saponification.

Adipocere is an artifact of the decomposition process, and because its formation requires that lipids (fats) be present, it is more commonly seen among animal remains containing comparatively high levels of fat. Among humans, this means that adipocere is found most frequently on the bodies of women, infants, and obese individuals of either sex. In addition, fatter individuals contain more moisture, and fats contain fatty acids that have an affinity to attach to sodium or potassium from the environment. Water assists in this process, and, indeed, adipocere is most often found among tissues that have been kept damp or moist, or even submerged.

It has been suggested that the formation of adipocere on a body may be useful as a guide for forensic scientists in estimating the length of time since death (the postmortem interval, or PMI), much like the appearance of algor, rigor, and livor mortis. However, because adipocere results from a chemical process, the speed with which the substance is formed is temperature-dependent, and, as is true for all other PMI indicators, the rate of formation varies. It appears that the formation of adipocere is speeded up by warmth, but temperature extremes, whether too warm or too cold, impede formation. In addition, because saponification produces a more durable substance than do other processes associated with decomposition, the formation of adipocere can result in a body's retaining facial and other anatomic features well after death.

*Turhon A. Murad*

## Further Reading

Gill-King, Herrell. "Chemical and Ultrastructural Aspects of Decomposition." In *Forensic Taphonomy: The Postmortem Fate of Human Remains*, edited by William D. Haglund and Marcella H. Sorg. Boca Raton, Fla.: CRC Press, 1997.

O'Brien, Tyler G., and Amy C. Kuehner. "Waxing Grave About Adipocere: Soft Tissue Change in an Aquatic Context." *Journal of Forensic Sciences* 52, no. 2 (2007): 294-301.

Spitz, Werner U., ed. *Spitz and Fisher's Medicolegal Investigation of Death: Guidelines for the Application of Pathology to Crime Investigation.* 4th ed. Springfield, Ill.: Charles C Thomas, 2006.

**See also:** Algor mortis; Decomposition of bodies; Forensic entomology; Livor mortis; Mummification; Rigor mortis; Taphonomy.

## Air and water purity

**Definition:** Extent to which natural water and air supplies are free of harmful forms of contamination.

**Significance:** Various forms of chemical and biological contaminants that pollute air and water supplies are responsible for death, disease, climate shifts, and the alteration of fragile ecosystems around the world. Techniques used to investigate the nature and causes of pollution are allied with forensic toxicology.

Although challenges to air and water purity have always existed, the assault has taken on forbidding aspects since the advent of the industrial age. So ubiquitous are the sources of air and water pollution that they have become woven into the fabric of everyday modern life. However, it is important to note that although much pollution comes from the processes of industry and commerce, pollution is also a product of natural biological and geographic processes. It should also be kept in mind that purity and pollution are relative. For example, although oxygen is necessary to animal life, it is highly toxic to certain organisms that flourish in an atmosphere of methane, which would be lethal to human beings.

Human-made pollutants come from the combustion of fuels that power ships, aircraft, motor vehicles, factories, and power-generating plants. Natural pollutants come from the discharges of wildfires and volcanoes. Pollutants also come from chemical discharges and landfill outgassing as well as military operations that generate nuclear fallout, pathogens, and toxic gases. Pollutants even ride the wind in the form of dust.

A notorious example of the damage inflicted when human activities alter the air's chemistry comes in the form of chlorofluorocarbons (CFCs), which find wide applications as refrigerants, insulating foams, and solvents. CFCs eventually make their way into the stratosphere, where the ultraviolet (UV) rays of sunlight break the CFCs' chemical bonds and release their chlorine atoms. As one chlorine atom is capable of breaking apart 100,000 ozone molecules, damage to Earth's ozone layer is great. The ozone layer protects Earth's surface from the damaging UV rays of the sun; without its protection, human beings are vulnerable to immune disorders, skin cancer, and cataracts. Additionally, increased UV radiation can reduce crop yields and cause serious dislocations in the marine food chain.

### Water Quality

The quality of naturally occurring freshwater may be degraded through natural sources such as bedrock salts or sediment containing organic material. Additional degradation of water quality may be caused by human manipulation, such as fertilizers and petroleum products. When water pollution comes from a single source such as a sewage-outflow pipe, it is called point-source pollution; when the exact source of pollution is not as clear, as in agricultural or urban runoff, it is called non-point-source pollution.

The principal water polluters are industry and agriculture. Rain helps to cleanse air of pollutant emissions from motor vehicles, factories, and heating boilers, but the pollutants ultimately find their way into groundwater and streams. More direct forms of water pollution come from industrial discharges, construction detritus, and agricultural runoff. All these forms of pollution change the chemistry of water, changing its acidity, conductivity, and temperature. Nitrogen runoff fertilizes water, causing it to be choked with new vegetation.

The consequences to human society of impure water are alarming. Intractable diarrhea is a leading cause of death around the world among children under five, and its main cause is degraded drinking water. Cholera, a potentially deadly bacterial infection that plagues much of the underdeveloped world, requires only clean drinking water and proper sanitation to be eliminated as a problem. Contaminated drinking water is responsible for up to fourteen thousand deaths every day in developing countries.

Sources of water pollution include sewage, industrial discharges, surface runoff from farms and construction sites, underground storage tank leakage, and acid rain. It is convenient to categorize water contaminants into subgroups: microorganisms, disinfectants, disinfection by-products, inorganic chemicals, organic chemicals, and radionuclides. The U.S. government's Environmental Protection Agency (EPA) lists eighty-six specific water contaminants, along with their sources and potential health effects.

Examples of specific pollutants include alachlor, an herbicide used in row crops that increases human risks of cancer and can also cause eye, liver, and kidney disease. Cadmium, which reaches water supplies from corroded galvanized pipes and discharges from metal refineries, can cause kidney damage. Dioxin is a chemical discharge from factories that causes cancer and reproductive disorders. *Giardia lamblia* is a protozoan parasite found in human and animal waste that often causes gastrointestinal disturbances. Toxaphene, an active

---

## Health Effects of Contaminated Drinking Water

*The U.S. Environmental Protection Agency (EPA) provides this information on acute and chronic health effects related to contaminants in drinking water.*

EPA has set standards for more than 80 contaminants that may occur in drinking water and pose a risk to human health. EPA sets these standards to protect the health of everybody, including vulnerable groups like children. The contaminants fall into two groups according to the health effects that they cause. . . .

Acute effects occur within hours or days of the time that a person consumes a contaminant. People can suffer acute health effects from almost any contaminant if they are exposed to extraordinarily high levels (as in the case of a spill). In drinking water, microbes, such as bacteria and viruses, are the contaminants with the greatest chance of reaching levels high enough to cause acute health effects. Most people's bodies can fight off these microbial contaminants the way they fight off germs, and these acute contaminants typically don't have permanent effects. Nonetheless, when high enough levels occur, they can make people ill, and can be dangerous or deadly for a person whose immune system is already weak due to HIV/AIDS, chemotherapy, steroid use, or another reason.

Chronic effects occur after people consume a contaminant at levels over EPA's safety standards for many years. The drinking water contaminants that can have chronic effects are chemicals (such as disinfection by-products, solvents, and pesticides), radionuclides (such as radium), and minerals (such as arsenic). Examples of the chronic effects of drinking water contaminants are cancer, liver or kidney problems, or reproductive difficulties.

ingredient in insecticides used in cotton farming and cattle production, increases cancer risk and can cause kidney, liver, and thyroid problems. Vinyl chlorides from plastics manufacturing discharges and leaching from polyvinyl chloride pipes also increase cancer risks.

## Air Quality

Air pollution not only threatens the health of human beings but also compromises the well-being of animal and plant life. It degrades bodies of freshwater, thins the atmosphere's protective ozone layer, and creates haze that shrouds the beauty of nature. The EPA attempts to sustain reasonable levels of air purity through regulatory enforcement and voluntary programs, such as Energy Star and Commuter Choice. Through the federal Clean Air Act of 1990, the EPA restricts the amounts of specific pollutants allowed into the atmosphere to help protect public health.

Under the surveillance of the EPA are these broad categories of atmospheric pollutants: aerosols, asbestos, carbon monoxide, chlorofluorocarbons, ground-level ozone, hazardous air pollutants, hydrochlorofluorocarbon refrigerants, lead, mercury, methane gas, nitrogen oxides, particulate matter, propellants, radon, refrigerants, sulfur oxides, and volatile organic compounds. The EPA is armed with government regulations. Through a cooperative effort that involves private industry and state and local governments, the agency calls for the discontinuation of ozone-depleting substances, the elimination of specified toxic chemicals, and the treatment of polluted areas.

To assess air quality, the EPA's Office of Air Quality Planning and Standards (OAQPS) monitors specific pollutants that can harm human health, the environment, and property. All common throughout the United States, these pollutants include sulfur dioxide, particulate matter, nitrogen dioxide, lead, and carbon monoxide. Based on national ambient air quality standards, geographic areas are designated as attainment or nonattainment areas. OAQPS gives the standards more meaning by subdividing them into primary and secondary standards. Primary standards are about issues of health, whereas secondary standards consider damage to crops, vegetation, or buildings. Further, they assess the health effects for their potential long- or short-term damage.

*Richard S. Spira*

## Further Reading

Friedlander, Sheldon K. *Smoke, Dust, and Haze: Fundamentals of Aerosol Dynamics.* 2d ed. New York: Oxford University Press, 2000. Written by a prominent authority on aerosols, this textbook designed for advanced undergraduates and graduate students covers basic concepts, lab techniques, and many practical applications.

Godish, Thad. *Air Quality.* 4th ed. Boca Raton, Fla.: Lewis, 2004. Up-to-date and comprehensive overview, appropriate for both undergraduate and graduate students, covers a wide variety of issues affecting air quality, with attention to atmospheric chemistry and the impact of polluted air on human health and the environment. Also covers public policy issues and risk assessment.

Heinsohn, R. J., and R. L. Kabel. *Sources and Control of Air Pollution.* Upper Saddle River, N.J.: Prentice Hall, 1998. Engineering textbook offers broad coverage of both natural and human-made sources of air pollution and methods for preventing or reducing pollution.

Nathanson, Jerry A. *Basic Environmental Technology: Water Supply, Waste Management, and Pollution Control.* 5th ed. Upper Saddle River, N.J.: Prentice Hall, 2007. Provides a clearly written introduction to water supply, waste management, and pollution control that is ideal for students with limited background in the hard sciences and engineering.

Novotny, Vladimir. *Water Quality: Diffuse Pollution and Watershed Management.* 2d ed. Hoboken, N.J.: John Wiley & Sons, 2003. Useful textbook focuses on all types of water-pollution problems. Especially strong on regulatory laws and judicial decisions.

Viessman, Warren, and Mark J. Hammer. *Water Supply and Pollution Control.* 7th ed. Upper Saddle River, N.J.: Prentice Hall, 2004. Authoritative standard textbook on modern water management issues stresses applications of scientific methods to problems that include pollution.

**See also:** Biodetectors; Biological Weapons Convention of 1972; Biosensors; Chemical Weapons Convention of 1993; Choking; Decontamination methods; Environmental Measurements Laboratory; Food and Drug Administration, U.S.; Forensic toxicology; International Association of Forensic Toxicologists; Lead; Mercury; Mycotoxins; Pathogen transmission.

# Airport security

**Definition:** All legal measures, law-enforcement activities, regulations, and forensic science applications needed to maintain the safety and security of passengers and operational facilities—including aircraft, terminals, and transportation facilities—associated with airline commerce.

**Significance:** As rates of world travel have increased and the threat of international terrorism has grown, airport security measures have evolved to keep pace. Forensic science has contributed a number of technologies and methodologies to the effort to keep airports safe.

Airport security measures have been operative since commercial airline traffic began during the 1920's. Initial measures included the establishment of rules for luggage, boarding, and other aspects of air travel intended to provide safe passage. As the volume and complexity of air traffic increased, so did the emphasis on rules and regulations governing air passengers, aircraft, and airport security. The most basic of these took the form of regulations regarding movement of passengers and their baggage within airports and their access to airport facilities, the airplanes, and the flight tarmac.

As airports grew larger and volumes of freight and passenger traffic increased during and following World War II, the movements of passengers within airport terminals and their access to operational infrastructure of air terminals were further restricted. Luggage restrictions and weight restrictions became routine, as

did requirements concerning passenger identification and boarding passes, but these rules were established to protect passengers from harm and to ensure airport efficiency rather than as deterrents to perceived threats.

The first important changes in airport security followed several incidents in the 1950's in which bombs were planted on aircraft to destroy them in flight for insurance purposes. These were followed with additional security measures taken in the 1960's in response to a number of high-profile hijackings, some of which led to the destruction of aircraft and crews as well as to passenger injuries and deaths. Airlines, agencies, and various governments around the world, including that of the United States, took the (at that time) extraordinary measure of instituting a program of sky marshals to fly on board aircraft. Sky marshals were armed and were charged with identifying and arresting potential menaces as well as with preventing incidents during flight.

Although the sky marshal program was well conceived and well designed for that time, it never received adequate funding to place marshals on every airplane. Hijackings continued to occur, necessitating additional airport security programs. In response, the U.S. Federal Aviation Administration (FAA) required that all passengers and their luggage be thoroughly screened beginning in January, 1973. The airlines contracted this work to private security companies that supplied equipment and trained personnel. The airlines maintained operational control over their airport and aircraft facilities, and the private security companies controlled the screening of carry-on baggage at designated checkpoints prior to passenger entry to the airport waiting rooms, all under the general oversight of FAA officials.

The terrorist attacks on the World Trade Center in New York City and on the Pentagon on September 11, 2001, precipitated immediate and drastic changes in airport security matters that have remained in place. Immediately following the attacks, the federal government mandated that the highest-priority emphasis be placed on the safety and security of passengers, airport facilities, and aircraft at all airports in the United States and most around the world as well. Dramatically increased levels of security were initially reflected in the presence of armed security guards, uniformed local police officers, and even National Guard and active-duty military personnel in some terminals. The military presence was discontinued after a few months; although some passengers were comforted by the open display of weapons, others had expressed alarm.

### Post-9/11 Airport Security

Long-term airport security measures that remain in place since the changes brought about after 9/11 include dramatically increased scrutiny of passengers and their carry-on luggage. This has led to the implementation of a number of measures aimed at passenger behavior. First, people are no longer permitted to leave cars unoccupied at terminals or to leave luggage unattended. Passengers must wait in long lines in which they and their luggage are checked with scanners, metal detectors, and, in some cases, substance-detection dogs. Each individual must present some form of personal identification with a photograph, such as a driver's license or passport, and must agree to extensive searching of luggage. These strictures sometimes lead to long waiting times and travel delays, all of which have been sanctioned by federal authorities; most such measures have met with general passenger approval.

Behind-the-scenes changes in airport security have been equally dramatic. Each airport, similar to a small town, now has a dedicated police force hired specifically to maintain airport security. Depending on locality, the airport force may be a private policing agency or a part of the local police force with a police station maintained at the airport. Most airport police forces also include dogs that have been trained to detect explosives and drugs.

Airports have tested and purchased a number of technologically advanced and very expensive apparatuses that permit rapid scanning of baggage and passengers. These include X-ray backscatter scanners that can detect hidden weapons and explosives on passengers as well as automated explosive detection system (EDS) machines that are able to scan hundreds of pieces of luggage per hour. New and improved computed axial tomography (CAT) scanners have been developed that provide three-dimensional images, thereby more effectively detailing luggage contents; this advancement promotes rapid and accurate identification of hidden weapons, bombs, and packets of chemicals.

### Forensic Applications in Airport Security

Airlines and airline facilities must be protected from all forms of terrorism, including bombs planted in luggage, airplane hijackers, and attacks using chemical or biological weapons. Since September 11, 2001, the U.S. government has poured millions of dollars per year into improving airport security, but security breaches still occur. For the most part, these involve identity fraud, drug trafficking, possession of explosives or weapons, or possession of

---

## Baggage-Screening Technology

*The Transportation Security Administration (TSA), a component of the U.S. Department of Homeland Security, is responsible for the security of the nation's transportation systems, including highways, railroads, buses, mass-transit systems, ports, and airports. The TSA provides this description of one of the security measures in place at American airports.*

Ever wonder what happens to your bag once you check it with your airline? We screen every bag—100% of all bags—placed on an airplane, whether taken as carry-on or checked with an airline. With nearly 2 million people flying each day, it's a Herculean task.

We are able to meet this requirement by relying on Explosive Detection System (EDS) machines, which work like the MRI machines in your doctor's office. Through a sophisticated analysis of each checked bag, the EDS machines can quickly determine if a bag contains a potential threat or not. If a weapon or explosive is detected, the machines alert our security officers so they can manage the bag appropriately. In some cases, the alarm is quickly resolved and in others law enforcement and the bomb squad may be called in.

international contraband, harmful chemicals, or biotoxins. Forensic science plays an important role in the prevention and investigation of such security breaches.

The first line of defense against terrorist threats to airport security involves a system of enclosure and screening that prevents access to aircraft and tarmacs. All airports in the United States are surrounded by tall fences or walls, making it nearly impossible for anyone to sneak in. In addition to constant video surveillance throughout airports, security personnel watch every checkpoint, entry, and exit. Upon entrance, both persons and luggage pass through metal detectors. Luggage is also exposed to X rays and may be searched. Individuals are also required to agree to noninvasive searches if asked to do so. Any person who is deemed a threat is subject to more intensive searches.

Modern airport security measures also involve more clandestine operations, such as profiling and the comparison of passenger names and identifications against lists of known terrorists. Airport security profiling involves generalizations about the personality types and physical characteristics of persons who may pose threats to other passengers. Security personnel are urged to be on the lookout for particular "types." Therefore, while random baggage and clothing checks are conducted, owing to the nature of many international terrorist attacks, ethnic profiling may also occur. Passengers on flights into the United States from overseas are also subject to profiling and comparison against terrorist "watch lists." If it is discovered that the passenger list of an inbound aircraft includes a known or suspected terrorist, the plane may be turned back, diverted to land at a designated high-security airport, or refused landing permission anywhere in the United States.

Anyone found to be carrying a weapon in an airport is immediately apprehended and the weapon removed. Forensic scientists then confirm and attest in court that the object was cause for the subject's arrest. In the case of gun possession, firearms analyses are performed in a laboratory to determine the model of the weapon and to recover the serial numbers if removed.

Hidden explosives may be detected using modern explosive detectors that use chromatography to detect volatile gases given off by explosive mixtures. Drug-detection and bomb-sniffing dogs are led by specialized teams at customs checkpoints and often can be seen roaming common rooms in airports as well. If a suitcase or other device is suspected of containing harmful material, it is often further tested with a mechanical "chemical sniffer." If hazardous material is found, be it illegal drugs, explosive material, chemicals, or other toxins, the individual is apprehended and held until forensic scientists can conduct toxicological and chemical composition tests to determine the identity of the substance. If the substance is determined to be an illicit one, the individual is further detained to face charges of possession of an illegal substance.

The detection of possible biological weapons is much more difficult than detection of other kinds of harmful substances. However, if airport security authorities are concerned, they can seize any suspicious substance and submit it for forensic analysis to determine what it is. Unfortunately, no standard procedure yet exists among airline or FAA officials for dealing with possible biological weapons.

A valid driver's license is sufficient identification for a person flying within the United States; a passport is needed to fly internationally. Both these forms of identification, however, provide merely photographs and some additional personal information about the appearance, age, and residence of the individual. The future of individual identification in respect to airport security is likely to involve screening systems based in biometrics—that is, human recognition based on physical traits, such as fingerprints. Biometric identification systems include fingerprint scanning, iris and retina scanning, and facial recognition technologies. In some cases, handwriting and voice recognition are also used to confirm identities.

Among the airport security measures that have been put in place in the United States since September 11, 2001, those involving biometric technologies have become particularly controversial. Some feel comforted by the prospect of being identified by their own fingerprints or retinal images, whereas others feel that these methods of identification are invasive and violate personal privacy. Also, many fear the damage that could be done if hackers or identity thieves gain access to the databases in which biometric data are stored.

Above all other matters related to airport security, Americans are often frustrated with the long lines, personal questions, baggage and clothing searches, and other time-consuming measures they are subject to when they fly. Many believe, however, that these inconveniences are a small price to pay for increased passenger safety. With increasing technological capabilities, the U.S. Department of Homeland Security and Department of Defense are working on measures to expedite the security process while ensuring efficiency, effectiveness, and accurate personal identification. The next decision that Americans who fly commercially will probably have to make is whether they would rather put up with the waiting and frustration or have their fingerprints and retinal scans stored in government databases.

*Dwight G. Smith*

**Further Reading**

Bullock, Jane, and George Haddow. *Introduction to Homeland Security*. 2d ed. Boston: Butterworth-Heinemann, 2006. Provides a basic introduction to the operations of the U.S. Department of Homeland Security. Outlines certain types of threats and their prevention, addresses responses to threats, discusses the uses of communication and other technologies in security measures, and speculates on the future evolution of such measures in the United States. Appendixes include a number of related legal documents.

Sweet, Kathleen M. *Aviation and Airport Security: Terrorism and Safety Concerns*. Upper Saddle River, N.J.: Pearson Prentice Hall, 2004. Provides a historical overview of aviation terrorism and discusses the changes in security measures through the years, particularly after September 11, 2001.

Thomas, Andrew R. *Aviation Insecurity: The New Challenges of Air Travel*. Amherst, N.Y.: Prometheus Books: 2003. An aviation security expert details the shortcomings of airport security systems from the days preceding September 11, 2001, through the implementation of changes following that terrorist attack.

Wilkinson, Paul, and Brian M. Jenkins, eds. *Aviation Terrorism and Security*. Portland, Oreg.: Frank Cass, 1999. Collection of essays includes a review of past incidents of aviation terrorism and discussion of the trends seen in security responses. Other chapters address the politics of aviation terrorism and security in the United States and the probable directions of global air security in the future.

**See also:** Biological terrorism; Biological weapon identification; Biometric eye scanners; Canine substance detection; Closed-circuit television surveillance; Facial recognition technology; Improvised explosive devices; Metal detectors; Racial profiling; September 11, 2001, victim identification.

---

## Alcohol-related offenses

**Definition**: Violations of the law in which consumption of alcohol is a fundamental component.

**Significance:** Alcohol is a legally available drug that has significant impairing effects on a number of aspects of human cognition and performance. Given that alcohol is used pervasively among the general population, alcohol consumption is a significant element in a wide range of criminal cases. Alcohol may play a contributory role in a variety of offenses, even when the presence of alcohol at concentrations associated with significant intoxication does not form the basis of the offenses.

Ethanol, commonly referred to as alcohol, is a drug whose effects include depression of the function of the central nervous system (CNS). As is true for other CNS depressants, the severity of alcohol's effects increases with dose, potentially causing significant impairment of psychomotor skills (such as those required for safe driving) and, ultimately, fatal respiratory depression or circulatory collapse.

### Effects of Alcohol

At low blood alcohol concentrations (BACs), the effects of alcohol consumption include euphoria, talkativeness, and reductions in anxiety and inhibitions. At progressively greater BACs, speech may become slurred, and dizziness or a significant loss of coordination may be observed. Further increases to BAC may be accompanied by drowsiness, emotional lability, confusion, and loss of consciousness. Uncontrolled overdose can result in fatal respiratory depression.

In addition to these relatively obvious symptoms, alcohol causes BAC-dependent impairment to a number of faculties related to psychomotor performance, including the ability to divide attention over multiple tasks, reaction time, risk or hazard perception, and motor coordination. All these faculties are essential for the safe operation of a motor vehicle. Consequently,

one of the most obvious offenses directly related to alcohol consumption is impaired driving, or operation of a motor vehicle with a BAC in excess of the legal limit. Despite the fact that the impairing effects of alcohol on the ability to drive safely have been studied extensively and publicized widely through various public education programs, the incidence of impaired driving offenses remains high in many jurisdictions. Driving under the influence of alcohol is an example of an offense for which the consumption of alcohol and the associated intoxication form the basis of the offense. In some jurisdictions, other legal offenses are also premised specifically on alcohol consumption; these include public intoxication and the consumption of alcohol by minors.

The consumption of alcohol may also be associated with an increased probability of occurrence of a number of other kinds of offenses. One such offense is sexual assault. A significant amount of research has examined the incidence of the use of drugs and alcohol in cases of sexual assault, especially those in which surreptitious

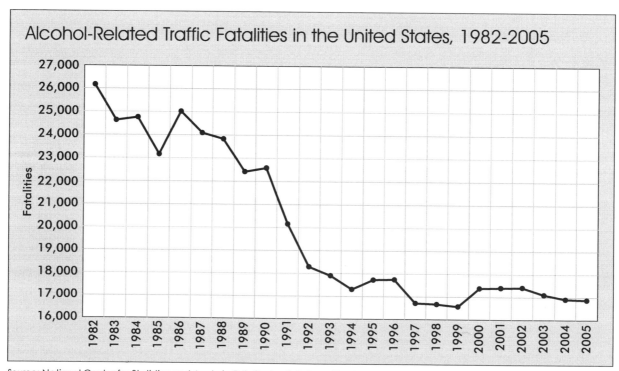

*Source:* National Center for Statistics and Analysis. Fatality Analysis Reporting System, 2008.

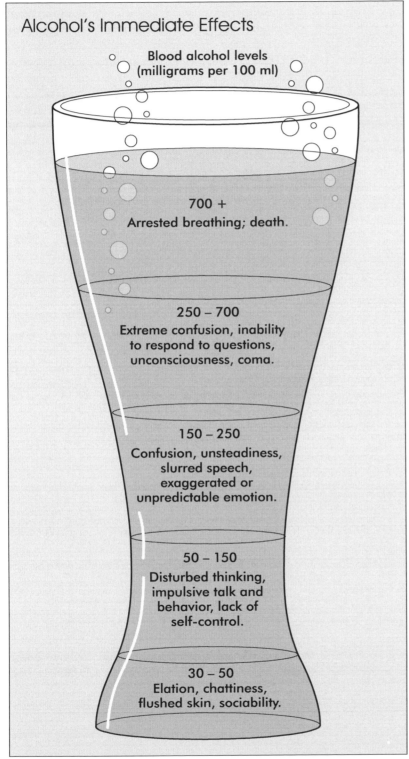

## Alcohol's Immediate Effects

Blood alcohol levels (milligrams per 100 ml)

**700 +**
Arrested breathing; death.

**250 – 700**
Extreme confusion, inability to respond to questions, unconsciousness, coma.

**150 – 250**
Confusion, unsteadiness, slurred speech, exaggerated or unpredictable emotion.

**50 – 150**
Disturbed thinking, impulsive talk and behavior, lack of self-control.

**30 – 50**
Elation, chattiness, flushed skin, sociability.

The presence of 30-50 milligrams of alcohol per every 100 milliliters of blood, which represents the effects of an average drink (a glass of beer or wine or an ounce of hard liquor), has immediate effects; as the amount increases, the effects progress toward death.

drug administration (so-called drink spiking) is suspected. Over a significant number of jurisdictions worldwide, the most common finding in such studies has been the presence of significant amounts of alcohol in the complainants. In cases of sexual assault, the consumption of alcohol by both complainant and assailant may be important. From the perspective of the complainant, alcohol suppresses behavioral inhibitions, possibly influencing decision-making skills or risk perception. Furthermore, excessive alcohol consumption often leads to substantial impairment and perhaps even unconsciousness, which can place an individual under considerable risk for attack. From the perspective of the assailant, alcohol's suppression of behavioral inhibitions may also be dangerous, but further complications may take the form of alcohol's interference with the perception of social cues.

### Forensic Analysis and Interpretation of Evidence

Forensic analysis of the role of alcohol in a particular case typically requires an understanding of the extent of intoxication or impairment, which, in turn, is reflected by the BAC at the time of the incident. In practice, measurement of BAC involves the collection of blood samples or breath measurements, depending on the type of offense (for example, breath analysis is typically done in driving-related offenses, whereas blood sampling is generally done in the course of the examination of victims of sexual assault). Breath alcohol analysis uses instrumentation specifically designed for that particular purpose; analysis of blood samples is generally done by enzymatic methods or gas chromatography. Once a BAC measurement is made, a correction is usually applied to account for the amount of alcohol eliminated from the blood through metabolism and other processes between the time of the incident and the time of sample collection. This provides an estimated BAC range at the time of the incident from which the likely extent of intoxication or impairment may be interpreted.

CNS function is enhanced when other depressant drugs are used in combination with alcohol, with potentially fatal consequences. Additionally, the combination of alcohol with other drugs not associated with CNS depression (such as cocaine or cannabis) may lead to significantly enhanced impairment or unexpected symptoms that may nonetheless contribute to some kinds of offenses. Consequently, more comprehensive forensic toxicological analysis may be warranted in some cases.

*James Watterson*

## Further Reading

Baselt, Randall C. *Drug Effects on Psychomotor Performance*. Foster City, Calif.: Biomedical Publications, 2001. Comprehensive reference work presents information on the impairing effects of a wide range of therapeutic and illicit drugs.

Brunton, Laurence L., John S. Lazo, and Keith L. Parker, eds. *Goodman and Gilman's The Pharmacological Basis of Therapeutics*. 11th ed. New York: McGraw-Hill, 2006. Authoritative advanced textbook explains basic pharmacological principles and the specific pharmacological features of therapeutic agents. Includes some discussion of illicit agents.

Garriott, James C., ed. *Medical-Legal Aspects of Alcohol*. 4th ed. Tucson, Ariz.: Lawyers & Judges Publishing, 2003. Comprehensive work covers all aspects of forensic alcohol toxicology, including analysis of biological samples, and alcohol pharmacology, including the physiological and psychomotor effects of alcohol consumption and the time course (pharmacokinetics) of alcohol within the body.

Karch, Steven B., ed. *Drug Abuse Handbook*. 2d ed. Boca Raton, Fla.: CRC Press, 2007. Describes the pharmacological, physiological, and pathological aspects of drug abuse in general, and individual chapters address specific compounds, such as alcohol, as well as specific issues related to drug abuse, such as workplace drug testing.

Levine, Barry, ed. *Principles of Forensic Toxicology*. 2d ed., rev. Washington, D.C.: American Association for Clinical Chemistry, 2006. Introductory textbook describes the analytical, chemical, and pharmacological aspects of a variety of drugs of forensic relevance.

**See also:** Actuarial risk assessment; Analytical instrumentation; Breathalyzer; Drug and alcohol evidence rules; Forensic toxicology; Gas chromatography; Halcion; Toxicological analysis.

## Algor mortis

**Definition:** Cooling of the body after death.

**Significance:** Because the temperature of the human body begins to cool at the moment of death, observation of algor mortis is one of the ways in which forensic scientists attempt to estimate the postmortem interval.

Investigators of homicides use various techniques to estimate the length of time since death, or the postmortem interval (PMI). It is likely that before the techniques employed by modern investigators gained wide acceptance, early hunters and gatherers distinguished the same stages of decomposition following death. Such stages include the fresh, bloat, active, and advanced decay stages versus the stage at which remains become dry or skeletonized. However, the indicators that modern forensic investigators consider classic for suggesting PMI are those of algor mortis (cooling of the body), rigor mortis (stiffening of the body), and livor mortis (discoloration of the body from gravitational blood seepage).

Because decomposition reflects chemical processes and all chemical processes are temperature-dependent, the acquisition of many of the conditions noticed after death is affected by temperature. That is, higher temperatures generally speed chemical reactions, and lower temperatures slow them. In algor mortis (the term derives from the Latin words *algor*, meaning "coolness," and *mortis*, meaning "death"), the body is expected to cool until its temperature matches that of the surrounding environment.

If a body cools at a uniform rate, the measure of its temperature decrease following death can assist in the accurate determination of the elapsed time since death. The formula used for making such an estimate, known as the Glaister equation, is based on the notion that a dead body is expected to lose 1.5 degrees Fahrenheit per hour. Because the metabolic processes associated with maintaining life among humans generates a normal body temperature of nearly 98.4 degrees Fahrenheit, the Glaister equation estimates the approximate postmortem interval in hours by subtracting the body temperature (measured in degrees Fahrenheit at the rectum or deep within the liver) from 98.4 degrees and dividing the result by 1.5. Thus, if a decedent's temperature is found to be 90.2 degrees Fahrenheit at the time of the body's discovery, the decedent would be suggested to have died approximately 5.5 hours earlier.

After death, a body cools by radiation, conduction, and convection, so many physical factors can influence algor mortis. One of these is ambient temperature, or, more precisely, the difference between ambient and body temperatures. If, for example, a body were to be discovered in a warm sauna, it might not have cooled at all. Furthermore, the body temperature of the decedent might not have been normal at the time of death owing to the effects of exercise, illness, or infection. Additionally, the amount of subcutaneous fat present, the lightness or heaviness of any clothing worn at the time of death, and any number of insulating coverings can alter the rate at which a body might be expected to cool. Any such variables can alter the effectiveness of employing the Glaister equation to estimate the postmortem interval.

*Turhon A. Murad*

**Further Reading**

Randall, Brad. *Death Investigation: The Basics*. Tucson, Ariz.: Galen Press, 1997.

Saferstein, Richard. *Criminalistics: An Introduction to Forensic Science*. 9th ed. Upper Saddle River, N.J.: Pearson Prentice Hall, 2007.

Spitz, Werner U., ed. *Spitz and Fisher's Medicolegal Investigation of Death: Guidelines for the Application of Pathology to Crime Investigation*. 4th ed. Springfield, Ill.: Charles C Thomas, 2006.

**See also:** Adipocere; Body farms; Decomposition of bodies; Forensic pathology; Livor mortis; Rigor mortis; Taphonomy.

## ALI standard

**Definition**: Statement of the insanity defense that has become widely accepted in federal and state jurisdictions throughout the United States.

**Significance:** The American Law Institute's carefully formulated insanity defense standard was created to overcome the shortcomings of earlier tests of insanity, such as the M'Naghten rule and the irresistible impulse rule.

During the 1950's and early 1960's, the American Law Institute (ALI) developed the Model Penal Code, the 1962 draft of which contained a statement of the insanity defense composed by a panel of judges, legal scholars, and behavioral scientists. It stated:

A person is not responsible for criminal conduct

if at the time of such conduct as a result of mental disease or defect he lacks substantial capacity either to appreciate the criminality (wrongfulness) of his conduct or to conform his conduct to the requirements of law. . . . the terms "mental disease or defect" do not include an abnormality manifested only by repeated criminal or otherwise antisocial conduct.

In the 1972 case of *United States v. Brawner*, the U.S. Court of Appeals for the District of Columbia adopted the ALI rule, and it became the standard used in almost all federal courts and in twenty-two U.S. state jurisdictions.

The ALI standard is considered a more precisely worded amalgam of two earlier insanity tests, namely, the M'Naghten rule and the irresistible impulse rule. The M'Naghten rule, developed in Great Britain in 1843, was the first formal test of legal insanity. As a test of legal insanity, it focused on whether the defendant's insanity deprived the defendant of a certain kind of cognitive ability, that of knowing what he or she was doing or knowing the difference between right and wrong. The ALI standard uses the broader term "appreciate" instead of "know" yet still retains the key idea of cognitive impairment.

Many jurisdictions had augmented the M'Naghten test with the irresistible impulse rule to allow for cases in which mental disease or defect impedes a person's power to choose. The ALI standard replaces the somewhat narrow and misleading phrase "irresistible impulse" with the person's not being able "to conform" his or her "conduct to the requirements of law," thus capturing the underlying idea of volitional impairment. In the federal Insanity Defense Reform Act of 1984, the volitional impairment part of the ALI standard was eliminated as part of the definition of the insanity defense.

The ALI rule was also drawn in such a way as to avoid the looseness of two similar legal insanity tests, the New Hampshire rule and the Durham rule. Both tests framed the issue of legal insanity in terms of whether the criminal act was a product of mental disease. They were criticized on the grounds that in practice they resulted in "undue dominance of experts" in the courtroom, specifically, that the testimony of forensic psychiatrists carried too much weight and encroached on the proper role of the jury.

*Mario Morelli*

**Further Reading**

Moore, Michael. *Law and Psychiatry: Rethinking the Relationship*. New York: Cambridge University Press, 1984.

Rogers, Richard, and Daniel W. Shuman. *Fundamentals of Forensic Practice: Mental Health and Criminal Law*. New York: Springer, 2005.

**See also:** Forensic psychiatry; Guilty but mentally ill plea; Insanity defense; Irresistible impulse rule; Legal competency; *Mens rea*.

# American Academy of Forensic Sciences

**Date:** Formed in 1948

**Identification:** Nonprofit professional organization created to improve, administer, and achieve justice through the application of science to the legal system.

**Significance:** With a membership made up of forensic scientists from all the field's major specialties, the American Academy of Forensic Sciences represents forensic science and its professionals to the public, offers credibility for their expert court testimony through board certification, and promotes educational and research opportunities for members.

In 1948, a small group of pathologists, psychiatrists, criminalists, and lawyers formed the American Academy of Forensic Sciences (AAFS) to apply science to the law. The AAFS has become the primary organization for professional forensic scientists, representing some six thousand members from across the United States, Canada, and more than fifty other countries. The society represents all the major forensic science disciplines, with sections including Criminalistics, Digital Forensics, Engineering Sciences, General, Odontology, Pathology/Biology, Physical Anthropology, Psychiatry and Behavioral Science, Questioned Documents, and Toxicology. AAFS members include physicians, pathologists, dentists, toxicologists, physicists, engineers, physical anthropologists, attorneys, and other forensic science specialists.

Functions of the society (in association with the Forensic Sciences Foundation) include the promotion of forensic science education through the publication of newsletters, symposia, and the flagship peer-reviewed journal the *Journal of Forensic Sciences*, which was launched in 1956, and through sponsorship of an annual meeting each February. The AAFS also administers board certification exams, continuing education credit (for physicians, dentists, chemists, nurses, and attorneys), and training seminars for members to advance their scientific accuracy and credibility. The AAFS offers job placement, scholarship, and grant opportunities for its members as well as career information for all persons interested in forensic science; the academy also supports research in the forensic science fields and provides ethical oversight in the practice of forensic science.

The AAFS oversees the Forensic Science Education Programs Accreditation Commission, known as FEPAC, which is dedicated to enhancing the quality of college-level academic forensic science education through a formal evaluation and recognition process. FEPAC sets quality standards for undergraduate and graduate forensic science programs and administers their accreditation.

Categories of membership in the AAFS are student affiliate, trainee affiliate, associate member, member, and fellow. The academy's stringent membership requirements include (for associate member and higher) proof of active engagement in and significant contributions to the field of forensic science as well as a minimum education of a baccalaureate degree from an accredited college or university. Each section within the AAFS also has its own additional requirements for membership. Applications for membership are approved only at the annual meeting each February.

*Donna C. Boyd*

**Further Reading**

Gaensslen, R. E., Howard A. Harris, and Henry C. Lee. *Introduction to Forensic Science and Criminalistics.* New York: McGraw-Hill, 2008.
Houck, Max M., and Jay A. Siegel. *Fundamentals of Forensic Science.* Burlington, Mass.: Elsevier Academic Press, 2006.

**See also:** American Society of Crime Laboratory Directors; Ethics; European Network of Forensic Science Institutes; Expert witnesses; Federal Bureau of Investigation Forensic Science Research and Training Center; Forensic Science Service; International Association for Identification; International Association of Forensic Nurses; International Association of Forensic Sciences; Training and licensing of forensic professionals.

# American Law Institute standard. *See ALI standard*

# American Journal of Forensic Medicine and Pathology

**Definition:** Attracting article submissions from prominent forensic pathologists, lawyers, and criminologists with associated expertise, *The American Journal of Forensic Medicine and Pathology* documents noteworthy current global protocols, and forensic medical practices.

**Significance:** Each issue of the journal features peer-reviewed articles on new examination and documentation procedures. In addition, stimulating discussions regarding the expanding role of forensic pathologists in human rights protection, drug abuse prevention, suicide, and occupational and environmental health, are among a multitude of diverse and intellectually challenging topics that satisfy the reader's curiosity. Articles embody original research and case reports that have not been formerly published and represent rigorous submission requirements.

*The American Journal of Forensic Medicine and Pathology* is published quarterly (4 issues/year) and individual subscriptions include full-text online access to all current and back issues. Journal articles are divided into four main headings: (1) introduction, (2) materials and methods, (3) results, and (4) discussion. The start year for the journal is 1980 and it is published in the United States.

Editorial board members include: Editor-in-Chief, Associate Editors, Honorary Editor, Editorial Board and an International Board of Editors. *The American Journal of Forensic Medicine and Pathology* offers electronic ahead-of-print articles online and prior to print publication that have been peer-reviewed and accepted for publication in the journal. These papers can be cited using the access date and unique DOI number. Any final changes in manuscripts are edited at print publication and reflect the final electronic version of the issue.

The journal offers a variety of features that include: case reports, technical notes on new examination devices, and reports of medicolegal practices abroad – including war crimes and natural disaster investigations. Abbreviations are defined at first mention in the passage to enhance readability, clarity, and understanding. Authors offer appropriate acknowledgement of all forms of contributor involvement that led to the article submission in an acknowledgements paragraph. *The American Journal of Forensic Medicine and Pathology* emphasizes that author responsibility includes assurance that patient anonymity is carefully protected and any human subject experimental investigation reported in the manuscript must be performed with informed consent. Guidelines are vigorously applied for experimental investigation with human subjects as required by the authors' affiliated institution(s). All identifying information is removed from the manuscript except content that otherwise has proof of informed consent from the patient. Another anonymity safeguard: a black bar placed across the eyes is not considered appropriate protocol to guarantee patient confidentiality.

Appropriate use of the English language is a requirement for publication. Authors who have difficulty in expressing their writing in English seek editorial support with grammar and style to enhance the clarity and readability of their manuscript. All figures include brief strategically placed and specific legends that offer readers timely image clarification. Additionally, the journal may present color images that enhance presentation.

Authors consult the *Council of Biology Editors Style Guide* (available from the Council of Science Editors, 9650 Rockville Pike, Bethesda, MD 20814) or other standard sources for universally accepted abbreviations. Full term notations are observed for each abbreviation at its first use, unless it is a standard unit of measure. The authors are responsible for the accuracy of references cited in manuscript submissions. *The American Medical Association Manual of Style* (9th edition). *Stedman's Medical Dictionary* (27th edition) and *Merriam Webster's Collegiate Dictionary* (10th edition) are recommended standard references.

Journal ranking commonly reflects the evaluation of an academic journal's contribution and distinction. The intent: to reflect the position of a journal within its discipline, the relative complexity of being published in that journal, and the prestige associated with that accomplishment. *The American Journal of Forensic Medicine and Pathology* has the following ranking: Medicine, Legal 15/16 and Pathology 72/76. The impact factor is .624, an annual Journal Citation Reports®*(SCI®)* calculation of the frequency with which the "average article" in a journal has been cited in a particular year or period.

*Thomas E. Baker and Jane Piland-Baker*

## Further Reading

www.amjforensicmedicine.com. This website is an official source of information for *The American Journal of Forensic Medicine and Pathology*. Notably, www.amjforensicmedicine.com offers readers a featured job search option for related employment opportunities.

# American Society of Crime Laboratory Directors

**Date:** Founded in 1974

**Identification:** Organization of forensic laboratory professionals that provides a forum for the discussion of laboratory management issues and promotes improvements in forensic techniques and services.

**Significance:** Through their interaction in the American Society of Crime Laboratory Directors, forensic laboratory managers advanced the standards of labs in North America and internationally and also secured public recognition for the need to require accredited laboratory analysis of forensic evidence.

Dr. Briggs Johnston White (1911-1994), a chemist who served as director of the Laboratory Division of the Federal Bureau of Investigation (FBI), envisioned forming the American Society of Crime Laboratory Directors (ASCLD) to encourage local, state, and federal managers of U.S. forensic laboratories and forensic science programs to share their experiences and suggestions for reinforcing the professionalism of forensic laboratories. In December, 1973, approximately thirty crime laboratory directors participated in a symposium at the FBI Academy in Quantico, Virginia, to discuss White's ideas. In fall, 1974, the laboratory directors returned to Quantico to organize ASCLD, designating White as chairman. Officers and a board of directors oversee ASCLD administration, with committees addressing specific needs. North American and international forensic professionals who oversee crime laboratories or associated scientific, educational, or legal work qualify for ASCLD membership categories. The ASCLD code of ethics outlines members' accountability to their profession and the public, and the organization's "Guidelines for Forensic Laboratory Management Practices" lists lab managers' duties, including the evaluation of employees and procedures.

ASCLD hosts meetings every year at which members and other forensic professionals can participate in workshops and discussions on topics relevant to the management of crime laboratories, such as personnel and accreditation. Also addressed are scientific and technological advances in forensic tests and techniques used to evaluate evidence in laboratories. Since 1994, ASCLD has presented the Briggs White Award annually to recognize notable forensic science laboratory leaders.

The association also distributes several publications, including *ASCLD News*, *Crime Laboratory Digest*, and *Crime Lab Minute*, which is posted on the ASCLD Web site. ASCLD guides outline forensic laboratory management practices for individual topics such as arson, and the association's laboratory accreditation manuals specify current standards. ASCLD established the National Forensic Science Technology Center (NFSTC) to improve laboratories by aiding crime laboratory directors and personnel to gain proficiency in forensics work. In 1981, the association's Committee on Laboratory Evaluation and Standards became the ASCLD Committee on Laboratory Accreditation and began evaluating U.S. state police laboratories. By 1993, the autonomous American Society of Crime Laboratory Directors/Laboratory Accreditation Board (ASCLD/LAB) was focused on examining North American and foreign laboratories because of complaints concerning inferior forensic work. The FBI Laboratory Division received accreditation from ASCLD/LAB in September, 1998. Approximately 350 laboratories, including other U.S. federal forensic laboratories, had secured accreditation by late 2006. Several states have passed legislation making the accreditation of government forensic laboratories a requirement for representatives of those labs to present evidence in courts.

As members of the Coalition of Forensic Science Organizations, ASCLD and ASCLD/LAB supported the National Forensic Science Improvement Act, which was enacted in December, 2000. This federal law provides for the distribution of federal funds to state and local crime laboratories. Starting in 2007, ASCLD representatives offered their insights to a National Academy of Sciences committee assessing how to advance and regulate scientific forensic investigations. In 2009, ASCLD president Dean Gialamas and successor Beth Greene detailed that organization's response to the resulting report, *Strengthening Forensic Science in the United States: A Path Forward*. ASCLD supported proposals to standardize crime laboratory practices, educate forensic science researchers regarding new technologies and processes, and secure sufficient, consistent funds to perform scientific investigations. In 2009, the ASCLD began publishing *Forensic Science Policy and Management: An International Journal*. The ASCLD prepares position statements regarding emerging issues such as the 2013 SAFER Act.

In February 2014, the ASCLD board of directors issued a statement regarding the National Commission on Forensic Science, requesting more crime laboratory leaders serve on that commission.

*Elizabeth D. Schafer*

## Further Reading

Carr, Andrew J. "Accrediting the Forensic Sciences: Computer Forensics." M.S. thesis, Utica College, 2012. Examines efforts to strengthen scientific aspects of forensic practices, focusing on issues associated with digital forensics, by the ASCLD standardizing crime laboratory requirements and accrediting labs. Discusses supporters and opponents of ASCLD.

Dao, James. "Lab's Errors in '82 Killing Force Review of Virginia DNA Cases." *The New York Times*, May 7, 2005, p. A1. Reports how Virginia central crime laboratory's DNA forensic investigators' mistakes impacted people who were convicted and imprisoned based on that laboratory's testing of DNA evidence. States that the ASCLD's assessment of how that laboratory's managers and personnel functioned and were influenced by political issues resulted in the retesting of evidence.

Lueck, Thomas J. "Sloppy Police Lab Work Leads to Retesting of Drug Evidence." *The New York Times*, December 4, 2007, p. B1. Criticizes New York Police Department crime laboratory for mishandling drug evidence, describing the state inspector general's examination of personnel and administrators. Comments that laboratory representatives did not tell the ASCLD regarding unscientific practices at that laboratory and notes efforts to restore professional testing methods.

National Research Council. *Strengthening Forensic Science in the United States: A Path Forward*. Washington, D.C: The National Academies Press, 2009. Comprehensive study outlining issues affecting the effective performance of forensic science professionals and the credibility of evidence they present in legal forums, citing results of flawed investigations. Incorporating ASCLD representatives' ideas, suggests how to achieve and regulate higher quality laboratories and scientific research and procedures in various forensic disciplines.

St. Clair, Jami J. *Crime Laboratory Management*. San Diego, CA: Academic Press, 2002. A former ASCLD president advises forensic science laboratory officials how to develop their workplaces to meet professional standards by maintaining competent employees who have credentials and knowledge to use the most precise, accurate, and current technology and scientific methods to evaluate evidence. Provides information regarding diverse aspects of overseeing crime laboratories.

Young, Tina, and Patrick J. Ortmeier. *Crime Scene Investigation: The Forensic Technician's Field Manual*. Upper Saddle River, NJ: Pearson/Prentice Hall, 2011. Educational text discusses the numerous roles associated with forensic personnel documenting and processing sites where crimes occurred with specific instructions for conducting this work based on ASCLD standards. Supplemented with illustrations, examples of situations people might encounter at scenes, and practice laboratory projects.

**See also:** American Academy of Forensic Sciences; Courts and forensic evidence; Crime laboratories; DNA fingerprinting; Ethics; European Network of Forensic Science Institutes; Federal Bureau of Investigation Laboratory; Forensic Science Service; Quality control of evidence; Training and licensing of forensic professionals.

# Amphetamines

**Definition**: Members of a class of drugs that contain an amphetamine base. These drugs are classified as stimulants, meaning they increase energy levels, reduce fatigue, and cause psychological exhilaration.

**Significance:** Despite intense effort on the part of both legislative and law-enforcement personnel, the number of users of amphetamines continues to rise. The popularity of these drugs is an ongoing concern because chronic use of amphetamines can produce severe mental and physical problems. These drugs are of particular interest to law enforcement because clandestine methamphetamine laboratories pose a threat to neighborhoods, the environment, and investigating officials.

In the United States, the use of controlled substances is governed at the federal level by the Controlled Substances Act of 1970. The most strongly controlled substances are listed in Schedule I of the act, and those under the least control are listed in Schedule V. Amphetamines, along with cocaine, morphine, and phencyclidine (PCP), are listed in Schedule II. Drugs in this class have a high potential for abuse and also have accepted medical uses within the United States (with severe restrictions). Abuse of Schedule II drugs may lead to severe psychological dependence, physical dependence, or both.

Amphetamines are easy to produce, cheap to buy, and cause effects in the body similar to those of cocaine. Most illicit, or "street," amphetamines are actually methamphetamine, which is particularly potent and has long-lasting effects. Street names for amphetamines and methamphetamine include meth, crank, krank, crystal, glass, ice, pep pills, speed, uppers, peanut brittle, and tweak. These names often reflect particular ways the drugs appear; for example, ice is a very pure form, whereas peanut brittle is less so. The street price for one gram of methamphetamine ranges from twenty to three hundred dollars.

## Manufacture

The high demand for methamphetamine, along with significant profit potential, has resulted in the production of the drug in thousands of clandestine laboratories, or "clan labs." "Super labs" are clan labs that are capable of producing seventy-five to one hundred pounds of methamphetamine in each production cycle. In comparison, "stove-top labs" typically produce only one to four ounces per batch. Production of one pound of the drug can result in from five to seven pounds of hazardous waste. Most of this waste ends up dumped on the ground or flushed into streams or sewage systems.

The synthetic route by which methamphetamine is prepared is widely known, and the required chemicals are readily available. The three most common production routes are the P2P (phenyl-2-propanone) amalgam method, the hydroiodic acid and red phosphorus reduction method, and the Birch reduction method. Ephedrine and pseudoephedrine, which can be found in many over-the-counter cold remedies, are key starting materials in the production of methamphetamine. Depending on the synthetic pathway, other important materials include iodine, red phosphorus, hydrogen chloride gas, and anhydrous ammonia. The U.S. government has regulated the sale and use of some of these chemicals in an effort to curb production of methamphetamine.

## Routes of Ingestion

Amphetamines may be smoked, snorted, injected, or taken orally in pill form. Methamphetamine is often smoked; the drug is placed in a glass pipe, heat is applied to the bowl, and the vapors are inhaled through the stem. Snorting the drug tends to cause irritation to the nasal lining. Heavy, long-term users generally prefer to inject the drug. Like cocaine, amphetamine can be dissolved in water and cooked to prepare it for injection.

The route of ingestion determines the onset

twenty-four hours.

### Forms

The appearance of amphetamine and methamphetamine depends on the synthetic process and quality control used in their production. High-quality street meth is generally a white crystalline powder. The color of lower-quality meth may range from dark yellow to brown. The drug may be crystalline, granular, or solid block, and it may have a sticky consistency. It may be packaged in plastic bags, paper bindles, or glass vials.

Ice is a very pure form of methamphetamine with an appearance similar to that of broken glass. It is usually ingested by smoking, and the effects can last up to fourteen hours. The price of one gram of ice ranges from two hundred to four hundred dollars.

### Effects

As stimulants that act on the central nervous system, amphetamines reduce fatigue and the need to sleep, increase confidence and energy levels, and in general cause psychological and physical exhilaration.

These effects are identical to those of cocaine, but the effects of cocaine last from twenty to eighty minutes, whereas those of amphetamines last for four to twelve hours. New users can rapidly develop psychological dependence on amphetamines.

Common effects displayed by people under the influence of amphetamines include alertness, anxiety, euphoria, reduced appetite, talkativeness, and teeth grinding. Chronic abuse of the drug can produce severe mental and physical problems, including delusions, visual and

of the drug's effects. Effects from oral ingestion are felt within thirty to sixty minutes. When snorted, the drug produces effects within five to twenty minutes. Injecting and smoking the drug both result in an intense "rush" within seconds of ingestion. The intensity of the effects, which can last from six to twelve hours, is related to both the dose of the drug and its purity. Regardless of the route of ingestion, tolerance to the drug may develop quickly, so that the user requires larger and larger doses of amphetamines to produce the desired effect. Whereas medical doses of amphetamines rarely exceed 100 milligrams per day, a super user on a binge may ingest more than 15,000 milligrams every auditory hallucinations, and violent behavior.

Long-term high-dose users of amphetamines may experience formication, which is the feeling that bugs are crawling under the skin. People in this state can severely injure themselves while trying to dig or cut the imagined bugs from their skin.

*Megan N. Bottegal*

**Further Reading**

Gano, Lila. *Hazardous Waste.* San Diego, Calif.: Lucent Books, 1991. Provides a good discussion of the health risks of the hazardous wastes generated by clandestine labs in the production of methamphetamine.

Hicks, John. *Drug Addiction: "No Way I'm an Addict."* Brookfield, Conn.: Millbrook Press, 1997. Focuses on drug-abuse treatment strategies, with an emphasis on amphetamine addiction.

Laci, Miklos. *Illegal Drugs: America's Anguish.* Detroit: Thomson/Gale, 2004. Comprehensive guide to illegal drugs in the United States includes discussion of the origins, uses, and effects of drug abuse. Of particular interest is the section on drug trafficking.

Menhard, Francha Roffé. *Drugs: Facts About Amphetamines.* Tarrytown, N.J.: Marshall Cavendish, 2006. Provides information on the characteristics, legal status, history, abuse, and treatment of addiction to amphetamines and methamphetamine.

Pellowski, Michael. *Amphetamine Drug Dangers.* Berkeley Heights, N.J.: Enslow, 2000. Discusses stimulant drugs in general and amphetamines in particular. Topics of interest include the signs and symptoms of amphetamine abuse.

**See also:** Club drugs; Controlled Substances Act of 1970; Drug abuse and dependence; Drug classification; Drug confirmation tests; Drug Enforcement Administration, U.S.; Drug paraphernalia; Meth labs; Stimulants.

# Anabolic Steroid Control Act of 2004

**Date:** Enacted on October 22, 2004

**The Law:** Federal legislation designed to clarify definitions of anabolic steroids, to provide for research and education activities relating to steroids and steroid precursors, and to expand regulatory and enforcement authority.

**Significance:** The Anabolic Steroid Control Act of 2004 represented an attempt by the U.S. government to address the growing problem of the use of anabolic steroids, particularly by young people. The law strengthened legal penalties for distribution and possession of these drugs while also encouraging increased education about their dangers for children and adolescents.

Anabolic steroids are synthetic chemicals that mimic the action of the hormone testosterone in the body. They originally found a valued use in maintaining tissue integrity in sufferers of chronic disease. Athletes, however, soon discovered that the muscle-promoting activity of anabolic steroids could enhance performance and give them decided advantages over other athletes in competition, and the use of these drugs became pervasive throughout the sporting world. When they found a place among American male teenagers craving larger muscles and better athletic performance, the U.S. Congress took note.

Congress first criminalized the nonmedical use of anabolic steroids by passing the Anabolic Steroid Control Act of 1990, which made it clear that anyone illegally possessing these drugs was subject to arrest and prosecution. Under the 1990 act, a first offense of simple possession was punishable by up to one year in prison, a minimum fine of $1,000, or both. The penalties increased for those with previous convictions related to narcotics crimes. The act reserved the most severe penalties for individuals who distributed or dispensed steroids. These activities carried a penalty of up to five years in prison, a fine of $250,000, or both. Penalties were higher for repeat offenders, and fines could rise to $1,000,000 for defendants that were other than individuals.

Although the 1990 act was an improvement over previous legislation, it did not go far enough. For example, the 1990 act listed only twenty-seven controlled substances; the Anabolic Steroid Control Act of 2004 act more than doubled that number in addition to stiffening penalties and providing for research and education regarding anabolic steroids. The 2004 act significantly increased the maximum term of imprisonment, fine, and length of supervised release for the manufacture or distribution of anabolic steroids. It also broadened the definition of an anabolic steroid to encompass any drug or hormonal substance chemically related to testosterone. The act specifically excluded estrogens, progestins, corticosteroids, and dehydroepiandrosterone from that list while designating fifty-nine specific drugs as anabolic steroids. Finally, the act encouraged the use of federal grants to carry out science-based education programs in elementary and secondary schools to highlight the harmful effects of anabolic steroids.

Although a great deal of debate continues regarding the negative effects of anabolic steroids, proponents of the 2004 legislation took their lead from studies that had found that these drugs may damage the liver, kidney, heart, and sexual organs. In addition, research has indicated that the use of anabolic steroids by children could prevent them from reaching their full height, and use of the drugs has been associated with outbursts of anger and violence (often referred to as "roid rage"). In recognition of anabolic steroids' potential for damage, U.S. president George W. Bush called for a "get-tough approach" to steroid abuse in his 2004 state of the union address. The Anabolic Steroid Control Act of 2004 was a step in that direction.

*Richard S. Spira*

## Further Reading

Aretha, David. *Steroids and Other Performance-Enhancing Drugs*. Berkeley Heights, N.J.: Enslow, 2005.

Gray, James. *Why Our Drug Laws Have Failed and What We Can Do About It: A Judicial Indictment of the War on Drugs*. Philadelphia: Temple University Press, 2001.

Monroe, Judy. *Steroids, Sports, and Body Image: The Risks of Performance-Enhancing Drugs*. Berkeley Heights, N.J.: Enslow, 2004.

Yesalis, Charles E. *Anabolic Steroids in Sport and Exercise*. Champaign, Ill.: Human Kinetics, 2000.

**See also:** Athlete drug testing; Drug confirmation tests; Drug Enforcement Administration, U.S.; Forensic toxicology; Performance-enhancing drugs; Toxicological analysis.

## Analytical instrumentation

**Definition**: Tools used during the chemical and physical investigation of physical evidence to identify components and their associated concentrations.

**Significance:** The scientific evaluation of forensic samples provides information that can be useful to law-enforcement investigators. The instruments employed by forensic scientists are designed to detect and measure small quantities and fine details, thus enabling comparisons of samples that can link suspects to crime scenes or eliminate persons from suspicion.

Advances in analytical instrumentation have significantly changed how forensic investigations are completed. Forensic scientists use many different types of analytical instruments, but all these tools serve the purpose of enabling the scientists to obtain more information on forensic samples. Analytical techniques have the ability to change a sample from one that was thought to have only class characteristics to one that has individual characteristics, making it more valuable in an investigation. This ability to detect individual characteristics is one reason analytical instrumentation has become an important part of forensic investigations.

Analytical instruments can be grouped according to the types of chemical and physical properties they measure. The analytical techniques most commonly used by forensic scientists are microscopy, chromatography, electrophoresis, spectrometry, and spectroscopy.

## Microscopy

Light microscopy, or the use of light microscopes, allows forensic analysts to magnify samples so the fine details can be viewed and evaluated. Light microscopes have the ability to magnify up to around 1,500× (that is, 1,500 times normal size). Light microscopy is useful for comparisons of samples and in the evaluation of specimens for similarities and differences. Common light microscopes used in forensic science include the compound microscope, the stereo microscope, and the comparison microscope. A comparison microscope allows an analyst to view two samples side by side, so they can easily be compared; fiber samples and bullets are among the kinds of forensic evidence often compared in this way.

An electron microscope uses a beam of electrons to probe a sample and allows a forensic scientist to view a sample at a greater magnification than is possible with a light microscope. A common type of electron microscope used in forensic applications is the scanning electron microscope (SEM), which can reach a magnification of 100,000× or greater. Another advantage of the SEM is that it enables the scientist to probe the elemental composition and elemental distribution of specimens using the X-ray fluorescence property of the microscope.

## Chromatography and Electrophoresis

Forensic scientists use chromatography and electrophoresis to analyze complex mixtures of chemicals. The term "chromatography" is used to refer to a range of techniques that allow the separation of the individual components of chemical mixtures through the use of either a gas or a liquid moving phase. Chromatographic analysis can be used to determine all the different chemical components that make up a sample and how much of each component is present.

The main types of chromatography used in forensic investigations are gas chromatography (GC) and high-performance liquid chroma-

tography (HPLC). GC separates, detects, and quantifies volatile species (atoms, molecules, or ions) or chemical compounds that can be converted to the gas phase by heating. Once in a gas phase, species move at different rates through a column, which results in a physical separation between components. This technique is very useful for arson investigations, in which fire accelerants often need to be evaluated. HPLC involves the analysis of mostly organic samples (molecules containing carbon) in a liquid state. The samples are dissolved in a suitable liquid solvent, such as water or an alcohol. This technique can be used to identify and determine the amounts of different drugs in samples collected at crime scenes.

Capillary electrophoresis is a technique used by forensic scientists to separate charged chemical species such as proteins and peptides. It uses an electric potential to cause positive and negative charged species to migrate and separate into components. The main forensic application of this technique is in DNA (deoxyribonucleic acid) analysis.

## Spectrometry and Spectroscopy

Forensic scientists use molecular spectrometry and spectrophotometry to look at the molecular or organic structure of chemical compounds. Techniques such as Fourier transform infrared (FTIR) spectrometry, ultraviolet and visible spectrometry (UV-Vis), and mass spectrometry (MS) allow analysts to classify and identify chemicals by their molecular spectra. FTIR spectrometry uses infrared light, and UV-Vis uses visible and ultraviolet light. A forensic scientist might compare an FTIR spectra of a forensic sample such as a white powder found at a crime scene with a spectral library of known compounds in order to identify the powder. FTIR can also be attached to a microscope to create a microspectrophotometer, which enables examination of the molecular structure of a sample. MS is often carried out in conjunction with gas or liquid chromatography to provide more detailed identification of components in a forensic sample.

Elemental spectroscopy is accomplished by techniques that measure the elemental composition and concentration in a sample. Atomic absorption (AA), inductively coupled plasma (ICP), X-ray fluorescence (XRF), X-ray diffraction (XRD), and neutron activation analysis (NAA) are typical instruments used in inorganic analysis. XRF can be used to determine the presence of lead and barium in gunshot residue. ICP can be used in finding out what elements are in a metal sample, such as a bullet; this allows the scientist to determine the alloy type, which then may be traced to a manufacturer.

*Dwight Tshudy*

## Further Reading

Bell, Suzanne. *Forensic Chemistry*. Upper Saddle River, N.J.: Pearson Prentice Hall, 2006. Chemistry-focused text presents discussion of the use of analytical instrumentation.

Girard, James E. *Criminalistics: Forensic Science and Crime*. Sudbury, Mass.: Jones & Bartlett, 2008. Textbook includes sections in which instruments and their uses are described.

Houck, Max M., and Jay A. Siegel. *Fundamentals of Forensic Science*. Burlington, Mass.: Elsevier Academic Press, 2006. Good general textbook includes a well-presented section on analytical tools.

James, Stuart H., and Jon J. Nordby, eds. *Forensic Science: An Introduction to Scientific and Investigative Techniques*. 2d ed. Boca Raton, Fla.: CRC Press, 2005. Covers analytical instrumentation in a section on forensic science in the laboratory.

Johll, Matthew. *Investigating Chemistry: A Forensic Science Approach*. New York: W. H. Freeman, 2007. Textbook designed for nonscience majors presents simple explanations of analytical instruments and their uses.

Saferstein, Richard. *Criminalistics: An Introduction to Forensic Science*. 9th ed. Upper Saddle River, N.J.: Pearson Prentice Hall, 2007. Introductory text describes and explains the uses of various analytical instruments and techniques.

**See also:** Atomic absorption spectrophotometry; Chromatography; Column chromatography; Crime laboratories; Electrophoresis; Fourier transform infrared spectrophotometer; Gas chromatography; High-performance liquid chromatography; Homogeneous enzyme immunoassay; Mass spectrometry; Microspectrophotometry; Scanning electron microscopy; Spectroscopy.

---

## Anaphylaxis

**Definition**: Anaphylaxis is a severe allergic reaction to substances referred to as allergens, in which contraction of smooth muscles in the bronchioles can result in suffocation. Anaphylaxis is synonymous with anaphylactic shock.

**Significance:** While allergic reactions to substances such as pollen, eggs and even antibiotics such as penicillin are common, and rarely more significant than simply a nuisance, severe anaphylactic shock may close off the breathing passages and even result in organ failure from circulatory damage. Unless the reaction is quickly reversed, the result may be death.

Anaphylaxis is considered an example of an immediate hypersensitivity reaction, classified as a Type 1 reaction in the classification scheme developed by Philip Gell and Robin Coombs in the 1960s. Their original scheme consisted of four forms of hypersensitivity reactions, differing either in the types of antibodies which trigger each of the types, or in the pathological changes which result. Unlike the other three hypersensitivities, Type 1 reactions, such as anaphylaxis, involve the interaction of a type of antibody known as IgE, and body cells known as basophils or mast cells.

### Discovery of Anaphylaxis

Anaphylaxis was first described by the French physiologists Charles Richet and Paul Portier in 1901, when, after sensitizing an animal with a protein, they observed that upon future exposure to that same protein the animal often reacted violently, in some cases dying within minutes. Richet termed the reaction anaphylaxis, meaning, "lack of protection;"

Richet was awarded the Nobel Prize in Physiology or Medicine in 1913 for the discovery.

The specific molecular mechanism underlying the reaction was not initially understood. During the 1890s, it had been demonstrated that when serum from an animal sensitized to an allergen was transferred to another animal, the recipient acquired the same sensitivity. The agent in serum was initially identified during the 1920s, and was termed a reagin. In 1966, the reagin was identified as an antibody, and designated IgE for the erythema, or reddening it produced when injected under the skin.

## Molecular Mechanism of Anaphylactic Shock

Immediate (Type 1) hypersensitivities in general, and anaphylaxis in particular, are associated with the specific class of antibody known as IgE. While the absence of an allergy, whether to pollen, peanut oil, or any other potential allergen, may be due to any number of reasons, the absence of IgE specific for an allergen means the individual will not be predisposed to anaphylactic shock upon exposure to that particular substance. Development of sensitivity is the result of a series of reactions involving the immune system. The reasons for an individual being predisposed to such reactions remain unclear, but do appear to have some genetic component. Two factors are involved: (1) IgE antibody; and basophils, a class of white blood cells, and mast cells, analogous to basophils but found in tissues. Both mast cells and basophils express surface receptors to which IgE is capable of binding, and contain internal pharmacologically active granules of vasoactive substances. Release of such chemicals results in the symptoms of allergies.

Sensitivity begins upon initial exposure to the allergen, which results in production of IgE antibody by the B lymphocytes of the immune system. During this sensitization phase the individual does not generally exhibit characteristics of the allergy. However, upon subsequent exposure to the same allergen, the response is immediate and enhanced. IgE connects with the allergen and the complex binds receptors on basophils or mast cells. The result is the release of intracellular granules – degranulation – with their vasoactive chemicals entering tissues and the circulation. Mediation of anaphylaxis is the direct result of the activity of the agents, which include chemicals such as histamine, leukotrienes and prostaglandins. A mild reaction may include a rash, or in the case of pollen, hay fever symptoms. More severe reactions, as in anaphylaxis, include the constriction of smooth muscles and possible circulatory collapse. The most common examples of these reactions are elicited by allergens expressed in insect bites or stings, or peanut allergies. The reaction begins within minutes, and may result in death unless the effects of the vasoactive agents are reversed, usually through injection of epinephrine.

Diagnosis of death due to anaphylactic shock is difficult when the allergy is unknown or if exposure to a known allergen has not been observed. Nevertheless, there are certain observations upon autopsy which may suggest anaphylaxis. An elevated level of IgE may be suggestive, but unless this can be shown to be specific for the suspected allergen, its presence may not be helpful. Among the vasoactive substances released by mast cells is the enzyme ?-tryptase. Significantly elevated levels of the enzyme in serum are suggestive of anaphylaxis, at least of exposure was other than in food. Unlike ?-tryptase, most of the other mediators have a short half-life in serum, and unless analysis is carried out within minutes after death, their absence is not significant. In general, therefore, diagnosis of death which resulted from anaphylactic shock, in the absence of witnesses to the actual event, requires first the elimination of any other cause.

*Richard Adler*

## Further Reading

Black, C. Allen. "A brief history of the discovery of the immunoglobulins and the origin of the modern immunoglobulin nomenclature." *Immunology and Cell Biology* (1997) 75: 65-68. Published to commemorate the 30th anniversary of IgE, the work summarizes the discovery and identification of function of the immunoglobulins, including that of IgE.

Sicherer, Scott. F*ood Allergies: A Complete*

*Guide for Eating When Your Life Depends on It.*" Baltimore, MD: Johns Hopkins University Press, 2013. Explanations for the average layperson of the basis of food allergies, including the most common examples. A portion of the book describes the causes and treatment of anaphylaxis.

Silverstein, Arthur. *A History of Immunology.* New York: Academic Press, 1989. The description of the evolution of thought about immunity includes a summary of Richet's work.

Smith, Roger. "Charles Richet." In Magill, Frank (ed.). *The Nobel Prize Winners: Physiology or Medicine*, Vol. 1. Pasadena, CA: Salem Press, Inc., 1991. Pp. 172-181. Biography of the physiologist who first identified anaphylaxis. Summaries of his career and Nobel lecture are included.

Tsokos, Michael. *Forensic Pathology Reviews,* Vol. 3. Totowa, NJ: Humana Press, 2005. Among the numerous topics are methods of analysis and descriptions of postmortem findings following death from anaphylactic shock.

**See also:** American Journal of Forensic Medicine and Pathology, The (Journal); Antibiotics; Asphyxiation; Autopsies; Forensic pathology; Journal of Forensic Sciences (Journal); Medicine; Poisons and antidotes; Serology.

---

## Anastasia remains identification

**Date:** Began in July, 1991

**The Event:** After Bolshevik revolutionaries executed the members of the Russian imperial family in 1918, rumors persisted—and the notion was popularized in books and films—that two of the czar's children, Anastasia and Alexei, survived. Numerous pretenders came forward claiming to be the missing Princess Anastasia. Beginning in 1991, forensic science was put to use in attempts to clarify which members of the family were in fact executed.

**Significance:** The forensic investigation undertaken to identify the remains of the Russian royal family, the Romanovs, was the first to employ both short tandem repeats and mitochondrial DNA for the identification of historical figures, portending the application of the same techniques in the identification of the remains of both well-known and obscure persons in future investigations.

On July 17, 1918, Czar Nicholas II of Russia, his family members (Czarina Alexandra, their four daughters—Olga, Tatiana, Maria, and Anastasia—and only son, Alexei), the family physician, and three servants were herded into a basement and executed by firing squad or by stab wounds from bayonets. Eyewitness accounts stated that most of the bodies were then placed in a shallow pit, and sulfuric acid was added to impede identification; the remains of Alexei and an unidentified daughter were burned separately.

In 1991, the Russian government authorized an investigation at the burial site. The July, 1991, exhumation of the grave near Yekaterinburg revealed that it contained nine corpses. A Russian forensic team did extensive work in determining the sexes of the bodies, in estimating ages, and in employing odontology and computer-assisted facial reconstruction to attempt identification, although the latter tests were limited because the facial areas of the skulls were destroyed. The scientists determined that the grave contained the remains of the czar, the czarina, three of the daughters, the physician, and the servants. However, a disagreement about the identification of the daughters developed between the Russian scientists and an American team of forensic anthropologists who had been hired by the city of Yekaterinburg. Relying on the same evidence, the Russian researchers argued that the missing daughter was Maria, whereas the Americans thought her to be Anastasia. No evidence of the allegedly burned children's bodies was found at the site or nearby.

To bolster the authenticity of the identification, a joint team of British and Russian scientists evaluated the remains using three DNA

The children of the last czar of Russia (from left): Tatiana, Maria, Anastasia, Olga, and Alexei. This photograph was taken sometime around 1916, approximately two years before the members of the Romanov family were executed. *(Library of Congress)*

(deoxyribonucleic acid) tests. The first confirmed that the mass grave contained five female and four male bodies. The second test was a short tandem repeat (STR) analysis; this type of test can establish whether individuals are closely related to one another. The second test showed that the remains included parents and three children. The third test was mitochondrial DNA (mtDNA) sequencing, which can be employed for identification even when the related persons are separated by many generations; mtDNA is passed directly from mothers to their children. DNA from the body believed to be that of the czar was compared with DNA samples from two of the czar's maternal grandmother's descendants; DNA from the czarina and the children was compared with DNA from Prince Philip, duke of Edinburgh, whose maternal grandmother was the czarina's sister. In both instances, matches were positive.

The researchers reported a 98.5 percent probability that the remains were those of the imperial family based on the anthropological, historical, and scientific evidence. They declined, however, to confirm the individual identities of the daughters. Both American and German authorities tested the DNA of Anna Anderson, the best known of the Anastasia pretenders, using STR analysis, and the DNA was not a match to the royal family.

In 2007, Russian archaeologists announced that they believed they had found the remains of the two missing children of the imperial family near the site where Nicholas, Alexandra, and the other three daughters were found. In April, 2008, Russian forensic scientists who had performed analyses on DNA extracted from teeth, bones, and other fragments of those remains announced their findings: The last two of the Romanov children, Alexei and Maria, had been identified. The remains found in the mass burial site examined beginning in 1991 thus included those of Anastasia.

*Susan Coleman*

## Further Reading

Gill, Peter, et al. "Identification of the Remains of the Romanov Family by DNA Analysis." *Nature Genetics* 6 (February, 1994): 130-135.

Jobling, Mark A., and Peter Gill. "Encoded Evidence: DNA in Forensic Analysis." *Nature Reviews Genetics* 5 (October, 2004): 739-751.

Klier, John, and Helen Mingay. *Quest for Anastasia: Solving the Mystery of the Lost Romanovs.* Secaucus, N.J.: Carol, 1997.

Rudin, Norah, and Keith Inman. *An Introduction to Forensic DNA Analysis.* 2d ed. Boca Raton, Fla.: CRC Press, 2002.

**See also:** Anthropometry; DNA analysis; Forensic odontology; Louis XVII remains identification; Mass graves; Mitochondrial DNA analysis and typing; Nicholas II remains identification; Short tandem repeat analysis; Skeletal analysis.

## Ancient criminal cases and mysteries

**Significance:** Many ancient humans engaged in illegal behaviors, ranging from theft to murder, that share elements with crimes that have been encountered by centuries of law enforcement personnel, who in turn developed effective forensic investigation techniques. Intrigued by certain unsolved ancient crimes, some modern investigators have applied the latest forensic methods and tools to the evaluation of the available evidence in those cases, and their work has sometimes led to improvements in modern forensic analysis.

In ancient times, legal systems and procedures were not standardized; they functioned distinctly in diverse locales and during various periods of time. Biblical accounts, particularly in the Old Testament, depict many crimes, beginning with Cain's killing of Abel. Ancient historians, including Herodotus (c. 484-425 b.c.e.) and Tacitus (c. 56-120 c.e ), recorded incidents of crime based on anecdotes they heard from contemporaries. The historical veracity of many of these accounts is questionable. Information regarding ancient crimes is often inconsistent, vague, and greatly distanced from eyewitnesses. Biased chroniclers often excluded information that countered their own beliefs or those of their patrons or incorporated incorrect details. In addition, wars and other disasters led to the loss of records that described crimes.

## Ancient Laws

The crimes committed in the ancient world were similar to the malicious actions humans have pursued in all eras. Ancient people robbed, abducted, and murdered much as modern people do, prompted by greed, revenge, and other motives. Rulers shaped most early laws to define crimes and establish punishments. The first known legal code was issued by Hammurabi during his reign as king of Babylon, from approximately 1792 to 1750 BCE. The behaviors defined as crimes in ancient times were those that violated the moral and social beliefs valued by the leaders who made the laws; these behaviors were often directed against royalty, governments, or temples, and they had negative impacts on communities. People were often considered criminal for disobeying rules and customs, especially those related to religious practices, as ancient theology and politics were often linked. Many ancient people perceived blasphemy to be a criminal activity.

Laws in particular areas changed as the ruling powers changed with invasions and wars, and the laws that were enforced varied depending on rulers' agendas, attitudes, and tolerance for criminality. Ancient philosophers, including Aristotle (384-322 BCE) and Plato (c. 427-347 BCE), contemplated the role of crime and punishment in societies and the need for justice.

The punishments for criminal behavior in ancient times included seizure of property, imprisonment, forced labor, mutilation, exile, and execution. Individuals usually dealt with personal crimes, such as embezzlement and extortion, by seeking compensation.

Just as the laws varied, the courts of the ancient world operated differently in different places and times. Most of the courts of ancient Rome were conducted by praetors, or magistrates, who chose the cases that would be heard. Juries came to decisions of acquittal, condemnation, or not proven after hearing cases in which alleged criminals were pitted against their accusers; in these courts, oratorical evidence was offered and witnesses testified. In ancient Greek courts, citizen juries, often consisting of several hundred men, ruled on the cases presented; both prosecutors and defenders in these cases used oratory rather than evidence to sway jurors' decisions.

## Murder

Ancient people committed homicide for many of the same reasons modern people do. Some murders were intentional, committed out of jealousy, rage, or vengeance; others were the unintentional result of other crimes, such as theft or assault. Assassinations of rulers occurred frequently throughout ancient history. Although most of the homicides that took place in ancient times remain anonymous, one that is widely known in the modern world is the assassination of the Roman ruler Julius Caesar (100-44 BCE), whose political actions provoked his rivals to conspire to kill him.

After he attained power in 49 BCE, Caesar instituted reforms that outraged his enemies, who feared losing the power and prestige that had been accorded their families for generations. On March 15, 44 BCE, Caesar went to the Theatre of Pompey, where the Roman senate was meeting. A group of senators led by Marcus Junius Brutus swarmed around Caesar and slashed him with knives. A physician who later examined Caesar's corpse noted that he had twenty-three stab wounds. Roman officials ordered that Caesar's assassins be apprehended and slain.

Other notorious ancient assassinations targeted Roman and Egyptian leaders. On September 18, 96 CE, Roman emperor Domitian was assassinated. Tired of Domitian's oppression, his chamberlain had devised a plot against him, involving Domitian's guards as accomplices. A steward named Stephanus fatally stabbed Domitian, whose supporters avenged his death by killing the assassins. In ancient Egypt, women living in the pharaoh's harem plotted to remove Ramses III from power in 1153 BCE. A judicial papyrus dating from that time indicates that numerous people were arrested for actions related to the crime, of whom twenty-four were declared guilty and probably executed.

## Poisoning

During ancient times, scientific techniques to detect poisons in bodies were nonexistent. This inability to trace toxins to fatalities benefited many people who relied on poisoning as the most effective method of eliminating enemies and rivals. Ancient poisoners derived toxins from organic sources, both plants and animal venoms, to contaminate food and drink or create deadly lotions. Arsenic, which was used to season foods and was incorporated in pharmaceuticals, proved lethal when concentrated in bodily tissues.

Among the notorious poisoners in ancient Rome (around 74 BCE) was a man named Oppianicus, whose criminal acts included poisoning but failing to kill Cluentius, whose stepfather Oppianicus had killed so he could marry Cluentius's mother, Sassia. Oppianicus schemed to acquire Cluentius's belongings, which his mother would inherit after his death. At Oppianicus's trial for attempting to kill Cluentius, his defense tried to discredit Cluentius by claiming that Cluentius had bribed judges. The tactic did not work, and Oppianicus was exiled. Sassia and Cluentius's sister later sought prosecution of Cluentius for allegedly attempting to poison Oppianicus, and Cluentius was acquitted. When Oppianicus was subsequently murdered, Cluentius, who was accused of the crime, benefited from the defense oratory of Roman statesman and philosopher Cicero. Cicero's strategy was not to stress Cluentius's innocence but to focus on the crimes

Oppianicus had committed to suggest that his death was justified. Cicero's persuasive statements resulted in Cluentius's exoneration.

Another ancient Roman poisoner, Locusta, was so well-known for her herbal expertise that prominent Romans sought her out for her poisoning services. Her influential clients included the wife of Emperor Claudius (10 b.c.e.-54 c.e.), Agrippina the Younger, who schemed for her son from an earlier marriage, Nero, to succeed Claudius as emperor rather than Britannicus, Claudius's son by a previous wife. Deciding to kill Claudius first, Agrippina contacted Locusta, who served Claudius a meal containing poisonous mushrooms. The physician who attended Claudius when he became ill was allied with Agrippina; he gave the emperor a poisonous enema, ensuring his death. Although Locusta was incarcerated for that murder, Nero, the new emperor, released her so that she could kill Britannicus with tainted wine.

## Theft and Civic Crimes

Theft was a common crime in ancient communities. Thieves picked pockets, stole goods from markets and homes, and embezzled. Papyrus records from ancient Egypt describe such notable heists as the Great Tomb Robbery. Royal tombs at Thebes were particularly vulnerable to robbery. Some corrupt officials aided thieves or stole from religious and royal sites. Records describe the plundering of the Karnak temple complex by a guard.

An example of the view that some ideas were criminal is found in the trial of the philosopher Socrates (470-399 BCE) in Athens. Many ancient communities deemed behavior that ignored or denounced tradition as criminal. Trials contemplated whether people should be punished for such sacrilegious acts as vandalizing statues related to gods. In 399 BCE, three prominent citizens of Athens—a poet, an artisan, and a politician—initiated a prosecution against Socrates, asserting that his crime was suggesting that people reject the city's gods. Also, Socrates had prompted Athenians, particularly young men, to examine their leaders' rules and conduct critically.

Because of his views, Socrates had alienated many Athenians who considered his behavior criminal and sought his conviction. Some people despised Socrates for criticizing their professions and demeaning them personally. A group of 280 jurors, out of a jury of approximately 500 men, declared Socrates guilty and sentenced him to death. They stressed that Socrates had endangered Athenians with his erratic religious views and his arguments that citizens should scrutinize their leaders. Socrates carried out his own execution by consuming hemlock.

## Death of Tutankhamen

The mysterious death of Eighteenth Dynasty Egyptian pharaoh Tutankhamen has intrigued people since Howard Carter and his archaeological team located the tomb of the "boy king" in 1922. The objects in the tomb, including the pharaoh's mummy, provoked speculation regarding why and how Tutankhamen died in 1323 BCE at the age of eighteen. The tomb's small size and arrangement were inconsistent with the stature accorded to other royal figures, suggesting that Tutankhamen's death was unexpected and required expeditious arrangements. In addition to suggesting that Tutankhamen may have succumbed to illness, archaeologists and historians have speculated that he may have been the victim of assassination by a rival.

For several decades, scientists lacked effective forensic methods and tools to evaluate hypotheses regarding Tutankhamen's premature demise. In 1968, Ronald Harrison, head of the Anatomy Department at the University of Liverpool, X-rayed Tutankhamen's mummy. He noted damage to the skull that suggested the pharaoh may have sustained a violent blow to the head. Harrison also observed that some of Tutankhamen's ribs and his breastbone were absent. Murder theorists identified four people who might have slain Tutankhamen to seize power: his adviser Ay, who became the next pharaoh; army commander Horemheb, who succeeded Ay and purged monuments of Tutankhamen references; his treasurer, Maya; or his wife, Ankhesenamun.

Investigation and speculation regarding Tutankhamen's death continued, and in January, 2005, Zahi Hawass, Egypt's chief archaeologist, oversaw a full digital evaluation of Tutankhamen's mummy through the use of a computed tomography (CT) scan. The approximately seventeen hundred images generated in the scan indicated that the pharaoh had been healthy and probably had not suffered fatal trauma, intensifying the mystery regarding his death. The scan revealed a fractured left femur (thighbone), causing scientists to ponder whether the bone had been broken before or after the pharaoh died. Many forensic experts interpreted the evidence provided by the CT scan as proof that Tutankhamen was probably not murdered, but many scientists have continued to seek definitive information that can point to the exact cause of his death. Appropriating advanced technology, often funded or supplied by corporate sponsors, Hawass and other investigators utilized new forensic procedures and insights to further examine King Tutankhamen's mummy. Hawass conducted the King Tutankhamun Family Project from 2007 through 2009, evaluating royal mummies' DNA and scanning their bodies to secure evidence concerning diseases, injuries, and any damages resulting from criminal actions. In addition to clarifying King Tutankhamen's lineage, Hawass declared that the pharaoh had contracted malaria and suffered from avascular necrosis which killed him, not murderers. Disagreeing with those findings, critics, including experts at laboratories specializing in ancient DNA, described them as problematic and suggested the DNA had been degraded or contaminated.

## Unresolved Cases

Several ancient murders have intrigued modern forensic investigators, some of whom have applied their techniques, tools, and knowledge to efforts to understand what happened. Discoveries of the preserved corpses of ancient persons, such as Kennewick man, discovered in the Pacific Northwest in 1996, and related artifacts have allowed scientists to gain insights into ancient lifestyles and communities. Although forensic methods have helped scientists develop plausible interpretations regarding specific ancient bodies, in cases where they have suspected murder they have been unable

to learn conclusively why particular individuals died or who might have killed them. Those crimes remain mysteries, although each advancement in forensic science offers continuing hope for resolution.

In September, 1991, mountain climbers found a frozen male corpse on a glacier in the Ötztal Alps near the border between Austria and Italy. When the clothing on the body and items adjacent to it were examined, the authorities realized the remains were ancient. The corpse, which later became known as Ötzi the Iceman, and the objects found with it were shipped to Innsbruck, Austria, where they were evaluated at the Forensic Medical Institute by Konrad Spindler, an archaeologist. Radiocarbon dating indicated that the remains were approximately 5,300 years old.

Scientists employed numerous methods, including CT scans, in attempting to solve the mystery of Ötzi's demise and whether it was criminal or accidental. In 1998, Ötzi was transported to Bolzano, Italy, where forensic pathologist Peter Vanezis studied the skull and performed a facial reconstruction. During June, 2001, Paul Gostner, a radiologist at Bolzano General Hospital, X-rayed the body and found that an arrowhead was lodged in Ötzi's shoulder. Stating that Ötzi had been murdered, forensic experts suggested various ways in which the death might have taken place. Some speculated that Ötzi may have been killed during warfare, that he may have been the victim of rival hunters, or that he may have been a human sacrifice.

Most researchers accept early twenty-first century revelations concerning analysis of ancient DNA taken from Ötzi's body which provided information about his eye color and health and affirmed genetic connections to his twenty-first century cousins several thousand generations removed. Similarly preserved ancient bodies found in northern Europe have also stimulated forensic analysis. Bodies immersed in peat bogs for centuries have retained evidence useful for forensic examination. Investigators have hypothesized that the so-called bog bodies were those of ancient murder victims, people whose lives were sacrificed to gods, or executed criminals. Radiometric dating has shown that some of those found in the bogs lived during the British Iron Age (seventh century BCE to fifth century BCE). Forensic scientists have evaluated their garments, wounds, and physical characteristics using techniques similar to those employed in the assessment of Ötzi. The evidence they have found, including fingerprints and preserved injuries, indicates that many of these ancient people met violent deaths—strangled with ropes, drowned, stabbed, or decapitated.

## Profiting from Ancient Crimes

The appeal of enigmatic ancient crimes, particularly mysteries associated with royalty, has abetted criminal activity in later centuries. Obscure information regarding historic individuals has often enabled criminals to carry out fraudulent schemes involving the deception of antiquities collectors.

In October, 2000, for example, information accompanying a mummy that was seized from the dwelling of a Karachi, Pakistan, chieftain stated that the remains were those of Rhodugune, young daughter of Persian king Xerxes I, who had lived in the fifth century BCE. Investigators noted the sloppy mummification procedures evidenced by the body and the odd usage of the Greek version of the princess's Persian name, Wardegauna. Scientists conducted X-ray and CT scans of the mummy at Pakistan's National Museum, and the results, along with further forensic examination, revealed that the mummy, although unusually short, was that of an adult woman in her twenties, not a child, and radiocarbon dating revealed she had died in 1996. Given that the woman's spine was fractured, authorities feared she had been murdered by people engaged in the marketing of counterfeit ancient mummies.

*Elizabeth D. Schafer*

## Further Reading

Aldhouse-Green, Miranda. *Bog Bodies Uncovered: Solving Europe's Ancient Mystery*. London: Thames & Hudson, 2015. Archaeologist applies forensic science investigation techniques to study individuals who were violently killed and whose bodies were preserved in bogs. Color illustrations supplement text.

Bolt, Hermann M. "Arsenic: An Ancient Toxicant of Continuous Public Health Impact, From Iceman Ötzi Until Now." *Archives of Toxicology* 86, no. 6 (2012): 825-830. Examines historical examples of humans using arsenic as a poison to murder victims, citing incidents in ancient Mediterranean communities. Describes symptoms people developed after being exposed.

Dando-Collins, Stephen. *Blood of the Caesars: How the Murder of Germanicus Led to the Fall of Rome*. Hoboken, N.J.: John Wiley & Sons, Inc., 2008. Explores how murder of Germanicus Julius Caesar—the grandson of Mark Antony, adopted son of emperor Tiberius, father of Caligula, and grandfather of Nero—may have been root cause of the empire's collapse four centuries later.

Emsley, John. *The Elements of Murder: A History of Poison*. New York: Oxford University Press, 2005. Presents details about how killers have used poisons throughout history. Features chapters on arsenic, lead, and other toxins.

Hawass, Zahi. *Tutankhamun: The Mystery of the Boy King*. Washington, D.C.: National Geographic Society, 2005. Egyptian archaeologist describes his experiences with forensic investigations regarding Tutankhamen's death. Features CT images.

Hawass, Zahi, et al. "Ancestry and Pathology in King Tutankamun's Family." *Journal of the American Medical Association* 303, no. 7 (2010): 638-647. Reports results of the King Tutankhamun Family Project which analyzed DNA secured from royal Egyptian mummies. Scans supplemented genetic investigations to determine physiological factors associated with diseases and infirmities that affected ancient people's health.

Marchant, Jo. *The Shadow King: The Bizarre Afterlife of King Tut's Mummy*. Boston, MA: Da Capo Press, 2013. Geneticist chronicles the numerous scientific investigations of King Tutankhamen's mummy, interviewing scientists and examining primary records and sites in an attempt to document facts and discredit incorrect theories popularized by media.

Redford, Susan. *The Harem Conspiracy: The Murder of Ramesses III*. De Kalb: Northern Illinois University Press, 2002. Archaeologist describes the women who plotted to kill the Egyptian king and their motivations based on temple and papyri resources.

Riggsby, Andrew M. *Roman Law and the Legal World of the Romans*. Cambridge: Cambridge University Press, 2010. Analysis of diverse legal topics and practitioners in ancient Rome includes a chapter focusing on criminal acts and punishment.

Williams, Robert C. *The Forensic Historian: Using Science to Reexamine the Past*. Armonk, N.Y.: M.E. Sharpe, 2013. Chapter on King Tutankhamen summarizes notable scientific, medical, and forensic evaluations utilizing CT scanning and innovative technology.

Wilson, Emily. *The Death of Socrates*. Cambridge, Mass.: Harvard University Press, 2007. Examines how Socrates' ideas were considered criminal in ancient Athens and how the philosopher's trial and execution influenced thought and culture.

Woolf, Greg. *Et Tu, Brute? The Murder of Caesar and Political Assassination*. Cambridge, Mass.: Harvard University Press, 2007. Presents comprehensive discussion of Caesar's death and the role of assassins in ancient history. Includes photographs of artifacts and artworks that portray the crime and its participants.

**See also:** Ancient science and forensics; Arsenic; Art forgery; Assassination; Food poisoning; Forensic archaeology; Homicide; Kennewick man; Knife wounds; Mummification; Peruvian Ice Maiden; Poisons and antidotes.

# Ancient science and forensics

**Significance:** Although ancient scientific techniques lacked the sophistication of modern forensic methods, individual examples of people applying science and technology to legal issues foreshadowed some of the basic concepts that forensic scientists recognized and developed centuries later.

The introduction of scientifically collected and examined evidence in legal proceedings is a relatively modern development. In ancient times, evidence presented in legal proceedings was generally limited to the oral arguments that prosecutors and defenders presented in courts. No concept of "forensic science" existed. Prosecutors and defenders relied primarily on words to convince officials and juries of the correctness of their cases. Most ancient legal personnel did not consider seeking such evidence as fibers, fingerprints, and hair or have techniques to evaluate them. The levels to which the hard sciences were developed varied among different ancient civilizations. Scientists typically shaped their pursuits to please patrons and rulers. Many people associated science with superstitions and magic, especially with the ancient world's fascination with the pseudoscience of alchemy, which sought to transform other elements into gold. Religious beliefs frequently influenced ancient science. Nevertheless, some people did pursue science for practical reasons, such as measuring land.

## Before Forensic Science

The absence of standardized forensic science practices throughout the ancient world aided criminals in escaping punishment. Without the input of scientifically collected and examined evidence, criminal investigations typically relied on force to secure confessions from suspects. In court trials, the only evidence that was usually considered was the testimonies of witnesses and the arguments of prosecutors and defenders. In rare instances, descriptions of the symptoms displayed by victims of poisoning or the physical damage inflicted by assaults might be presented. As scientific knowledge expanded, some people began applying common sense to evident connections between physical evidence and crimes. Some records of ancient legal proceedings include records of practices that resemble modern forensic techniques. However, many people were probably unaware of the scientific bases behind their methods. They tended to rely on common sense and practical approaches to solving problems related to problems they considered criminal or threatening. For example, a passage in the Bible's book of Judges describes a technique foreshadowing modern voice identification. Jephthah insisted people say the word *shibboleth* so he could identify his allies and detect his enemy Ephraimites who pronounced the word differently. Originating in this passage in the Bible, the ancient Hebrew word for stream, *shibboleth*, came to be used in English as a word or saying that might be used as a kind of password for a group while lacking any true meaning.

## Forensic Foreshadowing

Some early forensic scientific methods were based on accidental discoveries, or epiphanies, achieved while pursuing solutions to other problems. For example, the third century BCE Greek mathematician and inventor Archimedes was challenged to prove that a goldsmith had cheated King Hieron II of Syracuse by mixing inferior metals with the pure gold he had been given to make a crown for the king. Archimedes' investigation was constrained by the requirement that he not damage the royal crown in any way. According to legend, while Archimedes was taking a bath, he noticed that his body displaced an amount of water equal to his own weight. Drawing on that observation, he submerged both King Hieron's crown and an amount of gold equivalent to what the goldsmith was supposed to have used for the crown in water. When he determined than the crown displaced less water than the control sample, he proved that the goldsmith had committed fraud. Poisons had a special fascination for ancient scientists. However, physicians had a difficult time proving that apparent victims of poisoning crimes were actually poisoned, as the symptoms of poisoning and natural seizures were similar. Their attempts to devise methods to prove victims had been poisoned were simplistic compared to later toxicology developments. Around 200 BCE, the Middle Eastern physician and poet Nicander of Colophon studied poisons and their antidotes and wrote two books on the subject. *Alexipharmaca* describes many types of poisonings by animals, plants,

and inanimate agents and suggests antidotes and other treatments. *Theriaca* deals more narrowly with poisonings caused by animal bites, stings, and scratches. Nicander had a strong reputation during his time, but his books were not printed until 1499, when a joint edition appeared in Venice. The modern forensic science of odontology, which is used to identify bodies of victims by their teeth, has at least one ancient precursor. In 49 CE, the Roman emperor Nero's mother, Agrippina, sent for the head of her enemy Lollia Paulina after the woman reportedly committed suicide so that Agrippina could verify her death. The dead woman's face was distorted beyond easy recognition, but when Agrippina looked at the teeth in the head, she recognized a distinctively colored front tooth that she had previously noticed in Lollia Paulina's mouth.

## Detecting Fraud

Documents were frequently forged in ancient times, when most people were illiterate, so government officials sought effective methods to detect fraudulent wills, deeds, and contracts. In ancient Rome, legal officials used people considered to be experts in handwriting analysis to evaluate documents by comparing writing styles of known and suspect scribes. Seeking ways to detect lies, some ancients created primitive polygraph techniques. In contrast to modern polygraphs, which measure physiological responses, the techniques of the ancients were based solely on observations of the suspects' behavior, even though psychology was not yet an established scientific field. For example, around 500 BCE, priests in India tested people accused of thievery by placing them in darkened tents with donkeys whose tails were coated in soot. The priests would tell the suspected thieves to tug the animals' tails because the donkeys would bray when touched by thieves. Suspects who left the tents with their hands unsoiled by soot were considered guilty. Ancient Arabs conducted similar tests using grease instead of soot on the animals' tails. Ancient Chinese officials devised a different kind of lie-detecting test. They placed dried rice in the mouths of criminal suspects, whom they told to spit out the grains. Suspects with rice still sticking on their tongues were exposed as liars. This test actually had some scientific validity, as human bodies often respond to stress by being unable to produce the saliva necessary to spit. Because guilty suspects were more likely than the innocent to feel stress, they were less likely to be able to spit the rice out of their mouths.

### Prints

Throughout human history, every individual person has had fingerprints, palm prints, and footprints that are unique. These prints have always offered the potential for identifying criminal suspects but had to wait for a time when their forensic value was understood. The ancients were aware that the lines on their palms and fingertips formed distinct patterns and may have even recognized that those patterns were unique. However, they did not comprehend how prints left on objects could be used to identify criminal who touched things such as murder weapons and stolen items. They used fingerprints primarily to identify objects and documents, not for criminal investigations. Various hand and fingerprints were used for

signatures that were recognized in courts and business dealings. In Babylonia, for example, fingerprints were used to mark tablets related to business activities at least as early as 2000

In East Asia, ancient Chinese and Japanese officials and traders used thumbprints to distinguish legal seals and documents, and handprints were often used to sign divorce documents. A court case in which print evidence did prove significant occurred in Rome during the first century CE, when a Roman attorney named Quintilian defended a man accused of killing his mother. A talented speaker, Quintilian combined his oratorical skills with some scientific knowledge to build his legal strategy. He showed that a bloody palm print that had dried at the site of the murder was not compatible in size with the hand of his client. He went on to argue that the print had been placed at the crime scene by someone who wished to frame the murdered woman's son. Thanks to his comparison of handprints, he won his client's acquittal; however, the true murderer was never identified.

### Medical Evidence

Many ancient rulers and physicians recognized the importance of medical knowledge to legal systems. The eighteenth century BCE Babylonian king Hammurabi included laws relevant to medicine in the famous law code that he formulated. The early fourth century BCE Greek physician Hippocrates recommended that medical practitioners learn how to recognize injuries and poisonings inflicted by criminal assailants. Ancient physicians were often involved in investigations of crimes because of their specialized knowledge and their connections with rulers and officials. Medical autopsies go back at least as far as the early third millennium BCE As in modern times, they were performed to determine causes of deaths. However, members of many ancient societies opposed invasive examinations of dead people because they believed that bodies had to be intact for their transition to the afterlife. The word "autopsy" itself comes from ancient Greek, in which it means seeing with one's own eyes, even though the ancient Greeks seldom performed autopsies. During the third century        , the

Greek physicians Erasistratus and Herophilus of Chalcedon performed autopsies in Alexandria, Egypt, and may have explored how evidence of poisoning and injuries were linked to crimes. Perhaps the most notable autopsy in ancient history was that of the Roman ruler Julius Caesar, who was stabbed to death by assassins on March 15, 44 BCE at the Forum of Rome.

The physician who afterward examined Caesar's body reported to Roman officials that the second stab wound Caesar received was the fatal one. The word "forensic" comes from the Latin word *forum*. Some historians believe that the connection between the two words goes back to the autopsy performed after Caesar was killed at the Roman Forum.

## Modern Investigations of Ancient Crimes

Forensic investigators endeavor to attain more factual information in the early twenty-first century regarding ancient crimes, victims, and criminals. They seek to secure additional evidence from existing specimens and sites and to locate new sources of ancient human remains and artifacts that have yet to be discovered. Scientists representing diverse specialties and fields use advanced methods and powerful equipment with greater capabilities to reexamine evidence more precisely and accurately. For example, researchers secured a blood sample from the wound on Ötzi the Iceman's hand to assess it with an atomic force microscope and Raman spectroscopy. Their work inspired investigators to apply similar methods to study other ancient specimens.

To help comprehend sociopolitical and legal processes associated with ancient crimes, classical scholars enhance translations and annotations of court trial transcripts associated with cases involving prominent ancient people. They also seek new versions and undiscovered texts of trial speeches and contemporary accounts of criminal investigations.

*Elizabeth D. Schafer*

## Further Reading

Armit, Ian. "Violence and Society in the Deep Human Past." *The British Journal of Criminology* 51, no. 3 (2011): 499-517. Dis-

Portrait of the ancient Greek mathematician Archimedes by the early seventeenth century Spanish painter Jusepe de Ribera. All depictions of Archimedes are fanciful, as no contemporary pictures or sculptures of him are known to exist. *(Library of Congress)*

cusses how modern scientists' perceptions of ancient humans' criminal behavior have been impacted by discoveries of preserved bodies providing evidence of traumatic injuries resulting from physical assaults.

Carey, Christopher. *Trials from Classical Athens.* 2d ed. New York: Routledge, 2012. Provides annotated translations of speeches presented at trials for various crimes, including murder (featuring such homicide victims as Eratosthenes and Herodes) and theft. Appendices and illustrations supplement text.

Evans, Colin. *Murder Two: The Second Casebook of Forensic Detection.* New York: John Wiley & Sons, 2004. Discusses ancient efforts to detect liars, identify corpses, and determine cause of death through methods with scientific elements.

Gagarin, Michael. *Antiphon the Athenian: Oratory, Law, and Justice in the Age of the Sophists*. Austin: University of Texas Press, 2002. Provides examples of the forensic speeches, not scientific evidence, that ancient Greeks used strategically to win in court.

Janko, Marek; Robert W. Stark; and Albert Zink. "Preservation of 5300 Year Old Red Blood Cells in the Iceman." *Journal of the Royal Society Interface* 9, no. 75 (October 2012): 2581-2590. Asserts the importance of using modern technology to collect and evaluate forensic evidence associated with ancient crimes, focusing on the injury which killed Ötzi, and further developing those techniques for similar investigations.

Ramsland, Katherine. *Beating the Devil's Game: A History of Forensic Science and Criminal Investigation*. New York: Berkley Books, 2007. Discusses several significant uses of science in ancient Greek and Roman legal settings.

Ricciuti, Edward. *Science 101: Forensics*. New York: HarperCollins, 2007. Illustrations and text highlight early forensic precursors by ancient peoples, placing those achievements in context with later developments.

Riggsby, Andrew M. *Crime and Community in Ciceronian Rome*. Austin: University of Texas Press, 1999. Describes court procedures and verdict options for various ancient crimes. Explains that oratory was the primary evidence utilized.

**See also:** Ancient criminal cases and mysteries; Autopsies; Crime scene investigation; Document examination; Epidemiology; Forensic odontology; Forgery; Handwriting analysis; Knife wounds; Medicine; Poisons and antidotes; Ritual killing.

## Animal evidence

**Definition**: Organic materials from nonhumans, excluding insects, analyzed by forensic scientists for use in legal cases.

**Significance:** With advancements in DNA fingerprinting of dogs, cats, and other domesticated and wild animals, animal evidence has become much more useful in criminal and civil court cases than it was in the past, when individual animals, breeds or even species could not be identified.

The animal evidence involved in cases of crimes against humans most often consists of shed hairs and traces of blood, other body fluids (including saliva and urine), and excrement from either dogs or cats. Given that in the United States about 40 percent of households include at least one dog and 30 percent include at least one cat, crime scene investigators frequently encounter this kind of evidence.

### Animal Hair

In relation to crimes against humans, the most commonly analyzed type of animal evidence is shed hair. Research has shown that it is almost impossible for a person to enter a house where a dog or cat lives and not have some of the animal's hair transferred to his or her skin, shoes, or clothing. Criminal perpetrators who live with dogs or cats can thus transfer the hair of their animals to victims or crime scenes. Perpetrators can also pick up animal hairs from crime scenes, from victims' clothing, from household items, or directly from victims' pets.

In 1994, white hairs from a cat named Snowball were used to help convict a Canadian man of murdering his wife. Police investigators found the hairs on the husband's black leather jacket. This was the first evidentiary use of nonhuman DNA (deoxyribonucleic acid) to help solve a crime. In this case, the DNA analysis used feline microsatellite markers mapped by English geneticist Alec Jeffreys. Scientists have concluded that both feline and canine microsatellite markers are almost as discriminating as their human counterparts, not very much diminished by the inbreeding often seen in canines.

Because shed hair lacks a viable root, it usually does not contain enough nuclear DNA to allow short tandem repeat (STR, or microsatellite) fingerprinting of individuals. Instead, criminalists extract and amplify mitochondrial DNA (mtDNA) from the hair shaft, which contains thousands of mitochondria. This type of DNA identification of dogs and cats is most often used to add a layer of evidence rather than to provide a strong association to a particular animal, given that only a single locus is used for mtDNA profiling. In 2002, however, canine mtDNA was admitted into court during the prosecution of David Westerfield in the abduction and murder of seven-year-old Danielle van Dam, whose family owned a pet Weimaraner. This was the first trial in the U.S. to admit canine mtDNA analysis as evidence.

Forensic scientists also analyze the morphological (structural) characteristics of animal hair using compound light microscopy. Characteristic patterns of scales on the cuticle covering the shaft, for example, can be used to determine a particular species. Also, the medulla inside the shaft is informative for the identification of different species; for instance, the medullae of feline hairs show a typical "string of pearls" pattern. These features, among others, are usually used in conjunction with DNA profiling to identify particular animals.

## Other Types of Animal Evidence

Animal blood found at crime scenes usually contains enough viable nuclear DNA for STR analysis, which can be used to identify an individual animal. As early as 1998, STRs obtained from dried canine blood linked a suspect to the murder of a Seattle couple and the killing of their dog. Although the suspect was convicted, the canine DNA evidence was not admitted at trial because canine DNA typing was not considered reliable at the time. Since then, the reliability of canine and feline STR profiling has been well established in the scientific literature, and dog and cat DNA evidence is regularly admitted in legal proceedings.

Both urine and excrement from dogs have also provided nuclear DNA to help solve crimes and convict criminals. One example of using DNA from animal fecal matter outside the legal justice system is the identification of the Canadian lynx from scat found near the large cat's

paw prints in snow. This technique is being investigated as a way to track the health, distribution, and population densities of certain endangered animal species.

The National Fish and Wildlife Forensics Laboratory in Ashland, Oregon, is dedicated to the collection and analysis of evidence of crimes against wildlife. Law-enforcement agencies submit to the lab the types of animal evidence discussed above in addition to more unusual samples, such as hunting trophies (antlers), carved ivory, hides, furs, bones, teeth, leather goods, feathers, claws, talons, whole carcasses, stomach contents, and Asian medicinals, among other organic and inorganic materials usually investigated in criminal cases. Forensic experts at the facility extract and profile DNA from many of these items; they also employ other methodologies such as morphological and chemical analysis to determine whether samples come from particular species. Much of this work is concerned with supporting law-enforcement efforts to address crimes involving endangered species.

The emerging field of veterinary forensics is involved in identifying cases of animal abuse against domestic pets. In situations where abuse is suspected, veterinarians or veterinary pathologists most often obtain evidence from deceased whole animals, which are worked up in a manner similar to that employed during autopsies in homicide cases. These professionals look for specific patterns of injuries, telltale wounds, bullet holes, ballistic material, evidence of malnutrition or starvation, signs of torture, and incriminating human evidence (such as blood or hairs). Sometimes insects and maggots found on or in proximity to an animal carcass can be employed to determine the time of death or crime scene location.

*Lisa J. Shientag*

## Further Reading

Cassidy, Brandt G., and Robert A. Gonzales. "DNA Testing in Animal Forensics." *Journal of Wildlife Management* 69 (October, 2005): 1454-1462. Discusses how animal DNA is being used to solve human crimes. Gives examples from specific legal cases and notes the potential pitfalls related to DNA processing and collection methods.

Cooper, John E., and Margaret E. Cooper. *Introduction to Veterinary and Comparative Forensic Medicine*. Ames, Iowa: Blackwell, 2007. Includes discussion of wildlife conservation and links between cruelty to animals and violence toward humans. Intended for veterinarians and law-enforcement officials but written at a level understandable by interested laypersons.

Dorion, Robert B. J., ed. *Bitemark Evidence*. New York: Marcel Dekker, 2005. Comprehensive collection of essays on all aspects of the study of human and animal bite marks. Well illustrated.

Merck, Melinda D. *Veterinary Forensics: Animal Cruelty Investigations*. Ames, Iowa: Blackwell, 2007. Readable work discusses the handling of suspected animal cruelty cases.

Saferstein, Richard. *Criminalistics: An Introduction to Forensic Science*. 9th ed. Upper Saddle River, N.J.: Pearson Prentice Hall, 2007. Classic introductory text includes discussion of animal-related evidence.

**See also:** Biological terrorism; Bite-mark analysis; Canine substance detection; Crime scene investigation; DNA analysis; DNA banks for endangered animals; Evidence processing; Forensic entomology; Hair analysis; Mad cow disease investigation; Trace and transfer evidence; Wildlife forensics.

## Antemortem injuries

**Definition**: Injuries received before death.

**Significance:** In a death investigation, it is important to determine which injuries the person sustained before death as opposed to any injuries that occurred to the body postmortem (after death) because antemortem injuries may indicate the cause of death or factors that contributed to the death.

To determine cause of death accurately, a pa-

thologist must distinguish between the injuries to a body that were received before death and those that were received after death. The pathologist must also determine whether the body shows evidence of any injuries that occurred well before death. The most difficult determination to make involves which injuries were received immediately prior to death and which occurred immediately after death.

One significant difference between antemortem and postmortem injuries is in the ways in which the wounds have bled or bruised. It is possible for bleeding to occur after death, and, depending on the type of death, it is possible for bruising or pooling of the blood to occur postmortem, but a pathologist can generally tell by the way a wound has bled or bruised whether it is an antemortem injury.

A pathologist also looks at the type of tissue damage associated with injuries to determine when the injuries occurred. Tissues from antemortem injuries contain leukotriene B4, which living tissues produce in a chemical response to inflammation. Tissues that have been damaged by postmortem injuries do not contain this chemical. This information provides another way for the pathologist to determine exactly when injuries occurred.

In a case in which the body has been in water, the pathologist examines lung tissue to determine whether the person drowned or the body was put into the water after death. This tissue can show signs of whether the person struggled to breathe and began coughing before death or whether the lungs simply filled with water after death had already occurred.

The pathologist must also determine which antemortem injuries were the cause of the death as opposed to injuries that may have been received days, months, or even years before the death occurred. To do this, the pathologist looks for evidence of healing, such as wounds that have begun to close or bones that have begun to knit together, to eliminate those injuries as factors contributing to the death. Such older injuries can be significant clues in the determination of cause of death.

For example, in cases of deaths resulting from child abuse or domestic violence, bodies may evidence many injuries in various states of the healing process, showing a pattern that can help investigators establish the history of abuse. This pattern may also occur in victims who were tortured before death.

*Marianne M. Madsen*

## Further Reading

James, Stuart H., and Jon J. Nordby, eds. *Forensic Science: An Introduction to Scientific and Investigative Techniques.* 2d ed. Boca Raton, Fla.: CRC Press, 2005.

Shkrum, Michael J., and David A. Ramsay. *Forensic Pathology of Trauma: Common Problems for the Pathologist.* Totowa, N.J.: Humana Press, 2007.

Timmermans, Stefan. *Postmortem: How Medical Examiners Explain Suspicious Deaths.* Chicago: University of Chicago Press, 2006.

**See also:** Autopsies; Blunt force trauma; Body farms; Defensive wounds; Forensic anthropology; Forensic pathology; Forensic sculpture; Living forensics; Oral autopsy; Osteology and skeletal radiology.

## Anthrax

**Definition**: Deadly disease caused by the soil bacterium *Bacillus anthracis.*

**Significance:** Because anthrax is capable of debilitating and killing people and animals quickly, it is an attractive agent for use in biological warfare. The abilities to detect, treat, and neutralize anthrax efficiently are thus necessary to ensure public safety.

The bacterium *Bacillus anthracis* resides in soil, and, like other members of the bacterial genus *Bacillus*, can make a highly resistant resting cell known as an endospore. Endospores can withstand heat, desiccation, harsh chemicals, and ultraviolet radiation and can last in soils for centuries. Anthrax, the disease caused by *B. anthracis*, afflicts herbivorous animals, but human anthrax infections result from contact with infected animals or animal products.

## Types of Anthrax Infections

Anthrax is caused by the inhalation or ingestion of *B. anthracis* endospores or, in the case of cutaneous anthrax, by contact between damaged skin and *B. anthracis*. Inhalation of endospores causes inhalation anthrax, which typically occurs among workers in textile or tanning industries who handle contaminated animal products such as wool, hair, and hides. The incubation period of inhalation anthrax ranges from one to six days, and the disease follows a two-stage progression. After infection, the patient develops a dry cough, muscle weakness, tiredness, fever, and pressure in the middle of the chest. The second stage begins with the onset of respiratory distress and typically culminates in death within twenty-four hours. Inhalation anthrax has a mortality rate of 95 percent if untreated.

Gastrointestinal anthrax results from the ingestion of undercooked, contaminated meat. Two to seven days after ingestion, abdominal pain and fever occur, followed by vomiting, nausea, and diarrhea. Gastrointestinal bleeding is observed in some severe cases, and dissemination of the disease throughout the body also results. Fluid loss can result in shock and kidney failure. Approximately 50 percent of cases of gastrointestinal anthrax are lethal.

Cutaneous anthrax results from invasion of the skin by *B. anthracis*. If the skin is damaged by scrapes, cuts, or insect bites, endospores can breach the outer layers of the skin and infect it. After an incubation period of two to five days, small solid and conical elevations of the skin devoid of pus called papules form; these papules then swell, rupture, and blacken. Without treatment, anthrax skin infections can disseminate to other systems, and death occurs about 20 percent of the time.

## Detection of Anthrax

Growing *B. anthracis* from a blood sample is the best way to demonstrate an anthrax infection in patients who have not yet been given antibiotics. In patients who have begun antibiotic therapy, serological methods that detect antibodies made by the immune system against the bacterium are efficacious. Blood samples from a person who has died from anthrax should yield copious quantities of relatively large, rod-shaped bacteria that are encapsulated and easily visualized with polychrome methylene blue stains.

Automated detection systems (ADS's) can determine whether *B. anthracis* endospores have been released into a setting. The BSM-2000 (Universal Detection Technology), for example, continuously samples the air and heats it. Captured, heated spores release dipicolinic acid (DPA), a compound unique to bacterial endospores. DPA binds to terbium ions ($Tb^{3+}$), which, together, fluoresce green under ultraviolet light. Other ADS's use polymerase chain reaction (PCR) to test the air for DNA (deoxyribonucleic acid) sequences specific to *B. anthracis*.

### Treatment and Prevention of Anthrax

Several antibiotics are effective in the treatment of anthrax infections. High-dose intravenous penicillin G, ciprofloxacin, and doxycycline are typically quite effective. Preventive treatments with oral ciprofloxacin or doxycycline for six weeks are also effective. Anyone exposed to anthrax should begin treatment immediately because the disease can become untreatable with the passage of time.

BioThrax (made by Bioport Corporation) is a vaccine against anthrax. It consists of an extract prepared from a non-disease-causing strain of *B. anthracis*. It is administered as three inoculations given under the skin at two-week intervals, followed by booster injections at six, twelve, and eighteen months, after which yearly boosters are necessary to maintain immunity. BioThrax vaccinations are 93 percent effective in preventing anthrax infections.

When bodies or clothes are contaminated with *B. anthracis* endospores, personal contact can spread the disease. Washing with antibacterial soap and water and treating the wastewater with bleach can rid contaminated bodies of all endospores. Burning contaminated clothing and the corpses of those who have died from anthrax is an effective means of liquidating anthrax from the environment. Burial does not kill endospores. Endospores of *B. anthracis* released into the air are easily removed by means of high-efficiency particulate air (HEPA) or P100 filters.

Decontamination of areas that have been exposed to *B. anthracis* presents several challenges because the bacterial endospores are rather difficult to destroy. Ethylene oxide, chlorine dioxide, liquid bleach, and a decontamination foam created by Sandia National Laboratories kill *B. anthracis* endospores slowly. A cleanup method approved by the Environmental Protection Agency (EPA) that utilizes liquid bleach, water, and vinegar requires contact with a surface for at least sixty minutes. If chlorine dioxide is used in combination with an iron-based catalyst, sodium carbonate, and bicarbonate, disinfection requires only thirty minutes.

### Anthrax as a Biological Weapon

Many nations have examined the potential of *B. anthracis* as a biological weapon. Growing *B. anthracis* is extremely easy, but processing the endospores into a form that is easily disseminated is extremely difficult. The first attempts to use anthrax as a biological weapon utilized rather crude methods. During World War II (1942), the British military experimented with anthrax on Gruinard Island.

This experiment so thoroughly contaminated the site that it was quarantined for the next fifty years. Britain then manufactured some five million "N-bombs," which were anthrax-laced explosive devices, to attack German livestock, but the bombs were never used. In 1986, the British government hired a private company to disinfect the soil of Gruinard Island. The company first carted away the island's topsoil in sealed containers and then used 280 tons of formaldehyde mixed with 2,000 tons of seawater to disinfect the soil that remained. In 1990, the British defense minister declared the island safe.

At Fort Detrick in Frederick, Maryland, the U.S. Army developed a special form of anthrax endospores for use as a biological weapon. Such weaponized endospores lack the ionic charges that ordinarily cause them to stick together. Consequently, the spores are easily dispersed as a fine powder that can float for miles on the wind. On November 25, 1969, an executive order from President Richard M. Nixon outlawed offensive biological weapons research in the

United States. All existing U.S. stockpiles of biological weapons were subsequently destroyed.

Despite the fact that it was a signatory to the international Biological Weapons Convention of 1972, which was intended to end the production of biological weapons, the Soviet Union produced extensive quantities of weapons-grade anthrax endospores. On April 2, 1979, more than one million people in Sverdlovsk (now Yekaterinburg), Russia, were exposed to an accidental release of anthrax organisms from the local biological weapons plant. More than sixty people died from inhalation anthrax. An extensive KGB-sponsored cover-up from 1979 to 1992 prevented the international community from learning the truth of what happened until Russian president Boris Yeltsin admitted Soviet involvement in this incident. In Africa, South African intelligence services helped the Rhodesian government of Ian Smith use anthrax against humans and the cattle of the black nationalists who were fighting against his government during the late 1970's.

Weaponized endospores were used in the United States during the final four months of 2001, when spores of *B. anthracis* were mailed within the continental United States. Eleven cases of inhalation anthrax and eleven cases of cutaneous anthrax resulted from these attacks, and five people died.

### Anthrax and Microbial Forensics

Microbial forensics is concerned with the isolation and identification of any microbes used during bioterrorist attacks. Upon arrival at the site of an attack, the microbial forensics team must remove all persons from the site and decontaminate them. Sample collections taken from the air, vents, countertops, sinks, floors, and other surfaces can help the scientists to determine the source of the infection. All samples collected must be properly identified and stored in tamper-proof containers to preserve the chain of custody.

By identifying the exact strain of *B. anthracis* involved in an anthrax outbreak, experts can determine whether the disease has occurred as the result of a bioterrorism attack or as a naturally acquired infection. Various

## Risks of Anthrax Contamination in the Workplace

After the deaths of postal workers contaminated by anthrax bacteria sent through the mail by terrorists in late 2001, the U.S. Department of Labor's Office of Safety and Health Administration (OSHA) developed a matrix to help employers and workers understand the risks of anthrax exposure and to offer suggestions for preventive measures to avoid contamination. OSHA's matrix identified three levels of risk:

- **Green Zone:** Workplaces in which the risk of anthrax contamination is unlikely. This category encompasses the vast majority of workplaces in the United States.
- **Yellow Zone:** Workplaces in which anthrax contamination is considered possible. This category includes places that handle bulk mail, places handling mail from facilities known to be contaminated or that are close to such facilities, and places likely to be targeted by bioterrorists.
- **Red Zone:** Workplaces that authorities know or suspect to be contaminated.

strains of *B. anthracis* show very little DNA sequence variation, but because the entire genome of this organism has been completely sequenced, scientists are able to use PCR to detect single base differences between strains, called single nucleotide polymorphisms (SNPs), and thus provide a fingerprint for each *B. anthracis* strain. If the strains found at the scene of an attack and in the infected individuals are the same, then the agent used in the bioterrorism attack is confirmed.

This information can be used in determining both the source of the biological weapon employed and the best treatment options. Molecular forensics identified the strain used in the 2001 postal attacks on American soil as the Ames strain of *B. anthracis*, which was, ironically, developed at Fort Detrick.

*Michael A. Buratovich*

## Further Reading

Alibek, Ken, with Stephen Handelman. *Biohazard: The Chilling True Story of the Largest Covert Biological Weapons Program in the World—Told from Inside by the Man Who Ran It*. London: Hutchinson, 1999. Provides an insider's view of the extensive Soviet biological weapons program. Includes map and photographs.

Decker, Janet. *Anthrax*. New York: Chelsea House, 2003. Presents a detailed examination of the dynamics of anthrax epidemics and the influence that medical responses can have on them.

Guillemin, Jeanne. *Anthrax: The Investigation of a Deadly Outbreak*. Berkeley: University of California Press, 2001. Noted medical anthropologist discusses the Sverdlovsk anthrax tragedy in depth, including information on the Soviet Union's subsequent cover-up.

Holmes, Chris. *Spores, Plague, and History: The Story of Anthrax*. Dallas: Durban House, 2003. A medical epidemiologist surveys the historical effects of anthrax on human society.

Miller, Judith, Stephen Engelberg, and William Broad. *Germs: Biological Weapons and America's Secret War*. New York: Simon & Schuster, 2001. Three investigative journalists from *The New York Times* relate the deeply disturbing findings of their research into the history of biological weapons and the status of such weapons as of 2001.

Wheelis, Mark, Lajos Rózsa, and Malcolm Dando, eds. *Deadly Cultures: Biological Weapons Since 1945*. Cambridge, Mass.: Harvard University Press, 2006. Offers frank technical descriptions of the biological weapons programs of all the world's major countries.

**See also:** Anthrax letter attacks; Antibiotics; Bacteria; Bacterial biology; Bacterial resistance and response to antibacterial agents; Biological terrorism; Biological Weapons Convention of 1972; Centers for Disease Control and Prevention; Chemical Biological Incident Response Force, U.S.; Pathogen transmission; Polymerase chain reaction; U.S. Army Medical Research Institute of Infectious Diseases; Viral biology.

# Anthrax letter attacks

**Date:** September-November, 2001

**The Event:** One week after the terrorist attacks on New York City and the Pentagon of September 11, 2001, the discovery of the bacterium that causes the deadly disease anthrax in letters mailed to various parties in New York, Florida, and Washington, D.C., triggered a forensic investigation.

**Significance:** Beyond their human toll, infecting twenty-two people overall and killing five, the anthrax attacks that took place in September, 2001, caused heightened panic at a time when the United States was reeling from the tragedy of the terrorist attacks on the World Trade Center and the Pentagon. The 2001 anthrax attacks led to a number of policy changes surrounding preparations to combat biological terrorism in the United States.

On September 11, 2001, the United States endured the largest act of terrorism it had ever experienced when highjackers flew commercial airliners into the towers of the World Trade Center in New York City and into the Pentagon in Arlington, Virginia. These attacks led to a change in ideology within the country that was just getting under way when the United States was attacked again, this time by an unknown assailant using the naturally existing bioterrorism source known as anthrax.

## Anthrax

Anthrax is a life-threatening disease caused by the bacterium *Bacillus anthracis*. This bacterium is assiduous in that it turns dormant and into a spore stage when it does not have a host or is threatened by extreme temperatures, and it can survive in this state until it comes into contact with a new host. Then, even if it has been dormant for decades, it can spread very quickly.

Anthrax is most commonly found in agricultural areas, where it often infects cattle, sheep, goats, and other animals, but it can also occur among humans. Humans typically contract the disease through handling products from infected animals (cutaneous anthrax), by inhaling spores from contaminated products or animals (inhalation anthrax), or by eating the meat of infected animals (gastrointestinal anthrax). Anthrax is not known to spread from one person to another as do cold viruses; the large majority of people who become infected with anthrax experience cutaneous exposure. Anthrax outbreaks are rare in the United States, although they were more common in the eighteenth and nineteenth centuries; from the early twentieth century onward, anthrax has been most commonly encountered in developing countries.

Because anthrax kills humans through the multiplication of the *B. anthracis* bacterium within the body, it is most deadly when it reaches the lungs or the bloodstream. Cutaneous anthrax, the least dangerous form of the disease, typically results in blisters or ulcers on the skin. Indeed, more than three-fourths of people who contract cutaneous anthrax survive without medicinal treatment. Inhalation anthrax is the most dangerous of the three forms of the disease; more than half of those infected do not survive despite treatment. Treatment success is greatly influenced by how early the infection is uncovered and treated. People who come into contact with *B. anthracis* generally become sick within a week or ten days, but symptoms can take up to two months to appear.

Anthrax has been used in warfare since World War II, and a number of nations have developed biological weapons that include *B. anthracis*. Although some countries have destroyed their biological weapons facilities, others continue to test new strains of anthrax and conduct research seeking new antidotes for this disease.

## The Attacks

On October 1, 2001, Claire Fletcher, an employee at the Columbia Broadcasting System (CBS) news division in New York City began to develop facial swelling and nausea. Her symptoms were confirmed as cutaneous anthrax, and she was provided antibiotics and later recovered. On October 4, Robert Stevens, an employee at the tabloid newspaper *Sun*, contracted inhalation anthrax and died the next

day. *Sun* was published by American Media, Incorporated, located in Boca Raton, Florida

Although the first victim of the anthrax attacks was not identified until October 1, the attacks arguably began when the letters that contained the anthrax were first sent. Five such letters were postmarked in Trenton, New Jersey, on September 18, 2001, and sent to locations in New York City and Florida. Specifically, letters were sent to the news divisions of the American Broadcasting Company (ABC), the National Broadcasting Company (NBC), and CBS as well as the *New York Post* in New York City and to the *National Enquirer* and American Media in Boca Raton, Florida.

Two more letters containing anthrax were also postmarked in Trenton on October 9, 2001; these were addressed to the Washington, D.C., offices of Senator Tom Daschle of South Dakota and Senator Patrick Leahy of Vermont. After an aide at Daschle's office opened the letter, it was found to contain a more potent form of anthrax than had been used in the earlier mailings; initial news media reports referred to it as "weapons grade" anthrax. The U.S. government mail service was temporarily shut down in response to the attacks, and the letter addressed to Leahy was found a month later, on November 16, after it had been routed to the wrong ZIP Code and placed in an impounded mail bag.

In all, five people died as a result of the anthrax attacks and another seventeen were injured. Many of those who were injured continued to experience ill effects, including fatigue and memory loss, years later. Moreover, a few postal inspectors became ill during the massive cleanup effort that followed the attacks, which continued for two and one-half years. Including the costs of cleanup and replacement of equipment, as well as the investment of human resources, some estimates put the monetary figure for the total damage caused by the attacks at more than one billion dollars.

## The Investigation

After 2001, the anthrax attacks became known as Amerithrax, the case name given to them by the Federal Bureau of Investigation (FBI). The investigation that ensued relied on a combination of investigative police work and fo-

## Recognizing and Handling Suspicious Packages

*After the anthrax letter attacks in 2001, the Centers for Disease Control and Prevention developed the following guidelines for recognizing and handling suspicious packages.*

### Identifying Suspicious Packages and Envelopes

Some characteristics of suspicious packages and envelopes include the following:

**Inappropriate or unusual labeling**

- Excessive postage
- Handwritten or poorly typed addresses
- Misspellings of common words
- Strange return address or no return address
- Incorrect titles or title without a name
- Not addressed to a specific person
- Marked with restrictions, such as "Personal," "Confidential," or "Do not X-ray"
- Marked with any threatening language
- Postmarked from a city or state that does not match the return address

**Appearance**

- Powdery substance felt through or appearing on the package or envelope
- Oily stains, discolorations, or odor
- Lopsided or uneven envelope
- Excessive packaging material such as masking tape, string, etc.

**Other suspicious signs**

- Excessive weight
- Ticking sound
- Protruding wires or aluminum foil

**If a package or envelope appears suspicious, DO NOT OPEN IT.**

### Handling of Suspicious Packages or Envelopes

- Do not shake or empty the contents of any suspicious package or envelope.
- Do not carry the package or envelope, show it to others or allow others to examine it.
- Put the package or envelope down on a stable surface; do not sniff, touch, taste, or look closely at it or at any contents which may have spilled.
- Alert others in the area about the suspicious package or envelope. Leave the area, close any doors, and take actions to prevent others from entering the area. If possible, shut off the ventilation system.
- WASH hands with soap and water to prevent spreading potentially infectious material to face or skin. Seek additional instructions for exposed or potentially exposed persons.
- If at work, notify a supervisor, a security officer, or a law enforcement official. If at home, contact the local law enforcement agency.
- If possible, create a list of persons who were in the room or area when this suspicious letter or package was recognized and a list of persons who also may have handled this package or letter. Give this list to both the local public health authorities and law enforcement officials.

---

rensic testing. Investigators from the FBI, U.S. Postal Service, and other governmental agencies worked on the case, but through the seven ensuing years, no suspects were arrested.

Investigators observed that the anthrax used in the attacks was not all of the same grade. That mailed to television networks and the newspaper was of a brown granular form that caused only cutaneous anthrax, while that mailed to the senators and to Florida was a higher grade that caused inhalation anthrax. However, both types came from the same Ames strain that had been distributed to biological research labs across the United States and overseas.

Investigators narrowed the origin of the let-

ters to Princeton, New Jersey, after anthrax spores were found in a mailbox near Princeton University. Hundreds of mailboxes in the area were tested, and no others tested positive. After further testing of the anthrax used in the attacks, investigators backed away from referring to the higher-grade anthrax as "weapons grade." However, several scientists still thought that the anthrax spores had been combined with additives that rendered the material more easily inhaled. They argued that only someone with advanced expertise could have created such a mixture.

DNA (deoxyribonucleic acid) tests of the anthrax inhaled by the first victim, Robert

Stevens, ruled out laboratories in England as the source of the anthrax. Later testing found a DNA match with the original Ames strain of anthrax produced at Fort Detrick in Frederick, Maryland. Testing also indicated that the anthrax had been made within the two years preceding the attack, using a water source in the northeastern United States.

The person most closely scrutinized by investigators was Dr. Steven Hatfill, an American virologist and bioweapons expert who consistently denied any involvement. U.S. attorney general John Ashcroft labeled Hatfill a "person of interest," and significant amounts of government time and resources were invested in looking into possible connections between him and the anthrax attacks. Hatfill later sued several newspapers and magazines for libel and the FBI and U.S. Justice Department for violating his constitutional rights. In June, 2008, he was exonerated when he won a large settlement from the U.S. government.

Meanwhile, the investigation was moving in a different direction, as the government built a case against Bruce Ivins, a veteran biological-weapon researcher for the U.S. Army who had worked on the type of anthrax used in the attacks. Ivins had a history of suspicious behavior around the time of the attacks. In July, 2008, as the Justice Department was preparing to present its case against him to a grand jury, Ivins committed suicide. In early August, a federal prosecutor announced that Ivins was the sole culprit behind the 2001 anthrax attacks. Ivins clearly had the means and opportunity to perpetrate the attacks. Less certain was the question of what his motive may have been. One theory was the possibility that he stood to profit from his patents for a powerful anthrax vaccine.

*Brion Sever and Ryan Kelly*

**Further Reading**

Cole, Leonard A. *The Anthrax Letters: A Medical Detective Story.* Washington, D.C.: Joseph Henry Press, 2003. Presents an in-depth examination of the anthrax attacks and the media frenzy they created as well as the government's response to the attacks. Emphasizes the difficulties that investigators and scientists faced in reacting to the attacks and discusses the continuing threat posed by anthrax.

Graysmith, Robert. *Amerithrax: The Hunt for the Anthrax Killer.* New York: Berkley Books, 2003. Uses evidence from the official FBI investigation to guide an analysis of the anthrax case. Contends that the anthrax-contaminated letter opened at American Media in Florida on September 19, 2001, is the key to solving the case.

Hasan, Tahara. *Anthrax Attacks Around the World.* New York: Rosen, 2003. Brief volume presents details on the various anthrax attacks that have occurred around the world. Provides useful context for the 2001 attacks in the United States.

Thompson, Marilyn W. *The Killer Strain: Anthrax and the Government Exposed.* New York: HarperCollins, 2003. Focuses primarily on the U.S. government's reactions to the 2001 anthrax attacks. Analyzes the responses of doctors, politicians, scientists, and law-enforcement personnel in responding to the threat in the immediate days and weeks following the attacks.

**See also:** Anthrax; Bacteria; Bacterial resistance and response to antibacterial agents; Biological terrorism; Biological warfare diagnosis; Biological weapon identification; Biological Weapons Convention of 1972; Chemical Biological Incident Response Force, U.S.; Viral biology.

## Anthropometry

**Definition**: Systematic study of the dimensions of the human body and skeleton.

**Significance:** Anthropometry has a long history of use in criminalistics and medical sciences. Forensic anthropometry uses the methods and techniques of physical anthropology in a legal context to help law-enforcement agencies identify human remains specifically.

Anthropometry is the application of a quantified series of measures to the study of the human body with respect to origins, relationships, and individual identity. Forensic anthropometry is the application of anthropometrics to human remains—whether victims of accidents, catastrophes, or criminal acts—to identify characteristics and thus help establish personal identities. Anthropometry can be both objective and rigorous when conducted by trained scientists who are familiar with measurement techniques and their subsequent statistical interpretations.

## Scientific Basis

The science of anthropometry is based on several premises. First, the body dimensions of each individual represent a subset of unique features that can be used, like fingerprints, for identification purposes. Second, body dimensions provide information regarding additional characteristics such as gender, stature, and, in some cases, ethnicity. Third, body dimensions shed light on health, size, and morphology of internal tissues and organs. Fourth, certain body dimensions and skeletal remains can provide a record of health, accidents, and diseases and permit determination of health at time of death. All of these elements may aid the identification process.

Anthropometry is divided into two subfields: somatometry and osteometry. Somatometry is the measurement of dimensions of the living body, the cadaver, or body fragments. The measurement of the head and face constitutes a special field within somatometry termed cephalometry. Osteometry is the measurement of the bones and distinctive features of bones such as heads of ball joints, protuberances, condyles, articulations, and bone density of the human skeleton. Systematic measurement of the skull is sometimes termed craniometry. Both somatometry and osteometry have been proven useful in the comparison and identification of geographic variation and patterns among human populations in different areas of the world. Anthropometry is especially useful in the sciences of physical anthropology and the paleontological study of human ancestors and hominid relationships.

Collectively, anthropometric analysis of somatometry and osteometry can provide important information about an individual. De-pending on the extent of remains collected, anthropometrists can determine age, sex, stature, body shape, diet, work habits, and sometimes ancestry of an individual. Forensic anthropometry has proven especially useful in missing persons cases; the anthropometrics of discovered remains can be compared with information obtained from physicians, photographs, and other materials to determine the likelihood of a match between the remains and the missing person or persons. Anthropometric data on remains that do not match the missing persons of immediate interest are archived in an electronic database for future possible comparisons.

## History

Anthropometry traces its roots to French criminologist Alphonse Bertillon (1853-1914), who reasoned that because no two persons are exactly alike, an individual could be identified on the basis of his or her body dimensions. Beginning in 1882, Bertillon systematically measured various dimensions on the bodies of criminals in Paris jails, including height, length of ear, and length of foot. He laboriously compiled a vast archive of measurements that was successfully used as a guide to identify repeat criminal offenders. The Bertillon system, or *bertillonage*, as it came to be called, was widely adopted in France and several other European countries.English scientist Francis Galton (1822-1911) simplified the process originated by Bertillon by reducing the number of body dimensions measured. Galton also introduced the use of fingerprints to identify criminals. The reliability of fingerprints as a means of identification and the ease of fingerprinting were quickly recognized, and fingerprint analysis soon replaced Bertillon's laborious system of measuring body dimensions as a tool of the criminal justice system.

In the later years of the nineteenth century and well into the early years of the twentieth century, however, anthropologists adopted anthropometrics to compare human races. Although the method was useful at first, anthropometry took a darker turn as some used anthropometric data to suggest that morphological differences among groups of peoples implied superiority of some human groups over others. For example, anthropometry became a political tool in the eugenics policies of the Nazis, who used cranial measurements to distinguish Aryans from Jews. In a similar vein, social anthropologist William Herbert Sheldon contended that one could predict the mental, emotional, and social characteristics of a person, as well as personality and potential criminality, on the basis of the individual's body measurements alone. After the Holocaust, these schools of anthropometry went into decline, and the use of anthropometry to imply racial differences, personality traits, or criminal predisposition was largely discontinued.

### Forensic Applications

Although the use of anthropometry in foren-

sic science has been somewhat superseded by the use of DNA (deoxyribonucleic acid) analysis, anthropometry is still widely used to provide initial identification of human remains in cases of natural disasters, automobile accidents, and catastrophes such as airplane crashes or terrorist attacks. Anthropometry is also helpful in identifying remains that have been deliberately destroyed in an effort to make identification impossible.

Forensic anthropologists must be familiar with both field and laboratory techniques, as they are often among the first to arrive at a site to recover and gather remains for identification. These scientists combine expertise in comparative osteology, human osteology, craniometry, osteometry, and racial morphology as well as skeletal anatomy and function and skeletal pro-

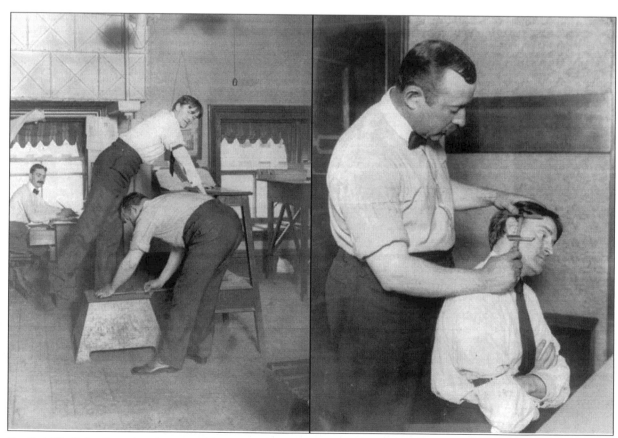

New York City Police Department personnel demonstrate the Bertillon measurement method of identification, an early use of anthropometry. These photographs, taken around 1908, show how measures were taken of two of the many body dimensions used in the Bertillon system, ears and feet. *(Library of Congress)*

portions characteristic of different geographic areas. Forensic anthropologists work with other crime scene investigators, such as forensic pathologists, to reconstruct the biological nature of individuals at the time of postmortem examinations; they also provide expertise in criminal cases.

Depending on the amount and nature of remains, forensic anthropometry continues to be useful in providing such information as age, gender, health, past injuries, and injuries that may have caused death. Forensic anthropometry has proven especially useful in cases in which only partial remains have been recovered. Examples of successful uses of forensic anthropometry include the identification of remains from the Vietnam War and other past conflicts, identification of the remains of victims of the 2001 terrorist attack on the World Trade Center, and identification of the skeletal fragments of the last two members of the family of Russian czar Nicholas II, who were murdered nearly one hundred years ago in a field in Siberia.

*Dwight G. Smith*

**Further Reading**

Krogman, Wilton Marion, and Mehmet Yasar Iscan. *The Human Skeleton in Forensic Medicine*. 2d ed. Springfield, Ill.: Charles C Thomas, 1986. Updated and expanded version of Krogman's classic work, which was first published in 1962.

Pheasant, Stephen, and Christine M. Haslegrave. *Bodyspace: Anthropometry, Ergonomics, and the Design of Work*. 3d ed. Boca Raton, Fla.: CRC Press, 2005. Details the many different applications of anthropometrics.

Reichs, Kathleen, ed. *Forensic Osteology: Advances in the Identification of Human Remains*. 2d ed. Springfield, Ill.: Charles C Thomas, 1998. Collection of essays includes discussions of the history, scope, and specialized methodologies of forensic anthropology, including anthropometry.

Ulijaszek, S. J., and C. G. N. Mascie-Taylor, eds. *Anthropometry: The Individual and the Population*. New York: Cambridge University Press, 1994. Collection of essays by anthropologists, biologists, clinical scientists, and other experts describes the many ways in which anthropometry is used.

White, Tim D., and Pieter A. Folkens. *The Human Bone Manual*. Burlington, Mass.: Elsevier Academic Press, 2005. Compact volume offers critical information about skeletal identifications and hundreds of illustrations and photographs. Intended for use by professional anthropologists, forensic scientists, and researchers.

**See also:** Autopsies; Biometric identification systems; Composite drawing; Crime scene investigation; Forensic anthropology; Forensic sculpture; Osteology and skeletal radiology; Sex determination of remains; Skeletal analysis.

# Antianxiety agents

**Definition**: Group of medications that relieve tension, reduce activity, induce relaxation, and produce drowsiness.

**Significance**: The use of antianxiety agents is routinely associated with high risk for dependence and abuse that can be associated with criminal activity, drug-seeking behaviors, and suicide. In addition, sexual predators are increasingly using antianxiety agents to reduce the capacity of their victims to react against assault.

The drugs classified as antianxiety agents are frequently prescribed for patients complaining of tension, muscle strain, sleep problems, panic attacks, and phobias. Among the drugs' effects are drowsiness, impaired social or occupational functioning, slurred speech, rapid mood changes, and impaired judgment; these effects become more pronounced with increased dosage. Because of the negative impact on occupational functioning that abuse of antianxiety agents can produce, many employment settings have implemented urine testing of employees to screen for these drugs.

## Benzodiazepines

The most commonly prescribed antianxiety agents are the benzodiazepines, which are classified as controlled substances by the U.S. Drug Enforcement Administration (DEA). These include such drugs as chlordiazepoxide (Librium), diazepam (Valium), alprazolam (Xanax), clonazepam (Klonopin), clorazepate (Tranxene), and lorazepam (Ativan). The benzodiazepines act on the central nervous system and produce intoxication and withdrawal symptoms. These drugs can produce physical and psychological dependence within two to four weeks of usage. The symptoms of withdrawal from antianxiety drugs can range form mild discomfort to severe reactions, including seizures. Some of the common symptoms include weakness, rapid pulse, tremor, insomnia, restlessness, nausea, hallucinations, and irritability. Sudden withdrawal from benzodiazepine dependence can lead to seizures and even death. Detoxification involves a gradual decrease of the drug over a period of weeks. Persons who are addicted to antianxiety medications often respond best to detoxification in residential treatment programs.

In medical practice, the benzodiazepines have replaced the usage of barbiturates for control of anxiety. Barbiturates were commonly used throughout the early to mid-twentieth century to induce relaxation, promote sleep, and quell tension, but they had a high abuse potential. Common barbiturates include amobarbital (Amytal), phenobarbital (Luminal), pentobarbital (Nembutal), seconbarbital (Seconal), and thiopental (Pentothal). Barbiturate drugs are still common among the chemical substances sold illegally. Colloquially they are frequently referred to as reds, red devils, yellow jackets, rainbows, downers, phennies, and nembies.

## Abuse and Negative Impacts

Although antianxiety agents are legitimately prescribed for the treatment of psychiatric disorders associated with anxiety, a large number of individuals use the drugs illicitly for their mood-altering relaxation effects. Some use only benzodiazepines, but others often use them in conjunction with other controlled sub-

stances, including stimulants and hallucinogens, to diminish anxious feelings; some use benzodiazepines with cocaine to reduce withdrawal symptoms or with heroin as a way to enhance the euphoric feelings heroin causes. Benzodiazepine abusers, the majority of whom are under forty years of age, account for approximately one-third of all substance-abuse-related hospital emergency room visits in the United States.

Benzodiazepine intoxication is associated with behavioral disinhibition that can result in heightened physical and sexual aggressiveness, especially when combined with alcohol use. The effects of benzodiazepines are additive to those of alcohol, and in combination the two can lead to respiratory depression that can result in death. In general, when the additive central nervous system depressant effects of alcohol are combined with a benzodiazepine, the results can include excessive sedation, cognitive impairment, and psychomotor slowing. The diagnosis of benzodiazepine intoxication is best confirmed through toxicological analysis of blood or urine samples.

Because of the disinhibition effects of the benzodiazepines, some sexual predators use these drugs to dose intended victims, often by surreptitiously introducing the drugs into liquids the victims are drinking. The drugs can reduce the potential victims' capacity to react strongly against sexual assault or may even render them unconscious. In order to prove a charge of a drug-facilitated criminal offense, law-enforcement officials must be able to prove detection of the substance in the victim during commission of the act. Research has shown that the antianxiety agents are detectable in oral fluid, blood, urine, and hair samples of those who ingest the drugs over the course of hours and days. The evidence of benzodiazepine ingestion in hair samples is significant in cases where long delays separate the time of the alleged crimes and the collection of blood and urine samples, which may be of little value after a certain period of time.

State and federal agencies in the United States have carried out a continuing effort to restrict the distribution of benzodiazepines through strict multiple-form reporting of prescriptions for these medications. Some U.S. states have created databases of the names of physicians who prescribe benzodiazepines, as well as the patients who receive the prescriptions, to monitor the distribution of these medications. Requirements for triplicate-form reporting of prescriptions have been found to reduce the use of the benzodiazepines for other than legitimate medical purposes.

*Frank J. Prerost*

## Further Reading

Galanter, Marc, and Herbert D. Kleber, eds. *Textbook of Substance Abuse Treatment.* Washington, D.C.: American Psychiatric Publishing, 2004. Extensive volume provides information concerning the effects of substance abuse in the workplace and describes strategies to overcome the problems.

Meyer, Robert G., and Christopher M. Weaver. *Law and Mental Health: A Case-Based Approach.* New York: Guilford Press, 2006. Focuses on the various legal issues surrounding drug abuse. Includes discussion of drug screening and informed consent.

Sales, Bruce, D., Michael Owen Miller, and Susan R. Hall. *Laws Affecting Clinical Practice.* Washington, D.C.: American Psychological Association, 2005. Describes the issues associated with mental health professionals' bringing evidence to trial in criminal and civil litigation.

Simon, Robert I. *Concise Guide to Psychiatry and Law for Clinicians.* 3d ed. Washington, D.C.: American Psychiatric Publishing, 2001. Brief volume aimed at mental health care professionals provides a good overview of the legal issues surrounding substance abuse.

Stern, Theodore A., et al., eds. *Massachusetts General Hospital Handbook of General Hospital Psychiatry.* 5th ed. St. Louis: C. V. Mosby, 2004. Handbook intended for health care professionals includes an extensive discussion of the screening process for abuse of controlled substances in health care settings that is relevant for investigators who gather forensic evidence in criminal cases.

**See also:** Amphetamines; Club drugs; Crack cocaine; Drug abuse and dependence; Halcion; Hallucinogens; Illicit substances; Opioids; Psychotropic drugs; Stimulants.

# Antibiotics

**Definition**: Therapeutic agents that kill or inhibit the growth of infectious microorganisms.

**Significance:** Antibiotics kill certain types of bacteria that cause diseases without severely hurting the patient. They can abate the progression of diseases and extensively reduce their effects on human populations. Effective use of antibiotics can also blunt the potential threat of microorganisms as biological weapons.

Microbial infections cause illnesses that diminish the quality of life, reduce productivity, and can cause long-term morbidity or death. Effective early treatment can reverse the progression of the disease, decrease the convalescence time, avert the onset of undesirable after-effects caused by some diseases, and potentially prevent the spread of the infection from one person to another. Antibiotics are the first-line treatments against infectious diseases.

## Antibiotic classification

Older antibiotics are derived from compounds made by various microorganisms to kill competing bacteria. The majority of antibiotics, however, are completely synthetic in their composition, even though their chemical structures are a variation of naturally-produced antibiotics.

Antibiotics are classified according to their chemical structures, and drugs with similar chemical structures are categorized in a common group. The largest group of antibiotics, the beta-lactams, consists of the penicillins, cephalosporins, monobactams, and carbapenems. Other antibiotic groups include the macrolides, tetracyclines, aminoglycosides, lincosamides, sulfonamides, quinolones/fluoroquinolones, polypeptides, glycopeptides, and the newer lipoglycopeptides.

Several antibiotic groups consist of only one drug. Such antibiotics include bacitracin, clindamycin, cycloserine, metronidazole, mupirocin, fusidic acid, and fosfomycin. Chloramphenicol and its structural derivative thiamphenicol are members of their own antibiotic group. Streptogramin A and dalfopristin are given as a combination, and these drugs are the only members of the streptogramin group. Quinupristin and dalfopristin are given in a combination product called *Synercid* and are in their own class. The oxazolidinones only contains one member, linezolid, and the diaminopyrimidines only contain trimethoprim. The antibiotic daptomycin is the sole member of the lipoproteins, tigecycline is the only representative of the glycylcyclines, and fidaxomicin is the only member of the macrocyclic antibiotics.

Finally a handful of antibiotics called antimycobacterials are specifically used to treat tuberculosis, leprosy or other diseases caused by other members of the genus *Mycobacterium*. Drugs like isoniazid, ethionamide, ethambutol, pyrazinamide, capreomycin, and rifampin and its derivatives are used to treat tuberculosis, which is caused by *Mycobacterium tuberculosis* (*M. tuberculosis*). Infections by *M. avium* and *M. intracellulare*, which are grouped together as the *M. avium* complex or MAC, are treated with anti-tuberculosis antibiotics in combination with aminoglycosides, fluoroquinolones, and macrolides. Dapsone and clofazimine are prescribed to treat leprosy, which is caused by *M. leprae*.

## Antibiotic mode of action

Several chemically unrelated groups of antibiotics can target similar biochemical processes in bacterial cells. The ability of distinct antibiotics to kill particular bacterial species varies extensively. Some antibiotics can only kill a few bacterial species (narrow-range) while others can eradicate many different types of bacteria (broad-spectrum). Some antibiotics kill bacteria (bactericidal) while others stop bacterial

growth without killing them (bacteriostatic).

Several antibiotics inhibit bacterial protein synthesis. These include the macrolides, tetracyclines, tigecycline, aminoglycosides, lincosamides, streptogramins, oxazolidinones, mupirocin, quinupristin/dalfopristin, fusidic acid, and chloramphenicol and its derivatives. These drugs inhibit protein synthesis at different stages of the process. Lincosamides are used to treat infections with anaerobic bacteria. Streptogramins and oxazolidinones are used for infections that resist other antibiotic treatments.

Many antibiotics inhibit the synthesis of the bacterial cell wall, which surrounds the bacterium and protects it. Without an intact cell wall, most bacterial cells quickly die or succumb to the host immune system. Antibiotics that inhibit bacterial cell wall synthesis include the beta-lactams, glycopeptides, bacitracin, cycloserine, and fosfomycin. These drugs are not effective against bacterial species that lack cell walls (e.g., *Mycoplasma*). The antituberculosis drugs isoniazid and ethionamide inhibit the synthesis of the specialized fatty acids (mycolic acids) required for the construction of the waxy cell walls of mycobacteria. Ethambutol, another anti-tuberculosis drug, hampers the synthesis of complex sugars in the cell wall of *M. tuberculosis*.

Beneath the bacterial cell wall is the cell membrane, and daptomycin disrupts bacterial membranes. Some bacteria (i.e., gram-negative bacteria) have a special membrane outside the cell wall (outer membrane). A few antibiotics, such as the polypeptides polymyxin B and colistin, specialize in attacking this outer membrane.

Some antibiotics interfere with the synthesis of essential molecules. Folic acid is a vital cofactor for the biosynthesis of the precursors of DNA and RNA, and without it bacteria die. Because humans cannot synthesize folic acid and solely acquire it from their diets, folic acid synthesis inhibitors do not adversely affect humans. The sulfonamides, the diaminopyrimidine trimethoprim, and the anti-leprosy drug dapsone impede the synthesis of folic acid.

Several antibiotics disrupt the synthesis of DNA or RNA. Rifampin and its derivatives, and fidaxomicin inhibit the synthesis of RNA and stop gene expression. The quinolones/fluoroquinolones kill bacteria by primarily hindering bacterial DNA replication, but these drugs also quell RNA synthesis as well. The antibiotic metronidazole, which is only active against anaerobic bacteria, is converted into a highly reactive molecule upon entering bacterial cells that damages bacterial DNA.

The anti-tuberculosis drug pyrazinamide inhibits the synthesis of fatty acids, which are used for the construction of biological membranes, and also hamstrings protein synthesis, which explains why this drug can kill dormant *M. tuberculosis* cells.

## New Antibiotics

Several new antibiotics are under development. Posizolid, radezolid, and torezolid are three new oxazolidinones still undergoing human tests. Platensimycin inhibits fatty acid synthesis and is still in the experimental stage. Teixobactin is a new agent that shows broad activity against several bacterial species and is effective in animals, but has yet to be tested in humans.

## Antibiotics and Forensics

The presence of antibiotics in bodily fluids such as urine or blood or tissue samples from the liver, stomach, or peripheral tissues obtained after death usually indicates the presence of an infection in the deceased. Detection of antibiotics or their break-down products in post-mortem tissues exploits the unique chemical structure of each antibiotic.

The prescription of antibiotics to prevent an impending infection is called antibiotic prophylaxis. Ciprofloxacin was given to approximately ten thousand people who were potentially exposed to *Bacillus anthracis*, the causative agent of anthrax, during the bioterrorism attacks in late October, 2001. Antibiotic prophylaxis probably saved many lives, and aggressive prophylactic use of antibiotics can potentially thwart a bioterrorism attack.

*Michael A. Buratovich*

## Further Reading

Blaser, Martin J. *Missing Microbes: How the Overuse of Antibiotics is Fueling our Modern Plagues*. New York: Picador, 2015. A research physician sounds the alarm over the misuse of antibiotics and the long-term consequences of this abuse.

Gallagher, Jason C. and Conan MacDougall. *Antibiotics Simplified*. 3rd ed. Burlington, MA: Jones & Bartlett Learning, 2013. A small, pocket-sized book that gives basic clinical facts about antibiotics and is easy to use and read.

Gilbert, David N., Henry F. Chambers, and George M. Eliopoulos. *Sanford Guide to Antimicrobial Therapy 2014*. 44th ed. Sperryville, VA: Sanford Guides, 2014. A classic, well-organized and accurate reference guide to antibiotic prescribing.

Hauser, Alan R. *Antibiotic Basics for Clinicians: The ABCs of Choosing the Right Antibacterial Agent*. 2d ed. Baltimore, MD: Lippincott Williams & Wilkins, 2012. Sound description of individual antibiotics, their mode of action, clinical use, and side effects.

Moffat, Anthony C. *Clarke's Analysis of Drugs and Poisons*. 4th ed. London: Pharmaceutical Press, 2011. An exhaustive reference of forensic analytical techniques for detecting antibiotics, poisons and other drugs in post-mortem material.

Sachs, Jessica Snyder. *Good Germs, Bad Germs: Health and Survival in a Bacterial World*. New York: Hill & Wang, 2007. Presents interesting discussion of the interrelationships between bacteria and our bodies and how antibiotic treatments can affect those relationships.

Scholar, Eric M., and William B. Pratt, eds. *The Antimicrobial Drugs*. New York: Oxford University Press, 2000. Detailed reference book on antibiotics offers wonderfully clear explanations.

Smith, Frederick P., ed. *Handbook of Forensic Drug Analysis*. Burlington, Mass.: Elsevier Academic Press, 2005. Provides precise, detailed discussions of the laboratory techniques used to detect substances in post-mortem tissue samples, including antibiotics.

Walsh, Christopher. *Antibiotics: Actions, Origins, Resistance*. Washington, D.C.: ASM Press, 2003. Offers encyclopedic treatment of the activities, structures, modes of resistance, and appropriate uses of antibiotics.

**See also:** Anthrax; Bacteria; Bacterial biology; Bacterial resistance and response to antibacterial agents; Biodetectors; Biological terrorism; Centers for Disease Control and Prevention; *Escherichia coli*; Parasitology; Pathogen transmission; Tularemia.

# Antidotes. *See Poisons and antidotes*

# Antipsychotics

**Definition**: Group of drugs used to treat psychotic disorders such as schizophrenia and mania.

**Significance:** Antipsychotic drugs have the ability to reduce psychotic symptoms without necessarily producing drowsiness and sedation. Forensic psychiatrists as well as law-enforcement personnel are familiar with antipsychotics because many criminals with mental illnesses use such drugs.

Antipsychotic drugs, also known as neuroleptic drugs or neuroleptics, were first discovered in the late 1940's by Henri Laborit, a French surgeon. Laborit found that when phenothiazines were used in conjunction with surgical anesthesia, the patients became less concerned about their surgery, and he thought that these drugs might be useful for reducing the emotionality of psychiatric patients. Since that time, the use of antipsychotics has become common in psychiatry. Initially, these drugs were called tranquilizers, but as that term seemed to imply sedation, its use was dropped.

All antipsychotic drugs tend to block dopamine receptors in the mesolimbic pathway of the brain; this accounts for their antipsychotic action. The drugs range in potency based on their ability to bind with dopamine receptors. High-potency antipsychotics such as haloperidol require lower dosage (usually a few milligrams) than do low-potency antipsychotics such as chlorpromazine (usually several hundred milligrams). Persons who are prescribed antipsychotics need to be monitored for regular intake, as compliance with drug therapy is an important aspect of treatment for psychotic disorders.

## Typical Antipsychotics

Antipsychotics are classified as typical or atypical. Typical, or conventional, antipsychotics (and some of the trade names under which they are sold) include chlorpromazine (Thorazine), thioridazine (Mellaril), mesoridazine (Serentil), loxapine (Loxitane), perphenazine (Trilafon), molindone (Moban), thiothixene (Navane), trifluoperazine (Stelazine), fluphenazine (Prolixin), haloperidol (Haldol), and pimozide (Orap). These kinds of drugs were the first antipsychotics to be developed. The efficacy of typical and atypical antipsychotics is comparable, but typical antipsychotics have the drawback of possibly severe side effects. The main side effects of typical antipsychotics are known as extrapyramidal symptoms—a name arising out of the part of the brain that is stimulated by the drugs. Akathisia, a syndrome involving a subjective desire to be in constant motion and an inability to sit still or stand still, with consequent pacing, is the most common side effect.

Side effects of typical antipsychotics may also take the form of facial tics. Sometimes Parkinson's disease (which is marked by tremors of the hands while they are at rest, muscular rigidity, a masklike face, and a shuffling walk) may be precipitated by antipsychotic drugs. Tardive dyskinesia—the term means "late-appearing abnormal movements"—is among the most serious complications of antipsychotic treatment. It involves repetitive sucking and smacking movements of the lips, thrusting in and out of the tongue, and movements of the arms, toes, or fingers.

Typical antipsychotics can also have several

anticholinergic side effects, such as dry mouth, blurred near vision, urinary retention, delayed emptying of the stomach, esophageal reflux, and precipitation of glaucoma. Often these drugs have metabolic and endocrine effects as well, such as weight gain, high blood glucose, temperature irregularities, and menstrual irregularities. Some allergic reactions may also occur, such as jaundice or skin rashes. Rarely, agranulocytosis, or low white blood cell count, can develop in the early stages of treatment.

## Atypical Antipsychotics

Atypical antipsychotic medications (and some of the trade names under which they are sold) include clozapine (Clozaril, Fazaclo), risperidone (Risperdal), olanzepine (Zyprexa), quetiapine (Seroquel), ziprasidone (Geodon), and aripiprazole (Abilify). These drugs have an advantage over typical antipsychotics in that they have no extrapyramidal side effects (such as Parkinsonism, akathisia, and tardive dyskinesia). Atypical antipsychotics are at least as effective as conventional or typical agents in inducing positive symptoms, and they also help to improve cognition and enhance mood.

Atypical antipsychotics are not completely free of side effects, however, and the side effects differ from drug to drug. Risperidone, for example, causes an increase in prolactin levels—a hormone that can lead to breast enlargement, production of breast milk, and irregular menses. In high doses, this drug can also cause extrapyramidal side effects. Olanzepine can cause weight gain and may produce modest prolactin elevation. Ziprasidone can cause drowsiness, dry mouth, runny nose, symptoms of high blood sugar, and allergic reactions. Quetiapine can cause drowsiness, dizziness, agitation, pain, and weakness. Clozapine can cause weight gain and sedation.

*Manoj Sharma*

## Further Reading

De Oliveira, Irismar R., and M. F. Juruena. "Treatment of Psychosis: Thirty Years of Progress." *Journal of Clinical Pharmacy and Therapeutics* 31, no. 6 (2006): 523-534. Discusses the evolution of antipsychotics, particularly the general replacement of typical antipsychotics with atypical antipsychotics, largely because the latter lack extrapyramidal side effects.

Parker, John, Jana De Villiers, and Samantha Churchward. "High-Dose Antipsychotic Drug Use in a Forensic Setting." *Journal of Forensic Psychiatry and Psychology* 13, no. 2 (2002): 407-415. Presents the results of a study of the application of antipsychotics in a forensic psychiatric setting.

Pinals, D. A., and P. F. Buckley. "Novel Antipsychotic Agents and Their Implications for Forensic Psychiatry." *Journal of the American Academy of Psychiatry and the Law* 27, no. 1 (1999): 7-22. Review of the literature on the clinical efficacy and mechanisms of action of atypical antipsychotics focuses on their use in forensic psychiatry. Concludes that use of these medications may reduce the risk of civil litigation.

Scherk, Harald, and Peter Falkai. "Effects of Antipsychotics on Brain Structure." *Current Opinion in Psychiatry* 19, no. 2 (2006): 145-150. Discusses the different effects of typical and atypical antipsychotics on brain structure and presents evidence that atypical antipsychotics might ameliorate structural changes caused by the disease process underlying schizophrenia.

Silverstone, Trevor, and Paul Turner. *Drug Treatment in Psychiatry*. 5th ed. New York: Routledge, 1995. Examines both general principles of psychiatric drug treatment and specific clinical applications of antipsychotic drugs.

Sinacola, Richard S., and Timothy Peters-Strickland. *Basic Psychopharmacology for Counselors and Psychotherapists*. Boston: Pearson, 2006. Basic text includes a chapter devoted to the treatment of psychotic disorders and the use of antipsychotics.

Stahl, Stephen M. *Essential Psychopharmacology: The Prescriber's Guide*. Rev ed. New York: Cambridge University Press, 2006. Guidebook for practitioners covers the most important and common drugs used for mood stabilization and treatment of psychosis. Includes information on the advantages and disadvantages of each drug, presented in easy-to-read and user-friendly style.

**See also:** Drug classification; Halcion; Hallucinogens; Nervous system; Psychopathic personality disorder; Psychotropic drugs; Stimulants.

## Argentine disappeared children

**Date:** Disappearances occurred between 1976 and 1983

**The Event:** From 1976 to 1983, a military dictatorship ruled Argentina. About thirty thousand people whom the government considered political dissidents or active opponents of the military were taken from their homes by force, interrogated, tortured, and killed. The "disappeared" included young children captured with their parents and pregnant women who were imprisoned until they gave birth. Many of these children were adopted by families associated with the military. Later, relatives of the disappeared filed inquiries with the courts to determine the fates of their children and grandchildren. An organization founded by grandmothers of disappeared children successfully lobbied for changes in Argentine laws to allow grandpaternity testing and to establish a national genetic database for identifying children who had been taken.

**Significance:** The efforts of the Asociación Civil Abuelas de Plaza de Mayo (known in English as the Grandmothers of the Plaza de Mayo) were essential in recruitment of help of international scientists in identifying children who had been separated from their families. The scientists established an Argentine national genetic database and confirmed the validity of tests for grandpaternity. By conducting genetic testing, scientists reunited a number of families.

In 1977, the women of the Asociación Madres de Plaza de Mayo (Mothers of the Plaza de Mayo) began to gather weekly in the main public square of Argentina's capital city, Buenos Aires, to protest the military government's practice of "disappearing" opponents. These women, mothers of missing sons and daughters taken by the government, succeeded in bringing international attention to Argentina's "dirty war."

Also in 1977, twelve grandmothers of children who had disappeared because of government actions formed the Grandmothers of the Plaza de Mayo. Although the military dictatorship was still in power, the Grandmothers began to protest and gather information about the disappearances of their children and grandchildren. Their focus was on locating the missing children; they launched an international campaign to gather support and met with human rights organizations from around the world. By 1982, the Grandmothers had collected information on some three hundred grandchildren whose parents had disappeared. They knew of the possible whereabouts of fifty grandchildren. Military rule ended December, 1983, with the election of president Raúl Alfonsín. He appointed the Comisión Nacional Sobre la Desaparición de Personas (National Commission on the Disappearance of Persons) to investigate what had happened to the disappeared. In 1986 Alfonsin passed a law (Full Stop) that ended investigation of violence during the dirty war. In 1987 the Due Obedience law indicated people could not be prosecuted for crimes committed while following orders. This resulted in the odd situation where captors of the babies could not be prosecuted, but the "adoptive" parents could. In 2003 both these laws were repealed and captors could be prosecuted.

### Application of Forensic Science

The Grandmothers sought help from international scientists. Among those who worked on the problem of identifying the missing children were Dr. Fred Allen, an expert on blood groups; Dr. Luigi Luca Cavalli-Sforza, a population geneticist; Dr. Mary-Claire King, a geneticist; and Pierre Darlu, a mathematician. The scientists took an approach never taken before when they applied the idea of grandpaternity testing—that is, they used the same methods used for standard paternity testing to determine the genetic relationships between children and their grandparents. For identification of related individuals, highly variable genetic markers passed from parent to child are studied. Initially, the scientists used immunological techniques to identify grandchildren; they examined blood samples from suspected stolen children, their possible grandparents, and other living relatives. No samples were available from the parents of the children because they had been murdered by the military. Genetic markers examined were blood group antigens from red blood cells, such as ABO, Rh, and Kelley, and from white blood cells, such as human leukocyte antigens (HLAs). King and other scientists also worked to determine what additional genetic markers could be used to identify the children. Mitochondrial DNA (deoxyribonucleic acid) is isolated from blood. The sequence of mitochondrial DNA is an excellent genetic marker for tracking grandpaternity because mitochondrial DNA is maternally inherited—that is, it is passed from a mother to all of her children. Fathers do not pass mitochondrial DNA to their children. One part of the mitochondrial genome that does not contain any genes is the most variable sequence of the human genome.

Because many copies of mitochondrial DNA exist in each cell, it can be easier to obtain mitochondrial DNA than it is to obtain nuclear DNA. Using mitochondrial DNA to identify individuals, the highly variable region of mitochondrial DNA is sequenced. The sequence is compared with sequences of known persons in a database. Some mitochondrial sequences are unique to particular maternal lineages and can be used to identify grandchildren in these lineages even if parents cannot be tested.

In the 1990's polymerase chain reaction (PCR), which amplifies even small amounts of DNA, greatly improved genetic testing. It even became possible to test small amounts of DNA collected from clothing people had worn (Shed-DNA). When scientists found genetic matches for suspected stolen children, the Grandmothers, the courts, and psychologists worked together to try to ensure the children were not subjected to further trauma. Some stolen children, now adults, felt loyalty to their "adoptive" parents and refused DNA testing. They were also concerned test results could

cause their "adoptive" parents ("appropriators") to go to prison. In some cases, courts ordered clothing confiscated for Shed-DNA testing. By 2014, 116 grandchildren of the estimated 500 people abducted as babies or young children had been identified and reunited with their relatives. While forming bonds with their newly found families, some grandchildren maintained a relationship with their "appropriators."

*Susan J. Karcher*

## Further Reading

Budowle, Bruce, Marc W. Allard, Mark R. Wilson, and Ranajit Chakraborty. "Forensics and Mitochondrial DNA: Applications, Debates, and Foundations." *Annual Review of Genomics and Human Genetics* 4 (September, 2003): 119-141. Describes the forensic applications of mitochondrial DNA analysis.

Goldman, Francisco. "Children of the Dirty War." *The New Yorker* March 19 (2012): 54-65. Relates cases of grandmothers who have not located their grandchildren.

Lazzara, Michael J. "Kidnapped Memories: Argentina's Stolen Children Tell Their Stories." *Journal of Human Rights* 12 (2013): 319-332. Individuals' stories illustrate there is not one answer for what is in the "best interest of the child."

Owens, Kelly N., Michelle Harvey-Blankenship, and Mary-Claire King. "Genomic Sequencing in the Service of Human Rights." *International Journal of Epidemiology* 31 (2002): 53-58. Describes use of genomic analysis in identification of victims of human rights abuses.

Penchaszadeh, Victor B. "Ethical, Legal and Social Issues in Restoring Genetic Identity After Forced Disappearance and Suppression of Identity in Argentina." *Journal of Community Genetics*. Epub February 18 (2015). Addresses interaction of genetics with historical and social factors.

_____. "Genetic Identification of Children of the Disappeared in Argentina." *Journal of the American Medical Women's Association* 52 (Winter, 1997): 16-22. Provides an overview of the historical events and the search for the children along with discussion of the genetic research used to identify the missing children.

Vaisman, Noa. "Relational Human Rights: Shed-DNA and the Identification of the 'Living Disappeared' in Argentina." *Journal of Law and Society* 41 (2014): 391-415. Focuses on use of Shed-DNA for testing.

**See also:** Child abduction and kidnapping; Croatian and Bosnian war victim identification; DNA analysis; DNA database controversies; DNA fingerprinting; DNA profiling; DNA typing; International Association for Identification; Mitochondrial DNA analysis and typing; Polymerase chain reaction

## Army Medical Research Institute of Infectious Diseases. *See* U.S. Army Medical Research Institute of Infectious Diseases

## Arsenic

**Definition**: Arsenic (element 33 in the periodic table) is a brittle, dense grey solid. Arsenic compounds are toxic, and are used industrially in the manufacture of glass, semiconductors and wood preservatives..

**Significance:** Because arsenic is widespread in soil and water, and has a number of industrial uses, there is a significant chance for human exposure, which can lead to toxic effects. The toxic effects and mechanisms of exposure can be subtle, and the symptoms of intoxication can be confused with those of other conditions. Modern methods of chemical analysis can easily reveal the presence of arsenic in body tissues and fluids, but this type of detection was not always as sensitive as it is today

Life- or health-threatening exposure to the toxic chemical arsenic can result from industrial contact, from deliberate poisoning, or from naturally contaminated food or drinking water. Arsenic poisoning may be acute or chronic, depending on whether a large dose is ingested at one time or smaller doses are taken over a lengthy period.

Acute arsenic poisoning is often associated with attempted murder of the victim. Ingestion of as little as two-tenths of a gram of arsenic trioxide (the arsenic compound most commonly used by poisoners, found in insecticides and weed killers) is followed by intense pain in the stomach and esophagus, followed by vomiting and diarrhea. Chronic poisoning by low levels of arsenic such as may be found in contaminated drinking water produces thickening of the skin (hyperkeratosis) of the hands and feet as well as white lines on the fingernails. Cancer of the bladder or other organs can result with long exposure. Neurological effects are also observed, including weakness in the hands and feet (peripheral neuropathy). These symptoms are not always recognized as arsenic-related unless suitable forensic tests are done.

Arsenic binds to proteins and exerts its toxic effects on the body by interfering with vital enzymes. The presence of arsenic in blood or urine can be confirmed through atomic absorption spectrophotometry, a method developed in the second half of the twentieth century. Previously, the primary method of detecting arsenic was a test developed in 1836 by James Marsh. The Marsh test was first used in Tulle, France, in the 1840 trial of Marie Lafarge, who was accused of murdering her husband.

Occasionally, arsenic poisoning may be suspected as the cause of death long after the person in question has died. In such a case, an expert can analyze a hair sample using neutron activation. In this process, the sample is subjected to a flux of neutrons in a nuclear reactor; the induced radioactivity can reveal arsenic, if it is present. This type of procedure has been used on samples from Napoleon I of France and U.S. president Zachary Taylor, both of whom died in the nineteenth century. Many other long-ago deaths have also been revisited in this way, but a complicating element in such cases is the fact that arsenic was sometimes used in embalming procedures in the past.

Quantitative determination of the arsenic

## Difficulty of Proving Arsenic Poisoning

The case of Marie Besnard of Loudun, France, provides some perspective on the difficulties that can arise in a trial for murder by arsenic. Besnard was arrested in 1949 on suspicion of having murdered two husbands, her mother, and several other individuals who had died suddenly. Several of the corpses were exhumed and were found to contain high levels of arsenic.

Besnard was brought to trial in 1952 but was not convicted. Her lawyer was able to use the fact that police had mislabeled some of the exhumed remains to impugn all of the forensic evidence, and the trial came to an end with no verdict. Besnard was tried again in 1954, and this time her attorney argued that the arsenic found in the corpses had in fact been carried there from the soil in the graveyard, perhaps by microbial action. Again, the jury could not reach a verdict. In a third trial in 1961, Besnard was acquitted for lack of proof. According to expert testimony, the neutron activation analysis of hair samples taken from the dead had involved too short a period of neutron irradiation, and therefore the results were unreliable. Testimony was also presented that arsenic could be lost from a long-buried body, raising doubt about the significance of the arsenic levels found.

level present in a given person's body is important because a certain amount of arsenic is to be expected from the naturally occurring traces of arsenic that appear in food and water. Elevation of a person's arsenic level above this threshold may indicate accidental or deliberate poisoning. It is estimated that, in the United States, the average person's diet contains 25-30 micrograms of arsenic per day. Excretion of more than 50 micrograms per day is cause for concern. Given that arsenic can exist in many forms of chemical combination, any urine analysis aimed at determining the body's level of arsenic should distinguish between organic arsenic compounds and inorganic ones. The latter are more dangerous.

### Arsenic Exposure

In the past, the dangers of arsenic were often treated casually, with the result that many people experienced unnecessary, sometimes dangerous, levels of exposure to the chemical. The use of arsenates as pesticides, now minimal in the United States, once was widespread. Fruit, vegetable, and tobacco crops were often sprayed with such pesticides, and high levels of arsenic were left in the soil and on the crops themselves. When humans suffered ill health as a result, forensic scientists needed to find the source of the trouble. In France, arsenate pesticide residues on grapes found their way into wine that poisoned hundreds of French sailors in 1932. Plants grown on contaminated soil can pick up enough arsenic content to be toxic for human or animal consumption, and residues on tobacco are eventually inhaled by smokers.

Chromated copper arsenate is still used as a wood preservative, but many products that formerly contained arsenic no longer do so. Arsenical pigments were long used in wallpaper and in paint, and this led to many poisonings. Research over many years revealed that wallpaper with pigments such as Paris green or Scheele's green (both arsenicals) could generate arsenic-containing vapors (known as Gosio gas, for Italian physician Bartolomeo Gosio, who published his research on the topic in 1893) if moisture and certain microorganisms were present. This type of vapor, which caused some mysterious deaths in the 1890's, was eventually identified as trimethylarsine during the 1930's. In the 1950's, the U.S. ambassador to Italy, Clare Boothe Luce, became the victim of arsenic poisoning when she absorbed a toxic dose from arsenic-contaminated chips of paint that fell from the ceiling of her bedroom in her embassy quarters. Her resulting health problems forced her to resign her post in 1956 and return to the United States.

Medicines based on arsenic are mostly of historical importance, with some exceptions. Arsenic trioxide has been approved for treatment of leukemia, and arsenicals continue to be used against some tropical parasitic diseases. All these remedies present some danger of arsenic poisoning, as do cosmetic preparations that contain arsenic.

Arsenic is probably an essential trace element in human nutrition in very small amounts. People in the Austrian state of Styria have been known to consume arsenic purposely for its supposed tonic effects. By habituating themselves to ever-increasing doses, they are eventually able to tolerate amounts that would normally be fatal.

## Murder by Arsenic

Foul play may be suspected in the death of an otherwise healthy person who develops the symptoms of arsenic poisoning. When such a person dies, forensic testing done postmortem can substantiate toxic levels of arsenic in the liver and other organs, in the stomach contents, and in the blood. If high levels are found, investigators must try to find the source of the poison and its mode of delivery. Accidental or environmental sources must be considered; for example, the victim may have used medicines containing arsenic or taken herbal supplements with arsenic content. If malicious intent is suspected, the dietary habits of the victim may suggest how the poison could have been administered. Any remnants of food or drink known to be ingested by the victim should be tested for arsenic, and anyone who has had access to the victim or the victim's food need should be investigated to see if they have obtained poison or are currently in possession of some.

*John R. Phillips*

## Further Reading

Emsley, John. *The Elements of Murder: A History of Poison.* New York: Oxford University Press, 2005. Discusses the use of arsenic and other poisons in murder. Describes a number of cases in detail, many of which involve one spouse poisoning the other.

Gerber, Samuel M., and Richard Saferstein, eds. *More Chemistry and Crime: From Marsh Arsenic Test to DNA Profile.* Washington, D.C.: American Chemical Society, 1997. Collection of chapters covers the history of forensic science as well as developments in the field through the 1990's. Includes chapters that focus on forensic toxicology, on the search for arsenic, and on the depiction of forensic science in detective fiction.

Jones, David. "The Singular Case of Napoleon's Wallpaper." *New Scientist*, October 14, 1982, 101-104. Discusses the case of Napoleon I, who, in exile on the island of Saint Helena, stayed in a house where the wallpaper contained toxic levels of arsenic. Modern scientists have found elevated arsenic levels in samples of Napoleon's hair, which could have been caused by the wallpaper through Gosio gas.

Meharg, Andrew A. *Venomous Earth: How Arsenic Caused the World's Worst Mass Poisoning.* New York: Macmillan, 2005. Focuses on the health consequences of the arsenic contamination of drinking water (from minerals near the water table) in Bangladesh. Also notes other areas of the world where the problem exists and includes examples of the dangers of arsenic-containing pigments, wallpaper, and other products.

Vilensky, Joel A. *Dew of Death: The Story of Lewisite, America's World War I Weapon of Mass Destruction.* Bloomington: Indiana University Press, 2005. Presents the history of the chemical weapon lewisite, an arsenical poison gas developed by the United States for use as a weapon of war. Notes that stockpiles of the compound still exist and may be hazardous.

White, Peter, ed. *Crime Scene to Court: The Essentials of Forensic Science.* 2d ed. Cambridge, England: Royal Society of Chemistry, 2004. General treatment of forensic science includes chapters on analysis of body fluids, forensic toxicology, and courtroom presentation of expert evidence.

**See also:** Analytical instrumentation; Ancient criminal cases and mysteries; Atomic absorption spectrophotometry; Blood agents; Chemical agents; Marsh test; Napoleon's death; Spectroscopy; Taylor exhumation.

# Arson

**Definition**: Deliberate setting of a fire with the intent to cause damage to a structure or other piece of property.

**Significance:** Arson is a destructive crime that often results in significant property and monetary losses. Investigations to determine whether fires were set intentionally or caused accidentally are notoriously difficult because of the high level of damage at most fire scenes. The forensic science of fire debris analysis, however, provides significant information that can help arson investigators make such determinations.

Arson has been committed throughout human history. Its definition as a crime originated in old English common law, where the term "arson" referred specifically to a fire set by one person against the dwelling of another. Since then, the definition of arson has developed to encompass fires deliberately set against any structure, inhabited or not, as well as vehicles or any other personal property. The penal consequences for the commission of arson have also progressed over time. In the United States, arson crimes are prosecuted based on the degree of damage inflicted, with the worst offense being first-degree felony arson—that is, the setting of a fire that results in the injury or death of one or more persons, whether purposely or accidentally.

## Prevalence and Perpetrators

Although the occurrence of and monetary damages caused by arson fires in the United States decreased steadily in the decade before, the U.S. Fire Administration (USFA) reported that more than thirty thousand structural fires were intentionally set across the nation in 2006. These cases of arson resulted in more than three hundred deaths and caused approximately $755 million in property damage. An estimated twenty thousand vehicle fires were also set in 2006, causing an additional $134 million in damages.

Based on the demographic patterns among those arrested for arson, most perpetrators are Caucasian males, the majority of whom are juveniles or young adults. The Federal Bureau of Investigation (FBI) reports that almost half of the people arrested for arson are under the age of eighteen, and up to two-thirds are younger than twenty-five. General trends show that between 80 and 90 percent of arson offenders are males, although the number of female arsonists has begun to increase. The FBI also reports that only a small percentage (15 to 20 percent) of arson cases, which are notoriously difficult to prosecute, result in an arrests or convictions. This meager success rate can be attributed to the loss of evidence caused not only by the intense heat of fires but also by firefighting efforts. By attempting to put out fires with pressurized water or fire suppression foam, firefighters often wash away any evidence that may point to arson.

## Motives

The people who set fires intentionally do so for many different reasons. Typically, arsonists are motivated by past events. For example, revenge is frequently a primary motive for arson—the arsonist believes that the damage caused by the fire is tantamount to whatever damage has been inflicted on the arsonist by the person targeted. Revenge arson is commonly committed by angry former spouses or significant others; some are committed by outraged students against their schools or by employees against their workplaces. Along similar lines, some arsonists commit their crimes to demonstrate their opposition to practices they deem offensive or immoral. These fires, usually initiated by radical activist groups, may target such organizations as companies that test their products on animals or genetic engineering research laboratories.

Other arsonists act with no prior instigation whatsoever. These people are considered pyromaniacs; they simply enjoy watching anything burn and set fires to satisfy their addiction. Fires set by juvenile offenders are frequently motivated by nothing more than the exciting sensation of pyromania. This infatuation with fire is classified as an impulse control disorder, but its causes and mechanisms of action are not

## Fire in Fiction

Don Winslow's *California Fire and Life* (1999) is a skillfully constructed novel about an insurance claims adjuster whose uncovering of an arson fire draws him into ever-deepening intrigue. Taking its title from the name of a fictional insurance company, the story provides a fascinating inside look at arson investigation that draws on Winslow's own long real-life experience in that field.

Another novel by an experienced arson investigator is John L. Orr's *Points of Origin . . . Playing with Fire* (1991). This story about a serial arsonist was written by a city fire captain and arson investigator who was himself convicted of three counts of arson soon after his book was published.

well understood.

Another motive for arson is the wish to conceal the evidence of other crimes. For example, a murderer may set fire to the homicide crime scene in an attempt to obliterate any incriminating evidence, including the victim's body, or even to make the death seem accidental. Both the Bureau of Alcohol, Tobacco, Firearms and Explosives (ATF) and the Drug Enforcement Administration (DEA) estimate that 30 percent of all arson fires in the United States are set in efforts to hide the effects of other crimes.

Insurance fraud is an increasingly common motive for arson. In old English common law, it was not considered arson for people to burn down their own houses or businesses, as they were allowed to destroy their own personal property as they saw fit. With the inception of property insurance, however, it became prudent for the law to define even the burning of one's own house or business as arson, to discourage the attempted fraudulent collection of insurance money. Arsonists who attempt to commit insurance fraud hope that the fires they set to destroy their homes or businesses will be ruled accidental, given that the determination of arson voids coverage by fire insurance policies.

## Methods

Arsonists use several different methods to set fires, although some are more common than others. The most common method involves the pouring of an accelerant—an ignitable liquid such as gasoline, kerosene, or lighter fluid—throughout the structure. The accelerant allows for easy ignition and also increases the rate and spread of the fire, which will follow the pour pattern of the accelerant. Many kinds of accelerants are readily available to arsonists; some are particularly dangerous because of their tendency to explode rather than just burn.

Some arsonists start fires by using incendiary devices, which can range from simple to very complex in their construction. Simple incendiary devices include lighted candles and flares, which can ignite their surroundings. Another frequently seen incendiary device is the Molotov cocktail: an ignitable liquid contained in a glass bottle along with a cloth soaked in the liquid that acts as a fuse. The cloth is ignited and the bottle is thrown at or into the structure, where, on impact, it shatters and the cloud of ignitable liquid vapor ignites a fireball that spreads to the surrounding areas.

Other chemical incendiary devices, such as those that utilize napalm, thermite, or white phosphorus, are rarely seen in civilian arson cases, although they are frequently used in military attacks. More complicated incendiary devices that operate on timers or other signals are seen occasionally in civilian arson cases. Fire investigators are careful to collect any evidence of incendiary devices found at fire scenes; such evidence may include shattered glass, burned cloth, wires, batteries, and other items that may have been used in timing mechanisms.

## Investigations

Arson investigators face difficult, and sometimes dangerous, work at scenes where intensive fires have taken place. At such scenes buildings are often reduced to ruins, making them dangerous to enter and also often making it difficult for investigators to discern the features of the structures themselves. The main job of an arson investigation team is to sift through the soot and charred debris at the fire scene and determine the point of origin of the fire. The origin, along with the evidence around it, plays a significant role in identifying whether the fire was accidental or intentional.

The origin of a fire is determined from the direction and intensity of the burn patterns that are observed along the remaining parts of the structure or in the charred debris itself. A fire tends to burn up and out from its point of origin, which results in the commonly observed V-shaped pattern in which the V typically points back to the source of ignition. Trailers, or pour patterns, are also commonly observed at arson scenes. Arsonists often pour accelerants throughout structures in order to maximize the spread of the fire, and areas of intense burning follow the pouring patterns.

After determining a fire's point of origin, the investigators can begin to hypothesize exactly what caused the fire. Evidence suggesting the presence of faulty wiring or a gas leak around the origin point may indicate that the fire was accidental in nature. If the area around the origin appears to have burned more significantly than it should have for the fuel load present, however, the fire may be determined to have been set intentionally. Other signs that point to arson include multiple sources of origin, accelerant pour patterns, and evidence of an incendiary device.

The area around the origin of a fire contains the most significant evidence about the cause of the fire. Arson investigators must collect and package as much debris from the scene as possible to be sent to the forensic laboratory so that more detailed analyses can be performed to corroborate the initial findings at the fire scene. If accelerant use is suspected, the investigators will usually focus on several types of debris around the origin, as well as any debris showing potential pour patterns, in collecting evidence. Control samples are also be taken for reference. For example, if burned carpet samples are col-

## Arson Fires in the United States, 1997-2006

| Year | Fires | Deaths | Direct Losses (millions) |
|---|---|---|---|
| 1997 | 78,500 | 445 | $1,309 |
| 1998 | 76,000 | 470 | $1,249 |
| 1999 | 72,000 | 370 | $1,281 |
| 2000 | 75,000 | 505 | $1,340 |
| 2001 | 45,500 | 330 | $1,013 |
| | | 2,451 | $33,440 |
| 2002 | 44,500 | 350 | $919 |
| 2003 | 37,500 | 305 | $692 |
| 2004 | 36,500 | 320 | $714 |
| 2005 | 31,500 | 315 | $664 |
| 2006 | 31,000 | 305 | $755 |

*Source:* U.S. Fire Administration, Federal Emergency Management Agency. Note that the first line for 2001 excludes the losses sustained in the terrorist attacks of September 11, 2001; the second line for that year includes those losses.

lected because they are suspected to contain accelerant residue, samples of carpet that are not burned, if available, are collected also so that forensic analysts can determine whether any potential accelerant identified in the burned carpet is actually inherent to the carpet itself.

The debris collected is stored in airtight containers, typically unused metal paint cans, for transport to the lab; such containers prevent any loss of the volatile components that are present in most commonly used accelerants.

## Forensic Analysis of Fire Debris Evidence

After the packaged evidence is received at the crime laboratory, it is analyzed for the presence of accelerants. Gas chromatography coupled with mass spectrometry (GC-MS) is the conventional analytical technique used to identify unknown liquids that are potential ignitable liquids, as well as ignitable liquid residues in fire debris. Before GC-MS analysis can be conducted, the ignitable liquid residue must be extracted from the fire debris. A variety of methods can be used to perform this extraction, the most popular of which is passive headspace adsorption/elution with activated charcoal strips.

Accelerants are identified from fire debris through chromatographic comparison of the pattern of the peaks present in the questioned sample to the pattern of peaks present in a known standard. Accelerants are classified according to a standard system developed and maintained by the American Society for Testing and Materials (ASTM). This classification scheme separates ignitable liquids based on chemical composition as well as boiling-point range.

Accelerant identification is subjective, and the experience of the analyst plays an important role. Identifying accelerants can be problematic because several materials commonly found in American homes contain ignitable liquid residues or compounds that are chemically very similar to such residues. Analysts must take these interferences into account when interpreting analytical results. Researchers who are examining methods of fire debris analysis are working on developing more objective methods for the identification of accelerants that are capable of placing a statistical confidence level on such identification.

*Lucas J. Marshall*

**Further Reading**

Almirall, José R., and Kenneth G. Furton, eds. *Analysis and Interpretation of Fire Scene Evidence*. Boca Raton, Fla.: CRC Press, 2004. Comprehensive collection addresses many aspects of fire scene investigation and the chemical analysis of fire debris.

DeHaan, John D. *Kirk's Fire Investigation*. 6th ed. Upper Saddle River, N.J.: Pearson Prentice Hall, 2007. Detailed volume covers the physical nature and chemistry of fire. Includes extensive discussion of arson fires.

Faith, Nicholas. *Blaze: The Forensics of Fire*. New York: St. Martin's Press, 2000. Describes how fire investigators work and the methods that forensic scientists use to contribute to solving the crime of arson.

Nic Daéid, Niamh, ed. *Fire Investigation*. Boca Raton, Fla.: CRC Press, 2004. Compilation provides material on the basics of fire investigation as well as informative discussion of laboratory reconstruction and analytical techniques.

Redsicker, David R., and John J. O'Connor. *Practical Fire and Arson Investigation*. 2d ed. Boca Raton, Fla.: CRC Press, 1997. Describes in detail the various steps involved in fire investigation, from scene investigation to courtroom testimony.

Saferstein, Richard. *Criminalistics: An Introduction to Forensic Science*. 9th ed. Upper Saddle River, N.J.: Pearson Prentice Hall, 2007. Textbook discusses all areas of the forensic sciences, including arson investigation.

**See also:** Accelerants; Bureau of Alcohol, Tobacco, Firearms and Explosives; Burn pattern analysis; Carbon monoxide poisoning; Fire debris; Gas chromatography; Mass spectrometry; National Church Arson Task Force; Smoke inhalation; Spectroscopy; Structural analysis.

## Arson Dogs

**Definition**: Canine and handler teams trained and certified to survey burned sites in order to detect odors of accelerants that might have ignited fires set by arsonists.

**Significance:** Because they have heightened scent capabilities, dogs can efficiently search sites damaged by fire and either locate flammable liquids that caused fires, enabling fire investigators to collect forensic samples for laboratory analysis, or indicate that no accelerants are present. Canines can search faster than humans and find chemical evidence in tiny amounts that people might not detect. Canine accelerant dogs' alerts confirm probable cause for investigators to secure search warrants and potentially arrest and prosecute arsonists.

Because of their intelligence and obedience, canines have historically been associated with firefighting in several roles, ranging from being mascots to rescuing people trapped inside burning buildings. In 1986, Connecticut State Police fire investigators needed better accelerant detection methods and trained a Labrador retriever guide dog named Mattie to detect accelerants. Her work as the initial accelerant detection canine in the United States inspired fire and police departments and insurance investigators to utilize dogs to search suspected arson scenes for forensic evidence.

By 1991, the Canine Accelerant Detection Association (http://cadafiredogs.com) set professional standards to certify dogs and handlers to perform arson investigations. Two years later, due to losses of over $30 billion annually to the insurance industry from fraudulent claims resulting from arson, the State Farm insurance company founded a training school for canine accelerant detection teams. The U.S. Bureau of Alcohol, Tobacco, Firearms and Explosives (ATF) has operated its Accelerant Detection Canine Program at Front Royal, Virginia since 1986 to train accelerant detection dogs for federal government uses. State agencies, such as forestry commissions, arrange for training of dogs, often bloodhounds, to find evidence associated with arsonists who set wildfires.

## Training and Certification

The primary duty of accelerant detection canines, the term endorsed by the CADA, which emphasizes dogs locate accelerants not decide if arson occurred, is to find sources that started fires at crime scenes. State Farm invests in the acquisition and training of accelerant detection canines at its State Farm Arson Dog Program training school in Alfred, Maine (http://www.arsondog.org) to work with fire investigators throughout North America. Approximately 350 teams of dogs and handlers have been certified through the State Farm program since 1993, with costs associated with training each team averaging $23,000 paid by State Farm.

Most accelerant detection canines are Labrador retrievers or mixes of that breed because their physiological, olfactory, and behavioral traits are favorable for detection training. The five-week training course prepares canines and handlers for situations they might encounter at fire scenes. The dogs learn to detect chemical odors of numerous accelerants that start fires and to ignore scents of objects that do not ignite fires. Canines communicate to handlers where accelerant samples need to be taken by sitting, staring, pointing their muzzles, or scratching. Most handlers reward dogs with food as motivation for successful performances. They vary the number of odors to be detected and sometimes stage searches without any accelerants to find.

The CADA "Testing Standards for Certification," revised in 2014, describes diverse tasks accelerant detection canines must master to the satisfaction of CADA representatives including chemists. The tests involve detection of twelve ignitable liquids categorized as light (such as paint remover), medium (gasoline), or heavy (kerosene). Test administrators place these liquids at testing sites, including buildings, vehicles, and open areas. Teams encounter distractions and are judged on their accuracy to detect the specified accelerants in varied amounts and percentages of evaporation and at different depths and heights. They also are expected to distinguish between containers filled with burned woods, plastic, rubber, or carpet and other containers with ignitable liquid accelerants. Certification of accelerant detection canine teams is essential for fire investigators to attain credibility. This professional status reinforces accelerant detection canines' accuracy and handlers' authority when they state they have probable cause to obtain search warrants to gather further evidence to connect suspects with fires or testify in trials. After certification, teams practice and enhance their skills. The CADA requires annual recertification of dogs and handlers to continue conducting accelerant detection work. Teams return to Maine where a chemist evaluates their scent skills. Dogs that do not qualify must successfully undergo additional training before they can resume searching assignments.

## Search and Detection

Fire investigations in buildings, houses, and factories occur when sites have cooled sufficiently. Accelerant detection canines wait until their handlers have assessed hazards such as debris, nails, and fallen beams. Handlers cover dogs' paws with protective boots if needed. If the accelerant detection canine smells an odor it has been trained to detect, the dog alerts the handler who gathers evidence of the accelerant to submit to a laboratory where chemists determine if that sample could start a fire by applying gas chromatography techniques. Sometimes accelerant detection canines alert to accelerants on clothing or shoes worn by arsonists or in vehicles, which may have carried accelerants to burned structures. At many fire scenes, the dogs do not detect accelerants, indicating arson did not occur. Handlers bathe dogs to remove toxic chemicals they were exposed to at fire scenes and provide first aid if needed.

The CADA emphasizes the National Fire Protection Association's *Guide for Fire and Explosion Investigations* states that only evidence that is gathered as a result of accelerant detection canine alerts and is laboratory verified, as accelerants will be credible forensic proof to support investigators' testimony in court. CADA encourages handlers to maintain records of training and searches throughout each dog's career. Some critics who claim the use of accelerant detection canines is expensive and inconsistent have focused on developing technological detectors as alternatives to dogs for searches at fire scenes.

Accelerant detection canines promote fire prevention and safety at community presentations. The American Humane Association presents its Hero Dog Award to outstanding arson dogs such as Sadie, an accelerant detection canine with the Colorado Bureau of Investigation, who won in 2011. In 2013, a national firedog monument, *Ashes to Answers*, depicting an accelerant detection canine with its handler, was dedicated in Washington, D.C.

*Elizabeth D. Schafer*

### Further Reading

Ballentine, Elishia. "Meet Ember, the Newest Canine in the AFC's 'Arson Dog' Program." *Alabama's Treasured Forests*, Summer 2013: 7. Comments how Alabama Forestry Commission's bloodhounds, Blaze and Ember, have reduced arson rates in state forests and enabled arrests of arsonists.

Chordas, Lori. "No Bones About It: State Farm's Arson Dog Program Trains and Funds Accelerant-Detection Dogs to Sniff Out Fraud." *Best's Review*, November 2011: 104. Summarizes basic information and provides statistics supplemented with quotations and examples of successful accelerant detection canines.

Ensminger, John J. *Police and Military Dogs: Criminal Detection, Forensic Evidence, and Judicial Admissibility*. Boca Raton, FL: CRC Press, 2012. Contains chapter discussing legal factors associated with accelerant detection dogs, including scientific standards for evidence presented at trials and credibility of alerts, samples, and laboratories.

Furton, Kenneth; Jessie Greb; and Howard Holness. *The Scientific Working Group on Dog and Orthogonal Detector Guidelines (SWGDOG)*. Miami, FL: U.S. Department of Justice/Florida International University, 2010. An appendix focuses on accelerant detection dogs, outlining training guidelines, certification criteria, maintenance training, accelerants handling, and record keeping.

Kelly, John. "Washington's Newest Memorial Honors Dogs Who Sniff Out Suspicious Fires." *The Washington Post*, October 29, 2013. Describes statue sculpted by Austin Weishel, a volunteer fireman, as a tribute to arson dogs.

Nowlan, Mark; Allan W. Stuart; Gene J. Basara; and P. Mark L. Sandercock. "Use of a Solid Absorbent and an Accelerant Detection Canine for the Detection of Ignitable Liquids Burned in a Structure Fire." *Journal of Forensic Sciences* 52, no. 3 (May 2007): 643-648. Compares performances of dogs and ignitable liquid absorbent™. Endnotes cite articles published during the initial years fire investigators used arson dogs.

Rogak, Lisa. *Dogs of Courage: The Heroism and Heart of Working Dogs Around the World*. New York: St. Martin's Press, 2012. Chapter titled "Fire Dogs" examines the history of canines and firefighting, particularly development of arson dogs.

**See also:** Counterfeiting; Forgery; Handwriting analysis; Paint; Paper; Questioned document analysis; Sports memorabilia fraud; X-ray diffraction.

# Art forgery

**Definition**: The deliberate manufacture and sale of misattributed works of art with intent to defraud.

**Significance:** With individual works of art by acknowledged masters selling for millions of dollars, art forgery is a high-stakes business involving finances, academic reputation and national pride. Despite advances in scientific analysis in the last fifty years, identification of the most meticulously crafted forgeries still depends upon the subjective aesthetic judgment of experts. Many fakes undoubtedly escape detection altogether. The authenticity of some works remains uncertain despite exhaustive study. Forensic analysis can also prove an item genuine. Because of the high level of skill required to forge fine art and lack of public sympathy for wealthy collectors, a successful art forger may attain the status of a public hero.

Art forgery is nearly as old as art. Archaeologists have unearthed objects with faked inscriptions from the ruins of ancient Babylon and Egypt. The Roman passion for Greek statuary produced numerous works in the style of classical Greek artists. During the Middle Ages, artists embellished religious relics to reinforce the impression that the object had a sacred origin. The Renaissance produced another flurry of reproductions of Greek and Roman statuary. However, commercial art forgery really blossomed in the eighteenth century. With the rise of private collectors and public collections of works of art, demand for examples of choice antiquities and works by popular artists greatly exceeded supply, prices skyrocketed, and unknown artists discovered the monetary advantages of passing off copies of masters as the real thing.

In the nineteenth and early twentieth century sentiment condemning art forgery as a threat to the integrity of art as a whole was widespread, but this attitude has diminished in recent years.

## Scope and Limits of Art Forgery

In general, a reproduction or modern work in historic style is not forgery unless it would deceive a knowledgeable buyer. Searching any flea market or low-end antique dealer will turn up numerous small art objects, purportedly old but bearing obvious signs, through materials and workmanship, of recent origin in Asian factories. Sometimes the deception is more elaborate, as with a scheme in which an importer not only commissioned bronze "Tiffany" belt buckles, but also a forged catalog, dated 1950, advising collectors on the scarcity and value of an item the Tiffany company never made.

Folk art is another gray area. An item newly handmade in the traditional manner assumes aspects of a forgery if deliberately altered to simulate age and traditional use. The country of origin may also be misrepresented, as with "African" carvings from Indonesia or Amish quilts from India. Fake antiques and folk art can usually be readily detected through analysis of materials (such as wood species) and telltale traces of artificial aging.

Some forgeries involve over-zealous restoration and/or addition of spurious elements to an otherwise authentic piece. A fad for collecting fifteenth and sixteenth century Majolica ware in the late nineteenth century spawned a whole industry, first of recreating missing parts of damaged excavated pottery, and then of fabricating entire pieces. Teodoro and Virgilio Ricardi, two brothers apprenticed to this trade, used their skill at faking antique ceramics to perpetrate one of the most notorious art frauds in history, the monumental Etruscan warriors displayed for three decades in New York's Metropolitan Museum of Art. Analysis of glazing and construction techniques raised suspicions; thermoluminescence confirmed the pieces as modern.

The most spectacular examples of art forgery consist of creating a completely new piece that passes as the work of a famous artist. Doing so requires a high degree of technical skill in the medium, knowledge of the materials and techniques appropriate to the period, careful study of comparable pieces by the same artist, and creation of a plausible chain of provenance explaining how a hitherto unknown work by an acknowledged master came to be on the market.

Most nations worldwide have enacted laws against exporting national art treasures and archaeological artifacts. Many countries also have internal laws, for example regulations prohibiting private excavation and sale of pre-Columbian ceramics in the United States. Such laws aid art forgers by making the origin of art difficult to trace and creating reluctance on the part of collectors to publicize their holdings or consult experts.

Wars and civil upheaval, for example the current chaos in the Middle East, create a window of opportunity for both art thieves and forgers. Multiple copies of authentic artifacts stolen from museums or private collections appear on the black market. When attempting return these items to their original owners, experts must distinguish original from replica, and may conclude that all of the recovered examples are fake, raising the possibility that the exhibit was a forgery to begin with.

## Detecting Art Forgery

The question of forgery usually arises when works of art are sold or transferred. Collectors and museums are understandably reluctant to amass evidence tending to show that their existing holdings, especially showpiece items, are fakes. If they engage experts to examine controversial pieces, it is usually to support authenticity.

To determine whether a work of art is genuine, the dealer or buyer first has it examined by an expert in the artist, art form, or period, who compares it with known authentic works and looks for telltale signs of the forger's art. A labored and hesitant technique indicates a copy, but not necessarily a deliberate forgery. Judgment concerning conformity of style is highly subjective. The same expert who praised the style and artistic quality of a piece, believing it to be genuine, may as vociferously point to its artistic worthlessness when it is exposed as the work of an imposter. Experts working for dealers may have a vested interest in overlooking subtle indications that something is not right, and a few are actually in league with the forgers. Experts also examine ownership and sales records to determine if the provenance has been falsified.

Use of computers to compare complex visual images is still in its infancy. A team at Dartmouth University has developed a program for analyzing the frequency and density of brush strokes in digitized images. Computer analysis does not require having the actual work of art in hand.

Most scientific detection of art forgeries relies on determining the age, chemical makeup and probable source of materials, and upon using various means to determine internal structure. For wooden sculptures and paintings on wood or canvas, carbon-14 dating of minute fragments places the substrate within a century, but will not distinguish an old copy or a modern fake executed with antique materials. The notorious Dutch forger Han Van Meegeren used seventeenth-century canvases from paintings by obscure artists. Eric Hebborn forged old master drawings on blank leaves removed from antique books. Both men mixed their own paints and inks from materials available in the seventeenth century; Hebborn also carefully reproduced period pens and brushes to ensure the right quality of line. Suspicion fell upon Manhattan art dealer Eli Sakhai when he purchased large numbers of inexpensive late 19th century paintings. Sakhai, who was convicted of fraud in U.S. Federal court in 2004, purchased genuine Impressionist paintings from auction houses, commissioned forgeries from an unknown artist, probably in China, and sold the fakes to Japanese collectors. The fraud came to light when he and one of his victims simultaneously tried to sell the "same" painting.

Dendrochronology can be used to date wooden objects. The pattern of rings indicates the years in which the tree was alive: a violin with a spruce sounding board from a tree felled after 1890 obviously cannot be an authentic Stradivarius.

Penetrating X rays reveal images covered by a final coat of paint, including the artist's preliminary sketches, portions that have been reworked, and entirely different pictures. Telltale signs of forgery include an under-image of obviously later date and retouching introducing characteristic stylistic peculiarities of a known

## Art Forgery as Defense

One of history's most notorious art forgers used his craft as a successful defense against treason.

Han Van Meeringen, a mediocre Dutch painter who adopted an archaic style in his own work, began turning out forgeries of paintings by Johannes Vermeer in the 1930's, using antique canvases, period paints, and an aging process undetectable at the time. The outbreak of the Second World War limited access to experts and added plausibility to stories of discovery of hitherto unknown art treasures. One of Van Meeringen's customers was the Nazi Air Marshall Hermann Göring.

Accused after the war of collaboration and selling national treasures, Van Meeringen confessed to having painted the picture himself, and, to prove this was possible, produced another fake Vermeer in his prison cell. Any admiration attached to Van Meeringen for having swindled Göring must be tempered by the fact that he also swindled a number of Dutchmen, was motivated entirely by greed, and produced clumsy forgeries that in retrospect should not have fooled anyone.

When listing his other forgeries for the court, he included paintings for which he was almost certainly not responsible, the authenticity of which is still disputed.

artist into a mediocre painting by an unknown hand

Thermoluminescence is a useful technique for determining when pottery was fired. Crystalline minerals stored at room temperature accumulate electrons in elevated energy states; subjecting them to high heat releases this energy in the form of light, the intensity of which is proportional to the time since the object was last heated.

X-ray emission and x-ray fluorescence are two recent techniques used to determine the chemical composition of objects without destructive sampling. When subjected to a high-energy beam of radiation, compounds re-emit radiation at a lower frequency in bands diagnostic of the elements and molecules present. The presence of certain compounds narrows the time frame in which a work could have been created. Compounds used in artificial aging can be detected in situ.

Trace element and stable isotope analyses are used to identify the source, and sometimes the age, of materials used in art work. Modern smelting methods generally produce purer metal than was available in earlier times. A competent art forger knows that lead carbonate, rather than titanium and zinc oxides, was the white pigment used by painters before 1920, but unless he has access to the same natural source used by Europeans in the 17th century, he will not be able to duplicate the profile of trace elements. Trace impurities help distinguish old silver from modern reproductions. Elements with more than one stable (nonradioactive) isotope can pinpoint the source quarry or mine. This will distinguish whether a white marble sculpture in classical Greek style is Greek, Roman, Renaissance Italian, or modern.

Sometimes scientific analysis vindicates the dealer and collector. A Roman marble bust, deemed a nineteenth century forgery on stylistic grounds, proved to be genuinely ancient. A nineteenth-century dealer in antiquities had "improved" upon it by sculpting away some of the original drapery. In 1914 the financier J. Pierpont Morgan purchased a collection of silver plates supposedly excavated in Cyprus and dated to the 3rd-4th centuries A.D. Experts labeled them modern forgeries. When reassessed by trace element analysis, production techniques and manufacturer's marks, they proved to be seventh century eastern Roman artifacts made in a deliberately archaic style.

### Art Forgery as a Criminal Defense

Art forgers themselves are rarely successfully prosecuted for creating fake art. Since the crime consists not of creating something indistinguishable from a valuable original, but in marketing it as such, the artist can argue that he was deceived by the dealer. Frank Kelley, a prolific forger of Impressionist paintings, protected himself by signing his forgeries in white lead, readily detectable in x-rays.

Creating and marketing bogus art treasures is simple commercial fraud, a less serious charge than theft, fencing stolen goods, clandestine archaeological excavations, or smuggling. Consequently, art forgery operations may be exposed when a party accused on one of these crimes confesses that the goods are fake.

*Martha Sherwood*

## Further Reading

Hebborn, Eric. *Drawn to Trouble: Confessions of a Master Forger.* New York: Random House, 1991. An insider's view describing how old master drawings are forged and marketed; compelling reading.

Hoving, Thomas. *False Impressions: The Hunt for Big-Time Art Fakes.* New York: Simon & Schuster, 1996. Part history, part vivid first-hand account by a former director of the Metropolitan Museum of Art.

Jones, Mark [ed.]. *Fake? The Art of Deception.* Berkeley, CA: University of California Press, 1990. Published as a companion to an exhibit of notorious forged art pieces, this copiously illustrated volume examines forgeries and their unmasking on a case by case basis.

Spencer, Ronald D. *The Expert Versus the Object. Judging Fakes and False Attributions in the Visual Arts.* Oxford, UK: Oxford University Press. 2004. Describes scientific methods for authentication and analyzes the psychological factors facilitating successful art forgery.

Thierry, Lenain. *Art Forgery: The History of a Modern Obsession.* London, UK:Reaktion Books, 2011. "Forgeries are Pollution. They taint art in general and the originals in particular." Traces changes in attitudes toward art forgery in modern times..

**See also:** Counterfeiting; Forgery; Handwriting analysis; Paint; Paper; Questioned document analysis; Sports memorabilia fraud; X-ray diffraction.

# Asian tsunami victim identification

**Date:** Tsunamis struck on December 26, 2004

**The Event:** An earthquake measuring 9.3 on the Richter scale triggered tsunamis that devastated the coastlines of several Asian countries. One of the worst mass-casualty disasters in history, the tsunamis killed as many as 250,000 people, including Asians living in coastal communities and many tourists from Western nations.

**Significance:** The Asian tsunamis of 2004 presented one of the biggest challenges ever faced by forensic teams in identifying the bodies of massive numbers of victims of a natural disaster. The identification effort drew experts from thirty different nations and produced successful collaboration among them.

On December 26, 2004, a massive earthquake struck in the ocean near the west coast of Sumatra, Indonesia, and triggered a series of deadly tsunamis. It has been estimated that up to 250,000 people became tsunami victims along the coasts of many countries bordering the Indian Ocean; victims included the citizens of eleven countries, many of them tourists who were spending time at Asian resorts. An estimated two million people lost their homes, and thousands were reported missing. The magnitude of the tragedy was unprecedented, and it created an unprecedented challenge for the forensic teams that came together to identify the dead.

## The Disaster Victim Identification Center

Following the tsunamis, many bereaved families sought assistance in identifying the dead. Despite their pleas for help, the rate at which the bodies were decomposing caused concerns about epidemics and forced local communities and national authorities to sanction mass burials without identification of the bodies. Many Western states, however, exerted every effort to ensure that their citizens who had died were identified before their remains were interred or cremated.

The challenges of identifying victims after the tsunami were daunting. High temperatures accelerated the rate of decomposition of the bodies, and the bloating and discoloration of faces made visual identification almost impossible after two days. Refrigeration was not immediately available to preserve the remains. In addition, no single country among those affected had sufficient forensic capacity to identify thousands of victims. Lack of national and local plans for mass fatalities further limited the quality and timeliness of the response, as did the absence of practical field guidelines or an international agency to provide technical support.

To respond to the problem of victim identification, Thai authorities set up a multinational disaster victim identification (DVI) center in Phuket, Thailand. The center drew the participation of three hundred investigators from thirty countries. Many of these investigators had expertise in DVI, having worked on teams that had identified mass fatalities from wars, natural disasters, and terrorist attacks.

The global effort to identify the victims of the tsunamis involved the participation of private corporations as well as individuals. Kenyon International Emergency Services, for example, conducted operations and eventually handed over a state-of-the-art identification tool kit worth ten million dollars to the Royal Thai Police's Thai Tsunami Victim Identification (TTVI) unit. Kenyon fielded more than one hundred employees to help create and run a comprehensive forensics database for use by analysts and Interpol experts who worked at the TTVI center in Phuket.

Identification of the tsunami victims was extremely difficult because many bodies recovered from the sea were badly decomposed. The scientists made positive identifications by analyzing dental records, fingerprints, or DNA (deoxyribonucleic acid); relatives of the deceased provided DNA samples and information that helped identify the bodies.

The Information Management Center at the DVI center processed several types of data, including postmortem data collected during victim examinations conducted in temporary morgues and antemortem data on possible victims gathered from the numerous countries involved. These data were entered into the PlassData system under standard operating procedures laid out by the Interpol Disaster Identification Manual. When the scientists were able to match dental, fingerprint, or DNA records with a body, they presented their findings to the Thai Reconciliation Commission, which, if satisfied, authorized the issuance of a Thai death certificate.

## Dental Records

The identification of tsunami victims through the use of dental information (forensic odontology) proved to be highly efficient, reliable, and fast. This method of victim identification, however, favored nationals of Western states, who typically had dental records that helped in the identification process. Dental data were generally unavailable for the Thai population, so this method led to the identification of only a small number of Thai victims. In contrast, for non-Thai victims the successful identification rate using dental data was about 80 percent.

Antemortem dental treatment data include X rays and treatment records as well as plaster models. In most cases, reliable identification of bodies using dental data depends on the availability of recent, high-quality data. If the dental data are scarce or old, investigators must utilize all available methods of identification and the assistance of experienced forensic odontologists to achieve reliable results. In the case of the tsunami victims, this was the case especially for children and adolescents, who had had no or very little dental treatment.

The reliability of dental records as a means of identification became evident early in the work with tsunami victims. After the first three months, 88 percent of the successful identifications of victims had been accomplished with the help of dental data. The large majority of those successfully identified were non-Thai victims.

## Unidentified Bodies

One year after the tsunamis struck, the TTVI center had identified all but 805 of the 3,750 bodies it had received for analysis. About 45 percent of the identifications had been made through dental records, 35 percent through fingerprint analysis, and the remaining 20 percent through DNA analysis. The remaining unidentified bodies were kept in refrigerated containers as efforts to identify them continued. Many of the unidentified were believed to be illegal immigrants, which could explain why their relatives were reluctant to claim them. One year after the tragedy, 160 non-Thais and 548 Thais remained missing.

Two years after the tsunamis, Thailand opened a cemetery for the last of the unidentified victims, about 400 bodies. The remains, mostly those of Burmese migrants, were buried in identical aluminum coffins. The graves are marked with concrete headstones that include registration numbers that will allow authorities to exhume the correct bodies if identifications are made in the future through the use of DNA samples taken from the bodies before burial.

*Dante B. Gatmaytan*

## Controversy in the Identification Process

Despite the progress made in victim identification following the Asian tsunamis, some complaints surfaced, particularly in regard to the use of funds in carrying out the identifications. In a joint letter sent to the Thai authorities in December, 2006, some Western countries demanded an audit, alleging that funds donated for the purpose of completing the identifications had been misused. The letter was signed by the ambassadors to Thailand from Finland, Germany, the Netherlands, Sweden, the United Kingdom, the United States, and France.

The letter noted that more than four hundred recovered bodies remained unidentified and that more than four hundred persons were still missing two years after the tsunamis. The diplomats stated their belief that among the two thousand bodies released to relatives shortly after the tsunamis struck (before the formal disaster victim identification center was established), some bodies had likely been misidentified. They urged the Thai authorities to complete the allegedly much-delayed analysis of the DNA samples taken from those bodies, to correct misidentifications and help identify the remaining bodies. The letter also raised the issue of suspected misuse of funds donated to support the identification work and requested a professional audit by a reputable private accountancy company to clear up the suspicions.

### Further Reading

Alonso, Antonio, et al. "Challenges of DNA Profiling in Mass Disaster Investigations." *Croatian Medical Journal* 46, no. 4 (2005): 540-548. Examines the different steps of DNA identification analysis and reviews the lessons learned and the scientific progress made in some mass-disaster cases described in the scientific literature.

Kieser, Jules A., et al., "Lessons Learned from Large-Scale Comparative Dental Analysis Following the South Asian Tsunami of 2004." *Journal of Forensic Sciences* 51, no. 1 (2006): 109-112. Examines the quality of the antemortem and postmortem dental data that were submitted for entry into the PlassData system in Thailand following the tsunami of December 26, 2004.

Knoppers, Bartha Maria, Madelaine Saginur, and Howard Cash. "Ethical Issues in Secondary Uses of Human Biological Materials from Mass Disasters." *Journal of Law, Medicine and Ethics* 34 (Summer, 2006): 352-365. Addresses the ethical issues of secondary uses of samples collected for identification purposes following mass disasters. Examines whether research is ethically permissible on these samples and, if so, what kind of research.

Schuller-Götzburg, P., and J. Suchanek. "Forensic Odontologists Successfully Identify Tsunami Victims in Phuket, Thailand." *Forensic Science International* 171, nos. 2/3 (2007): 204-207. Analyzes the success rates in the use of dental records in victim identification after this mass disaster.

Sumathipala, A., S. Siribaddana, and C. Perera. "Management of Dead Bodies as a Component of Psychosocial Interventions After the Tsunami: A View from Sri Lanka." *International Review of Psychiatry* 18, no. 3 (2006): 249-257. Discusses the need for the development of a comprehensive and efficient psychosocial intervention at the community level after a disaster. Focuses on the management of the bodies of the dead as an integral part of such an intervention.

**See also:** Beslan hostage crisis victim identification; Croatian and Bosnian war victim identification; DNA fingerprinting; Fingerprints; First responders; Forensic odontology; Mass graves; National Transportation Safety Board; September 11, 2001, victim identification; Tattoo identification.

# Asphyxiation

**Definition**: Act of causing death or unconsciousness by impairing normal breathing.

**Significance:** Immediately before death, the body enters a low-oxygen state as respiration slows. Forensically speaking, a death by asphyxiation is one in which the low-oxygen state happened in an unnatural manner, such as by suffocation or smothering.

Death by asphyxiation can occur in a number of ways: through airway obstruction, through displacement of oxygen, or through neck or chest compression. Forensic pathologists determine the types of asphyxiation in particular deaths by looking for certain signs.

In some cases, asphyxiation occurs when oxygen cannot get into the lungs because something is obstructing the airway. This could be a foreign object, such as food, that fills the throat or something from the body itself, such as the tongue or vomit. When oxygen cannot reach the lungs because the airway is swollen, whether as the result of an allergic reaction or heat, this is also classified as airway-obstruction asphyxiation. Hanging or garroting, in which the airway is physically pinched off by a rope or something else wrapped around the neck, is another type of airway-obstruction asphyxiation. This may occur during the practice of autoerotic asphyxiation, in which individuals enhance sexual plea-

sure by depriving the body of oxygen; this practice sometimes results in accidental death that may be mistaken for suicide.

Asphyxiation by displacement of oxygen is more commonly known as suffocation. It occurs when the oxygen in the air a person is breathing is replaced by something else, such as smoke, toxic fumes, or chemicals. Drowning also qualifies as this type of asphyxiation, as water replaces air in the lungs. In this type of death, pathologists generally observe no external signs of asphyxiation.

Compressing the chest or neck so that no air is able to enter the lungs is another type of asphyxiation. Neck compression, or strangling, also causes asphyxiation because the arteries leading to the brain are not able to provide oxygen to the brain.

A forensic pathologist looks for particular signs to determine whether asphyxiation was the cause of death and, if so, what type of asphyxiation occurred. One of these signs is cyanosis, or a bluish tinge to the skin caused by a decreased amount of oxygen in the blood at the time of death. Facial congestion or edema may occur in a strangling asphyxiation. Because blood is not able to return through the veins to the rest of the body, the face may be swollen. Petechial hemorrhages, which are small broken blood vessels, usually in the eyes, eyelids, or lining of the mouth and throat, may occur during a strangling or hanging type of death, when blood is not allowed to return to the body and the blood pressure causes the veins to rupture.

*Marianne M. Madsen*

## Further Reading

Dix, Jay, Michael Graham, and Randy Hanzlick. *Asphyxia and Drowning: An Atlas.* Boca Raton, Fla.: CRC Press, 2000.

Sheleg, Sergey, and Edwin Ehrlich. *Autoerotic Asphyxiation: Forensic, Medical, and Social Aspects.* Tucson, Ariz.: Wheatmark, 2006.

**See also:** Autoerotic and erotic asphyxiation; Choking; Drowning; Hanging; Inhalant abuse; Petechial hemorrhage; Smoke inhalation; Suffocation.

# Assassination

**Definition**: Intentional killing of a human being for political, moral, or ideological reasons.

**Significance:** The consequences of assassinations can often be greater than the consequences related to other murders because of the kinds of positions held by many of the targets of assassination; in cases of political assassination, for instance, wars or civil unrest may result. It is therefore critical that forensic investigations into such deaths determine the objective facts of these events.

Even a brief look at the history of assassination suggests the important role forensic science could have played in providing objective information as to cause of death in various assassinations. In ancient times, many assassinations were committed at very short range, as were many other murders. Victims were stabbed, strangled, or clubbed to death, and often the assassins, like other murderers, were quickly identified and apprehended. Philip II of Macedonia (382-336        ) and Julius Caesar (100-44        ) are only two of a long list of political leaders assassinated in ancient times.

Given the likely apprehension of assassins who used such short-range killing techniques as stabbing or strangling, poisoning became a widely used alternative. Although it required that the assassin gain immediate access to the target, poisoning constituted a much less obvious attack, and proving that someone had been poisoned was difficult after the fact. In the cases of such assassinations, better forensic science would have been helpful in the apprehension of the perpetrators. In modern times, the facts revealed through forensic science in the poisoning deaths of Bulgarian dissident Georgi Markov (poisoned with ricin) in 1978 and Russian dissident Alexander Litvinenko (poisoned with polonium 210) in 2006 pointed to the killers, implicating, in both cases, the secret police forces in Russia (under communist rule in 1978 and under the more "democratic" regime of Vladimir

Putin in 2006). The motivation for both killings was presumably a desire to silence the victims' criticisms of the regimes under which they lived.

## American Assassinations

The importance and the limitations of forensic science in the investigation of assassinations are clear in the modern era and in the United States, where law-enforcement resources make exhaustive investigations possible. In the cases of the assassinations of U.S. presidents James A. Garfield and William McKinley, in 1881 and 1901, respectively, the role of forensic science was small, as both were shot at close range by individuals who were captured immediately. The fact that the assassins of both presidents were obviously deranged obscured the political aspects of these events, but the questions raised by these assassinations later motivated attempts to use forensic psychology to construct profiles of persons who become assassins.

In the case of President Abraham Lincoln, dozens of spectators saw John Wilkes Booth, a well-known actor, leap from the president's box at Ford's Theatre after Booth fired the fatal shot. Better forensic science than was available in 1865 could have been helpful in resolving another aspect of the case, however. Booth escaped from the theater and from Washington, D.C., despite having injured his leg when he jumped from the president's box. Law-enforcement officials pursued Booth and eventually cornered him—or at least a person they believed to be him—in a barn in Virginia. Before they could take Booth into custody, the barn burned down, presumably with Booth inside. Although a corpse with an injured leg was recovered from the ashes, the body was too badly burned to be readily identified, and ever since that time, some commentators have raised the possibility that Booth may have escaped. If the techniques used by modern forensic scientists had been available then, the question of the burned man's identity would have been resolved.

Modern forensic science has sometimes been used in novel ways with regard to deaths of the past, including possible assassinations. For example, U.S. president Zachary Taylor was hated by certain political opponents, and his death in 1850, reputedly from food poisoning, was a boon to them. Although some suspicions were raised at the time, the primitive nature of forensic science precluded an effective analysis. In 1991, given the advances that had been made in forensic science, some researchers thought it might be possible to determine whether Taylor was in fact poisoned. His body was exhumed and examined by a team of experts who concluded that he had died of natural causes, most likely food poisoning.

## Uses and Limitations of Forensic Science

Three major assassinations in recent American history provide ample examples of the uses of a wide variety of forensic scientific techniques in attempts to find objective evidence about these crimes. In the 1968 assassinations of the Reverend Martin Luther King, Jr., and Senator Robert F. Kennedy, the purported assassins (James Earl Ray and Sirhan Sirhan, respectively) were apprehended, convicted of the crimes, and sentenced to imprisonment for life. A preponderance of the forensic evidence in each case clearly supports the conclusion that the accused man was involved in the assassination—probably by actually pulling the trigger. However, the forensic evidence available so far cannot reveal whether anyone else might have been involved in either case. Both Ray and Sirhan denied their guilt and sought new trials. Ray died in 1998 without achieving his goal of a new trial, and Sirhan has had no success in gaining a retrial.

In the case of James Earl Ray, the heart of the issue turned on Ray's contention that he was set up as a fall guy by other conspirators who have never been found. Ray was the principal witness to the existence of any conspirators. Sirhan's case is more complicated, as he clearly fired a gun in the direction of Senator Kennedy and was seized at the scene. Some conspiracy theorists, however, question whether any of the shots Sirhan fired at Kennedy actually struck him. They argue that there was a second gunman who fired two shots—one of which was the fatal shot to the head.

The conspiracy theorists gained a major

piece of supporting forensic evidence for their theory when a tape recording of the shooting was found. Three acoustical experts have concluded that the tape reveals that at least ten shots were fired at the scene. Given that Sirhan was apprehended with a single gun with only eight shells in it and that he had no time to reload, this points to the existence of a second gunman. The recording further reveals that some of the shots came too close together to have been fired by Sirhan's weapon. Whatever one makes of this evidence, the basic problem is that forensic science often cannot eliminate the possibility that persons other than the person who pulls the trigger may have been involved in an assassination.

Nowhere is this clearer than in the case of the assassination of President John F. Kennedy in 1963. The first major report on the assassination by the government investigative panel known as the Warren Commission claimed to provide a thorough review of the available forensic evidence, but subsequent research has shown a great deal of sloppiness in the commission's work—inadequacies that have fueled a plethora of conspiracy theories. The proponents of these theories advance different forensic evidence or arrive at strikingly different conclusions based on the same evidence. The greatest problem with the use of forensic science in the case of the Kennedy assassination has been the failure of various government agencies to maintain control of the evidence on which the forensic science relies. For example, if—as some contend—Kennedy's body was altered to make it appear that he was shot from the back when he was in fact shot from the front, then any subsequent autopsy would obviously be faulty.

Despite the advances that have been made in forensic science, forensic evidence often cannot answer every question related to a case of political assassination, including the question of whether anyone other than the direct assassin is involved.

*Richard L. Wilson*

## Further Reading

Ayton, Mel. *The Forgotten Terrorist: Sirhan Sirhan and the Assassination of Robert F. Kennedy.* Washington, D.C.: Potomac Books,

2007. Comprehensive review of the Robert F. Kennedy assassination supports the view that Sirhan, a Palestinian, was the assassin, motivated by his hatred of Kennedy's support of Israel.

Bugliosi, Vincent. *Reclaiming History: The Assassination of President John F. Kennedy.* New York: W. W. Norton, 2007. A major supporter of the Warren Commission's conclusion that Oswald was the lone assassin offers an exhaustive reexamination of the evidence from his point of view.

James, Stuart H., and Jon J. Nordby, eds. *Forensic Science: An Introduction to Scientific and Forensic Techniques.* 2d ed. Boca Raton, Fla.: CRC Press, 2005. Provides an excellent overview of forensic science for the general reader.

Kurtz, Michael L. *The JFK Assassination Debates: Lone Gunman Versus Conspiracy.* Lawrence: University Press of Kansas, 2006. Weighs the forensic evidence supporting the views of both sides of the main debate concerning the Kennedy assassination. One of the best sources available on the topic.

Lifton, David S. *Best Evidence: Disguise and Deception in the Assassination of John F. Kennedy.* New York: Signet, 1992. Argues that much of the forensic evidence used to prove Oswald was the lone assassin is faulty because Kennedy's body was altered before the official autopsy to prove that Kennedy was shot only from behind, whereas he was really shot from the front.

Posner, Gerald. *Case Closed: Lee Harvey Oswald and the Assassination of JFK.* New York: Random House, 1993. Carefully reviews the forensic evidence and concludes that Oswald—and Oswald alone—killed Kennedy.

_____. *Killing the Dream: James Earl Ray and the Assassination of Martin Luther King, Jr.* San Diego, Calif.: Harcourt Brace, 1999. Exhaustive account marshals all the forensic evidence to support the argument that James Earl Ray killed Martin Luther King while holding out the possibility that Ray may not have acted alone.

Sturdivan, Larry M. *The JFK Myths: A Scientific Investigation of the Kennedy Assassina-tion.* St. Paul, Minn.: Paragon House, 2005. Comprehensive account of the forensic evidence disposes of several myths about the assassination without conclusively resolving all potential conspiracies.

**See also:** Ancient criminal cases and mysteries; Ballistics; Eyewitness testimony; Federal Bureau of Investigation Laboratory; Fingerprints; Forensic psychology; Gunshot residue; Kennedy assassination; Markov murder; Silkwood/Kerr-McGee case; Taylor exhumation.

## ATF. *See* Bureau of Alcohol, Tobacco, Firearms and Explosives

## Athlete drug testing

**Definition**: Analyses conducted on athletes to determine if they have taken banned substances.

**Significance:** Athletes competing at high levels seek to gain advantages over their opponents. Some do so by using substances that they believe can improve athletic performance or the body's physical work capacity. Many of these substances are drugs and many are banned by various organizations that regulate sports, such as the National Collegiate Athletic Association and the International Olympic Committee. Despite such bans, some athletes still use these substances, making drug testing necessary to keep competition fair. Athletes who fail drug tests may be ruled ineligible for competition or may have their previously awarded medals or titles revoked.

The use of particular substances to improve athletic performance dates back to the ancient Greeks. It was not until 1928 that the International Amateur Athletic Federation became the first sports organization to ban athletes' use of certain substances. The federation, however, had no way to detect whether athletes were breaking the rules, and the use of performance-enhancing substances continued to increase. Drug testing of athletes for banned substances was first used in 1966 by the international federations governing the sports of soccer and cycling. By the 1970s, the widespread use of anabolic steroids among athletes forced the introduction of drug testing by most international sports organizations. The National Collegiate Athletic Association (NCAA) implemented a drug testing program in the fall of 1986 for all athletes participating in NCAA bowl games and national championships. By 1990, the NCAA had adopted year-round testing of athletes on teams within the association. In November 2007 the World Anti-Doping Code was approved and now guides testing worldwide.

## Drug-Testing Techniques

Common methods used to detect illicit drug use include the testing of blood, urine, hair, and saliva samples. The method chosen for a particular purpose must take into consideration the accuracy level provided by the test, the ease obtaining the sample, and the period of time for which the test can detect drugs in the sample. Urine testing is most commonly used for athletes because it is accurate, no cutting or piercing of the skin is involved, and it can detect drug use for the previous seven days or longer. To complete a urine test, an athlete must provide a fresh sample of urine collected in a clean vessel under supervision. Although this may be awkward for some, it is important that the tester be certain that the vessel contains that particular athlete's actual urine. After the vessel is appropriately labeled, it is sent to a laboratory for analysis.

The techniques used to examine urine for the presence of drugs include gas chromatography, mass spectrometry, and immunoassay. In gas chromatography, the urine sample is vaporized in the presence of a gaseous solvent as it travels through a machine called a gas chromatograph. Because the various substances in the urine dissolve in the solvent at different rates, they come out of the solvent at different times, leaving a pattern on a liquid or solid material. The pattern is analyzed by a detector, and a chromatogram is produced. Because different drugs produce different chromatograms, the analyst can compare the urine sample output with known drug outputs to identify the presence of specific drugs in the urine. A mass spectrometer is a machine with a long magnetic tube with a detector on the end. An electron beam blasts the urine sample and sends it down the tube to the detector. Every substance has a unique mass spectrometer output, so by comparing the outputs of known drugs with the urine output, the analyst can identify any specific drugs present in the urine. Immunoassay tests are used to detect the presence of hormone-like drugs in urine. A specific antibody (a protein that binds to particular substances) is tagged with a fluorescent dye or a radioactive marker and then mixed with the urine sample. The antibody binds to the drug (hormone), and the analyst measures the amount of fluorescent light or radioactivity in the sample to determine the amount of the drug or hormone present. Because this test also measures naturally occurring hormones in the urine, the analyst must know the athlete's natural hormone level to determine whether the athlete has taken a hormone-like drug. Despite precautions false positive tests do occur. Therefore appropriate follow-up testing and appeals processes must be in place.

## Challenges to Drug Testing

The ongoing challenge for athletic drug testing is the constant development of new drugs that existing methods and technologies are unable to detect. Athletes are continually looking for new advantages, and manufacturers are developing new drugs to improve athletic performance. After a new performance-enhancing substance becomes available, it often takes months or years for it to become popular enough to warrant the attention of sports officials. Then months or even years may elapse before scientists can develop new tests to determine whether athletes have used these drugs. During this lag of up to several years before a given drug is detectable, even more drugs are developed and the process begins again. This cycle creates a perpetual challenge to those who seek to keep sports competitions free from the use of banned performance-enhancing substances. To combat this problem and discourage athletes from trying to beat the current tests some agencies are testing and then preserving samples so they can be analyzed at a later date with new test procedures.

*Bradley R. A. Wilson*

### Further Reading

Cooper, Chris. *Run, Swim, Throw, Cheat: The Science Behind Drugs in Sport*. Oxford, UK: Oxford University Press, 2012. Chapter 10 discusses the science behind how to catch those who cheat.

Cotten, Doyice J., and John T. Wolohan. *Law for Recreation and Sport Managers*. 6th ed. Dubuque, IA: Kendall/Hunt, 2013. Comprehensive text on sports law includes information on drug testing of athletes in chapter 6.

Gardiner, Simon, John O'Leary, Roger Welch, Simon Boyles, and Urvasi Naidoo. *Sports Law*. 4th ed. New York: Routledge, 2012. Discusses the legal issues related to governing sports. Chapter 8 is devoted to the topic of illegal doping and includes discussion of drug testing.

Henne, Kthryn E. *Testing for Athlete Citizenship: Regulating Doping and Sex in Sport*. New Brunswick, NJ: Rutgers University Press, 2015. Comprehensive information about drug testing and gender verification in sports.

Ray, Richard and Jeff Konin. *Management Strategies in Athletic Training*. 4th ed. Champaign, Ill.: Human Kinetics, 2011. Chapter 10 provides an overview of existing programs concerned with athlete drug testing.

**See also:** Anabolic Steroid Control Act of 2004; Analytical instrumentation; Drug abuse and dependence; Drug classification; Drug confirmation tests; Gas chromatography; Mandatory drug testing; Mass spectrometry; Performance-enhancing drugs; Sports memorabilia fraud.

## Atomic absorption spectrophotometry

**Definition**: Technique used to determine the concentrations of metal elements in a sample based on the absorption of light energy by atoms.

**Significance:** By using atomic absorption spectrophotometry, forensic scientists can determine the concentrations of the elements that are present in evidence samples collected at crime scenes. Using this information, they may be able to match evidence samples with materials linked to suspects or found at other crime scenes.

The phenomenon of atomic absorption was discovered as the result of the observation of the dark absorption lines in the spectrum of the sun, which are caused by the absorption of light by elements existing as gaseous atoms being promoted from "ground" state to "excited" state in the sun's atmosphere. These dark lines were first observed by William Hyde Wollaston in 1802, then rediscovered by Joseph von Fraunhofer in 1814; they are now known as Fraunhofer lines. In 1953, Alan Walsh developed the first chemical analysis using atomic absorption.

### Atom-Light Relationship

Atoms absorb light energy based on electrons surrounding the atomic nuclei. Every atom of a specific element has a specific number of electrons in orbital positions. The most stable orbital configuration for an atom, called the "ground" state, possesses the lowest energy. The light energy resonates, or travels in space, like waves with specific wavelength. If light energy strikes an atom, the light is absorbed by the atom, and the electron in the outer orbital position is promoted to an unstable higher energy configuration, called the "excited" state. The excitation from ground to excited state is called atomic absorption; this absorption can be measured by the instrument known as the atomic absorption spectrophotometer. Because of the instability of the excited state, the electron decays and returns to the ground state; in doing so, it emits energy equivalent to the energy absorbed during the excitation process. The energy emitted during the decay process is not measured by the instrument.

## Instrumentation and Sample Analysis

The atomic absorption spectrophotometer has five basic features: a light source that emits a spectrum specific to the element of interest, an absorption cell in which gaseous atoms are produced during excitation, a monochromator that disperses light, a detector that measures absorption, and a readout system (printer or computer) that shows the results of the analysis. The spectrum emitted by the light source (for example, a hollow cathode lamp) is focused through the absorption cell leading to the monochromator. The lamp contains a specific metal element that emits a specific wavelength of light for the same element to be determined in the sample. For example, to determine the concentration of iron in the sample, the lamp used must contain iron. The light source must be modulated, or chopped, so that it is possible to distinguish between the emission from the lamp and the emission from the absorption cell. The monochromator disperses the modulated signal emitted from the lamp (not from the absorption cell) and isolates the specific wavelength of light that passes to the detector, which processes the light absorbed by the atoms. The absorption, which is proportional to the concentration of the element in a sample, is then displayed in the readout system.

A sample is introduced and atomized in the absorption cell in liquid or solid form (depending on atomizers) to accomplish the excitation process. If a liquid solution is required, elements are extracted by liquid reagents from solid materials. The liquid sample in the absorption cell is atomized, with thermal means (flame or graphite furnace) or chemical means (hydride or mercury vapor generator) used to excite the atoms. Flame produced by an air-acetylene mixture (2,100-2,400 degrees Celsius) is used for most metal elements (such as calcium or zinc) that do not form refractory compounds, which cannot be ionized or atomized at this temperature range. A hotter nitrous oxide-acetylene flame (2,600-2,800 degrees Celsius) is

used for elements (such as silicon or aluminum) forming refractory compounds (silicon dioxide or aluminum dioxide). A graphite furnace atomizer provides a wider range of temperatures (2,100-2,900 degrees Celsius) and handles liquid or solid samples.

A hydride or mercury vapor generator converts certain elements into gas. Elements that chemically react with sodium tetrahydridoborate (such as arsenic and selenium) are reduced to form hydride vapor. Mercury is reduced to mercury vapor. The vapors in the absorption cell are excited to absorb energy from the light source.

Not all elements are detected by atomic absorption. Elements with wavelengths of resonance lines below 190 nanometers, nonmetals (such as hydrogen, carbon, nitrogen, and oxygen), and noble gases are volatile, easily absorbed by air, immediately lost at temperatures greater than 2,100 degrees Celsius, and disappear before excitation. Elements that form very strong refractory compounds have extremely high melting points (greater than 2,900 degrees Celsius). Because these compounds cannot be atomized by flame or furnace, no atoms can be excited.

## Use in Forensics

In a criminal investigation, atomic absorption spectrophotometry can be used to discover the presence and the concentration of the elements in sample evidence. When explosives or poisons are used to kill, for example, they leave evidence that can be examined through chemical analysis. Some explosives contain platinum; others contain nickel, silver, cadmium, or mercury. The elements that are found in the residues of signature explosive products can be used to find the sources, manufacturers, and buyers of such explosives.

Atomic absorption spectrophotometry can also be used to detect concentrations of elements from poisons found in human victims. Poisoning is confirmed to have occurred (whether accidentally or intentionally) if concentrations of toxic elements—such as arsenic or mercury—exceed safe levels in the body. The atomic absorption spectrophometer enables analysts to determine whether poisoning has occurred by examining the levels of toxic elements appearing in a victim's blood, urine, and hair.

*Domingo Jariel*

## Further Reading

Caroli, Sergio. *The Determination of Chemical Elements in Food: Applications for Atomic and Mass Spectrometry.* Hoboken, N.J.: Wiley-Interscience, 2007. Covers the quantification of beneficial and toxic elements in food products.

Emsley, John. *Elements of Murder: A History of Poison.* New York: Oxford University Press, 2005. Describes the properties of five toxic elements (arsenic, antimony, lead, mercury, and thallium) and how they were used in some of the most famous murder cases in history.

Tsalev, Dimiter L. *Atomic Absorption Spectrometry in Occupational and Environmental Health Practice.* Boca Raton, Fla.: CRC Press, 1995. Covers fifty-five elements and provides almost eight hundred atomic absorption procedures for analysis of blood and other biological specimens.

Vandecasteele, C., and C. B. Block. *Modern Methods for Trace Element Determination.* New York: John Wiley & Sons, 1993. Describes the theory and usage of atomic absorption and other spectroscopy for element determination.

Welz, Bernhard, Helmut Becker-Ross, Stefan Florek, and Uwe Heitmann. *High-Resolution Continuum Source AAS: The Better Way to Do Atomic Absorption Spectrometry.* New York: John Wiley & Sons, 2005. Discusses both instrumentation and measurements of elements.

**See also:** Analytical instrumentation; Arsenic; Crime laboratories; Forensic toxicology; Quantitative and qualitative analysis of chemicals; Spectroscopy.

# Attention-deficit/ hyperactivity disorder medications

**Definition**: Pharmacologically produced agents used in the treatment of the syndrome of disruptive behavior known as attention-deficit/hyperactivity disorder.

**Significance:** Medication management of attention-deficit/hyperactivity disorder targets the areas of the disorder that contribute to the patient's impairment: inattention, hyperactivity, and impulsivity. These conditions can, at times, lead persons with the disorder to involvement with legal authorities. Researchers who have studied attention-deficit/hyperactivity disorder in prison populations have estimated its prevalence from as low as 20 percent to as high as 70 percent.

Most medications used in the treatment of attention-deficit/hyperactivity disorder (ADHD) are rudimentarily separated into stimulant and nonstimulant categories; further distinctions are made between those that are approved for treatment of the disorder by the U.S. Food and Drug Administration (FDA) and those that are nonapproved or used "off-label" by prescribing physicians. FDA-approved medications in the stimulant category comprise amphetamine preparations (brand names include Adderall and Dexedrine) and methylphenidate preparations (brand names include Ritalin, Metadate, Concerta, and Focalin). Although many nonstimulant medications are used to treat ADHD, only one, atomoxetine (brand name Strattera), has been approved by the FDA for use in children, adolescents, and adults.

## Stimulants

Although it may seem counterintuitive to treat a hyperactive patient with a stimulant, a simple explanation regarding the theory of ADHD is as follows: In the ADHD patient, the frontal lobe of the brain, which is responsible for executive functions (such as planning, organizing, and focusing attention) and other tasks (including controlling impulses, motivation, and movement), is deficient in the neurotransmitters that are restored to a more normative state with the use of stimulant medications. The main catecholamine neurotransmitters that are affected by the use of stimulants are dopamine and norepinephrine. These transmitters are involved in focusing attention, motivation, learning, and other cognitive functions that are adversely affected in patients with ADHD.

In general, the use of methylphenidate and amphetamine medications with patients who have ADHD leads to an approximation of a normal neurochemical state, both by blocking the reuptake of dopamine into and promoting the release of dopamine out of the nerve cells in the brain wherein dopamine is produced, stored, and released. The net effect is an increase in the amount of dopamine available to communicate between nerve cells. This area of communication between the cells is termed the synapse. Amphetamine preparations have the added effect of promoting release and blocking reuptake of norepinephrine.

When treatment is optimized, between 77 and 90 percent of patients with ADHD will have a favorable response to stimulant medications. This may be reflected in improvements in academic accuracy and grades, parent-child relations, and social functioning. However, although the stimulant medications have well-documented usefulness in the treatment of ADHD and are generally well tolerated, they may also be associated with side effects. These side effects include, but are not limited to, insomnia, weight loss, headaches, irritability, loss of appetite, stomach upset, and increases in blood pressure and heart rate. Other less common but potentially serious side effects include the development of undesired movements called tics, slowing of growth, the possibility of seizures, and the risk of developing psychotic symptoms such as hallucinations and paranoia. Often, side effects can be minimized or eliminated through the reduction of the medication dosage or through a change to a different type of stimulant that may be better tolerated.

## Atomoxetine

Atomoxetine is a selective norepinephrine reuptake inhibitor that is approved by the FDA for treatment of ADHD in children and adults. It is thought that atomoxetine blocks the norepinephrine transporter in nerve cells in the brain, thereby increasing the amount of norepinephrine in the synapse between nerve cells. It is further hypothesized that in the brain's frontal lobe, norepinephrine transporters may, to some extent, also be responsible for the reuptake of dopamine, not just norepinephrine. Research indicates that atomoxetine may be as effective in the treatment of ADHD as the stimulant methylphenidate, but atomoxetine may take a longer period of time to reach its full benefit.

Atomoxetine's side effects may include stomach upset, constipation, decreased appetite, headache, fatigue, irritability, and an inability to empty the bladder completely when urinating. More serious side effects include rare cases of liver toxicity and the concern, given that the chemical structure of atomoxetine is similar to that of certain antidepressants, that it could promote suicidal thinking and behavior in children and adolescents such as that seen clinically in 3-4 percent of patients in the population taking traditional antidepressants.

## Other Treatments

Typically, alternative medications have been used as second- or third-line options to treat ADHD. Although these approaches are not approved by the FDA, they still have usefulness for those patients who cannot tolerate or do not benefit from more traditional treatments. Further, these medications may be used in conjunction with other treatments to augment or boost a patient's response.

Tricyclic antidepressants, such as imipramine (brand names include Tofranil and Antideprin) and nortriptyline (brand names include Aventyl and Pamelor), have been used in the treatment of ADHD with some success. It is theorized that the beneficial effects of these antidepressants on ADHD symptoms are related to the blockade of norepinephrine reuptake into nerve cells. Use of these medications, however, has fallen out of favor with most treatment providers because of the limiting side effects associated with the drugs, the most concerning of which is the risk of sudden cardiac death if the medications are taken in overdose or if the blood levels of the medications get too high. Concerns also exist regarding an increase in suicidal thoughts and behaviors in child and adolescent patient populations. Nevertheless, in experienced hands and with proper monitoring, these medications can be prescribed safely and effectively for treatment of ADHD.

An alternative and structurally chemically different antidepressant with usefulness in treating ADHD is bupropion (brand names include Wellbutrin and Zyban). It is thought that bupropion helps patients with ADHD through its effects on norepinephrine and dopamine. This medication does not have the cardiac concerns that are present with tricyclic antidepressants, but, in high doses, it may make patients more prone to seizures. The suicide risk warnings with children and adolescents are the same as those applied to tricyclic antidepressants.

### Alpha-2 Adrenergic Agonists

The medications known as alpha-2 adrenergic agonists include clonidine (brand names Catapres and Disarit) and guanfacine (brand names Tenex and Intuniv). These drugs are used to treat high blood pressure and, through their effects on the central nervous system mediated by norepinephrine-containing nerve cells, are helpful in diminishing impulsivity, hyperactivity, and even aggression in patients with ADHD. They may also help with sleep disturbance and motor (movement) tics that are seen in some patients. The main side effects are dry mouth, headache, sedation, constipation, slowing of heart rate, and lowering of blood pressure.

*Neva E. J. Sanders-Dewey and Seth G. Dewey*

### Further Reading

Sadock, Benjamin James, and Virginia Alcott Sadock. *Kaplan and Sadock's Synopsis of Psychiatry: Behavioral Sciences/Clinical Psychiatry*. 10th ed. Philadelphia: Lippincott, Williams & Wilkins, 2007. General text aimed at mental health practitioners provides an overview of the entire field of psychiatry.

Schatzberg, Alan F., Jonathan O. Cole, and Charles DeBattista. *Manual of Clinical Psychopharmacology*. 6th ed. New York: American Psychiatric Publishing, 2007. Practical manual addresses the psychotropic management of psychiatric conditions.

Stahl, Stephen M. *Essential Psychopharmacology: Neuroscientific Basis and Practical Applications*. 3d ed. New York: Cambridge University Press, 2008. Good resource for readers seeking an understanding of the fundamentals of psychotropic interventions.

_____. *Essential Psychopharmacology: The Prescriber's Guide*. Rev. ed. New York: Cambridge University Press, 2006. Guidebook for practitioners provides information regarding the advantages and disadvantages of the various psychotropic medications.

**See also:** Bacterial resistance and response to antibacterial agents; Forensic psychiatry; Psychotropic drugs; Stimulants.

## Autoerotic and erotic asphyxiation

**Definition**: Potentially deadly practice of increasing sexual pleasure by restricting oxygen to the brain through hanging or suffocation during sex acts.

**Significance:** Deaths resulting from autoerotic and erotic asphyxiation are often mistaken for suicide (especially among teenagers) or homicide because many health care workers, emergency personnel, and police personnel are unfamiliar with the signs of these sexual practices. More widespread education about the dangers of these practices could save lives.

Erotic asphyxiation (EA) is the practice of depriving the brain of oxygen during sexual stimulation with a sex partner for purposes of increasing sexual pleasure and heightening orgasm. Autoerotic asphyxiation (AEA) is the same practice carried out by one person, without a sex partner; that is, autoerotic asphyxiators masturbate while voluntarily strangling themselves. Neck compression (strangulation), exclusion of oxygen (suffocation), airway obstruction (blocking the airway with a foreign object), and chest compression (restricting the movement of the chest) are all methods of depriving oxygen used during erotic asphyxiation.

During a normal breath, carbon dioxide is exhaled and oxygen is inhaled, keeping the brain's oxygen at an adequate level. In AEA and EA, oxygen deprivation is achieved in a variety of ways, including the use of a plastic bag over the head and self-strangulation using a ligature. When a person's supply of oxygen to the brain is too low and carbon dioxide is too high, some resulting effects may be a sense of euphoria, dizziness, lowered inhibitions, and even hallucinations.

## Statistics

Research indicates that some 70 percent of those who practice autoerotic or erotic asphyxiation are under the age of thirty. In the United States, AEA and EA are most common among single, white, middle-class, male teenagers and young adults (thirteen to twenty years of age). Teenagers are also the practitioners who most often die as the result of these practices. The most common reasons teenagers take part in AEA and EA are sexual experimentation, thrill seeking, and fantasies of masochistic bondage. No research has linked gender confusion, homosexuality, or transvestism with the practice of AEA or EA. Some psychologists believe that a history of child sexual abuse may influence later participation in these sexual practices.

Teenage girls and women also participate in AEA and EA, but to a much lesser extent than do young men. The techniques of AEA that women use tend to be less obvious than those used by men. Often a female practitioner will use a single neck ligature and only limited sexual props, such as a vibrator or a dildo. The small amount of evidence available when a woman dies as the result of AEA may be a cause of underreporting of AEA practices among women.

One study of autoerotic asphyxiation found that adult practitioners, in contrast with teenagers who participate in these acts, were often lonely and depressed. Other experts disputed this finding, however, noting that anecdotal reports indicate that adults who have died as a result of AEA have often been happily married men who were not deprived of sex or companionship.

Suicide is one of the leading causes of death among teenagers in the United States, and some researchers believe that many of the teen deaths labeled as suicide are actually accidental deaths from AEA or EA. According to estimates of the Federal Bureau of Investigation (FBI), some five hundred to one thousand deaths result from the practice of AEA and EA each year in the United States, but they are often misreported as suicide or homicide. Some experts theorize that in many cases embarrassed or shocked relatives of the deceased clean up AEA and EA death scenes before the police arrive. Additionally, emergency personnel and police are not always educated about the signs of AEA and so may easily misinterpret deaths resulting from this practice as suicide.

## AEA Syndrome

Although release mechanisms are often built into devices intended for use in autoerotic asphyxiation, the practice remains extremely dangerous. Death or permanent brain damage can result if a practitioner loses consciousness before removing the device used to deprive oxygen or if a release mechanism malfunctions.

The paraphernalia and practices of sexual bondage are common to both AEA and EA. Sometimes practitioners insert foreign bodies in the rectum for anal stimulation, and many place mirrors strategically to view themselves during the act of sexual asphyxiation. Some other signs of AEA and EA that may appear at death scenes, and of which investigators should be aware, include the presence of lubricants, sex toys, and pornographic pictures or literature and the binding of the body and genitals with chains, leather strips, or ropes. Items that may be found at such scenes include belts, cords, ropes, scarves, and neckties. Practitioners of AEA and EA also sometimes cover their heads with plastic bags to deprive their brains of oxygen.

Evidence of asphyxia by strangulation, protective padding around the neck, and evidence of trying to prevent marks on the body are all common elements of a death scene involving

AEA. In addition, the presence of devices with self-release mechanisms, sexual aids and props, and pornography is associated with an AEA death. Body position—with feet touching the floor, sitting in a chair or lying in bed, partially or totally nude, with arms and legs bound in chains or ropes—and evidence that masturbation occurred are also indicators of an AEA death. Another feature of the AEA death scene is what it lacks—no suicide letter or other evidence that the death resulted from a suicide attempt is found.

Some warning signs that a person may be participating in autoerotic asphyxiation include unexplained marks on the neck, bloodshot eyes, complaints of frequent headaches, and possession of knotted short ropes and neckties. Teenage boys who engage in AEA may install locks on their bedroom doors, keep women's clothing hidden in their rooms, and show a strong interest in sexual bondage and sadomasochism. Parents, teachers, and counselors of young people should be aware of all these signs. Each sign by itself is not necessarily indicative of AEA, but in combination these indicators should not be ignored. When parents and others involved with teenagers suspect the practice of autoerotic or erotic asphyxiation, they should investigate and communicate with these young people to inform them about the risks of such activities. Accidental deaths can be prevented when young people involved in these practices receive prompt counseling by professionals who are familiar with AEA and EA.

*Sharon W. Stark*

**Further Reading**

Boglioli, Lauren R., and Mark L. Taff. "The Medicolegal Investigation of Autoerotic Asphyxial Deaths." In *The Handbook of Forensic Sexology: Biological and Criminological Perspectives*, edited by James J. Krivacska and John Money. Amherst, N.Y.: Prometheus Books, 1994. Provides an overview of autoerotic asphyxiation, statistics, and description of the biological events that occur during AEA. Also discusses individual victims and death scenes.

Brody, Jane E. "'Autoerotic Death' of Youths Causes Widening Concern." *The New York Times*, March 27, 1984. Discusses growing concerns among members of the public about adolescents' experimentation with autoerotic asphyxiation. Offers information on the warning signs of AEA in young people.

Jenkins, A. "When Self-Pleasure Becomes Self-Destruction: Autoerotic Asphyxiation Paraphilia." *International Electronic Journal of Health Education* 3, no. 3 (2000): 208-216. Presents statistics and describes the characteristics of AEA participants.

Sheleg, Sergey, and Edwin Ehrlich. *Autoerotic Asphyxiation: Forensic, Medical, and Social Aspects*. Tucson, Ariz.: Wheatmark, 2006. Reviews the research regarding AEA and discusses the practice from the perspectives of both professionals and society.

Tournel, Gilles, et al. "Complete Autoerotic Asphyxiation: Suicide or Accident?" *American Journal of Forensic Medicine and Pathology* 22 (June, 2001): 180-183. Focuses on the topic of deaths associated with AEA.

**See also:** Asphyxiation; Choking; Hanging; Psychological autopsy; Strangulation; Suffocation; Suicide.

# Automated fingerprint identification systems. *See Integrated Automated Fingerprint Identification System*

# Autopsies

**Definition**: External and internal medical examinations of dead bodies to determine cause of death, identify decedents or their body parts, or study changes caused by disease.

**Significance:** An autopsy is a very important part of many forensic investigations, given that the body is usually the center of any death case. In a death investigation, the body is just as much a crime scene as the geographic area in which it was found. During the autopsy, evidence is collected from the body "scene." This evidence, along with the determination of the cause and manner of death, contributes greatly to the resolution of the investigation. It can also positively identify an otherwise visually unidentifiable person, making it possible for authorities to release the remains to the appropriate family.

Autopsies may be divided into two primary types: the clinical autopsies done at hospitals and the forensic autopsies executed by medical examiners or coroners. The aim of the clinical, or academic, autopsy is to determine, clarify, or confirm diagnoses that remained unknown or did not become sufficiently clear during the stay of a patient in a hospital or other health care facility. The forensic, or medicolegal, autopsy focuses primarily on violent death (death by accident, suicide, or homicide), suspicious and sudden death, death without medical assistance, or death that could result in a lawsuit, such as a death related to surgical or anesthetic procedures. The purposes of the forensic autopsy are to find the cause and manner of death and to identify the decedent.

## Cause, Manner, and Mechanism of Death

The term "cause of death" refers to the situation or illness that resulted in the loss of life. Examples of causes of death include heart disease, stroke, knife wound to the wrist, gunshot wound to the chest, and hanging. In assigning the cause of death, some medical examiners use the "but for" test, as in "But for the gunshot wound, the victim would still be alive." The cause of death is what brought about the person's death.

Manner of death is determined according to a classification system that coroners and medical examiners use to certify a death. Only five manners of death are possible: natural, accidental, homicide, suicide, and undetermined. Any doctor can pronounce death, but only a coroner or a medical examiner can certify a death as a manner other than natural. A natural death is one that results from the normal course of life. Death from heart disease would be a type of nat-

ural death. An accidental death is one that results from a mishap, such as a death resulting from a fall off a ladder.

Homicide, in this context, is a death that results from the actions of another person. This is a medical declaration only; it does not imply anything about the guilt or motives of the other person. A manner of death of homicide on a death certificate is not a legal assertion. The determination of the other party's culpability is made by the legal system, independent of the autopsy. Deaths that result from vehicle accidents that involve other vehicles are often classified as homicides. Accidental shootings also are often classified as homicides, although they do not warrant a verdict of murder. Aside from such exceptions, however, many cases with a manner of death of homicide are indeed the result of malicious actions that would constitute the legal determination of murder.

Suicide is the manner of death used to describe a death that resulted from the victim's own determined actions. Hangings and self-cuttings are both classified as suicide manners of death. A finding of undetermined manner of death simply means that enough evidence was not available for the pathologist to distinguish between two or more of the other manners of death. As an example, without proper investigative information, a medical examiner may have problems ruling between accidental death and suicide if the deceased took a few too many pills or mixed medications. The attending coroner or medical examiner makes every effort to gain as much information as possible to avoid the need to use the undetermined manner of death classification.

Laypersons often confuse the concept of mechanism of death with cause of death. Mechanism of death is much more specific than cause of death, however; it is the actual specific biological reason the person died. In a case where the cause of death is a gunshot wound to the chest, the mechanism of death might be exsanguination, meaning that the victim bled out; death was the result of the loss of blood caused by the gunshot wound. Chronic alcoholism and cirrhosis are causes of death, whereas hepatic encephalopathy (the impairment of the brain cells caused by the release of liver toxins into the body) would be the actual mechanism of death in such cases. Cardiac arrest is often a stated mechanism of death, but many coroners and medical examiners disapprove of this determination, as heart failure (meaning the heart stopped) is a result of every death and may not be the true mechanism of death.

### Identification of the Deceased

In addition to establishing cause and manner of death, the forensic autopsy positively identifies the deceased. Visual identification is not considered sufficiently accurate to be counted as positive identification. The body goes through many physical changes during decomposition that can make recognizing an individual difficult. Also, the person who is asked to identify the deceased visually is often in a highly emotional state, which can lead to mistakes and misidentification.

The clothing on the body, likewise, is not a positive identifier. For example, members of the U.S. military have their last names on every uniform they are required to wear, and they also must wear dog tags that bear their names, but even these precautions do not guarantee that a dead soldier will be correctly identified by these items. Sometimes people do not wear their own clothes, and, in some documented cases, good friends in the military have exchanged dog tags in particularly dire situations as a means of encouraging each other or lifting morale. Reliance on clothing and dog tags has occasionally resulted in the misidentification of deceased military personnel.

To make a positive identification of a deceased person, investigators use one of three main recognized methods. The first is fingerprint examination. If the decedent was part of the military, ever served time in prison, worked for the government, or participated in a local "Protect Our Children" or similar drive, he or she likely had fingerprints taken. These antemortem (prior to death) records can be compared with fingerprints taken from the body at autopsy to identify the decedent with certainty.

Another positive identification technique is forensic odontology, in which the decedent's teeth are compared with antemortem dental records. To carry out the comparison, a forensic odontologist takes X rays and castings of the decedent's teeth and then compares tooth positions, shapes of fillings, root lengths, and other factors with those found in the dental records of the person suspected to be the deceased.

The third method used for positive identification of a body involves the examination of DNA (deoxyribonucleic acid). DNA comparison methods are of two types. One uses nuclear DNA, which is in the blood and tissue; this DNA is somewhat fragile and can be damaged by decomposition. Identification using this DNA involves strict comparison of the DNA found in the blood and tissue of the deceased to antemortem material. If the nuclear DNA cannot be used, it is possible to use mitochondrial DNA, which is much sturdier and can withstand decomposition changes. Mitochondrial DNA is a

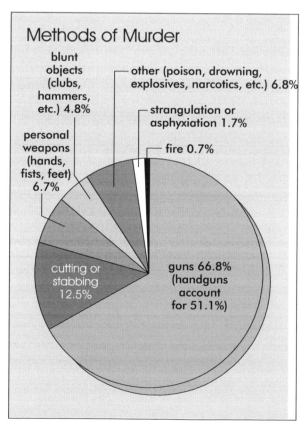

*Source:* Federal Bureau of Investigation, *Crime in the United States.* Figures are based on 14,274 murders in the United States in 2002.

## The Autopsy Through History

The term "autopsy" comes from *autopsia*, a Greek word meaning "to see with one's own eyes." Around 3000    , the Egyptians practiced mummification—removing organs through tiny slits in the body so that the body itself remained whole—and the Greek Herophilus broke religious taboos by dissecting bodies to learn how the inner organs worked. By around 150    , autopsy results had legal parameters in the Roman Empire. In 1761, the Italian anatomist Giovanni Battista Morgagni published *De Sedibus et Causis Morborum per Anatomen Indagatis* (*The Seats and Causes of Diseases Investigated by Anatomy*, 1769), the first exhaustive written work on pathology.

The nineteenth century Austrian anatomy professor Karl Rokitansky is regarded as the founder of the modern autopsy. Rokitansky personally performed or supervised more than one hundred thousand autopsies and was also one of the world's first pathologists. Under his leadership, all autopsies were carried out equally so that every part of the body in question could be studied exactly the same way.

*Kelly Rothenberg*

bit trickier in its comparison because this type of DNA is passed on only from the mother to the child, so a family member from the mother's side of the family is needed for comparison.

Other methods of positive victim identification are also available. A radiologist can compare X rays of the body to X rays from any previous injuries in the medical records of the person believed to be the deceased. If evidence of previously documented injuries can be found on the postmortem (after death) X rays, the pathologist can identify the victim. If antemortem facial X rays exist, a radiologist can compare how the sinuses line up, as well as their sizes and shapes. Evidence of some type of extreme medical procedure, such as the attachment of a metal plate to a bone to aid in the healing of a serious injury, can also be an identifier. These methods, however, are used relatively rarely because they rely on the presence of previous X rays in the suspected victim's medical records and on the uniqueness of those X rays.

### Initial External Examination

Significant examination of the body occurs during an autopsy prior to any cutting. This initial procedure may vary a bit from practitioner

to practitioner, but the same basic principles are always followed. The first and most important step in any autopsy is photography. Pictures of the body are taken before the body is removed from the body bag, to document exactly how the remains appeared when they came into the care of the coroner or medical examiner. Typically, a few shots of the body bag are taken, with any identifying tags visible, and then the bag is opened and the first shots of the body are taken, still in the body bag. In cases of mass disasters and severe commingling of bodies, these initial shots are very important to show what exactly was received and then later put together as related remains.

In another external stage of the autopsy, full-body X rays are taken of the remains so that when the body is ready for postmortem examination, the pathologist can get an idea of what is inside prior to cutting. Broken bones and other injuries are documented, as these may help to guide the pathologist in determining the cause of death. X rays are essential in shooting cases because they allow the pathologist to document and count the bullets that remain in the body before cutting and provide information on where the bullets will be when the cutting begins, thereby saving a search that could otherwise take hours.

The coroner or medical examiner also typically allows any law-enforcement personnel attending the autopsy to take the fingerprints of the deceased at this time. Some medical examiner offices have their own investigators who work as liaisons between the medical examiners and law-enforcement agents. These in-house investigators may be the ones who routinely take decedents' fingerprints.

Forensic odontology may be done before the pathologist cuts or after, depending on the procedures set up for that office. The forensic

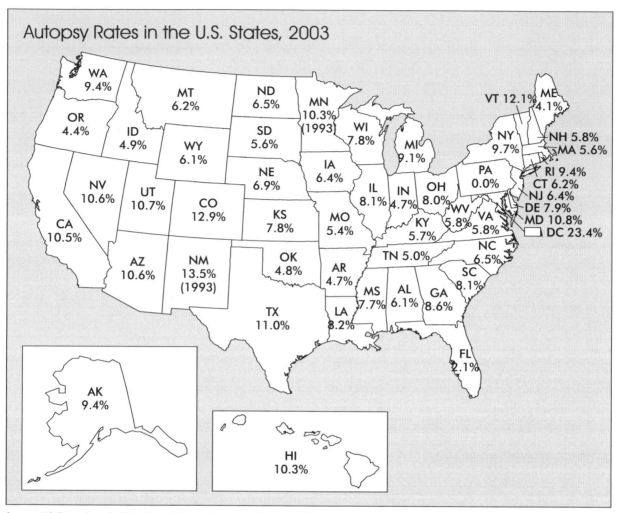

Autopsy Rates in the U.S. States, 2003

WA 9.4%
MT 6.2%
ND 6.5%
MN 10.3% (1993)
VT 12.1%
ME 4.1%
OR 4.4%
ID 4.9%
WY 6.1%
SD 5.6%
WI 7.8%
NY 9.7%
NH 5.8%
MA 5.6%
NV 10.6%
UT 10.7%
CO 12.9%
NE 6.9%
IA 6.4%
MI 9.1%
PA 0.0%
RI 9.4%
CT 6.2%
NJ 6.4%
CA 10.5%
KS 7.8%
IL 8.1%
IN 4.7%
OH 8.0%
WV 5.8%
VA 5.8%
DE 7.9%
MD 10.8%
DC 23.4%
AZ 10.6%
NM 13.5% (1993)
OK 4.8%
MO 5.4%
KY 5.7%
AR 4.7%
TN 5.0%
NC 6.5%
SC 8.1%
TX 11.0%
MS 7.7%
AL 6.1%
GA 8.6%
LA 8.2%
FL 2.1%
AK 9.4%
HI 10.3%

*Source:* U.S. Department of Health and Human Services, Centers for Disease Control and Prevention, 2007. Figures indicate percentages of deaths for which autopsies were reported in 2003, except in Minnesota and New Mexico, whose figures are from 1993.

odontologist makes a thorough postmortem dental examination and compares the findings to antemortem dental records. Dental X rays are taken, casts are made, and, if necessary, sometimes the jaw is removed from the body for examination. (The jaw is removed only in specialized cases, however, and only when it has already been determined with certainty that there will be no open-casket funeral.)

After all of the steps described above have taken place, the pathologist does an external examination as well. The body is taken out of the body bag, and pictures are once again taken. The doctor then carefully removes the clothing and jewelry from the body while noting any cuts, tears, or other indicators of injury or struggle shown by these items. These personal effects are then set aside and photographed separately for documentation. The doctor may refer back to the clothes if they have any cuts in them to marry up the cuts with injuries on the body or perhaps to find marks on the body that are not readily visible. If there are other marks on the body, the doctor may also refer to the clothing to see if the marks may have been made by it.

All salvageable personal effects that are not going to be kept as evidence are set aside for return to the family of the deceased. The doctor tries not to add further damage to any salvageable effects; for example, if possible, the clothes are unbuttoned or unzipped as opposed to cut away from the body. If the clothes are not salvageable, whether because they are saturated in blood or somehow destroyed, they are usually cut off. If a garment is covered with body fluid, it is dried prior to packaging to prevent spoilage from bacteria activity.

The doctor then examines the body itself, documenting any and all injuries as well as any unusual markings (birthmarks or tattoos), noting their placement on the body, their shapes, and their measurements. References to placement on the body are always made from the decedent's perspective. That is, an injury on the right side of the body's chest is described as such, although the injury appears on the left as the doctor views the body from above.

Sometimes, depending on the type of case, the pathologist will also take fingernail scrapings or clippings from the body for evidence; materials of interest to investigators may include soil samples and blood or skin that may have been left on the body by a suspect. The naked body is then washed, and the wounds are cleaned. The corpse is photographed once again, with separate shots taken of all identified injuries.

## Internal Examination

After all the external evidence is recorded and set aside for possible further examination, the process of dissection begins. As a rule, a forensic pathologist begins an autopsy at the upper portion of the body and works downward. Some pathologists may open the head at a later step, but initial examination always starts there. First, the scalp is searched for hidden wounds or artifacts, and hair samples are taken if needed. The mouth is examined for tooth damage, tongue lacerations, chemicals or toxic substances, and cuts on the lip and inner mouth, and the nose and ears are examined for any blood accumulations.

The inner eyelids are examined for petechiae, which are tiny pinpoint blood specks that may suggest asphyxiation. Whether at the beginning or at the end of the autopsy, when the pathologist opens the head to gain access to the brain, an incision is made that reaches from behind one ear to behind the other. The scalp is then inverted until it rests over the face and the outer skull is accessible. A bone saw is used to open the skull so that the brain can be removed, weighed, and sampled and the cranium can be inspected for injuries. In some cases the cranium is also sawed at various angles to expose the sinuses, jawbone, or other parts of the skull that require scrutiny.

The standard American autopsy begins with a cut known as a Y incision (the cut looks like the letter Y when it is completed). A cut is made from each shoulder, and the two cuts meet at the lower part of the sternum (breastbone), although some pathologists intersect these cuts as low as the stomach. A straight cut is then made from the intersection down to the pubic bone. The skin and muscle are then cut back, revealing the rib cage beneath. The ribs are examined for any breaks or healing injuries before each rib is cut so that the breastplate—beneath which many of the body's organs are housed—can be removed.

Each organ (the heart, lungs, liver, kidneys, spleen, stomach, and testicles) is removed, weighed, and examined for injury. Each organ is then sliced, and samples are preserved for toxicology screens (tests for any drug use or poison) and histology analysis (study of the organ on a microscopic level). Samples are also preserved in case they are needed for reexamination at some point in the future. Blood, bile, and urine are also taken, examined, and preserved, along with fluids from the lungs and pleural cavity. The contents of the stomach are also inspected.

The autopsy ends in the pelvic cavity. The external and internal anus and genitalia are inspected, the bladder is removed and studied, and, in cases of suspected sexual assault, vaginal and anal swabs are made.

Upon completion of the examination, all organs (including the brain) are placed in a bag that is put into the chest cavity. The piece of the skull that has been removed is put back into place, and the scalp is pulled back down to hold it in place. The scalp and chest incisions are sewn shut, so that when the body is dressed for viewing, no cuts are visible and open-casket viewing is possible.

After all else is completed, including any toxicology, DNA, and histology analyses, the pathologist writes a full report that describes the autopsy procedures and findings in detail. Included in the report is a brief history of the case; a death scene description; a list of all persons present at the scene; an X-ray description of the body; descriptions of the clothing found on the body, of the naked body prior to dissection, of the condition of the organs at autopsy, and of the wounds; the toxicological findings; and the cause and manner of death.

*Russell S. Strasser*

### Further Reading

DiMaio, Vincent J., and Dominick DiMaio. *Forensic Pathology.* 2d ed. Boca Raton, Fla.: CRC Press, 2001. One of the best reference sources available in the field of forensic pathology. Covers autopsies in detail as well as certain techniques for specific kinds of deaths.

Mann, Robert, William Bass, and Lee Meadows. "Time Since Death and Decomposition of the Human Body: Variables and Observations in Case and Experimental Field Studies." *Journal of Forensic Sciences* 35, no. 1 (1990): 103-111. Excellent comprehensive study focuses primarily on the decomposition of a body but gives a good idea of what to expect at autopsy from certain types of cases. Discusses the difficulty of determining time of death.

Sheaff, Michael T., and Deborah J. Hopster. *Post Mortem Technique Handbook.* London: Springer, 2001. Provides a very good in-depth look at postmortem examinations. Thorough discussion covers every step of an autopsy extensively.

Shkrum, Michael J., and David A. Ramsay. *Forensic Pathology of Trauma: Common Problems for the Pathologist.* Totowa, N.J.: Humana Press, 2007. Excellent technical reference work discusses how trauma affects a body and the problems that forensic pathologists face in conducting trauma autopsies.

Spitz, Werner U., ed. *Spitz and Fisher's Medicolegal Investigation of Death: Guidelines for the Application of Pathology to Crime Investigation.* 4th ed. Springfield, Ill.: Charles C Thomas, 2006. Indispensable volume for those conducting forensic investigations and forensic pathology. Includes comprehensive sections on specific cases along with their pathological findings.

Timmermans, Stefan. *Postmortem: How Medical Examiners Explain Suspicious Deaths.* Chicago: University of Chicago Press, 2006. Outstanding work on forensic pathology explains the autopsy process and gives case study examples.

Zugibe, Frederick, and David L. Carroll. *Dissecting Death: Secrets of a Medical Examiner.* New York: Broadway Books, 2005. A forensic pathologist discusses some of his cases and how he performed the autopsies. Interesting book aimed at readers who like the popular *CSI* television shows.

**See also:** Antemortem injuries; Coroners; DNA analysis; Fingerprints; Forensic odontology; Forensic pathology; Forensic toxicology; Gunshot wounds; Oral autopsy; Petechial hemorrhage; Psychological autopsy; Puncture wounds; Suicide; Thanatology; Toxicological analysis.

# B

## Back-spatter

**Definition:** Biological and non-biological traces represent a primary significance in firearms crime scene investigations. Back-spatter or "blowback" results when a weapon discharges, producing high-velocity retrograde biological and gunpowder trace evidence. The transfer of trace evidence between shooter and victim occurs at the moment of the firearms discharge. Back-spatter is redirected back toward the source of energy and shooter.

**Significance:** Back-spatter patterns produce valuable transfer evidence that serve investigators in their search for suspects. Gunpowder residue, lesions on hands, as well as blood, bone fragments, or brain tissue spatters on the trigger hand or the supporting hand serve as scientific evidence. The basic theory of transfer applies mathematical probability and rarity equations that eliminate as well as identify suspects and prove cases. The distance analysis of back-spatter is particularly significant in forensic investigations. Investigative results from back-spatter reenactment testing enhance crime scene reconstruction accuracy and efforts.

Three possible explanations unfold in death scene investigations: (1) accidental, (2) suicide, and (3) homicide. Crime scene reconstruction requires critical thinking and problem solving. The end result is excellent decision-making that points investigators in a more precise direction toward viable suspects. Forensic pathologists and homicide investigators reason, with some certainty, a plausible explanation for what the death scene account describes. The autopsy report assists in linking back-spatter trace evidence from the victim, the scene, and offender.

Excellent homicide investigators understand the value of back-spatter trace evidence. Firearms back-spatter applications originate from research that dates back prior to 1920's. Back-spatter on the firearm or shooter assists in crime scene reconstruction. The transfer of trace evidence may be disclosed on countless locations that include: the shooter, skin, clothing, hands, forearms, fingernails, and anterior parts of the body. The possibilities are too numerous to mention; investigators and the scientific community understand the importance of securing minuscule evidence that at first glance appears insignificant.

Investigators apply scientific analysis to reconstruct an accurate sequence of blood spatter events. Crime scene interpretation is the result of a hypothesis, laboratory examination, experimentation, and logical back-spatter associative trace evidence. Physical evidence, such as blood spatter may determine how the homicide transpired and provide insight into the dynamics of the shooter's movements.

### Processing Blood Back-Spatter

Blood back-spatter requires maintaining meticulous evidence collection procedures, chain of custody documentation, and control. Investigators photograph, collect, and preserve the trace evidence for scientific laboratory examination and court room testimony. Evidence team members train to focus on blood stain patterns before the victim's hands are treated and bagged. Most importantly, blood stain evidence is videotaped and photographed as a first priority. Back-spatter blood trace examination and victim assessment protocols are initiated before crime scene investigators and support teams bag both hands and transport the body.

Investigators typically use luminol at crime scenes where no blood is visible. They spray the chemical over a wide area in near-total darkness, so any reaction is obvious. Luminol is a chemical that glows greenish-blue when it comes into contact with blood — even traces that are years old. Blood reacts to hemoglobin, an oxygen-carrying protein in red-blood cells.

Luminol is so sensitive, it can detect blood at 1 part per million. In addition, luminol reacts to some metals, paints, cleaning products and plant matter. Luminol can detect blood traces that the human eye can miss.

It is preferable to have a forensic pathologist examine and document back-spatter blood trace evidence at the on-site crime scene. Wrapping the hands in paper bags can destroy or smear fragile blood traces. The bagging of hands for transportation is accomplished after securing all obtainable blood evidence. Following predetermined and precise scientific procedures helps protect blood evidence. Gunpowder and fingerprint examination testing only takes place after protecting the fragile blood evidence.

### Biological Back-Spatter

DNA applications for back-scatter biological trace evidence are the most valuable sources for shooter identification. DNA evidence supports the theory that offenders bring something to the crime scene, and upon their departure, unknowingly take evidence with them. A desire to commit a perfect crime fails because of the transfer of blood back-spatter evidence.

Forward spatter or back-spatter impact stains occur when blood receives some impact and is divided into smaller droplets or exclamation mark droplets. Back-spatter shooting patterns are the result of blood droplets expelled from the entry wound. The consequence is *medium* or *high* velocity blood striking the shooter's trigger hand and supporting hand. Back-spatter evidence is important in estimating the distance between the shooter and victim.

The most convincing and sometimes missed back-spatter evidence may be detected inside the shooter's sleeve, especially when combined with gunshot residue and DNA biological materials. Traces of back-spatter in the gun barrel post-homicide indicate a contact wound. Generally, the contact pattern forms a star pattern and may also be of value in suicide cases.

The application of rarity and mathematical probability to high-velocity DNA back-spatters links the shooter and victim. The genetic code continues to unlock new opportunities for solving crimes and accurate case closure. DNA evidence is extremely important in forensic investigation. DNA evidence continues to evolve and develop; it represents the prime crime fighting tool. Biological back-spatter on the shooter remains the most convincing element of proof. New developments in DNA technologies and DNA finger printing continue to expand the scope of forensic investigations. DNA blood back-spatter meets the reliability, material and relevance evidence tests.

### Processing Gun Shot Residue

When a shooter fires a weapon at a crime scene, the search begins for gunshot residue (GSR). The primer chemical reaction leads to the detonation of smokeless gunpowder in the cartridge. The reaction in the primer typically releases three elements: lead, barium, and antimony. Some cartridges have primers that do not use antimony and barium. These cartridges are mostly .22 calibers and are marked "lead free" and "clean fire." Less frequent elements in the primer include: aluminum, sulfur, tin, calcium, potassium, chlorine, silicone, and mercury (from mercury-fulminate, used in Eastern Europe cartridges).

In numerous cases, trace evidence of GSR pattern dispersal will not identify the shooter. The discharge of a firearm, specially a revolver, can scatter GSR on all nearby objects. Gunshot residues are useful for a relatively short time, approximately 3 to 48 hours.. This form of trace evidence dissipates with normal activity and requires timely and specific collection protocols. Gunshot Residue Collection Kits should be available for immediate use.

### In Summary

The success or failure of any criminal investigation depends on the recognition of physical evidence left at a crime scene and the proper analysis of that evidence. Excellent evidence gathering procedures result in competent, material, and reliable evidence for presentation in court. In numerous cases, back-spatter traces are the only evidence that can differentiate between a murder, manslaughter, suicide, or self-defense death. The purpose of back-spatter evidence is the exoneration of the innocent or conviction of the guilty. GSR and DNA back- spatter trace evidence enhances a "guilty beyond a reasonable doubt" verdict.

*Thomas E. Baker*

**Further Reading**

Gardner, Beverley T. *Bloodstain Pattern Analysis.* Boca Raton, Fl: CRC Press, 2002.

Girard, James E. *Criminalistics: Forensic Science, Crime, and Terrorism.* 2ded. Sudbury, MA: Jones and Bartlett, 2011.

Swanson, Charles R. et al. *Criminal Investigation.* 10th ed. Boston, MA: McGraw-Hill, 2012.

**See also:** Blood residue and bloodstains; Crime scene investigation; DNA isolation methods; DNA profiling; Gunshot residue; Firearms analysis; DNA analysis; Homicide; Suicide.

# Bacteria

**Definition:** Single-celled organisms lacking a nucleus, found in and on humans and widespread in the environment.

**Significance:** Bacteria are ubiquitous on Earth, and some species can cause disease in humans. An understanding of the classification of bacteria as well as the ways in which bacterial populations grow and reproduce is useful to the identification, diagnosis, and treatment of bacterial diseases.

The tiny unicellular organisms known as bacteria define the biosphere on Earth—that is, if bacteria do not inhabit a particular environment, no living things reside there. Bacteria are extremely adaptable and have managed to exploit a wide variety of habitats successfully. One niche exploited by bacteria is the human body. Humans support a population of more than two hundred species of bacteria in numbers greater than the cells that make up an individual human host. These members of the normal flora are found on the skin and in the digestive, urinary, reproductive, and upper respiratory tracts of humans.

Although some species of bacteria can cause disease in humans, other animals, and plants, the majority of bacterial species are not pathogenic (disease-causing). Bacteria are key players in the ecology of the Earth, functioning in important roles in global chemical cycles. Perhaps most important, bacteria are the only organisms on Earth that possess the ability to fix nitrogen—that is, to convert the nitrogen gas in the atmosphere to a form that is usable by other organisms.

Disease-causing bacteria have attracted the most interest and study since the confirmation of the germ theory of disease by Louis Pasteur and Robert Koch in the 1870's. It is interesting to note that Koch's proof that germs cause disease involved the bacterium *Bacillus anthracis*, which causes anthrax, an organism that has been used as a biological weapon.

The first sixty years of the study of medical bacteriology focused on identification and diagnosis, with little attention to the basic biology of bacteria. The discovery and development of antibiotics led to an overly optimistic view that infectious disease had been conquered. The emergence of antibiotic-resistant strains of bacteria as well as outbreaks of previously unknown pathogens stimulated a renewed interest in bacteriology.

## Classification and Taxonomy

Bacteria are classified as prokaryotic cells—that is, the genetic material of a bacterium is not enclosed in a nucleus. This lack of a nucleus distinguishes bacterial cells from the cells that make up plants and animals, which are classified as eukaryotic. Additional differences between bacterial cells and eukaryotic cells include the types of molecules found in the cell walls, organization and expression of genes, and sensitivity to certain antibiotics.

Bacteria themselves have been classified in several ways. In 1923, the first edition of *Bergey's Manual of Determinative Bacteriology* offered descriptions of all the species of bacteria then identified, an outline of the taxonomic relationships among bacteria, and keys for diagnosis of diseases caused by bacteria. The ninth edition of *Bergey's Manual*, published in 1994, focuses primarily on identification of bacteria and uses taxonomic divisions that do not necessarily reflect evolutionary relationships.

During the 1980's, *Bergey's Manual of Systematic Bacteriology* was published in an attempt to organize bacterial species into the type of hierarchical classification schemes that have been applied to eukaryotic organisms. This manual later underwent revision to include new species and to cover the progress that had been made in molecular classification methods.

The International Committee on Systematics of Prokaryotes (ICSP) is the organization that oversees the nomenclature of prokaryotes and issues opinions concerning related taxonomic matters. When a researcher discovers a previously undescribed bacterium, the ICSP must approve the researcher's proposed name for the newly described species as well as the taxonomic classification of the species.

Clinically, classification of bacteria is performed primarily to diagnose particular diseases. Identification of bacteria in a clinical specimen can be accomplished through direct microscopic examination, isolation and culture of the responsible bacteria, and biochemical and immunological tests. Researchers have developed and marketed a number of automated microbial diagnosis systems that allow rapid diagnosis without the need to isolate the organisms of interest.

Dr. Robert Koch with his wife in 1908, three years after he won the Nobel Prize in Physiology or Medicine for his work on tuberculosis. During the 1870's, Koch and French biologist Louis Pasteur proved the germ theory of disease that laid the foundation for modern bacteriology. *(Library of Congress)*

### Cell and Population Growth

In discussing the growth of living organisms, one can focus on the growth of an individual or the growth of a population. Because bacteria are single-celled organisms, growth of an individual bacterium does not include development of organs or other body parts, but rather just enlargement of the cell itself.

Discussion of the growth of bacterial species is usually concerned with the growth of a population of cells. Because almost all bacteria reproduce through the division of one cell into two, the growth of a population of bacterial cells is geometric—that is, the population doubles in size with each round of cell division. The length of time required for a population of bacterial cells to double varies depending on the species and strain of bacteria as well as on the environmental conditions, including temperature, pH, nutrient availability, and waste accumulation.

Some bacteria, such as *Escherichia coli*, have a maximum doubling rate of less than thirty minutes. At this rate, a single cell could generate a population of one million cells in less than ten hours. In fact, if the environmental conditions remained optimal, with ready nutrients and regular waste removal, a culture of maximally reproducing *E. coli* bacteria would equal the mass of the planet Earth within one week. Other bacteria, such as *Mycobacterium tuberculosis*, divide much more slowly, taking twelve to eighteen hours under optimal conditions for one round of binary fission. The optimal growth rates estimated for many bacteria are merely speculative because the majority of species have not yet been cultured on defined or artificial media.

Even slowly dividing bacteria can reproduce in far less time than nearly every other type of organism. Because of their rapid reproductive rates and omnipresence in the living world, bacteria can rapidly overwhelm any unpreserved biological sample. Unrefrigerated food, blood and tissue samples, and other biological specimens can quickly become host to a diverse, rapidly growing population of bacteria.

## Reproduction

Most bacteria reproduce by binary fission. One cell grows by manufacturing more cellular components. The genome is replicated, and the single cell divides into two essentially identical cells. This type of reproduction is termed asexual because it does not involve the recombination of genetic material from two parents. Because the cells that result from binary fission are virtually identical genetically, the individual cells in a group or colony of bacteria all descended from a single ancestral cell could well be clones of the original cell.

The cellular machinery involved in replicating the genetic material does not perform this replication with perfect fidelity. At each round of replication, there is a finite probability of errors occurring. These errors lead to changes in the genetic material known as mutations. These mutations may result in cells with characteristics that are different from those of the other cells in the population. These altered characteristics may lead to cells that are better adapted to a particular environment—perhaps the ability to metabolize a new nutrient or survive in the presence of an antibiotic. Because bacterial cells reproduce by simple cell division, altered characteristics are transmitted to all offspring of the altered cell (barring further mutation).

Although bacteria do not reproduce sexually by recombination of genetic material from two parents, many bacteria are capable of obtaining genetic material from other cells through various methods. Some bacteria can take up DNA (deoxyribonucleic acid) from the environment (probably released from decomposing cells), can receive DNA through viral infections, and can transfer DNA directly from one living cell to another. These genetic recombination processes allow genes (such as those that confer antibiotic resistance) to be spread throughout a bacterial population rapidly.

*Lisa M. Sardinia*

## Further Reading

Betsy, Tom, and James Keogh. *Microbiology Demystified.* New York: McGraw-Hill, 2005. This alternative to hefty textbooks is intended as a review for allied health students having difficulty understanding concepts in microbiology. Clearly written.

Madigan, Michael T., John M. Martinko, Paul V. Dunlap, and David P. Clark. *Brock Biology of Microorganisms.* 12th ed. Upper Saddle River, N.J.: Pearson Prentice Hall, 2008. The industry standard for introductory microbiology textbooks. Contains extensive information on bacterial classification and diversity.

Nester, Eugene W., Denise G. Anderson, Jr., C. Evans Roberts, and Martha T. Nester. *Microbiology: A Human Perspective.* 5th ed. New York: McGraw-Hill, 2007. Introductory textbook intended for nonscience majors and allied health students includes frequent discussion of real-world applications of concepts.

Pommerville, Jeffrey C. *Alcamo's Fundamentals of Microbiology.* 8th ed. Sudbury, Mass.: Jones & Bartlett, 2007. Accessible textbook is designed for introductory college students, particularly those in the health sciences. Includes numerous sidebars and case studies.

Willey, Joanne, Linda Sherwood, and Chris Woolverton. *Prescott, Harley, and Klein's Microbiology.* 7th ed. New York: McGraw-Hill, 2007. Comprehensive textbook has sections on bacterial growth (including techniques) and diversity (several chapters describe various categories of bacteria). The organization is clear and logical; introductory discussions of topics are accessible to readers with little scientific background.

**See also:** Anthrax; Anthrax letter attacks; Antibiotics; Bacterial biology; Bacterial resistance and response to antibacterial agents; Biological terrorism; Biological warfare diagnosis; Biotoxins; Bubonic plague; Centers for Disease Control and Prevention; Decomposition of bodies; *Escherichia coli*; Food and Drug Administration, U.S.; Parasitology; Pathogen genomic sequencing; Pathogen transmission; Tularemia.

## Bacterial biology

**Definition:** Study of prokaryotic organisms lacking membrane-bound organelles and nuclei—simple, single-celled microscopic organisms growing by cell division to produce identical daughter cells.

**Significance:** Forensic scientists are sometimes called upon to identify bacterial strains causing such problems as hospital-acquired infections, food-borne infections, or microbial diseases; they may also need to identify biological agents used in bioterrorism. Bacteria have different DNA polymorphisms (variations in DNA sequence between individual bacteria or bacterial strains) that serve as markers for typing bacteria.

Several types of polymorphisms are used for DNA (deoxyribonucleic acid) profiling, including single nucleotide polymorphisms (SNPs), in which only a single nucleotide in a sequence varies, and variable number of tandem repeats (VNTRs). A sequence of DNA is tandemly (end-to-end) repeated, with the number of repeats differing between individual bacteria. An example is a sequence of thirty nucleotides that is repeated twenty to one hundred times in different bacterial cells. To identify VNTRs, polymerase chain reaction (PCR) primers are designed for both sides of the VNTR locus. With PCR, the sequence between the two primers is amplified, giving a large amount of this specific DNA, which is then separated by gel electrophoresis to determine the size (number of repeats) of the region amplified. The different numbers of tandem repeats are thought to arise from mistakes in DNA replication generating INDEL (insertion or deletion of DNA) mutations. Another polymorphism is short tandem repeats (STRs) — short sequence elements (usually three to seven bases) — repeating to be less than five hundred bases long.

Other types of markers used to identify bacteria are the sequences of 16S rRNA (ribosomal ribonucleic acid) and the spacer between the 16 and 23S rRNAs. Ribosomal RNA is part of the ribosome that translates messenger RNA into proteins. By comparing rRNA sequences, types of bacteria are identified. PCR amplifies the specific DNA coding for 16S rRNA. For example, 16S rRNA can be used to identify the bacterial pathogen causing disease in different persons.

### Forensic Applications

The ability to identify bacteria is important in many kinds of cases. Extensive use of antibiotics and the development of antibiotic-resistant bacterial strains, such as methicillin-resistant Staphylococcus aureus, can cause hospital-acquired infections. Different strains of Staphylococcus can be identified through DNA typing. Identification of an antibiotic-resistant strain of a bacterium leads to a more effective type of antibiotic treatment for the patient. Also, in some cases infections may be caused by inadequate hygienic precautions taken during surgery or in postoperative care. DNA analysis is important to identify the source of such infection-causing bacterial strains.

In cases of food-borne infections, it is important to trace the microbes causing them to the sources—whether companies, farms, or persons—to determine the origin of the microbes. Scientists use DNA analysis to track food-borne infections caused by Salmonella or the Esherichia coli strain O157:H7 to identify the types of bacteria causing the problems.

Molecular techniques are used to follow outbreaks of microbial diseases. The U.S. Centers for Disease Control and Prevention (CDC) maintains a database of microbial DNA fingerprints (PulseNet). Scientists have examined some thirty-one VNTR loci to compare strains of Mycobacterium tuberculosis, the bacterium that causes tuberculosis. It is also important to identify bacteria in cases of biological terrorism. For example, in 2001, letters containing Bacillus anthracis, the bacterium that causes anthrax, were sent through the mail in the eastern United States, and five people died of inhalation anthrax. Because B. anthracis spores are commonly found in soil, it was essential that prosecutors prove spores found in a suspect's home or laboratory were the same strain that was found on the material mailed to the victims. In 2002, the American Academy of Microbiology formulated standards for evidence collection and analysis of molecular tests for microbial forensics.

Bacteria can also be used to estimate time of death. After death, the action of bacteria destroys the soft tissues of the body. The bacteria generally found are those normally present in the respiratory and intestinal tracts, such as bacilli, coliform, and clostridiuim. The temperature of the environment surrounding the body determines the rate of bacterial growth. The postmortem interval can be studied by analyzing the microbes around the grave site, which change rapidly. Rapid next generation DNA sequencing is used to sequence many microbial genomes to identify the microbes present.

*Susan J. Karcher*

### Further Reading

Budowle, Bruce, Steven E. Schutzer, Roger G. Breeze, Paul S. Keim, and Stephen A. Morse, eds. *Microbial Forensics*. 2d ed. Burlington, MA: Elsevier Academic Press, 2010. Details the importance of forensic microbiology and discusses its uses.

Butler, John M. *Advanced Topics in Forensic DNA Typing: Methodology*. Waltham, MA: Elsevier Academic Press, 2011. Accessible textbook provides detailed overview of DNA methodologies used by forensic scientists.

Cho, Mildred K., and Pamela Sankar. "Forensic Genetics and Ethical, Legal, and Social Implications Beyond the Clinic." *Nature Genetics* 36 (2004): S8-S12. Discusses the ethical considerations related to DNA profiling and genetic analysis.

Finley, Sheree, M. Eric Benbow, Gulnaz T. Javan. "Potential Applications of Soil Microbial Ecology and Next-Generation Sequencing in Criminal Investigations." *Applied Soil Ecology* 88 (2015): 69-78. Review of analysis of soil bacteria around grave site using next generation DNA sequencing.

Jobling, Mark A., and Peter Gill. "Encoded Evidence: DNA in Forensic Analysis." *Nature Reviews Genetics* 5 (October, 2004): 739-751. Informative summary of DNA forensics.

Madigan, Michael T., John M. Martinko, Kelly S. Bender, and David H. Buckley, David A. Stahl, and Thomas Brock. *Brock Biology of Microorganisms*. 14th ed. Boston, MA: Benjamin-Cummings Publishing Company, 2014. Widely respected basic microbiology textbook includes information about biological weapons and methods of microbial identification.

**See also:** Anthrax; Antibiotics; Bacteria; Bacterial resistance and response to antibacterial agents; Biological terrorism; Biological warfare diagnosis; Biological weapon identification; Biotoxins; Centers for Disease Control and Prevention; Escherichia coli; Food poisoning; Pathogen genomic sequencing; Pathogen transmission; Short tandem repeat analysis.

## Bacterial resistance and response to antibacterial agents

**Definition:** Ability of some bacteria to resist

or entirely withstand the effects of anti-microbial agents.

**Significance:** Although most bacteria are be-nign, a small percentage are pathogenic, or disease-causing. Bacteria rank among the most important of all disease-causing organisms in humans, and bacterial infec-tions are countered by a wide variety of an-tibiotic and antibacterial agents. Re-peated use of such agents results in bacterial resistance, necessitating the de-velopment of stronger antibacterial agents. Increasing fears that antibiotic-re-sistant strains of bacteria may be used as bioweapons add urgency to efforts to de-velop new antibacterial agents.

Less than 10 percent of all bacteria threaten hu-man health. These disease-causing species are notorious for such diseases as cholera, typhus, and syphilis. The most common and some of the most deadly forms of bacterial diseases are respiratory infections, such as tuberculosis, which kill millions of people every year. Coun-tries around the world have used antibiotic drugs to treat bacterial infections for more than fifty years. The initial introduction of antibiot-ics was markedly successful, but continued and widespread use has resulted in a phenomenon in which microbial adaptation is making tar-geted bacteria increasingly difficult to control. This bacterial resistance to antibiotics is of spe-cial concern, as ever more powerful antibiotics must be developed.

## Antibiotics and Antibacterials

In its broadest definition, an antibacterial is an agent that interferes with the growth and re-production of bacteria. Although antibiotics and antibacterials both attack bacteria, these terms have evolved over the years to mean two differ-ent things. The term "antibacterials" is most commonly applied to agents that are used to dis-infect surfaces and eliminate potentially harm-ful bacteria. The term "antibiotics" is commonly reserved for medicines given to humans or ani-mals to treat infections or diseases.

Bacteria become resistant to antibacterial agents in one of three ways: natural resistance, vertical evolution, and horizontal evolution.

Therefore, bacteria exhibit either inherited or acquired resistance to antibacterial agents. Natural resistance occurs when bacteria are in-herently resistant to an antibacterial. For ex-ample, a gram-negative bacterium has an outer membrane that establishes an impermeability barrier against the antibiotic it manufactures, so it does not self-destruct.

Acquired resistance occurs when bacteria de-velop resistance to an antibacterial agent to which the population has been exposed. This may occur through mutation and selection (ver-tical evolution) or exchange of genes between strains and species (horizontal evolution) of the bacteria exposed to the antibacterial agent.

Vertical evolution represents an example of Darwinian evolution driven by principles of natural selection. Genetic mutations in the bac-teria population create new genes or combina-tions of genes that are resistant to the antibac-terial agent. While the nonmutant, sensitive bacteria are killed, bacteria containing the mu-tated genes survive, and their progeny populate the increasingly resistant colony.

Another form of acquired resistance, horizon-tal evolution, is the transfer of resistant genes from one bacterium to another in the popula-tion. For example, *Escherichia coli* or *Shigella* may acquire a gene from a streptomycete that is resistant to the antibiotic streptomycin. Fol-lowing this transfer, the population contains a mutant *E. coli* bacterium now resistant to strep-tomycin. Then, through the process of selection, it donates these genes to further generations, creating a resistant strain.

Transfer of genes in bacteria occurs in one of three ways: conjugation, transduction, or trans-formation. In conjugation, the gene-containing DNA (deoxyribonucleic acid) crosses a connect-ing structure, called a pilus, from a donor bacte-rium to recipient bacteria. In transduction, a vi-rus may transfer genes between bacteria. In transformation, DNA is acquired directly from the environment, having been released from an-other bacterium. Following transfer, the combi-nation of the newly acquired gene or genes re-sults in a process called genetic recombination that may lead to the emergence of a new geno-type. The combination of transfers and genetic recombination promotes rapid spread of antibacterial resistance through a species population and also between strains and other bacterial species.

The combined effects of fast growth rates, high concentrations of cells, genetic processes of mutation and selection, and genetic recombination account for the extraordinary rates of adaptation and evolution observed in bacteria populations. For these reasons, bacterial resistance to antibacterials is a common occurrence and one that promises to be of increasing concern in the future.

## Bacterial Resistance and Forensic Science

The importance of bacteriology in forensic science is recognized in diverse areas, including DNA profiling, toxicology studies, fingerprinting, and the tracing of violence stemming from or potentially relating to murders. Bacteria have been used as weapons and can be the causes of violence, but they may also serve as tools in the investigation of crimes.

The most serious threat posed by bacteria is their possible use in biological warfare, especially in acts of bioterrorism. For example, *Bacillus anthracis*, which causes anthrax, has become a preferred bacterial strain used by terrorists. Strains of deadly bacteria selected especially for their antibody resistance can pose health threats of enormous proportions at both local and global levels.

Some research has suggested that bacterial infections can lead to criminal behavior. For example, *Streptococcus* infections have been linked to hyperactivity, and hyperactivity has been linked to criminal behavior. Some defense lawyers have used such research findings in

## Facts About Antibiotic Resistance

*The Centers for Disease Control and Prevention provides the following information about the growing problem of antibiotic resistance.*

- Antibiotic resistance has been called one of the world's most pressing public health problems.
- The number of bacteria resistant to antibiotics has increased in the last decade. Nearly all significant bacterial infections in the world are becoming resistant to the most commonly prescribed antibiotic treatments.
- Every time a person takes antibiotics, sensitive bacteria are killed, but resistant germs may be left to grow and multiply. Repeated and improper uses of antibiotics are primary causes of the increase in drug-resistant bacteria.
- Misuse of antibiotics jeopardizes the usefulness of essential drugs. Decreasing inappropriate antibiotic use is the best way to control resistance.
- Children are of particular concern because they have the highest rates of antibiotic use. They also have the highest rate of infections caused by antibiotic-resistant pathogens.
- Parent pressure makes a difference. For pediatric care, a recent study showed that doctors prescribe antibiotics 65% of the time if they perceive parents expect them, and 12% of the time if they feel parents do not expect them.
- Antibiotic resistance can cause significant danger and suffering for people who have common infections that once were easily treatable with antibiotics. When antibiotics fail to work, the consequences are longer-lasting illnesses; more doctor visits or extended hospital stays; and the need for more expensive and toxic medications. Some resistant infections can cause death.

attempts to explain their clients' actions, connecting criminal behavior with infection-caused states of delirium.

In some cases, the bacteria present at the site of a crime can give important clues about the crime itself. For instance, bacteria can reveal how long a person has been dead or the temperature the body was subjected to after death. Heart and spleen blood cultures may be taken at autopsy to identify any possible infections or diseases the deceased may have had.

*Dwight G. Smith*

## Further Reading
Bartelt, Margaret A. *Diagnostic Bacteriology. A Study Guide.* Philadelphia: F. A. Davis, 2000. Provides a comprehensive, user-

friendly introduction to bacteriology for general readers.

Breeze, Roger G., Bruce Budowle, and Steven E. Schutzer, eds. *Microbial Forensics.* Burlington, Mass.: Elsevier Academic Press, 2005. Details the importance of forensic microbiology and discusses its uses.

Cummings, Craig A., and David A. Relman. "Microbial Forensics: When Pathogens Are 'Cross-Examined.'" *Science* 296 (2002): 1976-1979. Discusses the science involved in inferring the origin and transmission route of a microbial strain that has caused an infectious disease outbreak.

Larkin, Marilynn. "Microbial Forensics Aims to Link Pathogen, Crime, and Perpetrator." *The Lancet Infectious Diseases* 3, no. 4 (April, 2003): 180-181. Brief discussion of microbial forensics covers basic information on the field.

Tsokos, Michael, ed. *Forensic Pathology Reviews.* Vol. 4. Totowa, N.J.: Humana Press, 2006. Collection of articles by forensic pathologists includes valuable information on advances in forensic work concerned with bacteria.

**See also:** Anthrax; Antibiotics; Bacteria; Bacterial biology; Biological warfare diagnosis; Biotoxins; Bubonic plague; Pathogen genomic sequencing.

## Ballistic fingerprints

**Definition:** Marks that are etched on a rifle or handgun bullet as it is pushed through the gun's barrel.

**Significance:** The analysis of ballistic fingerprints is used in criminal investigations to gain information about the models of guns as well as the individual guns that fired bullets recovered from crime scenes. By comparing the marks that guns leave on bullets, experts can often identify the weapons used in crimes.

The examination of ballistic fingerprints is part of the field of internal ballistics, which is the study of events that begin when the firing pin of a rifle or handgun strikes the cartridge and end when the bullet exits the barrel. Ballistic fingerprinting is not a new science. In June, 1900, Dr. Albert Llewellyn Hall published an article titled "The Missile and the Weapon" in the *Buffalo Medical Journal*, in which he presented the first analysis of bullet marks imparted by rifling in a gun barrel.

The interior of the barrel of a rifle or handgun has raised and lowered spirals, called rifling, that impart spin to the bullets as they are fired, making them more aerodynamically stable. As a bullet is pushed down a gun's barrel by the gas that is generated by burning gunpowder, it is etched with fine lines, or striations, from the rifling. Under microscopic examination, these striations look something like the parallel lines of a universal product code. In addition, "skid marks" may be left on a bullet in the short period after it leaves the firing chamber and before it is fully engaged by the rifling.

The striations common to all guns of a particular model are known as class characteristics. Individual characteristics are the striations unique to a particular gun; these result from tiny imperfections in the rifling process and in the rifling tools used as well as from the wear and tear caused by the particular usage of that gun. Individual characteristics change over time. Criminals sometimes deliberately change a gun's individual characteristics; common techniques include shortening the barrel and rubbing the interior of the barrel with a steel brush.

Different types of ammunition fired through the same gun will produce very different striations. Even the small natural variations from one cartridge to another in the same box of commercial ammunition can produce some differences in patterns.

The analysis of ballistic fingerprints produces its most accurate results when the cartridge case (which holds the bullet, gunpowder, and primer before firing) as well as the bullet has been recovered; the firing pin, extractor, magazine, and other parts of the gun often leave distinctive marks on the case. Ballistic fingerprinting cannot be used on shotgun pellets because shotgun bores are smooth rather than rifled. However, shotgun cases can still be examined for firing pin marks and the like.

Several databases of digitized ballistic fingerprints of bullets recovered from crime scenes are available to criminal investigators. Forensic experts who conduct ballistic fingerprinting can use these databases to narrow their selection of bullets for microscopic examination. Binocular microscopic comparison of two bullets can take many hours.

A few jurisdictions require that ballistic fingerprint samples from new, lawfully sold handguns be put into a digitized database, but the efficacy of such efforts is the source of ongoing debate.

*David B. Kopel*

**Further Reading**

Burnett, Sterling, and David B. Kopel. *Ballistic Imaging: Not Ready for Prime Time.* Dallas: National Center for Policy Analysis, 2003.

Heard, Brian J. *Handbook of Firearms and Ballistics: Examining and Interpreting Forensic Evidence.* New York: John Wiley & Sons, 1997.

Warlow, Tom. *Firearms, the Law, and Forensic Ballistics.* 2d ed. Boca Raton, Fla.: CRC Press, 2005.

**See also:** Ballistics; Bullet-lead analysis; Class versus individual evidence; Firearms analysis; Gunshot residue; Integrated Ballistics Identification System; Microscopes.

## Ballistics

**Definition:** Study of the motion, behaviors, effects, and impact signatures of projectiles.

**Significance:** When projectiles—whether bullets, bombs, or missiles—are involved in crimes, ballistics experts play a vital role in the investigations. Forensic scientists trained in ballistics can identify the specific types of firearms used in crimes based on bullets, shell casings, and other evidence found at crime scenes. By comparing this information with weapons belonging to possible suspects, they can confirm individual weapons as those used in the crimes.

A ballistic body is any object used to exert force to make another object move or change in form, state, or direction. A bullet, for example, is a ballistic body when it is propelled by the sudden increase of pressure that takes place within a handgun or other firearm when the trigger is pulled and a discharge of explosive powder propels the bullet forward in a direction dictated by the barrel of the weapon. When the bullet exits the weapon, it is subject to the laws of ballistics. As the projectile reaches its target, its velocity and trajectory cause distinctive entry and exit wounds.

The science of firearms ballistics is divided into four components: internal ballistics, transition ballistics, external ballistics, and terminal ballistics. Internal ballistics is the study of the forces that cause the acceleration of ballistic bodies; in the case of a bullet fired from a gun, internal ballistics is concerned with the detonation of the bullet, its discharge from the chamber, and its pathway through the barrel. Transition, or intermediate, ballistics is the study of the immediate effects on ballistic bodies as they leave the barrels of weapons; this area of ballistics focuses on forces such as air pressure, gravity, and air density, which act collectively on projectiles as their initial acceleratory force is reduced.

External ballistics is the study of projectiles' flight through the air. This includes the examination of changes in velocity and trajectory of ballistic bodies during the time they are in flight from weapons to targets. The last component of basic ballistics, terminal ballistics, is concerned with the impacts of projectiles on the objects with which they come in contact. This includes the effects of impacts on projectiles themselves and the ways in which bullets penetrate various surfaces (including human flesh).

### Criminal Cases

Because the barrels of firearms are rifled (that is, they have raised and lowered spiral surfaces) to impart spin to bullets, distinctive marks (striations) are left on bullets as they swirl down the shafts of barrels after firing. The first recorded use of such marks as evidence in a criminal case took place in 1835. It was found that bullets fired from a weapon taken from the home of the primary suspect had a distinctive ridge that was identical to the ridge seen on a bullet recovered from the scene of the crime. When confronted with this evidence during questioning, the suspect confessed to the crime. Nearly seventy years later, in 1902, attorney Oliver Wendell Holmes, Jr., introduced ballistics evidence in a court of law. In a murder case, Holmes had a local gunsmith test fire a weapon belonging to the suspect into a wad of cotton stuffing. Under magnification, the marks on the test-fired bullet were seen to match those on the bullet retrieved from the crime scene, and this evidence was presented to the jury.

Shortly thereafter, two ballistics experts of that time, Calvin Goddard and Charles Waite, began compiling a database of information on all known gun manufacturers and on specific types of handguns as well as the marks made on bullets fired from them. Waite later invented the comparison microscope, which forensic scientists use to make side-by-side comparisons of the marks on two bullets at a time.

In the twenty-first century, forensic ballistics examinations are undertaken in virtually every criminal case involving firearms in the United States. The two basic types of weapons involved in forensic ballistics cases are handheld weapons (handguns or pistols) and shoulder weapons (rifles). The two types of firearms produce unique marks on bullets and shell casings when fired. Even after a weapon has fired hundreds of rounds, a bullet from that weapon will still match the first bullet from its barrel. For experts in forensic ballistics, bullet marks are like fingerprints; each firearm leaves marks that are unique to that weapon.

## Forensic Techniques

Experts in forensic ballistics perform many different kinds of analyses, including making bullet comparisons, matching projectiles to weapons, and estimating the lengths of projectile flights, which enables them to determine the types of weapons used and the locations

of the operators of weapons when they were fired. During investigations of crime scenes involving shootings, ballistics experts analyze the impacts of bullets on victims, whether wounded or dead, to determine the types and sizes of projectiles fired and the types of weapons used, the distances from the shooters to the victims, and the angles at which the shots were fired.

If bullets, cartridges, or cartridge cases are not found at the scene of a fatal shooting, a forensic pathologist will usually analyze the victim's wounds to determine information about the type of weapon used. Entry wounds are generally smaller than exit wounds and have dark rings around the injured surfaces, and by examining these, experts can often determine the width and thus the likely caliber of the bullets that made the wounds. This technique is referred to as wound ballistics.

When bullets are recovered from crime scenes, ballistics experts compare the striations on the bullets to those on other bullets from known sources. If the firearm suspected to have been used in a given crime is available, a test bullet is shot from that weapon and then the marks on that bullet are compared with the marks on the bullets found at the crime scene. The bullets found at crime scenes are also often compared with thousands of images of bullets stored in law-enforcement databases. Matches to bullets in such databases can give investigators important information about the histories of the weapons that fired the bullets.

The identification of specific weapons is another important aspect of the forensic investigation of crimes involving firearms. Many criminals remove the serial numbers from the guns they use—by filing the numbers off or using acid washes—because they believe this will make the weapons untraceable. Forensic scientists, however, are able to reclaim obliterated serial numbers using sophisticated techniques. To recover a gun's missing serial number, the examiner files down the metal that carried the serial number to retrieve a strip of highly polished and hardened metal located beneath where the original serial number was stamped. By adding a solution of copper salts and hydrochloric acid to the area, the scientist can dissolve the weaker metal below where the numbers were stamped to reveal an imprint of the original serial number. This imprint is then photographed before the metal dissolves completely, and the photograph serves as documentation of the weapon's serial number.

Related to the work of ballistics experts is the detection and evaluation of gunshot residue, which figures importantly in forensic investigations. The amount and scatter of gunshot residue provides information about the proximity of a victim to a weapon as it was fired. In addition, gunshot residue on the hands, skin, hair, and clothing of persons who were present at the time of a crime can reveal how close those individuals were to the weapon. Firearms give off a back-spray of gunpowder when discharged, and this hot and sticky substance adheres to most items of clothing and skin with which it comes in contact. It may remain embedded in objects during subsequent and sometimes repeated washings or cleanings. Forensic scientists sometimes use electron scanning techniques to detect minute particles of gunshot residue on watches and other jewelry worn by people suspected of having used guns in crimes.

*Dwight G. Smith*

**Further Reading**

Carlucci, Donald E., and Sidney S. Jacobson. *Ballistics: Theory and Design of Guns and Ammunition*. Boca Raton, Fla.: CRC Press, 2008. Comprehensive work covers all aspects of the topic, including the theory and fundamental physics of ballistics, design techniques for firearms and ammunition, and the tools used to investigate firearms-related crimes.

Heard, Brian J. *Handbook of Firearms and Ballistics: Examining and Interpreting Forensic Evidence*. New York: John Wiley & Sons, 1997. Thorough volume focuses on the science of forensic firearms analysis.

Rinker, Robert A. *Understanding Firearm Ballistics: Basic to Advanced Ballistics, Simplified, Illustrated, and Explained*. 6th ed. Clarksville, Ind.: Mulberry House, 2005. Provides an easy-to-understand general introduction to theory of weapons ballistics.

Zukas, Jonas A., and William P. Walters, eds. *Explosive Effects and Applications*. New York: Springer, 1998. Collection of essays by experts focuses on the component of ballistics concerned with the explosive impacts of bullets.

**See also:** Ballistic fingerprints; Bullet-lead analysis; Bureau of Alcohol, Tobacco, Firearms and Explosives; Firearms analysis; Gunshot residue; Improvised explosive devices; Integrated Ballistics Identification System; Sacco and Vanzetti case.

# Barbiturates

**Definition:** Family of chemically related drugs belonging to the sedative-hypnotic class.

**Significance:** The habit-forming drugs known as barbiturates have a variety of therapeutic applications and have been used as drugs of abuse. Barbiturates depress the central nervous system and can cause significant psychomotor performance impairment as well as fatal toxicity. The potential for toxic interactions with other drugs, including alcohol, is significant. Forensic toxicologists are often called upon to measure barbiturate concentrations in biological samples.

The barbiturates are a family of drugs with related chemical structures derived from barbituric acid. In the past, barbiturates were used extensively as sedative-hypnotics—that is, drugs that reduce anxiety and induce sleep. Barbiturates are also used as anticonvulsants and in anesthesia. Because of barbiturates' significant potential for toxicity, their use has been largely replaced by the safer benzodiazepines, but selected barbiturates are still used in specific applications.

**Effects**

Barbiturates depress central nervous system (CNS) function in general rather than specific CNS functions. The severity of CNS depression increases with dose, potentially causing significant impairment of psychomotor skills (such as those required for safe driving) and, ultimately, fatal respiratory depression. Dose-dependent effects also extend to the peripheral nervous system, where they manifest primarily as reductions in blood pressure and heart rate. However, at appropriate sedative-hypnotic doses, these latter effects are not hazardous.

At subanesthetic doses, barbiturate effects may include euphoria, reduced anxiety and inhibitions, slurred speech, loss of coordination, and dizziness. CNS depression intensifies with increasing dose; sedation becomes more pronounced, and significant stupor, drowsiness, and loss of coordination may ensue. Anesthetic doses produce coma as well as depressed respiration and blood pressure. Uncontrolled overdose can result in fatal respiratory depression. These effects are intensified in combination with other CNS depressants (such as alcohol or benzodiazepines), and significant impairment or death may occur at lower barbiturate doses (or blood concentrations) when such drugs are coadministered.

Chronic barbiturate use results in the development of tolerance—that is, progressively larger doses are required to achieve a given effect. Repeated administration of and tolerance to the effects of one barbiturate confers tolerance to the effects of the others as well as to other depressant compounds with similar mechanisms of action (for example, alcohol and benzodiazepines). Chronic use can lead to physical dependence and corresponding withdrawal symptoms upon cessation of use. Symptoms of barbiturate withdrawal range from minor symptoms—nausea, vomiting, agitation, and confusion—to more severe symptoms including seizures, hallucinations, delirium tremens, very high fevers (hyperpyrexia), and death.

### Other Chemical and Pharmacological Properties

Barbiturates are weakly acidic and are often prepared as the sodium salts. Their weakly acidic nature becomes important in the design of analytical methods requiring extraction of the drug from a complex forensic sample (for example, blood or tissue). Alteration of the chemi-

cal structure results in variation in drug potency (the magnitude of effect at a given dose) and time course of action.

Even in cases where the drug effects last a short time, barbiturates have a relatively long time course within the body. One indicator of this is the half-life of the drug, or the time required for the reduction of drug concentration to 50 percent of its original value. Half-life values for the various barbiturates range from approximately 3 hours to 80 hours. Any drug with a long half-life poses the risk of accumulation in the blood if dosing regimens are not carefully monitored, creating the potential for toxicity. Half-life is also related to the duration of drug action: Typically, a drug with a shorter half-life has a shorter duration of action. This is relevant to forensic investigation, as the half-life is indicative of the time window over which a drug may be detected in the blood; generally, a drug is essentially completely eliminated from the blood within five elimination half-lives.

Duration of action and half-life are important considerations in the choice of a barbiturate for a particular therapeutic action. For example, thiopental is an ultrafast-acting barbiturate, typically used in induction of anesthesia. Due to its high lipid solubility, it is rapidly and extensively distributed into the central nervous system, wherein it exerts its anesthetic effect through depression of various functions. The elimination half-life for thiopental is 8 to 10 hours, although its ability to diffuse into and out of the CNS results in anesthetic action lasting only minutes following a single intravenous dose. Conversely, phenobarbital, a barbiturate used as an anticonvulsant and as a sedative-hypnotic, is significantly longer acting, with a half-life of 80 to 120 hours.

The route of administration of the drug is also dependent on the desired therapeutic action. Barbiturates used as sedative-hypnotics or anticonvulsants may be administered orally and have a slower onset of action than those given by parenteral (for example, intravenous) administration, where the onset of drug action is very rapid. Accordingly, parenteral administration is typically used in the treatment of status epilepticus (a condition in which the brain is in a state of persistent seizure) and for general anesthesia. The route of administration is ultimately related to the maximum blood drug concentration achieved, and therefore the magnitude of drug effect, at a given dose. Consequently, knowledge of the route of administration is valuable to toxicological interpretation. It should be noted, however, that some drugs intended for oral administration—in tablet form—are illicitly administered by parenteral routes, potentially leading to greater toxic effects.

The metabolism of most barbiturates occurs primarily in the liver, where the drugs undergo various biotransformation reactions (such as oxidation) that reduce or eliminate pharmacological activity. In a few cases (for example, aprobarbital, phenobarbital), renal elimination of unchanged drug into the urine also occurs to a significant extent. Consequently, barbiturate metabolism may be affected by processes that affect hepatic metabolism (for example, liver disease or drug interactions). Inhibited barbiturate metabolism may result in the development of significant toxicity.

### Forensic Analysis and Interpretation of Evidence

Law-enforcement personnel may encounter barbiturates in the form of suspicious materials (for example, tablets) requiring identification or quantitative analysis. Forensic scientists may analyze biological samples (such as blood, tissues, urine, or stomach contents) to establish exposure to barbiturates. Correlation of toxic symptoms with measured barbiturate concentration is done in both clinical and forensic settings and in attempts to establish a toxicological cause of death.

Methods used for forensic barbiturate analysis include immunoassay, spectrophotometry, gas or liquid chromatography, and mass spectrometry. Usually, the analysis of biological samples for barbiturates requires preparatory steps to extract the drug from the complex matrix and minimize or eliminate other compounds (such as lipids or proteins) that may be present in those samples that may interfere with analysis, leading to spurious results. The exact nature of the sample preparation steps taken is determined by the nature of the sample being analyzed. Solid samples typically require dissolution or digestion as a first step.

Extraction of drugs from complex samples may be accomplished through the manipulation of chemical conditions (such as pH adjustment) and subsequent partition into a suitable organic solvent system or into a solid phase with subsequent recovery. Following extraction, analysis is typically done using gas chromatography or liquid chromatography to separate extracted constituents for accurate quantitative analysis.

The interpretation of measurements requires consideration of the nature of the sample analyzed as well as the measured drug concentration. Drug concentrations in blood may allow estimation of toxic effect, with consideration given to the potential for tolerance to drug action. Conversely, detection of a barbiturate in hair under properly controlled conditions is indicative of drug exposure only, but it may be useful in establishing an approximate time line of drug exposure.

The forensic detection of a particular barbiturate must be considered in the context of the case under investigation. The tolerance of the individual must be considered in the interpretation of measured barbiturate concentrations as well. For example, in toxicological analysis of blood samples from a known epileptic, the detection of phenobarbital may be consistent with a therapeutic regimen, and some degree of tolerance may often be assumed. In routine forensic practice, tolerance is difficult or impossible to quantify, so interpretation is difficult. Correlation of a measured blood concentration with toxicity or fatality requires comparison of the result to other similar cases that have been previously reported, giving due consideration to the history of use of barbiturates and other drugs by the subject, the detection of other relevant drugs in the sample (such as CNS depressants), and any observed symptoms (such as shallow breathing, impaired coordination, or slurred speech).

*James Watterson*

### Further Reading

Baselt, Randall C. *Disposition of Drugs and Chemicals in Man*. 7th ed. Foster City, Calif.:

Biomedical Publications, 2004. Describes the properties and associated tissue concentrations of a wide range of toxic compounds and discusses the techniques used to analyze these chemicals.

_____. *Drug Effects on Psychomotor Performance*. Foster City, Calif.: Biomedical Publications, 2001. Comprehensive reference work presents information on the impairing effects of a wide range of therapeutic and illicit drugs, including barbiturates.

Brunton, Laurence L., John S. Lazo, and Keith L. Parker, eds. *Goodman and Gilman's the Pharmacological Basis of Therapeutics*. 11th ed. New York: McGraw-Hill, 2006. Authoritative advanced textbook explains basic pharmacological principles and the specific pharmacological features of therapeutic agents. Includes some discussion of barbiturates.

Karch, Steven B., ed. *Drug Abuse Handbook*. 2d ed. Boca Raton, Fla.: CRC Press, 2007. Describes the pharmacological, physiological, and pathological aspects of drug abuse in general, and individual chapters address specific compounds, such as alcohol, as well as specific issues related to drug abuse, such as workplace drug testing.

Levine, Barry, ed. *Principles of Forensic Toxicology*. 2d ed., rev. Washington, D.C.: American Association for Clinical Chemistry, 2006. Introductory textbook describes the analytical, chemical, and pharmacological aspects of a variety of drugs of forensic relevance.

**See also:** Analytical instrumentation; Antianxiety agents; Controlled Substances Act of 1970; Drug abuse and dependence; Forensic toxicology; Gas chromatography; High-performance liquid chromatography; Homogeneous enzyme immunoassay; Illicit substances; Mass spectrometry; Nervous system; Pseudoscience in forensic practice; Truth serum; Ultraviolet spectrophotometry.

**BATFE.** *See* Bureau of Alcohol, Tobacco, Firearms and Explosives

## Beethoven's death

**Date:** March 26, 1827

**The Event:** Ludwig van Beethoven suffered from many chronic ailments during his life, and the precise cause of his death has long been a topic of debate. Dr. William Walsh, director of the Beethoven Research Project, announced at a press conference on October 17, 2000, that samples of Beethoven's hair revealed extremely heavy lead deposits, indicating that lead poisoning may have caused the great composer's many illnesses and death.

**Significance:** The forensic investigation into the death of Beethoven proves both the achievements of forensic technology in historical investigation and the limitations of such technology. Analyses of hair and bone fragments have shed light on Beethoven's many illnesses, but researchers still question whether lead poisoning or lead poisoning alone caused Beethoven's problems.

Born in Bonn, Germany, in mid-December, 1770, Ludwig van Beethoven died on March 26, 1827, in Vienna, Austria, where he had lived since 1792. Ferdinand V. Hiller, a German admirer who visited the composer's deathbed, received a lock of Beethoven's hair that was later enclosed in a locket inscribed with names and date. This keepsake remained in the Hiller family until the 1930's, when the family, which was Jewish, was forced to flee Adolf Hitler's Nazi regime. The lock of hair then became the property of a Danish physician who aided Jewish refugees; the physician's family had possession of the hair until 1994, when it was offered for auction.

The hair was purchased by a consortium of members of the American Beethoven Society.

Arizona urological surgeon Dr. Alfredo Guevara, the principal purchaser, retained 27 percent of the hair (160 individual hairs), and the remaining 422 strands were donated to the Ira F. Brilliant Center for Beethoven Studies at San Jose State University in Northern California. Guevara wanted to know if forensic technology could show the cause of Beethoven's poor health and death. In addition to becoming totally deaf, Beethoven suffered from eye disorders, liver disease, and a broad range of gastrointestinal and respiratory symptoms. When an autopsy was performed on his body on March 27, 1827, visual inspection showed abnormalities of the liver, gallbladder, spleen, pancreas, and kidneys.

### Forensic Analysis

Dr. Werner Baumgartner of Psychemedics Corporation's laboratories in Los Angeles examined twenty hairs to determine whether Beethoven received relief from opiates during his final illness. A radioimmunoassay found no evidence of opiates. William Walsh speculated that Beethoven, who continued to compose music until very near the time of his death, rejected substances that would dull his mind.

McCrone Research Center in Chicago performed side-by-side analyses of two hairs from Beethoven and three samples from living subjects, using a scanning electron microscope, energy-dispersive spectroscopy, and scanning ion microscope-mass spectrometry. Using nondestructive synchrotron X-ray beams, the U.S. Department of Energy's Argonne National Laboratory tested six Beethoven hair strands in a side-by-side comparison with hair from a control group and a glass film of known lead composition. Both facilities found heavy lead concentrations. Beethoven's hair revealed an average lead content of 60 parts per million; living Americans, in comparison, average 0.6 parts per million. Researchers concluded that Beethoven suffered from lead poisoning, or plumbism.

In Beethoven's time, lead was used in pewter cups and dinnerware as well as in paint, cosmetics, medical preparations, and food coloring. Wine bottles were sealed (plumbed) with lead to keep the contents from turning sour. In

an online interview on December 6, 2005, on *Online NewsHour*, Walsh offered an explanation for Beethoven's exceptionally poor health, speculating that the composer may have been among the 5 percent of people who are extremely sensitive to heavy metals and cannot excrete lead.

Scientists who examined Beethoven's hair found no traces of mercury, which led them to conclude that Beethoven had not been treated for syphilis, given that mercury was the most common treatment for the disease in Beethoven's time.

Because some of the hairs in the Beethoven sample included partial bulbs, DNA (deoxyribonucleic acid) examination was possible. In 2005, researchers at the Argonne National Laboratory's Advanced Photon Source facilities conducted additional testing using elemental X-ray fluorescence analysis on hair and fragments of Beethoven's skull made available after the original research was completed. DNA testing positively identified the bone and hair as Beethoven's. Researchers used microimaging to calculate the distribution of lead in the bone and hair fragments and again found substantial lead deposits. Mitochondrial DNA testing was also performed at the University of Münster in Germany.

### Controversy

A number of researchers have noted that not all questions concerning Beethoven's death can be answered through hair and bone analysis. They question whether lead poisoning or any single problem explains Beethoven's ill health, which was markedly worse than that of most of his contemporaries, or could be conclusively named as the sole, primary, or immediate cause of the composer's death. Concerns about the relatively simple explanation of lead poisoning begin with Beethoven's family history. In his early years, Beethoven was exposed to the tuberculosis that killed his mother and one brother. His father and his paternal grandmother were incapacitated by alcohol abuse, suggesting inherited alcohol intolerance. Some have speculated that Beethoven may have overused alcohol; observers at the time were divided, but consumption of alcoholic beverages was high in his

## A Finding of Lead Poisoning

*In a press release dated December 6, 2005, the U.S. Department of Energy's Argonne National Laboratory announced the findings of research conducted on fragments of bone from Ludwig van Beethoven's skull:*

The bone fragments, confirmed by DNA testing to have come from Beethoven's body, were scanned by X-rays from the Advanced Photon Source at Argonne, which provides the most brilliant X-rays in the Western Hemisphere. A control bone fragment sample from the same historic period was also examined. Both bone fragments were from the parietal section—the top—of the skull.

"The testing indicated large amounts of lead in the Beethoven bone sample, compared to the control," said Bill Walsh, chief scientist at the Pfeiffer Treatment Center in Warrenville, Ill., and director of the Beethoven Research Project. . . .

"The finding of elevated lead in Beethoven's skull, along with DNA results indicating authenticity of the bone/hair relics, provides solid evidence that Beethoven suffered from a toxic overload of lead," Walsh said. "In addition, the presence of lead in the skull suggests that his exposure to lead was not a recent event, but may have been present for many years."

time, and physicians did not wash their hands between patients, as the possibilities of contagion and fatal infection were not recognized. Surgery was conducted hastily for the patient's sake, but, as Davies has noted, rapid fluid drainage may cause shock or acute renal failure. Effective diuretics were unknown during Beethoven's lifetime.

*Betty Richardson*

### Further Reading

Davies, Peter J. *Beethoven in Person: His Deafness, Illnesses, and Death*. Westport, Conn.: Greenwood Press, 2001. Includes a time line of the composer's symptoms, information on the credentials of his physicians, critiques of the various suggested possible causes for his many symptoms, and a glossary of medical terms.

Emsley, John. *Elements of Murder: A History of Poison*. New York: Oxford University Press, 2005. Volume devoted to the use of poisons in murder includes a brief account of the Beethoven findings. Also discusses the historical use of lead in common substances and the effects of lead exposure on the human body.

Hayden, Deborah. *Pox: Genius, Madness, and the Mysteries of Syphilis*. New York: Basic Books, 2003. Argues that Beethoven may have had both lead poisoning and syphilis.

Mai, François Martin. *Diagnosing Genius: The Life and Death of Beethoven*. Montreal: McGill-Queen's University Press, 2007. Includes information about Beethoven's physicians and treatment and a timetable of his symptoms. Suggests the possibility that the conductor suffered from liver cirrhosis or infectious hepatitis and bacterial peritonitis, among other disorders.

Martin, Russell. *Beethoven's Hair: An Extraordinary Historical Odyssey and a Scientific*

lifetime, a period when urban water supplies, including Vienna's Danube River, were badly contaminated with human and animal waste. (No connection had yet been made between contaminated water and disease.)

Peter J. Davies has raised the possibility that Beethoven suffered from adult-onset diabetes mellitus, which was then uncontrollable. Deborah Hayden has noted that if Beethoven had been treated for syphilis in early manhood, the treatment would leave no evidence at his death decades later. In 1796, Beethoven contracted typhus, and this illness may have undermined his general health; his hearing loss began soon afterward.

The medical treatment that Beethoven received may have been immediately responsible for his death. He consulted at least a dozen physicians, usually insisting on receiving unknown medications and altering dosages. Four times in a period of three months, Dr. Johann Seibert, chief surgeon of the Vienna General Hospital, tapped Beethoven's abdomen to drain fluid. Neither anesthesia, other than opiates, nor the need for sterile conditions was known at that

*Mystery Solved.* New York: Broadway Books, 2000. Describes the history of the famous lock of hair, from Beethoven's deathbed through the research results announced in 2000.

**See also:** DNA analysis; Exhumation; Hair analysis; Lead; Mitochondrial DNA analysis and typing; Napoleon's death; Opioids; Scanning electron microscopy; Taylor exhumation.

# Benzidine

**Definition:** Chemical formerly used in the standard presumptive test for blood at crime scenes.

**Significance:** A positive reaction to benzidine or tetramethylbenzidine of a stain found at a crime scene suggests that the stain is probably blood; such information can facilitate an initial reconstruction of a crime and prompt follow-up.

For most of the twentieth century, benzidine was the standard chemical used in presumptive testing for blood at crime scenes. In the presence of heme iron and hydrogen peroxide, benzidine, which is clear in the reduced state, is converted to the oxidized state, which is deep blue. Because heme iron is present in hemoglobin, the protein that carries oxygen in the blood, a positive test can indicate the presence of blood. This test does not distinguish between human blood and animal blood, however; further testing is necessary to make that distinction and, if the blood is human, to determine whose blood it is. In addition, constituents of some plants, such as potatoes and horseradish, as well as oxidizing agents found in some cleansers, can catalyze the reaction. Accordingly, a benzidine test is only presumptive of blood; a positive result must be confirmed by laboratory test.

Developed in 1904, the benzidine test became the most popular presumptive test for blood because of its high sensitivity, specificity, and reliability. Benzidine, however, which was also used for the synthesis of dyes in the textile industry, proved to be highly carcinogenic, and its use and manufacture in the United States was banned by the Environmental Protection Agency in 1974. At that time, 3,3',5,5' tetramethylbenzidine (TMB) was developed as a presumptive test for blood. It is not as sensitive as benzidine, but it is much safer to use, although it is a probable carcinogen.

Typically, a forensic investigator performs the TMB test by moistening a cotton swab with deionized water and rubbing the swab on the suspect stain, adding a drop of TMB solution to the swab, waiting thirty seconds, and then adding a drop of 3 percent hydrogen peroxide to the swab. A positive reaction will turn the swab a blue-green color within fifteen seconds. Often a swab taken from near the stain is used as a control. If the swab turns blue-green before the hydrogen peroxide is added, the test is invalid. Validation of the reagents using a known blood standard is usually conducted.

The TMB reagent in a colloidal mixture can also be used to spray an area in order to raise faint bloodstains, such as might be left by handprints or shoe prints. Like luminol, this substance can allow investigators to see evidence of attempts to clean up blood from crime scenes. The standard TMB test does not destroy the sample, which can be subsequently tested for blood type and DNA, but the spray reagent, like luminol, fixes a stain so that it cannot be tested further; investigators must thus take care to limit the use of the reagent.

*James L. Robinson*

**Further Reading**

Lee, Henry C., Timothy Palmbach, and Marilyn T. Miller. *Henry Lee's Crime Scene Handbook.* San Diego, CA: Academic Press, 2001.

Tilstone, William J., Kathleen A. Savage, and Leigh A. Clark. *Forensic Science: An Encyclopedia of History, Methods, and Techniques.* Santa Barbara, CA: ABC-CLIO, 2006.

**See also:** Acid-base indicators; Blood residue and bloodstains; DNA recognition instruments; DNA typing; Luminol; Orthotolidine; Phenolphthalein; Presumptive tests for blood; Reagents; Serology.

# Beslan hostage crisis victim identification

**Date:** Hostage siege occurred between September 1 and 3, 2004

**The Event:** On September 1, 2004, a group of about thirty men and women, who were reportedly Muslim Chechen separatists, took over School Number One in the town of Beslan in the Russian Federation republic of North Ossetia-Alania, and held nine hundred students and fifty-nine teachers hostage. A three-day siege ended when Russian special forces and civilian volunteers attacked the school. This resulted in a violent confrontation in which the hostages were caught in the middle of gunfire and explosions; when it was over, nearly four hundred people were dead. The incident contributed to a growth in the power of the Russian government, which instituted new security measures, at the same time it heightened public mistrust of Russian authorities, who were suspected of covering up official incompetence in the handling of the incident and of censoring press coverage about it.

**Significance:** Forensic scientists played an important role in the aftermath of the tragedy in efforts to identify the dead as well as in the investigation of the motivations and the actions of the terrorists.

Since the dissolution of the Soviet Union in 1991, the region of Chechnya, located between the Black Sea and the Caspian Sea on part of the northern border of Georgia, has fought for independence from the Russian Federation. The Chechens are Muslim, and the separatist struggle has given rise to radicalism that is based both in nationalism and in Islamic ex-

tremism. The terrorists who took over School Number One in Beslan identified themselves as Chechen separatists, and most were indeed later found to be Chechens.

The hostage takers seized the school on the traditional first day of the Russian school year. After a brief exchange of gunfire with the police, the terrorists forced their hostages to crowd into the school's gymnasium. The terrorists then shot a number of men who appeared to be most capable of resistance and forced other hostages to throw out the bodies and clean up the blood.

The perpetrators may have hidden weapons and explosives in the school before their attack, but this point is denied by official reports and remains open to question. As security forces surrounded the school, the terrorists mined the gym and set up wires that, if tripped, would cause the explosives to go off. They also announced that if anyone attempted to intervene forcefully, they would kill fifty hostages for every one of their own number killed and twenty hostages for every one of their group injured.

## The Tragedy

On the afternoon of the second day of the siege, the hostage takers allowed Ruslan Aushev, the president of the Russian republic of Ingushetia, to enter the school. Several of the hostage takers were later revealed to be Ingushetians, an ethnic group closely related to the Chechens. Aushev was allowed to bring twenty-six hostages out of the school with him. The terrorists also gave Aushev a list of demands, apparently authored by Chechen rebel leader Shamil Basayev, who reportedly had ordered the seizure of the school but was not present. One of the demands was that Russia recognize the independence of Chechnya.

The events that took place on September 3 are still not entirely clear. Some members of the Russian military were allowed to approach the school to take away bodies, and as they did so, bombs went off in the gymnasium and the hostage takers began firing, killing two of the servicemen. About thirty hostages were able to escape in the chaos. Then Russian special forces, along with civilian volunteers, began to attack the school, and a pitched battle ensued. Explosions and gunfire continued for the rest of the night, and when the fighting was over, 334 hostages, 31 hostage takers, and more than 20 other people were dead.

## The Application of Forensic Science

The primary use of forensic science in relation to the Beslan incident was in the identification of the dead, both victims and hostage takers. After the tragedy, family members initially attempted to identify children and other victims from their clothing or by looking for distinguishing physical features. Many of those who died had been badly burned, however, so investigators had to use more sophisticated approaches. More than one hundred of the corpses were so badly damaged that DNA (deoxyribonucleic acid) analysis was necessary to establish positive identification. This involved comparison of the DNA of the victims with the DNA of existing family members; investigators took blood samples from the bodies of the dead and from relatives of those lost in the event and sent the samples to Moscow for matching. In many cases, the bodies were so badly damaged that the extraction of DNA for testing was very difficult. Researchers used the technique of polymerase chain reaction (PCR) to amplify pieces of DNA to provide sufficient material for testing. Forensic investigators also helped to examine the motivations and behavior of the terrorists. Along with identification of the thirty-one attackers who died in the incident, the investigation revealed that drug use appeared to be an element in the Beslan tragedy. Moscow researchers reported that toxicological analyses of the hostage takers' bodies showed that the blood of several of them showed high levels of the narcotics heroin and morphine, and several showed signs of other drugs in their systems. Moreover, the hostage takers who had been drug users had apparently not taken in these substances in several days, and so they were likely in states of drug withdrawal. Some observers have suggested that the experience of withdrawal may have accounted for the remarkable brutality and callousness with which the hostage takers treated children and other innocent victims at the school.

*Carl L. Bankston III*

## Further Reading

Giduck, John. *Terror at Beslan: A Russian Tragedy with Lessons for America's Schools.* Golden, Colo.: Archangel Group, 2005. Describes the background, events, and aftermath of the Beslan incident and provides a good description of the investigation. Asserts that similar events could happen in the United States and draws on the Beslan example to suggest how American schools should prepare for this possibility.

Kornienko I. V., V. V. Kolkutin, and A. V. Volkov. "Molecular-Genetic Identification of the Hostages Killed in the Terror Act on September 1-3, 2004, in Beslan." *Forensic Medical Examination* 5 (2006): 31-35. Examines the technical forensic issues involved in the identification of the Beslan victims and notes the importance of the precise staging of the investigation.

Lansford, Lynn Milburn. *Beslan: Shattered Innocence.* Charleston, S.C.: Booksurge, 2006. Addresses the needs of the Beslan survivors for support and assistance following the tragedy. Lansford has worked with children's relief programs and was involved in helping the Beslan survivors.

Phillips, Timothy. *Beslan: The Tragedy of School No. 1.* London: Granta Books, 2007. Account of the ordeal at Beslan includes testimony by the people of the town and a critique of the Russian government's response.

**See also:** Asian tsunami victim identification; Autopsies; Croatian and Bosnian war victim identification; DNA extraction from hair, bodily fluids, and tissues; DNA fingerprinting; Forensic toxicology; Hostage negotiations; Mass graves; Osteology and skeletal radiology; Police psychology; September 11, 2001, victim identification.

## Biodetectors

**Definition:** Devices comprising highly specific sensing components—such as biolayers of DNA, proteins, or enzymes— immobilized on surfaces that serve as transducers that measure electrical signals produced by interactions between the biomolecules of interest and the biolayers.

**Significance:** Combining the ability to process data with the selectivity of biological systems, biodetectors are powerful analytical tools employed in forensic science. They can be used to counter the growing threat of biocrimes or acts of bioterrorism because of their ability to detect even minute levels of colorless and odorless harmful agents (such as pathogenic viruses, fungi, bacteria, and other noxious substances) days before concentrations of the agents are high enough to cause medical symptoms.

Following a biocrime, responses based on data obtained from biodetection may include forensic investigation, medical diagnoses, and crisis management. In 2001, the importance of timely forensic investigation of surface contamination was demonstrated following identification of the anthrax bacterium found in letters sent to the Hart Senate Office Building in Washington, D.C.; early detection allowed for prophylactic treatment with antibiotics, thus saving the lives of those exposed to the pathogen. For highly contagious diseases such as smallpox, it may be crucial to institute immediate measures such as vaccination or quarantine to halt the spread of the disease.

The significance of early detection of harmful biological agents cannot be overemphasized. At first, medical symptoms may seem mild, and outbreaks may be mistaken for ordinary influenza; this can delay necessary remedial actions that could lessen, or even prevent, morbidity and mortality. The greatest benefit of biodetectors may be to protect against highly lethal pathogens such as Ebola and Marburg viruses, for which no vaccines, treatments, or cures have been developed.

In the mid-1960's, Leland C. Clark, considered the "father of biosensors," developed the first enzyme electrodes, which eventually led to creation of more advanced versions for applications in biotechnology and forensic science, especially as the latter pertains to countering acts of bioterrorism. Biosensors of this type, employed to detect DNA and related biomolecules, are also known as biodetectors; they are key players in the investigation of events leading up to and following exposure to such pathogenic agents as ricin (a highly toxic protein derived from the castor bean) and *Bacillus anthracis*, the bacterium that causes anthrax. Biodetectors may also be employed for continuous monitoring of the environment, surveillance of medical symptoms, and ancillary intelligence activities that may be put in place to mitigate or prevent the aftereffects associated with biocrimes and acts of bioterrorism.

Ideally, biodetectors should be networked—that is, decentralized—during an attack involving biological weapons so that they can be used to define the perimeter of the assault. Portability is another desirable characteristic for biodetectors; such devices could be moved quickly to the locations of biocrimes to perform evaluation and monitoring. Although the task of building a system of networked biodetectors is fraught with complexity, the future of emerging biosensor technology lies in scientists' ability to develop networks of sophisticated alarm-bearing biodetectors that can differentiate between harmful and benign entities and can be used anywhere, with wireless and remote capabilities.

*Cynthia Racer*

**Further Reading**

Behnisch, Peter A. "Biodetectors in Environmental Chemistry. Are We at a Turning Point?" *Environment International* 27 (December, 2001): 441-442.

Cooper, Jon, and Tony Cass, eds. *Biosensors: A Practical Approach.* 2d ed. New York: Oxford University Press, 2004.

Malhotra, Bansi D., et al. "Recent Trends in Biosensors." *Current Applied Physics* 5 (February, 2005): 92-97.

**See also:** Air and water purity; Biological terrorism; Biological warfare diagnosis; Biological weapon identification; Biosensors; Breathalyzer; Cadaver dogs; Canine substance detection; Chemical Biological Incident Response Force, U.S.; DNA recognition instruments.

## Biohazard bags

**Definition:** Containers used by laboratories for the safe disposal of blood and other potentially infectious wastes.

**Significance:** Forensic, clinical, and research laboratories, as well as publicly and privately owned health care establishments such as hospitals, medical clinics, long-term care facilities, dental clinics, and blood banks, are required to use safety containers known as biohazard bags when disposing of blood or other potentially infectious materials. Forensic laboratories often analyze such materials when they are obtained as evidence in various crimes.

The use of biohazard bags, as an element of the Hazard Communication Standard (HCS) is one of the key provisions in the Standard on Occupational Exposure to Bloodborne Pathogens issued by the U.S. Occupational Safety and Health Administration (OSHA) [29 CFR 1910.1030] on December 6, 1991. The HCS is now aligned with the Globally Harmonized System of Classification and Labeling of Chemicals (GHS), which is an international mechanism of hazard communication, effective December 1, 2013. This alignment allows workers the right to know and the right to understand hazard information in their workplace.

OSHA promotes worker's safety and health by establishing guidelines and standards, and by providing resources for training and education, in every workplace in the United States. Biohazard bags meet OSHA's requirements for disposing of materials that are potentially harmful to humans, animals or the environment. The biohazard bags are labeled with symbols and precautions, to communicate the presence of blood or other potentially infectious materials (OPIM); these disposable bags serve to warn workers who may be exposed to potentially hazardous and harmful materials. Facilities that use biohazard bags must train their workers to use universal precautions in handling the bags and their contents.

According to OSHA, OPIM include human body fluids (semen, vaginal secretions, saliva, any body fluid visibly contaminated with blood, and all body fluids that are difficult or impossible to differentiate) and any unfixed tissue or organ from a human being (dead or alive). OSHA also considers as OPIM any materials containing human immunodeficiency virus (HIV) or hepatitis B virus (HBV), such as blood, liquids, solutions, and cell, tissue, and organ cultures used in clinical, research, and forensic laboratories. The Medical Waste Tracking Act of 1988 amended the Solid Waste Disposal Act, and included material wastes generated in healthcare, research and laboratory facilities. This Act defined medical waste as "any solid waste that is generated in the diagnosis, treatment, or immunization of human beings or animals, in research pertaining thereto, or in the production or testing of biological." Forensic laboratories often conduct evidence analyses on blood and OPIM.

OSHA's Bloodborne Pathogens Standard also uses the term "regulated waste," which refers to "liquid or semi-liquid blood, OPIM, and contaminated materials or wastes that would release blood or other potentially infectious materials in a liquid or semi-liquid state if compressed; items that are caked with dried blood or other potentially infectious materials and are capable of releasing these materials during handling; contaminated sharps; and pathological and microbiological wastes containing blood or other potentially infectious materials."[29 CFR 1910.1030 (d)(4)(b)]. Regulated waste requires special handling, including placement in containers with biohazard warnings (that is, biohazard bags) and safe disposal in accordance to the Environmental Protection Agency (EPA) and federal, state, and local regulations. OSHA also requires employers to have a protection program for employees, minimizing or eliminating exposure to regulated waste in the workplace.

Biohazard bags are color-coded red (sometimes red-orange) and generally display the universal biohazard symbol and precautionary procedures in four languages (English, French, German and Spanish) to warn individuals that the materials contained are potentially infectious. As part of the special handling of regulated waste, before disposal, biohazard bags are often sterilized in an autoclave, a device that uses high pressure and high temperature steam to eradicate bacteria, viruses, and other microbes. OSHA thus requires that biohazard bags be made of substances—such as thick blended polymers—that can withstand high pressure and high temperature, and that are resistant to leakage and tears. Biohazard bags also have indicators that change color after exposure to steam and thus indicate that the materials contained inside have been subjected to sterilization or decontamination.

*Miriam E. Schwartz and Charlene F. Barroga*

**Further Reading**

Acello, Barbara. *The OSHA Handbook: Guidelines for Compliance in Health Care Facilities and Interpretive Guidelines for the Bloodborne Pathogens Standard*. Clifton Park, NY: Thomson/Delmar Learning, 2002.

Barker, Kathy. *At the Bench: A Laboratory Navigator*. Cold Spring Harbor, NY: Cold Spring Harbor Laboratory Press, 2004.

Chao, Elaine L. and John L. Henshaw. Model Plans and Programs for the OSHA Bloodborne Pathogens and Hazard Communications Standards (OSHA Publication 3186). Washington, DC: U.S. Department of Labor Printing Office, 2003.

O'Neal, Jon T. *The Bloodborne Pathogens Standard: A Pragmatic Approach*. New York: Van Nostrand Reinhold, 1996.

Ruskin, Maureen, Deana Holmes, and Darlene Susa-Anderson. Hazard Communication 2012 – The Revised Standard and What Changes You Can Expect in the Workplace [PDF document]. Retrieved from Lecture Notes from a Live Webinar Event Held August 13, 2012: http://urban.csuohio.edu/cep/docs/OSHA_Haz_Com_2012_Revised_Standards.pdf

United Nations. Globally Harmonized System of Classification and Labelling of Chemicals (GHS). New York:United Nations, 2011.United States Department of Labor. (n.d.). OSHA Fact Sheet.Hazard Communication Standard Final Rule. Retrieved from https://www.osha.gov/dsg/hazcom/HCSFactsheet.html. Accessed March 21, 2015.

United States Enviromental Protection Agency. (n.d.). Wastes. Website last updated March 23, 2015. Retrieved from http://www.epa.gov/epawaste/index.htm.

United States Government Publishing Office. (1999). 29 CFR 1910.1030 - Bloodborne pathogens. Retrieved from http://www.gpo.gov/fdsys/granule/CFR-1999-title29-vol6/CFR-1999-title29-vol6-sec1910-1030. Accessed March 21, 2015.

World Health Organization. *Laboratory Biosafety Manual*. Geneva: World Health Organization, 2005

**See also:** Blood residue and bloodstains; Blood spatter analysis; Crime laboratories; Crime scene cleaning; Decontamination methods; Forensic pathology; Saliva; Semen and sperm; U.S. Army Medical Research Institute of Infectious Diseases.

# Biological terrorism

**Definition:** Spread of dangerous biological agents within civilian populations or agricultural areas with the intent of causing disorder and intense fear.

**Significance:** A bioterrorist attack is perhaps one of the events most feared by emergency responders and government officials in the field of counterterrorism, in large part because, although the probability of a wide-scale attack is rather low, in the event of such an attack, the potential for catastrophic results is high.

Ever since the influenza pandemic of 1918-1919 (a natural event), which killed some forty million people around the world, a heightened awareness has existed of the potential for the spread of harmful, even lethal, biological cultures among human populations. Among the purposeful biological attacks that have been perpetrated, perhaps the one with which the most Americans are familiar is the case in which letters containing the bacterium that causes anthrax were sent to addresses in New York City, Washington, D.C., and Boca Raton, Florida, in October and November of 2001, shortly following the September 11 terrorist attacks on the World Trade Center and the Pentagon. This case, which remains unsolved, greatly increased awareness of the need for government agencies (including the U.S. Postal Service) to learn how to identify and respond effectively to any biological crisis. The outbreak of severe acute respiratory syndrome (SARS) in Canada in 2002-2003, which quickly spread from one to more than two hundred persons in Toronto-area hospitals and resulted in thirty-three deaths among patients and health workers, also demonstrated the need for improvements in government and health care responses to epidemic and pandemic disease outbreaks. The investigation and prevention of biological terrorism have become foremost components of nations' efforts to improve their homeland security.

Bioterrorist attacks can target human populations directly or indirectly, through food and water supplies. Agroterrorism—biological terrorism that targets agricultural food sources—is a very real threat to national security in some countries because modern agricultural systems are tightly integrated, and many points in the harvesting, processing, and distribution systems represent potentially "soft" targets for terrorists and difficult targets to defend from terrorist acts. The routine transport and commingling of production and processing systems greatly aid the dissemination of any biological pathogens. It is estimated that 75 percent of the value production in U.S. agriculture occurs on just 6.7 percent (143,500) of U.S. farms, so a successful attack on any of these locations would be catastrophic.

## History

The use of biological weapons can be easily traced back to ancient times. Soldiers used to dip their weapons in animal excrement or known plant toxins before battle so as to cause infection in whomever they stabbed or shot with arrows. In both ancient and medieval times, poisoning water supplies with dead animals was a favorite tactic, as was slinging or firing dead animal or human carcasses over defender walls in the hopes of spreading disease. Although few records exist to prove that European settlers in the New World purposely spread disease among Native Americans, sufficient evidence is found in the form of a letter from Colonel Henry Bouquet to Lord Jeffrey Amherst in 1763 to suggest that the British attempted to spread smallpox to their Native American opponents during the French and Indian War. Emperor Napoleon I drew on the expertise of French scientists to visit swamp fever on his opponents in the eighteenth century, and Confederate soldiers were known to poison ponds as they retreated from the advancing Union Army during the American Civil War.

By the time World War I began in 1914, science was sufficiently advanced that the mechanisms of the spread of disease were understood, and serious consideration was given to making use of biological agents during this global conflict. The German government formally and repeatedly refused to deploy biological agents against humans during the war, however, and the Allied Powers followed Germany's lead in this regard. Nevertheless, German saboteurs deployed anthrax against horses and mules that were to be sent to Allied soldiers on the front lines. During World War II, as ample surviving film footage and written evidence shows, the Japanese tested biological agents extensively on Chinese prisoners and Chinese civilians. Whether the Japanese employed these agents as weapons of war, as some scholars allege, has not been proved. The Geneva Protocol, signed by various nations in 1925, outlaws the use of biological weapons, but such prohibitions are only as good as the resolve of nations to follow the protocol.

A number of terrorist organizations have at least discussed the use of biological weapons, including the Italian Brigate Rosse (Red Brigades) and the German Rote Armee Fraktion (Red Army Faction), earlier known as the Baader-Meinhof Gang. Members of cults in the United States have poisoned restaurants with agents such as salmonella to cause sickness. The Japanese group Aum Shinrikyo (known as Aleph since 2000) actively acquired and cultured *Bacillus anthracis* (the bacterium that causes anthrax) and Ebola virus, both of which were found in significant quantities when police raided the group's headquarters in 1995 following its sarin gas attack on the Tokyo subway. The group purportedly released botulinum toxin as well as anthrax in the same period, but these attempts were not successful. Experts are not sure why these attacks failed; possible reasons include the method of delivery, manufacturing problems, and that the group may have released an anthrax vaccine and a slowly reproducing botulinum toxin rather than more potent varieties of these pathogens.

Since 1996, the Federal Bureau of Investigation (FBI) has opened numerous cases involving the potential use of biological agents. Many have amounted to mere threats, but some have included attempts to produce such pathogens as botulinum toxin, anthrax, and ricin.

## Types of Agents

Because the variety of biological agents available for use in terrorist acts is quite extensive, stockpiling vaccines that may be needed in the event of biological attacks is extremely difficult; it is virtually impossible to have safeguards in place against every potential type of biological agent. Some of the most dangerous pathogens that may potentially be used by bioterrorists, as categorized by the Centers for Disease Control and Prevention, are anthrax, pneumonic plague, botulinum toxin, smallpox, and ricin.

Anthrax is perhaps the biological pathogen most likely to be used in a bioterrorist attack. It is relatively easy to cultivate the spores of *B. anthracis*, and the spores are fairly stable under a variety of conditions, so dissemination of the pathogen is not particularly difficult. When inhaled, the agent works into the lungs and causes fever, shock, and, ultimately, death. Anthrax can also cause sores on the skin of people working with infected livestock, which can result in other bodily infections. Approximately ten thousand spores of *B. anthracis* must be inhaled to prove deadly, but a mere gram of the bacterium contains millions of lethal doses.

The possibility of the use of pneumonic plague in a biological attack is high on the list of such threats maintained by first responders be-

cause this disease is incredibly virulent. Its killing potential in an uninoculated population is extremely high, close to 90 percent, and lethal exposure requires far fewer spores (around three thousand) than does anthrax. Pneumonic plague first appears as a fever accompanied by coughing, which progresses into hemorrhaging in the lungs. If left untreated for a relatively short period, the disease is almost always fatal.

Botulinum toxin is also fairly easy to cultivate. The potential of this toxin for use in aerosol form makes it very attractive as a biological weapon because the pathogen can be spread rapidly over a wide area. Botulinum toxin attacks the muscle nerves, paralyzing the nerve endings and preventing the muscles from responding to the brain. The paralysis begins near the head and works its way down through the body.

Smallpox is considered to be high on the list of potential bioterrorism pathogens because many people in the United States and around the world are no longer immunized against the disease, ever since aggressive vaccination programs let to its global eradication, which was verified and announced in December, 1979. The *Variola major* virus, which causes the most deadly form of smallpox, is relatively easy to cultivate and is easily spread using aerosols. Smallpox is contracted through inhalation, and after it incubates, the infected person normally experiences headache, fever, and other common signs of the flu. Next a rash develops, followed by pus-filled bumps on the skin. The mortality rate is approximately 30 percent for victims who have not been inoculated.

Ricin is a toxic protein found in castor beans; it is extracted from the waste produced in the manufacture of castor oil. Ricin is relatively easy to acquire and also much easier to stockpile than most other biological pathogens. A large dose is required to kill, but the toxin can be either ingested or inhaled.

When employed in conjunction with other pathogens, ricin can enable other pathogens to attack an already afflicted body. Ricin can cause respiratory problems, fever, cough, abdominal pain, and, when ingested, damage to organs such as the liver and kidneys. Ricin prevents cells in the body from making protein, which causes the cells to die off.

## Methods of Investigation

Perhaps the greatest difficulty in the investigation of biological attacks is the fact that many of the initial symptoms caused by intentionally introduced agents are very similar to the symptoms of common diseases, such as influenza. Most often, the only way first responders are even aware that a biological attack has potentially taken place is the presence of a massive influx of people with the same symptoms. Such attacks are not usually discovered until after the pathogens have been widely disseminated and have infected large numbers of people.

The teams that investigate biological attacks need to include persons with knowledge of both biology and chemistry, who can understand the interplay between the body and the pathogen. Other areas of knowledge that are extremely important in the investigation of such attacks include the disciplines of anthropology and geography. An understanding of human living, interaction, and moving patterns, combined with meteorological data, can help investigators to track a disease back to where it may have originated, particularly in the case of aerosol dissemination.

Much of the investigative strategy used in determining whether biological agents have been intentionally spread involves the review of medical diagnoses and the employment of effective vaccines against the various agents. Investigators usually trace such agents back to their sources by comparing strains of genetic material with a database that catalogs various strains and the laboratories or environments in which the strains originated. Many materials used in the manufacture of biological agents are sold commercially, and investigators try to

> ## The Danger of Developing Biological Weapons
>
> In April of 1979, Sverdlovsk, Russia, was afflicted by an outbreak of anthrax during which at least sixty people died. At the time, the government of the Soviet Union claimed that the deaths and illness were caused by tainted meat, thoroughly denying any connection between the outbreak and the development of biological weapons.
>
> In 1992, after the dissolution of the Soviet Union, a team of experts in pathology, biology, anthropology, and veterinary science traveled to Sverdlovsk, now known as Yekaterinburg, to ascertain what had happened there in 1979. In the course of the team's investigation, anthropologist Jeanne Guillemin discovered, through interviews with victims' families, a pattern regarding those who became infected with the anthrax virus. Guillemin ascertained where each victim had been on April 2, 1979, when the outbreak began, and subsequently compared this information with data on wind direction for that day. She found that the wind was blowing only from the northwest and that the victims' positions on that day placed them in the path of the wind. A biological weapons factory operated by the Soviet government was also directly in line with the wind, northwest of the city. Given this information, Guillemin concluded that the anthrax deaths did not result from tainted meat; the specific pattern of illness in Sverdlovsk pointed to the biological weapons factory as the source of the anthrax outbreak.

track where such materials may have been purchased and by whom. Scientists have been working on developing a system of biological agent detection that will be able to identify pathogens through size, nucleic acid sequence, and antigen recognition.

It is clear that the modern world has seen neither the end of bioterrorist activities nor the full range of bioterrorism possibilities yet displayed. It is equally certain that just as formal counterterrorism measures evolve and successfully propogate, so will the methods, means, and modes of bioterrorism.

*Michael W. Cheek and Dennis W. Cheek*

## Further Reading

Anderson, Burt, Herman Freedman, and Mauro Bendinelli, eds. *Microorganisms and Bioterrorism.* New York: Springer, 2006. Provides comprehensive coverage of infectious diseases, including smallpox, anthrax, tularemia, brucellosis, pneumonic plague, Q fever (caused by *Coxiella bernetii*), and rickets.

Cordesman, Anthony H. *Terrorism, Asymmetric Warfare, and Weapons of Mass Destruction: Defending the U.S. Homeland.* Westport, Conn.: Praeger, 2002. Extremely comprehensive work addresses potential terrorist attacks. Includes sections on specific biological weapons as well as extensive suggestions for improvements in the area of homeland security. Provides a good overview of the difficulties in responding to biological attacks.

Foster, George T., ed. *Focus on Bioterrorism.* New York: Nova Science, 2006. Presents a well-written overview of the topic with discussion of attention to vaccine stockpiles, the U.S. Postal Service, responses to bioterrorism, and existing laws on proliferation sanctions in the United States and internationally.

Katz, Linda B., ed. *Agroterrorism: Another Domino?* New York: Novinka Books, 2005. Surveys threats, preparedness, and continuing challenges of biological actions against American agriculture. Topics include the specific challenges that the tightly interlocking system of modern agriculture presents to counterterrorism efforts and the ease with which various aspects of the food supply could be assaulted with biological weapons.

Pilch, Richard F., and Raymond A. Zilinskas, eds. *Encyclopedia of Bioterrorism Defense.* Hoboken, N.J.: Wiley-Liss, 2005. Large reference work includes essays by noted experts on the many dimensions of bioterrorism and how various strategies, organizations, and individuals are used to counter the many different types of bioterrorist threats in the modern world.

Ursano, Robert J., Anne E. Norwood, and Carol S. Fullerton, eds. *Bioterrorism: Psychological and Public Health Intervention.* New York: Cambridge University Press, 2004. Provides an excellent overview of the psychological and public health dimensions of bioterrorism. Includes an extensive case study of the 1918 influenza pandemic as well as chapters that discuss the psychological effects of bioterrorism on individuals and communities and the role of public health in communication, prevention, and management

response.

Wagner, Viqi, ed. *Do Infectious Diseases Pose a Serious Threat?* New Haven, Conn.: Greenhaven Press, 2005. Collection of essays addresses the potential use of infectious diseases in terrorism and which agents are the most serious threat to the United States.

Wheelis, Mark, Lajos Rózsa, and Malcolm Dando, eds. *Deadly Cultures: Biological Weapons Since 1945.* Cambridge, Mass.: Harvard University Press, 2006. Discusses developments in biological warfare since World War II and addresses the issue of why states acquire biological weapons.

**See also:** Airport security; Anthrax; Anthrax letter attacks; Bacterial biology; Biodetectors; Biological warfare diagnosis; Biological Weapons Convention of 1972; Biosensors; Bubonic plague; Centers for Disease Control and Prevention; Chemical Biological Incident Response Force, U.S.; Chemical terrorism; Decontamination methods; Pathogen transmission; U.S. Army Medical Research Institute of Infectious Diseases; Viral biology.

## Biological warfare diagnosis

**Definition:** Determination of the specific nature of disease-producing agents used as weapons.

**Significance:** The use of deadly organisms as weapons is perhaps more feared than chemical warfare because biotoxins have the potential of wreaking havoc on plants, animals, and humans. Detailed genomic determinations of these agents are critical parts of forensic analyses for the detection, diagnosis, and prosecution of biocrimes, bioterrorism, and biological warfare.

A large number of infectious organisms exist in nature, and many of them can be pathogenic (disease-causing) to humans. Microbiologists have developed bioengineering tools to increase the numbers and virulence of these organisms. Because biological weapons could cause catastrophic harm to a nation's population and economy, some political and military leaders have confessed that they fear the use of biological weapons more than the use of nuclear weapons. This anxiety has led several countries to develop techniques for detecting the use and diagnosing the nature of biological weapons in order to assist in the medical treatment of victims as well as in the prosecution of those who use these weapons.

The ideal agent of biological warfare is easy and cheap to produce, aerosolizable for effective delivery, and highly infectious for rapid person-to-person transmission. Although microbiologists have not yet developed the perfect biological weapon, they have discovered ways of manufacturing microorganisms that have the potential for creating mass casualties. For example, the following microbes have been developed into biological weapons: *Bacillus anthracis*, the bacterium that causes anthrax; *Variola major*, the virus that causes smallpox; *Yersinia pestis*, the bacterium that causes pneumonic (or bubonic) plague; *Francisella tularensis*, the bacterium that causes tularemia; and viruses that cause hemorrhagic fevers. Because of the secrecy surrounding research on potential biological weapons, specific examples of new, highly virulent strains of naturally occurring organisms or artificial pathogens are hard to come by.

### Detection and Diagnosis

By the early twenty-first century, more than 140 nations had signed and ratified the 1972 Biological Weapons Convention, which prohibits the development, manufacture, and stockpiling of bacteriological weapons. Although this treaty did lead some countries to destroy their stockpiles of biological weapons, the advent of modern bioengineering made several of the convention's provisions obsolete.

After an exercise simulating a germ attack on Denver in 2000 revealed weaknesses in state and federal responses to such a threat, and particularly after the terrorist attacks against the United States on September 11, 2001, the U.S. government developed new organizations to deal with the assessment of and reaction to threats of biological warfare. The Department of Homeland Security established the National

Biodefense Analysis and Countermeasures Center to help Americans anticipate, prevent, respond to, and recover from biological attack (previous countermeasures had been erroneously based on models for chemical warfare).

Because of the necessity of medical involvement in diagnostics and forensics, the National Response Plan developed in 2004 focused on the U.S. Department of Health and Human Services as the primary agency to deal with bioterrorist events. The Centers for Disease Control and Prevention developed the Laboratory Response Network to detect and diagnose biological agents. Also, because biological attacks cause more fatalities the longer they remain undetected, the U.S. government established BioWatch, a network of air samplers around metropolitan areas, and BioShield, a program designed to accelerate medical countermeasures against biological hazards. The information gathered from these and other organizations and programs is also intended to be used by experts at the National Bioforensic Analysis Center to discover the sources of any biological agents used in attacks.

### Forensic Analysis

A bioterrorist attack creates problems not only for early and rapid detection and diagnosis but also for forensic analysis. To deal with such problems, the Federal Bureau of Investigation (FBI) established the Scientific Working Group for Microbial Genetics and Forensics in 2002 to facilitate the identification of any organism used in a biocrime or bioterrorist attack.

Because the diagnostic requirements of microbial forensics are much more stringent than those of public health, experts at the location of a biological attack and in laboratories have to document sample collection with great care and perform detailed genomic analyses of the biological agent while maintaining a clear chain of custody for all evidence to be used in future legal proceedings.

Advanced technologies, such as miniaturized immunoassay devices that can collect data in the area of an attack, have improved the chances for convictions of the attackers, but the cooperation of medical professionals, military personnel, law-enforcement officials, and foren-

## The Laboratory Response Network

*The Centers for Disease Control and Prevention provides the following information about the Laboratory Response Network (LRN).*

The LRN's purpose is to run a network of labs that can respond to biological and chemical terrorism, and other public health emergencies. The LRN has grown since its inception. It now includes state and local public health, veterinary, military, and international labs. . . .

### The LRN Structure for Bioterrorism

LRN labs are designated as either national, reference, or sentinel. Designation depends on the types of tests a laboratory can perform and how it handles infectious agents to protect workers and the public.

**National labs** have unique resources to handle highly infectious agents and the ability to identify specific agent strains.

**Reference labs**, sometimes referred to as "confirmatory reference," can perform tests to detect and confirm the presence of a threat agent. These labs ensure a timely local response in the event of a terrorist incident. Rather than having to rely on confirmation from labs at CDC, reference labs are capable of producing conclusive results. This allows local authorities to respond quickly to emergencies.

**Sentinel labs** represent the thousands of hospital-based labs that are on the front lines. Sentinel labs have direct contact with patients. In an unannounced or covert terrorist attack, patients provide specimens during routine patient care. A sentinel lab could be the first facility to spot a suspicious specimen. A sentinel laboratory's responsibility is to refer a suspicious sample to the right reference lab.

---

sic scientists is necessary to minimize deaths immediately after an attack as well as in the later identification and conviction of those responsible for it.

*Robert J. Paradowski*

### Further Reading

*Clinics in Laboratory Medicine* 26 (June, 2006). Special issue titled "Biological Weapons and Bioterrorism" includes articles that examine the laboratory and forensic aspects of deadly biological agents.

Croddy, Eric A., with Clarisa Perez-Armendariz and John Hart. *Chemical and Biological Warfare: A Comprehensive Survey for the Concerned Citizen.* New York: Copernicus Books, 2002. Detailed overview for the layperson includes sections on the nature, history, detection, and control of biological weapons.

Dudley, William, ed. *Biological Warfare: Opposing Viewpoints.* Farmington Hills, Miss.: Greenhaven Press, 2004. Collection discusses differences of opinion among scientists and other experts on how to understand, prepare for, and prevent biological warfare.

Lederberg, Joshua, ed. *Biological Weapons: Limiting the Threat.* Cambridge, Mass.: MIT Press, 1999. Compendium of historical and technical essays includes information on the detection of biological agents and responses to biological attack. Intended for both doctors and students.

Mauroni, Al. *Chemical and Biological Warfare: A Reference Handbook.* 2d ed. Santa Barbara, Calif.: ABC-CLIO, 2007. Addresses the history of chemical and biological weaponry and presents information on experts and related organizations as well as case studies.

**See also:** Anthrax; Anthrax letter attacks; Bacteria; Biodetectors; Biological terrorism; Biological weapon identification; Biological Weapons Convention of 1972; Biotoxins; Blood agents; Chemical warfare.

---

## Biological weapon identification

**Definition:** Identification of weapons of mass destruction that are based on bacteria, viruses, fungi, and toxins produced by these microorganisms.

**Significance:** Heightened concerns regarding the possibility of bioterrorist attacks have led to increased emphasis on microbial forensic science. Microbial forensic data may be presented in court as evidence in cases of terrorist attacks.

Virtually all disease-causing microorganisms are potentially useful as biological weapons. The most important candidates for biological weapons are microorganisms, which cause diseases with the highest human mortality rates such as anthrax, smallpox, plague, encephalitis, and hemorrhagic fever (*e.g.*, Ebola).

In 2001, the general public in the United States became aware of biological weapons such as the bacterium *Bacillus anthracis* (agent of anthrax) which was used in a series of bioterrorism attacks. Biological weapons have become a great concern due to the fact that they can be easily produced and spread by terrorists.

Since 2001, in response to the threat of terrorist attacks, there have been mounted efforts led by the U.S. government to develop quick and efficient methods of biological weapon identification, ultimately leading to establishment of the new scientific discipline of microbial forensics. Microbial forensics is based on techniques that rely on the microscopic examination of microbes, analysis of growth and metabolic functions of the microbes (growth-dependent and biochemical tests) and immunological and molecular diagnostics tests.

### Growth-Dependent and Biochemical Tests

Classical methods of microbial identification involve preliminary examination of stained specimens under a microscope, followed by growth-dependent tests. Growth-dependent tests are based on the growth patterns of microorganisms on artificial food sources (media). Particular medium can be selected that will produce microbial populations, known as colonies, that have distinctive appearance and color. By comparing the reactions on these media with the known characteristics of different species of microorganisms, it is usually possible to identify which microbe is present. However, most growth-dependent tests do not provide results that are species specific.

To aid in definitive microorganism identification, scientists have developed a series of biochemical tests that can be used to identify species. These tests are based on the identification of various metabolic reactions and products of different microbes. A number of rapid identification tests are available that allow several (approximately 20) biochemical tests to be performed quickly on a particular microorganism.

To identify microorganisms at sub-species level known as strains, the strain typing methods are usually done. Strain typing techniques are based also on biochemical differences, ether on enzyme profiles or on antibiotic resistance patterns.

### Immunological Tests

Immunological tests utilize antibodies that are produced in response to the presence of a specific microorganism; actually, they respond to the presence of specific molecules, called antigens, on the microorganism cell surfaces. Antibodies are proteins produced by the body that recognize and bind to those antigens. Specific antibodies for many known disease-causing microorganisms are commercially available. Immunological tests vary in the ways they make the antigen-antibody reaction visible; some show obvious clumps and precipitates, whereas others show color changes or the release of fluorescence.

An example of an immunological test is the agglutination test, which is performed routinely in hospitals to determine blood types. In an agglutination test, antibody-antigen complexes form visible clumps on a test glass slide. Extremely sensitive immunological tests called immunoassays permit rapid and accurate measurement of trace bioweapon agents. A good example of such an immunoassay is the enzyme-linked immunosorbent assay (ELISA). A positive result in this immunoassay is the appearance of a colored product.

### Molecular diagnostics tests

Molecular diagnostics tests are based on the detection of the unique DNA (deoxyribonucleic acid) sequences of potential weapon microorganisms. Certain viruses maintain their genetic material in the form of RNA (ribonucleic acid), which can be converted into corresponding DNA for detection purposes. Molecular diagnostics tests, which provide rapid and specific identification of microorganisms, are especially useful for microbes, which do not grow or grow slowly in laboratory conditions. One particular technique that has been widely used for identifying microorganisms based on their DNA sequences is the polymerase chain reaction (PCR). The test utilizes specific sets of primers (short DNA sequences) to amplify and detect DNA sequences unique to a particular microorganism. In PCR, amplified DNA sequences are subjected to separation by electrophoresis, where negatively charged DNA fragments move toward the positive pole. Separated DNA fragments can be classified by the distance they traveled depending upon their molecular size. Each microorganism exhibits a characteristic DNA moving pattern by which it can be identified. Officials of the United Nations used portable PCR detectors when they conducted their 2002-2003 inspections of Iraqi facilities for weapons of mass destruction. These detectors can identify a single *B. anthracis* bacterium in an average kitchen-sized room. The United States Postal Service has a PCR-based fully automated system in place since 2006 to detect anthrax bacteria in letters and packages. This system takes samples from random mail items every hour and processes it in less than 30 min. A similar system is employed by the U.S. government in its BioWatch Program in 30 major cities. There is a big difference between the BioWatch system and the post office device; the BioWatch system can not only check for anthrax but many other disease-causing microbes.

Another commonly used molecular diagnostic test is the nucleic acid (DNA or RNA) hybridization assay. Nucleic acid hybridization (or hybridization for short) assay is based on the formation of hybrid molecules between a sequence-known single-stranded nucleic acid, which is called the probe, and nucleic acid from an identified microbe, which is known as the target. The probe is a DNA or RNA fragment with an attached chemical that can be visualized by a color or by using an instrument.

## Ongoing Challenges

Although, in most cases, agents used as biological weapons could be identified easily within twenty-four hours, prosecutors may have difficulty proving that microorganisms identified in the homes or laboratories of suspects are in fact the same microorganisms used as weapons or intended for such use. One problem with making legal arguments based on weapon microbe identification is that some potentially dangerous microorganisms, such as *B. anthracis*, are found widely in soil. A prosecutor thus must prove that the microbes submitted as evidence in a given case are the same microbes used in the attack in question, and not simply microorganisms that have been transported into the suspect's home or lab accidentally.

*Sergei A. Markov*

## Further Reading

Alibek, Ken and Stephen Handelman. *Biohazard: The Chilling True Story of the Largest Covert Biological Weapons Program in the World—Told from the Inside by the Man Who Ran It.* New York: Dell Publishing, 1999. Book describes 21st century bioterrorism and germ weapons including anthrax, smallpox, plague, Ebola, toxins, delivery methods, identification, symptoms, treatment, and equipment.

Cowan, Marjorie K. *Microbiology: A System Approach.* 4th ed. Boston, MA: McGraw-Hill, 2014. Health sciences-related general microbiology text. An entire ,chapter in this textbook describes microbial identification techniques

Lindler, Luther E., Frank J. Lebeda *and George W. Korch. Biological Weapons Defense: Infectious Disease and Counterbioterrorism.* Totowa, NJ: Humana Press, 2005. Prominent experts in biodefense research - many from the US Army Medical Research Institute of Infectious Diseases describe how to identify the presence of biological weapons by proteomic and genomic analysis as a gateway to better diagnostics and forensics.

Madigan, Michael T., John M. Martinko, Paul V. Dunlap, and David P. Clark. *Brock Biology of Microorganisms.* 12th ed. Upper Saddle

River, N.J.: Pearson Prentice Hall, 2008. Widely respected basic microbiology textbook includes information about biological weapons and methods of microbial identification.

Mahon, Connie R., Donald C. Lehman, George Manuselis. *Diagnostic Microbiology*. 5th ed. St. Louis, MO: Saunders Elsevier, 2014. This book provides the essentials of diagnostic microbiology, full-color text helps students to develop skills in identification of microorganisms.

Peruski, Anne Harwood, and Leonard F. Peruski, Jr. "Immunological Methods for Detection and Identification of Infectious Disease and Biological Warfare Agents." *Clinical and Diagnostic Laboratory Immunology* 10 (July, 2003): 506-513. Technical article describes immunological methods of biological weapon identification.

**See also:** Anthrax; Bacterial biology; Biological warfare diagnosis; Biosensors; Biotoxins; Bubonic plaque; DNA analysis; Ebola virus; PCR (Polymerase chain reaction); Smallpox; Tularemia; Viral biology.

---

# Biological Weapons Convention of 1972

**Dates:** Opened for signature April 10, 1972; entered into force March 26, 1975

**The Convention:** International agreement designed to ban the development, production, and stockpiling of a variety of biological weapons.

**Significance:** Seeking to increase international security, the Biological Weapons Convention of 1972 outlawed all biological weapons and delivery systems for such weapons. The openness required by this treaty can assist forensic scientists who investigate crimes that involve such organisms.

Early in human history, people in certain hunting societies learned how to use plant or animal poisons to make their weapons more deadly. As human beings gained more detailed knowledge of diseases and biological processes, they developed other, more efficient, means of using biological agents to infect or kill their enemies. After more than one million casualties in World War I, mainly from chemical weapons, the international community adopted the Geneva Protocol in 1925; this agreement limited the first use of chemical or biological weapons in future wars. The method of conducting warfare was thus recognized as being subject to international law.

The United States researched and developed biological weapons on a large scale until 1969, when President Richard M. Nixon ordered a halt to these programs and instructed the Department of Defense to design a plan to dispose of the weapons. Around the same time, the British govenment proposed international negotiations on banning biological weapons. In 1971, an agreement was reached, and in 1972, the process of signing and ratification of the Convention on the Prohibition of the Development, Production and Stockpiling of Bacteriological (Biological) and Toxin Weapons and on Their Destruction began. According to the convention, also known as the Biological and Toxin Weapons Convention or simply the Biological Weapons Convention, biological weapons were supposed to be destroyed beginning in 1975. This was at the height of the Cold War, however, and verification procedures that required countries to allow international observers into their military facilities were not acceptable to many signatories. Enforcement of the provisions of the convention was impossible because no system existed for verifying that countries were adhering to those provisions.

Adding to the enforcement problem since the convention entered into force in March, 1975, has been the fact that virtually everything that is needed to develop biological weapons also has a peaceful use. The existence of sealed biological research facilities, for instance, does not necessarily indicate that biological weapons research is being conducted. Sealing such a facility is a common procedure to keep contamination, in either direction, from affecting a biology experiment. Those who seek to enforce the terms of the treaty must use indirect means to verify that nations are following those terms. A series of Review Conferences have been held to clarify certain aspects of the treaty and generally assist with its implementation in an ever-changing world. The Fourth Review Conference directed a working group to develop a protocol for a mandatory multinational verification process. In 2002, at the last meeting prior to the protocol's going to the Fifth Review Conference for adoption, the United States effectively vetoed the proposed protocol as not being strong enough to guarantee that it would be completely effective.

## Posttreaty Incidents

Although the Biological Weapons Convention allows countries to keep small quantities of biological agents for medical or defensive purposes, the treaty prohibits active work on the development of such agents. Many people were surprised when, in April, 1979, an outbreak of anthrax killed more than sixty people in the Soviet city of Sverdlovsk (now Yekaterinburg, Russia). Soviet authorities denied any relationship of the outbreak to biological weapons, but given that anthrax is a commonly produced biological agent and the disease has been virtually wiped out, the rest of the world was certain that the anthrax deaths had resulted from an accident at a biological research facility. Without a mandatory inspection process in place, however, international observers were unable to investigate the situation fully and determine the cause of the outbreak with complete certainty.

The possible use of biological agents by terrorists was dramatically demonstrated in September and October, 2001, when letters containing anthrax spores were mailed to five news media operations in New York City and Boca Raton, Florida, and later to two U.S. senators. As a result of these attacks, twenty-two people became ill, five of whom died. Although law-enforcement investigators were eventually able

---

## First Four Articles of the Biological Weapons Convention

### Article I

Each State Party to this Convention undertakes never in any circumstances to develop, produce, stockpile or otherwise acquire or retain:

1. Microbial or other biological agents, or toxins whatever their origin or method of production, of types and in quantities that have no justification for prophylactic, protective or other peaceful purposes;
2. Weapons, equipment or means of delivery designed to use such agents or toxins for hostile purposes or in armed conflict.

### Article II

Each State Party to this Convention undertakes to destroy, or to divert to peaceful purposes, as soon as possible but not later than nine months after entry into force of the Convention, all agents, toxins, weapons, equipment and means of delivery specified in article I of the Convention, which are in its possession or under its jurisdiction or control. In implementing the provisions of this article all necessary safety precautions shall be observed to protect populations and the environment.

### Article III

Each State Party to this Convention undertakes not to transfer to any recipient whatsoever, directly or indirectly, and not in any way to assist, encourage, or induce any State, group of States or international organizations to manufacture or otherwise acquire any of the agents, toxins, weapons, equipment or means of delivery specified in article I of this Convention.

### Article IV

Each State Party to this Convention shall, in accordance with its constitutional processes, take any necessary measures to prohibit and prevent the development, production, stockpiling, acquisition, or retention of the agents, toxins, weapons, equipment and means of delivery specified in article I of the Convention, within the territory of such State, under its jurisdiction or under its control anywhere.

President Richard M. Nixon at his first inauguration in January, 1969. Later that same year, Nixon ordered the discontinuation of biological weapon development in the United States. As other world powers followed suit, a movement began that led to an international ban on such weapons. *(NARA)*

to track the letters to a specific mailbox in New Jersey, the case remains unsolved. Forensic scientists have spent countless hours trying to determine the source of the anthrax, focusing on the slight differences that distinguish the various samples of anthrax spores stored at different locations. One early analysis indicated that the anthrax used in the attacks came from a U.S. military base, although this was never officially confirmed, and dozens of sites have been searched.

As a result of the possible contamination of multiple sites owing to the method the terrorist used, sending the anthrax spores through the mail, the U.S. government has spent hundreds of millions of dollars cleaning up various locations, especially postal facilities. The fact that even after years of intensive investigation the perpetrator of the crime has not been found in-

dicates how difficult it is to track weapons of this type. If the signatories of the Biological Weapons Convention follow the intent of the treaty and reduce the amount of stored biological materials available for misuse by terrorists and closely guard what remains, incidents such as the 2001 anthrax attacks may not happen in the future.

*Donald A. Watt*

### Further Reading

Cirincione, Joseph, Jon B. Wolfsthal, and Miriam Rajkumar. *Deadly Arsenals: Nuclear, Biological, and Chemical Threats*. Rev. ed. Washington, D.C.: Carnegie Endowment for International Peace, 2005. Provides an overview of the range of chemical weapon threats facing the United States.
Gillemin, Jeanne. *Biological Weapons: From*

*the Invention of State-Sponsored Programs to Contemporary Bioterrorism.* New York: Columbia University Press, 2006. Discusses biological weapon programs from before World War II through the 1990's, with special attention to the remnants of those programs that later became "available" to terrorists.

Hoover Institution on War. *The New Terror: Facing the Threat of Biological and Chemical Weapons.* Palo Alto, Calif.: Hoover Institution Press, 1999. Covers a wide range of issues, including the constitutional constraints on U.S. law enforcement in combating chemical weapons and suggestions for reducing the damage from such weapons.

Lederberg, Joshua, ed. *Biological Weapons: Limiting the Threat.* Cambridge, Mass.: MIT Press, 1999. Examines the dangers posed by biological weapons as well as the ways in which the United States has tried to decrease those dangers.

Tucker, Jonathan B., ed. *Toxic Terror: Assessing Terrorist Use of Chemical and Biological Weapons.* Cambridge, Mass.: MIT Press, 2000. Presents twelve case studies of the use of chemical and biological agents by terrorist groups. Identifies terrorists' patterns of behavior and discusses strategies to combat them.

**See also:** Anthrax; Anthrax letter attacks; Biological terrorism; Biological warfare diagnosis; Biological weapon identification; Biotoxins; Chemical Weapons Convention of 1993; Pathogen genomic sequencing; Smallpox; U.S. Army Medical Research Institute of Infectious Diseases.

## Biometric eye scanners

**Definition:** Imaging technologies that use the iris or retina of the eye to identify individuals.

**Significance:** Biometric eye scanning can facilitate the automated control of access to areas where high levels of security must be maintained, such as correctional institutions and military and government installations that house sensitive materials.

The goal of biometric identification systems is to provide automated identity assurance—that is, the capability to recognize individuals accurately—with reliability, speed, and convenience. The complex nature of the human eye provides two of the most accurate biometric measures available. The iris and the retina, located on the front and back of the eye, respectively, are individually distinguishing structures. Retinal recognition became commercially available in the early 1980's, preceding iris recognition systems by about five years.

The iris is the round, pigmented membrane that surrounds the pupil of the eye. The intricate pattern of furrows and ridges in the iris is randomly formed prior to birth and remains stable from early childhood until death. In a typical iris scan, the person being identified aligns one eye close to a wall-mounted scanner for a few seconds. The scanner uses a near-infrared light to scan an image of the eye, and computer software then isolates the iris in the image and performs size and contrast corrections. Computer software then compares the final digital image with other iris images stored in a database; when a match is made, the person is identified.

Prisons throughout the United States use iris-scanning technology to verify the identities of convicts before release. Correctional facilities also enroll visitors in their iris image databases and scan the irises of people leaving the facilities to be certain they are visitors, not inmates. Some organizations use small, semiportable iris scanners to control access to sensitive computer files and information.

Retina biometric identification is based on the individually distinguishing characteristics of blood vessel patterns on the back of the eye. These patterns are thought to be created by a random biological process and remain unchanged throughout life in a healthy individual. During retina scanning, the person being identified aligns one eye with a wall-mounted scanner for several seconds. The scanner illuminates the retina with a low-intensity infrared light and creates an image of the patterns formed by the major blood vessels. The image is then digitally encoded, stored, and compared using computer software.

Because the retina is located on the back of the eye, this type of scan requires a high degree of cooperation from the user to ensure proper illumination and alignment. Given that retina scanning is more complex than the iris-scanning process, retina-scanning technology is best deployed in high-security, controlled-access environments where user convenience is not a priority. Employees in military weapons facilities, power plants, and sensitive laboratory environments are commonly required to undergo retina scanning to gain access.

*Ruth N. Udey*

### Further Reading

Coats, William Sloan, et al. *The Practitioner's Guide to Biometrics*. Chicago: American Bar Association Publishing, 2007.

Nanavati, Samir, Michael Thieme, and Raj Nanavati. *Biometrics: Identity Verification in a Networked World*. New York: John Wiley & Sons, 2002.

Woodward, John D., Jr., Nicholas M. Orlans, and Peter T. Higgins. *Biometrics*. New York: McGraw-Hill, 2003.

**See also:** Airport security; Biometric identification systems; Facial recognition technology; Imaging; Iris recognition systems.

---

## Biometric identification systems

**Definition:** Technologies that use automated measurements and database comparisons of physiological and behavioral characteristics to identify target individuals.

**Significance:** Biometric identification systems are becoming increasingly important given heightened concerns with security in many contexts. Compared with many other means of authorization and authentication, including password recognition, biometric technologies represent a significant advance in terms of ease of use, reliability, and validity.

The constantly evolving science of biometrics has produced a wide variety of systems capable of comparing hand, facial, eye, signature, vocal, and DNA and brain measures of given individuals against profiles of such measures stored in large data-bases. The applications of this technology for law enforcement purposes are extensive. Biometric systems have been used to identify offenders who are using aliases, fight illegal immigration, and identify inmates as they are moved through various phases of the correctional system. Biometric data can be used to verify identity claims or screen for persons who have been identified as potential security risks.

### Accuracy

Biometric identification systems represent a huge improvement over the traditional "token" (credit card or document) and password systems. Credit cards can be lost or stolen and then used as false identification. Similarly, passwords can be "cracked," forgotten, or stolen. Biometric characteristics, on the other hand, are much more stable and permanent. Their inherent complexity renders them difficult or impossible to replicate, and the person being identified usually needs to be physically present at the time of the verification attempt. In addition, biometric systems can couple identifying information with other important background data, such as health or employment records (a fact that has led some to criticize the use of these systems as infringing on civil liberties).

The components of the typical biometric system are relatively straightforward; they consist of a sensor and a computer. The sensor is the device that gathers the biometric data from the individual being evaluated. The computer then processes the data collected; in some cases, the computer may refine the data by removing irrelevant information and background "noise" that can interfere with the interpretation of the results. The computer captures the biometric features being measured and creates a template, which it then compares to a database of biometric information on known individuals, looking for an identification match, or "hit." The consequences of a successful identification are as varied as the systems themselves. At the point of identification, an individual might be allowed into a restricted area, picked up for further questioning in a specific investigation, or observed further for any suspicious behavior.

The accuracy of a biometric system is typically assessed using one or more of the following measures: the failure-to-acquire rate (a measure of the percentage of unsuccessful attempts by the system to obtain specific biometric information from subjects), the false accept rate (also known as the false positive rate, a measure of the percentage of incorrect matches of subjects' biometric profiles to profiles already included in the database), and the false reject rate (also known as the false negative rate, the percentage of failures to match subjects' biometric profiles with identical profiles already included in the database). Minimization of all these kinds of error rates reduces the numbers of suspects who are needlessly detained, restricted from air travel, or otherwise affected by law enforcement "false alarms" while maximizing the appropriate identification of true security threats.

## Applications

Law enforcement agencies employ biometric technologies in many ways, including fingerprint and DNA identification and facial, iris and voice recognition. Facial recognition systems use specific aspects of facial features from scanned photographs to make identifications. The features analyzed may include the physical distance between specific parts of the face, skin color, thermal patterns of blood flow, and facial lines. One application of facial recognition technology is the establishment by police departments of archives containing many thousands of offender photographs. These are matched with suspects' pictures or used to produce photo lineups that can be shown to crime victims or witnesses.

Numerous evaluations of facial recognition technology have produced mixed results. One Australian system, for example, tested in the Sydney airport, was found to have a false reject rate of 2 percent. This rate was confirmed by tests sponsored by the U.S. government. Al though this error rate seems low, major world airports typically service several million passengers annually, which means that the sys-

tems could potentially falsely reject many thousands of people. On the other hand, with the advent of the newest technologies such as 3D scanners, current recognition rates frequently exceed 90%. Factors affecting accuracy include lighting, the quality of the photographs taken, movements of the subjects, the angles of the poses in the photographs, and the presence of eyeglasses on subjects. In general, male subjects and older persons were more easily recognized than female and younger subjects. An inverse relationship was also found between accuracy and the size of the database against which the subjects' facial features were compared. With the ubiquity of CCTV monitoring, difficult ethical issues arise in terms of possibly capturing faces for databases when those photographed have no knowledge of their inclusion.

Fingerprint identification is the oldest form of biometrics, having been in use for more than one hundred years. The Federal Bureau of Investigation (FBI) established a central database of fingerprints in 1924 against which law-enforcement agencies can seek to match the prints of crime suspects and victims.

With modern electronic and laser technology, fingerprint images are often taken and transmitted "live" to a database. Efforts to automate the analysis and identification of fingerprints began in the 1960's. Using today's sophisticated computer systems, up to 800,000 fingerprints in a database can be analyzed in one second.

Fingerprint identification systems use electronic fingerprint readers to locate where the ridges of fingerprints start, end, or split up. These areas, known as minutiae points, form the basis for the identification. Each fingerprint typically contains thirty to forty minutiae points, and no two people's prints will match on more than eight such points.

In terms of accuracy, the false accept rates of fingerprint identification systems have generally been less than one in one million, and false reject rates have been 2 percent or less. The accuracy of the analysis of fingerprints taken from crime scenes, however, is often reduced because of the poor quality of the prints themselves. In addition, although it is often as-

## Mark Twain and Fingerprints

Although Mark Twain never knew the word "biometrics," he might fairly be credited with introducing that science to fiction in *Pudd'nhead Wilson* (1894)—the first novel to use fingerprint evidence as a plot device. During the mid-nineteenth century, the novel's title character, attorney David Wilson, mystifies and amuses the simple people of Dawson's Landing, Missouri, by collecting their fingerprints on glass slides.

For years, the villagers dismiss him as a "pudding-headed" fool—until the final chapter, when he displays his legal brilliance in a murder trial. Wilson creates a sensation by using his slides to prove the innocence of the murder suspect whom he is defending. That revelation is minor, however, compared to his second use of fingerprint evidence at the trial. Drawing on glass slides he has collected over more than two decades, he proves that the culprit in the murder case is a man who was born a slave and somehow got switched with the infant son of his master in infancy. The theme of switched identities that are sorted out by fingerprint evidence gives the novel a strong claim to being called the first application of biometrics in fiction.

David Wilson examining his fingerprint collection in the first edition of *Pudd'nhead Wilson*.

sumed that fingerprints are stable over a lifetime, research has shown that they in fact can change in response to physiological growth, activity, or intentional alteration. It has also been shown that many fingerprint matching systems can be "spoofed." Despite some limitations, fingerprinting is less controversial and more highly developed than many other types of biometric identification systems. This is reflected in court acceptance of fingerprinting evidence.

In iris recognition systems, an image of the iris of the eye of the person to be identified (the colored ring surrounding the pupil) is recorded by a digital camera and then converted into a template, which is checked for matches against an existing database. False positive rates for such systems have averaged .1 percent, and false negative rates have averaged 1.5 percent. An advantage of using this biometric is that, unlike fingerprints, the structure of the iris is permanent by the age of one and is unique for each person (this includes comparisons between identical twins and even between the left and right eyes of the same person). A review of six iris databases ranging greatly in size (from 384

to 16,000 images) showed that each of them had one or more "noise factors." The latter most commonly included eyelid or eyelash obstructions. It should be noted that iris evidence is not left at crime scenes. In addition, failure rates as high as 15 percent have been found when iris-scanning technology is used in brightly lit settings. This technology has many potential applications, including security screening at airports and borders, passport and immigration control, and identification for banking and issuance of drivers' licenses. Iris recognition biometrics has also been scored jointly with face recognition to achieve greater accuracy than through either biometric alone.

Voice recognition systems use physical and behavioral aspects of the voice to identify individuals. The features measured are based on the physiology of the windpipe, nasal cavity, and vocal cords. A digital "voice signature" is recorded, and a computer measures the features and compares them against known samples for identification and verification. One drawback to the use of voice biometrics is that patterns can vary with age. They can also be affected by med-

137

ical problems (including even a cold) and the emotional state of the examinee. Background noise can also be a problem with the use of this identification technology.

Another biometric identification technology that has been investigated is hand geometry scanning, which involves more than ninety measurements of different parts of the hand. To detect forgery, dynamic signature identification has been developed. In this system, the specific dimensions of the pen strokes a person makes while writing his or her signature (including pressure, speed, and direction) are recorded and stored for later matching. This technology is prone to high false negative rates, however, because even though signatures are ubiquitous in daily transactions, only specific parts of a person's signature remain constant across every signing. Gait analysis, which focuses on people's unique walking patterns, is another type of biometric technique. Limitations to gait analysis include the fact that making gait measurements may be invasive. Gait can also be affected by injury or a change in shoes. CCTV footage has been systematically analyzed for suitability in terms of gait analysis. This is obviously less invasive but it would be subject to the same ethical dilemma mentioned in connection with facial recognition analysis through CCTV as the data source.

The future of biometric identification systems will likely be characterized by diverse measures collected simultaneously and interactively. The data will be shared across law enforcement agencies and their social welfare counterparts, both nationally and internationally. Social scientists have documented the use of relatively sophisticated biometric programs in developing counties, with half the applications donor-supported. This largely represents an effort to develop efficient, broad-based national identity systems in countries whose poorer population segments have lacked the rights and services afforded citizens with more "officially-recorded" identities. For many, privacy concerns related to the invasive nature of many of these measures are frequently of secondary importance in a global society increasingly preoccupied with defending itself against the threat of sophisticated terrorist attacks.

*Eric Metchik*

## Further Reading

Eskadari, M. and T. Onsen. "A New Approach for Face-Iris Multimodal Biometric Recognition Using Score Fusion." *International Journal of Pattern Recognition and Artificial Intelligence,* 27, No. 3 (2013): 1-15. Methodology presented for conjoint analysis of iris and facial recognition biometrics, including an analysis comparing accuracy in unimodal models.

Gelb, A. and J. Clark. "Identification for Development: The Biometrics Revolution." Working Paper 315, Center for Global Development, www.cgdev.org (2013). A review of specific biometric technologies as they have been used by developing countries.

Jain, Anil K., Arun Russ, and Sharath Pankanti. "Biometrics: A Tool for Information Security." *IEEE Transactions on Information Forensics and Security* Vol. 1, no. 2 (2006): 125-143. Provides a comprehensive technical analysis of several of the major biometric approaches.

Krishnan, K. N., with D. R. Berwick. *Developing a Police Perspective and Exploring the Use of Biometrics and Other Emerging Technologies as an Investigative Tool in Identity Crimes.* Payneham, SA: Australasian Centre for Policing Research, 2004. International review of basic biometric technology use includes recommendations for law-enforcement applications.

Kumar, M.J. "Facial Recognition by Machines: Is it an Effective Surveillance Tactic?" *IETE Technical Review, Vol.* Vol. 30, No. 2, (2013): 93-94. An editorial concerning the efficacy of law enforcement applications of the most recent facial recognition technology.

Parashar, R. and J. Sandeep. "Comparative Study of Iris Databases and UBIRIS Database for Iris Recognition Methods for Noncooperative Environment" *International Journal of Engineering, Research and Technology,* Vol. 1, No. 5 (2012):1-6. Insightful review of extant iris databases as well as sources of "noise" which can impede their analysis.

Peralta, D., I. TrigueroI., R. Sanchez-Reillo,

F. Herrera, and J. Benitez. "Fast Fingerprint Identification for Large Databases." *Pattern Recognition*, Vol. 47, No. 2 (2014): 588-602. A review of the problem of analyzing large fingerprint databases, presenting a suggested solution.

Vacca, John R. *Biometric Technologies and Verification Systems*. Burlington, MA: Elsevier, 2007. Comprehensive, well-organized text includes discussion of how biometrics works, analysis of biometric data, and uses of biometric data.

**See also:** Airport security; Anthropometry; Biometric eye scanners; Biosensors; Brain-wave scanners; Ear prints; Electronic voice alteration; Facial recognition technology; Fingerprints; Integrated Automated Fingerprint Identification System; Iris recognition systems; National Institute of Justice; Voiceprints.

# Biosensors

**Definition:** Devices that use biological molecules or cells to detect and measure chemicals, biological agents, or physical conditions and then use nonbiological components to convert the data into signals or readouts.

**Significance:** Biosensors have attracted a lot of interest for their potential in countering the use of chemical and biological weapons by terrorists and for their applications as on-site forensic analytical devices at crime scenes. Biosensors potentially offer sensitive and rapid detection of harmful organisms and substances in food and water supplies. Such instruments have demonstrated usefulness for measuring many substances that are of interest to forensic science, such as toxins, drugs of abuse, poisonous chemicals, and DNA.

Biosensor devices differ in the biological components they use for sensing chemicals. Examples are enzymes, antibodies, receptors, and whole cells. The most common biological components used in biosensors are enzymes and antibodies. Different types of biological components result in different types of signals that must be converted into readouts.

Biosensors can be classified according to the ways in which the detection that is mediated by their biological components is converted into measurable signals. After the initial recognition of a chemical species by the biological component, a biosensor generates a readout signal in a process called transduction. At least five different kinds of transducers are used in biosensors: Amperometric transducers involve the movement of electrons resulting from a biorecognition event among three electrodes; potentiometric transducers exploit biological sensor-induced changes in the movement of ions, which results in the generation of an electric potential; thermal transducers utilize heat from biorecognition events that are endothermic reactions; optical transducers make use of the production or absorption of light resulting from biological recognition of detected chemicals or biological molecules; and piezoelectric transducers react to changes in mass produced by biological recognition of target chemicals or biological molecules.

The physical component of a biosensor's transducer, which is in contact with the biological sensor, may comprise electrodes, semiconductors, and optical constructions such as fiber optics and nanoparticles. Most biosensors use electrochemical types of transduction, such as amperometric and potentiometric methods, and enzymatic, antibody, or DNA biological recognition components.

## Working and Organization

A biosensor contains an external and an internal interface. In the first step, at the external interface of the device, the substance being measured (analyte) binds with the biological recognition component of the biosensor. In the second step, at the internal interface, the biological recognition system interacts with the transducer component, and this produces a physical or chemical response. This response may involve the production of hydrogen ions, other ions, or electrons for amperometric, potentiometric, and conductimetric biosensors. A second type of transducer response may involve the biologically coupled production or absorption of light (fluorescence, chemiluminescence, or visible wavelength). A third type of transducer response would be a change in mass at the transducer such as occurs in piezoelectric (or microelectromechanical) systems. A fourth type of transducer response involves changes in temperature for thermal or calorimetric systems. The physical or chemical response produced by the transducer is processed and amplified to produce a readout signal that serves to indicate the presence and amount of a substance of interest.

## Applications

Nanotechnology—that is, the application and study of the structuring and behavior of materials at nanometer scale—has also been used in making biosensors. Gold, cadmium selenide, and zinc selenide nanoparticles and single-walled carbon nanotubes are among the nanoscale substances that are being used to make biosensors to detect metal ions, biological molecules, and even viruses such as those responsible for strains of influenza (such as influenza A and the avian flu virus H5N1).

Challenges in the uses of biosensors arise from the need for small, portable devices, the inherent instability of most biological molecules and cells, and the need for highly sensitive devices that can measure a wide range of substances simultaneously. Biosensors used at crime scenes by forensic investigators and in national defense applications must perform reliably and produce quick results under field conditions. In the United States, in addition to their uses by law-enforcement personnel and by national security agencies for the detection and prevention of bioterrorist attacks, biosensors are used for environmental monitoring, for quality control during food processing and the processing of pharmaceuticals, and for monitoring of agriculture.

*Oluseyi A. Vanderpuye*

## Further Reading

Cooper, Jon, and Tony Cass, eds. *Biosensors: A Practical Approach*. 2d ed. New York: Oxford University Press, 2004. Provides multidisciplinary coverage of biosensor research, construction, and operation, with descriptions of practical methods in the field.

Eggins, Brian R. *Biosensors: An Introduction*. New York: John Wiley & Sons, 1996. Offers an overview of the various classes of biosensors and describes the methods used in their manufacture.

Hall, Elizabeth A.H. *Biosensors*. Englewood Cliffs, N.J.: Prentice Hall, 1991. Provides an approachable introduction to the concepts behind biosensors as well as information on their construction and applications.

Kress-Rogers, Erika, ed. *Handbook of Biosensors and Electronic Noses: Medicine, Food, and the Environment*. Boca Raton, Fla.: CRC Press, 1997. Discusses both the design and the practical uses of biosensors. Includes informative figures and tables.

**See also:** Air and water purity; Biodetectors; Biological terrorism; Biological warfare diagnosis; Biological weapon identification; Immune system; Pathogen genomic sequencing; Toxicological analysis; Tularemia.

# Bioterrorism. *See Biological terrorism*

# Biotoxins

**Definition:** Toxic substances that originate from biological sources, including viruses, bacteria, fungi, algae, and plants.

**Significance:** Biocrimes present law-enforcement agencies with serious challenges, as the perpetrators of such crimes can use numerous pathogens that exist naturally and do not require sophisticated expertise or technology to prepare. Further, because the effects of biotoxins are as diverse as the substances' multiple origins, it can be difficult for investigators to ascertain the types of biotoxins employed in particular crimes or terrorist attacks.

The use of biological agents and their toxins in criminal acts and as weapons of war has a long history. In the Far East, opium was the poison used for murder and suicide for several centuries. In the fourteenth century, Mongol warriors used plague-infected bodies as weapons of war, triggering an outbreak that killed thousands. During the French and Indian War (1754-1763), the British approved a plan to distribute to Native American tribes blankets contaminated with smallpox. These examples, however, pale in comparison with the chilling prospects of modern bioterrorism aided by a rapidly expanding knowledge of biological agents, biotoxins, and their potential to wreak havoc in complex, interdependent societies.

## Common Microbial Agents

Various microbes can be the sources of biotoxins, including viruses, bacteria, and fungi. It is relatively easy to propagate bacteria and fungi with small samples, but the propagation of viruses for use in biocrimes requires certain training and access to specific technologies. Some of the common viruses that produce devastating effects include smallpox, Ebola, and Marburg. Smallpox, a highly contagious virus, is transmitted easily and carries a high mortality rate. By the 1970's, a worldwide vaccination program had eradicated smallpox. Three decades later, only two places in the world still officially maintained live cultures of the virus: a laboratory of the Centers for Disease Control and Prevention (CDC) in the United States and a lab in Russia. The Ebola and Marburg viruses are also extremely lethal; both cause hemorrhagic fever and profuse bleeding from bodily orifices. No cure or effective treatments for either virus have yet been found.

Bacterial biotoxins include anthrax, botulism, plague, and tularemia. *Bacillus anthracis*, the bacterium that causes anthrax, produces spores that are extremely resistant to the environment and are highly infectious when inhaled. Botulism is caused by a potent neurotoxin produced by the bacterium *Clostridium botulinum*. Once inhaled or ingested, the toxin causes respiratory failure and paralysis. Plague is also highly contagious; it causes a type of pneumonia and can be fatal if not treated early.

*Francisella tularensis* causes tularemia, a generally nonlethal disease that is extremely incapacitating; symptoms include weight loss, fever, and headaches.

Many fungi produce remarkable amounts of toxic secondary metabolites, some of which are toxins. Fungal toxins are grouped into two categories: mycotoxins, which are produced by common molds, and mushroom toxins, which are formed in the fleshy fruiting bodies of sac or club fungi. Mycotoxins are major contributing factors to many cases of food poisoning. Some mycotoxins, such as aflatoxins, are believed to be among the most potent known carcinogens. Ingestion of even minute amounts of aflatoxins over long periods of time through contaminated food can cause liver cancer. In 1974, hundreds of people were poisoned by aflatoxin-contaminated corn in India; more than one hundred died. Several members of the mushroom genus *Amanita* contain amanitin, one of the deadliest poisons found in nature. The poison contained in false morels, monomethyl hydrazine (MMH), can cause diarrhea, vomiting, and severe headaches; ingestion of this poison occasionally results in death.

## Marine and Plant Biotoxins

Many plants produce poisonous secondary metabolites that induce toxic effects when the plants or their extracts are consumed. Although sensitivity to plant toxins may vary among individuals, a good correlation generally exists between the amount of poison ingested and the severity of the clinical symptoms. Some highly toxic substances derived from plants include ricin (derived from castor beans), aconitine (from monkshood), strychnine (from the vomit nut), and huratoxin (from jimsonweed, also known as thorn apple). Ricin has been employed as a murder weapon in many cultures. In South America, native tribes have long used various plants to prepare curare, a common name for a deadly poison used on the tips of arrows or darts.

Harmful algal blooms represent a real threat to virtually all U.S. coastal and fresh waters. Potential impacts range from devastating economic effects to public health risks to ecosystem alterations. The phenomena commonly known as "red tides" produce extremely potent biotoxins. When such toxins accumulate in marine food chains, they cause mass mortalities of birds, fish, and marine mammals and often lead to closures of commercial and recreational fisheries. When humans accidentally consume seafood contaminated with algal toxins, illness develops and even death occurs in extreme cases. Two classes of algal toxins have been well studied: the paralytic shellfish poisoning (PSP) toxins and domoic acid, both of which act on nerve systems.

## Microbial Forensics

Criminal investigations involving biotoxins rely on forensic scientists who work in the cross-discipline known as microbial forensics. It can be challenging at times to distinguish symptoms and signs that may be caused by toxins from those that are just variants of normal health.

Physicians and forensic scientists may not be able to recognize early symptoms associated with particular pathogens or biotoxins. Often, the identification of particular biotoxins requires the careful study of highly skilled professionals using sophisticated analytical instruments.

Furthermore, confirmation of the presence of biological agents or toxins in evidence samples

*The Cow Pock — or — the Wonderful Effects of the New Inoculation! — Vide the Publications of ý Anti Vaccine Society*

Although smallpox is one of the most virulent and most easily transmitted viruses known to humankind, it was also one of the first biotoxins to be eradicated. During the 1790's, the British physician Edward Jenner developed a vaccine from material taken from infected cows that effectively protected people against smallpox. Despite the early success of Jenner's procedure, it was slow to win public acceptance. This British cartoon from 1802 caricatures a scene at a public hospital in which Jenner is vaccinating a frightened woman as cows emerge from the bodies of people already vaccinated. *(Library of Congress)* is generally not enough to guarantee conviction of a suspect without other supporting evidence.

*Ming Y. Zheng*

## Further Reading

Beasley, Val Richard, et al. "Diagnostic and Clinically Important Aspects of Cyanobacterial (Blue-Green Algae) Toxicoses." *Journal of Veterinary Diagnostic Investigation* 1 (October, 1989): 359-365. Scholarly article focuses on the diagnosis of biotoxins in animals.

Breeze, Roger G., Bruce Budowle, and Steven E. Schutzer, eds. *Microbial Forensics.* Burlington, Mass.: Elsevier Academic Press, 2005. Reviews the relationships between microbe physiology and forensics.

Cooper, Marion R., Anthony W. Johnson, and Elizabeth A. Dauncey. *Poisonous Plants and Fungi: An Illustrated Guide.* 2d ed. London: TSO, 2003. Comprehensive volume describes the many varieties of poisonous plants and fungi.

Garrett, Laurie. *The Coming Plague: Newly Emerging Diseases in a World Out of Balance.* New York: Farrar, Straus and Giroux, 1994. Discusses the increase in outbreaks of infectious diseases in the late twentieth century as well as ways to prevent such outbreaks.

Nelson, Lewis S., Richard D. Shih, and Michael J. Balick. *Handbook of Poisonous and Injurious Plants.* 2d ed. New York: Springer, 2007. Provides useful information on many different plant biotoxins.

**See also:** Bacterial resistance and response to antibacterial agents; Biological terrorism; Biological warfare diagnosis; Biological weapon identification; Biological Weapons Convention of 1972; Botulinum toxin; Centers for Disease Control and Prevention; Chemical agents; Mycotoxins; Poisons and antidotes; Ricin; Smallpox; Toxicological analysis; Viral biology.

# Bite-mark analysis

**Definition:** Examination and comparison of wounds caused by biting during physical attacks.

**Significance:** The bite marks analyzed by forensic scientists may include marks made by attackers on victims and marks made by victims on attackers. Also, in some cases, crime victims and the perpetrators of crimes leave bite marks on objects found at crime scenes. Bite-mark analysis can sometimes provide important physical evidence linking an offender to a victim or crime scene.

The reliability of the evidence resulting from bite-mark analysis depends greatly on the skill and experience of the forensic odontologist who conducts the analysis. The occurrence of bite marks in criminal cases is not common; when bite marks are found, they are seen most often in cases of violent sexual crimes or child abuse.

## Procedures

When investigators suspect that a particular wound is a bite mark, they record every detail about it, including its appearance, color, location on the body, and size, and whether the bite seems to be human or animal. They also photograph the mark from all possible angles, laying a ruler alongside the mark in each photo to show both the mark's length and its width. If a ruler is not available, another object of known size, such as a coin, is included in the photographs to clarify the size of the mark.

If the indentation of the bite mark is sufficient, an impression is made of the mark before the skin is able to smooth over or change shape.

Obtaining a good impression of a bite mark can be difficult, particularly if the skin was distorted before being bitten or the teeth slid across the skin while biting. The suspected bite-mark area is also wiped with sterile cotton swabs to collect any saliva or other evidence left behind by the biter that might yield DNA (deoxyribonucleic acid) for analysis; the swabs are placed in sterile tubes to preserve the evidence.

If a suspect has been identified, a dentist or forensic odontologist then makes an impression of the suspect's teeth. From this impression, a transparency or computer image of the bite mark that would be left by that suspect's teeth is created. The dentist also examines the suspect's bone and muscle structure to determine if any unusual factors are present that would affect the suspect's bite. Also taken into account in the analysis of a suspect's bite are factors such as fillings, lost teeth, the curve of the teeth, and any spaces between teeth.

The American Board of Forensic Odontology has set specific guidelines regarding the presentation of bite-mark evidence in court. In testifying as expert witnesses regarding such evidence, forensic odontologists are held to the standard of "reasonable medical certainty," which means that they must be confident in their conclusions.

## Questionable Evidence?

In a study conducted in 1999, a member of the American Board of Forensic Odontology found that bite-mark analyses wrongly identified the persons who made the bite marks about 63 percent of the time. This study concluded that bite-mark analysis is always subjective and that no standards are accepted across the forensic odontology field.

Some widely publicized cases of men wrongly convicted based at least in part on bite-mark evidence include those of Ray Krone, Roy Brown, and Ricky Amolsch. Krone was convicted of murdering a woman based on a bite mark on the victim's breast; he was later released when DNA evidence showed another man had left the bite mark. Brown was also convicted of murder but was freed after serving fifteen years in prison when DNA analysis of the saliva left in the bite marks on the murder victim showed that the saliva was not his. Based on the flawed testimony of a forensic dentist, Amolsch spent ten months in jail, during which time he lost his life savings, his home, and his children. He was freed when the work of the same dentist was called into question in another case involving bite-mark evidence.

*Marianne M. Madsen*

## Ted Bundy and Bite Marks

When the infamous serial rapist and murderer Ted Bundy was finally convicted, his conviction owed a great deal to bite-mark analysis. During the attack and murder of two young women at Florida State University, distinctive bite marks were left on the breast and buttocks of one of the women. After Bundy was arrested and charged with the murders, investigators asked Bundy to submit to the making of a dental impression for a forensic odontologist to use for comparison with the bite marks. Bundy refused, but the investigators were given a search warrant to get Bundy's dental impression in any way possible, as he was suspected of attempting to grind his teeth in a way that would eventually make a match impossible. Dr. Richard Souviron, a dentist, took photos of Bundy's teeth and gums, noting that he had an unusually uneven bite pattern that could improve the likelihood of matching his teeth to bite marks.

At Bundy's trial, Souviron was able to show how the bite marks matched Bundy's unusual teeth. During his testimony, Souviron placed a transparent overlay showing an impression of Bundy's bite mark on top of an enlarged photograph of the bite mark left on the victim's buttock, leaving no doubt in the minds of the jurors that Bundy had left the mark. Souviron had an unusual amount of evidence with which to work: The attacker had bit, turned sideways, and bit again. These two bite marks left plenty of evidence to match with Bundy's teeth, and he was convicted and sentenced to death.

## Further Reading

Bowers, C. Michael. *Forensic Dental Evidence: An Investigator's Handbook.* San Diego, Calif.: Elsevier Academic Press, 2004. Discusses the management of dental evidence, including the collection and documentation of bite-mark evidence.

Dorion, Robert B. J., ed. *Bitemark Evidence.* New York: Marcel Dekker, 2005. Focuses on the anatomy and physiology of bite marks and on the process of bite-mark analysis. Includes information on landmark cases involving bite-mark evidence.

Johansen, Raymond J., and C. Michael Bowers. *Digital Analysis of Bite Mark Evidence.* Santa Barbara, Calif.: Forensic Imaging Institute, 2000. Hands-on reference book for forensic scientists discusses how to use and understand digital photography and computer imaging in bite-mark analysis.

Libal, Angela. *Fingerprints, Bite Marks, Ear Prints: Human Signposts.* Philadelphia: Mason Crest, 2006. Brief work discusses bite marks along with other types of evidence that may be found at crime scenes and used to identify suspects.

**See also:** Animal evidence; Child abuse; Crime scene documentation; Crime scene measurement; DNA analysis; DNA fingerprinting; Evidence processing; Forensic odontology; Innocence Project; Rape kit; Saliva; Tool marks.

# Blast seat

**Definition:** Point of detonation of an explosive device.

**Significance:** The blast seat is generally the area that suffers the most damage when an explosion takes place. It is very important that the investigators at an explosion scene locate the blast seat, because that area provides many clues about the nature of the explosion.

After an explosion, prompt identification of the blast seat (also known as the seat of explosion, blast hole, or epicenter) makes it possible for investigators to locate evidence quickly and to determine the type of explosion that occurred. The type of crater formed at the blast seat depends on the type and quantity of explosives used, how the device was placed, and whether the explosives were in a container, such as in a pipe. Depending on the magnitude of the explosion and the amount of explosives used, the process of finding the crater can be easy or difficult.

Blast seats are characterized as either point source, such as when a large crater is produced, or diffuse. This characterization is one of the most important determinations for investigators to make when a major explosion occurs, because it can provide information about what caused the blast, such as whether the explosive materials were concentrated or dispersed. A concentrated explosive will typically excavate the blast seat and form a crater. In fact, a distinct crater is usually a very good indication that an explosive device was used. In such a case, thermal imaging cameras can detect a thermal effect surrounding the blast seat. Other types of explosions, such as those that are caused by fuel gas, vapors, or dust explosives, do not produce craters or have definite blast seats. With dispersed explosives, a thermal effect near the immediate blast seat is also absent.

The type of surface on which an explosion takes place can affect the blast seat that forms. When an explosion occurs on the ground, dirt, rock, and other debris are blasted out to form a crater. These materials land near the top of the crater, with some rock and debris falling back into the crater. When a blast is caused by large amounts of explosives, the debris that falls back into the crater can cover it completely, making it difficult for investigators to find the blast seat. Explosions that take place on hard surfaces such as concrete also produce craters, but these are generally not as deep as the craters formed by explosions on open ground.

*C. J. Walsh*

**Further Reading**

Beveridge, Alexander, ed. *Forensic Investigation of Explosions.* New York: Taylor & Francis, 1998.

Ellis, John W. *Police Analysis and Planning for Homicide Bombings: Prevention, Defense, and Response.* Springfield, Ill.: Charles C Thomas, 2007.

Horswell, John, ed. *The Practice of Crime Scene Investigation.* Boca Raton, Fla.: CRC Press, 2004.

National Institute of Justice. *A Guide for Explosion and Bombing Scene Investigation.* Washington, D.C.: Author, 2000.

Thurman, James T. *Practical Bomb Scene In-*

*vestigation*. Boca Raton, Fla.: CRC Press, 2006.

**See also:** Bomb damage assessment; Bombings; Bureau of Alcohol, Tobacco, Firearms and Explosives; Crime scene investigation; National Church Arson Task Force; Oklahoma City bombing; Structural analysis; World Trade Center bombing.

# Blood agents

**Definition:** Chemical agents that affect the body by being absorbed into the blood.
**Significance:** Forensic investigators must be aware of the signs and symptoms of the presence of blood agents when these chemical substances are involved in homicides or other deaths. The possibility that such agents may be used in terrorist attacks is also of concern to law-enforcement agencies.

Chemical agents are toxic substances that are classified by their primary sites of effect; blood agents are thus chemical agents that exert their primary effects in the blood. Known blood agents are either cyanide- or arsenic-based. Examples of cyanide-based blood agents include hydrogen cyanide and cyanogen chloride. Arsine is an example of an arsenic-based blood agent.

## Characteristics

Blood agents are fast-acting, potentially deadly chemicals. Cyanide can be a highly volatile colorless gas, such as hydrogen cyanide or cyanogen chloride, or can exist in crystal forms, such as sodium or potassium cyanide. Cyanogen chloride is slightly less volatile than hydrogen cyanide. Arsine exists as a colorless gas. As gases, blood agents are lighter than air and quickly dissipate. Consequently, these agents are more toxic in confined areas than in open areas. Blood agents typically have a slight odor detectable at higher concentrations. Cyanide gas, for example, may have a smell of peach kernels or bitter almonds, but the odor can be faint

and many people cannot detect it—only about half of all persons have the ability to smell cyanide gas. Arsine has a mild garlic odor that can be detected only at concentrations greater than those that are fatal.

## Exposure Routes

Blood agents are difficult to detect, volatile, and fast-acting, features that render such compounds potentially useful in chemical warfare. When these agents are used as chemical weapons, they are typically disseminated as aerosols, and inhalation is one of the deadliest exposure routes.

Cyanide occurs naturally in the environment, and small amounts are present in certain foods and in cigarette smoke. Both cyanide and arsine are used in various manufacturing processes, so some people may be exposed at their workplaces. Cyanide is present in the chemicals used to make paper, textiles, and plastics and to develop photographs; it is also used in metallurgy, electroplating, and mining.

Because cyanide gas can be released when synthetic fabrics and polyurethane burn, cyanide poisoning may contribute to fire-related deaths.

Cyanide gas has been used to exterminate pests. Arsine, which was developed initially as an insecticide, is used in the manufacture of computer chips. Arsine gas forms when arsenic encounters an acid, and most common reports of arsine exposure have resulted from accidental formation of arsine in the workplace.

## Effects

Blood agents poison the blood quickly and can result in very rapid death. Often, powerful gasping for breath occurs, followed by violent convulsions. Death from cyanide poisoning is painful, and it takes a few minutes to die from blood agent poisoning.

Blood agents are taken into the body either by ingestion or by inhalation. Cyanide-based blood agents irritate the eyes and respiratory tract. Arsine, in contrast, is nonirritating. Respiratory failure is usually the cause of death. Blood agents interfere with oxygen utilization at the cellular level by preventing exchange of oxygen and carbon dioxide between blood and

## Blood Agents in Chemical Warfare

The cyanide-based blood agents hydrogen cyanide and cyanogen chloride were studied extensively as potential chemical weapons and used sporadically during World War I. In practice, these compounds were rarely used in military situations because their effectiveness was limited by quick dispersion. Arsine was considered as a potential warfare agent during World War I, but because of the substance's high volatility and chemical instability, weaponization of arsine was abandoned, and arsine has never been used in chemical warfare. During World War II, Nazi Germany used hydrogen cyanide, under the name Zyklon B, as a genocidal agent. Hydrogen cyanide gas, along with other chemical agents, may also have been used during the Iran-Iraq War (1980-1988).

tissues, causing cells to suffocate from lack of oxygen. Arsine works by damaging red blood cells, which also impairs the ability of cells to deliver oxygen throughout the body. The lack of oxygen to tissues and cells can quickly lead to death unless the victim is immediately removed from the toxic atmosphere.

Symptoms of blood agent exposure depend on concentration and duration. Breathing in or ingesting very small amounts of cyanide may have no effects, whereas exposure to somewhat higher concentrations may result in dizziness, weakness, and nausea. If removed from exposure, the person generally will begin to feel better. Over time, exposure to low concentrations can produce mild symptoms followed by permanent brain damage and muscle paralysis. Moderate exposure can result in headache, dizziness, and nausea, symptoms that can last for several hours, and may be followed by convulsions and possible coma. Higher concentrations or longer exposure may also result in convulsions and coma. With very high concentrations, severe toxic effects begin in seconds, and death occurs rapidly.

### Detecting Blood Agents as Causes of Death

Because blood agents prevent adequate utilization of oxygen, the blood of persons exposed to these chemicals is a rich red rather than blue-red. Cyanogen chloride injures the respiratory tract, which results in severe congestion and in-

flammation in the lung. A smell of bitter almonds may be detected. The presence of thiocyanate or cyanide in the blood can also be used to detect cyanide poisoning. Arsine may leave a garlic smell on the victim's breath, but no specific tests have been developed to determine arsine poisoning.

*C. J. Walsh*

### Further Reading

Crippen, James B. *Explosives and Chemical Weapons Identification*. Boca Raton, Fla.: CRC Press, 2005. Provides useful information for first responders on identifying chemical weapons.

Ellison, D. Hank. *Handbook of Chemical and Biological Warfare Agents*. 2d ed. Boca Raton, Fla.: CRC Press, 2007. Excellent reference source for information on agents used in chemical and biological warfare, including blood agents.

Hoenig, Steven L. *Compendium of Chemical Warfare Agents*. New York: Springer, 2007. Describes and discusses the use of various agents that may be employed in chemical warfare, including how they can be identified at scenes of release and in the laboratory.

Wecht, Cyril H., ed. *Forensic Aspects of Chemical and Biological Terrorism*. Tucson, Ariz.: Lawyers & Judges Publishing, 2004. Resource designed for personnel involved in public health and safety includes discussion of the symptoms of chemical exposure.

**See also:** Blood residue and bloodstains; Chemical agents; Chemical terrorism; Chemical warfare; Chemical Weapons Convention of 1993; Crime scene cleaning; Nerve agents; Presumptive tests for blood.

# Blood residue and bloodstains

**Definition:** Wet or dry remnants and areas of discoloration on surfaces resulting from the shedding of blood.

**Significance:** Analysis of bloodstains and other blood residue found at a crime scene can help investigators identify objects used as weapons, reconstruct the events that took place at the scene, and link suspects to the crime.

Blood consists principally of plasma and blood cells. Plasma is the yellowish fluid that carries suspended blood cells called erythrocytes and leukocytes. Erythrocytes, commonly known as red blood cells, get their color from the hemoglobin that carries oxygen from the lungs to the organs and periphery of the body. Mammalian red blood cells do not have nuclei and do not contain DNA (deoxyribonucleic acid), but they do have antigens on their outer membranes that can be used to type the blood. Leukocytes, commonly known as white blood cells, do contain nuclei and do contain DNA that is unique to an individual (with the exception of identical twins, who carry identical DNA); this DNA can be isolated and characterized to identify the source of the blood.

**Because** blood accounts for 8 percent of a healthy person's weight, typically 5 liters (a little more than 5 quarts), and it circulates near the surface of the skin, almost all kinds of trauma to the body result in the loss of blood. At crime scenes, blood's red color generally makes it readily apparent; in cases where attempts have been made to remove it, residues are difficult to eliminate completely. Blood residue has been identified on 100,000-year-old stone tools, and bloodstains left by Confederate soldiers wounded at the Battle of Gettysburg in 1863 have been recovered from between the floorboards of an attic where the soldiers had been hiding.

## Examining a Crime Scene

A dried, but relatively fresh, bloodstain is generally reddish-brown in color and glossy. The gloss eventually disappears under the action of sunlight, wet weather, or attempts to remove the stain, and the color turns gray. The color and gloss of blood may also be affected by the surface on which it is found.

At a crime scene, investigators' search for bloodstains is facilitated by the use of flashlights, which are held so that the light falls at an angle to the surfaces being examined. Presumptive tests for blood are sometimes used when small quantities of fluids suspected to be blood are present, especially if it appears that an attempt has been made to clean the area; these tests are also used to differentiate blood from other stains, such as rust, ketchup, or chocolate syrup.

A crime scene search for blood extends beyond the immediate area of the crime, because bloody fingerprints may have been left in other areas, such as on doorknobs, drawers, or sinks. Towels, draperies, or other fabrics may have been used to wipe blood off hands. If a floor has been cleaned, blood may be found in the cracks or joints in the floor or under the edges of carpets or linoleum. Investigators must search clothing at the scene carefully; even clothes that have been cleaned can contain blood residue in seams or linings, or inside sleeves or pockets. Persons who were present at the scene during the crime may also have bloodstains on their bodies.

Compared with indoor crime scenes, crime scenes that are open to the elements pose many more difficulties for the search for blood. Blood residues may have been obliterated by the weather or may have changed color in contact with soil. At outdoor crime scenes, investigators need to pay special attention to damp areas on the ground and to surfaces such as blades of grass, leaves, and tree branches.

## Description and Recording of Bloodstains

Crime scene investigators record descriptions of all bloodstains found, including information on their forms, colors, sizes, and positions. Information on the physical appearance of bloodstains is best preserved through photography; photographs are usually taken at wide range, medium range, and close up. A scale is included in all close-up shots to show the sizes of the bloodstains or drops pictured.

A rough sketch of the crime scene is also often created to show the relationship of the bloodstains and other blood residue to other elements of the scene. At violent crime scenes, blood spatter evidence is often present, and its analysis can be invaluable in reconstructing how the crime occurred.

## Collection and Preservation

After crime scene bloodstain patterns and distribution have been well documented, the collection and preservation of blood residue and stains may proceed. Because these substances present the possibility of blood-borne disease, such as hepatitis or human immunodeficiency virus (HIV), investigators must be careful to protect themselves from infection. Also, they must take proper care to avoid contaminating the scene or cross-contaminating the samples collected. For collecting blood and other biological samples, investigators wear multiple layers of latex gloves, which they change frequently. Clean equipment is also essential to prevent contamination.

Blood is fragile, and to maintain its properties, investigators must ensure that blood evidence samples are properly preserved. If wet or damp bloodstains are stored in airtight containers, the blood will putrefy and be useless for forensic examination in a matter of days. In contrast, air-dried samples stored at room temperature or, better, under refrigeration will retain their usefulness for a much longer period. Ideally, biological samples should be stored in a frozen state, especially if they cannot be analyzed immediately.

Wet blood may be collected with a sterile disposable pipette or syringe and placed in a tube containing an anticoagulant to keep it from clotting any further. Alternatively, wet blood may be collected from pools of liquid blood with pieces of absorbent material such as filter paper, cotton fabric, or cotton-tipped applicators. Each swab with absorbed blood is placed inside a clean, unstoppered tube to permit it to air-dry. With large bloodstained items, such as carpets or mattresses, investigators may cut out bloodstained areas to transport them to the lab for analysis. As with all evidence collected at a crime scene, each sample must be clearly labeled with information on who collected it and when. An investigator may collect dried blood by scraping the surface on which it is found with a clean razor blade, scalpel, or pocketknife, placing the scrapings in a clean tube. If dried blood cannot be scraped, it may be collected with a fabric swab or cotton-tipped applicator moistened with distilled water (or saline solution). The area of interest is swabbed, and the sample is placed in a clean tube that is left unstoppered to allow the swab to air-dry. The investigator swabs an unaffected area nearby as well, to provide a control sample for analysis. Bloodstains may also be "lifted" using gel lifter or fingerprint tape, if it is determined that the gel or tape will not interfere with subsequent tests.

Bloodstained clothing and other items, such as possible weapons, that can be transported from the scene are often best submitted to the laboratory whole for analysis. Investigators generally air-dry such objects and pack them in wrapping paper or paper bags for transport. They should never be tightly rolled or stored in plastic bags, as this may result in cross-contamination.

## Blood Typing

If presumptive tests indicate the presence of blood at a crime scene, further tests are performed to establish whether it is of human or animal origin. Reaction to appropriate antibody serum definitely establishes the species of origin. In addition, the blood group to which a human blood sample belongs can be established. Although more than twenty-nine human blood group systems are known, the ABO and Rh (or rhesus) groups are commonly used. With respect to the former, blood may be typed as A, B, AB, or O, characterized by the presence of antigen A, antigen B, both antigens, or neither antigen on the surface of red blood cells, respectively. With respect to the Rh group, a sample is either positive or negative for Rh antigen. A person's blood type is inherited and hence unchangeable. Although ABO and Rh blood group analysis does not link a sample to a particular person, it can enable investigators to include or exclude a person of interest as a suspect or victim. Because blood group antigens deteriorate with age or improper storage, samples that have not been collected and stored with care often cannot be typed.

Blood also contains DNA, however, which is less subject to deterioration. Given that DNA testing of bloodstains and other blood residues can provide positive identification of the source of the blood, law-enforcement agencies around the world rely on DNA analysis of any blood and other biological samples recovered from crime scenes.

*James L. Robinson*

## Further Reading

Fisher, Barry A. J. and David R. Fisher. *Techniques of Crime Scene Investigation*. 8th ed. Boca Raton, FL: CRC Press, 2012. Standard text in the field includes a chapter on blood and other biological evidence.

Geberth, Vernon J. *Practical Homicide Investigation: Tactics, Procedures, and Forensic Techniques*. 4th ed. Boca Raton, FL: CRC Press, 2006. Text used in many U.S. police academies provides full coverage of all aspects of homicide investigations, including the collection of blood evidence.

Lee, Henry C., Timothy Palmbach, and Marilyn T. Miller. *Henry Lee's Crime Scene Handbook*. San Diego, Calif.: Academic Press, 2001. Practical guide to crime scene procedures includes a section on the collection, preservation, and analysis of blood.

Lyle, D. P. *Forensic Science*. Chicago, IL: American Bar Association, 2012. Written for lawyers, this book describes the strengths and weaknesses of evidence, including that involving blood and bloodstains.

Tilstone, William J., Kathleen A. Savage, and Leigh A. Clark. *Forensic Science: An Encyclopedia of History, Methods, and Techniques*. Santa Barbara, CA: ABC-CLIO, 2006. Comprehensive work covers the role of blood analysis in forensic investigations, including blood groups, bloodstain identification, blood spatter analysis, and presumptive tests for blood.

Young, Tina and P. J. Ortmeier. *Crime Scene Investigation: the Forensic Technician's Field Guide*. Upper Saddle River, NJ: Pearson/Prentice Hall, 2011. Uses a case study approach to illustrate effective and flawed crime scene investigation, including the collection of blood evidence and its analysis.

**See also:** Biohazard bags; Blood agents; Blood spatter analysis; Blood volume testing; Control samples; Crime scene cleaning; Crime scene investigation; Crime scene protective gear; Crime scene search patterns; DNA typing; Luminol; Multisystem method; Petechial hemorrhage; Presumptive tests for blood; Trace and transfer evidence.

## Blood spatter analysis

**Definition:** Application of the principles of projectile motion to the examination of patterns of human bloodstains.

**Significance:** By analyzing bloodstain patterns (blood spatter) found at crime scenes, forensic scientists can determine such details of crimes as where victims were located when they received the wounds that produced the blood spatter, whether victims were standing or seated when the wounds were inflicted, and even sometimes whether the assailants wielded the weapons in their right or left hands.

Blood spatter analysis is a valuable tool of forensic investigators in the determination of the events that transpired during crimes in which victims received wounds that resulted in bloodstains. Investigators can apply the physical principles of the motion of blood through the air to the patterns of blood droplets found at crime scenes, as well as the droplets' overall shapes, to ascertain the exact locations where victims' wounds were received.

### Blood Spatter Ballistics

Blood is a fluid of constant density that is not affected by temperature, pressure, or other atmospheric conditions when it is in flight. The large surface tension of blood drops holds them together during their time of flight, and as they move through the air, the drops assume a spherical shape. Blood spatter patterns are influenced by the distance the blood travels through the air and the material with which it comes in contact.

A blood drop that falls straight down from its ejection point will project a circular stain on the material that absorbs it. In contrast, a blood drop that travels an extended distance from the source of the wound will follow a parabolic path, striking any surface it meets at an angle. When this angle of impact is not 90 degrees measured with respect to the horizontal surface (which would be a straight-down motion), the blood drop will leave an elongated (elliptical-shape) stain on the surface that it strikes. The more pointed end of the stain will be in the direction the blood drop was traveling.

## Analysis of Blood Spatter

The patterns of bloodstains observed on surfaces provide evidence of the points of impact of wounds and the force of the punctures. Crime scene investigators can use the directionality of bloodstain patterns to work backward toward the two-dimensional point on the surface level with the blood spatter to identify the point of ejection and distance from the wound. (Given that the pointed ends of blood drops indicate the direction of travel, the more rounded ends converge toward the point of origin.) In the early days of blood spatter analysis, crime scene investigators laid out series of strings or wooden rods in the diverging direction of a blood spatter pattern to determine the convergent point. Modern forensic tools include computer software packages that use the data of the coordinates of blood spatter to determine the point of emergence of the blood drops.

In addition to the two-dimensional determination of the victim's position when the injury occurred, the blood spatter analyst can estimate the vertical position of the wound from the angle of impact of the blood spatter. This can provide evidence in terms of whether the victim was standing, sitting, or lying down at the time of the injury.

In examining a bloodstain, a forensic investigator measures its length and width. The angle of impact is then determined by the

trigonometric relation involving the sine of the angle:

$$\mathrm{Sin}(a) = w/l,$$

where $w$ is the width of the bloodstain, $l$ is its length, and $a$ is the angle of impact. Solving this equation for the angle $a$ (inverse sine) can determine where above the surface level the wound was inflicted. Using the results from the two-dimensional analysis that identifies how far away the victim was from the blood spatter pattern, the analyst can use this equation to solve for the height (third coordinate) where the point of puncture occurred. (In actuality, this can determine only the maximum height the victim was at the moment the wound occurred, because the action of gravity tends to change the shape of the blood's trajectory from straight-line motion.)

Analysis of bloodstains that are determined to have come from the tip of a weapon, such as a knife, can provide another kind of evidence. Passive bloodstains are drops caused only by the action of gravity, with no external force projecting the droplets forward. Such blood spatter appears as small circular drops. If these drops show a rotational sense (that is, if they curve either right or left), this directionality can indicate which of the assailant's hands the weapon was in at the time of the assault, providing information on whether the attacker was right-handed or left-handed.

## Obstacles to Useful Analysis

The major problem faced by forensic scientists attempting to conduct blood spatter analysis is that many crime scenes lack well-defined blood spatter patterns even when blood is present. Difficulties may arise because of the effects of blood on different surfaces, because smaller blood droplets have broken off from larger droplets, because the victim moved after the injury and disturbed the initial spatter pattern, or simply because of the overall chaos of an environment where a violent crime has been committed. In such cases, often the only substantive evidence that can be gained from bloodstains involves identification of victims and possibly assailants through the blood types found at the crime scene and through analysis of DNA (deoxyribonucleic acid) extracted from the blood found.

*Joseph Di Rienzi*

### Further Reading

Adams, Thomas F., Alan G. Caddell, and Jeffery L. Krutsinger. *Crime Scene Investigation.* 2d ed. Upper Saddle River, N.J.: Prentice Hall, 2004. Handbook for law-enforcement professionals includes a chapter titled "Evidence Collection" that has an informative section on blood and blood analysis.

Bennett, Wayne W., and Kären M. Hess. *Criminal Investigation.* 8th ed. Belmont, Calif.: Wadsworth/Thomson Learning, 2007. Comprehensive textbook provides in-depth discussion of forensic techniques and procedures. Includes checklists and questions at the ends of chapters to highlight the most important ideas presented.

Camenson, Blythe. *Opportunities in Forensic Science Careers.* Chicago: VGM Career Books, 2001. Presents accounts of professionals working in forensic science and identifies the education needed and the job responsibilities related to various disciplines within forensics.

James, Stuart H., and Jon J. Nordby, eds. *Forensic Science: An Introduction to Scientific and Investigative Techniques.* 2d ed. Boca Raton, Fla.: CRC Press, 2005. Comprehensive introductory textbook uses many case studies to illustrate crime investigation methodologies. Includes a section on recognition of bloodstain patterns.

Nickell, Joe, and John F. Fischer. *Crime Science: Methods of Forensic Detection.* Lexington: University Press of Kentucky, 1999. Very thorough examination of forensic investigative work includes discussion of blood spatter analysis.

**See also:** Ballistics; Biohazard bags; Blood residue and bloodstains; Blood volume testing; Crime scene investigation; Crime scene sketching and diagramming; Defensive wounds; Gunshot wounds; Knife wounds; Luminol; Presumptive tests for blood; Puncture wounds; Serology; Simpson murder trial.

## Blood volume testing

**Definition:** Technique used to determine how much blood has been shed at crime scenes and accident scenes.

**Significance:** Forensic examiners can learn much about the wounds inflicted on victims of crimes from the volume of blood found at crime scenes. Blood volume testing may also be used to determine whether wounds were inflicted on victims at locations other than where the victims were ultimately found.

When blood is present at a crime or accident scene, a forensic team attempts to collect the blood or at least to determine how much blood was spilled at the scene. The human body generally contains about 5 liters (a little more than 5 quarts) of blood, but this amount is affected by factors such as body size and amount of fat tissue. The volume of blood present at a crime scene—and, sometimes, the blood spatter pattern—can inform investigators as to the types, depths, and seriousness of the wounds that caused the blood loss. Blood volume testing may also help to determine whether a victim has been moved—that is, if the amount of blood found at the scene is not consistent with the victim's loss of blood, it is likely the victim was moved after the wounds were inflicted.

Any blood present at a crime scene is collected (or collection is at least attempted) and sent to a forensic laboratory for typing and identification. Fresh blood is collected in plastic containers. Dried blood may be collected in various ways: Fabrics with dried bloodstains may be transported to the lab, and sticky tape, such as fingerprint tape, may be used to peel spots of dried blood away from hard surfaces. Dried blood may also be collected with swabs or pieces of sterile cloth that have been moistened with distilled water or saline solution.

At the laboratory, a forensic scientist can estimate the blood volume found at the crime scene by determining how many red blood cells are present in the collected blood and then calculating how much whole blood would contain that many red blood cells. Alternatively, the scientist can determine how much plasma was left behind and calculate a blood volume from that figure.

When no body or victim is found at a crime scene where blood is present, knowing the volume of blood shed at the scene can help investigators determine what kind of wound was inflicted; for example, a minor cut produces only a small volume of blood, whereas a deep stab wound or an arterial puncture is likely to produce copious amounts of blood. A blood volume test can also help determine how much time was necessary for the amount of blood present to be left behind.

*Marianne M. Madsen*

### Further Reading

Geberth, Vernon J. *Practical Homicide Investigation: Tactics, Procedures, and Forensic Techniques*. 4th ed. Boca Raton, Fla.: CRC Press, 2006.

Genge, N. E. *The Forensic Casebook: The Science of Crime Scene Investigation*. New York: Ballantine, 2002.

Platt, Richard. *Crime Scene: The Ultimate Guide to Forensic Science*. New York: Dorling Kindersley, 2003.

**See also:** Blood residue and bloodstains; Blood spatter analysis; Crime scene investigation; Crime scene search patterns; Crime scene sketching and diagramming; Presumptive tests for blood.

## Bloody Sunday

**Date:** January 30, 1972

**The Event:** During a civil rights march in the Roman Catholic section of Londonderry, Northern Ireland, British army troops shot twenty-six marchers, thirteen of whom died immediately. A fourteenth shooting victim died several months later.

**Significance:** One of the most significant episodes in the long, violent conflict between the Catholic and Protestant factions in Northern Ireland, Bloody Sunday was met with outrage in both local and international communities and led to a dramatic increase in support for the Irish Republican Army (IRA) in Northern Ireland. Meanwhile, in response to charges that the British soldiers had fired without provocation, the British government quickly launched an investigation to determine who had fired the first shots. The official report that came from the investigation exonerated the soldiers, but its findings were criticized because of the commission's questionable handling of forensic evidence.

Two days after the Bloody Sunday shootings, the British parliament ordered an investigation under Baron Widgery, the lord chief justice of England and Wales. The report of the Widgery Tribunal supported the account of the event given by the army, which claimed that marchers began the incident by firing weapons and hurling explosives at the soldiers. The evidence considered by the tribunal included the results of paraffin tests used to identify bullet-lead residues from the weapons that fired the fatal shots, along with nail bombs that had been recovered from one of the bodies. Preliminary tests for traces of explosives on the clothes of all but one of the victims of the shootings proved negative. The clothes of the remaining victim could not be tested as they had already been compromised by careless handling. The report offered no analyses of the individual shots fired by the soldiers.

The Bloody Sunday massacre intensified the campaign of the Provisional Irish Republican Army (PIRA) against British occupation of Northern Ireland and helped to win more public support for PIRA among Roman Catholics. The massacre helped to aggravate two decades of anti-British rioting in Northern Ireland and attacks on British economic targets and social institutions.

The findings of the Widgery Tribunal remained controversial in the 1990's. In 1998, British prime minister Tony Blair ordered the formation of a second commission of inquiry to reevaluate evidence from Bloody Sunday. Assembled under the chairmanship of Lord Saville, the new commission completed its hearings in November, 2004. Although the full report of the Saville Inquiry was not published as late as mid-2008, it is considered to be a more comprehensive study than that of the Widgery Tribunal. Its evidence, which included witness testimonies from local residents, soldiers, journalists, and politicians, appears to call into question the credibility of the Widgery Tribunal's report. At the center of the controversy is the new report's finding that forensic evidence collected from shooting victims' bodies may have been contaminated when bodies of shooting victims were placed alongside weapons and explosives. That finding appears to contradict the original report's conclusion that trace evidence found on the bodies indicated that the shooting victims had themselves used firearms or explosives.

## Investigations

The march that ended in the Bloody Sunday shootings began as a protest rally organized in Londonderry by the Northern Ireland Civil Rights Association to demand an end to the internment without trial of suspected IRA terrorists. Reports of the number of participants in the march are conflicting. Some observers estimated there were twenty thousand marchers; however, the Widgery Report estimated there were only three to five thousand marchers.

The marchers initially walked toward the Bogside area of Londonderry (which is also known as Derry). There, local residents joined the protest, and the marchers were redirected to another street to avoid army blockades. A planned highlight of the march was to have been a speech by the Irish nationalist Bernadette Devlin, who then held a Northern Ireland seat in Great Britain's Parliament. Around 3:30 ., however, a small number of young men began throwing stones and hurling insults at troops manning the army barricades that had been erected to contain the march. The troops initially responded with tear gas grenades, fire hoses, and rubber bullets. When the paratroopers began crossing the barricades to arrest demonstrators, they met such strong resistance that

they feared for their own safety and began firing real bullets into the crowd. Within twenty minutes, thirteen young, unarmed men were dead. At least eighteen other people were seriously injured. The paratroopers later justified their actions by claiming that they had been fired on, but evidence in support of their claim was controversial.

## Forensic Issues

The central question in the Bloody Sunday massacre that remains to be resolved is whether the solders who shot the marchers were attacked by firearms and nail bombs before they began shooting into the marchers. The weight of known evidence says no. Eyewitness accounts by civilians do not support that finding; no soldiers were injured during the confrontation, and no civilian firearms were found. Additionally, the initial investigation into the shootings found no conclusive proof that the marchers who were shot had even handled firearms. Moreover, there was no evidence that the Irish Republican Army was then planning to provoke the British military. Nevertheless, the initial investigation did not call eyewitnesses and did not take testimony from survivors. The investigation's interpretation of forensic evidence was believed to be inaccurate and incomplete. Nonetheless, Lord Widgery concluded from the traces of firearm residue found on the bodies of the men who had been shot to death that some of them, at least, had been in close contact with firearms or explosives.

*Elizabeth K. Hayden*

## Further Reading

Coates, Tim. *Bloody Sunday: Lord Widgery's Report 1972.* London: Stationary Office Books, 2001. Reprints the report of the first government commission to investigate the shootings.

Dunn, Seamus, ed. *Facets of the Conflict in Northern Ireland.* New York: St. Martin's Press, 1995. Collection of scholarly articles highlights fundamentals of politics in Northern Ireland. Selected authors—funded by the Centre for the Study of Conflict, University of Ulster—address the social, legal, political, and economic ramifications of the events that have shaped Irish history.

Hayes, Patrick Joseph, and Jim Campbell. *Bloody Sunday: Trauma, Pain, and Politics.* Ann Arbor, Mich.: Pluto Press, 2005. Covers the political and psychological aspects of the incident. Based on interviews with families of those killed by British soldiers.

Holland, Jack. *Hope Against History: The Course of Conflict in Northern Ireland.* New York: Henry Holt, 1999. Engaging narrative covers the origins of IRA and loyalist paramilitary groups, the events of Bloody Sunday, the Northern Ireland civil rights movement, and attempts to settle the conflict. Illuminates the experiences of both Protestant and Catholic communities in Northern Ireland.

McClean, Raymond. *The Road to Bloody Sunday.* 2d ed. Londonderry, Northern Ireland: Guildhall Press, 1997. Presents the eyewitness account of a medical doctor who treated shooting victims on Bloody Sunday.

Mullan, Don, and John Scally, eds. *Eyewitness: Bloody Sunday.* Rev. ed. Dublin, Ireland: Merlin, 2002. Contains testimonies by both soldiers and marchers at the incident. Many of the eyewitness accounts in this collection dispute the conclusions of the Widgery Report. Includes a foreword written by film director Paul Greengrass, whose 2002 film *Bloody Sunday* is based on this work.

**See also:** Ballistic fingerprints; Ballistics; Bombings; Bullet-lead analysis; Firearms analysis; Gunshot residue; Improvised explosive devices; Interrogation.

# Blunt force trauma

**Definition:** Trauma caused to a body part by a blunt instrument or surface through physical impact, injury, or attack.

**Significance:** By examining the types of injuries incurred by a victim of blunt force trauma, forensic scientists may be able to determine the cause of the accident or crime that resulted in the injuries as well as what type of instrument caused the injuries.

"Blunt force trauma" is a general term that covers trauma to the body from a variety of sources. Blunt force trauma, also known as blunt trauma, results when the body is struck by an object or when the body strikes an object. When a forensic scientist is asked to investigate blunt force trauma, it is usually to determine what instrument or event caused the injuries—for example, to determine whether the injuries resulted from a beating as opposed to a fall. Blunt force trauma to the body is not always life-threatening (unless organs or blood vessels rupture), but blunt force trauma to the head may cause death. Injuries that indicate blunt force trauma include lacerated blood vessels (including major vessels such as the aorta), lacerated or crushed organs, hematomas, contusions, crushed or fractured bones, and severed spinal cord.

## Causes

Blunt force trauma is often caused by motor vehicle accidents in which the body is slammed into a steering wheel or dashboard. This slamming action, caused by the rapid deceleration of the vehicle, may cause contusions or rupturing of internal organs. Another common type of blunt force trauma is an accidental fall. The many other possible causes of blunt force trauma include assault by another person (through clubbing with an object, hitting, kicking, or punching) and sporting accidents.

When blunt force trauma is caused by a beating or clubbing, the type of weapon used by the assailant can often be identified by the characteristics of the wound. If the wound shows characteristics that can identify only a class of instrument (as opposed to the specific type of instrument) as the weapon, such as a bone fracture showing smooth, curved lines that could have been made by any smooth weapon, these are called "class characteristics" of the weapon. At times, however, a specific weapon can be identified by the distinctive marks it has left on skin, bone, or other tissues. For instance, a hammer that had individualized marks of wear on it before it was used to inflict wounds could leave those specific marks on the victim. These are called "individual characteristics" of the weapon.

A single weapon can also cause a variety of wounds. For example, if a shovel is used as a weapon, it may cause a large flat wound if the back of the shovel is used. The same shovel wielded so that its side or blade struck the victim would produce a sharp, linear wound.

In addition to examination of the victim's injuries, blood spatter analysis can provide clues as to the type of weapon used in a situation involving blunt force trauma, the strength of the person wielding the weapon, and the relative spacing of the victim and the attacker.

## Injuries

Abdominal trauma is the most common type of blunt force trauma, and the liver, spleen, and small intestine can be affected. This often happens during a car accident, which may cause organ rupture.

Abrasions, or scrapes, are also often seen in cases of blunt force trauma. These injuries result when the skin is forcefully rubbed away by a rough surface, such as asphalt. Abrasions are usually only surface injuries. Lacerations may also occur; these can be either external or internal injuries, damaging the skin and penetrating into other tissues deeper within the body, such as muscles or organs.

In addition to other head injuries, such as skull fracture, that can result from blunt force trauma, the brain can also be damaged by the force of the blow. This can cause damage to the nerve cells deep inside the brain, even when there is no breaking of the skin.

Contusions, or bruises, from blunt force trauma can be either internal or external injuries. Bruises happen when blood vessels are damaged and begin to leak blood into surrounding tissues. Bruising on the skin surface shows up as swelling of the tissues and dark shades of color (blue, red, or purple). The amount of discoloration can vary with a person's age and weight: Older people and those who are heavier may show more bruising than younger and less heavy people. Deep bruising caused by extreme blunt force can occur so far inside the body that nothing shows on the surface; such injuries can

be seen only with the aid of technologies such as magnetic resonance imaging (MRI). Contusions of the brain may not be noticeable at all from surface injuries; they may manifest themselves only through neurological symptoms such as confusion and weakness.

*Marianne M. Madsen*

## Further Reading

DiMaio, Vincent J. M., and Suzanna E. Dana. *Handbook of Forensic Pathology.* 2d ed. Boca Raton, Fla.: CRC Press, 2007. Comprehensive volume discusses common issues in forensic pathology, including determination of instruments in blunt force trauma situations.

Ferllini, Roxana, ed. *Forensic Archaeology and Human Rights Violations.* Springfield, Ill.: Charles C Thomas, 2007. Collection of essays by experts in various disciplines includes discussion of the forensic examination of bodies subjected to blunt force trauma and other deadly injuries in human rights violation cases.

Moore, Ernest E., Kenneth L. Mattox, and David V. Feliciano. *Trauma Manual.* 4th ed. New York: McGraw-Hill, 2003. Focuses mostly on trauma surgery, but discusses blunt force trauma in surgical situations.

Shkrum, Michael J., and David A. Ramsay. *Forensic Pathology of Trauma: Common Problems for the Pathologist.* Totowa, N.J.: Humana Press, 2007. Addresses common trauma patterns, including determination of blunt force trauma, in forensic settings.

Wilson, William C., Christopher M. Grande, and David B. Hoyt, eds. *Trauma: Critical Care.* Vol. 2. New York: Informa Healthcare, 2007. Discusses the determination of types of blunt force trauma and wound analysis.

**See also:** Antemortem injuries; Blood residue and bloodstains; Blood spatter analysis; Child abuse; Crime scene investigation; Defensive wounds; Driving injuries; Forensic anthropology; Osteology and skeletal radiology; Peruvian Ice Maiden; Physical evidence; Skeletal analysis.

# Body farms

**Definition:** Outdoor facilities that allow forensic anthropologists to study postmortem decomposition of human remains.

**Significance:** Research conducted at body farms helps the practitioners of a number of forensic disciplines—including medical examiners, crime scene investigators, and law-enforcement personnel—with the identification of human remains.

The first body farm was established in 1972 by Dr. William M. Bass at the University of Tennessee in Knoxville. Shortly after he moved to Tennessee, Bass was asked to join the staff of the state's medical examiner's office as state forensic anthropologist. Part of Bass's duties in this position included consulting on death investigations being conducted by federal, state, and local law-enforcement agencies. Although Bass had extensive training in forensic anthropology, he did not have a lot of knowledge about or experience with the decomposition of human remains. In addition, research in this area was nearly nonexistent. This need led Bass and his colleagues to open the University of Tennessee Anthropological Research Facility, which came to be known as the Body Farm.

## Purpose of Body Farms

The research conducted on body farms allows forensic anthropologists to study the postmortem decomposition of human remains. This work is important for a number of reasons. First, it helps scientists to gain a more comprehensive understanding of what occurs to the body after death and thus to develop better methods of determining the "time since death" in specific cases. Time since death, or the postmortem interval, is a critical element in homicide investigations, as law-enforcement officers or crime scene investigators must often confirm or disprove the alibis of potential suspects.

Second, the research on body farms provides information that is useful to forensic anthropologists and medical examiners who must identify bodies from skeletal remains. By examining a set of skeletal remains, a forensic anthropolo-

gist or medical examiner can determine a great deal about the decedent, including age, sex, stature, ancestry, and the presence of unique features. Body farm research also provides information that can help examiners to determine the cause of death in individual cases. In homicide investigations, law-enforcement officers or crime scene investigators need to know whether the decedents have died of natural causes or whether they have been the victims of foul play.

When the University of Tennessee's Anthropological Research Facility first began its work, almost no research had been done documenting what happens to the human body after death. Even the most rudimentary questions—for example, When do blowflies show up on a body? How long does it take for a corpse to become a skeleton?—could not be answered. As the Body Farm's studies progressed, the questions became more sophisticated: How do decomposition rates differ between sunshine and shade? How do climate differences (cool versus hot) affect decomposition rates? How is decomposition affected when bodies are buried in shallow graves as opposed to left on top of the ground? Do bodies decompose faster in water than they do on land? How do bodies decompose in vehicles? What effects do other variables—such as clothing, body weight, and condition of the body—have on rates of decomposition?

## What Happens to Bodies

The University of Tennessee's body farm occupies a three-acre tract of land situated near the University of Tennessee Medical Center; it is surrounded by razor wire and a wooden privacy fence. When a corpse arrives at the facility, it is assigned an identification number to ensure the confidentiality of the donor. The body is then examined and its condition is thoroughly documented. Bodies are placed in various environmental conditions across the property. For example, some bodies are placed in car trunks, some are left lying in the sun or shade, some are buried in shallow graves, some are covered with brush, and some are submerged in water.

Two things happen when a body decays. At death, enzymes in the digestive system, having no more nutrition, begin to eat on the body and the tissues liquefy. This process is known as putrefaction. Insects gather on the body, and maggots consume the rotting flesh. At the University of Tennessee, forensic anthropologists Dr. Richard Jantz and his wife, Dr. Lee Meadow Jantz, document such insect activity and how long it takes the insects to do their work. Most of the characteristics used to determine time since death are related to insect activity.

After the bodies at the Tennessee facility have completed the decomposition process, the bones are cleaned and measured, and the data are entered into the University of Tennessee's Forensic Anthropology Data Bank, which was created by Dr. Richard Jantz. This database is the primary tool that forensic anthropologists use to determine age, sex, stature, ancestry, and other unique characteristics from skeletal remains. The database is the central component of a computer program called FORDISC (for Forensic Discrimination). The FORDISC software is used all over the world as a tool to assist in the identification of bodies. For example, a medical examiner or anthropologist can enter a few skeletal measurements and the program can predict with a fairly high degree of accuracy the age, race, sex, height, and ancestry of the decedent. The bones are then cataloged and added to the William M. Bass Donated Skeletal Collection, which is the largest modern bone collection in the United States.

## Sources of Bodies

The bodies studied at body farms come from three primary sources. First, bodies are often donated through state medical examiners' offices. For instance, if a body comes through a county medical examiner's office and it ends up unclaimed—either because the decedent is never identified or because the decedent had no friends or relatives to claim the body—the medical examiner may choose to send it to a body farm for decomposition research or for addition to the facility's skeletal collection. Second, family members who are aware of the valuable research conducted at body farms and who are genuinely interested in furthering the cause of science may choose to donate the bodies of loved ones. Third, some people make the decision before their deaths to donate their bodies to body farms; by completing donor consent forms, they

ensure that their wishes are carried out.

Body farms do not accept the corpses of persons who were infected with the human immunodeficiency virus (HIV), with hepatitis, or with antibiotic-resistant bacteria. These facilities will accept the donation of anyone's bones, however.

## Impact of the University of Tennessee's Body Farm

The success of the research conducted at the Body Farm in Tennessee inspired the opening of other body farms in the United States and abroad. Western Carolina University in Cullowhee, North Carolina, created a body farm in 2006 as part of the Western Carolina Human Identification Laboratory. The facility is run by the university's forensic anthropology program on several acres of land near the campus. Like the original Body Farm, the North Carolina facility studies the decomposition of human remains. Researchers at the facility hope to learn more about the decomposition of bodies in the western Carolina mountain terrain, which is very different from the terrain of eastern Tennessee. They are interested in discovering whether these differences may affect rates of decomposition and suggest that it is important to study postmortem decomposition in a variety of geographic locations.

Texas State University planned to have a body farm operational by the fall of 2007, but completion of the facility, which will be run by the San Marcos Department of Anthropology, part of the Forensic Anthropology Center at Texas State, was delayed by objections from residents in the area and concerns about the presence of buzzards, which might interfere with flight operations at a nearby airport. Researchers at Texas State are interested in learning about rates of decomposition in Texas, where both geography and climate are significantly different from those of western Carolina and eastern Tennessee. Differences in climates may well be found to affect the rates of decomposition in human remains.

Other body farms are in various stages of planning and development across the United States, including in California, Florida, Kansas, and Iowa. In India, a student, Roma Kahn,

## The Body Farm in Popular Culture

The University of Tennessee's Anthropological Research Facility came to widespread public attention, and gained its nickname, with the 1994 publication of Patricia Cornwell's novel *The Body Farm*. In 2003, the nonfiction book *Death's Acre: Inside the Legendary Forensic Lab the Body Farm Where the Dead Do Tell Tales*, by Bill Bass and Jon Jefferson, increased the public's knowledge of the work done on body farms. In addition, author Mary Roach visited the Tennessee facility and included discussion of its work in a chapter of her 2003 nonfiction book *Stiff: The Curious Lives of Human Cadavers*. Since coming to the attention of television writers, body farms have figured as settings in several episodes of crime and suspense shows, including *CSI: Crime Scene Investigation*, *Law & Order: Special Victims Unit*, and *The Dead Zone*.

who received a master's degree in forensic archaeology from Bournemouth University in England, has been conducting preliminary work on the decomposition of cattle. She hopes to open a facility to study human decomposition in India, modeled along the lines of the body farms operating in the United States.

Dr. Bass and the faculty of the University of Tennessee's Department of Anthropology have played a key role in shaping the field of forensic anthropology. It has been estimated that as of 2007, the University of Tennessee was responsible for the education of some 25 percent of the board-certified forensic anthropologists in the United States. Entry into the forensic anthropology program at the University of Tennessee is highly competitive, with roughly sixty students applying for the fewer than ten doctoral positions available annually. The University of Tennessee's Forensic Anthropology Center also inspired the formation of the National Forensic Academy (NFA), one of the leading law-enforcement investigation training centers in the United States. The NFA offers an intensive ten-week training program designed to educate law-enforcement agents in evidence identification, collection, and preservation. The primary goal of the NFA is to prepare law-enforcement officers to recognize crucial components of crime scenes and improve the process of evidence recovery and submission.

## Opposition to Body Farms

Although the research conducted at body farms has undoubtedly contributed a great deal to the field of forensic anthropology, some people are disturbed by the idea of such facilities in their neighborhoods. At the heart of many debates is the placement of body farms. Residents who live near proposed sites often protest the opening of these facilities for a variety of reasons, including fears that insects will be attracted to the area or that scavenging animals will carry off body parts, perhaps dropping them in residents' backyards.

When Texas State University proposed placing its body farm about two miles from the San Marcos Outlet Mall, one of the biggest tourist attractions in the area, local government officials objected, saying that the mall's businesses would likely be hurt by their proximity to such a facility. The University of Tennessee's Body Farm was subject to similar opposition in its early days. Members of a local health care advocacy group called Solutions to Issues of Concern to Knoxvillians (SICK) protested at the research facility, holding up signs proclaiming, "This makes us SICK." A number of local residents also complained about the odor emitted from the Body Farm. The primary point of contention, however, was that the facility was not completely fenced in, and some people could see the decaying bodies from their homes. The university solved this problem by agreeing to install a privacy fence.

*Kimberly D. Dodson*

## Further Reading

Bass, Bill, and Jon Jefferson. *Beyond the Body Farm: A Legendary Bone Detective Explores Murders, Mysteries, and the Revolution in Forensic Science*. New York: William Morrow, 2007. Examines the forensic science employed in a number of cases and discusses advances in forensic anthropology.

_____. *Death's Acre: Inside the Legendary Forensic Lab the Body Farm Where the Dead Do Tell Tales.* New York: G. P. Putnam's Sons, 2003. Traces the development of the University of Tennessee's body farm and presents real-life accounts of forensic cases.

Hallcox, Jarrett, and Amy Welch. *Bodies We've Buried: Inside the National Forensic Academy, the World's Top CSI Training School.* New York: Berkley Books, 2006. Describes the National Forensic Academy's ten-week training course for law-enforcement agents. Topics of the training include the identification, collection, and preservation of evidence.

Roach, Mary. *Stiff: The Curious Lives of Human Cadavers.* New York: W. W. Norton, 2003. Discusses the evolution of the study of human decomposition as well as the use and handling of corpses. Profiles the University of Tennessee's Anthropological Research Facility.

**See also:** Adipocere; Autopsies; Crime scene investigation; *CSI: Crime Scene Investigation*; Decomposition of bodies; Evidence processing; Forensic anthropology; Forensic entomology; Forensic pathology; Osteology and skeletal radiology; Skeletal analysis; Taphonomy; University of Tennessee Anthropological Research Facility.

---

## Body Fluid Trace Analysis

**Definition:** The identification of trace amounts of body fluids.

**Significance:** Body fluids are commonly encountered at crime scenes and represent important evidence, although they are often present in trace amounts. Historically, most serological and DNA tests required relatively large amounts of body fluid, however advances in technology have resulted in much more sensitive tests, allowing for the analysis of trace samples.

Body fluid found at a crime scene can be valuable evidence, as it may provide information indicating both the events that occurred (e.g. blood stains indicate a violent incident; semen suggests a sexual encounter/assault), and the identity of the individuals involved.

Many body fluids are not visible, and require enhancement to locate and identify them. Body fluids encountered at crime scenes include blood, semen, vaginal fluid, and saliva.

### Traditional Approaches for Identifying Body Fluids

There are many well-established serological methods for body fluid identification, including chemical tests, catalytic activity assays, immunological tests, and microscopy, most of which can be categorized as either presumptive or confirmatory. Presumptive tests are designed to be fast and simple so they can be conducted at the crime scene, giving a quick indication of whether or not a body fluid may be present, however they may react with other substances resulting in a false positive. Confirmatory tests are more involved and are generally performed at the crime laboratory to positively confirm the identification of a body fluid.

Presumptive tests are typically more sensitive than confirmatory tests, and are therefore more likely to succeed when testing trace samples. Common presumptive tests for blood include tetramethylbenzidine (TMB) and phenolphthalein. Both are colorimetric tests, in which a chemical reaction with iron in blood results in the appearance of a blue or pink color respectively. TMB and phenolphthalein are both sensitive tests, capable of reacting with dilutions of blood as low as 1:10,000 to 1:1,000,000. These types of dilutions may be encountered at a crime scene when an assailant attempts to clean up visible bloodstains.

The most common presumptive test for semen detects acid phosphatase, an enzyme present at high levels in seminal fluid. This enzyme catalyzes a chemical reaction that can be combined with a color developer to produce a color change. Using the traditional method of acid phosphatase testing, in which potential seminal stains are first transferred to a cotton swab or piece of filter paper, dilutions of 1:1000 can produce a positive result. A more recent method of applying the reagents directly to the stain has proven to be even more sensitive, capable of detecting dilutions of 1:3000.

The microscopic visualization of spermatozoa is the most common confirmatory test for semen, in which the detection of even one sperm is considered a positive result. In trace samples, microscopically locating sperm on a slide can be difficult and time consuming using traditional techniques. A newer method employing fluorescent staining, in which sperm appear bright against a dark background, can greatly aid in the identification of a single sperm.

## Emerging Approaches for Identifying Body Fluids

A relatively new and now commonly used method to quickly identify body fluids is through the use of immunological test strips. These tests use antibodies to target proteins found in specific body fluids; a positive result is indicated by the appearance of a colored line at the test site, similar to a home pregnancy test. The strips are favored for their low limits of detection, which are often below 1 ìL of body fluid, as well as their specificity for human samples.

Many highly sensitive methods for identifying body fluids are being developed which utilize RNA. Though generally considered unstable, one study showed that messenger RNA markers from blood and saliva stains were stable after 18 months (depending on heat and humidity). Several assays have been developed that utilize a number of body tissue specific RNAs to identify blood, semen, saliva, vaginal fluid, and menstrual blood. Such assays are highly specific and sensitive, capable of detecting as little as 200 pg input RNA. However, these assays typically target RNAs that are 200 – 300 nucleotides in length, and are therefore not optimal for highly degraded samples.

The use of micro RNA as a forensic biomarker for body fluid identification is also being considered. Micro RNAs are small non-coding RNAs, 20 – 25 nucleotides in length, which makes them promising targets for degraded samples. Micro RNA assays are extremely sensitive, requiring as little as 50 pg input RNA to obtain a positive result. Several real time PCR assays have been developed for use with forensic samples, utilizing hundreds of different micro RNAs, however because reproducibility remains a problem these tests are not yet ready for use in forensic laboratories.

New methods for identifying body fluids have also been developed that make use of tissue specific DNA methylation patterns. These extremely sensitive techniques have been used to identify blood, menstrual blood, semen, vaginal fluid, and saliva from as little as 31 pg of DNA.

*David R. Foran*

## Further Reading

An, J.H., K. Shin, W.I. Yang, and H.Y. Lee. "Body Fluid Identification in Forensics." *Biochemistry and Molecular Biology Reports* 45 (2012): 545 – 553. Review of current and emerging techniques for the identification of body fluids.

Cox, M. "A Study of the Sensitivity and Specificity of Four Presumptive Blood Tests." *Journal of Forensic Sciences* 36 (1991): 1503 – 1511. A comparison of the sensitivity of four presumptive blood tests.

Lewis, J., et al. "Analysis of Body Fluids for Forensic Purposes: From Laboratory Testing to Non-Destructive Rapid Confirmatory Identification at a Crime Scene." *Science and Justice* 53 (2013): 385 – 394. A comparison of direct and indirect acid phosphatase testing methods and sensitivity.

Silva, Sarah S., et al. "Forensic miRNA: Potential Biomarker for Body Fluids?." *Forensic Science International: Genetics* 14 (2015): 1 – 10. Overview of research in the use of miRNA in forensic body fluid identification.

**See Also:** Blood residue and bloodstains; DNA analysis; Rape; Saliva; Semen and sperm.

## Bomb damage assessment

**Definition:** Assessment of the severity of blast effects caused by explosions.

**Significance:** By conducting bomb damage assessment, investigators can aid in the identification of explosive devices or explosive propellants. Such analysis can also provide information on bomb delivery systems and their targeting accuracy.

An explosive device is designed to release large amounts of energy quickly from a concentrated source. The explosion results from the reaction of a solid or liquid chemical or vapor that forms highly pressurized gases, propagating an outward-moving pressure wave. In a high-explosive detonation, the speed of the reaction is faster than the speed of sound, 5,000 to 8,000 meters (about 16,000 to 26,000 feet) per second. Such an explosion produces an intense shock wave that expands within milliseconds of detonation. The effects of explosions vary, but the initial destructive effects on targets are directly related to stress-wave propagation, pressure-driven phenomena resulting in the impact and penetration of propelled objects, ground-transmitted shock, and explosion-generated effects such as fire, smoke, dust, and pressure damage to organs and tissue.

A bomb detonation can have catastrophic effects, destroying or severely damaging its intended human or material targets. The amount of damage done by a detonated bomb depends on the nature and size of the explosive device and its location relative to its target. Additional factors relate to specifics of the target, such as materials and construction, surroundings, and the proximity of potential victims. Bomb damage to targets is the direct result of explosive detonation involving shock-wave blast pressure and high-speed impact from ejected target materials, shrapnel, and debris. The postdetonation distribution of these materials reflects physical processes and properties that can be measured and correlated directly to the initiating explosive device.

The physical and chemical characteristics of explosions and their structural by-products are well defined by known scaling laws and equations of state, and any explosion can ultimately be referenced by its geometry, density, and temperature. As the result of more than one hundred years of testing, a large cross-referenced database has been compiled regarding the major and minor damage potential of shock waves generated by explosions. Most blast data come

from unclassified war documentation, industrial records, scientific and engineering research, and forensic analyses. These data correlate explosive type and quantity to blast pressure, detonation velocity, target strata, ground shock, atmospheric conditions, target distance, target materials, above- or below-ground penetration, and confined or unconfined conditions. Blast injuries from explosive shock waves include body displacement, dismemberment, ruptured eardrums and internal organs, and tissue destruction from propelled objects; the extent of such injuries has been well documented, cataloged, and correlated according to detonation proximity.

As explosions involve predictable quantitative chemical and physical signatures, after a bombing forensic scientists can determine the size and type of device detonated and its effectiveness. In addition to conducting trace chemical analyses to identify the explosives used, the scientists examine such elements as the dimensions of the blast area and crater, the target's materials, weather conditions at the time of the explosion, the fallout distance of blast-propelled objects, and the extent of bodily harm caused by the blast.

*Randall L. Milstein*

## Further Reading

Cooper, Paul W. *Explosives Engineering.* New York: Wiley-VCH, 1996.

Fannelöp, Torstein K. *Fluid Mechanics for Industrial Safety and Environmental Protection.* New York: Elsevier, 1994.

Thurman, James T. *Practical Bomb Scene Investigation.* Boca Raton, Fla.: CRC Press, 2006.

Zukas, Jonas A., and William P. Walters, eds. *Explosive Effects and Applications.* New York: Springer, 1998.

**See also:** Ballistics; Blast seat; Bombings; Bureau of Alcohol, Tobacco, Firearms and Explosives; Crime scene reconstruction and staging; Improvised explosive devices; Oklahoma City bombing; Structural analysis; World Trade Center bombing.

# Bombings

Definition: Incidents involving weapons that explode and release destructive shock waves and shrapnel that damage buildings and other property and injure and kill people.

**Significance:** In modern society, law-enforcement agencies are increasingly faced with the investigation of crimes involving explosives. Forensic scientists and law-enforcement officers use a number of different techniques to detect explosives before they can be used in bombs, and, after bombings have taken place, they examine the resulting debris for evidence that can link the explosions to the perpetrators.

Bombs create destructive shock waves, flying shrapnel, and intense heat and flame capable of destroying objects and killing people. As the materials needed for bomb making (especially such dual-use products as fertilizer) and the technical information needed to construct and detonate bombs have become more readily available than in the past, in large part because of the advent of the Internet, bombings have increased in frequency. The availability of potentially explosive chemicals, dynamite, and, in some countries, military explosives has provided the criminally disposed with the ability to wield very destructive and deadly weapons. Furthermore, the news coverage that inevitably follows bombing incidents may inadvertently embolden those so inclined to carry out additional bombing attacks.

## Types of Explosives

Every bomb has an igniter, a primer or detonator, and a main charge. Most kinds of bombs are confined within some sort of shell, such as a pipe or a box. The igniter may be either a fuse or a primer. A primer is a small explosive charge that may be ignited by flame, electrical spark, or friction. When the primer is ignited, it explodes, causing the bomb's main charge to detonate. A firearm cartridge, for example, is an explosive that is set off when a shock-sensitive primer located at one end of the cartridge is struck by a pin. When a gun's firing pin strikes the primer on a firearm cartridge, the primer explodes and ignites the main charge, the smokeless black powder located behind the bullet. The explosion of the main charge is what forces the bullet to travel through the barrel of the gun and downrange.

The speed at which an explosive detonates determines whether it is classified as a low or high explosive. Low explosives, such as black and smokeless powder, are typically used as propellants for ammunition and rockets because they burn relatively slowly. Most homemade bombs tend to be low explosives because they are often constructed with black powder, which is easy to obtain from gun stores. High explosives such as dynamite and C-4, in contrast, produce more of a smashing, shattering effect.

High explosives may be divided into two types, primary and secondary. Primary high explosives tend to be sensitive to heat, shock, and friction and detonate very easily. Because of this, they are generally used in primer devices to set off larger, secondary explosives. Secondary high explosives tend to be relatively insensitive to heat, shock, and friction and usually require a primary charge explosion to detonate. In most cases, this involves the use of a blasting cap, initiated by a burning fuse or by an electrical current. Homemade bombs are usually initiated by an electronic blasting cap wired to a battery that is switched on by a device such as a clock, mercury switch, vehicle ignition switch, or cell phone ring.

Dynamite is a high explosive known for producing a quick shattering effect. It is mainly used for construction, mining, and demolition. When it was first developed in 1866, it was made from nitroglycerin, diatomaceous earth (soft, chalklike sedimentary rock), and sodium carbonate wrapped in distinctive red paper. The "kick" that is produced by dynamite is derived from the nitroglycerin it contains. Nitroglycerin is a very powerful shock-sensitive explosive, meaning that vibrations may cause it to explode. This makes it very dangerous to handle. However, when diatomaceous earth and sodium carbonate are combined with nitroglycerin to create dynamite, the nitroglycerin becomes more stable and safe to handle.

The explosive strength of a stick of dynamite is designated by the percentage of nitroglycerin it contains; for example, in a 60 percent grade stick of dynamite, 60 percent of the stick consists of nitroglycerin. The actual blasting power of a stick of dynamite, however, is not in proportion to its grade percentage markings. That is, a 60 percent grade stick of dynamite is not three times as powerful as a 20 percent grade stick; it is only about one and one-half times as strong.

By the early years of the twenty-first century, the use of nitroglycerin-based dynamite had all but disappeared. Dynamite was replaced by ammonium nitrate-based explosives, which are more stable and useful in wet conditions. Ammonium nitrate/fuel oil (ANFO) explosives are high explosives that are often used in the mining and construction industries. They consist of ammonium nitrate soaked in fuel oil and require a primer explosive to detonate. About 80 percent of the explosives used in North America are ANFO explosives. The availability of ammonium nitrate in the form of fertilizer makes it a readily obtainable ingredient for homemade explosives, and its use in bombs has become a trademark of various criminal and terrorist groups around the globe. Timothy McVeigh used a variation of an ANFO bomb when he attacked the Alfred P. Murrah Federal Building in Oklahoma City in 1995, killing 168 people and injuring hundreds more.

The explosive known as RDX is currently the high explosive most commonly used by the U.S. military. It is second in strength only to nitroglycerin. RDX is widely used in plastic explosives, detonators, artillery rounds, Claymore mines, and demolition kits. It is combined with plasticizers to make C-4, which is a pliable, puttylike explosive that can be molded into a variety of shapes and has a long shelf life. It is believed that al-Qaeda used C-4 in 1996 to blow up the Khobar Towers (a military housing complex) in Saudi Arabia and again in 2000 in its attack on the military destroyer the USS *Cole*. In the Khobar Towers bombing, nineteen U.S. service personnel were killed. In the bombing of the *Cole*, seventeen sailors were killed and thirty-nine others were injured.

Triacetone triperoxide (TATP) is an explosive created through the combination of the common ingredients of acetone and hydrogen peroxide with a catalyst such as hydrochloric acid. Persons who are so inclined can purchase its base ingredients (drain cleaner, bleach, and acetone) easily and without attracting suspicion, and instructions for making TATP can be found on the Internet. In its finished form, this explosive is almost undetectable by substance-detection dogs or by conventional bomb-detection systems. Because of this, the Palestinian militant organization Hamas has favored TATP for use by suicide bombers sent into Israel. Al-Qaeda has also used it when conducting terror missions abroad. TATP was included as a trigger in the shoe bomb that Richard Reid intended to detonate on a flight from Paris, France, to Miami, Florida, in 2001. It is also the type of explosive that was used in the 2005 public transit bombings in London, England, which killed fifty-two commuters and injured seven hundred people. The drawback of TATP, from a criminal or terrorist's point of view, is that it is highly unstable and sensitive to heat and friction.

### Detecting Explosives at Airports

Terrorists around the globe have successfully used explosives to end lives and undermine public confidence in air travel. In response to such threats, airports and their cargo terminals employ a number of different techniques and technologies to aid in the identification and interdiction of explosives.

X-ray machines are used to scan large numbers of people and items to identify hidden suspicious shapes that could indicate the presence of bombs. Because it is possible that such explosive devices could be hidden inside electronic equipment, such as laptop computers, security measures often include chemical analyses. In such a test, a swab is wiped across a piece of electronic equipment, such as a laptop, and is then placed into a device that heats it up and performs a spectrographic analysis of the resulting vapors. The machine searches for traces of nitrogen, which is found in the majority of explosives.

Trace-detection machines (sniffers), which look like metal detectors, search for explosives by blowing air over persons or their luggage.

The blowing air releases particles from the surface of the person or object of interest, and the machine then processes the air and analyzes it for traces of known explosives. Airport security measures also include the use of dogs that have been trained to alert their handlers by sitting near any objects or persons that give off the telltale odors of explosives.

## Responding to Bomb Threats

Most bomb threats turn out to be nothing more than prank phone calls from misguided individuals who take pleasure in causing others fear and inconvenience. Unfortunately, those whose true intent is to kill, maim, and destroy are unlikely to notify their intended victims prior to the detonation of their bombs. When a bombing does occur, individuals who have specialized training in bomb disposal, bomb-site investigation, forensic analysis, and criminal investigation work together to determine what happened so that those who are responsible may be apprehended.

When a bomb threat is called in, the authorities who are given the task of responding to the scene (the first responders) need to enlist the assistance of people who are familiar with the area, such as building managers and employees, because such persons may be more adept at determining whether something is out of place than someone who is not as familiar with the surroundings. Those participating in a search for a bomb must turn off all their radios and transmitters before they begin the search, because the signals these devices emit may set off an explosion. When searchers first enter a room in a location where a bomb may have been planted, they pay special attention to items such as unattended bags, boxes, baby carriers, briefcases, trash cans, flowerpots, incoming mail, and panels in the ceiling that may be easily pushed up. Experts also recommend that when searchers enter a room, they should stand quietly in the room's center, close their eyes for several seconds, and listen. Unusual noises may indicate the location of a bomb.

If a bomb is found, the searchers are careful not to touch it, because contact may cause it to explode. Only bomb disposal personnel are tasked with handling any suspected devices that are located. Bomb squads in larger police departments use robots to approach and detonate certain bombs. After a bomb is found, the area is cleared and the crime scene is secured to prevent further contamination. Emergency services are requested from bomb technicians, firefighters, emergency medical personnel, and law-enforcement officers, and a search for secondary explosive devices is then conducted.

## Investigating Bomb Explosions

When an explosion occurs, law-enforcement personnel must identify scene hazards such as the possibility of building collapse, hazardous chemicals, and secondary explosives. Bombing scenes may contain secondary explosive devices specifically designed to kill or maim public safety responders. If a suspected secondary device is located, the area must be evacuated immediately and bomb disposal personnel must be contacted. As soon as conditions permit, investigators need to establish a security perimeter that restricts access into and out of the scene; they also begin documenting the scene (taking notes, identifying witnesses, and videotaping bystanders).

During an initial scene walk-through, investigators pay special attention to various safety concerns, such as structural damage, the possibility of the presence of secondary devices and unconsumed explosive materials, failed utilities, and hazardous materials. Following this walk-through, the investigators meet with available emergency responders and investigative personnel to determine what resources, equipment, and additional personnel may be needed.

The search for evidence typically starts at the seat of the blast, which is usually indicated by a crater, and spirals out in ever-increasing circles. The scene is documented with both written and photographic records before anything is removed or disturbed. The material at the scene is then sorted in an attempt to recover the materials that were used to construct the bomb. All of the personnel involved in the search must wear disposable gloves, shoe covers, and overalls so that they do not contaminate evidence and compromise the investigation.

To uncover clues to the construction and thus

the origin of a bomb, investigators usually sift material from the blast scene through a series of increasingly finer mesh screens to collect portions of the explosive device for analysis. For instance, if a pipe bomb was used, a forensic investigator may find the bomb's end cap; in many cases, this part of a pipe bomb will retain small specks of unexploded material that becomes trapped in the threading. These small specks of explosive may then be used to trace the origins of the materials used to construct the bomb. Investigative leads may also develop from tool marks left on a pipe from a vise used in cutting and threading. Other clues that may aid an investigation include the type of wire that was used, the type of timing device used, the particular type of wrapper paper (indicating the origin of a piece of dynamite), or a unique method of bomb construction.

The materials from the scene that are collected for laboratory examination are placed in sealed containers and labeled. Soil and other soft materials are placed in metal containers or plastic bags. Evidence samples that are packaged in plastic bags must not be kept next to each other, because it has been demonstrated that some explosives can diffuse through plastic and contaminate nearby containers.

Bombing victims should also be examined for evidence, as bomb component fragments may be found on or in their clothing or bodies. Autopsies should include full-body X rays.

When the debris evidence from a bomb scene arrives at the laboratory, it is examined microscopically, and an acetone wash is often used to extract explosives from the debris. Chromatographic techniques (which can separate and identify the components in chemical mixtures) may then be used to determine the types of explosives that were used.

Explosive residues are often collected at bomb scenes with a portable machine called an ion mobility spectrometer (IMS). The IMS uses a vacuum to suck in explosive residues from surfaces. Depending on the types of surfaces found at a bomb scene, however, investigators may collect explo-

## Bomb Scene Equipment

Because first responders and investigators may not know the details of a situation involving explosives until they arrive at the scene, prior preparation is vital. The following is a list of the kinds of tools and other equipment frequently used by investigative teams at bombing scenes. This list is not exhaustive, and all of the items listed may be not applicable to every situation.

- First-aid kit
- Biohazard materials (bags, tags, labels)
- Respiratory equipment
- Hard hats, safety glasses, protective safety boots, and kneepads
- Protective outerwear (disposable suits, shoe covers)
- Heavy, disposable cotton gloves
- Barrier tape
- Flashlights, flares, and auxiliary lighting
- Hand tools (rakes, shovels, trowels, screwdrivers, crowbars, hammers)
- Brushes and brooms
- Ladders
- Sifters/screens
- Swabbing kits
- Vacuum
- Evidence collection kits
- Writing equipment (notebooks, pens, permanent markers)
- Drawing equipment (sketchbooks, pencils)
- Measuring equipment (tape measure, tape wheel)
- Photography and video equipment
- Computer and computer-aided design program
- Consent-to-search forms
- Audio recorders
- Evidence flags or cones, placards, and tags
- Bags and corrugated or fiberboard boxes
- Chemical test kits and vapor detectors
- Trace explosives detectors (sniffers) and detection canines

## Explosive Incidents Investigated by ATF, 2000-2003

| | 2000 | 2001 | 2002 | 2003 |
|---|---|---|---|---|
| Incidents | 807 | 763 | 711 | 386 |
| Persons injured | 81 | 98 | 80 | 55 |
| Persons killed | 19 | 12 | 13 | 7 |
| Damage | $5,634,681 | $7,279,023 | $5,153,448 | $267,000 |

*Source:* Bureau of Alcohol, Tobacco, Firearms and Explosives.

sive residues more efficiently by wiping the surfaces down with paper disks and then using the IMS to collect the residues off the disks. Once the residues are in the IMS, they are vaporized into electronically charged molecules or ions. Identification of the size and structure of the molecules and ions enables investigators to determine the types of explosives that were detonated at the bomb scene.

Investigators often examine bomb blast craters using an ultraviolet light and magnetic probe in the hope of finding small particles, called taggants, that are sometimes put into explosives by manufacturers. Taggants are tiny color-coded magnetic fluorescent chips the size of sand grains. The color of the fluorescent chips indicates where an explosive was made and when it was produced. Switzerland requires all explosives manufacturers in that nation to add taggants to their products. The U.S. government has not taken such a step, but increasing concerns about terrorism may eventually result in a similar requirement for American manufacturers.

*Daniel Pontzer*

### Further Reading

Bennett, Wayne W., and Kären M. Hess. *Criminal Investigation.* 8th ed. Belmont, Calif.: Wadsworth/Thomson Learning, 2007. Introduces the challenges encountered by criminal investigators and discusses investigators' basic responsibilities. Details the work involved in the investigation of violent crimes such as death, assault, rape, and robbery as well as property offenses such as burglary, arson, and crimes using explosives.

Gaensslen, R. E., Howard A. Harris, and Henry C. Lee. *Introduction to Forensic Science and Criminalistics.* New York: McGraw-Hill, 2008. Addresses the types of forensic science techniques used in crime laboratories in criminal cases and by private examiners in civil cases. Discusses various crime scene procedures and analyses, physical pattern evidence, biological evidence, and chemical and materials evidence.

Martin, Gus. *Essentials of Terrorism: Concepts and Controversies.* Thousand Oaks, Calif.: Sage, 2008. Addresses the topic of modern-day terrorism by reviewing different types of terrorism and the nations, movements, and individuals who have engaged in terrorist violence.

National Institute of Justice. *A Guide for Explosion and Bombing Scene Investigation.* Washington, D.C.: Author, 2000. Outlines the tasks that investigators should consider at every explosion scene and provides guidance on the procurement of equipment and tools, prioritization of initial response efforts, evaluation of the scene, documentation of the scene, and processing of evidence at the scene.

Saferstein, Richard. *Criminalistics: An Introduction to Forensic Science.* 9th ed. Upper Saddle River, N.J.: Pearson Prentice Hall, 2007. Comprehensive introductory textbook addresses the role of science in the criminal justice system. Includes in-depth discussion of the technologies that law-enforcement agencies use to apprehend criminals and the use of trace evidence to link perpetrators to crime scenes.

Simonsen, Clifford E., and Jeremy R. Spindlove. *Terrorism Today: The Past, the Players, the Future.* 3d ed. Upper Saddle River, N.J.: Pearson Prentice Hall, 2007. Provides background on the history and legal issues associated with terrorism and discusses the types of terrorism and terrorist groups found around the world. Includes suggestions regarding counterterrorism tactics and speculation on the directions terrorism may take in the future.

Trimm, Harold H. *Forensics the Easy Way.* Hauppauge, N.Y.: Barron's, 2005. Presents information on the applications of physics and chemistry in the criminal justice system by focusing on forensics, including discussion of physical evidence, body fluids, explosives and incendiaries, firearms, fingerprints, and DNA evidence.

**See also:** Atomic absorption spectrophotometry; Blast seat; Bomb damage assessment; Bureau of Alcohol, Tobacco, Firearms and Explosives; Canine substance detection; Chromatography; Driving injuries; Illicit substances; Improvised explosive devices; Mass spectrometry; National Church Arson Task Force; Oklahoma City bombing; Unabomber case; World Trade Center bombing.

---

## Borderline personality disorder

**Definition:** Disorder in which personality characteristics are maladaptive in nature, including chronic difficulties in maintaining stable interpersonal relationships, severe mood swings that are reactive in nature, impulsivity, hostility, feelings of emptiness, and propensity to engage in self-harm behaviors.

**Significance:** Persons with borderline personality disorder are at high risk for engaging in criminal and antisocial behavior and tend to be overrepresented in prison populations. Because of their often violent and aggressive demeanor, such individuals are extremely disruptive to forensic settings and tend to pose additional risks to themselves and others when placed

within these environments.

It has been estimated that from 1 to 2 percent of the world's population qualify for a diagnosis of borderline personality disorder (BPD) based on the guidelines in the fourth edition, text revision, of the American Psychiatric Association's *Diagnostic and Statistical Manual of Mental Disorders* (*DSM-IV-TR*). A disproportionate number of the people diagnosed with BPD found in psychiatric inpatient, psychiatric outpatient, and forensic settings are female.

Individuals with BPD exhibit enduring patterns of emotional and behavioral instability. The pervasive and often inflexible nature of their behavior can result in actions that are harmful and, sometimes, criminal in nature. These erratic behaviors are believed to result from a dangerous combination of extreme affective instability and high levels of impulsivity. Although self-destructive in nature, these behaviors—including reckless driving, sexual promiscuity, substance abuse, and aggressive acts—may result in legal repercussions. People with BPD are highly likely to exhibit symptoms of additional psychopathology and often warrant additional comorbid diagnoses of depression, anxiety, and other Axis II personality disorders (disorders classified in the *DSM-IV-TR* as underlying pervasive or personality conditions), most predominantly of the histrionic or antisocial types.

An intense fear of abandonment, often stemming from psychosocial factors during development (such as sexual abuse, neglect, separation or loss, or parental psychopathology), is believed to contribute to the manipulative behaviors exhibited by persons with BPD. To avoid either real or imagined abandonment, persons with BPD put forth significant effort to thwart others' attempts to leave them. In these situations, they may engage in flagrantly manipulative behaviors, including significant threats of self-harm or attempts at suicide. These behaviors, although intended to keep others from departing, can result in life-threatening or lethal injuries. In addition to such self-harm behaviors, persons with BPD often engage in self-mutilating acts such as repetitive cutting or burning; most often, they perform these acts on their forearms or legs, but sometimes they may mutilate their faces, chests, or genitals.

In addition to exhibiting unstable behavior, individuals with BPD tend to have extreme difficulty with interpersonal relationships, self-image, and moods. They often report histories of intense but stormy relationships, typically involving severe fluctuations between overidealization of friends or lovers and bitter disappointment, frustration, and disillusionment with these persons, which, at times, may lead to violence. These drastic mood shifts and difficulties modulating and controlling anger can lead individuals with BPD to display intense behavioral and emotional outbursts with little provocation.

*Neva E. J. Sanders-Dewey and Seth G. Dewey*

### Further Reading

Friedel, Robert O. *Borderline Personality Disorder Demystified: An Essential Guide for Understanding and Living with BPD*. New York: Marlowe, 2004.

Kreisman, Jerold J., and Hal Straus. *Sometimes I Act Crazy: Living with Borderline Personality Disorder*. Hoboken, N.J.: John Wiley & Sons, 2004.

Mason, Paul T., and Randi Kreger. *Stop Walking on Eggshells: Taking Your Life Back When Someone You Care About Has Borderline Personality Disorder*. Oakland, Calif.: New Harbinger, 1998.

**See also:** ALI standard; Child abuse; *Diagnostic and Statistical Manual of Mental Disorders*; Forensic psychiatry; Guilty but mentally ill plea; Insanity defense; Irresistible impulse rule; Minnesota Multiphasic Personality Inventory; Psychopathic personality disorder; Suicide.

# Bosnian war victim identification. *See* Croatian and Bosnian war victim identification

# Botulinum toxin

**Definition:** Highly toxic substance produced by the *Clostridium botulinum* bacterium that targets nerve tissue and blocks neuromuscular transmission of impulses in the body, causing the paralytic disease botulism.

**Significance:** Botulinum toxin is one of the most lethal known toxic substances; a few grams of the toxin introduced into the food supply could kill millions of people, making it an attractive agent for potential use as a biological weapon. In addition to that possibility, nonintentional poisonings sometimes occur through the consumption of food containing the toxin or through contamination of wounds with the toxin. Whenever botulinum toxin is suspected in cases of poisoning, law-enforcement agencies are concerned with identifying the toxin and its source.

Although the possibility that botulinum toxin could be used in biological warfare has been acknowledged for many years, no uses of the poison as a weapon have been reported in any major wars. Despite the Biological Weapons Convention of 1972, however, it is generally believed that many countries have stockpiles of the *Clostridium botulinum* bacterium and toxin as part of their biological warfare programs.

The most common form of botulinum poisoning occurs through the ingestion of foods containing the toxin. Food products contaminated with *C. botulinum* spores that are stored at room temperature can cause poisoning if they are consumed without first being adequately heated. Canned cheeses, ham, and sausage are common sources of the toxin. In a typical incident that took place in Italy in 1996, eight people contracted the poison by eating commercial cream cheese. One died, and the others had prolonged medical recoveries. In a 1995 incident in Canada, a sixteen-year-old girl was poisoned when she ate smoked fish. She died a few months later despite having received intensive medical treatment. In September, 2006, four cases of botulism in the United States and two cases in Canada were traced to the consumption of contaminated carrot juice.

## Mechanism of Toxicity

The toxin, which was first isolated from *C. botulinum* in 1944 by Edward Schantz, must come into contact with nerve tissue to cause damage. The toxin attaches to the axon terminal of nerve endings, where it blocks the release of the principal neurotransmitter in the body, acetylcholine. This blockage prevents transmission of nerve impulses, resulting in loss of muscle contractility and flaccid paralysis.

In food-related poisoning, symptoms occur six to thirty-six hours after ingestion of food containing the toxin. Symptoms include excessive dry mouth, diarrhea, and vomiting. These may be followed by blurred vision, droopy eyelids, generalized muscle weakness, and progressive difficulty in breathing. Death may occur as a result of paralysis of the respiratory muscles. Symptoms of botulinum poisoning may occur more rapidly if the toxin is inhaled rather than ingested.

## Medical and Cosmetic Uses

Some medical treatments have been developed that take advantage of the botulinum toxin's neuromuscular blocking action; tiny concentrations of the toxin are used, for example, in the treatment of involuntary eye muscle contractions (blepharospasm). The toxin is also used in the treatment of migraine headaches and cervical dystonia, a neuromuscular condition involving the head and neck. Another important medical use of the toxin is in the treatment of excessive underarm perspiration (severe primary axillary hyperhidrosis). The toxin has also been employed at times in the treatment of the following ailments and symptoms, although it is not approved by the U.S. Food and Drug Administration (FDA) for these

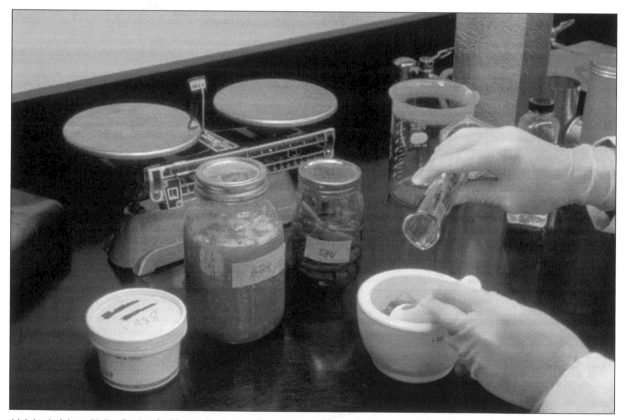

A lab technician with the Centers for Disease Control and Prevention grinds food with a mortar and pestle to enable the extraction of botulinum toxin. The CDC treats every case of food-borne botulism as a public health emergency. *(Centers for Disease Control and Prevention)*

uses: overactive bladder, anal fissure, stroke, multiple sclerosis, Parkinson's disease, excessive salivation, neurological complications of diabetes mellitus, and muscle problems affecting the limbs, face, jaw, and vocal cords.

Commercial botulinum toxins, marketed under the names Botox and Dysport, among others, are used cosmetically to remove facial wrinkles and improve facial appearance. The toxin works on wrinkle lines that have been formed in the upper part of the face, particularly the forehead and around the eyes. Because very low concentrations of the toxin are used in these cosmetic preparations, treatment is usually safe. However, occasional adverse effects—such as allergic reactions and paralysis of the wrong muscles—have been reported. Four cases of poisoning caused by cosmetic use of a type of botulinum toxin that had not been approved by the FDA were reported in Florida in 2004.

### Investigation of Botulinum Poisoning

When deaths or illnesses are suspected to be attributable to botulinum toxin poisoning, both forensic scientists and public health experts are usually involved in investigating the incidents. The immediate goal in any case is to identify the source of the toxin as quickly as possible to prevent any further harm. In the United States, law-enforcement agencies are required to report all cases of such poisoning to the Centers for Disease Control and Prevention (CDC).

Evidence at the suspected poisoning site must be preserved so that it can be analyzed for clues that may point to the source of the toxin. Apart from food, botulinum toxin and the toxin-producing *C. botulinum* bacterium may be found in the blood and feces of patients suffering from botulinum poisoning. In some fatal cases, forensic examination of tissue samples and suspensions of body fluids have been used to demonstrate the presence of the toxin even after advanced putrefaction.

*Edward C. Nwanegbo*

### Further Reading

Balkin, Karen F., ed. *Food-Borne Illnesses*. San Diego, Calif.: Greenhaven Press, 2004. Collection of essays offers a variety of perspectives on issues of food safety.

Breeze, Roger G., Bruce Budowle, and Steven E. Schutzer, eds. *Microbial Forensics*. Burlington, Mass.: Elsevier Academic Press, 2005. Details the importance of forensic microbiology and discusses its uses. Includes discussion of botulism.

Scott, Elizabeth, and Paul Sockett. *How to Prevent Food Poisoning: A Practical Guide to Safe Cooking, Eating, and Food Handling*. Hoboken, N.J.: John Wiley & Sons, 1998. Provides thorough information on the causes and symptoms of food poisoning, including botulism.

Smith, Louis D. S., and Hiroshi Sugiyama. *Botulism: The Organism, Its Toxins, the Disease*. 2d ed. Springfield, Ill.: Charles C Thomas, 1988. Textbook covers virtually every aspect of botulism.

Tucker, Jonathan B., ed. *Toxic Terror: Assessing Terrorist Use of Chemical and Biological Weapons*. Cambridge, Mass.: MIT Press,

## Diagnosing Botulism

*The U.S. Centers for Disease Control and Prevention (CDC) provides this information on the diagnosis of botulinum poisoning.*

Physicians may consider the diagnosis if the patient's history and physical examination suggest botulism. However, these clues are usually not enough to allow a diagnosis of botulism. Other diseases such as Guillain-Barré syndrome, stroke, and myasthenia gravis can appear similar to botulism, and special tests may be needed to exclude these other conditions. These tests may include a brain scan, spinal fluid examination, nerve conduction test (electromyography, or EMG), and a tensilon test for myasthenia gravis. The most direct way to confirm the diagnosis is to demonstrate the botulinum toxin in the patient's serum or stool by injecting serum or stool into mice and looking for signs of botulism. The bacteria can also be isolated from the stool of persons with food-borne and infant botulism. These tests can be performed at some state health department laboratories and at CDC.

2000. Collection of case studies discusses various uses of chemical and biological agents by terrorist groups. Identifies terrorists' patterns of behavior and discusses strategies to combat them.

**See also:** Biological terrorism; Biological Weapons Convention of 1972; Chemical agents; Chemical terrorism; Food poisoning; Food supply protection; Forensic toxicology; Poisons and antidotes.

Bovine spongiform encephalopathy. *See Mad cow disease investigation*

## Brain-wave scanners

**Definition:** Instruments used to map regions of the brain or to measure brain responses to stimuli.

**Significance:** Brain-wave scanners can be used to monitor brain activity to determine whether or not a person is telling the truth and to perform postmortem mapping of the brain to determine whether death may have resulted from trauma to the head.

Brain-wave scanners are used to map activity in the brain. The patterns seen in the three-dimensional images produced by brain-wave scanning are indicative of whether or not a person is lying. The images are formed using magnetic resonance imaging (MRI). When experts examine the images to determine which areas of a person's brain become active in response to questions, pictures, or other stimuli, this method is referred to as functional magnetic resonance imaging (fMRI). The subject is placed inside the scanning machine and allowed to interact with a computer screen to answer specific questions related to a crime. The MRI machine is interfaced with special computer software

that recognizes specific brain patterns. When a person is telling a lie, the brain has to expend more energy than it does when the person is telling the truth. Even when a lie has been rehearsed in the mind of the subject, the subject uses more brain energy to think beyond the truth and access the lie. The extra brain activity shows up as a "bright" region on the brain-scanned image. In tested case studies, the fMRI method has shown an accuracy of more than 90 percent in detecting lies.

Although still undergoing development and refinement, the fMRI technique has many possible forensic applications. These include situations that involve libel, slander, fraud, or terrorist activities; the technology may also be useful in the security screening of potential employees for important government positions. The technique might be used in the interrogation of criminal suspects or in the assessment of the intentions of prisoners before they are released. Because individuals involved in terrorist plots have detailed knowledge of plans and activities that innocent persons do not have, brain scans might be used to identify persons who have terrorist training and knowledge of terrorist activities.

The primary ethical issue that needs to be addressed in regard to the use of brain-wave scanners as lie detectors is that of the invasion of personal privacy. This problem may be resolved by safeguards that ensure that subjects are fully informed about brain-wave scanning and agree to be examined in this way.

For examination of the brain after death, postmortem multislice computed tomography (PMSCT) provides detailed in situ images of the brain. These are useful for screening corpses for foreign matter in the brain or for identifying whether head trauma resulting in skull fractures or cerebral hemorrhaging was the cause of death.

Both two-dimensional cross-sectional images and postprocessed three-dimensional images of the skull can be made. Postmortem computed tomographic (PMCT) scans of an infant's brain can reveal signs that are indicative of shaken baby syndrome. This type of child abuse is accompanied by subdural hemorrhage of ruptured cerebral bridging veins, which can be identified in PMCT images but is difficult, if not impossible, to detect in a typical autopsy.

*Alvin K. Benson*

**Further Reading**

Saferstein, Richard. *Criminalistics: An Introduction to Forensic Science.* 9th ed. Upper Saddle River, N.J.: Pearson Prentice Hall, 2007.

Tilstone, William J., Kathleen A. Savage, and Leigh A. Clark. *Forensic Science: An Encyclopedia of History, Methods, and Techniques.* Santa Barbara, Calif.: ABC-CLIO, 2006.

White, Peter, ed. *Crime Scene to Court: The Essentials of Forensic Science.* 2d ed. Cambridge, England: Royal Society of Chemistry, 2004.

**See also:** Biometric identification systems; Forensic psychiatry; Forensic psychology; Interrogation; Nervous system; Polygraph analysis; Psychological autopsy.

## Breathalyzer

**Definition:** Device used to measure ethanol in the breath of a subject as an indication of blood alcohol concentration. Breathalyzer is also the trade name of a series of instruments designed to analyze breath alcohol.

**Significance:** Police officers commonly conduct analyses of the breath of drivers suspected of driving under the influence of alcohol, and Breathalyzer results are often used as grounds for arrest in cases of impaired driving. Such analyses are increasingly used also in workplace drug-testing and research applications. The accuracy and precision of the measurements produced by Breathalyzer testing, which are related to physiological and instrumental variables, are often debated in court.

Police officers often ask drivers whom they suspect are under the influence of alcohol to provide samples of their breath by blowing into instruments—at the roadside or at police de-

tachments—that can determine the concentration of alcohol in their breath. Such breath analysis is valuable because the sample collection is minimally invasive, especially in comparison with direct analysis of blood. Breath samples are analyzed upon collection, which establishes sample continuity. When the results are properly documented, and when the instrument is properly calibrated and in good working order, the measurements are typically used as evidence in court.

The instruments used in breath alcohol analysis are based on a variety of designs. The Breathalyzer 900/900A uses oxidation of ethyl alcohol (ethanol) in a fixed volume of breath by potassium dichromate in a standard solution to cause a shift in the solution absorbance spectrum (that is, a color change); the change in absorbance is correlated with the alcohol concentration in the breath sample. Newer instrument designs typically rely on ethanol detection based on absorbance of infrared radiation at selected wavelengths or on electrochemical reaction of the ethanol in the breath sample. Some instruments are portable, and small, handheld units are often used as screening devices; that is, law-enforcement personnel use them to determine whether alcohol is present in subjects within a concentration range that warrants further evidentiary breath testing. Different designs often vary in terms of accuracy and in their susceptibility to other interfering compounds in the breath.

Breath alcohol concentration (BrAC) is correlated with blood alcohol concentration (BAC). Henry's law states that, at a given temperature, the ratio of the concentration of a volatile substance in solution to that of the substance in the vapor above the solution is fixed. Physiologically, such a system exists in the capillaries within the alveoli (air sacs) of the lungs. Volatile compounds, including alcohol, are exchanged between the alveolar air and the blood within these capillaries. BAC is thus determined by multiplication of the measured BrAC by this ratio, termed the blood/breath ratio (BBR). Reported BBR averages typically fall within the range 2,200-2,500.

To be detected in the breath, a compound must be sufficiently volatile, present at sufficient blood concentrations, and measurable by the detection scheme of the instrument. To characterize potential interferences, the response of evidentiary instruments to volatile compounds (such as acetone, isopropanol, methanol, and toluene) should be measured in vitro at toxicologically relevant fluid concentrations (that is, those associated with occupational or environmental exposure, a disease state such as diabetes mellitus, or nonfatal substance abuse). The influence of such compounds on BrAC measurements depends on their chemical properties and the detection scheme of the instrument.

Further safeguards against falsely elevated results are provided by careful observation of the subject by the test administrator and by the collection of a detailed history of the subject being tested.

*James Watterson*

**Further Reading**

Garriott, James C., ed. *Medical-Legal Aspects of Alcohol*. 4th ed. Tucson, Ariz.: Lawyers & Judges Publishing, 2003.

Karch, Steven B., ed. *Forensic Issues in Alcohol Testing*. Boca Raton, Fla.: CRC Press, 2007.

Levine, Barry, ed. *Principles of Forensic Toxicology*. 2d ed., rev. Washington, D.C.: American Association for Clinical Chemistry, 2006.

**See also:** Alcohol-related offenses; Analytical instrumentation; Chain of custody; Drug and alcohol evidence rules; Forensic toxicology; Infrared detection devices; Sobriety testing; Toxicological analysis.

## Brockovich-PG&E case

**Date:** Settled out of court in 1996

**The Event:** A law firm filing clerk instigated an investigation into the contamination of a small California town's water supply with a chemical toxin known as chromium 6 by the Pacific Gas and Electric Company (PG&E) that led to the largest settlement ever paid in a lawsuit in the United States up to that time.

**Significance:** Because the terms of the PG&E settlement have never been made public, details of the forensic investigation leading to that settlement are mostly unknown. Nevertheless, the commercial and critical success of the motion picture *Erin Brockovich* (2000) helped elevate public awareness of the importance of forensic science in identifying toxic pollutants in the environment. The case itself was regarded as a precedent for future litigation for similar cases.

Thanks to a major Hollywood film using her name for its title, Erin Brockovich is indelibly associated with one of the biggest water-contamination cases in U.S. history. While working as a filing clerk in a Southern California law firm, she investigated medical records connected with a real estate case and found evidence that a PG&E facility connected with a natural gas pipeline had contaminated the drinking water of the tiny Mojave Desert community of Hinkley, California, from the 1960's through the 1980's. Brockovich's investigation helped trigger the class-action suit brought against PG&E, and she received a significant share of the money that came out of the case's settlement. However, much of the impetus for the case was provided by residents of Hinkley themselves. Brockovich's name is closely tied to the case largely because of the unusual circumstances of her personal involvement, which was magnified by the film made about the case.

Brockovich's interest in environment cases began after she had been seriously injured in a traffic accident in Nevada. To represent her interests in the legal suit emerging from that accident, she engaged the Thousand Oaks, California, law firm of Masry & Vititoe. Soon afterward, the firm hired her to work as a file clerk, although she was not a college graduate and had no legal training.

While filing papers for a real estate case concerning the community of Hinkley during the early 1990's, Brockovich found information in medical records of Hinkley residents that piqued her curiosity. With her employer's permission, she began researching the matter. Her investigation found that the health of many people who lived in and around Hinkley during the three preceding decades had been damaged by exposure to hexavalent chromium, also known as chromium 6, a suspected carcinogen that had leaked into the groundwater from PG&E's nearby repressurization station. Brockovich's investigation eventually led to a class-action lawsuit against PG&E, which settled most of the cases out of court by paying $333 million in damages to more than six hundred Hinkley residents.

## Background

Hinkley, California, is the site of a repressurization, or compressor, station built by PG&E in 1952 to help push natural gas through a long pipeline that connects Texas with Northern California. As gas moves through pipelines, friction causes it to lose the pressure it requires to keep it moving. Compressor stations like that of Hinkley raise the pressure within pipelines to facilitate the transmission of the gas. The gas compressors themselves require cooling, which is done with oil and water. To prevent rust from corroding the cooling system PG&E, PG&E put chromium 6 in the water. Chromium 6 is one of the cheapest and most efficient corrosion inhibitors but is also a highly toxic chemical that many scientists believe is a carcinogen. Between 1952 and 1966 alone, the runoff of fluids from Hinkley's pumping station's cooling system poured about 370 million gallons of chromium-tainted water into the open and unlined ponds near the community.

During an environmental assessment in 1987, PG&E discovered that chromium 6 had entered Hinkley's groundwater supply and contaminated ten private drinking wells with concentrations of the chemical that exceeded the safety standard set by the state. In December, 1987, PG&E notified the Lahontan Regional Water Quality Board (LRWQB), which managed local water sources, about the contamination. The LRWQB quickly ordered PG&E to clean up the contaminated groundwater. PG&E began to comply, but, after spending

$12.5 million on the effort, it approached the owners of three farms and ten houses drawing on the groundwater to inquire about buying their property. When the company offered to pay ten times fair market value for one property, other Hinkley residents became suspicious and took measures to file suit against PG&E.

For the first time, Hinkley residents began to believe that PG&E's use of chromium 6 was causing severe health problems within their town. Many residents cited such health problems as cancer, tumors, and birth defects. PG&E countered by arguing that the incident rates of the health problems the residents cited were not statistically significant in a population the size of Hinkley, even though residents were drinking, bathing in, and inhaling vapor from water contaminated with chromium 6 every day.

Eventually, with the help of Brockovich and the firm for which she worked, approximately 650 plaintiffs claimed that PG&E had failed to warn them adequately of the potential health risks associated with the chromium 6 exuded by the company's compressor plant. Their lawyers also alleged that two PG&E employees who had become whistle-blowers had been instructed by PG&E to dispose of all records from the Hinkley compressor station. The lawsuit the residents filed in 1993 was eventually settled for a $333 million payment in an undisclosed arbitration agreement. Other cash settlements were made over the ensuing decade.

PG&E's out-of-court settlement may have allowed the company to escape a finding of liability by a court, as settlement offers cannot be used in court as evidence of one party's wrongdoing. Because the arbitration was closed to the public, it remains unclear exactly what scientific proof of harm plaintiffs in the case presented or whether PG&E's actions actually damaged the health of Hinkley residents. However, in the public's perception, PG&E's $333 million settlement was equivalent to a conviction. PG&E's alleged cover-up of its activities and the sheer size of the settlement dramatically increased the intrigue of the story and helped to focus public attention on the potential dangers of chromium 6. Despite the size of the

## The Complex Geography of PG&E

The Brockovich-PG&E case revolved around the Southern California community of Hinkley, a tiny, unincorporated town about fourteen miles west of Barstow, on the fringes of the Mojave Desert. One of the largest energy utilities in the United States, PG&E services Northern California and supplies no energy to the southern part of the state. However, much of the natural gas that the company supplies to its Northern California customers comes to it from the Texas Panhandle, through long pipelines that pass through Southern California. To move the gas the great distances it must travel, PG&E maintains repressurization, or pumping, stations every several hundred miles. Leakage of water mixed with chromium 6, a rust inhibitor, from the station near Hinkley contaminated the town's underground water supplies.

settlement, the Hinkley case and the dangers of chromium 6 might have been quietly forgotten, had the story not become the subject of a major Hollywood film.

### The *Erin Brockovich* Film

Erin Brockovich's role in the PG&E case inspired a film in the year 2000 that used her name for its title and starred Julia Roberts as Brockovich. The film was an instant box-office hit and eventually grossed almost as much money as PG&E had paid out in its 1996 settlement. The film also received many major awards, including five Academy Award nominations, and won Roberts the Oscar for Best Actress in a Leading Role. More important, the film did a great deal to raise public awareness of the dangers of chromium 6 but did not do so without controversy. PG&E downplayed the film's message, claiming that the story had been highly dramatized for entertainment value, and it sent a memo to its employees warning them that not everything in the film was true. Regardless of the film's historical accuracy, however, it clearly increased public awareness of the importance of water quality and the role that forensic scientists play in uncovering environmental crimes. It also opened up discussion for proponents of more stringent water regulation by creating a media forum in which broader issues of water quality were addressed.

*Erin Brockovich* led to several concrete changes in government policies regarding environmental health. For example, the state of California passed two bills requiring assessment of chromium 6 levels in drinking water in its San Fernando Basin aquifer and setting limits for chromium 6 in drinking water sources. The federal government allocated $3 million for a treatment plant and technology to remove chromium 6 from drinking water.

Despite the critical acclaim and commercial success enjoyed by the film *Erin Brockovich*, the Brockovich-PG&E case has continued to generate controversy. Some scientists have concluded that chromium 6 is not, after all, a carcinogen. In 2001, the Chromate Toxicity Review Committee, a panel made up of university scientists that had been formed at the request of the California Environmental Protection Agency's Office of Environmental Health Hazard Assessment (OEHHA) concluded that there was no basis for concluding that chromium could cause cancer when ingested through water. Although the panel's report posed a serious challenge to future lawsuits concerning water contamination, some critics suggested that the panel's composition was suspect and its report had been skewed to protect the utility industry's interests.

*Dante B. Gatmaytan*

### Further Reading

Banks, Sedina. "The 'Erin Brockovich Effect': How Media Shapes Toxics Policy." *Environs: Environmental Law and Policy Journal* 26 (2003): 219-251. Presents an interesting exploration of the impact of the film *Erin Brockovich* on public policy decisions.

Brockovich, Erin, and Marc Eliot. *Take It from Me: Life's a Struggle but You Can Win.* New York: McGraw-Hill, 2002. Motivational autobiography in which Brockovich recounts the events in her life that led to her involvement in the PG&E case.

Egilman, David. "Corporate Corruption of Science: The Case of Chromium (VI)." *International Journal of Occupational Environmental Health* 12 (2006): 169-176. Scholarly discussion addresses the controversy over the suspected health hazards of chromium 6.

Ellis, Erin Brockovich, and Dan Levine. "*Erin Brockovich.*" *Conservation Matters* 8 (June 22, 2001): 12. Views the film *Erin Brockovich* in the broader context of the impacts on the environment of PG&E's practices.

Grant, Samantha. *"Erin Brockovich": The Shooting Script.* New York: Newmarket Press, 2001. Complete script of the Hollywood film based on the Brockovich-PG&E case; edited, with notes, by the original screenwriter, Samantha Grant.

Martens, Daniel L. "Chromium, Cancer, and Causation: Has a Death-Blow Been Dealt Chromium Cases in California?" *Natural Resources and Environment* 16 (2002): 264-266. Focuses on the possible legal impacts of the Brockovich case.

Pellerin, Cheryl, and Susan M. Booker. "Reflections on Hexavalent Chromium: Health Hazards of an Industrial Heavyweight." *Environmental Health Perspectives* 108 (2000): A402-A407. Discusses the potential hazard posed to the environment by chromium 6.

**See also:** Air and water purity; Chemical terrorism; Decontamination methods; Nuclear detection devices; Nuclear spectroscopy; Toxicological analysis.

## Bubonic plague

**Definition:** Highly contagious human bacterial disease with a very high rate of mortality.

**Significance:** Natural outbreaks of bubonic plague still occur periodically, with an average of about 5 cases in the United States and 4000 cases worldwide per year, mostly in Africa. A larger cause for concern, however, is the possibility that weaponized plague bacteria could be used in biological terrorism.

Bubonic plague is caused by a gram-negative, facultative anaerobe bacterial species, Yersinia pestis, acting as an intracellular parasite. The disease is transmitted primarily by fleas from infected hosts, including more than two hundred species of rodents as well as domestic cats, dogs, rabbits, and even sheep or camels. Transmission may also occur through contact with infected bodily fluids or tissues as well as through aerosol exposure from a coughing patient.

The bubonic plague is also known as the Black Death because it results in buboes, infected and inflamed lymph nodes that turn black as they become necrotic and hemorrhagic. Three forms of plague are known. The skin form of the disease, bubonic plague, has a mortality rate of 50-90 percent if untreated and up to 15 percent if treated. A second form, pneumonic plague, results when the bacteria invade the lungs. Pneumonic plague is especially virulent, with mortality of 100 percent if not treated within twenty-four hours. Moreover, it causes bronchial pneumonia, which leads to coughing of highly infective aerosols of bacteria. The third form of plague is septicemic plague, in which blood-borne bacteria are widespread throughout the body, invading almost all organs. Septicemic plague is 100 percent fatal if untreated, and some 40 percent of those who contract it die even with treatment. Incubation time for plague before symptoms appear is one to six days. Symptoms of bubonic plague include fever (as high at 105 degrees Fahrenheit), chills, muscular pain, sore throat, headache, severe weakness, extreme malaise, and enlarged, painful lymph nodes especially in the groin, armpits, and neck. In later stages, accelerated heart rate, accelerated breathing, and low blood pressure ensue. The normal course of treatment is antibiotics of the tetracycline or sulfonamide families.

A vaccine does exist, but it is no longer available in the United States; it is used to contain local outbreaks in other parts of the world. Because of the highly contagious nature of *Y.*

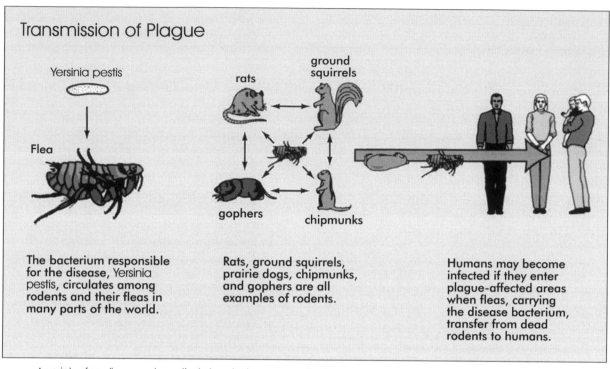

## Transmission of Plague

Yersinia pestis

Flea

rats

ground squirrels

gophers

chipmunks

The bacterium responsible for the disease, Yersinia pestis, circulates among rodents and their fleas in many parts of the world.

Rats, ground squirrels, prairie dogs, chipmunks, and gophers are all examples of rodents.

Humans may become infected if they enter plague-affected areas when fleas, carrying the disease bacterium, transfer from dead rodents to humans.

A variety of small mammals, particularly rodents, may carry the flea that transmits the plague bacterium *Yersinia pestis.*

*pestis*, this organism poses a grave danger as an agent in a biological terrorism attack. Aerosolized plague organisms as well as antibiotic- resistant strains of plague have been developed in former biological weapons facilities in Russia and the United States. Rapid identification of the agent is essential in any bioterrorism event.

*Ralph R. Meyer*

### Further Reading

Brubaker, Bob. "*Yersinia pestis* and the Bubonic Plague." In *The Prokaryotes*, edited by Martin Dworkin et al. 3rd ed. Vol. 6. New York: Springer, 2006. An excellent, if somewhat dated, review of the plague organism.

Bos, Kirsten, et al. "A Draft Genome of *Yersinia pestis* from Victims of the Black Death." *Clinical Microbiology and Infection* 18 (2012): 224-230. These authors extracted and sequenced DNA from the dental pulp of victims of the 14th century Black Plague buried in a plague cemetery in East Smithfield, England. The ancient DNA sequences were similar to contemporary strains of *Y. pestis*. The DNA sequence can be accessed in GenBank by accession #SRA 045745.1.

Raoult, Didier, et al. "Plague: History and Contemporary Analysis." *Journal of Infection* 66 (2013): 18-26. This provides a brief review of the history and current outbreaks of plague, including epidemiology, geographic distribution, transmission, microbiology, clinical symptoms, diagnosis, treatment and prevention.

Zhou, Dongsheng and Ruifu Yang. "*Yersinia pestis*." Ch. 36, pp. 403-412, In *Manual of Security Sensitive Microbes and Toxins*, edited by Dongyou Liu. Boca Raton, FL: CRC Press, 2014. This volume addresses possible organisms that could be developed into biological weapons. This chapter deals specifically with the plague bacterium *Y. pestis*

**See also:** Bacteria; Bacterial biology; Bacterial resistance and response to antibacterial agents; Biological terrorism; Biological warfare diagnosis; Biological weapon identification; Biotoxins; Centers for Disease Control and Prevention;

Chemical Biological Incident Response Force, U.S.; Hemorrhagic fevers; Parasitology; Pathogen transmission; Smallpox; Tularemia.

## Bugs. *See* Electronic bugs

## Bullet-lead analysis

**Definition:** Examination of the amounts of trace elements in lead bullets to enable comparison of bullets and determination of their sources.

**Significance:** Analysis of the trace elements present in bullets can be conducted on bullet fragments found at a shooting scene and on any bullets found in the possession of suspects; comparison of the findings can link a suspect to a crime.

Bullets found at crime scenes may be compared with test bullets fired from weapons suspected to have been used in the crimes, but such analysis is not possible when only bullet fragments are recovered or no weapons are found. To address such situations, the technique of bullet-lead analysis was developed during the 1960's. In this process, a fragment of a bullet is dissolved, the solution is vaporized, and the vapor is heated until it glows. By examining the spectrum of light from the glowing vapor, the analyst can determine what trace elements are present in the lead and the amount of each element. Lead typically has traces (1 percent or less) of antimony, arsenic, bismuth, cadmium, copper, silver, and tin. The amounts of these elements vary with where the lead was mined and what kinds of scrap lead have been added. (Most modern bullets are made from recycled lead taken from automobile batteries.)

The use of bullet-lead analysis has been criticized by some. In one case involving the analysis of bullet lead, Michael Behm was convicted in 1997 of murdering a man in South River, New Jersey. The only physical evidence presented in court that linked Behm to the murder was a chemical match between the amounts of trace elements found in bullet fragments from the crime scene and the amounts of those elements found in ammunition recovered from Behm's home. The prosecution led the jury to believe that this meant that the crime scene bullet fragments must have come from the box of ammunition in Behm's possession. This was a serious misuse of bullet-lead analysis because such a match does not necessarily pinpoint a bullet's source. A large batch (or melt) of lead might produce millions of bullets, so hundreds of people in each of dozens of towns might have had bullets matching the crime scene fragments.

Another serious problem with bullet-lead analysis is the question of how the level of experimental error should be calculated. For example, the amount of antimony in a sample might be reported as 0.85 percent ± 0.15 percent, meaning that the amount of antimony is between 0.70 percent and 1.0 percent. If the level of experimental error (in this instance ±0.15 percent) is estimated from too few measurements, confusion can result. Suppose that the antimony content of a different lead sample is reported as 0.51 percent ± 0.20 percent, so that it lies between 0.31 percent and 0.71 percent.

Because this range overlaps with the antimony range given for the first lead sample, it appears that the antimony contents in the two lead samples "match" or are "analytically indistinguishable." Had the second measurement been reported as 0.51 percent ± 0.10 percent, no overlap, and thus no match, would have resulted. A questionable practice sometimes used in the presentation of evidence involving bullet-lead analysis is called chaining:

Because bullet A is found to be a chemical match to bullet B, which in turn matches bullet C, the claim is made that bullet C matches bullet A, regardless of whether A and C are chemical matches. Chaining was used in convicting Behm.

On March 7, 2005, an appellate judge ruled this interpretation of the bullet-lead analysis results invalid and overturned Behm's conviction. On September 1, 2005, after extensive review, the Federal Bureau of Investigation (FBI) announced that it would discontinue the use of bullet-lead analysis.

*Charles W. Rogers*

### Further Reading

Boyce, Nell. "Do Bullets Tell Tales?" *U.S. News & World Report*, November 24, 2003, 60-61.

Goho, Alexandra. "Forensics on Trial: Chemical Matching of Bullets Comes Under Fire." *Science News*, March 27, 2004, 202.

**See also:** Atomic absorption spectrophotometry; Ballistic fingerprints; Ballistics; Firearms analysis; Gunshot residue; Gunshot wounds; Integrated Ballistics Identification System; Lead; Nuclear spectroscopy.

## Bureau of Alcohol, Tobacco, Firearms and Explosives

**Date:** Established in 1972 as the Bureau of Alcohol, Tobacco and Firearms, an independent division of the U.S. Department of the Treasury

**Identification:** Regulatory and law-enforcement unit of the U.S. Department of Justice.

**Significance:** The lead agency for much of the U.S. government's forensic work involving firearms, explosives, and arson.

The bulk of the work of the Bureau of Alcohol, Tobacco, Firearms and Explosives (ATF, also sometimes known as BATFE) involves the regulation of lawful firearms and explosives businesses in the United States as well as some regulation of alcohol (for example, labeling laws) and tobacco. The bureau also enforces federal criminal laws related to these products and, accordingly, conducts forensic investigations involving firearms and explosives as well as illegal sales of alcohol and tobacco.

### Firearms

Pursuant to U.S. law, all firearms must have serial numbers, and persons who sell firearms (whether as manufacturers, wholesalers, or re-

tailers) must keep written records of the sales. Starting in the 1990's, many manufacturers and wholesalers of firearms began providing ATF's National Tracing Center with computerized records of all their sales. In conjunction with local law-enforcement agencies, ATF frequently uses serial numbers to trace the histories of recovered crime guns. In some cases, ATF agents conduct fieldwork to attempt to find out what happened to particular guns after their retail sale.

ATF's National Integrated Ballistic Information Network (NIBIN) uses the Integrated Ballistics Identification System (IBIS) to supply 182 federal, state, and local law-enforcement agencies with ditigized images of bullets and cartridge cases recovered from crime scenes. These images can be used in ballistic fingerprinting—for example, to investigate whether the same gun might have been used in crimes in two different states.

### Arson and Explosives

Federal law regulates the manufacture, sale, and possession of explosives in the United States and provides penalties for the misuse of explosive materials. Under the theory that some fires are started with accelerants that might legally be considered explosives, ATF has become the leading federal agency involved in arson investigation. In 1978, the bureau created its National Response Team (NRT), which assists local authorities in investigating significant arson fires. The NRT comprises four units, each assigned to a different region of the United States. Each NRT unit includes ATF agents with expertise in arson or bombing investigation, forensic chemists, dogs trained in the detection of explosives or accelerants, and various support personnel.

The main purpose of the NRT is to assist in local investigations of major commercial arson fires, but the NRT also provides help to local law-enforcement agencies that must investigate bombings. The NRT was involved with the investigations of the 1993 World Trade Center bombing, the 1995 Oklahoma City bombing, and the 1996 Atlanta Summer Olympics bombing. The NRT also supports ATF's regulatory role by participating in investigations of illegal explosives manufacturing and by responding to explosions at lawful ammunition and fireworks factories. ATF's International Response Team (IRT) assists in arson and explosives investigations in foreign countries, with the approval of the U.S. ambassadors to the particular nations. The IRT has participated in the investigation of Islamist terrorist bombings in Argentina as well as in investigations involving improvised explosive devices (IEDs) in other nations.

In 1996, many news media outlets in the United States reported on what some observers described as a massive wave of racist arson attacks on black churches in the South. Although no actual increase in church arson attacks had occurred, in response to the perceived need the U.S. Congress and President Bill Clinton created the National Church Arson Task Force (NCATF), a multiagency federal organization in which ATF assisted with church-related arson and bombing investigations.

### Research and Training

In its database known as the Arson and Explosives National Repository, ATF compiles information about arson and explosives crimes and suspected crimes. The bureau uses the Advanced Serial Case Management (ASCMe) system to manage the collection and organization of data from arson scenes. In 1986, ATF and the Federal Bureau of Investigation (FBI) began a joint program to profile at-large criminals who are perpetrating arson or bombings. The Arson and Bombing Investigative Services (ABIS) subunit is part of the FBI's National Center for the Analysis of Violent Crime (NCAVC) in Quantico, Virginia. The U.S. Bomb Data Center

> ## ATF's Stated Mission, Vision, and Values
>
> ### Mission
> The Bureau of Alcohol, Tobacco, Firearms and Explosives (ATF) is a principal law enforcement agency within the United States Department of Justice dedicated to preventing terrorism, reducing violent crime, and protecting our Nation. The men and women of ATF perform the dual responsibilities of enforcing Federal criminal laws and regulating the firearms and explosives industries. We are committed to working directly, and through partnerships, to investigate and reduce crime involving firearms and explosives, acts of arson, and illegal trafficking of alcohol and tobacco products.
>
> ### Vision
> The Bureau of Alcohol, Tobacco, Firearms and Explosives must protect the public against crime, violence, and other threats to public safety. Our vision will help us chart the course to improve the way we serve and protect the public, provide leadership and expertise, and achieve new levels of effectiveness and teamwork.
>
> ### Values
> We value each other and those we serve. We will:
> - Uphold the highest standards of excellence and integrity;
> - Provide high quality service and promote strong external partnerships;
> - Develop a diverse, innovative, and well-trained work force to achieve our goals; and
> - Embrace learning and change in order to meet the challenges of the future.

was created by Congress in 1996. Led by ATF, the center compiles data about arson and explosives crimes from various agencies and makes those data available for statistical research by scholars and law-enforcement personnel. ATF also operates three laboratories (in Atlanta, San Francisco, and suburban Maryland) that work on cases involving alcohol, tobacco, firearms, explosives, and fire debris.

The ATF National Laboratory Center in Maryland has a facility where scientists researching arson can re-create the circumstances of particular fires under controlled conditions. Each of the three ATF labs has a Rapid Response Laboratory that can join on-scene investigations.

ATF conducts many training programs for other law-enforcement agencies, covering topics such as arson investigation, recovery of defaced serial numbers on firearms, and postblast explosives investigation.

*David B. Kopel*

## Further Reading

Kopel, David B., and Paul H. Blackman. *No More Wacos: What's Wrong with Federal Law Enforcement and How to Fix It.* Amherst, N.Y.: Prometheus Books, 1997. Offers a close analysis of the disastrous 1993 raid on the Branch Davidians compound in Waco in the context of broader problems with the Bureau of Alcohol, Tobacco and Firearms.

Moore, James. *Very Special Agents: The Inside Story of America's Most Controversial Law Enforcement Agency—The Bureau of Alcohol, Tobacco, and Firearms.* Champaign: University of Illinois Press, 2001. Presents a fervent and heartfelt defense of the bureau. Includes several informative appendixes.

National Learning Corporation. *Alcohol, Tobacco and Firearms (ATF) Inspector: Test Preparation Study Guide—Questions and Answers.* Syosset, N.Y.: Author, 2005. Volume designed to prepare students to pass a qualifying test to become an ATF inspector. Focuses on the bureau's regulatory side.

U.S. Bureau of Alcohol, Tobacco, Firearms and Explosives. *2008 Essential Guide to the ATF: Complete Coverage of Firearms Publications, Laws, Forms.* Washington, D.C.: Author, 2007. This guide on CD-ROM, published annually, provides all the material available on the ATF Web site as well as many other public documents related to the bureau.

Vizzard, William J. *In the Cross Fire: A Political History of the Bureau of Alcohol, Tobacco, and Firearms.* Boulder, Colo.: Lynne Rienner, 1997. A retired ATF supervisor criticizes the bureau's institutional weaknesses.

**See also:** Accelerants; Arson; Ballistic fingerprints; Body farms; Bombings; Canine substance detection; Exhumation; Federal Bureau of Investigation; Firearms analysis; Improvised explosive devices; Integrated Ballistics Identification System; National Church Arson Task Force; World Trade Center bombing.

# Buried body locating

**Definition:** Determination of the placement of human remains that are obscured from view—whether by water, soil, or other intervening materials—for the purpose of their recovery.

**Significance:** Law-enforcement authorities are concerned with the systematic and efficient location of human remains in cases of crimes, accidents, and natural disasters, as location of the remains is the vital first stage in the recovery and identification of the victims, the investigation of the manner of their death, and the return of the remains to surviving relatives.

Human remains may be obscured from view, or buried, as the result of intentional human acts, accidents, or natural events. Bodies can be buried in a variety of settings, depending on the circumstances preceding death and at the time of death. Bodies may be obscured by water, soil, building debris, or other materials. Different burial environments require different methods of body location.

## Possible Locations of Bodies

Human remains in bodies of water may be trapped in sunken ships, automobiles, or aircraft, or they may be entangled in or obscured by trees, brush, or logs floating in the water or along the banks of rivers or lakes. In the case of a disaster such as a bridge collapse over water, bodies may be further obscured by debris from the fallen structure.

Bodies buried in soil may be found at various depths, depending on the circumstances of their death. Perpetrators of homicides might bury victims covertly only a few inches below the surface.

Bodies buried by mudslides might be several feet deep, and victims of an airplane crash over land might be interred deeply as a result of the force of impact. Victims of a building collapse will be obscured from view by tons of construction debris, as was the case for many of the deceased from the Haitian earthquake in 2010. Victims of floods or tornadoes might also be hidden under debris, whether from buildings or natural materials.

## Methods

The method of body location applied is specific to the particular case at hand. When bodies are believed to be in a body of water, physical searches may be conducted by certified divers, although in some instances, floating sediment or algae can obscure visibility. Small, localized bodies of water, such as ponds, may be drained or dredged to enhance exposure of any human remains. Side-scan sonar, which produces sound pulses that reflect off of submerged objects and are recorded, is a remote sensing technology that has been used with success to identify sunken vessels, crashed airplanes, and even individual drowning victims. Computer simulations may also be conducted to predict the locations of drowning victims, given sufficient hydrological data for a body of water.

For bodies buried under soil, a variety of location methods may be used. A walkover line survey, wherein several searchers are aligned and move in unison across the search area, is effective in identifying the disturbed soil or vegetation indicative of a covert or clandestine grave, which might be close to the surface. Even though this method works best in open areas, some modified form of walkover survey is a useful first step even in an urban disaster (such as the aftermath of a tornado). In such a setting, individual remains will often be partially covered but may be detected through the close inspection of a walkover survey.

Remote sensing techniques such as infrared aerial photography and geophysical remote sensing devices like ground penetrating radar (GPR), soil resistivity or conductivity meters, and metal detectors are also useful. Infrared aerial photography is most useful in identifying large buried features, such as mass graves from violent conflicts, based on the different heat signals of disturbed and undisturbed soil. GPR is considered the best ground survey tool for identifying graves, although it works best in well-drained soils. Resistivity or conductivity meters and metal detectors can locate buried metallic objects that may be associated with buried bodies. These remote sensing devices identify anomalies (unusual patterns) in the electromagnetic signals coming from the ground, but their effectiveness may vary, given different soil and moisture conditions. With the information from these devices, investigators can then narrow their focus on identified anomalies as potential locations of buried remains. Actual controlled excavation of these anomalies is necessary to confirm their forensic significance.

When bodies are obscured by vegetation debris or debris from destroyed structures following natural or human-made disasters (like Hurricane Katrina or the September 11, 2001, terrorist attacks on the World Trade Center in New York City), special measures may be needed to locate them. In relatively small, localized events, cadaver dogs can help locate bodies under debris by scent. When large mass disasters occur, local authorities may be overwhelmed and may require outside assistance. In 1993, the U. S. government established ten regional Disaster Mortuary Operational Response Teams (DMORTs) to provide local agencies with added expertise in the location, recovery, and identification of deceased individuals after such disasters. These teams, under the direction of the U. S. Department of Health and Human Services (National Disaster Medical System), are made up of pathologists, forensic anthropologists, forensic odontologists, medical technicians, medical examiners, nurses, counselors, and funeral home directors. Team members are skilled private citizens who, when deployed upon request of local authorities dealing with a disaster, have the initial goal of location and recovery of remains in complex settings and, ultimately, their positive identification.

*Cliff Boyd*

## Further Reading

Buck, Sabrina. "Searching for Graves Using Geophysical Technology: Field Tests with Ground penetrating Radar, Magnetometry, and Electrical Resistivity." *Journal of Forensic*, 48, no. 1(2003): 5-11. Reports on the results of tests of the efficiency of three remote sensing techniques in a variety of settings, including cemeteries and in a murder investigation. Discusses the limitations of each method in detail.

Congram, Derek R. "A Clandestine Burial in Costa Rica: Prospection and Excavation." *Journal of Forensic Sciences,* 53, no. 4 (2008): 793-796. Excellent case study that describes the search and recovery of remains from a covert burial in a tropical environment.

Dupras, Tosha L., John J. Schultz, Sandra M. Wheeler, and Lana J. Williams. *Forensic Recovery of Human Remains: Archaeological Approaches.* 2d ed. Boca Raton, FL.: CRC Press, 2012. Provides detailed descriptions of search and recovery methods and the equipment used for such purposes in forensic scene investigations. Includes standardized recording forms and conversion tables in appendices.

Haglund, William D., and Marcella H. Sorg, eds. *Advances in Forensic Taphonomy: Method, Theory, and Archaeological Perspectives.* Boca Raton, FL.: CRC Press, 2002. Extensive edited volume presents several case studies of the recovery of human remains in a variety of settings, including remains found in water, in burned structures, and in mass graves.

Killam, Edward W. *The Detection of Human Remains.* 2d ed. Springfield, IL: Charles C. Thomas, 2004. Presents thorough descriptions of nonintrusive and intrusive forensic search methods, including various forms of remote sensing.

**See also:** Cadaver dogs; Crime scene investigation; Decomposition of bodies; Exhumation; Homicide; Mass graves; Skeletal analysis; Soil

## Burn pattern analysis

**Definition:** Analysis of the spread of a fire from its site of origin, along with the type of burn damage and extent of destruction, to determine the cause of the fire.

**Significance:** Burn pattern analysis helps investigators to determine whether fires were started by natural events (such as lightning strikes) or by human activity and, if the latter, whether they were caused accidentally (for example, by cooking fires or welding sparks) or intentionally. Determining the causes of fires is important to both law-enforcement and insurance investigators because arson is the most common cause of major structure fires (houses, schools, warehouses) and accounts for greater monetary losses than any other category of fires.

Every twenty seconds, a fire department somewhere in the United States responds to a fire. According to the National Fire Protection Association, in 2013 more than 1.42 million fires caused 3,204 civilian and 89 firefighter deaths and $11.5 billion in property damage. More than 282,600 of these fires were intentionally set, about half of them by juveniles. Nevertheless, despite the high rate of arson fires, few arsonists are successfully prosecuted.

In the past, much of the information investigators had about how different types of fires behave and the burn patterns they leave behind was gleaned from firefighter observation. In the twenty-first century, however, the desire to improve the rates of arson convictions has combined with advances in technology to create a movement to develop a better and more scientific understanding of how fires behave under specific conditions. Researchers at educational agencies such as the Maryland Fire and Rescue Institute at the University of Maryland use controlled experiments to demonstrate that different types of fires create different burn patterns and to validate what burn pattern analysis reveals about the origin, type of fuel, and other factors that characterize a fire.

### Point of Origin and Ignition

Every fire starts somewhere. Burn pattern analysis begins with an attempt to determine the site or origin of the fire. When a fire ignites simultaneously in several locations within a building, for example, this pattern suggests that the fire was intentionally set. A single point of origin does not by itself rule out arson, however. Investigators also consider whether the fire started inside or outside the structure or vehicle, if it started in a location where one might normally expect to find an ignition source (such as in a kitchen or workshop), and what type of fuel was likely to be available. In determining the point of origin, investigators may not only examine the physical remains of the structure or vehicle but may also request a chemical analysis of the remains and interview witnesses for information about the early stages of the fire.

## Spread and Intensity

Once a fire has ignited, how it behaves is determined by three factors: availability of fuel, availability of oxygen, and the heat these produce. These factors are in turn influenced by such elements as the type of fuel available, weather conditions, ventilation systems, drafts from open windows and doors, functioning of installed fire suppression equipment within a building, and firefighter intervention. Although most fires follow a characteristic pattern of development, the constellation of conditions surrounding each fire is unique, and a burn pattern analysis must consider all these factors.

Investigators know that certain materials burn in predictable ways and leave particular telltale signs. Burn pattern analysis involves putting all these signs together to explain the behavior of the fire. Examples of signs that fire investigators might look for that can become part of their burn pattern analyses include the following:

- V-shaped charring patterns on walls, which can give clues to the intensity of fires
- Spalling, or flaking, patterns on concrete or stone floors, which may indicate that accelerant liquids were dribbled across the floors and ignited
- Large, shiny char blisters, which are more likely to form when accelerant liquids are present (small, dull blisters are more characteristic of slow-igniting accidental fires)
- Atypical burn rates for specific materials, which may suggest that accelerants were used
- Abnormal or atypical continuity of burn patterns

Because of the many factors that influence the behavior of any given fire, burn pattern analysis evidence is often successfully challenged in court. Only 2 percent of arson cases result in conviction. Since the late 1990's, the federal Building and Fire Research Laboratory (BFRL) has conducted research to gather scientific documentation on specific burn patterns. For example, researchers have started experimental fires under precisely the same conditions but using different types of accelerants; they have also started fires in rooms that are identical except for having different types of flooring. The burn patterns and other data from these experiments are documented and made available to fire investigators. In addition, the BFRL has developed computer simulations of fire scenarios to assist in training fire investigators and to help explain the results of burn pattern analyses to jurors.

*Martiscia Davidson*

## Further Reading

Icove, David J., and John D. DeHaan. *Forensic Fire Scene Reconstruction.* 3rd ed. Upper Sad- dle River, N.J.: Pearson Prentice Hall, 2012. Shows how investigators trace the history of a fire by using physical evidence of human ac- tivity and knowledge of burn patterns

Lentini, John. *Scientific Protocols for Fire Investigation.* 2nd ed. Boca Raton, FL: Taylor & Francis, 2013. An introduction to arson investigations written in a way that is accessible to both fire professionals and other interested parties.

National Fire Protection Association. <http://www.nfpa.org>

Redsicker, David R., and John J. O'Connor. *Practical Fire and Arson Investigation.* 3rd ed. Boca Raton, Fla.: CRC Press, 2010. Provides comprehensive coverage of all aspects of fire investigations, with emphasis on fires that cause death.

Saferstein, Richard. *Forensic Science: from the Crime Scene to the Crime Lab.* 2nd ed. Boston: Pearson/Prentice Hall, 2013. An introduction to crime scene analysis for those with a limted science background.

**See also:** Accelerants; American Academy of Forensic Sciences; Arson;  Bureau of Alcohol, Tobacco, Firearms and Explosives; Crime scene documentation; Electrical injuries and  deaths; Fire debris; National Church Arson Task Force; Physical evidence; Structural analysis.

# *C*

## Cadaver dogs

**Definition:** Dogs that are specially trained to find the scents associated with decomposing human remains.

**Significance:** Although dogs have been used for many years to aid in crime detection, their use in more highly specialized investigative techniques is a relatively recent development. During the last two decades of the twentieth century, law-enforcement agencies and dog trainers increasingly focused on training dogs to search out human remains in addition to the already established use of dogs to track living humans.

Cadaver dogs constitute a subcategory of search-and-rescue dogs, which are used to help law-enforcement officials find missing people. Cadaver dogs differ from other kinds of search-and-rescue dogs in that cadaver dogs search only for human remains; they are not used to find living humans or other kinds of evidence. Training dogs for the purpose of finding human remains is a fairly recent development in law enforcement's use of dogs. In addition to their use by law enforcement at crime scenes, cadaver dogs are used to find bodies following natural and human-caused disasters.

Cadaver dogs receive specialized training in which they are cross-trained for use both in trailing living humans and in detecting the scents of decomposing human remains. These dogs are trained to differentiate among a variety of scents and to recognize the difference between decomposing human flesh and other scents. In addition to identifying the locations of recent human remains, cadaver dogs can detect the presence of bones and blood as well as other residual scents.

Most cadaver dogs are first trained as trailing and air-scenting dogs, which are used in tracking lost and injured people. After their initial training in tracking general scents, they begin their training as cadaver dogs. In this stage, trainers use special chemicals that mimic the smells of decomposing human flesh to familiarize the dogs with the scents associated with human remains. Careful screening is necessary to identify those dogs that are likely to become good cadaver dogs; trainers must attempt to determine the dogs' abilities to track the necessary scents and whether the dogs are attracted to those scents.

The Institute for Canine Forensics and other organizations draw distinctions among different kinds of search-and-rescue dogs. Subcategories of dogs used by law enforcement, in addition to cadaver dogs, include search dogs, area search dogs, trailing dogs, forensic evidence dogs, water search dogs, and human remains detection dogs. The last of these are similar to cadaver dogs but more specialized, in that human remains detection dogs are trained only to scent decomposing human flesh; they have never been trained to track living humans. The training of human remains detection dogs includes training in the ability to rule out the scent of live human flesh and other animal scents.

The science of canine forensics is a fairly new discipline in law enforcement. As more dogs are used successfully in new capacities, the idea of using dogs for many law-enforcement purposes is gaining popularity. Highly trained dogs such as cadaver dogs are becoming an indispensable part of many law-enforcement agencies.

*Kimberley M. Holloway*

### Further Reading

Bulanda, Susan. *Ready! The Training of the Search and Rescue Dog*. Irvine, Calif.: Doral Publishing, 1994.

Rebmann, Andrew, and Edward David. *Cadaver Dog Handbook: Forensic Training and Tactics for the Recovery of Human Remains*. Boca Raton, Fla.: CRC Press, 2000.

Snovak, Angela Eaton. *Guide to Search and Rescue Dogs*. New York: Barron's Educational Series, 2004.

**See also:** Animal evidence; Buried body locating; Canine substance detection; Crime scene investigation; Decomposition of bodies; Fire debris; Forensic archaeology; Scent identification.

# Canine substance detection

**Definition:** Work carried out by trained dog and handler teams to discover contraband items and hazardous materials associated with criminal activities or security threats.

**Significance:** Well-trained dogs, with their natural scent abilities, are able to locate illegal narcotics and explosive and flammable chemicals expeditiously, whereas humans and technological search devices might overlook these materials or discover them only slowly. Canine substance detection has proven useful in the apprehension and prosecution of lawbreakers.

For several centuries, dogs have assisted humans in seeking forensic evidence related to crimes, including tracking missing people and finding human remains. Law enforcement agencies' use of canines to detect illegal drugs, explosives, and accelerants intensified during the late twentieth century. Although other animals, such as rats, also have keen smelling abilities, law enforcement personnel prefer dogs because of their appeal to many people, their ability to work in congested areas and shift quickly to additional sites, and their willingness to obey commands.

The scent capabilities of canines significantly exceed those of humans. A dog's sense of smell is enhanced by the presence of approximately 220 olfactory receptors in the nose. Mucus covers these receptors, enabling them to capture molecules released by chemicals when the dog sniffs nearby. Information from these molecules reaches the dog's brain through a nerve, alerting it to the presence of specific substances. These qualities make dogs ideal for law enforcement use in detecting various illegal and dangerous substances.

## Training and Certification

Law enforcement personnel procure detection dogs from various sources. The Australian Customs Service Detector Dog Breeding Program provides stock for U.S. detection dog breeders, particularly the Transportation Security Administration (TSA) Explosive Detection Dog Program and Auburn University's Canine Detection Training Center (CDTC) at McClellan, Alabama, which supply detection dogs for governments at various levels. As the sole training program of its kind affiliated with a veterinary school, the CDTC benefits from studies conducted by veterinarians and scientists at the Canine and Detection Research Institute. The government and university programs focus on refining detection qualities in Labrador retrievers, Belgian Malinois, and shepherd breeds considered to be behaviorally reliable and physically sturdy. Detector dog selection and training are rigorous, and only the most competent canines are approved for deployment to law-enforcement agencies. Several government facilities, the CDTC, and private businesses train canines and handlers for substance-detection duties. The Bureau of Alcohol, Tobacco, Firearms and Explosives (ATF) Canine Training Center at Front Royal, Virginia, where the U.S. Customs and Border Protection (CBP) also has a canine training site, certifies dogs that complete successfully national odor recognition testing. The U.S. Drug Enforcement Administration (DEA) licenses the use of drugs at government and approved private training facilities.

ATF also trains canines to detect explosives, working with forensic chemists to choose appropriate explosives for effective training. According to their individual intended purposes, the dogs are trained to detect and distinguish the scents of many substances, ranging from chemicals found in heroin, cocaine, marijuana, and methamphetamine to explosive nitroglycerin, trinitrotoluene (TNT), and smokeless powders. In ATF training for arson dogs, the dogs learn to

## ATF-Trained Detection Dogs

*In a press release dated March 12, 2008, the Bureau of Alcohol, Tobacco, Firearms and Explosives announced the graduation of seven canine teams from its Canine Training Center:*

The Bureau of Alcohol, Tobacco, Firearms and Explosives (ATF) graduated a new class of canine handlers today at its Canine Training Center in Front Royal, Va. The ceremony was the culmination of an intensive, 10-week training course completed by federal officers from the CIA, Department of Defense, U.S. Marshals Service and the Federal Protective Service, in which ATF canine trainers spent six weeks "imprinting" the dogs, giving them the capability to locate 19,000 explosive odors—including peroxide-based explosives.

These handlers and their ATF-trained canine partners will be deployed throughout the Washington, D.C. metropolitan area and other parts of the country, where they will be used for criminal investigations, protective search and sweep oper-

ations, and safeguarding national special events such as the Republican and Democratic National Conventions, G-8 summits, the World Series and the Super Bowl. . . .

The handlers and their canines train extensively together for 10 weeks, learning how to search out explosives in vehicles, schools, train stations, concert venues, warehouses and retail stores. The dogs can also detect firearms and ammunition. Prior to graduation, each canine must pass an odor recognition test with 100 percent accuracy. This certification test is conducted by a forensic chemist using the National Odor Recognition Test developed by ATF.

ATF trains approximately 90 new canine teams each year and places them, without cost, with local, state, federal or foreign law enforcement agencies. Teams are recertified each year and receive continuous support from ATF throughout the approximate eight-year working life of the dogs.

detect specified odors of gasoline, kerosene, and other accelerants.

### Detection and Effectiveness

Many law enforcement officials consider the use of canines to be the most efficient and effective method of detecting narcotic substances, resulting in arrests of suspects. Substance detection dogs are taken to public and private locations, including schools, businesses, prisons, stadiums, and motor vehicles, where they seek the scents they are directed to detect; they alert their handlers to any substance finds by scratching, barking, or sitting. At border checkpoints, CBP and U.S. Department of Agriculture detection dogs search for illegal substances, including harmful agricultural products.

For example, in 2004, U.S. customs authorities using substance-detection dogs conducted 11,600 narcotics seizures totaling approximately 1.8 million pounds of narcotics as well as 6,500 pounds of illegal plant and animal products. Substance-detection dogs that locate ex-

plosives effectively defuse potentially hazardous situations. The U.S. Department of Homeland Security oversees canine substance detection in its antiterrorism work; this work is conducted by CBP and TSA dogs that are trained to locate dangerous chemicals and bombs. Because such substances are often hidden in sealed containers and in concealed areas, dogs can swiftly find them where humans might not easily detect them.

Explosives experts provide information on the chemicals that have previously been used by terrorists, and the dogs are trained to detect those substances. As part of enhanced security measures in the United States and elsewhere, canines sniff luggage, packages, mail, and cargo for illegal substances, explosives, and bombs at airports, train stations, ports, and crowded areas that could be terrorist targets. Dogs are used to examine industrial sites for potential sabotage.

The ability of dogs to detect explosive chemicals has also led to their use in arson investigations to find accelerants at sites of suspicious fires. As new chemical threats emerge, researchers and trainers are constantly refining their training procedures to expand the abilities of substance detection dogs to detect chemical and narcotic substances.

Despite detector dogs' high accuracy rates, many courts disregard evidence located by dogs through scent detection because this method lacks a sufficient scientific basis. Some judges, however, have ruled that search warrants can be issued based on detection dogs' alerts, as in the finding in *United States v. Trayer* (1990), a case that involved a dog alerting to drugs at the door of a train compartment. To reinforce legal acceptance of the forensic contributions of detector dogs, researchers are attempting to gain a better scientific understanding of canine scent-detection capabilities. Scientists study handler-canine interactions, canine behavior, and environmental factors to try to find ways to improve dogs' scent-detection training and performance. Law-enforcement agencies consistently evaluate and recertify substance-detection canines and their handlers, removing from service those that do not perform adequately and might discredit canine substance detection as a forensic tool.

## Legal Challenges and Changes

As of 2013, more than seven thousand teams of North American canines and law enforcement handlers performed drug detection work according to the United States Police Canine Association (www.uspcak9.com). The use of substance detection canines in the early twenty-first century often was controversial. In Illinois, reporters evaluated records to show that because of handler cues some dogs alerted more frequently to vehicles driven by minorities, providing probable cause for searches to be conducted. In many cases, no drugs were found because the dog had falsely alerted.

Critics sought standardized training by professional instructors. In 2012, the Illinois legislature passed a law requiring drug detection dogs and handlers to earn a state certificate by undergoing training procedures approved by the Illinois Law Enforcement Training and Standards Board. Dogs and handlers also participate in supplementary training exercises to reinforce and update the reliability and competency of their performances. Handlers must report every alert and results of searches to the Illinois Department of Transportation.

In 2013, the U.S. Supreme Court considered when alerts by drug detection dogs gave handlers probable cause for searches and did not violate people's Fourth Amendment rights. Revised state laws legalizing marijuana impact detection dogs trained to alert on previously illegal substances. Retraining involves adjusting how dogs alert to specific drugs in an attempt to prevent unconstitutional searches.

*Elizabeth D. Schafer*

## Further Reading

Bidner, Jen. *Dog Heroes: Saving Lives and Protecting* America. Guilford, CT: Lyons Press/Globe Pequot Press, 2002. Presents examples of canines performing police and customs work, including ATF detection dogs that search for drugs and bombs.

Bryson, Sandy. *Police Dog Tactics*. New York: McGraw-Hill, 1996. Comprehensive text written by a police dog trainer and handler. Includes sections on drug searches and the detection of explosives and accelerants.

Derr, Mark. "With Dog Detectives, Mistakes Can Happen." *The New York Times*, December 24, 2002, F1. Relates some incidents in which detection canines falsely alerted to locating substances and examines the reasons for dogs' scenting errors.

Furton, Kenneth; Jessie Greb; and Howard Holness. *The Scientific Working Group on Dog and Orthogonal Detector Guidelines (SWGDOG)*. Miami, FL: U.S. Department of Justice/Florida International University, 2010. Appendix 11 summarizes essential information regarding training, substances utilized to train canines, certification, maintenance training, and records and documentation associated with narcotics detection dogs.

Hinkel, Dan "Tighter Leash for Drug-sniffing Dogs." *Chicago Tribune*, January 2, 2012. Reports details of state legislation passed in response to criticisms of how canine drug detection was conducted, requiring new standards and procedures regarding training and monitoring of police handlers and dogs.

Hinkel, Dan, and Joe Mahr. "Tribune Analysis: Drug-sniffing Dogs in Traffic Stops Often Wrong." *Chicago Tribune*, January 6, 2011. Reveals inconsistencies in canine detection performances which resulted in higher percentages of searches for illegal substances in vehicles operated by minorities. Comments regarding demands for laws to enforce standardized training requirements for dogs and handlers.

Jezierski, Tadeusz; Ewa Adamkiewicz; Marta Walczak; Magdalena Sobczyñska; Aleksandra Górecka-Bruzda; John Ensminger; and Eugene Papet. "Efficacy of Drug Detection by Fully Trained Police Dogs Varies by Breed, Training Level, Type of Drug and Search Environment." *Forensic Science International* 237 (2014): 112-118. Details tests replicating training and detecting practices by the Polish police and involving 164 dogs representing retrievers, German shepherds, terriers, and spaniels to assess how well the canines performed and whether drug users' criticisms regarding the dogs' detection abilities were valid.

Lee, Jane J. "Detection Dogs: Learning to Pass the Sniff Test." *National Geographic* April 7, 2013 http://news.nationalgeographic.com/news/2013/04/130407/detection-dogs-learning-to-pass-the-sniff-test/. Notes how changes in laws legalizing marijuana in some states affect detection dogs that were trained to alert on drugs that had been illegal. Addresses retraining techniques and situations handlers and dogs might encounter and prepare for in order to minimize false alerts.

Lit, Lisa; Julie B. Schweitzer; and Anita M. Oberbauer. "Handler Beliefs Affect Scent Detection Dog Outcomes." *Animal Cognition* 14, no. 3 (2011): 387-394. Describes tests involving eighteen pairs of detection dogs and handlers searching for drugs and explosives the handlers were told had been concealed in a specific area. Although none of those items were actually present, the dogs made over two hundred false alerts, responding to handlers' cues.

Needles, Colleen, and Kit Carlson. *Working Dogs: Tales from Animal Planet's K-9 to 5 World*. Photographs by Kim Levin. New York: Discovery Books, 2000. Profiles several drug enforcement, arson, police, and customs inspector dogs.

Ross, Darrell L. "Probable Cause and the Sniff Factor: *Florida v. Harris* and *Florida v. Jardines*." *Criminal Justice Review* 38, no. 3 (September 2013): 412-422. Focuses on legal concerns regarding the role of detection dogs and the Fourth Amendment in searches for contraband in two cases which were debated in state courts and appealed to the U.S. Supreme Court.

U.S. Congress. House. Committee on Homeland Security. *Sniffing Out Terrorism: The Use of Dogs in Homeland Security*. Washington, D.C.: Government Printing Office, 2007. Transcript of statements made by canine detection trainers, handlers, scientists, and law enforcement representatives at a congressional hearing held on September 28, 2005.

**See also:** Airport security; Arson dogs; Bombings; Bureau of Alcohol, Tobacco, Firearms and Explosives; Cadaver dogs; Courts and forensic evidence; Drug Enforcement Administration, U.S.; Fire debris; Narcotics; Scent identification; Training and licensing of forensic professionals.

## Carbon monoxide poisoning

**Definition:** Poisoning caused by exposure to toxic levels of carbon monoxide, a colorless, odorless, and tasteless gas derived from incomplete burning of carbon- containing organic materials, such as gasoline, natural gas, oil, propane, coal, and wood.

**Significance:** Carbon monoxide (CO) poisoning is the most common type of accidental poisoning that occurs in the United States. Undetected, unsuspected, or undiagnosed, carbon monoxide poisoning can result in death. Hospital emergency departments treat thousands of patients with confirmed and probable CO poisoning yearly, and hundreds of fatalities occur as the result of unintentional, non-fire-related CO exposure. It is estimated that the incidence of intentional CO poisoning, such as suicide and homicide, is even higher.

Carbon monoxide is known as the "silent cold-weather killer" and as "the Great Imitator" because the manifestations of its toxicity are nonspecific. If CO is not considered as a cause when CO poisoning occurs, health care personnel can easily misdiagnose the victim. CO is a ubiquitous gas that is present in workplaces, recreational areas, and homes.

The most common sources of carbon monoxide include motor vehicle exhaust, smoke from fires, portable kerosene heaters, charcoal grills, propane stoves, and tobacco smoke. Chemical sources include spray paints, solvents, degreasers, and paint removers containing methylene chloride, which is processed in the liver and changed into CO.

## Casting

The annual incidence of fatal and nonfatal toxic exposure to carbon monoxide is highest during the winter months, when many homes are closed for protection against cold weather [or insulated due to cold weather]; cases of CO poisoning are fewest during the summer months. More than two hundred CO poisoning fatalities are caused annually in the United States by fuel-burning appliances such as furnaces, gas ranges, water heaters, and kerosene space heaters. CO poisoning occurs at low levels in susceptible individuals, such as infants, pregnant women, the elderly, and those with anemia or heart and lung diseases.

The symptoms of CO poisoning are vague; in many ways they are similar to those of viral illnesses, and victims may be misdiagnosed. The most common symptoms are headache, dizziness, nausea, and fatigue. More severe symptoms include loss of consciousness, shortness of breath, confusion, and loss of muscle control. Some patients develop delayed symptoms of the nervous system, such as memory loss, personality changes, and movement disorders. All of these symptoms arise because CO binds tightly

to hemoglobin, a protein found in red blood cells; this binding causes a decrease in the ability of red blood cells to deliver oxygen to the vital organs, especially the heart and the brain. Medical personnel should be suspicious if anyone displaying such symptoms reports circumstances of the illness that could relate to possible CO exposure. An important point for the medical personnel is that a commonly used method of checking oxygen in the blood referred to as pulse oximetry is misleading; an arterial blood gas measurement is required to make the diagnosis.

The diagnosis of CO poisoning is made through the measurement of the CO bound to hemoglobin by arterial blood gas measurement mentioned above. Treatment consists of providing supplemental oxygen to dissociate the CO-hemoglobin binding. Oxygen may be delivered through a face mask, through hyperbaric oxygen therapy, or through mechanical ventilation.

Preventive measures to avoid CO poisoning include having heating and ventilation systems, water heaters, and other similar devices serviced yearly by qualified technicians. Generators, charcoal grills, camp stoves, and other similar appliances should not be used indoors or near buildings, and gas ovens should not be used to heat homes. In addition to these precautions, many experts recommend the installation of home CO detectors, which should be checked regularly. Finally, medical attention should be obtained immediately if CO poisoning is suspected.

*Miriam E. Schwartz and*
*Shawkat Dhanani*

## Further Reading

Guzman, Jorge A. "Carbon Monoxide Poisoning." *Critical Care Clinics* 28, no. 4 (2012):537-548.

Occupational Safety and Health Administration. *Carbon Monoxide Poisoning Fact Sheet.* Washington, DC: Government Printing Office, 2002.

Penny, David G., ed. *Carbon Monoxide Poisoning.* Boca Raton, FL: CRC Press, 2008.

Piantadosi, Claude A. "Perspective: Carbon Monoxide Poisoning." *New England Journal of Medicine* 347, no. 14 (2002): 1054-1055.

Smollin, Craig and Kent Olson. "Carbon Monoxide Poisoning (Acute)." *British Medical Journal (BMJ) Clinical Evidence* (2010): October 12.

Weaver, Lindell K. "Carbon Monoxide Poisoning." *New England Journal of Medicine* 360, no. 12 (2009): 1217-1225.

Wu, Peter E. and David N. Juurlink. "Five Things to Know About...: Carbon Monoxide Poisoning." *Canadian Medical Association Journal* 186, no. 8 (2014): 611.

United States Consumer Product Safety Commission. Carbon Monoxide Information Center. http://www.cpsc.gov/en/Safety-Education/Safety-Education-Centers/Carbon-Monoxide-Information-Center.

United States Environmental Protection Agency. An Introduction to Indoor Air Quality (IAQ)

Carbon Monoxide (CO). http://www.epa.gov/iaq/co.html.

**See also:** See also: Air and water purity; Arson; Centers for Disease Control and Prevention; Chemical agents; Food poisoning; Forensic toxicology; Livor mortis; Nervous system; Poisons and anti-dotes; Smoke inhalation; Suffocation; Suicide.

# Casting

**Definition:** Production of three-dimensional models of impressions left by footwear, tires, or tools at crime scenes.

**Significance:** Forensic scientists use casts, permanent physical records of marks left at crime scenes, to compare with the vehicle tires, footwear, or tools found in the possession of possible suspects.

Perpetrators often leave traces of their presence at crime scenes in the form of tire impressions or footprints in dust, soil, mud, or snow. The tools used by perpetrators also leave distinctive impressions, such as the marks left on a door by a crowbar. Casting is a way of making permanent three-dimensional records of these impressions. Because tires, footwear, and tools do not wear evenly, they develop unique use patterns. Using a cast made from an impression found at a crime scene, a forensic scientist can compare the unique wear pattern shown by that impression with the wear patterns on the possessions of any suspects. Casts often show marks with a degree of accuracy that either confirms or eliminates the presence of some persons at the crime scene. In court, casts are used as physical evidence to show a link between the accused and the crime.

## Casting in Soil

Castings in mud, dirt, and sand are made with a product known as dental stone. Dental stone creates a crisper, more detailed cast than does plaster of paris or other plasters and is less likely to be damaged during cleaning. Dental stone comes in powder form, and water is added at the crime scene to make a runny, batterlike mixture that is used to fill the impression. Photographs are taken to locate the impression within the scene, and a plastic frame is placed around the impression before the cast is made. In loose soil or sand, the impression may be sprayed with a chemical that hardens the surface before casting.

To prevent distortion of the impression, the technician fills it with dental stone gently. After the impression is filled, the dental stone is allowed to harden for at least half an hour in warm weather and longer in cold or very humid conditions. Before hardening is complete, the technician inscribes the cast with identifying information. Once the cast has solidified, it is removed from the soil and is allowed to air-dry for several days, after which it is cleaned of clinging soil and examined.

## Casting in Snow

Casting in snow creates special problems because of the fragility of the impression. This is especially true when the impression has been made in very dry, nonpacking, or windblown snow, or in snow that has begun to melt. Two techniques can be used to cast in snow. In one, before the dental stone cast is made, several layers of a product called Snow Print Wax are sprayed over the snow to stabilize the impression. The impression is then cast in the same way as an impression in soil. Cold conditions substantially slow the hardening of the cast, and it may be several hours before the cast can be removed from the snow.

Another way of casting in snow involves the use of Snow Print Wax and prill sulfur, a pellet form of sulfur that is a by-product of natural gas refining. The pellets are melted and then cooled so that the sulfur will not melt the snow. The impression is first sprayed with Snow Print Wax and then filled with the melted sulfur. Pouring the sulfur when it is at the correct temperature—not hot enough to melt the snow yet not so cold that it starts to form crystals before it is poured—is a critical step in creating a good prill sulfur cast. After about twenty minutes, the cast is hard enough to remove. Because prill sulfur casts are brittle and easily broken, they are often embedded in a protective layer of dental stone.

In 2003, the Royal Canadian Mounted Police tested both methods of casting in snow and found that prill sulfur casting produced sharper, more detailed casts than did Snow Print Wax casting alone.

### Casting Tool Marks

Tools that are used to pry, scrape, cut, or drill hard surfaces leave marks that can be cast. For example, a hammer hitting a nail leaves a reproducible and distinctive mark. When tool marks found at a crime scene are on objects too large to move to the laboratory (such as on a safe or a door frame), photographs are taken to locate the marks within the scene and casts are then made with sprayable silicone rubber or a similar silicone resin. This material dries quickly and accurately reproduces the unique indentations and ridges made by tools. Tool marks are more difficult to match than are tire or footwear marks, and the marks made by a tool may change over time if the tool is heavily used.

*Martiscia Davidson*

### Further Reading

Bodziak, William J. *Footwear Impression Evidence: Detection, Recovery, and Examination.* 3rd ed. Boca Raton, FL: CRC Press, 2015. Comprehensive guide to handling footwear evidence includes information on casting both footwear and barefoot impressions.

Bodziak, William. *Tire Tread and Tire Track Evidence: Recovery and Forensic Examination.* Boca Raton, FL: CRC Press, 2015. Comprehensive guide to handling tire track impressions in the field and in the laboratory.

Hilderbrand, Dwane S. *Footwear, the Missed Evidence: A Field Guide to the Collection and Preservation of Forensic Footwear Impression Evidence.* 3rd ed. Wildomar, Calif.: Staggs, 2013. Provides information about all aspects of preserving, collecting, and interpreting footwear impressions, including detailed information on how to cast impressions under a variety of conditions.

James, Stuart H., and Jon J. Nordby, eds. *Forensic Science: An Introduction to Scientific and Investigative Techniques.* 4th ed. Boca Raton, FL: CRC Press, 2011. Easy-to-read introductory textbook covers all aspects of forensics, including the casting of footwear and tire impressions.

Srihari, Sargur. "Analysis of Footwear Impression Evidence," *US DoJ Report,* March 2011. <https://www.ncjrs.gov/pdffiles1/nij/grants/233981.pdf> Technical use of computers to analyze footwear impressions.

**See also:** Autopsies; Bite-mark analysis; Disturbed evidence; Evidence processing; Footprints and shoe prints; Oral autopsy; Prints; Tire tracks; Tool marks.

## Celebrity cases

**Definition:** Forensic investigations of accidents and alleged crimes involving well-known persons.

**Significance:** Whenever a celebrity is involved in an incident requiring law-enforcement investigation, the event receives widespread coverage in the news media. The in-depth reporting on these cases by some media outlets brings public attention to the uses of forensic science and demonstrates the need for investigators to follow correct procedures in the collection of evidence.

Tragedies among the rich and famous typically garner significant attention from the general public. Among others, the cases described below involving entertainment industry celebrities have drawn public attention to the use of forensic techniques in law-enforcement investigations.

### Robert Blake

Best known for his role as the star of the television series *Baretta* (1975-1978), Robert Blake, who had also been a member of the cast of the Our Gang series of comedy shorts in the 1930's and 1940's, gained renewed notoriety in 2001 as the prime suspect in the murder of his wife, Bonny Lee Bakley.

Bakley was shot and killed as she sat in a car outside a Los Angeles restaurant, and Blake was charged with one count of murder, two counts of solicitation of murder, and one count of murder conspiracy. He was accused of trying to hire two Hollywood stuntmen to kill his wife. Blake was tried for and acquitted of the murder charge and of one count of solicitation of murder; the other charges against him were dropped. In 2005, however, Blake was found liable for Bakley's wrongful death by a jury in a civil suit filed by Bakley's four children and was ordered to pay the family thirty million dollars.

Among the forensic evidence introduced during Blake's criminal trial was the finding from an analysis of the amount of gunshot residue (GSR)—particles emitted when a gun is fired—found on Blake's hands after Bakley was shot. An independent scientist testified that she found only five particles of GSR on the actor's hands and that the killer would likely have had ninety-seven to ninety-eight particles; the GSR found on Blake could have been a result of Blake's handling his own gun, which was not the murder weapon. Other experts testified that the source of the GSR on Blake's hands could not be confirmed. Additionally, no latent fingerprints could be found on the murder weapon.

Another area of suspicion for both the prosecution and the defense was the fact that Blake had no blood on his clothes immediately after the shooting. A forensics expert who analyzed the blood-spray patterns in the car where Bakley was killed said that the killer would not necessarily have been sprayed by blood because of the angle of the shooting. Other forensic testimony was presented in the case by a psychopharmacologist, who testified that frequent methamphetamine and cocaine use could cause delusions, paranoia, and hallucinations; this testimony was used to discredit the claims of the two stuntmen Blake was alleged to have tried to hire to kill his wife.

### Christian Brando

Known for having a bad temper fueled by frequent drug and alcohol abuse, Christian Brando, the son of actor Marlon Brando, had an especially close relationship with his sister, Cheyenne, who also had drug and alcohol problems. In 1990, Christian Brando was accused of murdering his sister's longtime boyfriend, Dag Drollet, whom Cheyenne had accused of abusing her. After a night of drinking, Christian, carrying a handgun, confronted Drollet in a bungalow on the Brando estate. Drollet was shot and killed; Brando claimed that the gun had gone off accidentally.

Evidence reports, as well as two autopsies, called into question Brando's story that the two men were struggling for the gun when it went off. Forensic analyses indicated that Drollet had died from a bullet to the back of the head, not in the face, as Brando originally reported. Further, investigators found that the scene of the death did not indicate that a struggle had taken place.

Forensic psychologists who testified for the prosecution characterized Christian Brando as a violence-prone threat to society, whereas defense experts described him as chronically depressed with diminished capacity as the result of long-term drug abuse. Key witnesses were not available to testify at the trial, and the court ruled that Brando's Miranda warning was inadequately administered, rendering his earlier confession inadmissible. Eventually, Brando pleaded guilty to voluntary manslaughter and was sentenced to ten years in prison.

### Bob Crane

The 1978 murder of Bob Crane, who is best known as the star of the television series *Hogan's Heroes* (1965-1971), remains a mystery. After Crane was found brutally beaten to death in a Scottsdale, Arizona, apartment, investigators determined that he had been bludgeoned while he slept. The murder weapon was never found, but it was believed to be a camera tripod. The prime suspect was a video expert, John Henry Carpenter, who frequently participated in group sex parties that Crane organized. Criminologists found blood in Carpenter's car that matched Crane's relatively rare blood type, but at the time, the source of the blood could not be confirmed; DNA (deoxyribonucleic acid) typing did not yet exist. The case was closed for lack of evidence. When it was reopened in 1992, it was discovered that improper storage of the evidence made DNA analysis of the blood impossible. Nonetheless, Carpenter was indicted, and forensic photography experts were called to testify as to the authenticity of photos of an unknown material found in Carpenter's car. Despite these attempts, Carpenter was acquitted.

### John Holmes

Dubbed the "Sultan of Smut," John Holmes starred in more than two thousand pornographic movies and was the template for one of the characters in the 1997 film *Boogie Nights*. By the 1980's, he had become debilitated by drug use, and his career had collapsed. Holmes came under suspicion of being one of the three masked thugs who committed the brutal 1981 quadruple homicide that became known as the "Wonderland murders," named for the street on which the killings occurred. The murders were later confirmed to be drug-related retaliation killings. From a forensic standpoint, the Wonderland murders marked a turning point in courtroom evidence. The first law-enforcement investigators at the crime scene were so appalled by the amount of blood they found—the victims had all been beaten to death—that they videotaped the scene, and the prosecutors used the tape at trial.

This marked the first time video evidence was admitted in court. Despite significant evidence pointing to Holmes's involvement in the killings, he was acquitted in 1982.

### Manson Family

In August, 1969, starlet Sharon Tate was eight months pregnant by her husband, film director Roman Polanski. On a warm Saturday evening, Tate gathered with friends at her home near Beverly Hills. Early the next morning, Tate's housekeeper discovered a gruesome scene: five bodies, including Tate's. Investigators found that the victims had been shot, beaten, strangled, and mutilated. The word "pig" had been scribbled in blood on a door, and the broken grip of a .22 caliber revolver was discovered at the scene.

The next day, in another part of town, Leno and Rosemary LaBianca were discovered stabbed and strangled. The word "war" had been carved into Leno's body, and "death to pigs," "rise," and "healther skelter" (misspelled this way) had been scrawled in blood. A few days earlier, music teacher Gary Hinman had been stabbed to death, and "political piggy" had been written on his wall in his own blood.

Initially, the Los Angeles Police Department (LAPD) refused to draw connections among the three crimes, claiming that the Tate murders were a result of a drug deal gone bad. Two weeks after the murders, a .22 revolver with a broken grip was found in another Los Angeles suburb, but police failed to connect it to the earlier crimes. The Los Angeles County Sheriff's Department and the LAPD continued to pursue the cases separately for three months. In October, 1969, the two departments began to work together on the cases, and investigations led to a commune run by Charles Manson; Manson and his followers were known as the Manson Family.

A key piece of evidence in the Tate case was a fingerprint found in Tate's home that belonged to one of Manson's followers. In addition, bullets matching those found at the crime scene were discovered in the Manson compound. The .22 revolver in LAPD custody was finally rediscovered and matched to the bullets. In March, 1971, Manson was found guilty of first-degree murder. Several of his followers were later convicted.

In the years since the Manson murders, forensic historians have frequently referred to these cases in terms of "what not to do" for crime scene investigators. For example, the bodies found at the scenes were initially covered with household sheets, which could have contaminated evidence with unrelated fibers. Blood that had been left by the killers on the security gate button at the Tate estate was smeared by police officers who used the button. Police also smeared possible fingerprints on the .22 revolver when they received it, and pieces of the broken gun grip were inadvertently kicked under a chair. In addition, investigators tracked blood throughout the Tate house, and insufficient blood samples were taken from the crime scene and from the victims.

### Marilyn Monroe

Officially, Marilyn Monroe died of an accidental overdose of sleeping pills, but some experts have suggested that Monroe was actually murdered, speculating that her death may have been related to her involvement with President John F. Kennedy and his brother, Robert F. Kennedy. Several elements of the August 5, 1962, death have raised questions. For example, Monroe's housekeeper found her unconscious at about 3:30    and called Monroe's psychiatrist and her physician. Despite confirming the death upon their arrival, the two doctors then waited at least a half hour to call the police. Further, although toxicologists found Nembutal (a barbiturate) in her system (the drug had been prescribed for Monroe as a sleep aid), they also found high levels of chloral hydrate of unknown origin.

The initial autopsy was performed by Dr. Thomas Noguchi of the Los Angeles County Coroner's Office, who would go on to become somewhat famous as the "coroner to the stars."

Although later investigation would deem his autopsy to have been thorough, Noguchi wanted to investigate further. Shortly after his initial autopsy, he tried to reexamine the tissue samples, but they were missing. In addition, one of the nation's top forensic pathologists deemed the toxicology report incomplete.

Other evidence suggested that Robert Kennedy had visited Monroe in the evening before her death; it has been asserted that he went there to break off contact between Monroe and the Kennedy brothers. Additionally, it has been alleged by some that actor Peter Lawford, who was the brother-in-law of John and Robert Kennedy, may have removed from Monroe's house any evidence suggesting her involvement with the Kennedys. The Los Angeles District Attorney's Office reopened the case in 1982, but after a lengthy examination of the evidence, investigators again concluded that Monroe's death was a probable suicide.

### George Reeves

George Reeves, star of the 1950's television show *Adventures of Superman*, died of a gunshot wound to the head in his California home on June 16, 1959. The death was ruled a suicide; it was believed to have been the result of Reeves's despondency over the cancellation of his television series and his waning career. Much later, unofficial investigations into Reeves's death raised questions about this ruling, citing forensic evidence that appears to contradict a finding of suicide. For example, no fingerprints were found on the gun, no gunpowder burns were present around the entry wound, and no record exists of any test for gunshot residue on Reeves's hands. Forensics experts have noted, however, that the gun was too well oiled to retain fingerprints, that gunpowder stippling frequently does not occur when a gun is held directly against the skin, and that tests for gunshot residue were not commonly performed in the 1950's.

### Elizabeth Short

The case of the "Black Dahlia" is still considered one of the most notorious Hollywood murders. Nicknamed perhaps for her penchant for black clothes, Elizabeth Short was an aspiring starlet. On January 15, 1947, her nude body was found in a weed-covered lot by a pedestrian. Her remains had been slashed and stabbed, and the body was neatly cut in half. Further, the young woman had been posed spread-eagle with the two halves set a foot apart, and the letters "BD" were carved into her thigh. Perhaps most disturbing, her face had been slashed to resemble a clownish death grin. The body appeared to be washed clean and there was little blood at the scene, leading investigators to surmise that Short had been killed elsewhere.

Forensic technicians working for the Federal Bureau of Investigation (FBI) used fingerprint analysis to identify the body as Short's. The Los Angeles Coroner's Office reported that Short had died of massive internal hemorrhaging caused by blows to the head, and no traces of sexual activity were found. The clean bisection of her body led some investigators to believe the murder might have been the work of a medical student or butcher. The young woman's shoes and purse were found in a trash receptacle several miles away from the scene where her body was discovered.

Although "confessions" began pouring in to the LAPD and the FBI, and investigators eventually interviewed more than one thousand people, it was all to no avail. Nine days after Short's body was found, the *Los Angeles Examiner* newspaper office received a package containing Short's belongings, including photos, her birth certificate and Social Security card, and an address book containing the names of seventy-five men—none of whom could be connected to the murder. The sender had soaked the package in gasoline, apparently to remove any fingerprints or other identifying materials.

One key suspect, Robert Manley, had been the last to see Short alive, but the police released him after he passed a polygraph test. Later, he was committed to a mental institution; he was questioned again there after being dosed with sodium thiopental—a so-called truth serum—and he still denied the murder. Over a period of years following Short's death, police and various news media outlets received thirteen letters thought to be written by the murderer, but they produced no identifying evidence. The case remains unsolved.

## O. J. Simpson

O. J. Simpson's murder trial became one of the most highly publicized trials in American history and brought DNA evidence to the forefront of public awareness. Nicole Brown Simpson, the former wife of sometime actor and

retired professional football star O. J. Simpson, was stabbed to death outside her home on the night of June 12, 1994, along with an acquaintance, Ronald Goldman.

After police responded to the crime scene, detectives immediately went to Simpson's home, where they found a bloodstain on the door of his Ford Bronco along with a trail of blood leading up to his house. As they questioned Simpson, the investigators noticed a cut on his left hand. Crime scene investigators had already concluded that the killer also had been cut on his left hand. In addition, analysis of drops of blood found at the crime scene indicated that they had DNA factors that pointed toward Simpson. Investigators also found footprints in Simpson's size at the crime scene and determined that they had been left by an exotic brand of shoe that Simpson owned. They also discovered a bloodstained glove on his property that matched one taken from the crime scene. Finally, investigators found traces of Nicole Brown Simpson's blood in Simpson's car and house, intermingled with Simpson's blood.

During the trial, Simpson's defense attorneys called forensic witnesses who asserted that the blood samples used as evidence by the prosecution had been mishandled, raising the possibility that they were contaminated or too degraded to produce accurate DNA analysis results. The prosecution produced other criminologists to refute these claims, but Simpson was eventually acquitted on all counts. In 1997, the jury in a civil suit brought by Ronald Goldman's father found Simpson responsible for the deaths of Brown Simpson and Goldman.

## Phil Spector

Phil Spector, a well-known music producer who had worked with the Righteous Brothers, the Beatles, and many other famous recording artists, was arrested on February 3, 2005, when police discovered the body of actress Lana Clarkson in the foyer of Spector's home in Alhambra, California. Although Spector initially told police, "I think I killed someone," he later claimed the shooting was an "accidental suicide."

Spector's 2007 murder trial was surrounded by controversy. Famed forensic expert Henry C.

Lee was accused by the district attorney of hiding evidence that proved Spector's guilt. In addition, a coroner concluded that bruises on Clarkson's tongue indicated that the gun had been forced into her mouth. The defense got a break when a DNA expert testified that only Clarkson's DNA was found on the murder weapon and that none of Spector's DNA was found under Clarkson's fingernails. In addition, a forensic pathologist testified for the defense that Clarkson had mental problems that could have led to suicide.

During the trial, forensic witnesses for the defense used a sophisticated three-dimensional plexiglass bust of the victim to demonstrate how the bullet went through her head and into her spine. The defense ended its arguments by presenting a computer-animated demonstration of the shooting as Spector asserted it took place. The trial ended in a hung jury, resulting in a mistrial, and the Los Angeles District Attorney's Office began preparing for a new trial.

### Cheryl Turner

Cheryl Turner, daughter of movie queen Lana Turner, was fourteen years old when police investigated her role in the 1958 death of her mother's boyfriend, Johnny Stompanato. Lana and Johnny had a tempestuous relationship, and Cheryl had witnessed several incidents in which Stompanato had been violent toward her mother. During one of these episodes, Cheryl apparently intervened and stabbed Stompanato with a knife.

At a grand jury inquest during which Lana Turner gave what was described as a stunning performance, the Los Angeles coroner introduced an autopsy report outlining the extent of Stompanato's injuries. Further testimony indicated some confusion over details such as the lack of fingerprints on the knife, strange fibers in the blood on the knife, and a lack of blood on Lana Turner's clothes. Nonetheless, the jurors deemed the death justifiable homicide, and the prosecutor decided not to file charges. Stompanato's family subsequently brought a wrongful-death suit against Lana Turner; it was eventually settled out of court.

*Cheryl Pawlowski*

### Further Reading

Bugliosi, Vincent. *Outrage: The Five Reasons Why O. J. Simpson Got Away with Murder*. New York: W. W. Norton, 1996. Famous former Los Angeles prosecutor presents a compendium of alleged mistakes by the legal system that resulted in the acquittal of O. J. Simpson.

Bugliosi, Vincent, with Curt Gentry. *Helter Skelter: The True Story of the Manson Murders*. 25th anniversary ed. New York: W. W. Norton, 1994. Best-selling book by the chief prosecutor in the case tells in graphic detail the story of the investigation and prosecution of Charles Manson and his followers.

Gilmore, John. *Severed: The True Story of the Black Dahlia Murder*. Los Angeles: Amok Books, 1994. Luridly detailed account of the investigation into the death of aspiring starlet Elizabeth Short, written by the son of a Los Angeles police officer who helped investigate the case.

Graysmith, Robert. *Auto Focus: The Murder of Bob Crane*. New York: Berkley Books, 2002. Examines Crane's life and discusses how the investigation into his murder was marred by conflicts and the inexperience of the investigators.

Noguchi, Thomas T., with Joseph DiMona. *Coroner*. New York: Simon & Schuster, 1983. Los Angeles coroner Noguchi explores some of the more famous cases in which he was involved, including the deaths of Robert Kennedy, Sharon Tate, and Marilyn Monroe.

**See also:** *Cold Case*; *CSI: Crime Scene Investigation*; DNA extraction from hair, bodily fluids, and tissues; Fingerprints; *Forensic Files*; Forensic photography; Homicide; Journalism; Misconceptions fostered by media; Prints; Pseudoscience in forensic practice; Simpson murder trial; Sports memorabilia fraud.

# Centers for Disease Control and Prevention

**Date:** Founded in 1946 as the Communicable Disease Center

**Identification:** Agency of the U.S. Department of Health and Human Services that promotes a higher quality of human life through the prevention and control of disease, injury, and disability in the United States and globally.

**Significance:** The Centers for Disease Control and Prevention, the highest-level governmental health organization in the United States, employs forensic and public health experts who can efficiently investigate outbreaks of disease, mass-casualty events, and biological, chemical, nuclear, and radiological terrorist attacks domestically and elsewhere. Because of the organization's vast resources and expertise, all public health institutions in the United States as well as institutions in many other countries look to the Centers for Disease Control for training and investigation of mysterious diseases and deaths.

The agency now known as the Centers for Disease Control and Prevention (CDC) was called the Communicable Disease Center when it was organized in Atlanta, Georgia, during World War II. At that time, its major mission was to assist in the prevention and control of malaria in the southeastern United States and in war zones with endemic malaria. The agency was organized by Dr. Joseph W. Mountin, a visionary public health official. Within a few years, the center eradicated malaria in the southeastern United States. The success of this project was confirmed through the disease surveillance programs that the agency established in 1949. With the outbreak of the Korean War in 1950 and the threat of biological warfare, the CDC launched the Epidemic Intelligence Service (EIS) to carry out biological warfare surveillance. This program trained "disease detectives" to be deployed throughout the world to monitor outbreaks of diseases and to investigate suspected biological warfare-induced conditions.

## Late Twentieth Century Achievements

The credibility of the CDC in disease investigation was bolstered after the successful control of poliomyelitis outbreaks among recipients of the new Salk polio vaccine in 1955. This success was followed by the successful tracing of the course of an influenza epidemic that led to the CDC's development of a flu vaccine in 1957. During the early 1960's, the CDC expanded its mission to work involving surveillance of chronic diseases, nutrition, occupational safety, quarantine services, and immunizations against measles, rubella, and smallpox. The agency also joined international efforts to control malaria and expanded its disease control programs globally.

To combat the menace of smallpox, the CDC developed and tested the jet-gun immunization device, which was used successfully in immunizing people in South America and Central and West Africa in 1966. Following increasing involvement in international projects, in 1970 the agency's name was changed to the Center for Disease Control; it was renamed the Centers for Disease Control in 1980.

In collaboration with the World Health Organization, the CDC assisted in the global eradication of smallpox, which was declared accomplished in 1977. The CDC was also involved in the identification of Ebola virus, isolation of hepatitis C, and the first description of the sexual transmission of hepatitis B. In another investigation, the agency successfully described the association between Reye's syndrome and aspirin. The agency also helped to explain the relationship between occupational exposure to vinyl chloride and liver cancer, and, after a thorough investigation, the agency reported the harmful effects of a popular liquid protein diet.

From 1970 through early 1980, the CDC investigated mysterious deaths that occurred in the United States and found their causes in toxic shock syndrome and Legionnaires' disease; the agency both described health hazards and applied appropriate preventive measures to combat them. The CDC also described the first case of acquired immunodeficiency syndrome (AIDS) in 1981 and published information on the disease's associated risk factors and control measures. In collaboration with the National Center for Health Statistics, the CDC identified the dangers to human health of lead, which was subsequently removed from gasoline.

During the 1980's the CDC also investigated the use of estrogen replacement therapy and oral contraceptives and the relationship of such use to risks of breast, cervical, and ovarian cancers. At the request of the U.S. Congress, the agency investigated the effects of service in Vietnam on the health of Vietnam War veterans and their offspring. This led to the development of a serum test for a toxin called dioxin, which was identified as a potential cancer-inducing chemical. In the 1990's, the CDC participated in the investigation of an outbreak of hantavirus pulmonary syndrome in the United States. In addition, the agency played major roles in global efforts to eradicate polio and to prevent neural tube defects among unborn babies. In recognition of the CDC's diverse roles in both disease control and prevention, the U.S. Congress changed the agency's official name to the Centers for Disease Control and Prevention in 1992.

Dr. Jonas Salk speaks to the press during a visit to the Centers for Disease Control in 1988. The credibility of the CDC in disease investigation was bolstered by the successful control of poliomyelitis outbreaks among recipients of the polio vaccine created by Salk in 1955. *(Centers for Disease Control and Prevention)*

## Twenty-first Century Missions

The CDC's role in monitoring the use of biological and chemical weapons intensified in the twenty-first century. Following the September 11, 2001, terrorist attacks on Washington, D.C., and New York City and the anthrax bioterror mail attacks that occurred shortly thereafter, the agency embarked on policies that would improve its ability to respond to similar events in the future. In addition, the Emergency Operation Center (EOC) of the CDC collaborated with law-enforcement agencies and state and local health departments in an investigation of the source of the anthrax used in the 2001 attacks and the hunt for victims of the attacks.

When Hurricane Katrina struck the U.S. Gulf coast in August, 2005, the CDC's disaster response team was involved in attempting to help manage the crisis. The agency also provided support to the National Disaster Medical System and the Federal Emergency Management Agency (FEMA). The CDC played similar roles during the Hurricane Rita disaster of September, 2005.

As part of its ongoing work, the CDC maintains constant surveillance for new infectious diseases and signs of biological and chemical terrorist attacks. The agency also coordinates training aimed at enhancing its responses to future attacks through its strategic plan for bioterrorism preparedness and response, which was developed in conjunction with other federal agencies responsible for public health and safety.

## CDC Partners and Investigations

The CDC works with many other domestic agencies, as well as agencies of foreign governments, to carry out disease surveillance around the world. It is also involved in the detection and investigation of health problems and the management of disaster events involving mass casualties. Furthermore, the CDC conducts research to determine the best ways to enhance efforts to prevent such problems. In addition, the center fosters the training of public health leaders while assisting in the development of sound public health policies and the implementation of prevention strategies.

Among the CDC's notable external partners is the World Health Organization, with which it works to control and prevent infectious diseases. In addition to collaborating with public health institutions and laboratories in other countries, the CDC maintains its own laboratories in other parts of the world. Through these networks, the CDC plays a crucial role in world health. Because it operates the finest health laboratories in the world, the agency serves as an international center for training and disease investigation. Law-enforcement agencies employ its services in investigations of homicides, terrorist attacks, and unusual deaths.

CDC investigations focus on identifying the causes, current victims, and potential victims of major public health problems, including both natural and human-made disasters. The agency's experts collaborate with officials of local and national law-enforcement agencies in conducting investigations of particular events.

## Chronic and Infectious Diseases

Investigations of health problems involve isolating the agents or risk factors responsible. For example, in cases of chronic disease, investigators seek to establish the association between agents and diseases, such as in the CDC's work that connected aspirin consumption by young children with Reye's syndrome. The CDC frequently carries out investigations of suspected relationships between toxic agents and exposure to special occupational and environmental conditions. Forensic toxicologists are often involved in such investigations.

When it began during World War II, the CDC was concerned primarily with the control of malaria. It gradually evolved to become one of the most important institutions in the world in the investigation of infectious diseases. Apart from employing a large number of highly trained public health experts, the agency maintains one of the best laboratories devoted to the study of infectious diseases in the world. CDC investigators examine outbreaks of infectious diseases by isolating the infectious agents responsible, characterizing those agents, identifying possible vectors and reservoirs of the organisms, and mapping transmission patterns.

In some cases involving fatalities, the CDC uses forensic samples to identify or isolate the infective agents. Samples from body fluids and suspected harbingers of infectious agents may also be used in CDC investigations. The CDC has identified, isolated, and characterized a number of infectious agents in this way. The agency's Special Pathogens Branch studies highly infectious viruses that cause human diseases. This group's laboratory studies such dangerous microorganisms as hantaviruses and Ebola, Lassa, and Nipah viruses. All outbreaks of infectious disease in the United States are reported to the CDC, and many foreign governments engage the CDC to investigate disease outbreaks in their countries.

## Bioterrorism

The investigation of biological attacks has become an increasingly important part of the CDC's work, as the U.S. government has recognized the potential for such attacks to produce mass casualties. Organisms used in biological attacks may be dispersed through the atmosphere or introduced into domestic food and water supplies.

In late 2001, the CDC was involved in the investigation of attacks in several American cities in which the bacterium that causes anthrax was sent through the U.S. mails. The investigation identified eleven cases of inhalation anthrax and eleven cases of cutaneous anthrax. Organisms were isolated from samples of blood, cerebrospinal fluids, and wound and skin biopsies taken from victims of the attacks. In seeking to identify the sources of the organisms, investigators recovered four letters that had been sprayed with powder containing the anthrax bacterium and were able to trace the paths of the envelopes. Further investigation revealed the presence of the organism in facilities where U.S. mail was sorted. Although the perpetrator of the attacks was not identified, this investigation was helpful in identifying the attack agents and the victims. Because the potential sources of the anthrax were identified, people who were exposed to anthrax were promptly treated, and others were protected from potential infection.

Among the many other infectious agents that bioterrorists may disseminate are smallpox virus, plague bacteria, and the Ebola, Marbug, and Lassa viruses. The CDC classifies such viruses, which can cause high mortality and can be disseminated relatively easily, as Category A agents. The CDC has also recognized the dangers posed by agents causing lower mortality rates that may be used by terrorists. Category B agents include *Coxiella burnetii* (the bacterium that causes Q fever), alphaviruses, ricin (a toxin derived from castor beans), *Clostridium perfringens* (a bacterium involved in food-borne illnesses), and bacteria such as *Salmonella, Shigella*, and *Escherichia coli*.

Category C organisms include emerging infectious agents and other pathogens that are readily available and may be engineered for mass dissemination. Members of this group include hantaviruses, Nipah virus, tick-borne hemorrhagic fevers and encephalitis viruses, and multidrug-resistant tuberculosis.

## Chemical Agents

The CDC maintains a nationwide surveillance system for the detection of possible terrorist attacks with a wide range of dangerous chemical agents. These include nerve agents such as tabun, sarin, soman, cyclosarin (GF), and VX; blood agents such as hydrogen cyanide; blister agents such as lewisite and mustard gas; volatile toxins such as benzene, chloroform, and trihalomethanes; pulmonary agents such as phosgene, vinyl chloride, and chlorine; poisonous industrial gases such as cyanides and nitriles; and incapacitating agents such as BZ. The CDC provides guidelines for local health authorities to help them manage possible chem-

ical attacks. As poisons are often used as murder weapons, all cases of suspected poisoning in the United States are reported to both local health authorities and the CDC, which has helped solve many cases of murder by poison.

*Edward C. Nwanegbo*

## Further Reading

Fong, I. W., and Ken Alibek, eds. *Bioterrorism and Infectious Agents: A New Dilemma for the Twenty-first Century*. New York: Springer, 2005. Provides information on bioterror agents and emerging infectious diseases that will foster understanding, treatment, and protection against these agents.

Hogan, David E., and Jonathan L. Burstein. *Disaster Medicine*. 2d ed. Philadelphia: Lippincott, Williams & Wilkins, 2007. Presents excellent coverage of human-made and natural disasters in different parts of the world and steps to be taken in managing medical emergency situations. Discusses the allocation of resources during disasters as well as treatment of the individuals affected.

Landesman, Linda Young. *Public Health Management of Disasters: The Practice Guide*. 2d ed. Washington, D.C.: American Public Health Association, 2005. Comprehensive discussion of natural and human-made disasters in the United States takes a practical approach to disaster response and management.

Lashley, Felissa R., and Jerry D. Durham, eds. *Emerging Infectious Diseases: Trends and Issues*. 2d ed. New York: Springer, 2007. Collection of essays provides information on the epidemiologies and clinical manifestations of various infectious diseases and discusses prevention and treatment of those diseases. Includes chapters on bioterror agents and avian influenza.

McQueen, David V., and Pekka Puska, eds. *Global Behavioral Risk Factor Surveillance*. New York: Kluwer Academic/Plenum, 2003. Excellent collection presents information on lifestyle behaviors in different parts of the world that foster development of chronic diseases such as diabetes, cancer, cardiovascular disease, and chronic obstructive airway diseases. An important resource for readers interested in understanding the roles of alcohol, tobacco, unhealthy diet, and inactivity in the development of chronic diseases.

Roy, Michael J. *Physician's Guide to Terrorist Attack.* Totowa, N.J.: Humana Press, 2003. Provides an informative review of the infectious and chemical agents that potentially can be used in terrorist attacks. Includes diagnostic and therapeutic guides to assist physicians in recognizing and managing the problems caused by such agents as well as information on the treatment of blast injuries.

Tucker, Jonathan B., ed. *Toxic Terror: Assessing the Terrorist Use of Chemical and Biological Weapons.* Cambridge, Mass.: MIT Press, 2000. Presents twelve case studies of the use of chemical and biological agents by terrorist groups. Identifies terrorists' patterns of behavior and discusses strategies to combat them.

Veenema, Tener Goodwin, ed. *Disaster Nursing and Emergency Preparedness: For Chemical, Biological, and Radiological Terrorism and Other Hazards.* 2d ed. New York: Springer, 2007. Nursing management guide addresses emergency needs for different categories of terrorist attacks as well as postdisaster care and psychological support for victims and their families.

**See also:** Autopsies; Bacterial biology; Biological terrorism; Biological warfare diagnosis; Biotoxins; Chemical Biological Incident Response Force, U.S.; Chemical terrorism; Chemical warfare; Food poisoning; Food supply protection; Forensic toxicology; Mustard gas; September 11, 2001, victim identification; U.S. Army Medical Research Institute of Infectious Diseases; Viral biology.

## Chain of custody

**Definition:** Documentation of the location of physical evidence from the time it is collected until the time it is introduced at trial.

**Significance:** The establishment of chain of custody is important for all physical evidence collected in criminal investigations, but it is particularly crucial when items of evidence might become confused with other evidence or when there is a possibility that someone could have tampered with the evidence.

In criminal investigations, the identification of an object as one found at a certain place involves the establishment of a proper chain of custody, or paper trail. Each piece of physical evidence must be authenticated or identified by a witness or through other means.

### Authentication

Authentication involves proof that the evidence is what it purports to be. Rule 901 of the Federal Rules of Evidence sets out methods of authenticating or identifying evidence. According to the rule, authentication or identification may be established by any of the following means: testimony of a witness with knowledge that a matter is what it is claimed to be, a nonexpert opinion as to the genuineness of handwriting based on familiarity, comparison by the trier of fact (jury) or expert witness with specimens that have been authenticated, distinctive characteristics, voice identification, telephone conversations showing that a call was made to a certain number and the identification of the person who answered the phone individually or on behalf of a business, ancient document or data compilation in existence twenty years or more at the time it is offered, evidence describing a process or system used to produce a particular result, or a method provided by act of Congress or by other rules pursuant to statutory authority.

### Proper Chain of Custody

The first clause of Rule 901 addresses proper chain of custody. A weapon found next to a victim and then taken by the police and put into a bag that is sealed and marked with identification can later be identified by an officer on the stand at trial as the one found next to the victim. If more than one person had access to the bag, however, the role of each must be accounted for to ensure that the evidence is truly the object it is claimed to be. Similarly, when a powder is put into an evidence bag that is then sealed and checked in to the evidence room, the bag may later be checked out and sent to a laboratory for analysis of the contents. The laboratory technician has the responsibility of keeping track of the substance while testing it. The technician can then take the stand and testify about the identity of the substance.

It should be noted that minor gaps in the chain of custody are permissible and do not destroy the chain of custody. The evidence can be considered by the jury, which will determine its reliability and its probative value, if any, given the missing links in the chain. If, however, the evidence is not what the proponent claims it to be because of tampering in the chain of custody, the judge may prevent the jury from seeing or considering the evidence.

### Chain of Custody in Court

It is important that law-enforcement personnel document the seizure, custody, control, transfer, analysis, and disposition of physical and electronic evidence. Because evidence can be used in court to convict persons of crimes, it must be handled carefully to avoid later allegations of tampering or misconduct that can compromise cases. Establishing a chain of custody is especially significant when the evidence takes the form of fungible goods—that is, goods that can easily be substituted for other items in the same category. This applies to illegal drugs seized by law enforcement.

An identifiable person must always have custody of the evidence. Therefore, when a police officer or detective takes charge of a piece of evidence, the officer or detective must document the item and give it to an evidence clerk for secure storage. This transaction and every succeeding transaction affecting that evidence, from its collection to its appearance in court, should be completely documented so that the evidence can withstand any challenges to its authenticity. Properly detailed documentation includes the conditions under which the evidence was gathered, the identities of all those who handled the evidence and how long they had it in their possession, the security conditions that

existed during handling and storing of the evidence, and the manners in which the evidence was transferred to subsequent custodians.

In the case of the recovery of a bloody weapon at a murder scene, for example, every transfer of the weapon from person to person must be documented, from the time the weapon is picked up at the scene to the time it is presented in court. Law-enforcement personnel must be able to prove that only persons with legitimate reasons to inspect, test, or otherwise examine the weapon have had access to it. In cases involving chemical sampling, proper chain of custody ensures maintenance of the condition of samples by providing documentation of their control, transfer, and analysis.

*Marcia J. Weiss*

### Further Reading

Broun, Kenneth S., ed. *McCormick on Evidence.* 6th ed. St. Paul, Minn.: Thomson/West, 2006. Considered to be the ultimate standard reference on the law of evidence. Contains detailed explanations and case references.

Mauet, Thomas A. *Trial Techniques.* 7th ed. New York: Aspen, 2007. Handbook covering all aspects of the trial process includes extensive examples of patterns of questions that attorneys use in examining expert witnesses.

Rothstein, Paul F., Myrna S. Raeder, and David Crump. *Evidence in a Nutshell.* 5th ed. St. Paul, Minn.: West, 2007. Provides a succinct summary of the law of evidence. Useful for both students and practitioners.

Stopp, Margaret T. *Evidence Law in the Trial Process.* Albany, N.Y.: West/Delmar, 1999. Undergraduate textbook intended primarily for paralegals discusses the principles of the law of evidence. A chapter on lay and expert witnesses includes cases and examples.

**See also:** Biological warfare diagnosis; Crime scene documentation; Disturbed evidence; Drug and alcohol evidence rules; Drug confirmation tests; Evidence processing; Handwriting analysis; Locard's exchange principle; Quality control of evidence; Rape kit; Toxicological analysis.

# *Challenger* and *Columbia* accident investigations

**Dates:** *Challenger* accident took place January 28, 1986; *Columbia* accident took place February 1, 2003

**The Event:** After the accidents that destroyed the *Challenger* and *Columbia* space shuttles, investigators began the difficult tasks of finding and identifying evidence that would allow scientists to understand what had happened and allow the families of the dead crew members to bury their loved ones.

**Significance:** High-profile, widely publicized, multiple-casualty disasters create particular complexities in the search, collection, and identification portions of the investigation process. The investigations of the *Challenger* and *Columbia* tragedies required the use of many forensic tools.

The National Aeronautics and Space Administration (NASA) began the space shuttle program with *Columbia*, which launched for the first time in April, 1981. *Challenger* was the next shuttle to be launched, after *Columbia* had completed five missions. *Challenger* made its maiden flight in April, 1983.

On January 28, 1986, seventy-three seconds after it lifted off for its tenth mission, the space shuttle *Challenger* disintegrated. Investigators would later determine that the disaster was caused by the failure of an O-ring seal in the craft's right solid rocket booster. This failure caused a flame leak that engulfed the fuel tank and resulted in structural breakdown. With the structure compromised, aerodynamic forces broke the shuttle apart.

On January 16, 2003, as it was lifting off for its twenty-eighth mission, the space shuttle *Columbia* sustained damage when a piece of foam insulation broke off the main propellant tank and struck the shuttle's left wing, damaging the thermal protection system. The crew continued and completed their mission, but the damage was enough to compromise the wing's structure, and the shuttle began to fall apart during reentry into Earth's atmosphere on February 1. Eyewitnesses on the ground reported seeing debris break off the shuttle prior to its disintegration above Texas and Louisiana.

Government-appointed review boards were commissioned to look into the two shuttle disasters, and both found that the accidents were caused by malfunctions of which NASA officials were already aware. Both boards cited NASA administrators' insensitivity to the true potential risks posed by these documented issues as the main contribution to the tragedies.

Forensically speaking, every investigative scene analysis is intended to answer the same basic questions: How does the scene fit into what really happened, and what evidence within the scene supports the conclusions about what happened? Forensic scene searches are concerned with the identification, collection, and preservation of evidence. Scenes of the magnitude of the two shuttle destructions are no different from smaller scenes; they are simply amplified. When everything from the number of people involved to the amount of evidence available is on a grand scale, it becomes essential for investigators to establish a system to keep track of every detail.

## Jurisdiction

The first thing that must be established in any type of law-enforcement investigation is which agency has the proper jurisdiction to investigate the case—that is, which agency is going to take charge of the investigation based on its legal authority over the crime or event, the geographic area, or the laws of the area. Sometimes jurisdictions can overlap, such as when both state and federal agencies have interests in particular cases. In these cases, agencies can share authority; this known as concurrent jurisdiction. It is always better, however, for one agency to take the lead in an investigation so that the work is not hampered by any competing goals and agendas the different agencies may have.

The investigators of both the space shuttle accidents had to contend immediately with jurisdictional issues. The agencies and other entities involved in the *Challenger* investigation included NASA, the Federal Bureau of Investigation (FBI), a specially appointed presidential commission chaired by former U.S. secretary of state William P. Rogers (known as the Rogers Commission), and the U.S. Air Force, Navy, and Coast Guard. The *Columbia* investigation included personnel from NASA, the FBI, the National Transportation Safety Board, the Secret Service, the U.S. Marshals Service, the Air Force, the Office of the Armed Forces Medical Examiner (OAFME), many Texas and Louisiana state and local agencies, and, later, the North American Aerospace Defense Command (NORAD). The *Columbia* incident was also reviewed by a presidential commission known as the *Columbia* Accident Investigation Board.

NASA took the lead in the *Challenger* investigation, confiscating tapes and pictures of the incident and making decisions to release little information to the news media. The FBI conducted an investigation to determine whether sabotage was involved, but eventually the Rogers Commission took jurisdiction to direct the investigation. In the *Columbia* incident, the FBI initially guided the search for shuttle parts and human remains on the ground, but NASA and the OAFME soon became the two main agencies involved. All recovered parts of the shuttle were sent to NASA for technical analysis, and the astronauts' remains and uniforms were sent to the OAFME for identification and examination.

### Searching the Scenes

When *Challenger* broke apart, it was about 10 miles above the Atlantic Ocean, approximately 18 miles offshore. Pieces of the shuttle continued to fall for an hour, making it dangerous for search crews to enter the area immediately. *Challenger*'s nose section, with the crew cabin inside, was blown free from the rest of craft. NASA later learned from flight-deck intercom recordings and the apparent use of some emergency oxygen packs that at least three of the astronauts were alive during *Challenger*'s fall. The nose section shattered upon hitting the ocean at what is estimated to be about 200 miles per hour. The wreckage scene covered approximately 93,000 square miles of ocean that included depths of up to 1,200 feet.

An hour after the incident, search-and-recov-ery planes and ships began the search for survivors and wreckage. Although some pieces of the shuttle floated on the surface of the ocean, most of the debris had sunk to the bottom. The bodies of the crew were not found right away, despite a search effort that included twenty-two ships, six submersibles, and thirty-three aircraft. Over the next few months, pieces amounting to about 50 percent of the shuttle were recovered, including parts of the external tank, both solid rocket boosters, and the orbiter. About 45 percent of the orbiter itself was found, including all three main engines, which were recovered intact, leading investigators to believe the engines were not involved in the incident.

On March 8, 1986, thirty-nine days after the search began, search teams found the crew cabin, which had not been destroyed. The bodies of all seven crew members were found inside, still strapped into their seats. The bodies were transported to the OAFME mortuary at Dover Air Force Base in Delaware for autopsy.

On the morning of February 1, 2003, NASA officials lost contact with the crew of the space shuttle *Columbia* about fifteen minutes prior to its scheduled landing. Video evidence depicts the shuttle breaking apart over Texas, approximately 39 miles above the ground. It has been estimated that the shuttle was traveling at approximately 12,500 miles per hour. The debris covered a rectangular area nearly 60 miles wide by 250 miles long over East Texas and Louisiana, in terrain that ranged from arid ground to bogs.

In contrast with the *Challenger* scene, which, as it was in the ocean, was relatively isolated from the public, the *Columbia* scene was accessible to anyone within the vicinity. Control of the scene became an immediate concern for investigators, and they found such control nearly impossible to achieve. Within the first few hours after the accident, materials alleged to be parts of the shuttle were being offered for sale on the auction Web site eBay. Authorities quickly shut down the auctions, and the posters were charged with tampering with an investigative scene and evidence.

The *Columbia* scene was so large that no single investigative agency could handle the search independently. All local law-enforcement agencies were contacted and asked to help within their areas of responsibility. If searchers came across anything they thought could possibly be related to the *Columbia* or its crew, they were told to collect it, note the appropriate location and time, and send it to NASA officials. NASA held all the recovered mechanical debris at Barksdale Air Force Base in Louisiana, and all organic materials found were sent to the OAFME mortuary at Dover Air Force Base for identification.

## Autopsies and Victim Identification

A question often arises concerning autopsies conducted on persons who died as the result of a known disaster: What can such autopsies prove beyond what is already known? In both of the space shuttle tragedies, the deaths of all fourteen crew members were obviously the result of the shuttles' disintegration. Forensic pathology, however, can shed light on other important aspects of cases in addition to cause and manner of death, including incident analysis and victim identification. Remains may be identified through the analysis of DNA (deoxyribonucleic acid), fingerprints, or dental records. It is important to identify remains positively for the sakes of the families of the deceased.

In the case of *Challenger*, all seven crew members were found in their uniforms and strapped into their seats, so presumptive identification was easily accomplished. The news media and the crew members' families, however, also wanted to know when the crew died and whether they had suffered before their deaths. The autopsy findings in this case were inconclusive, largely because the remains had been submerged in the ocean for more than a month, and severe decomposition had set in. NASA officials found evidence that some of the crew may have survived the initial breakup of the craft, but then the crew cabin fell more than 50,000 feet and hit the water at approximately 200 miles per hour—no one could have survived such an impact.

Victim identification was an extremely important element of the investigation of the *Columbia* incident. The remains of the *Columbia* crew were found in parts, scattered with the shuttle debris over a very large search area.

Identification of every body part was essential, so that the family of each crew member could be presented with as complete a body as possible for burial.

## Findings

The Rogers Commission concluded that the space shuttle *Challenger* did not explode; rather, it was torn apart by aerodynamic stress after the structural failure of an external tank. The condition of the shuttle's three main engines showed no signs that they contributed in any way to the incident. An assessment of the external tank debris suggested that the tank itself was not responsible for the accident; rather, the failure of an O-ring used to seal joints in the solid rocket booster compromised the structure.

The *Columbia* Accident Investigation Board concluded that a puncture in the leading edge of the shuttle's left wing was caused by a piece of insulation foam that peeled off the external tank at launch. The hot gases formed during reentry into Earth's atmosphere expanded inside the wing, causing the shuttle to break apart on its final approach.

*Russell S. Strasser*

## Further Reading

Cabbage, Michael, and William Harwood. *Comm Check . . . : The Final Flight of Shuttle Columbia.* New York: Free Press, 2004. Offers a good summary of the ethics of *Columbia*'s mission and the debate among engineers on the ground concerning whether it was safe for the shuttle to return. Notes that opportunities to learn the extent of the spacecraft's problems were missed and that repeated warning signs were ignored.

Feynman, Richard P. "Richard P. Feynman's Minority Report to the Space Shuttle *Challenger* Inquiry." In *The Pleasure of Finding Things Out: The Best Short Works of Richard P. Feynman*, edited by Jeffrey Robbins. Cambridge, Mass.: Perseus, 1999. One presidential commission member—a Nobel laureate in physics and widely renowned scientist and teacher—presents his explanation of what caused the *Challenger* accident.

Kubey, Robert W., and Thea Peluso. "Emotional Response as a Cause of Interpersonal News

Diffusion: The Case of the Space Shuttle Tragedy." *Journal of Broadcasting and Electronic Media* 34, no. 1 (1990): 69-76. Good post-*Challenger* look at how NASA dealt with the media and the visual depictions of the *Challenger* incident. Discusses how these factors may have affected the investigation.

Langewiesche, William. "*Columbia*'s Last Flight." *The Atlantic Monthly*, November, 2003, 58-87. Excellent overview of the investigation that followed the *Columbia* tragedy, with good explanations of the findings of the *Columbia* Accident Investigation Board.

Lighthall, F. F. "Launching the Space Shuttle *Challenger*: Disciplinary Deficiencies in the Analysis of Engineering Data." *IEEE Transactions on Engineering Management* 38 (February, 1991): 63-74. Analyzes the field data acquired before the launch and compares them with the results of the investigation. Somewhat technical, but very informative.

McDanels, S. J. "Space Shuttle *Columbia* Post-accident Analysis and Investigation." *Strain: An International Journal for Experimental Mechanics* 42 (August, 2006): 159-163. Presents a thourough, technical review of the *Columbia* incident and investigation.

*Report of the Presidential Commission on the Space Shuttle Challenger Accident.* Springfield, Va.: National Aeronautics and Space Administration, 1986. Provides a comprehensive view of what caused the *Challenger* accident and the tragedy's repercussions.

Vaughan, Diane. "Autonomy, Interdependence, and Social Control: NASA and the Space Shuttle *Challenger*." *Administrative Science Quarterly* 35 (June, 1990): 225-257. Provides informative discussion of NASA's failure to identify legitimate risks, which resulted in the *Challenger* tragedy.

**See also:** Accident investigation and reconstruction; Crime scene search patterns; Evidence processing; Flight data recorders; Mitochondrial DNA analysis and typing; Oral autopsy; ValuJet Flight 592 crash investigation.

## Check alteration and washing

**Definition:** Process of changing checks intended for others, by simple alteration or exposure to chemical substances, to collect funds from bank accounts fraudulently.

**Significance:** The fraudulent cashing of stolen checks costs individuals and businesses in the United States hundreds of millions of dollars each year. Unfortunately, many altered checks are not detected until funds have already been transferred and the criminals are long gone. Security features are constantly evolving to combat this problem.

Check alteration is a very common problem in the United States, causing losses to victims of many millions of dollars each year. A common scenario is as follows: Someone writes a check to pay a bill and places the envelope containing the check in a residential mailbox, raising the box's red flag so that the letter carrier will pick up the outgoing mail. Unfortunately, the red flag also alerts a criminal that outgoing mail is in the box, and when no one is around the criminal rifles through the mail and takes anything that looks like it might contain a check. After collecting checks from a number of different mailboxes in the neighborhood, the criminal alters them, either by washing and rewriting them or by using simpler methods, so that he or she can cash them using a false identity. By the time the victims discover the withdrawal of funds from their accounts, the criminal has moved on to another identity or another town.

### How Checks Are Changed

In the most basic type of check alteration, the perpetrator simply makes small changes to a check using a pen or other writing instrument similar enough to the one that was used to write the check to avoid detection. Examples of this include an individual changing a check for five dollars to a check for five thousand dollars by adding extra zeros and the word "thousand." Another example involves checks made out to the IRS (Internal Revenue Service). A criminal can take these checks and by adding two pen strokes change "IRS" to read "MRS." The criminal can then add a last name, making the check payable to "MRS. SMITH" or something similar, and then uses false identification to cash the check.

More complex check alteration involves actually removing the writing on the "payable to" line of the check, along with the amount. When this is done through the submersion of the check in a bath of fluid to dissolve the ink, it is known as check washing. Practiced criminals, and even some amateurs, can use a variety of household products to remove the inks of many commonly used pens from handwritten checks.

Common substances such as acetone (found in many products, including nail polish remover), bleach, and isopropyl alcohol can be used to wash checks. Different chemicals are often effective at removing different types of ink, and seasoned check washers can recognize many inks and choose just the right solutions to accomplish their goal. Check washers protect the signatures on the checks during the washing process, either by covering them with tape or by holding them out of the wash solution, so that after the chemicals have done their work, they have blank, signed checks that they can rewrite for any amount. Check washers often have many false identities supported by false driver's licenses, identification cards, and other documentation to help them cash checks without raising suspicion. After the checks are cashed, the victims often remain ignorant of the fraud for days or weeks, and by the time they report the crimes, the criminals have usually moved on.

### Detection and Prevention

The most basic types of check alteration, those involving the simple addition or modification of writing on the payee line or in the amount of the check, can often be detected through close visual inspection or examination of the check with a magnifying glass or microscope. Very rarely is it possible for a criminal to find exactly the same type of pen used to write the check originally or to match the handwriting of the original check writer perfectly. Unfortunately, bank tellers, store clerks, and others in the first line of defense against check fraud rarely have the training, or the time, to do significant examination of each check that is presented for cashing. Because of this, most of even the most basic types of check alteration can slip through undetected; they are not caught until it is too late, when the victims whose accounts were charged receive their bank statements.

It can be difficult to detect check washing, but careful examination of a check can often reveal clues. In some cases, especially when the check washer is an amateur, some traces of the original ink markings may be visible. One problem with detecting check washing is that when the process does not work well, the criminal usually will simply not attempt to pass that particular check. This is good for the person whose check was stolen; instead of losing hundreds or even thousands of dollars, the individual is simply inconvenienced by the apparent disappearance of a check that never made it to where it was intended to go. Checks that seem to have been lost in the mail may have been stolen by individuals who planned to wash them; thus persons who realize that checks they have written are missing should be extremely vigilant.

Increasingly, security measures are being built into checks, especially high-security checks that make it more difficult for criminals to copy or wash the checks and also make it easier for professionals to detect check alteration. Features of checks that can deter attempts to pass photocopied versions include watermarks, thermal verification seals, and the use of colored fibers woven into the paper. These features do not necessarily protect against washing, however. The best protection against check washing that is offered by check manufacturers involves the treatment of checks with chemicals that cause the paper to change color if it is submerged in any of the solutions commonly used by check washers.Some simpler means of protecting against check alteration and washing are also available. One of these is the use of gel pens, instead of ballpoints or other pens, to write and sign checks. Gel inks are much more difficult to wash successfully because these inks enter the paper fibers of checks and become trapped. Another way to prevent check washing is to prevent the stealing of mail containing checks.

People can help to protect themselves from check fraud by mailing bill payments only at post offices or by handing such mail directly to letter carriers. If they must place mail containing checks in home or business mailboxes for pickup, they should be careful to put the mail out as close to the pickup time as possible. In many cases it is possible to pay bills electronically rather than by mailing a check. Paying bills online using secure bank websites can reduce the number of checks an individual mails, reducing the chance that he or she will be a victim of check fraud.

*Helen Colby*

## Further Reading

Abagnale, Frank W., with Stan Redding. *Catch Me If You Can*. New York: Grosset & Dunlap, 1980. True story of a master of check alteration and washing, who passed more than $2.5 million in fraudulent checks in only five years.

Allen, Michael John. *Foundations of Forensic Document Analysis: Theory and Practice*. Hoboken, NJ: John Wiley & Sons, 2015. A look at how experts use a variety of techniques to determine whether documents are authentic.

Lewis, Jane. *Forensic Document Examination: Fundamentals and Current Trends*. San Diego, CA: Academic Press, 2014. A comprehensive look at the most common methods used in the forensic examination of documents of all kinds.

Ramamoorti, Sridhar, et al. *A.B.C's of Behavioral Forensics: Applying Psychology to Financial Fraud Prevention and Detection*. Hoboken, NJ: Wiley, 2013. A behavioral approach covering many types of financial fraud.

**See also:** Document examination; Fax machine, copier, and printer analysis; Forensic accounting; Handwriting analysis; Hughes will hoax; Identity theft; Microscopes; Paper; Questioned document analysis; Secret Service, U.S.; Sports memorabilia fraud; Typewriter analysis; Writing instrument analysis.

# Chemical agents

**Definition:** Chemical compounds with toxic properties that can be used to cause harm to humans, plants, and animals.

**Significance:** Chemical agents are classified as weapons of mass destruction and have the capability of inflicting massive amounts of damage and death. Given that some domestic terrorist groups have attempted to deploy chemical agents within the United States, it is important that forensic investigators have a thorough understanding of these compounds, their effects on the human body, and effective ways to combat chemical attacks.

Since their first use as weapons during World War I, chemical agents have been deployed numerous times. Large stockpiles of these agents are maintained in different parts of the world, largely because of nations' needs to develop chemical programs for research purposes.

The U.S. Department of Homeland Security lists six main categories of chemical agents: biotoxins, blister agents, blood agents, choking agents, nerve agents, and incapacitating agents. Biotoxins are agents that come from plants or animals; these include compounds such as ricin and nicotine. Blister agents, also known as vesicants, are among the agents most commonly associated with the term "chemical weapons"; these cause blistering to the skin, eyes, and respiratory system on contact. Mustard gas, perhaps the most widely known blister agent, was first employed by Germany in 1917, during World War I. Blood agents, which include cyanide and carbon monoxide, enter the body through the bloodstream.

Choking agents, when inhaled, damage the membrane of the respiratory tract and cause asphyxiation from pulmonary edema. Chlorine and phosgene are both choking agents. Nerve agents are some of the most recently used chemical weapons (during the Iran-Iraq War, 1980-1988); these compounds are designed to disrupt the nervous system and keep it from functioning properly. The nerve agent sarin was employed in the Tokyo subway attack perpetrated by the religious cult Aum Shinrikyo in 1995. Nerve agents can kill within minutes of exposure to a lethal dosage. Incapacitating agents, in contrast with other chemical agents, are not generally lethal; they produce mental or physiological effects that inhibit normal functioning. Law-enforcement agencies sometimes use such highly irritating agents for purposes of crowd control; tear gas is the most widely known example.

Numerous chemical detection devices are in common use by law-enforcement and emergency medical personnel who respond to scenes where chemical contamination may be suspected. One type consists of a glass tube that contains reagents (substances designed to foster a reaction with another substance) that will react chemically with a suspected agent in a predetermined volume of air. By measuring the stain produced, the user can determine which agent was detected. Among the least effective methods of detecting chemical agents is the use of pH test strips. When chemicals come into contact with such strips, they indicate the alkalinity or acidity of the chemicals through a change of color. A gas chromatograph-mass spectrometer (GC-MS) is a device made of two separate tools that are most effective in combination. A GC-MS separates the various elements that make up compounds and measures their quantity to identify the compounds. Many of the devices that first responders use to detect chemical agents are most reliable when they are employed in conjunction with other tools of forensic science.

*Michael W. Cheek*

## Further Reading

Bevelacqua, Armando, and Richard Stilp. *Terrorism Handbook for Operational Responders.* 2d ed. Albany, N.Y.: Delmar, 2004.

Croddy, Eric A., with Clarisa Perez-Armendariz and John Hart. *Chemical and Biological Warfare: A Comprehensive Survey for the Concerned Citizen.* New York: Copernicus Books, 2002.

Hoenig, Steven L. *Handbook of Chemical Warfare and Terrorism.* Westport, Conn.: Greenwood Press, 2002.

**See also:** Blood agents; Centers for Disease Control and Prevention; Chemical Biological Incident Response Force, U.S.; Chemical terrorism; Chemical warfare; Chemical Weapons Convention of 1993; Decontamination methods; Mustard gas; Nerve agents; Sarin; Soman; Tabun.

## Chemical Biological Incident Response Force, U.S.

**Date:** Activated on April 4, 1996
**Identification:** Branch of the U.S. Marine Corps designed to respond rapidly to terrorist-initiated chemical and biological threats against the United States.
**Significance:** Developed in response to growing threats of terrorist attacks during the mid-1990's, the U.S. Chemical Biological Incident Response Force is designed to work with other federal, local, and state emergency response agencies. The force's services include chemical and biological agent detection, emergency medical care, casualty search and rescue, and personnel decontamination.

A self-sustaining unit under the command of the U.S. Marine Corps, the Chemical Biological Incident Response Force, or CBIRF, is part of the Fourth Marine Expeditionary Brigade. It is headquartered at Indian Head, Maryland, twenty-seven miles from Washington, D.C. Its personnel represent a variety of military occupational specialties. The CBIRF owns and maintains commercially available radiological, biological, and chemical defense equipment; general support equipment; and medical equipment used in support of its quick-response mandate to terrorist incidents occurring throughout the world.

Although the CBIRF is not directly involved in counterterrorist operations, its personnel are trained to deal with the consequences of chemical and biological attacks. Other government agencies have expertise and responsibilities that overlap those of the CBIRF. What makes the CBIRF exceptional is that it is a completely self-contained unit capable of handling all its mandated responsibilities on its own.

## Background

Creation of the CBIRF was a response to such terrorist events as the bombing of Oklahoma City's federal office building and the Aum Shinrikyo cult's nerve gas attack on a Tokyo subway station—both of which occurred in 1995. In the aftermath of those events, U.S. president Bill Clinton issued a directive on counterterrorism policy calling for specific efforts to deter deadly terrorist attacks in both the United States and allied nations. The most tangible outcome of that presidential directive was the establishment of the CBIRF within the U.S. Marine Corps in April, 1996.

Shortly after its creation, the CBIRF was deployed to assist in a series of high-profile events. One of the first of these was the Summer Olympic Games in Atlanta, Georgia, during 1996. Less than ten minutes after a pipe bomb exploded in the Olympic Village, a CBIRF unit on standby only one mile away went into action. Since that time, CBIRF units have been deployed to serve at presidential inauguration ceremonies, subsequent presidential state of the union addresses in Congress, papal visits to the United States, and the 1999 summit meeting of the North Atlantic Treaty Organization (NATO).

Since the terrorist attacks on the United States of September 11, 2001, CBIRF units have been active in collecting biological samples and screening congressional mail and office equipment. In December of 2001, the CBIRF sent a one-hundred-member initial-response team into the Dirksen Senate Office Building in

---

## CBIRF Teams in Action

At any given moment, CBIRF units are ready for rapid deployment in large diesel vans. These vans are specially equipped with onboard analytical systems designed to provide early detection and identification of chemical and biological agents used in terrorist attacks. When the units must be deployed rapidly to remote locations, the vans are loaded into C-130 aircraft.

During suspected terrorist attacks, the personnel of the CBIRF recon and rapid intervention group are typically first on the scene. There, they provide security, area isolation, and assistance to local medical authorities and service support. They assess the types of chemical agents present and determine the levels of protective clothing required for greatest safety:

- **Level C clothing:** full suits and gas masks
- **Level B clothing:** biological suits with air tanks
- **Level A clothing:** sealed, domelike environments

After donning the requisite clothing, casualty search teams enter the scene to locate and assess victims. They are soon followed by extract teams, which remove the casualties to decontamination tents, where up to thirty victims may receive attention. In assembly-line fashion, victims are placed on rollers that facilitate their movement from station to station within the tents as they progress through levels of assessment and treatment.

Meanwhile, Marines in full decontamination suits work to remove all clothing material for proper disposal. Victims are then sponged with decon solutions, rinsed with water, and sent to the final stations, where medical corpsmen tag them for appropriate medical attention.

---

Washington, D.C., to detect and remove anthrax. CBIRF units have also supported overseas exercises in such countries as Bahrain, France, Iceland, Italy, Jordan, the Philippines, and Japan.

## The Five CBIRF Elements

The CBIRF is organized to operate through five areas of responsibility called "elements": reconnaissance, decontamination, medical, security, and service support. After the nuclear, biological, and chemical (NBC) reconnaissance element defines the locations of incident sites, the decontamination element decontaminates personnel and equipment exposed to chemical or biological agents. Meanwhile, the medical element provides triage support to casualties, the security element provides security for the contaminated site, and the service support element provides shelter, food, and water.

Members of the reconnaissance elements are always the first to enter affected areas. They are trained and equipped to detect, classify, and identify all known chemical and biological agents. This element has two reconnaissance vehicles equipped to detect vapor and liquid contamination. The unit's twenty Marines, ten corpsmen, and one medical officer also provide emergency casualty evacuation teams capable of stabilizing and extracting casualties from the affected area.

Decontamination elements made up of twenty-seven Marines and sailors are responsible for the decontamination of personnel and casualties, and they stabilize casualties waiting for further treatment. Decontamination elements establish themselves at the edges of contaminated areas, near the medical elements' triage stations. There, personnel and casualties, both ambulatory and nonambulatory, are processed through a series of stations derived from NBC decontamination standards.

As contaminated individuals enter the areas, their personal effects and equipment are collected, and clothing items are removed. The individuals themselves are then sprayed and sponged with a 0.5 percent bleach solution and led through showers that rinse off the decontaminating liquid. The personal effects and equipment of the contaminated individuals are also processed through the cycle.

Individuals are then monitored with hand-held chemical agent monitors (CAMs) to determine whether traces of contamination are still present. Those found still to be contaminated are again sent through the full decontamination cycle. After all casualties are decontaminated, element members change their bandages and dressings as needed and transport the individuals to waiting medical personnel. Although the decontamination element's personnel includes Marines with a variety of occupational specialties, more than half of the Marines are NBC defense specialists who have undergone nine-week training courses at Fort McClellan, Alabama.

## Equipment

When the CBIRF was first organized, it used "off-the-shelf" equipment, such as chemical-protective overgarments and gas masks. Other items included NBC reconnaissance vehicles capable of detecting both vapor and liquid contamination, chemical agent monitors, vapor and liquid agent detection kits, remote chemical agent sensing alarms, and decontamination kits. As the CBIRF has developed, it has played an increasing role in testing innovative concepts in equipment, techniques, and procedures used in its mandated tasks.

During the fall of 2004, CBIRF personnel began conducting exercises with a naval hovercraft on the Potomac and Anacostia rivers. Thanks to its air-cushion technology, the hovercraft is able to land on more than 70 percent of the world's coastlines. This is a huge increase over the approximately 15 percent of coastlines accessible by conventional landing craft. Capable of carrying payloads of up to seventy-five tons, the hovercraft significantly increases the CBIRF's ability to move quickly and efficiently into future emergency situations.

*Richard S. Spira*

## Further Reading

Bolz, Frank, Jr., Kenneth J. Dudonis, and David P. Schulz. *The Counterterrorism Handbook: Tactics, Procedures, and Techniques.* 3d ed. Boca Raton, Fla.: CRC Press, 2005. Practical handbook describes the procedures that should be followed during and after terrorist attacks. Includes many of the procedures used by the CBIRF.

Boss, Martha J., and Dennis W. Day, eds. *Biological Risk Engineering Handbook: Infection Control and Decontamination.* Boca Raton, Fla.: CRC Press, 2003. Provides extensive coverage of the kinds of biological contaminants with which the CBIRF deals.

Cirincione, Joseph, Jon B. Wolfsthal, and Miriam Rajkumar. *Deadly Arsenals: Nuclear, Biological, and Chemical Threats.* Rev. ed. Washington, D.C.: Carnegie Endowment for International Peace, 2005. Presents an authoritative overview of the range of biological, chemical, and nuclear threats that the United States faces from terrorist attacks.

Environmental Protection Agency. *Compilation of Available Data on Building Decontamination Alternatives.* Washington, D.C.: Author, 2005. Provides information on the various technologies employed to decontaminate buildings affected by chemical and biological attacks.

Sauter, Mark A., and James Jay Carafano. *Homeland Security: A Complete Guide to Understanding, Preventing, and Surviving Terrorism.* New York: McGraw-Hill, 2005. Comprehensive textbook discusses the nature, methods, and dangers of terrorism and offers practical advice on dealing with terrorist threats at both national and individual levels.

Tucker, Jonathan B., ed. *Toxic Terror: Assessing the Terrorist Use of Chemical and Biological Weapons.* Cambridge, Mass.: MIT Press, 2000. Presents twelve case studies of the use of chemical and biological agents by terrorist groups. Identifies terrorists' patterns of behavior and discusses strategies to combat them.

**See also:** Anthrax; Anthrax letter attacks; Biodetectors; Biological terrorism; Biological warfare diagnosis; Biological weapon identification; Centers for Disease Control and Prevention; Chemical agents; Chemical terrorism; Environmental Measurements Laboratory; Quantitative and qualitative analysis of chemicals.

## Chemical microscopy. *See* Polarized light microscopy

## Chemical terrorism

**Definition:** Use of dangerous toxic chemicals that cause mass casualties and economic damage to achieve the objectives of terrorist groups.

**Significance:** The dangers posed to public health by attacks with lethal toxic chemicals are potentially catastrophic. When such attacks occur or are threatened, forensic toxicologists, public health officials, and law-enforcement agencies work together closely to identify the toxins involved, treat victims, decontaminate affected areas, bring perpetrators to justice, and provide protection to the public against future attacks.

Chemical agents capable of causing life-threatening injuries and death present serious threats to human communities. Many agents can be easily produced and disseminated in the atmosphere or public water and food supplies. When they make contact with human skin, mucous membranes, eyes, and respiratory and digestive systems, they can have harmful and even lethal effects. The dangers posed by chemical weapons are made greater by the ready availability of information on how to produce them in printed publications and on the Internet. Would-be terrorists with little or no chemistry training can produce dangerous chemicals easily and cheaply.

### Chemical Toxins in History

Although potential uses of chemicals as poison weapons have been known for several centuries, they were not used as important weapons until World War I (1914-1918). In that European conflict, Germany, which then had the world's largest chemical industry, introduced poison gases into combat against Allied ground troops. The numbers of casualties from gas attacks were small in comparison with the overall casualty rates that troops suffered in that war. Nevertheless, the disruptions caused by fear of gas attacks and the need for troops to adopt protective equipment and procedures made poison gas an effective weapon. New lethal chemicals were produced during World War II but were not used as extensively in that conflict as in the earlier war, partly because of conventions against their use that the combatants honored.

After World War II, research and development on chemical weapons accelerated. By the late twentieth century, chemical weapons remained integral parts of many countries' secret military programs. Proliferation of these weapons gave many nations reason for concern that some of them might fall into the hands of terrorist organizations and be used in attacks that would overwhelm public health care delivery systems and cause high fatality rates and general chaos. By the early twenty-first century, no terrorist group had yet successfully mounted a large-scale chemical attack, but numerous small-scale attacks had occurred, and evidence that some groups have planned larger attacks has been found.

During the 1970's, a radical political group known as the Weather Underground Organization, or Weathermen, threatened to use chemical toxins during its series of terrorist attacks on institutions of the U.S. government. In 1984, an animal liberation group claimed it had laced candy bars manufactured by Mars, Incorporated, with rat poison. That claim moved the company to recall millions of chocolate bars and sustain a hefty economic loss. In 1985, federal agents found large quantities of potassium cyanide when they raided the Arkansas headquarters of an extremist organization called The Covenant, the Sword and the Arm of the Lord. That organization's apparent intention was to poison the water supply of several large cities. In 1989, Israeli forces found a stockpile of toxic chemicals in a Tel Aviv hideout of the Palestinian Liberation Organization. Three years later, a German neo-Nazi group attempted to pump hydrogen cyanide gas into a synagogue.

Two widely publicized atrocities involving chemical toxins occurred in Iraq and Japan. During the 1990's, the Iraqi government used chemical weapons against its own Kurdish citizens. In Japan, members of the Aum Shinrikyo religious cult attacked civilians in the Tokyo subway system with the nerve gas sarin in 1995. When police afterward raided the headquarters of the cult, which was later renamed Aleph, they found significant quantities of dangerous biological agents.

## Combating Chemical Terrorism

The success of chemical terrorist attacks depends on the types of agent used, the ports of introduction of those agents, the methods of disseminating the agents, and the weather conditions. Nerve gas agents such as sarin and VX are strongly toxic and associated with high fatality rates. When such agents are disseminated in the open air, high humidity, high air temperatures, and strong winds can affect their potency and diminish their effectiveness. By contrast, when such agents are disseminated within enclosed buildings, fatality rates are likely to be high. Similarly, the dissemination of such agents with rockets or explosive ammunition in any almost environment can cause massive casualties. Poisoning an entire city's water supply is unlikely to be a practical method of chemical attack because of the massive amounts of toxic chemicals needed to make them effective in a large water system. Chemicals such as cyanide are most dangerous when they are used to target patrons of individual eating places or they are introduced into commercially sold beverages or foods.

Collaboration among the forensic experts and security agents of law-enforcement agencies, such as the Federal Bureau of Investigation (FBI) in the United States, and public health agencies is especially important in investigations of suspected chemical agent attacks. The first task of any investigation is to determine exactly what has happened and whether, in fact, chemical or biological agents have been used. The investigators then work to identify the toxic agents and their source.

Forensic scientists are assisted by security agents in collecting samples from crime scenes. The identification of any chemical agents that are collected assists health care professionals to provide treatment for survivors of the attacks. Public health officials also use forensic investigators' findings to plan and execute environmental decontamination of such crime scenes. Public health officials also work to identify everyone who has been exposed to the toxic agents, provide needed treatment, and monitor their health in case complications later emerge.

## Terrorist Incidents in Japan

Immediately after a chemical attack in the Japanese city of Matsumoto in 1994, local police were alerted to a strange illness that claimed the lives of 7 victims and hospitalized 274 others. An initial investigation of the area that had been attacked found dead animals and abnormal changes in vegetation of the area. Autopsies found similarly unusual pathologies in the organs of human victims. Finally, a forensic analysis of the water in a pond within the area found traces of sarin nerve gas, conclusive proof of a deliberate chemical attack.

Japan suffered another, similar attack in March, 1995, during the midst of rush-hour commuter traffic in a Tokyo subway station. This attack exposed more than five thousand people to the dangerous sarin gas. The survivors of this attack who were checked by medical teams demonstrated symptoms similar to those of victims in the previous year's incident. Likewise, forensic pathological examinations of the dead revealed pathologies similar to those of the previous year's victims. Evidence collected from the subway attack confirmed the presence of sarin.

These events demonstrated the importance of close collaboration between security agencies and forensic experts in the investigation of suspected chemical terrorist attacks. The role of security agents is crucial in secluding the area affected by an attack, both to preserve evidence and to prevent more people from becoming exposed to any noxious agents. Security agents also serve important functions during rescue efforts, particularly in the management of mass-casualty disasters such as the Tokyo subway chemical terrorist attack.

*Edward C. Nwanegbo*

### Further Reading

Charles, Daniel. *Master Mind: The Rise and*

---

## Classification of Chemical Toxins

*The Centers for Disease Control and Prevention defines the following basic categories of chemical toxins.*

- **Biotoxins:** Poisons derived from plants and animals, such as ricin, a poisonous protein extracted from castor beans.
- **Blister agents:** Also known as vesicants, chemicals that cause severe blisters on contact with eyes, the respiratory tract, and skin. An important member of this group is mustard gas.
- **Blood agents:** Chemical agents that cause pathological changes when absorbed into the bloodstream. Important members of this group include arsine and cyanide.
- **Caustics:** Chemicals that cause severe burns or corrosion on contact with the skin, eyes, and mucous membranes. Hydrogen fluoride is an important example.
- **Choking and pulmonary agents:** Chemicals that attack the respiratory tract, causing severe irritation and swelling of the tract and the lungs. Examples include ammonia, chlorine, methyl isocyanate, phosgene, and phosphine.
- **Incapacitating agents:** Chemicals that alter the consciousness of victims, such as BZ and opioids, which include natural and synthetic derivatives of opium.
- **Long-acting anticoagulants:** Toxins that prevent blood clotting, such as warfarin, which was originally developed as a medication for heart patients.
- **Metallic poisons:** Naturally occurring substances such as the chemical compound arsenic and the element mercury.
- **Nerve agents:** Powerful toxins that inhibit nerve functions, such as sarin and VX.
- **Toxic alcohols:** Poisonous alcohols that attack the heart, the kidneys, and the nervous system. An important member of this group is ethylene glycol, which is chemically similar to the ethyl alcohol consumed in liquor, wine, and beer products. Ethyl alcohol itself can also be toxic when consumed in large quantities.

---

*Fall of Fritz Haber, the Nobel Laureate Who Launched the Age of Chemical Warfare.* New York: HarperCollins, 2005. Biography of the scientist who led the German chemical weapons effort during World War I places Haber's work in the context of his times. Includes bibliography and index.

Coleman, Kim. *A History of Chemical Warfare.* New York: Palgrave Macmillan, 2005. Describes the development and use of chemical weapons from 700      . to the beginning of the twenty-first century, with extensive discussion of World War I. Also assesses current attempts to control the use and proliferation of such weapons and analyzes their potential use by terrorist groups.

Keyes, Daniel C., ed. *Medical Response to Terrorism: Preparedness and Clinical Practice.* Philadelphia: Lippincott Williams & Wilkins, 2005. Provides a review of clinical treatments for exposure to biological and chemical agents. Also discusses health care organizations' readiness for responding to terrorist attacks.

Roy, Michael J. *Physician's Guide to Terrorist Attack.* Totowa, N.J.: Humana Press, 2003. Provides an informative review of the infectious and chemical agents that potentially can be used in terrorist attacks.

Tucker, Jonathan B., ed. *Toxic Terror: Assessing the Terrorist Use of Chemical and Biological Weapons.* Cambridge, Mass.: MIT Press, 2000. Presents twelve case studies of the use of chemical and biological agents by terrorist groups. Identifies terrorists' patterns of behavior and discusses strategies to combat them.

Veenema, Tener Goodwin, ed. *Disaster Nursing and Emergency Preparedness: For Chemical, Biological, and Radiological Terrorism and Other Hazards.* 2d ed. New York: Springer, 2007. Nursing management guide addresses emergency needs for different categories of terrorist attacks as well as postdisaster care and psychological support for victims and their families.

Von Lubitz, Dag K. J. E. *Bioterrorism: Field Guide to Disease Identification and Initial Patient Management.* Boca Raton, Fla.: CRC Press, 2004. Volume aimed at medical professionals focuses on rapid recognition of the symptoms of exposure to biological or chemical weapons and on first steps in treatment for such exposure.

**See also:** Biological terrorism; Biosensors; Biotoxins; Botulinum toxin; Centers for Disease Control and Prevention; Chemical agents; Chemical Biological Incident Response Force, U.S.; Chemical warfare; Chemical Weapons Convention of 1993; Decontamination methods; Forensic toxicology; Mustard gas.

## Chemical warfare

**Definition:** Use of toxic chemical substances to increase military and civilian casualties or to make habitat conditions unsuitable for military use by opponents during war.

**Significance:** Following the widespread use of chemical weapons during World War I, a number of countries tested and maintained stocks of such weapons as supplements to their stockpiles of more traditional military weapons. This work produced new chemical warfare agents as well as increasingly sophisticated ways to deliver and disseminate them, which led in turn to the development of better means of early detection of these agents and prevention of their spread. Forensic science is concerned with detecting and tracing specific chemicals used in the manufacture of chemical weapons, locating facilities that manufacture and store chemical weapons, and identifying nations with military programs that include chemical weapons in their arsenals.

Rudimentary forms of chemical warfare have been employed for millennia. Poisons of different kinds have been used to destroy livestock and armies' food supplies, with varying degrees of success, through the centuries. New World versions of chemical warfare measures include the arming of arrows, darts, and spears with batrachotoxins extracted from the poison dart frog in the tropics of Latin America. Modern chemical warfare was introduced during the early years of World War I, when French chemists loaded tear gas into small, hand-thrown bombs to be used by French troops to drive German soldiers out of their trenches. In response, German chemists manufactured chlorine gas, which was released from canisters downwind of the Russian army on the eastern front, marking the first time that lethal chemical weapons were used on a massive scale by any army. France responded with phosgene gas loaded in artillery shells, and before the end of the war all the major combatants were using chemical weapons. Gas masks became standard issue for soldiers of all sides on all fronts.

Since World War I, many countries have experimented with and stockpiled chemical weapons, and some have promoted chemical warfare, either openly or secretly. Modern chemical warfare involves the production of several types of chemical weapons, which may be classified according to their form (fluids, vapors, gases, or powders) or their persistence (that is, the length of time they maintain their toxic properties after dissemination). Chemical weapons can be further categorized based on how they affect human beings. Some recognized classes include lachrymatory (tear-causing) agents, such as chlorine gas and tear gas; nerve gases, such as sarin, which disrupt the nervous system; cyanides, which poison the digestive system; and agents containing acids that damage the skin or respiratory system.

When chemical substances are the cause of military and civilian casualties in war, specially trained forensic scientists are often called upon to collect and test evidence to determine the substances involved. Such scientists are trained in the detection of the chemicals used in weapons and in locating the sites where such weapons are manufactured. Their first objective is to collect chemical samples from corpses and from the scenes where the chemicals were deployed so that they can conduct tests to determine precisely what chemicals are present. Most substances used in chemical weapons have origin signatures or contain toxins that must be manufactured using specific types of equipment and techniques. By pinpointing the chemicals used, investigators may be able track the weapons from the chemicals' points of origin to the sites where the weapons were manufactured and to any storage locations. The evidence collected in this manner may aid in the investigation of war crimes and may be presented in national and international courts of law when accused perpetrators face trial.

*Dwight G. Smith*

### Further Reading

Harris, Robert, and Jeremy Paxman. *A Higher Form of Killing: The Secret History of Chemical and Biological Warfare.* New York: Random House, 2002.

Marrs, Timothy C., Robert L. Maynard, and Frederick R. Sidell, eds. *Chemical Warfare Agents: Toxicology and Treatment.* 2d ed. Hoboken, N.J.: John Wiley & Sons, 2007.

Romano, James A., Jr., Brian J. Lukey, and Harry Salem. *Chemical Warfare Agents: Chemistry, Pharmacology, Toxicology, and Therapeutics.* 2d ed. Boca Raton, Fla.: CRC Press, 2008.

Somani, Satu M., and James A. Romano, Jr., eds. *Chemical Warfare Agents: Toxicity at Low Levels.* Boca Raton, Fla.: CRC Press, 2001.

Sun, Yin, and Kwok Y. Ong. *Detection Technologies for Chemical Warfare Agents and Toxic Vapors.* Boca Raton, Fla.: CRC Press, 2004.

Tucker, Jonathan B. *War of Nerves: Chemical Warfare from World War I to al-Qaeda.* New York: Pantheon Books, 2006.

**See also:** Blood agents; Chemical agents; Chemical Biological Incident Response Force, U.S.; Chemical terrorism; Chemical Weapons Convention of 1993; Decontamination methods; Mustard gas; Nerve agents; Poisons and antidotes; Sarin; Soman; Tabun.

## Chemical Weapons Convention of 1993

**Dates:** Opened for signature January 13, 1993; entered into force April 29, 1997

**The Convention:** International agreement designed to outlaw the production, stockpiling, and use of chemical weapons.

**Significance:** In addition to contributing to international security, the Chemical Weapons Convention mandated that signatory nations declare all chemical agents they had developed for possible military use and all production facilities for such agents. This information was made publicly available, assisting forensic scientists in their efforts to investigate crimes involving these or similar compounds.

Although crude types of poisonous and other

## Article I of the Chemical Weapons Convention

General Obligations

1. Each State Party to this Convention undertakes never under any circumstances:
   a. To develop, produce, otherwise acquire, stockpile or retain chemical weapons, or transfer, directly or indirectly, chemical weapons to anyone;
   b. To use chemical weapons;
   c. To engage in any military preparations to use chemical weapons;
   d. To assist, encourage or induce, in any way, anyone to engage in any activity prohibited to a State Party under this Convention.
2. Each State Party undertakes to destroy chemical weapons it owns or possesses, or that are located in any place under its jurisdiction or control, in accordance with the provisions of this Convention.
3. Each State Party undertakes to destroy all chemical weapons it abandoned on the territory of another State Party, in accordance with the provisions of this Convention.
4. Each State Party undertakes to destroy any chemical weapons production facilities it owns or possesses, or that are located in any place under its jurisdiction or control, in accordance with the provisions of this Convention.
5. Each State Party undertakes not to use riot control agents as a method of warfare.

chemical weapons have been known since the Spartans burned sulfur and pitch to create toxic fumes during the Peloponnesian War, it was not until the industrial age that massive quantities of chemical weapons could be produced. The use of substances such as mustard gas and chlorine gas in World War I caused massive deaths and brought chemical weapons to the attention of the world. The 1925 Geneva Protocol sought to limit the use of such weapons, but it did not outlaw the possession of chemical substances that might become weapons. Given that the violation of international law is most likely to happen during wars, at which time the enforcement of the law is least likely, chemical weapons continued to be used at various times throughout the twentieth century, although on a lesser scale than in World War I and often more hidden from public view.

### Terms of the Agreement

During the early 1980's, negotiators representing various national governments began seeking to reach an agreement to go beyond the Geneva Protocol and outlaw the possession of chemical weapons. Finally, in 1992, a formal agreement was reached, and the Convention on the Prohibition of the Development, Production, Stockpiling and Use of Chemical Weapons and on Their Destruction, also known simply as the Chemical Weapons Convention, was signed in January of the following year. As the name indicates, the convention broadened international law to prohibit not just the use but also the possession of virtually all chemical substances used as weapons.

The agreement mandated that all countries that signed the new law had to declare all their chemical weapons and production facilities publicly. The convention also included a long-term schedule for the destruction of stocks of weapons. An independent entity, the Organization for the Prohibition of Chemical Weapons, was created to oversee the provisions of the treaty. Of the 71,300 metric tons of chemical weapons declared by the more than 180 nations that have signed the treaty, more than 23,000 tons were destroyed during the first decade after the treaty entered into force. All the sixty-five production facilities declared were either destroyed or converted to peaceful purposes.

The international law has thus been upheld, which should have decreased the possibility that illegal groups can obtain chemical weapons, but this has not necessarily been the result. After the technology to create a chemical weapon has been developed, others can copy what had previously been done only in government laboratories.

### Sarin Attack and Its Aftermath

Although rare, attempts to use chemical substances as weapons on a large scale have been made by individuals and nongovernmental groups. One of the most widely publicized attempts to use a chemical weapon as a tool of terrorism took place in 1995, when members of the Japanese religious cult Aum Shinrikyo released sarin gas, a nerve agent, in the Tokyo subway system. Owing to the relatively small amount of the gas released in the subway cars and an inefficient system of circulating the gas, the death toll was very low in this case, with only twelve people killed. Some fifty-five hundred others were injured by the gas, however. It was later found that the sect had legally purchased tons of materials capable of being used in the production of chemical weapons.

The laws in Japan concerning such materials have since changed, as this incident brought vividly into focus the scope of the potential dangers posed by chemical weapons. The fact that one group had used a chemical agent to push its agenda of destruction made law-enforcement agencies much more vigilant around the world. When the Chemical Weapons Convention had been ratified by enough countries to go into force in 1997, law-enforcement officials gained significant knowledge regarding chemical weapons. As nations declared their weapons stockpiles and production facilities, it became clearer what types of chemical agents might be available and from what sources. After the secrecy surrounding chemical weapons was removed, law-enforcment agencies could make better plans for responding to the threats that did exist. This also facilitated investigation into the possible use of these agents, as law-enforcement personnel could be better prepared to watch for activities that might indicate that criminal groups were trying to create such weapons. One other aspect of the treaty that affected law-enforcement practices in some countries is the provision limiting the types of chemical agents that can be used for crowd control and other domestic concerns. Unlike some other international treaties, the Chemical Weapons Convention includes provisions that are binding on domestic law-enforcement agencies in signatory nations. Police are not allowed to use chemicals that are on the convention's list of prohibited agents and "have irritation or dis-

abling physical effects which disappear within a short time following termination of exposure."

*Donald A. Watt*

## Further Reading

Cirincione, Joseph, Jon B. Wolfsthal, and Miriam Rajkumar. *Deadly Arsenals: Nuclear, Biological, and Chemical Threats.* 2d ed. Washington, D.C.: Carnegie Endowment for International Peace, 2005. Provides an overview of the range of chemical weapon threats facing the United States.

Drell, Sidney D., Abraham D. Sofaer, and George D. Wilson, eds. *The New Terror: Facing the Threat of Biological and Chemical Weapons.* Palo Alto, Calif.: Hoover Institution Press, 1999. Collection of essays with commentary covers a wide range of issues, including the constitutional constraints on U.S. law-enforcement agencies combating chemical weapons and methods for minimizing the damage caused by such weapons.

Kirby, Reid D., and U.S. Army Chemical School. *Potential Military Chemical / Biological Agents and Compounds.* Wentzeville, Mo.: Eximdyne, 2005. U.S. military field manual identifies various chemical agents and their properties. Includes additional information on industrial chemicals.

Sun, Yin, and Kwok Y. Ong. *Detection Technologies for Chemical Warfare Agents and Toxic Vapors.* Boca Raton, Fla.: CRC Press, 2004. Covers the means for detecting both military and industrial chemicals that might be used by terrorists and discusses steps that should be taken to prepare for such attacks or for accidents.

Tucker, Jonathan B., ed. *Toxic Terror: Assessing the Terrorist Use of Chemical and Biological Weapons.* Cambridge, Mass.: MIT Press, 2000. Presents twelve case studies of the use of chemical and biological agents by terrorist groups, identifying terrorists' patterns of behavior and strategies to combat them.

**See also:** Blood agents; Chemical agents; Chemical terrorism; Chemical warfare; Mustard gas; Nerve agents; Quantitative and qualitative analysis of chemicals; Sarin; Soman; Tabun.

## Chicago nightclub stampede

**Date:** February 17, 2003

**The Event:** Twelve women and nine men, ages twenty-one to forty-three, were killed and more than fifty other persons were injured when they were trampled or crushed as a panicked crowd attempted to flee Chicago's E2 nightclub through a single exit after pepper spray was used inside the club to break up a fight.

**Significance:** Situations in which surging crowds of people cause injuries and deaths are of great concern to law-enforcement officials and public safety authorities. When such events occur, coroners and medical examiners must perform autopsies to determine the specific causes of any deaths.

The E2 nightclub occupied the second floor of a building above the Epitome restaurant on South Michigan Avenue in Chicago, Illinois. E2 was frequented by celebrity figures and was considered by many in the local African American community to be the place to be seen. On the night of Monday, February 17, 2003, a party promoted by Envy Entertainment was in progress in the nightclub. The promoter had hired ten security guards to maintain order and assist patrons. When one of the security guards used pepper spray to attempt to stop a fight among some patrons, some people in the crowd began choking on the chemicals and then some began to shout, "Poison gas!" It was later reported also that someone said, "I bet it's Bin Laden."

The panicked crowd scrambled to get to the club's only open staircase leading outside. In the stampede, some smaller people were pushed and trampled by others as they tried to get to the door. The crowd got stuck on the restricted stairway, but people continued to pile on top of those already trapped. Some were literally squeezed to death or asphyxiated by crushing; many sustained broken bones. By the time police and fire officers arrived, even though security guards had been trying to remove fallen victims from below, the crush was so tight

that significant exertion was required to begin to disentangle individuals from the pile of patrons. Following the incident, the Cook County medical examiner's office performed routine after-death activities. The office certified the causes of death and held bodies at the morgue, where, even after several days, families and friends came looking for loved ones. Much of the investigation into the incident itself was assigned to the Chicago Fire Department. A deputy medical examiner eventually testified at a hearing that "all E2 victims were crushed."

The deaths triggered a series of investigations and disputes involving licensing of the club and permits issued by the city of Chicago. Prominent African Americans spoke out in support of the club owners, and the owners of the club and their attorneys maneuvered to avoid criminal charges by attempting to discredit Chicago city officials. Significant civil damages were eventually paid.

*David R. Struckhoff*

### Further Reading

Horan, Deborah, and Sean Hamill. "It Was People on Top of People." *Chicago Tribune*, February 18, 2003.

Sadovi, Carlos. "All E2 Victims Were Crushed." *Chicago Tribune*, January 26, 2007.

"Stampede at Chicago Nightclub Leaves Twenty-one Dead." *USA Today*, February 19, 2003.

**See also:** Asphyxiation; Autopsies; Choking; Fire debris; Forensic pathology; Smoke inhalation; Suffocation.

## Child abduction and kidnapping

**Definition:** Unlawful seizing and detaining of children, through force or enticement, with the intent of keeping the children permanently or with the intent of harming the children or concealing them from their legal parents or guardians until ransoms are paid.

**Significance:** State and federal law-enforcement agencies working to solve child abduction and kidnapping cases often draw upon the tools of forensic science to locate missing children and to identify children when they are recovered or when their bodies are found.

Distinctions between "child abduction" and "child kidnapping" are not always clear-cut, as the terms are not always used consistently in the news media, the sociological literature, and statutory law. Generally, however, "child abduction" is the more inclusive term and is almost always the term applied to the unlawful seizing or detaining of children by their own close relatives. Abductions by family members are also the most common form of child abduction. The word "kidnapping" tends to be applied more to abductions by nonrelatives, particularly people who are strangers to their youthful victims. That term is generally applied to cases in which perpetrators abduct children with the intention of demanding ransoms for their return, physically abusing or harming the children, or keeping them permanently separated from their legal guardians for other reasons.

In the popular public perception, many if not most abductions of children are perpetrated by strangers or by little-known acquaintances of the victims. However, most nonrelative abductions are actually perpetrated by people with whom the victims' families are well acquainted. Nevertheless, fear of kidnapping by strangers is behind public campaigns to alert families to what is called "stranger danger" and efforts to have children carry identification cards, to collect fingerprints and DNA (deoxyribonucleic acid) samples of children for possible future need, and to have current photos available. Public awareness of the danger of child abduction has been kept alive by such practices as advertising missing children on milk cartons and the broadcasting of AMBER Alerts. Taking their name from "America's Missing: Broadcast Emergency Response," AMBER Alerts are designed to disseminate information on missing children as widely and quickly as possible. In many regions, the alerts interrupt television programs and are broadcast on electronic traffic signs over freeways. These and other practices help to dramatize the dangers of child abduction and foster the perception that most abductions are perpetrated by dangerous criminals.

**Abduction and the Law**

The abduction of children is everywhere regarded as a horrendous crime against society and has prompted legislation and law-enforcement efforts to prevent its occurrence. Highly publicized kidnapping cases typically prompt fresh legislation and new antikidnapping campaigns. One of the most famous child kidnapping cases in American history was the 1932 abduction and murder of the infant son of Charles A. Lindbergh, a famous aviator who was regarded as a national hero. The widespread public revulsion against that crime prompted the U.S. Congress to pass legislation, the Federal Kidnapping Act, popularly known as the Lindbergh Law. This law was significant because it authorized the investigation of kidnapping cases by the Federal Bureau of Investigation (FBI), which draws on the largest databases and most advanced forensic tools available to law enforcement.

In 1980, Congress enacted the Federal Parental Kidnapping Prevention Act to address the lack of uniformity in state laws regarding kidnapping. Disparities in the laws among different states encouraged some noncustodial parents forcibly to take their children to states with less stringent requirements or to refuse to return their children to the custodial parents' states so they could retain custody themselves. The new federal law gave the home states of abducted children priority in the resolution of custody disputes.

Several federal agencies provide assistance to local law-enforcement agencies that are investigating abducted children. In addition to the FBI, these agencies include the National Center for Missing and Exploited Children and the Forensic Services Division of the U.S. Secret Service. The services the agencies provide include on-site investigators, access to handwriting and fingerprint databases, and laboratory analyses of evidence and written reports. In addition, they make available consultations with forensic experts in such fields as computer forensics, forensic photography, graphic arts, video production, imaging, voice analysis, and computer modeling, and they provide experts to testify in court proceedings.

## Prevalence

Among the various violent crimes perpetrated against children and juveniles in the United States, abduction is comparatively rare. In a study published in 2000, David Finkelhor and Richard K. Ormrod found that child abduction was responsible for less than 2 percent of all violent crimes against juveniles that were reported to law enforcement. Although large numbers of children are annually abducted, most abductees are returned to their families within short periods of time. However, parents and other family members are themselves responsible for most child abductions. In the year 1999, for example, roughly 78 percent of the approximately 262,100 children abducted throughout the United States were taken by relatives. Slightly fewer than 1,000 of the abductions were perpetrated by parents who were citizens of other countries.

Kidnapping and abductions by nonrelatives, both family acquaintances and strangers, accounted for about 22 percent of child abductions in 1999. In contrast to popular belief, the most frequent victims of nonfamily kidnapping—about 80 percent—are not young children but youths age twelve and older. Children from fifteen to seventeen years old make up nearly 60 percent of acquaintance and stranger kidnapping.

## Family and Acquaintance Abductions

"Parental abduction" is generally defined as taking and not returning a child in violation of the custodial rights of the child's parent or guardian by another member of the family or someone acting on behalf of a family member. Indeed, any form of concealment of a child to prevent return, contact, or visitation is considered be unlawful abduction. Likewise, transporting a child out of a state or country with the intent to deprive the caretaker of custodial rights or contact is also unlawful abduct in order for the act to be considered abduction. In cases involving children who are fifteen years of age or older and considered mentally competent, unlawful abduction occurs only when the perpetrators use physical force or threats of bodily harm to the children who are hidden or are taken from the state. Most parental abductions involve children six years or younger, with two-year-olds being the most frequently abducted. Such abductions typically occur at the children's homes.

Gender appears to have little bearing on parental child abduction. Statistics show that girls and boys are equally at risk of being abducted by their parents. Moreover, both mothers and fathers abduct children. However, although some studies find that noncustodial mothers and fathers are equally likely to abduct their children, others find that noncustodial fathers are more likely than mothers to be perpetrators.

Statistics for other types of abduction do show patterns that are more clearly gender-related. For example, almost three-quarters of acquaintance abductions of teenagers involve female victims. In general, teenage girls are more likely to be abducted by acquaintances than by strangers. Almost one-third of perpetrators are teenage boys. Moreover, boyfriends and former boyfriends account for nearly one-fifth of teenage girl abductions.

## Stranger Abductions

Although the media often publicize stranger kidnapping, Finkelhor and Ormrod's study of juvenile kidnapping found that stranger and nonfamily child kidnapping is rare. A comparatively small percentage of juvenile abductions conform to the stereotypical model of kidnapping—that is, the taking of children and holding them for extended periods of time, whether to attempt to extort ransom or to subject the children to sexual assault and murder. The majority of perpetrators of that kind of abduction are strangers to their victims. Most stranger kidnappings occur in outdoor settings. Nearly 60 percent of the crimes occur in such outdoor public places as parks, streets, and parking lots. Kidnappings rarely occur on school grounds.

Some gender and age patterns can be seen in stranger abductions. For example, girls are twice as likely as boys to be victims of nonfamily kidnapping. Teenagers account for more than half the victims, elementary school-age children account for just over one-third of the victims, and preschoolers are rarely targeted. About 95 percent of perpetrators of stranger kidnapping are male. About 20 percent of the abductions are connected with other violent crimes, such as sexual assault, which is most commonly inflicted on girls. When kidnapping is connected with robberies, boys are more likely to be victims, and firearms are often involved in the kidnapping.

Among infants between six and twelve months old, boys and girls are equally at risk of being abducted by strangers, and most perpetrators kidnap infants of the same race. Infants who are kidnapped tend to be in good health, and their risk of being physically injured during their abductions is low. However, the risk of harm to the parents—especially mothers—during kidnapping is high when infants are taken from their homes. Mothers are occasionally killed by kidnappers; in some instances, unborn babies are taken from their mothers' wombs.

### Forensic Techniques Used in Investigations

As with investigations into any specialized field of crime, child abduction and kidnapping investigations draw on specialized forensic tools and procedures. One of the most important aspects of many child kidnapping investigations is identifying recovered children who have not been seen by their families for many years. The method most frequently used to identify kidnap victims is simple visual recognition by their parents. However, that method may not work in cases involving children who have been away from their parents so long that their physical appearance and voices have changed and their memories have faded. Such cases generally call for advanced forensic techniques. For example, photographic manipulation and age regression techniques may be used. These techniques entail manipulating old photographs artificially to age the faces of children so they will appear to match the current ages of the kidnapped children.

Some of the methods used to identify abducted infants after they are returned employ evidence that may have been collected when the children were born. For example, matching footprints to prints recorded on birth documents is the second-most-frequently used method of identification. Other evidence that is

## Megan's and Jessica's Laws

In 1994, a seven-year-old girl named Megan Kanka was kidnapped, raped, and brutally killed by a man who lived across the street from her family home in New Jersey. Unbeknownst to her parents up until that time, her murderer and his two housemates were all convicted sexual predators. After Megan's death, her parents created the Megan Nicole Kanka Foundation to put pressure on New Jersey's government to enact legislation requiring public notification of the residences of known sex offenders. The state legislature responded quickly, making New Jersey the first state to pass such legislation. Most other states soon followed New Jersey's lead. Details of legislation requiring community notification regarding persons convicted of sex crimes against children vary widely among the states, but all such legislation has become popularly known as "Megan's

Law." The federal government also enacted similar legislation. The Jacob Wetterling Crimes Against Children and Sexually Violent Offender Registration Act of 1994 requires convicted sex offenders to notify local law enforcement of any changes in their addresses or employment.

Another horrific case of kidnapping occurred in Florida in 1995, when a nine-year-old named Jessica Lunsford was kidnapped, raped, and murdered by a forty-seven-year-old man. Public outrage against this crime led Florida's legislature to pass a law setting mandatory minimum prison sentences on adults convicted of sex crimes against children under thirteen years of age. Florida's law and those of the many other states that passed similar legislation are popularly known as "Jessica's Law."

used includes blood tests, photographs, birth-marks, hospital wristbands, and DNA samples.

In kidnapping cases, it is vital that the initial investigators collect as much evidence as possible from the crime scenes, especially when children are abducted by nonfamily members and there is a possibility of their being held for ransom or becoming targets of sexual or violent crimes. Blood samples, hair samples, fibers, and other forensic evidence must be collected as soon as possible and properly stored. Such evidence often proves crucial in tracking victims' movements and identifying young victims after they are recovered.

Analysis of latent fingerprints is frequently an important tool in investigations of child abductions and missing children. Fingerprints often reveal the specific locations where children have been or the vehicles in which they have been transported. Latent prints also can be used to identify the child. A special problem in using fingerprint evidence in child abduction cases is that the latent prints of children may not last as long as those of adults, possibly because children's fingers secrete less oily residue.

DNA samples taken at birth from an infant or provided by the guardians of the missing child can be very helpful in identifying a missing child. Also, DNA can place a child at a scene or in an area or in a vehicle, and this information can help authorities to track the child's movements.

### Identifying Dead Kidnap Victims

In the unfortunate cases in which kidnapping victims die, a primary task of forensic investigators is to identify the remains of whatever bodies have been recovered. The basic techniques used to identify children's remains are the same as those used to identify remains of adults. However, the remains of juveniles do present some special problems. For example, juvenile skulls are not as fully developed as skulls of adult human beings. The shapes of skulls change considerably as individuals grow older, making it more difficult to identify the remains of children who have been missing for long periods. Changes in skull shape are particularly great during the first few years of children's

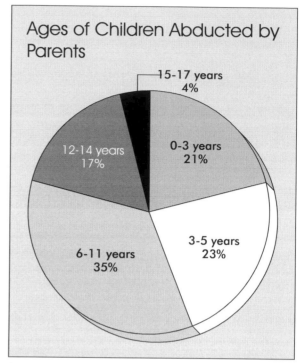

*Source:* Office of Justice Programs, Office of Juvenile Justice and Delinquency Prevention, 2002. Figures are based on 203,900 incidents of child abduction in the United States in 1999.

lives. The length of an infant skull is about one-quarter the full height of the body. Adult skulls are only about one-eighth of full body height. As children grow older, their skulls and bodies gradually assume adult proportions. Meanwhile, the proportions of their facial features to their heads change. For example, the nasal and dental areas become larger relative to the rest of their faces. Other physical changes occur in the pigmentation and elasticity of their skin and the distribution of fatty tissue in their faces. The forensic reconstruction of juvenile faces must take into account these and other differences between juvenile and adult faces.

Some changes in skulls of children may actually assist in estimating the children's ages. For example, there is a consistent and predictable sequence for the formation, eruption, and loss of a child's first teeth—or baby teeth—and their replacement with permanent teeth. Thus, the age of a preadolescent child can be estimated by

## Characteristics of Strangers Who Kidnap Children

- Most are male.
- Most are white.
- Most are under thirty years of age.
- Most are single.
- About half are employed.
- Employed male kidnappers typically work in unskilled and blue-collar occupations.
- About two-thirds of male kidnappers have prior arrest records, mostly for violent crimes, especially sexual assault against children.
- Female kidnappers are less violent than their male counterparts and rarely murder their victims.
- Female kidnappers are often motivated by revenge, the desire to have a child, or other emotional reasons.

examining how many of its teeth have emerged, the extent of calcification of the first molars, and the calcification of the dentition in its entirety.

*Judy L. Porter*

## Further Reading

Bartol, Curt R., and Anne M. Bartol. *Introduction to Forensic Psychology*. Thousand Oaks, Calif.: Sage, 2004. Comprehensive work provides an easily understood guide to forensic psychology.

Beyer, Kristen R., and James O. Beasley. "Nonfamily Child Abductors Who Murder Their Victims: Offender Demographics from Interviews with Incarcerated Offenders." *Journal of Interpersonal Violence* 18 (October, 2003): 1167-1188. Presents the results of an analysis of data gleaned from personal interviews with offenders who have kidnapped and murdered children.

Blasdell, Raleigh. "The Longevity of the Latent Fingerprints of Children Versus Adults." *Policing: An International Journal of Police Strategies and Management* 24, no. 3 (2001): 363-370. Presents evidence from a study that found that children's latent fingerprints do not last as long as those of adults and discusses the implications of this finding for forensic science and law enforcement.

Burgess, Ann Wolbert, and Kenneth V. Lanning. *An Analysis of Infant Abductions*. Washington, D.C.: National Center for Missing and Exploited Children, 2003. Discusses in depth the national data on infant abductions.

Finkelhor, David, and Richard K. Ormrod. *Kidnaping of Juveniles: Patterns from NIBRS*. OJJDP Bulletin NCJ 181161. Washington, D.C.: U.S. Department of Justice, 2000. Brief work presents an analysis of the patterns found in the data concerning child abductions collected by the National Incident-Based Reporting System.

Hammer, Heather, David Finkelhor, and Andrea J. Sedlak. *Children Abducted by Family Members: National Estimates and Characteristics*. Washington, D.C.: U.S. Department of Justice, 2002. Brief work reports on data collected on family abductions by the National Incidence Studies of Missing, Abducted, Runaway, and Thrownaway Children.

James, Stuart H., and Jon J. Nordby, eds. *Forensic Science: An Introduction to Scientific and Investigative Techniques*. 2d ed. Boca Raton, Fla.: CRC Press, 2005. Provides an overview of forensic science procedures, including those involved in the investigation of cases of kidnapping. Informative for both practitioners and students.

Steadman, Dawnie Wolfe. *Hard Evidence: Case Studies in Forensic Anthropology*. Upper Saddle River, N.J.: Prentice Hall, 2003. Presents constructive case studies that demonstrate the scientific foundations of forensic anthropology as well the broad scope of its modern applications.

Wilkinson, Caroline. *Forensic Facial Reconstruction*. New York: Cambridge University Press, 2004. Provides detailed description of the procedures involved in reconstructing faces and addresses the problems related to the determination of age, sex, and race using only the skull. Notes the particular problems of reconstructing the faces of children.

**See also:** Argentine disappeared children; Child abuse; DNA fingerprinting; Federal Bureau of Investigation Laboratory; Fingerprints; Forensic anthropology; Hostage negotiations; Lindbergh baby kidnapping; Megan's Law; Ritual killing.

# Child abuse

**Definition:** Mistreatment of children that encompasses sexual molestation, infliction of physical injuries, emotional and psychological maltreatment, neglect, forced isolation, and threats of inflicting harm and other forms of intimidation.

**Significance:** Child abuse, long one of the most underreported and underinvestigated forms of violent crime, is among the most difficult crimes to uncover and prosecute. In the past, investigations were typically relegated to child protective workers who were untrained in crime scene investigation and evidence collection and processing. With increasing frequency, however, child abuse investigations are being conducted by trained law-enforcement officers and by technicians who draw heavily on the tools of forensic science.

Child abuse is a serious crime whose victims' psychological and physical scars often last for years. Child abuse cases are typically difficult to investigate and prosecute, but the tools of modern forensic science are making important contributions in identifying and convicting offenders.

Teamwork plays a special role in these investigations, which typically involve not only law-enforcement professionals but also social workers, mental health providers, physicians, and others.

## Forms of Abuse

Both sociological and legal definitions of child abuse and molestation have varied over time. "Child abuse" and "child molestation" can be subsumed under the more inclusive phrase "child maltreatment," which encompasses neglect, child endangerment, emotional and psychological abuse, physical abuse, and sexual abuse. Perhaps the most common form of child maltreatment is neglect—the failure to provide minor children with the most basic needs of food, shelter, clothing, education, and medical care.

Legal definitions of child abuse and subtypes of abuse are codified in state statutes and vary among jurisdictions. In contrast to sociological definitions, which may be vague and open to different interpretations, legal definitions and individual statutes spell out exactly what behaviors are illegal. For example, when adults who are legally responsible for the care of children expose those children to dangerous conditions, the adults are guilty of child endangerment. Examples of endangerment range from leaving young children unattended in parked cars while running errands to leaving minors completely alone in their homes for extended periods.

Physical abuse takes many forms that are easy to define—hitting, slapping, punching, kicking, beating, striking with objects, stabbing, cutting, burning, and choking. Somewhat less obviously abusive but equally serious is the violent shaking of infants or toddlers, which often manifests itself in shaken baby syndrome. Severe instances of physical abuse can lead to death.

Physical abuse may be one of the most underreported crimes against children. Part of the reason is that very young children lack the ability to communicate the abuse. Also, some abused children may regard what their parents do to them as normal behavior. They may even think that they deserve to be hit because of their own misbehavior. Forms of emotional and psychological abuse are less easy to define legally. They include verbally abusing or deriding children and threatening or terrorizing them.

Laws against the sexual abuse of children generally provide precise definitions of illegal behavior. Such abuse encompasses any or all forms of sexual contact between minors and adults, from improper touching and fondling to forced vaginal, oral, or anal intercourse. Consensual sexual contact between two minors can be considered sexual abuse when a significant age difference exists between them. In some jurisdictions, a difference of only three or four years in the ages of sexual partners may be regarded as significant. Sexual abuse also includes involving minors in the making of pornography.

## Criminal Investigations

The gathering and preservation of evidence in child abuse investigations can be a daunting job. Police investigators must find out what has happened, how it happened, and other information in order to make arrests and bring offenders to justice. The forensic sciences provide important tools for collecting evidence in these crimes.

The first step in collecting evidence of abuse in cases that are reported is to determine when the crimes occurred and how much time has elapsed since the crimes took place. When child abuse is reported immediately after incidents occur, police can usually collect more physical evidence than in cases in which longer periods of time have elapsed.

The clothing worn by victims during times when they have been abused often provides valuable physical evidence. Hairs and traces of tears, dirt, blood, and semen found on clothing can be used as direct evidence of crimes. Investigators also comb the crime scenes, which often contain such physical evidence as bloodstains, hair samples, semen stains, and fragments of damaged clothing. All items that are collected must be carefully packaged, labeled, analyzed, and protected for use in court.

## Medical Evidence of Abuse

Most injury evidence can be documented through medical procedures. Ideally, victims of child abuse should receive physical examinations by qualified physicians as quickly as possible. Indeed, in most cases of physical abuse of children, physicians discover evidence that maltreatment has occurred in the injuries themselves. For example, spiral arm fractures provide almost conclusive evidence of abuse, as such fractures are caused by arm twisting and can occur in almost no other way.

Another almost conclusive sign of child abuse that may be detected by physicians is traumatic alopecia—the forceful pulling of hair or breaking of hair shafts by friction, traction, or other forms of physical trauma. Traumatic alopecia occurs when abusers deliberately pull the hair of their child victims. Hair pulling can cause hemorrhaging under the scalp, which has a rich supply of blood vessels. Accumulations of blood under the scalp are often important clues in differentiating between abusive and nonabusive hair loss. Medical evaluations can discover evidence of shaken baby syndrome, which is responsible for at least half the deaths of victims of child abuse. Vigorous shaking of an infant or toddler causes a number of medical conditions that physicians can read as signs of the syndrome. These include closed-head injuries that are evidenced by altered levels of consciousness, coma, convulsions, or death; central nervous system injuries that are evidenced by central nervous system hemorrhaging, lacerations, contusions, and concussions; and retinal hemorrhages. Central nervous system injuries can be identified through magnetic resonance imaging (MRI) and computed tomography (CT) scans. Both of these techniques are used to discover a variety of injuries that reveal abuse, such as intracranial and intra-abdominal abnormalities. Ultrasound, a technique that creates two-dimensional images and is used for examining internal body structures, can be used to detect physical abnormalities. It is especially useful for detecting intracranial hemorrhaging in children under the age of two.

Techniques for determining the age of skeletal injuries are also valuable in abuse investigations because they can help differentiate between accidental and intentionally inflicted injuries. For example, radiology studies that determine the ages of bone injuries make it possible to identify patterns of physical abuse over long periods of time. Among all types of cases involving physical injuries, human bites are the most common and easily recognized form of physical maltreatment. The ability to recognize injuries as human bite marks is thus particularly important, and forensic dentistry (also known as forensic odontology) contributes a great deal to the investigation of such injuries. By analyzing bite marks, forensic dentists can often help to identify the individuals who made them.

## DNA Evidence

Although many proven forensic science techniques are helpful in the investigation of child abuse, perhaps nothing has helped solve more crimes in this area than DNA (deoxyribonucleic acid) testing. DNA carries coded genetic information that determines individual traits. Analyses of DNA samples can be used to identify the persons from whom the samples come. DNA testing was first used in criminal investigations during the early 1980's and almost immediately became one of the most valuable tools available to forensic science. Many parts of human DNA are the same in different persons; however, the parts found in nonfunctioning sequences vary greatly. The variable parts can be matched to single individuals. In criminal child abuse cases, investigators often collect samples of fluids, hairs, and tissues left behind on victims by their abusers. These samples are then compared with samples taken from suspected perpetrators. When samples are found to match, the possibilities of misidentification are remote. DNA testing requires only small amounts of sample material. Bloodstains the size of a dime and semen samples the size of a quarter are usually sufficient. Results of analyses are usually obtained within four to six weeks. DNA evi-

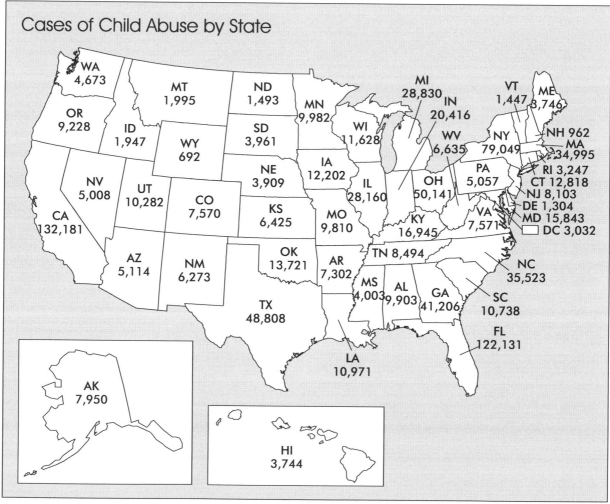

Cases of Child Abuse by State

*Source:* U.S. Department of Health and Human Services, 2004. Figures represent substantiated cases of child maltreatment in 2002. Total number of cases for the entire United States in 2002 was 897,168.

dence has been used successfully in the prosecution of many perpetrators of child abuse.

*Jerry W. Hollingsworth and the Editors*

### Further Reading

Barkan, Steven E. *Criminology: A Sociological Understanding*. 3d ed. Upper Saddle River, N.J.: Pearson Prentice Hall, 2006. Examines criminal justice issues from a sociological perspective. Includes discussion of child abuse.

Buzawa, Eve S., and Carl G. Buzawa. *Domestic Violence: The Criminal Justice Response*. 3d ed. Thousand Oaks, Calif.: Sage, 2003. Presents information on how law-enforcement agencies and the courts approach cases of child and spousal abuse.

Fontes, Lisa Aronson, ed. *Sexual Abuse in Nine North American Cultures: Treatment and Prevention*. Thousand Oaks, Calif.: Sage, 1995. Collection of essays discusses the characteristics of child sexual abuse in various cultural communities in North America.

Monteleone, James A. *A Parent's and Teacher's Handbook on Identifying and Preventing Child Abuse*. St. Louis: G. W. Medical Publishing, 1998. Provides valuable information on the signs and symptoms of child abuse for lay readers.

_____, ed. *Child Abuse: Quick Reference for Healthcare Professionals, Social Services, and Law Enforcement*. St. Louis: G. W. Medical Publishing, 1998. Illustrated guide is designed to help those who might come into contact with abused children in their professional capacities.

Walker, Lenore E. A., and David L. Shapiro. *Introduction to Forensic Psychology: Clinical and Social Psychological Perspectives*. New York: Kluwer Academic/Plenum, 2003. Presents an overview of the applications of psychology to the law. Includes case examples.

**See also:** Bite-mark analysis; Blunt force trauma; Child abduction and kidnapping; DNA extraction from hair, bodily fluids, and tissues; False memories; Parental alienation syndrome; Rape; Rape kit; Semen and sperm; Shaken baby syndrome; Strangulation.

## Choking

**Definition:** Medical emergency that occurs when partial or complete obstruction of the airway interferes with breathing, depriving the body of the oxygen necessary to maintain life.

**Significance:** Appropriate actions may be taken to prevent death in choking victims if others present recognize the signs of choking. Choking deaths may be mistaken for other types of deaths, such as suffocation, strangulation, or asphyxia, which may be intentional or accidental.

Choking is almost always accidental and preventable. The signs of active choking vary depending on the age of the person and the type of choking (partial or complete) involved. In adults, choking on food is most commonly found in situations of alcohol intoxication. Children often choke as the result of putting small objects, such as coins or small toys, into their mouths and then unintentionally inhaling them into the trachea (airway). Children also sometimes choke because they have put large amounts of food into their mouths and have not chewed the food properly before swallowing; the objects enter the airway rather than the esophagus.

A choking victim who is able to cough or speak is receiving adequate oxygenation to sustain life; the only action needed in such a situation is observation. The person should be allowed to cough in an attempt to dislodge the object.

A partial airway blockage, however, may progress to a complete blockage. When the airway is completely blocked, the victim is not taking in adequate oxygen and is unable to speak or cough. A blue discoloration of the mouth and fingernails may become apparent.

A person who is choking may panic because of the lack of oxygen and fear of death. An adult may avoid seeking help in public owing to embarrassment, whereas a child may run from help out of fear. If the blockage is not quickly resolved, the individual will lose consciousness because of the lack of oxygen to the brain. At that point, the muscles in the airway will relax, but the object will remain in the airway unless the victim receives assistance from another person. If choking continues, the victim's heart will eventually stop beating and death will occur.

Medical and police personnel need to be aware of the signs of choking that may be present at the scene of a death. By thoroughly examining the scene and interviewing witnesses, emergency responders and police officers may aid the medical examiner in determination of the cause and manner of death. Bruising of the neck should not be seen in a choking victim. A person who has died from choking may have scratch marks at the neck from grabbing at the throat; if any skin is found under the fingernails, it will be the victim's own. The eyes of a choking victim may be bloodshot from vigorous coughing or from straining to relieve the blockage. As death occurs, the muscles relax. The bladder also relaxes, and urine may be present at the scene.

*Amy Webb Bull*

**Further Reading**

American Red Cross. *American Red Cross First Aid: Responding to Emergencies.* 5th ed. Yardley, Pa.: StayWell, 2006.

Lynch, Virginia A. *Forensic Nursing.* St. Louis: C. V. Mosby, 2006.

**See also:** Air and water purity; Asphyxiation; Autoerotic and erotic asphyxiation; Chemical agents; Epilepsy; Hanging; Petechial hemorrhage; Smoke inhalation; Strangulation; Suffocation.

## Chromatography

**Definition:** Laboratory techniques used to separate chemical mixtures into their individual components and to quantify and identify the isolated components.

**Significance:** Chromatography techniques are useful for a variety of purposes in the forensic sciences, including determining causes of death, linking individuals to spe-

cific crime scenes, and analyzing the residues from explosives to identify possible suspects.

Chromatography was invented in 1903 by the Russian botanist Mikhail Semyonovich Tsvet, who used it to separate plant pigments, the various colored components of plants. It has been suggested that Tsvet arrived at the name "chromatography" for this process by combining the Greek words *chroma* and *graphein*, literally meaning "color writing." The uses of chromatography are not limited to colored substances, however.

The various forms of chromatography all share certain characteristics. For example, the sample to be analyzed is dissolved in a mobile phase, typically a liquid or a gas, which then comes into contact with a stationary phase, typically a solid or a liquid. As the mobile phase flows over the stationary phase, the various components of the sample are attracted to each phase to different extents, based on their physical characteristics. Those components that are attracted more to the stationary phase will move less quickly than those that are attracted more to the mobile phase, so the components separate from each other.

Chromatographic techniques may be categorized based on the nature of the mobile phase. In liquid chromatography, the mobile phase is a liquid. In gas chromatography, the mobile phase is a gas. Additionally, many of these techniques use columns containing the stationary phase; the mobile phase flows through the column after the sample has been dissolved in the mobile phase and applied to the column. When the components of the chemical mixture have been separated, they may be identified through the use of a detector attached to the chromatographic system. The detector, which may include one of several instruments used in chemical analysis, records various physical properties of the components. When a column is used, the detector is attached to the end of the column where the components are released.

Chromatography is used in the forensic sciences whenever it is necessary to separate the chemical components of a sample to determine the identity or the quantity of one or more of those components. The uses of chromatography include detecting the presence of explosives in airport baggage, analyzing explosives residues to identify the sources as well as possible suspects, and determining cause of death in autopsies through the screening of biological samples (such as blood, hair, and skin) for drugs or poisons. Chromatography is also used to identify the chemical makeup of seized illicit drugs and to determine blood alcohol levels in persons accused of driving under the influence of alcohol. Using chromatography techniques, analysts can determine the composition and quantity of the dyes in textile fibers left at a crime scene and thus help identify the potential source of the fibers, examine the ink on legal documents to determine whether any information has been fraudulently inserted, compare small amounts of soil to link suspects to a crime scene, determine the likely factory source of automobile paint left at the scene of a hit-and-run accident, detect the presence of accelerants at the scene of an arson investigation, and screen foods to determine whether they have been contaminated with dangerous chemicals.

*Jason J. Schwartz*

### Further Reading

Bogusz, M. J., ed. *Handbook of Analytical Separations*. Vol. 6 in *Forensic Science*, edited by Roger M. Smith. 2d ed. New York: Elsevier, 2007.One of a multi-volume series that provides detailed reviews of analytical separation methods. This volume focuses on separation methods applicable to the forensic sciences, including chromatography.

Lundanes, E., L. Reubsaet, and T. Greibrokk. *Chromatography: Basic Principles, Sample Preparations and Related Methods*. Weinhiem, Germany: Wiley VCH Verlage GmbH & Co. KGaA, 2014. Discusses various types of chromatography and related techniques.

**See also:** Analytical instrumentation; Column chromatography; Forensic toxicology; Gas chromatography; High-performance liquid chromatography; Hit-and-run vehicle offenses; Homogeneous enzyme immunoassay; Mass spectrometry; Quantitative and qualitative analysis of chemicals; Separation tests; Spectroscopy; Thin-layer chromatography; Toxicological analysis.

## Class versus individual evidence

**Definitions:** Class evidence is evidence that can be linked to a type (or class) of items; individual evidence is evidence that can be linked to a specific individual or item.

**Significance:** Because the majority of evidence at crime scenes is class evidence and not individual evidence, it would be difficult to link objects at crime scenes to specific suspects were it not for the fact that many objects pick up individual characteristics.

Class evidence makes up the vast majority of all evidence in forensic cases. For example, a glass fragment can be analyzed to determine its refractive index and chemical makeup. The resultant laboratory report can tell investigators that the fragment's properties are consistent with a certain type of glass, such as that from windowpanes or car headlights. What the analysis usually cannot reveal is from which particular window or which particular car headlight the fragment comes.

By contrast, individual evidence can be linked to specific objects, such as fingerprints, no two of which have ever been found to be exactly alike. For this reason, any fingerprint that is found must have been made by one, and only one, person. Other examples of individual evidence include human lip prints, ear prints, and sole prints. Researchers have also found through X-ray analyses of skulls that sinus prints—the unique patterns of bone and space in sinus cavities—are also individual. Forensic anthropologists can use this information to identify bodies of long-dead people. Surprisingly, DNA (deoxyribonucleic acid) evidence is not individual, as identical twins have identical DNA.

Many objects that would otherwise fall under the heading of class evidence pick up individual characteristics. For example, the soles of all shoes of a specific model and size come out of their factories looking exactly the same. After they have undergone some substantial wear, however, they develop distinctive wear patterns. The ways in which different users distribute their weight, the feet that they favor, and many other factors, including chemical and biological materials on which they step, contribute to making the soles of their shoes take on individual characteristics.

The individuation of characteristics can be seen in many different types of evidence. For example, tools can develop distinctive wear patterns and leave distinctive marks when they are used. Vehicle tires develop distinctive wear patterns over time, just as shoes do. Firearms can leave distinctive marks on the bullets they discharge. Glass may fracture in ways that make it possible for investigators to reassemble the broken pieces, much like a jigsaw puzzle. In forensic investigations, considerable time is devoted to looking at how class evidence becomes individualized.

*Ayn Embar-Seddon and Allan D. Pass*

## Further Reading

Beavan, Colin. *Fingerprints: The Origins of Crime Detection and the Murder Case That Launched Forensic Science.* New York: Hyperion, 2001.

Platt, Richard. *Crime Scene: The Ultimate Guide to Forensic Science.* New York: Dorling Kindersley, 2003.

**See also:** Ballistic fingerprints; Chain of custody; Courts and forensic evidence; Crime scene reconstruction and staging; Cross-contamination of evidence; Direct versus circumstantial evidence; Disturbed evidence; DNA fingerprinting; Ear prints; Evidence processing; Federal Rules of Evidence; Fingerprints; Footprints and shoe prints; Physical evidence; Prints; Sinus prints; Trace and transfer evidence; Voiceprints.

# Closed-circuit television surveillance

**Definition:** Monitoring of activities in public or private spaces conducted through the use of video cameras that transmit to limited sets of monitors.

**Significance:** As a tool of crime deterrence and detection, closed-circuit television technology is used extensively to monitor movement in public areas. With improvements in video technology and growing fears of terrorism around the world, increasing numbers of law enforcement agencies are employing closed-circuit television surveillance. There are, however, serious questions this form of surveillance raises regarding civil liberties.

Combating crime committed in public locations has long been an important law enforcement priority, and closed-circuit television (CCTV) has become an integral part of the technologies used in this effort. CCTV surveillance of public movements is especially pervasive in England, where hundreds of thousands of video cameras are already mounted and the numbers continue to grow, requiring an enormous expenditure of public funds. The use of CCTV surveillance in England has attracted widespread attention in high-publicity cases, such as the 2005 London subway bombings, when several of the suspects were caught after they appeared on CCTV cameras. CCTV was also part of an organized public response in the wake of the 2011 riots in Manchester. Other European countries that are heavily involved in CCTV monitoring include Ireland, France, Belgium, Finland and Scotland. Latin American countries such as Brazil have shown a huge increase in the use of CCTV monitoring, especially in private, residential areas. Often, however, this increase has not been accompanied by legislation addressing accompanying civil liberties implications.

## Methods and Results

Logistically, the monitoring of the images captured by CCTV cameras is conducted remotely. In England, monitoring is conducted from central stations, which are frequently found in police headquarters. The personnel who monitor CCTV feeds may be police or civilians. Across departments, variations are found in terms of the staff time allotted to live monitoring or post hoc monitoring of surveillance tapes and in the periods of time for which the tapes are kept. The empirical results of the implementation of CCTV surveillance have been mixed, ranging from reports of crime reduction as large as 90 percent to reports of crime increases up to 20 percent.

Any interpretation of crime expansion must be made in terms of two basic goals of CCTV use: crime deterrence and crime detection/clearance. An increase in crime might actually be viewed as a success if the presence of CCTV enhanced crime detection. In terms of property crime, the studies that have found the most positive results have reported long-term reductions in burglary, car theft, and general theft in CCTV areas, with concomitant increases in non-CCTV zones. CCTV may have a displacement effect, whereby the total volume of crime remains fairly constant but much of it is shifted to areas that lack video monitoring. Other studies have found that reported crime reductions in areas with CCTV surveillance could not be isolated from reductions that might have come about because of the large amount of publicity given to the CCTV program itself. Some property crime studies have reported no substantial crime reductions as the result of CCTV surveillance, but it is possible that the monitoring had an impact by holding down projected crime increases. In studies of elderly populations, CCTV tapes were found to provide records useful for identifying suspects (a task in which elderly persons are typically weak).

In another group of studies, CCTV reduced the volume of some crimes, particularly those whose commission took long enough to be recorded by cameras, such as auto theft. However, the frequency of relatively "quick" crimes, such as burglary and shoplifting, increased. Studies have also found a "fading effect" associated with the implementation of CCTV surveillance— that is, crime rates decline initially but then begin to rise again, after the novelty of the moni-

toring wears off and its deterrent impact on would-be offenders recedes. Researchers have also found it difficult at times to separate the effects of CCTV monitoring from other simultaneous changes in the areas being studied, such as better lighting or overall security. Little research has addressed the effects of CCTV implementation on crime trends for violent offenses such as robbery and assault. Because violent offenses are generally more impulsive than property offenses, violent crime is less amenable to preventive measures, but CCTV surveillance could allow police to intervene faster when these offenses take place.

While there has been a tendency in many jurisdictions to spread a large number of CCTV cameras over broad areas without regard to crime trends, recent research has shown that the largest reductions in crime occur when smaller numbers of cameras are placed in high crime areas. The exact reasons for this effect await further explication through studies incorporating more extensive control comparisons. Recent research has also demonstrated that the effects of CCTV in terms crime reductions, including violent attacks, are greatly enhanced when the monitoring is accompanied by proactive policing strategies. These strategies include increased monitoring personnel: camera ratios as well as higher prioritization of prompt responses to CCTV detection of crime in real time.

## Public Responses

Often, governmental responses to the question of CCTV proliferation are driven by high profile violent crime. In New Delhi, for example, which has the highest rate of rape in India, several recent horrific instances of gang rape resulted in calls to increase the number of surveillance cameras from 4000 to one million. Some have claimed, however that such a massive increase would be undertaken as a proxy for remedying inherent weaknesses in the legal system which have allowed this crime to proliferate with apparent impunity for the offenders.

Anti-CCTV advocates have even gone so far as to claim that the technology would be used by those with a "blaming the victim" mentality to document allegations that these women were wearing "provocative" clothing or were frequenting questionable locations where (in their view) they should not have been alone. Researchers have also looked at the effects of CCTV surveillance on fear of crime. In some studies, the majority of the people who were surveyed thought that the use of CCTV would reduce crime in their jurisdictions, but actual fear levels did not decline. Results of such studies have varied depending on the populations involved and the exact crimes and camera locations.

In a survey of elderly persons residing in sheltered housing, for example, reduced fear of burglary was found, as the respondents widely believed that the cameras made stranger entry into their homes more difficult. Studies have found that fears of crime are reduced more by CCTV cameras located in parking lots than by the presence of cameras in shopping centers or on the streets. A sex effect has also been noted regarding fear of crime, with some studies indicating that women are particularly fearful at night in bus and train stations even with CCTV monitoring. Subjects in one study felt that CCTV surveillance was superior to other police crime detection strategies, but they also said that they preferred retaining police foot patrols in order to feel safer. They felt that foot patrols facilitated quicker law enforcement response if needed in any given situation. This "back to the basics" approach would seem to be in sync with some studies that found little or no actual impact on crime rates from CCTV implementation.

In part, such a finding may reflect staffing difficulties in certain jurisdictions. There are an inadequate number of personnel to actually monitor the cameras, either in real time or retrospectively. These studies have sometimes found that the cameras are used more often to monitor the whereabouts of (limited) police personnel, as opposed to the deterrence or detection of crime.

Given the current clamor in many quarters for police body cameras to monitor officers' activities, a related role for CCTV may now have increased salience. CCTV surveillance is generally appealing in terms of its potential to deter and detect crime. It may also help to revive busi-

nesses located in high crime areas and increase the numbers of guilty pleas made by defendants who know their crimes were caught on tape. The use of CCTV surveillance raises several concerns regarding civil rights, however.

Some critics have asserted that members of minority groups are disproportionately targeted for observation and that the police or others may use the monitoring videotapes for purposes that exceed the original scope of the surveillance. Members of the public may not always know when they are being monitored. The actions seen on the tapes (which include images of varying clarity and frequently lack auditory information) may sometimes be misinterpreted. Nevertheless, the use of CCTV surveillance is growing steadily, and the refinement of video technology is expected to become increasingly important in helping law enforcement authorities meet crime deterrence and investigatory goals.

*Eric Metchik*

## Further Reading

Firmino, R., M. Kanashiro, F. Bruno, R. Evangelista, and L. Nascimento. "Fear, Security, and the Spread of CCTV in Brazilian Cities: Legislation and the Market." Journal of Urban Technology, 20, no. 3, (2013): 65-84. A study which contrasts the marketing appeal of CCTV systems in Brazil with the lag in legislative attention to concomitant civil liberties implications.

Germain, S. "A Prosperous 'Business': The Success of CCTV Through the Eyes of International Literature. Surveillance and Society, 11, No. ½ (2013), 134-147. The growth of CCTV is highlighted, apart from its actual effect on detecting and deterring crime. Rather, a confluence of business and political interests are sited as having important roles supporting this trend.

Goold, Benjamin. "Open to All? Regulating Open Street CCTV and the Case for 'Symmetrical Surveillance.'" Criminal Justice Ethics 25, no. 1 (2006): 3-17. Provides a legally oriented analysis of the increasing use of CCTV surveillance of public spaces in the United States.

Menichelli, F. "Technology, Context, Users: A

Conceptual Model of CCTV." Policing: An International Journal of Police Strategies and Management, 37, No. 2 (2014), 389-403. A study of CCTV implementation in two Italian jurisdictions. Emphases include implementation issues in light of limited personnel and other resources, as well a priority given to using the technology to track police officers instead of the traditional crime detection/prevention rationales.

Piza, E., J. Caplan, L. Kennedy, and A. Gilchist. "The Effects of Merging Proactive CCTV Monitoring with Directed Police Patrol: A Randomized Controlled Trial." Journal of Experimental Criminology, 11 (2015): 43-69. An experiment testing the effects of proactive policing strategies and greater dispatch responsivity on the effectiveness of CCTV monitoring.

Shah, R. and J. Braithwaite. "Spread Too Thin: Analyzing the Effectiveness of the Chicago Camera Network on Crime. Police Practice and Research, 14, No. 5, (2013) 415-427. An analysis of CCTV impact in Chicago which focuses on crime density differentiations.

**See also:** Airport security; Crime analysis; Electronic bugs; Facial recognition technology; Forensic photography; Night vision devices; Racial profiling; Satellite surveillance technology; Video surveillance.

# Club drugs

**Definition:** Licit and illicit substances with hallucinogenic properties often used in social situations and resulting in excitation and/or sedation of users

**Significance:** These unregulated street drugs are part of an underground economy and may put the drug consumers in dangerous situations, such as falling unconscious, exhibiting risky sexual behavior, or experiencing sudden death.

Club drugs also go by the name designer drugs. These are substances typically created by man-

ufacturers to make a profit producing drugs and/or who are interested in finding substances that are technically legal for use in clubs and at raves to facilitate enjoyment. The manufacturer chemically modifies these unregulated substances and/or illegal chemical substances technically to make them legal and suitable for such purposes. Once problems emerge, however, relevant authorities and legal systems classify the new substances and assign legal consequences for inappropriate use. To this end, club drugs are a moving target. They represent a large number of different substances by a variety of names. New drugs emerge every day. Users in many countries may not realize their dangers. In fact, online purchasing is common, further sanitizing the image of the drugs and distancing users from their dangers. As such, the users of these drugs may not fit the usual stereotype of a person seeking treatment for substance use. Instead, these individuals may present after a first use of the drug and will present across a range of treatment settings, including sexual health services and emergency rooms, creating some unique public health cnces in sexual crimes.

Many club drugs are variants of what users historically call psychedelic drugs. Psychedelic drugs are substances that alter perception and thinking. A more established drug known as a club drug is lysergic acid diethylamid (LSD). Slang names for LSD include acid and blotter. Other popular contemporary club drugs include substances described as bath salts (synthetic Cathinones), Mephedrone, Purple Drank, synthetic cannabinoids, Salvia Divinorum, and opium tea.

One of the most popular club drugs, historically, is methylenedioxymethamphetamine, or MDMA. MDMA abbreviates the name of its components: methylene-dioxy-meth-amphetamine. MDMA has many slang names as well: Adam, ecstasy, and X, among others. It is important to know that MDMA is different from the club drug herbal ecstasy (also known as cloud nine, herbal bliss, herbal X). While MDMA is a derivative of methamphetamine, herbal ecstasy is from ephedrine or pseudoephedrine and caffeine. Other historically well-known club drugs include ketamine

## Street Names for Club Drugs

**GHB (gamma-hydroxybutyrate)**
- G
- Georgia home boy
- grievous bodily harm
- liquid ecstasy

**Ketamine**
- bump
- cat Valium
- green
- honey oil
- jet
- K
- purple
- Special K
- special la coke
- super acid
- super C
- vitamin K

**LSD (lysergic acid diethylamide)**
- acid
- blotter
- blotter acid
- boomers
- dots
- microdot
- pane
- paper acid
- sugar
- sugar cubes
- trip
- window glass
- windowpane
- yellow sunshine
- Zen

**Methamphetamine**
- chalk
- crank
- crystal
- fire
- glass
- ice
- meth
- speed

**Methylenedioxy-methamphetamine (MDMA)**
- Adam
- Clarity
- ecstasy
- Lover's Speed
- X
- XTC

**Rohypnol**
- forget-me pill
- roche
- roofies
- rophies

hydrochloride (ketamine, special K), gamma-hydroxybutyrate (GHB, Georgia Home Boy, Liquid X), and rohypnol (roach, roche, roofies).

Though the effects of these drugs vary, club drugs generally have no medical use. There are, however, some researchers with interests in examining these drugs for the treatment of trauma. On the positive side, many of these substances may elicit positive reactions, such as happiness, euphoria, and a general feeling of well-being. Users also may experience feelings of emotional clarity, a decreased sense of personal boundaries, and/or feelings of empathy and increased closeness to others. They may also talk about pleasant psychedelic effects where they experience changes in their way of thinking about themselves, others, and their surroundings. On the negative side, however, they are known to cause chills, high blood pressure, rapid heartbeat, respiratory distress, sweating, and tremors. In some cases, convulsions may result. They also may impair judgment, memory, and motor control, cause un-

pleasant hallucinations, irrational behavior, insomnia, and trigger violence, panic, paranoia, or amnesia. Use may also cause blackouts and lead to flashbacks. As such experimentation with such drugs in the treatment of serious conditions has some very large potential risks, particularly if it takes place in circumstances that are not highly controlled, such as in a clinical trial.

Professional health experts expect the experiences described in individuals considered normal and not suffering from any mental, emotional, or physical health problems. Reactions may magnify, however, in individuals compromised by other physical or mental problems. Additionally, it can be very dangerous for individuals to mix these drugs with alcohol, energy drinks, herbal remedies, prescription medications, or other drugs — even over the- counter drugs. This is because combining drugs may result in synergistic effects. Synergistic effects result when drugs interact with each other. They may not simply be additive, but multiplicative, making any of the drugs consumed much more pronounced in its effects. Further, because these are street drugs (e.g., not manufactured by a regulated pharmaceutical lab), the purity of the drugs may vary widely. Street drugs can contain contaminants, or may look alike but deliver unknown or very different drug effects. As such, risk to users can increase.

How and where these substances are used also dictates effects. In a medical or lab setting, or in one's home under observation, fewer risks may be present. In crowded situations, emotionally charged situations, and/or situations where use is taking place in the company of strangers, risks may be pronounced. In clubs, for instance, individuals may be dancing and physically active for long periods of time. Significant dehydration may occur in these circumstances; so much so that it can be life-threatening. In fact, due to the drug's effects, the club drug users may not realize they are dehydrated. This is one reason why problems related to club drug use often end up in emergency rooms. The proximity of strangers may add to the problems as well, as not all club attendees may have the best intentions in mind. In some cases, individuals add club drugs such as rohypnol to a person's drink to subdue the individual. In such circumstances, physical harm may come to the user through physical, sexual (date rape), or property crimes. When such substances are used away from home, driving under the influence also may be an issue, as can the potential to experience a loss of consciousness. In both cases, serious accidents are a concern.

Beyond the short-term risks associated with use, club drugs may also expose users to risks related to substance-related disorders. Substance use problems may come in the form of repeated use leading to problems with functioning at work, home, or school. For instance, the user may be so exhausted from the use of the club drugs that they miss work or school, or do not perform expected duties at home. They may also experience problems with using in dangerous situations and problems with significant others over the consequences of one's substance use. Similarly, they may have problems related to increases in time spent obtaining, using, or recovering from the drug, giving up other activities to use, and exacerbating other psychologi-

cal or physical problems. For some users, these drugs may interact with other states of mind or conditions, for instance, anxiety or depression, and trigger sustained problems with anxiety or mood. Users may also unwittingly place themselves in dangerous situations while under the influence, such that they may suffer significant dehydration, sexual assault or coercion, participate in unprotected sex, or otherwise be vulnerable to crime due to a diminished sense of boundaries.

The scope of legal matters related to club drugs is very broad. Manufacturers of these drugs are entrepreneurs chemically designing the substances to avoid status as a controlled or illicit substance. As such, they bring drug identification, classification, and enforcement challenges related to manufacturing, distribution, and use. Because they are largely unregulated, the sale of such drugs contributes to a primarily underground economy. They also create direct and indirect harm for users. Impaired judgment and behavior among users contribute to accidents and related crimes, such as drunken driving, assault, and property damage. They are also used by victimizers to facilitate date rape, abduction, and other sexual crimes. The fact that these drugs are popular among both high school and college-aged youth emphasizes their negative social impact and the numerous public health and safety challenges they present.

*Nancy A. Piotrowski*

## Further Reading

Dargan, Paul and David Wood, eds. *Novel Psychoactive Substances: Classification, Pharmacology, and Toxicology.* London: Elsevier Academic Press, 2013. An international, multidisciplinary perspective on classification, availability, and problems of "legal highs."

Kuhn, Cynthia, Scott Swartzwelder, and Wilkie Wilson. *Buzzed: The Straight Facts About the Most Used and Abused Drugs from Alcohol to Ecstasy.* 4th ed. New York: W. W. Norton, 2014. Easy to read basic information on commonly used drugs.

Levine, Barry. *Principles of Forensic Toxicology.* 4th ed. American Association for Clinical Chemistry. 2013. Review of concerns and methods for testing substances for their toxic effects.

Substance Abuse and Mental Health Services Administration. *Results from the 2013 National Survey on Drug Use and Health: Summary of National Findings*, NSDUH Series H-48, HHS Publication No. (SMA) 14-4863. Rockville, MD: Substance Abuse and Mental Health Services Administration, 2014. Technical survey results of drug usage as of 2013.

United States Department of Justice. *Situation Report, Cathinones (Bath Salts): An Emerging Threat,* NDIC Product Number 2011-S0787-004. Johnstown, PA: National Drug Intelligence Center, 2011. Government report describing problems associated with designer drugs such as synthetic cathinones, also known as bath salts.

**See also:** Amphetamines; Bath Salts; Cannabis; Drug abuse and dependence; DSM-V; Ecstasy; Hallucinogens; Illicit drugs; Rape; Stimulants; Substance use disorders.

# CODIS

**Date:** Established in 1990

**Identification:** Database maintained by the Federal Bureau of Investigation that stores DNA profiles for comparison purposes, used by federal, state, and local crime laboratories.

**Significance:** CODIS allows forensic laboratories to compare DNA profiles related to crimes (forensic profiles) to those obtained from other crimes or from individuals previously convicted of a felony. Through such comparisons, links may be found between crime scenes, and repeat offenders may be identified.

The Combined DNA Index System, better known as CODIS, was established as the result of a suggestion from the Technical Working Group on DNA Analysis Methods; the intent was to create a national database of DNA (de-

oxyribonucleic acid) profiles collected from convicted criminals. When CODIS was initiated in 1990 as a pilot project of the Federal Bureau of Investigation (FBI), it included fourteen state and local laboratories.

The DNA Identification Act of 1994 allowed the formation of a national DNA database and clarified which types of DNA evidence could be stored in it. DNA profiles from persons convicted of crimes, evidentiary items obtained from crime scenes, and unidentified human remains were to be included, as well as profiles voluntarily submitted by relatives of missing persons. In 1998, the national database became operational, and by 2003 it was accepted by all fifty states. Qualified city, county, regional, state, and federal crime laboratories, as well as laboratories in several other countries, now contribute to this powerful crime-solving tool.

## Structure of the Database

CODIS is operational at three tiers: the National DNA Index System (NDIS), the State DNA Index System (SDIS), and the Local DNA Index System (LDIS) levels. A DNA profile originates locally and then migrates to the state and national levels. This approach allows each state access to a database that is concurrent with its individual legislation, including what crimes will result in submission of a DNA profile (for example, sexual assault, any violent crime, all felonies).

CODIS consists of several databases, including the forensic index and the convicted offender index. The forensic index contains data on DNA profiles obtained from victims or crime scenes, whereas the convicted offender index includes the profiles of those convicted of offenses. Using the two indexing systems, it is possible to link crimes together for the purpose of identifying a repeat perpetrator or to link a crime to a person who is or was in prison. Other databases existing in CODIS include the arrestees index, the missing persons index, the unidentified human remains index, and the biological relatives of missing persons index. Whether an individual state participates in these at the national level depends on state policy or law. In order for a state to be eligible to participate in CODIS, the appropriate state authority must sign a memorandum indicating that the state's laboratory (or laboratories) adheres to FBI quality assurance standards; the laboratory must also pass a series of inspections and subsequent reviews.

A DNA profile found in CODIS contains only the following: an identification code for the submitting agency, an identification number for the specimen, the DNA profile itself, and the name of the person who submitted the information. Only the submitting laboratory can place a name on a DNA profile. The limited data ensure that the DNA profiles are not exploited and that the identities of those whose profiles are submitted to the database are protected. CODIS is accessible only to those working within the field of law enforcement. Participating laboratories submit their information through a secure intranet called the Criminal Justice Information Services Wide Area Network (CJIS WAN), which is located in Clarksburg, West Virginia. It is also important to note that the profiles do not contain any information about medical conditions

## Putting a DNA Sample Through CODIS

DNA samples can be taken from convicted persons in several different ways. Blood or buccal swabs (swabs of the inside of the cheek) are generally collected, although in theory almost any tissue could be used. Forensic samples come from a huge variety of sources, the most common being semen from sexual assault cases, but blood, hair, saliva, bone, or virtually any other tissue or body fluid can be tested. New developments have allowed for touch samples—samples extracted from items that have come into direct contact with the persons of interest (such as held objects)—to also be used as potential sources of profiles.

DNA profile information is submitted to CODIS in the form of short tandem repeats (STRs). Thirteen core STR loci were chosen for use with CODIS; the profiles of convicted offenders must contain all thirteen of these loci to be uploaded to CODIS, whereas forensic profiles, which often originate from less-than-ideal sources, are required to have at least ten loci.

At the local level, analysts have some leeway when searching the database. For instance, a laboratory may require that a complete match be made at a locus for that locus to be considered, whereas another laboratory, recognizing that degraded DNA from a crime scene can result in the loss of part of a profile, might find a partial profile probative. Likewise, the minimum number of loci needed to be considered informative can vary from case to case.

After a potential match has been found in CODIS, the laboratories responsible for the corresponding profiles must contact each other to authenticate the results. The samples are often then retested to ensure the validity of the match. Upon confirmation that the two profiles are consistent with each other, the laboratories exchange any additional information they need.

## The Future of CODIS

In recent years, there has been a push to increase the number of core CODIS loci. There are three main reasons for this: to increase discriminating power, to increase international compatibility, and to aid in missing persons cases. In 2010, the CODIS Core Loci Working Group was developed by the FBI to evaluate the 13 core loci and determine if additional loci were

## Indexes Within CODIS

- **Convicted offender index:** Contains profiles of individuals who have been convicted of crimes
- **Forensic index:** Contains DNA profiles developed from crime scene evidence, such as semen stains or blood
- **Arrestees index:** Contains profiles of arrested persons (from those states in which laws permit the collection of arrestee samples)
- **Missing persons index:** Contains DNA reference profiles from missing persons
- **Unidentified human remains index:** Contains DNA profiles developed from unidentified human remains
- **Biological relatives of missing persons index:** Contains DNA profiles voluntarily contributed by relatives of missing persons

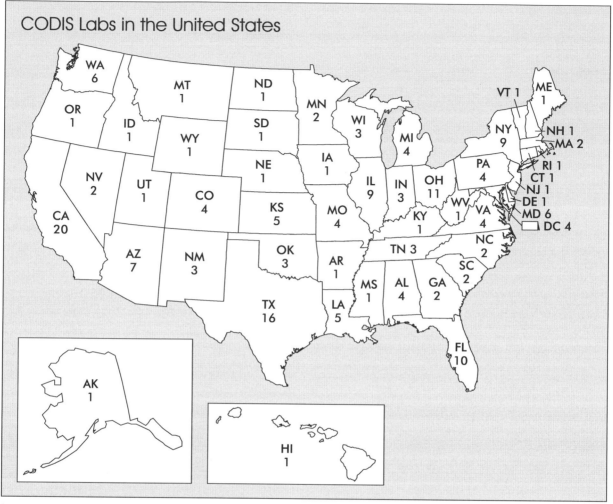

CODIS Labs in the United States

WA 6
OR 1
MT 1
ID 1
WY 1
ND 1
SD 1
NE 1
MN 2
WI 3
MI 4
VT 1
ME 1
NY 9
NH 1
MA 2
RI 1
CT 1
NJ 1
DE 1
MD 6
DC 4
NV 2
UT 1
CO 4
KS 5
IA 1
IL 9
IN 3
OH 11
PA 4
WV 1
VA 4
CA 20
AZ 7
NM 3
OK 3
MO 4
AR 1
KY 1
TN 3
NC 2
SC 2
MS 1
AL 4
GA 2
TX 16
LA 5
FL 10
AK 1
HI 1

*Source:* Federal Bureau of Investigation, 2008.

needed. The Working Group identified criteria for the acceptance of any new loci, such as a low mutation rate and no known association with medical conditions/defects. While maintaining the importance of the continued use of the original 13 CODIS loci, the Working Group proposed a number of additional loci that could be added to the database following laboratory validation. Additional information including mitochondrial DNA and Y-STR data (which are already accepted by the NDIS system), will also be utilized in future generations of CODIS, as well as information such as sex, age, and date of last sighting for missing persons.

*David R. Foran and Rebecca L. Ray*

**Further Reading**

Balding, D. J., and P. J. Donnelly. "Evaluating DNA Profile Evidence When the Suspect Is Identified Through a Database Search." *Journal of Forensic Sciences* 41 (1996): 603 – 607. Leads the reader through the process of entering a DNA profile into a database and discusses the population genetics associated with such a profile.

Butler, John M. Forensic *DNA Typing: Biology, Technology, and Genetics of STR Markers.* 2nd ed. Burlington, MA: Elsevier Academic Press, 2005. Provides a detailed overview of short tandem repeats and their applicability to forensic science.

Hares, D.R. "Expanding the CODIS Core Loci in the United States." *Forensic Science International: Genetics* 6 (2012): e52–e54. Presents suggestions made by the CODIS Core Loci Working Group for increasing the number of core loci in CODIS.

National Research Council. *The Evaluation of Forensic DNA Evidence.* Washington, D.C.: National Academy Press, 1996. Spells out the guidelines on methods of DNA analysis that are accepted in the courtroom.

Walton, Richard H. Cold *Case Homicides: Practical Investigative Techniques.* Boca Raton, FL: CRC Press, 2006. Examination of cold cases includes a section on applying CODIS to the investigation of old, unsolved crimes.

**See also:** DNA analysis; DNA database controversies; DNA fingerprinting; DNA profiling; DNA typing; Ethics of DNA analysis; Federal Bureau of Investigation DNA Analysis Units; Federal Bureau of Investigation Laboratory; National Crime Information Center; National DNA Index System; Rape; Restriction fragment length polymorphisms; Short tandem repeat analysis.

---

# Coffin birth

**Definition:** Spontaneous delivery of a fetus from the uterus of a dead woman.

**Significance:** When a fetus is found outside the dead body of the mother, it may be necessary for forensic scientists to determine whether the mother died while the fetus was still in the uterus, the fetus later expelled by the buildup of decomposing gases in the mother's body, or whether the fetus was delivered before the mother's death and died separately. The distinction may be important when charges are brought against a suspect for the murder of a pregnant woman.

Although it has always been rare, the phenomenon of coffin birth, or postmortem birth, has occurred throughout history. Paleopathologists have discovered evidence of coffin birth (or *Sarggeburt* in German, the language in which it was first described) in archaeological digs in ancient graveyards. With modern embalming techniques, it has become even more unusual, although it still may occur in cases of accidental death, murder, or incorrect embalming practices.

Coffin birth is truly the birth of a fetus, not a case of the fetus being expelled through the body through the abdomen, such as with a wound mimicking a birth by cesarean section. The buildup of gases in the decomposing body of a pregnant woman may put pressure on the uterus to the point of expelling an unborn fetus through the birth canal. Scientists believe that this buildup could take weeks or months to happen, and the possibility of a coffin birth occurring depends on many outside factors, such as the air temperature and whether the woman's body is in water or buried in the ground.

Coffin birth is so rare that it does not often appear in the medical literature. The topic came into the news spotlight in 2003, however, in the case of Laci Peterson. Peterson was about seven and one-half months pregnant when she disappeared in December, 2002, leading to speculation that her husband, Scott Peterson, had murdered her. Later, when her body and the body of her late-term fetus were found separately on the shores of the San Francisco Bay, coffin birth was raised as the possible reason that the fetus was no longer in her uterus. Coffin birth was only one possibility of many, but it was thought a strong possibility, partly because Laci Peterson had no external wounds consistent with the fetus's exiting her body other than through the birth canal. Despite the confusion over whether she was still pregnant when she was killed or whether the baby was born before her death, charges were filed against Scott Peterson for the murder of both his wife and son. He was convicted in March, 2005, and sentenced to death for the murders.

*Marianne M. Madsen*

**Further Reading**

Fleeman, Michael. *Laci: Inside the Laci Peterson Murder.* New York: St. Martin's Press, 2003.

Lyle, D. P. *Forensics and Fiction: Clever, Intriguing, and Downright Odd Questions from Crime Writers.* New York: St. Martin's Press, 2007.

**See also:** Autopsies; Decomposition of bodies; Forensic archaeology; Paternity evidence.

## Cognitive interview techniques

**Definition:** Interviewing protocols based on the science of cognitive psychology.

**Significance:** Because eyewitness evidence is critical to solving many crimes, it is important that law enforcement personnel employ interviewing techniques that elicit extensive and accurate information from witnesses. The use of cognitive interview techniques can maximize the effectiveness of witness interviews.

Evidence collected from cooperative witnesses is critical for solving many crimes and for determining what happened at accident scenes. Nevertheless, many police and accident investigators receive only minimal or no training in techniques to use when interviewing cooperative witnesses. Often the only training they get comes from on-the-job experience or from observing senior investigators conduct interviews— whether done effectively or poorly. Police and other investigative interviewers therefore often make avoidable errors and collect less information than is potentially available. Even worse, through poor questioning techniques, interviewers may unintentionally entice witnesses to recall or describe events incorrectly.

A common error that many interviewers make is to ask too many questions, thereby inducing witnesses to adopt the role of answering questions rather than generating information. Compounding this error, the interviewer's questions are often closed-ended (*cf.* open-ended) and suggestive (*cf.* neutral). To remedy this problem, two research psychologists, Ronald P. Fisher and R. Edward Geiselman, began

work during the 1980s to develop an improved interviewing technique, the cognitive interview (CI), to increase the amount of accurate information collected from cooperative witnesses.

CI techniques incorporate the theoretical principles of cognitive and social psychology and borrow elements and techniques from other investigative domains, including journalism, medicine, and social work. Part of the training in CI techniques involves modeling the differences between effective and ineffective police interviewers.

### Principles of the Cognitive Interview

Cognitive interview techniques were developed to improve three psychological processes: the social dynamics between the witness and the interviewer, the thought processes of both the witness and the interviewer, and the communication between the witness and the interviewer. Interviewers can create more favorable social dynamics for interviews by developing personal rapport with respondents. This is especially true when they are interviewing victims and suspects. Interviewers should also instruct witnesses to take an active role within the interview and not merely answer questions with brief responses. Interviewers can accomplish this by instructing witnesses to generate detailed narrative descriptions without waiting for more questions, by asking mainly open-ended questions, and by not interrupting witnesses during their narrative responses.

At times, witnesses cannot recall critical details even though they have the information stored in their memories. Interviewers can help witnesses search through their memories more efficiently by instructing them to re-create the context of the original event (asking, for example, "What were you thinking about at the time?"), to search through their memories repeatedly, and to use all of their senses. Interviewers, too, make cognitive errors, as they have to do many mental tasks at the same time, including listening to and making notes on the witness' answers, formulating hypotheses about the critical event, and asking follow-up questions. Interviewers can improve their own thought processes by encouraging witnesses to generate information without waiting for questions and by developing more efficient methods to record witnesses' answers.

Interviewers often fail to communicate to witnesses their investigative needs for detailed and extensive information. As a result, witnesses do not report all of their available knowledge. Interviewers should inform witnesses explicitly that they need to provide detailed and informative answers. In addition, interviewers should understand that witnesses may have much information that is stored nonverbally (for example, a mental picture of the crime scene) and should facilitate witnesses' communicatin such information by encouraging nonverbal responses (such as making a sketch). The sequence of the cognitive interview is based on two principles. First, the interviewer should try to develop a general understanding of the witness' cognitive map of the event— that is, how the witness mentally represents the event—and then ask questions that are compatible with the witness' cognitive map. Second, questioning should generally proceed in a funnel-like fashion, from more global, open-ended questions to more specific, closed-ended questions.

The cognitive interview is not a set of specific questions that are posed in the same fashion to all witnesses. Rather, CI techniques comprise a collection of many tools that should be used flexibly, depending on the specific factors of the case, such as the amount of time that has passed since the event and the witness' state of anxiety and verbal skills.

## Scientific Testing of the Cognitive Interview

CI techniques have been tested repeatedly in laboratory and field studies. In a typical laboratory study, volunteer witnesses—often college students—see a videotape of a simulated crime or accident or view a live, innocuous event. Shortly thereafter, each witness is interviewed by someone trained to use CI techniques or by someone using a more conventional technique (for example, a typical police interview). Researchers have introduced many variations in the basic laboratory study by testing different types of witnesses (children, elderly, learning disabled, autistic, lay people and law enforcement personnel), types of events (crimes, vehic-

ular and industrial accidents and medical procedures), and time intervals (immediately after the event, hours later, weeks later, and up to thirty-five years later). Field studies have also been conducted with victims and witnesses of real crimes (e.g., robbery, sexual assault).

More than one hundred such validation studies have been conducted in the United States, England, Germany, Spain, Australia, France, and elsewhere. Generally, CI techniques have been found to elicit between 25 percent and 75 percent more correct statements than the conventional technique and at comparable or slightly higher accuracy rates. Only one kind of witness task has not shown the cognitive interview to be superior to conventional interview techniques; identifying a perpetrator from a lineup.

## Practical and Legal Concerns

CI techniques are taught and used in some police departments and investigative agencies, but the techniques are not employed universally. Within the United States, CI techniques are more likely to be taught at major investigative agencies (such as the Federal Bureau of Investigation, the Federal Law Enforcement Training Center, and the National Transportation Safety Board) than at smaller police departments. Internationally, CI techniques are taught and used extensively in England, Australia, Canada, Sweden, and Israel, but less so in other countries. More time is required to conduct a cognitive interview than a conventional police interview, so CI techniques are most likely to be used in relation to major crimes and accident investigations and by follow-up detectives (rather than first responders). Feedback from investigators credits the cognitive interview with generating extensive witness information to solve several types of high-profile cases, including kidnappings, terrorist bombings, military attacks, and accidents at sea. Although CI techniques were developed for interviews with cooperative witnesses, some component techniques have proven valuable for interviewing suspects (such as establishing rapport, drawing sketches, and reporting events in different orders). When these techniques are applied, detecting deception is improved.

CI techniques have been challenged unsuccessfully in a few court cases. In England, an appeals court overturned an earlier decision on the basis of information obtained with CI techniques. Although the court did not explicitly mention the cognitive interview in its ruling, the ultimate decision was consistent with the information elicited by the interview. In a California case, a prosecutor used evidence that had been elicited by a police officer trained in CI techniques. The defense attorney argued that the cognitive interview was similar to hypnosis and that it promoted inaccurate eyewitness testimony. The judge, however, found the CI-elicited testimony admissible at trial. A Nebraska court evaluated CI techniques for reliability according to the *Daubert* standard (a standard set by the U.S. Supreme Court concerning expert witness testimony) and found these techniques to meet the standards of scientific testing, peer review and publication, known (and acceptably low) error rates, and general acceptance, as required under Daubert.

*Ronald P. Fisher , Alexandra E. Mosser, Peter Molinaro, and Geri E. Satin*

This work was funded by a Florida International University Presidential Fellowship award to Geri E. Satin.

---

## Cognitive Interview Versus Hypnosis

The use of cognitive interview techniques with crime witnesses has been criticized as similar to the use of hypnosis, which can raise legal issues. CI techniques and hypnosis do have some elements in common; for instance, in both, interviewers need to develop rapport with witnesses, witnesses are instructed to close their eyes, and witnesses are asked to re-create in their minds the contexts of the original events. Scientific research shows, however, that the cognitive interview and hypnosis function differently: The cognitive interview enhances recall more reliably than does hypnosis; the accuracy of the information collected during cognitive interviews is relatively high, whereas hypnosis may promote fabrication; the cognitive interview does not influence witness confidence, whereas hypnosis elevates confidence; and the cognitive interview reduces witness suggestibility to leading and suggestive questions, whereas hypnosis increases suggestibility. The legal problems associated with hypnosis thus do not plague the cognitive interview.

---

### Further Reading

Fisher, Ronald P. and R. Edward Geiselman. *Memory-Enhancing Techniques in Investigative Interviewing: The Cognitive Interview.* Springfield, IL: Charles C Thomas, 1992. Written for investigative interviewers; describes in detail how to conduct the CI. Also includes chapters on training and learning the CI technique as well as sample interviews to illustrate good and poor interviewing techniques.

Fisher, Ronald P., R. Edward Geiselman, and Michael Amador. "Field Test of the Cognitive Interview: Enhancing the Recollection of Actual Victims and Witnesses of Crime." *Journal of Applied Psychology,* 74 (1989): 722-727. Describes a scientific field study comparing the effectiveness of CI-trained police interviewers with other untrained (but experienced) robbery investigators. Aimed at forensic researchers.

Geiselman, R. Edward and Fisher, Ronald P. "Interviewing Witnesses and Victims." Chapter in St.-Yves, Michel (Editor) *Investigative Interviewing: The Essentials.* Toronto: Carswell 29-62. Written for investigative interviewers; describes the most recent research on the CI, including use for interviewing suspects.

Kebbell, Mark R., and Graham F. Wagstaff. "Hypnotic Interviewing: The Best Way to Interview Eyewitnesses?" *Behavioral Sciences and the Law,* 16 (1998): 115-129. Compares the effectiveness of hypnosis and the CI as methods for eliciting information from witnesses.

Memon, Amina, Christian A. Meissner and Joanne Fraser. "The Cognitive Interview: A Meta-analytic Review and Study-space Analysis of the past 25 Years." *Psychology, Public Policy, and Law, 16 (2010): 340-372.* Applies the statistical technique of meta-analysis to examine the data on the effectiveness of the CI gathered in more than fifty laboratory and field studies.

**See also:** Accident investigation and reconstruction; Composite drawing; *Daubert v. Merrell Dow Pharmaceuticals*; Eyewitness testimony; Forensic psychology; Interrogation; National Institute of Justice; *People v. Lee*; Police psychology.

## Cold Case

**Date:** First aired on September 28, 2003

**Identification:** Television series that focuses on Philadelphia detectives who solve cold cases in part through the examination of forensic evidence.

**Significance:** By immersing viewers in the scientific context of each case it depicts, *Cold Case* demonstrates the relevance and application of forensic science within the criminal justice system.

*Cold Case* focuses on a fictional special investigative team located in Philadelphia, with particular emphasis on the lead investigator, Detective Lilly Rush (played by Kathryn Morris). Rush and her coworkers investigate cold cases—that is, cases that have gone unsolved, often for long periods, and on which active investigation has ceased because the leads or evidence trails have gone cold—that are brought to their attention for various reasons. Sometimes new evidence is found that relates to an old case or a witness presents new information; sometimes a body is discovered that has a connection to an unsolved case.

The show's format revisits each unsolved case through the utilization of flashbacks that feature music specific to the year of the case. Cases on the show have ranged from a murder that took place in 1919 to current cases that have no leads. Although the resolutions of some cases rely on

witness recall, the majority of the cases are solved through the introduction of new forensic evidence or the reanalysis of evidence that was tainted or misused when it was examined previously. The types of forensic evidence that have figured into the program's plots have included fingerprint analysis, DNA (deoxyribonucleic acid) analysis, ballistics, and blood evidence. *Cold Case* often showcases new forensic technologies that are used to solve criminal cases.

Examples of *Cold Case* episodes in which forensic evidence played an important role include one in which blood evidence on a policeman's nightstick linked the officer to the murder of a college baseball player. In another episode, a skull with a bullet in it was found beneath the remains of an old nightclub, and subsequent ballistics analysis and examination of arson evidence showed that a murder at the scene had been covered up by arson; this information also led to the discovery of twenty-three new murder cases.

An episode about the drowning of a military academy's swim coach featured the use of DNA evidence and handwriting analysis, which indicated that children at the academy whom the coach had molested were responsible for his death. DNA evidence was important in an episode in which the detectives found that an innocent man had been convicted of the murder of a fifteen-year-old girl; DNA evidence also identified the correct killer. Skeletal analysis and DNA evidence were featured in an episode that involved the misidentification of some human remains left outside a prison, and in an episode in which the detectives investigated a drive-by shooting, ballistics evidence and fingerprint analysis were important elements.

*Alana Van Gundy-Yoder*

### Further Reading

Ramsland, Katherine. *The Science of "Cold Case Files."* New York: Berkley Books, 2004.

Walton, Richard H. *Cold Case Homicides: Practical Investigative Techniques.* Boca Raton, Fla.: CRC Press, 2006.

**See also:** Blood spatter analysis; Bullet-lead analysis; Celebrity cases; *CSI: Crime Scene Investigation*; DNA analysis; DNA fingerprinting;

Fingerprints; *Forensic Files*; Handwriting analysis; Literature and forensic science; Misconceptions fostered by media.

## Columbus remains identification

**Date:** Began in 2002

**The Event:** The cities of Seville, Spain, and Santo Domingo, Dominican Republic, have long debated which of them is the resting place of the authentic remains of Christopher Columbus. Modern DNA analysis techniques have been put to use in the examination of the remains in Seville, but efforts to settle the issue conclusively have not been successful because the Dominican Republic has refused to allow the remains in its possession to be tested.

**Significance:** The use of DNA analysis to test the remains held in Seville that were reputed to be those of Columbus brought international attention to the use of such techniques for the positive identification of individuals. For the countries involved in the debate over Columbus's burial site, national and regional pride are at stake, but tourism and other financial benefits are also major factors.

Christopher Columbus was born in 1451 and died on May 20, 1506, at age fifty-five. He died, from a variety of ailments and exhaustion, in Valladolid, Spain, while pursuing a successful effort to secure financial benefits for his heirs from King Ferdinand II. He was buried in Valladolid, his temporary residence. Although Columbus died surrounded by his close loved ones, the death of the great explorer went almost unnoticed in Spain.

A few years after Columbus died, one of his sons, Diego, had his body transferred to the Carthusian monastery of Santa María de las Cuevas, near Seville, more than three hundred miles from Valladolid, where Columbus had rested for months after returning from his fourth voyage in 1504. In 1526, the bones of his son Diego were also buried there. Christopher

Columbus had asked to be buried in Santo Domingo, his favorite island, and in 1537, his and Diego's remains were transferred to Santo Domingo, to a temporary location and then to the cathedral. In 1796, to avoid French control when Hispaniola was ceded to France, the Spanish government had Columbus's body moved again, this time to Havana, Cuba. When Spain lost Cuba to independence in 1898, Columbus's body was again transferred, this time to the Cathedral of Seville.

Meanwhile, in 1877, during renovation of the cathedral in Santo Domingo, a lead box had been found that was inscribed with Columbus's name; the box contained thirteen large and twenty-eight small bone fragments. Despite questions about the location of the lead box, Santo Domingo claimed that the wrong remains (perhaps those of Columbus's son Diego) had been sent to Havana, and that it had the true remains of Columbus. In 2002, Marcial Castro, a historian and teacher from the Seville area, began a project that would perform DNA (deoxyribonucleic acid) analysis on the reputed Columbus remains held at the Cathedral of Seville. José Antonio Lorente, a forensic geneticist who had worked on criminal cases and had helped to identify the bodies of victims of brutal Latin American regimes of the 1970's, was enlisted as the leader of a team of genetic experts. By June, 2003, the researchers had obtained fragments of the remains believed to be those of Christopher Columbus as well as fragments from known relatives of Columbus: his son Hernando and his brother Diego, both of whom had been buried in Seville. Comparison of the Y (male) chromosomes of the remains attributed to Columbus and those of Hernando proved impossible because of deteriorated conditions.

In January, 2005, the researchers gained permission to view the purported Columbus remains in Santo Domingo, but Dominican authorities then withdrew permission and refused to allow any attempt to extract DNA from the bones, citing religious objections. In May, 2006, the researchers announced that they had matched the mitochondrial (maternally inherited) DNA of the remains in Seville claimed to be those of Columbus with the mitochondrial DNA of Columbus's brother Diego, proving that the two sets of remains were those of brothers. Despite this evidence, controversy about the true burial site of Christopher Columbus remains because of Santo Domingo's refusal to allow testing on the remains in its possession.

*Abraham D. Lavender*

**Further Reading**

Dugard, Martin. *The Last Voyage of Columbus.* New York: Little, Brown, 2005.

Wilford, John Noble. *The Mysterious History of Columbus: An Exploration of the Man, the Myth, the Legacy.* New York: Alfred A. Knopf, 1991.

**See also:** Anastasia remains identification; Anthropometry; Buried body locating; DNA analysis; DNA extraction from hair, bodily fluids, and tissues; DNA typing; Exhumation; Louis XVII remains identification; Mitochondrial DNA analysis and typing; Nicholas II remains identification; Y chromosome analysis.

## Column chromatography

**Definition:** Technique used to analyze complex samples by separating the mixture of chemical species into individual components so their identities and concentrations can be determined.

**Significance:** Forensic samples can be complex mixtures of components, and determination of the individual components in a sample may provide investigators with valuable information. The components, once separated, are normally evaluated by a detector that is able to determine specific chemical or physical information about each component. The similarity between samples or the likelihood that samples have a common origin may be determined after individual components are evaluated.

The term "column chromatography" is applied to variety of techniques that can be classified by the phase of the material that is moving through the column. When this mobile phase is a gas, the technique is called gas chromatography (GC); when the phase is a liquid, it is called liquid chromatography. The column can be filled with particles, which is called a stationary phase, that allow a separation of individual components to take place. Instrumentation is often used to push the mobile phase through the column at higher pressures, allowing faster and improved separation of components.

Capillary GC is a common technique that requires that chemical components be analyzed in their gas state. It uses narrow glass columns that can be as long as 100 meters (roughly 330 feet). The insides of the columns can be coated with different chemical polymers so different types of chemical species can be separated. These columns are coiled for easy placement in an oven so the temperature can be controlled accurately. By changing the temperature, the scientist can analyze different chemical species. GC is commonly used to analyze samples taken from fire scenes in arson investigations.

High-performance liquid chromatography (HPLC) is a widely used analysis technique that employs high-pressure pumps to force a liquid phase through columns packed with small particles. Columns come in a variety of sizes, with inside dimensions smaller than 0.10 millimeters (0.004 inches) to as large as a few centimeters.

To handle the high pressure, the columns are commonly made of stainless steel, but they may be made out of plastic for specific applications such as ion chromatography. Solvents such as methanol and water are commonly used as mobile phases. HPLC can be used to separate and analyze a range of forensically important samples; it is commonly used to determine the presence of illegal drugs and to determine what substances were used in suspected poisonings.

Solid phase extraction (SPE) is a specific type of column chromatography designed for sample preparation. It uses plastic columns filled with particles specifically designed to either attract or ignore different chemical compounds that would be found in a sample. For example, it can be used to concentrate drugs of abuse from urine.

*Dwight Tshudy*

## Further Reading

Dong, Michael. *Modern HPLC for Practicing Scientists*. Hoboken, N.J.: Wiley-Interscience, 2006.

Grob, Robert L., and Eugene F. Barry, eds. *Modern Practice of Gas Chromatography*. 4th ed. Hoboken, N.J.: Wiley-Interscience; 2004.

Telepchak, Michael. *Forensic and Clinical Applications of Solid Phase Extraction*. Totowa, N.J.: Humana Press, 2004.

**See also:** Accelerants; Analytical instrumentation; Chromatography; Fax machine, copier, and printer analysis; Forensic toxicology; Gas chromatography; High-performance liquid chromatography; Micro-Fourier transform infrared spectrometry; Quantitative and qualitative analysis of chemicals; Questioned document analysis; Separation tests; Thin-layer chromatography.

## Combined DNA Index System. *See* CODIS

## Competency. *See* Legal competency

## Competency evaluation and assessment instruments

**Definition:** Psychological evaluation instruments that assess the ability of persons to function meaningfully and knowingly, without serious deficiencies, in understanding legal proceedings, communicating with attorneys, understanding their roles in proceedings, and making legally relevant decisions.

**Significance:** Legal competency is the capacity to understand the nature and purposes of legal rights, obligations, and proceedings. Forensic psychiatrists are often in-

volved in conducting competency evaluations, which assist in protecting the rights of those being evaluated by determining the subjects' competency to stand trial.

In 1960, the U.S. Supreme Court established a law based on an appeal filed by a man named Milton Dusky, who was diagnosed with schizophrenia, after he received a forty-five-year jail sentence for kidnapping and assisting two teenagers in carrying out the rape of a sixteen-year-old girl. In its decision in *Dusky v. United States*, the Court ruled that to be deemed competent to stand trial, individuals must have a minimum level of understanding of the legal proceedings and the ability to assist their attorneys in their own defense. As a result, Dusky's sentence was reduced to twenty years.

The perception of competency is related to a defendant's ability to understand charges, relevant facts, legal issues and procedures, potential legal defenses, and possible dispositions, pleas, and penalties as well as the roles of the lawyers, judge, jury, witnesses, and defendant. Also important are the individual's abilities to identify witnesses, to communicate rationally with counsel, to comprehend instructions and advice, to make decisions, to help plan legal strategy, to follow testimony for contradictions or errors, to testify and be cross-examined, to challenge prosecution witnesses, to tolerate stress at trial and while awaiting trial, to refrain from irrational behavior during trial, to disclose pertinent facts surrounding alleged offenses, and to use available legal safeguards.

Aside from competency, two other areas of defense are related to mental capacity: diminished capacity and mitigating circumstances. Diminished capacity evaluations focus on the ability of defendants to intend to commit the crimes of which they are accused. Evaluations of mitigating circumstances focus on defendants' ability to understand that their behavior was wrong.

### Evaluation Process

An evaluation of a defendant's competency to stand trial can be ordered by the defense, the prosecution, or the judge. Competency to stand trial involves the defendant's ability to understand the legal proceedings, the charges, the roles of court personnel, the difference between pleas of guilty and not guilty, and the meaning of a plea bargain. It also encompasses the defendant's ability to assist in his or her defense, to work with the attorney, and to take an active part in the defense.

A psychological evaluation of an individual's competency to stand trial includes a review of the person's medical and psychological histories as provided by the individual being evaluated as well as by that person's family members. Assessment for brain damage caused by head injuries, dementias, and acute or chronic alcohol and drug abuse may also be included. A clinical interview follows and includes assessments regarding orientation, short-term memory, and ability to reason. After the clinical interview, psychological testing is performed based on the results of the interview.

In criminal court, a defendant must be competent to waive Miranda rights if a confession is being used, to stand trial, to be sentenced, and to serve a sentence if found guilty. Additionally, the defendant must have been competent at the time of the offense and must be competent to be executed if a death penalty is ruled. Individual competency determinations do not automatically lead to determinations of competency in other areas. For example, competency at the time of the offense does not guarantee that the defendant will be competent to stand trial later. The courts can dismiss charges against individuals if there is no indication that competency will return following treatment.

Competencies to waive constitutional rights and to waive the right to counsel are addressed in the evaluator's report on competency to stand trial. Such a report includes the following elements: information regarding the source of the referral; date, place, and time of evaluation; nonconfidentiality statement; references and interviews used to prepare the report; criteria for competency to stand trial; background information on the defendant; information on the defendant's history of psychiatric and medical treatment and substance abuse; results of the mental status exam; the evaluator's findings on the defendant's level of mental function and ability to understand the proceedings; and

statements from the defendant that demonstrate the defendant's understanding of the issues of the case (charges, legal situation, roles of courtroom personnel, differences between pleas, and range of possible verdicts). The report also assesses the defendant's ability to assist in the defense (based on the defendant's ability to recount his or her whereabouts and activities at the time of the offense) and to interact with the defense attorney and behave in an acceptable manner in the courtroom. Some reasons that defendants are deemed incompetent to stand trial are low intelligence, dementia, depression, mania, and paranoid delusions.

## Assessment Instruments

Many psychological tests have been developed for use in evaluating mental competency. Among those most frequently employed by forensic psychiatrists are the Competency Screening Test, the Competency Assessment Instrument, the Interdisciplinary Fitness Interview, and the Georgia Court Competency Test.

The long form of the Competency Screening Test (CST), developed by a group of Harvard psychologists, comprises twenty-two sentence stems concerning hypothetical legal situations; the person being evaluated is asked to complete each sentence. An example item is "When I go to court, the lawyer will _____." The evaluator scores each answer as indicating competency, questionable competency, or incompetency. A short form of the CST is also sometimes used; the short form comprises just five sentence stems.

The Competency Assessment Instrument (CAI), developed by the same group of psychologists who created the CST, requires a one-hour structured clinical interview that explores the thoughts and feelings of the person being evaluated in thirteen topic areas, including coping with stress and sense of optimism as well as an understanding of legal proceedings. The CAI provides sample questions for each topic area, and the evaluator scores the responses of the person being evaluated using a five-point scale of competency.

The Interdisciplinary Fitness Interview (IFI) is administered jointly by a mental health professional and an attorney. The IFI, which takes thirty minutes, addresses both legal and mental health issues, with greater focus on mental illness than some other instruments.

The Georgia Court Competency Test (GCCT) consists of twenty-one questions related to the client's general legal knowledge and knowledge of such specifics as the judge's job and the lawyers' job. This tool is particularly useful for measuring behavioral aspects of competency.

Other competency tests that have shown promise but have not yet been determined to be both reliable and valid include the MacArthur Competence Assessment Tool-Criminal Adjudication, the Computer-Assisted Determination of Competence to Proceed, and the Competence Assessment for Standing Trial for Defendants with Mental Retardation.

*Sharon W. Stark*

### Further Reading

Bardwell, Mark C., and Bruce A. Arrigo. *Criminal Competency on Trial: The Case of Colin Ferguson*. Durham, N.C.: Carolina Academic Press, 2002. Case study of a notorious mass murderer examines the legal and psychological issues associated with his competency to stand trial.

Dagher-Margosian, Jeanice. "Representing the Cognitively Disabled Client in a Criminal Case." *Disabilities Project Newsletter* (State Bar of Michigan) 2 (March, 2006). Presents an overview of the types of mental incapacities that may be reviewed in considering a person's competency to stand trial.

Grisso, Thomas. *Evaluating Competencies: Forensic Assessments and Instruments*. 2d ed. New York: Springer. 2002. Offers useful tools for evaluating legal competency in both criminal and civil cases.

Resnick, Phillip J., and Stephen Noffsinger. "Competency to Stand Trial and the Insanity Defense." In *Textbook of Forensic Psychiatry*, edited by Robert I. Simon and Liza H. Gold. Arlington, Va.: American Psychiatric Publishing, 2003. Uses case vignettes to illustrate various aspects of the determination of competency to stand trial.

Rogers, Richard, and Daniel W. Shuman. *Fundamentals of Criminal Practice: Mental Health and Criminal Law*. New York: Springer, 2005. Textbook covers all aspects of criminal law as it applies to issues of mental health, including competency to stand trial.

Swerdlow-Freed, Daniel H. "Assessment of Competency to Stand Trial and Criminal Responsibility." *Michigan Criminal Law Annual Journal* (2003). Discusses the protocols and procedures involved in legal proceedings concerning the evaluation of a defendant's mental competency to stand trial.

**See also:** *Diagnostic and Statistical Manual of Mental Disorders*; Forensic linguistics and stylistics; Forensic psychiatry; Forensic psychology; Innocence Project; Insanity defense; Legal competency; Living forensics; Trial consultants.

## Composite drawing

**Definition:** Artistic rendering of the facial features of unknown persons, often crime suspects, based on eyewitness information for use in narrowing law-enforcement searches.

**Significance:** The ability of law-enforcement officials to solve a crime depends largely on the cooperation and participation of private citizens in the investigatory process. Without eyewitness identification, many offenders remain at large and are never brought to justice for their crimes. Police sketch artists often contribute to investigations by creating composite drawings of the perpetrators of crimes based on descriptions provided by victims or other eyewitnesses. The productions of sketch artists have been instrumental in the capture of many notorious criminals, including the serial killer Ted Bundy and Richard Allen Davis, the kidnapper and murderer of twelve-year-old Polly Klaas.

Forensic artists, also known as police artists or sketch artists, are specially trained professionals whose work assists law-enforcement investigators in the identification, apprehension, and conviction of unknown suspects in unsolved criminal cases. Certified by the Forensic Art Certification Board of the International Association for Identification, forensic artists contribute to the investigatory process primarily through their creation of composite drawings or sketches, called composite imagery.

Forensic artists create composite drawings of unknown suspects on the basis of reports from victims or other witnesses (informants) about the perpetrators of unsolved crimes. From memory, an informant provides a sketch artist with a description of a suspect, and the artist creates a composite drawing that emerges as the artist obtains increasingly specific information about the suspect's facial features. With the exception of the largest police departments in the United States, few American law-enforcement agencies employ full-time sketch artists. Most share the services of police artists with other agencies or hire local professional artists on an ad hoc basis to create composite imagery.

## Beginnings of Forensic Art

The field of forensic art has a long history. In the United States, the earliest practitioners were the artists of the Old West who created the posters depicting wanted criminals that were displayed in a wide range of public settings, including in churches, schools, saloons, and post offices. During the late nineteenth century, French criminologist Alphonse Bertillon created the first formal system of criminal identification, which included techniques that became the forerunners of forensic art. Bertillon's book on anthropometry (the study of the dimensions of the human body), *Identification anthropométrique; instructions signalétiques* (1893; *Signaletic Instructions Including the Theory and Practice of Anthropometrical Identification*, 1896), laid the groundwork for the basic procedures of composite drawing that continue to influence practitioners of the art.

During the 1950's, a kit designed to aid in the creation of composite imagery, the Identi-Kit, became a huge commercial success. Use of the Identi-Kit became standard practice among U.S. law-enforcement agencies, especially in cases involving multiple victims or other witnesses. The kit contained a large collection of hand-drawn facial features (hairlines, mouths, cheekbones, eyes, noses, ears, and so on) from which informants could choose in building composite faces. By the 1970's, police sketch artists had replaced the use of the Identi-Kit with composite drawings, which produced richer and less contrived portraits of unknown suspects.

## Uses of Composite Imagery

Composite drawings can be used in several ways. In most cases, a composite drawing is created to capture the facial appearance of an unknown suspect so that law-enforcement investigators can begin to narrow the pool of viable suspects and better target their search for the unknown offender. Although composite drawings are usually of faces, forensic artists also sometimes provide useful visual depictions of evidence in criminal cases, such as stolen property or automobiles, or of actions that transpired at crime scenes. All of these kinds of images can be submitted as demonstrative evidence in the trial process.

Composite drawings can be modified to simulate how suspects might appear as they naturally change or age or as they might attempt to alter their appearance by adopting various disguises. For example, a sketch artist can modify the original image of a suspect by adding or subtracting weight or by adding signs of aging. Other image modifications might include the addition of various types of facial hair (mustaches, beards, sideburns) and different types of glasses, hats, or piercings.

## Creating the Drawings

Forensic artists can create two-dimensional depictions of suspects by hand or with the aid of computer-imaging software. The success of either technique depends largely on the ability of the informant to describe the suspect accurately and on the talent of the police artist in translating the informant's description into a precise recreation of the suspect's facial features.

Police sketch artists must possess not only artistic ability but also effective interviewing, listening, and intuitive skills. The creation of a composite drawing necessitates close communication between the informant and the sketch artist. To jog the informant's memory, the artist asks the informant a series of questions covering all aspects of the crime incident, including questions about the length of time the perpetrator was observed, the lighting conditions at the crime scene, the distance between the perpetrator and the informant during the incident, and any obstacles that obstructed the informant's view of the perpetrator.

Helping the informant return to the crime scene in his or her mind's eye is a critical first step in the composite-drawing process. A well-executed rendering based on inaccurate information about a suspect's appearance can be costly to a criminal investigation, wasting police time and resources and allowing an offender to remain at large to commit subsequent crimes. The sketch artist must take care to elicit precise details from the informant that will enable the creation of a successful drawing.

The process of creating the composite image continues with the sketch artist showing the informant a series of photographs that depict various face shapes as well as various types of eyes, noses, hair, ears, and so on. The informant selects from those choices the characteristics that most closely resemble those of the perpetrator, and the police artist assembles the selected features to create the first draft of the composite. The artist then carefully refines the drawing through several iterations until the informant decides that the artist has achieved a match.

The most common type of composite image is a freehand drawing that represents the artist's attempt to reproduce the informant's reports as closely as possible. The drawing's approximation of the suspect's actual appearance might be close enough to generate productive leads for police investigation, and it might also be close enough to jog the memories of other possible witnesses among the general public.

Some law-enforcement agencies employ computer-based assemblages of features in creating composite drawings, instead of or in tandem with the renderings of sketch artists. Although such software packages are useful, they do have shortcomings.

For example, basic packages are restricted in the variations they can generate in terms of human features, which in reality are virtually limitless in their shapes, sizes, and shades of color. Stocking such programs with greater numbers of features is costly and makes the programs more challenging to operate; in addition, it takes more time to find the correct feature when the pool is large. Even with an abundant stock of features, an image program might lack a particular feature or combination of features that fits a given unknown suspect, especially one with an uncommon profile (for example, a middle-aged Asian woman).

## Identifying the Dead

In addition to creating images of suspects for use in criminal investigations, police sketch artists are sometimes called upon to lend their skills to the identification of unknown deceased persons whose faces are unrecognizable because of suicide-related trauma, homicide, or accident, or as a result of decay, decomposition, or skeletonization. In such facial reconstruction or approximation, tissue depth markers and special drawing techniques are used to produce three-dimensional images.

A thorough examination of the human skull by a forensic anthropologist can reveal a great deal of information about the deceased, including the unknown person's gender, approximate age, race, and overall size. A forensic artist can then use existing knowledge about the likely depths of tissue covering various parts of the face to fill in missing areas or to correct facial distortions in front- and profile-angle portraits or models so that the decedent's re-created face can be used for postmortem identification.

In some cases, forensic artists use clay to build three-dimensional faces on casts of the skulls of unidentified deceased persons. Facial reconstruction is usually employed only after other avenues of identifying an individual—such as by matching fingerprints, DNA (deoxyribonucleic acid), or dental records have failed.

*Arthur J. Lurigio*

## Further Reading

Boylan, Jeanne. *Portraits of Guilt: The Woman Who Profiles the Faces of America's Deadliest Criminals*. New York: Pocket Books, 2001. Provides a behind-the-scenes look at the career of Boylan, a nationally renowned police sketch artist. Dramatic narrative relates the author's participation in several high-profile cases, including the searches for the Unabomber and for the perpetrators of the bombing of the Alfred P. Murrah Federal Building in Oklahoma City. Enables readers with no law-enforcement background to understand the painstaking work of criminal investigations.

Clement, John G., and Murray K. Marks. *Computer-Graphic Facial Reconstruction*. New York: Academic Press, 2005. Focuses on a variety of approaches to computer-aided identification of deceased persons based on skull structure.

Fridell, Ron. *Forensic Science*. Minneapolis: Lerner, 2007. Brief volume intended for young readers includes an outstanding chapter on identification that describes methods of forensic facial reconstruction.

Gibson, Lois, and Deanie Francis Mills. *Faces of Evil: Kidnappers, Murderers, Rapists, and the Forensic Artist Who Puts Them Behind Bars*. Liberty Corner, N.J.: New Horizon Press, 2005. Interesting volume intended for a general audience discusses the work of Gibson, a forensic artist, on thirteen individual cases.

Taylor, Karen T. *Forensic Art and Illustration*. Boca Raton, Fla.: CRC Press, 2001. Definitive compendium on the subject by an internationally recognized forensic artist and in-demand instructor in law-enforcement agencies and universities. Highly illustrated work covers all aspects of the field, including chapters on the history of forensic art, lessons in human anatomy, and step-by-step descriptions of the practical methods and techniques that are used by top practitioners in the investigatory process. Features numerous interesting case studies that show how forensic artistry is used in solving crimes and identifying dead persons.

**See also:** Anthropometry; Biometric identification systems; Child abduction and kidnapping; Cognitive interview techniques; *Cold Case*; Crime scene investigation; Crime scene sketching and diagramming; Facial recognition technology; Forensic anthropology; Forensic sculpture; Tattoo identification.

## Computer crimes

**Definition:** Crimes in which computers, computer networks or databases, digital devices, or the Internet have been attacked or infiltrated as well as crimes that are facilitated by computers, wireless Web devices, or the Internet.

**Significance:** The investigation and prosecution of computer crimes are concerns for the private, public, and government sectors responsible for information security. Computer crime, also called cybercrime, is ranked third in priority by the Federal Bureau of Investigation, behind terrorism and espionage.

Computer-based crimes caused an estimated $14.2 billion in damages to businesses throughout the world in 2005, including the cost of repairing systems and lost business. Costs to individuals who were victims of identity theft were also tremendous. Criminals are committing traditional and high-tech crimes using their own computers, hijacked computers, cellular telephones, personal digital assistants (PDAs), credit card readers, iPods, and BlackBerry devices.

Because computer crime can be committed anonymously from anywhere in the world, and because it is difficult to prove who was at the keyboard in any given case, the number of computer criminals successfully captured and prosecuted remains very low. The people who carry out such crimes are difficult to identify or locate in part because they work hard to hide the electronic tracks left by their activities. They can disguise or hide their identities by hacking into and taking control of Internet-connected computers anywhere in the world and routing their activities through them.

With few effective deterrents in place, traditional criminals such as con artists, extortionists, child pornographers, money launderers, industrial spies, and drug dealers have been able to increase the scope and frequency of their crimes by using computer and communication technologies. In addition, with increasing numbers of users connected to the Internet, particularly in developing countries, geographic barriers to entry into criminal activity have been eliminated. One of the greatest financial threats in computer crime comes from spyware programs sent from developing countries that secretly record passwords, banking information, or other keystrokes. These confidential data are then sent to data thieves who sell them to money launderers or other criminals.

Serious crimes involving the exploitation of children have moved online. Pedophiles cultivate relationships with children using social network Web sites and then arrange to meet them in public places. Child pornographers use file servers, chat rooms, and e-mail to distribute images.

Computer crimes do leave electronic evidence on individual computers, on computer networks, and in log files. The downloading, storage, and distribution of images or files leave electronic evidence. Because spyware programs get installed on victims' computers, evidence of their existence can be found in the receiving computers' registries. Although different types of computer crimes are investigated differently, a number of generally accepted policies and procedures, if strictly followed, can help investigators to locate, acquire, and recover electronic evidence that is admissible in court.

### History

In its earliest forms, cybercrime was carried out with hacker tools that required computer expertise to use. During the 1970's, most computer criminals were hackers who were highly motivated people with technical knowledge; some worked at universities or computer centers. In 1988, Robert Morris, Jr., a graduate student at Cornell University and son of a chief scientist at the U.S. National Security Agency, developed an Internet worm that infected thousands of computers and cost an estimated $100 million in cleanup.

In 1992, the Federal Bureau of Investigation (FBI) proposed expanding federal wiretapping laws to require all public and private networks in the United States to be capable of intercepting an intruder's or suspect's activities. The FBI wanted real-time remote access to all data, fax, voice, and video traffic in the United States.

Civil liberties groups contested this proposal, however, and were able to defeat it.

The first federal computer crime statute was the Computer Fraud and Abuse Act of 1984 (CFAA). Only one indictment was made under the CFAA before it was amended in 1986. By the mid-1990's, almost every U.S. state had enacted a computer crime statute. These statutes criminalize any wrongful access into a computer, regardless of whether any damage occurs as a result. Other statutes under which the FBI investigates computer-related crimes include the Economic Espionage Act and the Trade Secrets Act.

Many countries have adopted similar statutes designed to protect electronic commerce, the financial industry, and information stored on computers. An ongoing challenge for those investigating computer crime is keeping up with hardware and software advances that can affect forensic analysis.

### Computer Crime and Physical Investigations

Because considerable overlap exists between computer crimes and traditional physical and financial crimes, traditional criminal personality profiling is valuable in computer forensic investigations, where computers and the Internet are the electronic crime scenes. For example, fraud and extortion are age-old crimes that are more easily committed using computer technology. Cyberterrorists have extorted millions of British pounds by threatening to knock out computer-dependent financial systems, and extortionists have hacked into corporate databases and demanded huge payoffs in exchange for not destroying or publishing the data stored there. Investigators should assess how they would investigate particular crimes or criminals in the physical world and then apply that knowledge to the digital world. By examining the similarities between crimes committed through physical methods and those committed using electronic methods, investigators can better understand the perpetrators and where to search for evidence.

Given the dramatic increase in the incidence of computer crimes, prosecutors and law-enforcement agents must be knowledgeable concerning how to go about obtaining the electronic evidence stored in computers. Electronic records such as computer network logs, e-mails, word-processing files, and electronic picture files increasingly provide authorities with essential evidence in criminal cases. Computer hard drives and other storage media are the digital equivalents of filing cabinets holding information that investigators can turn into proof of a variety of crimes, including the distribution of child pornography, embezzlement, drug trafficking, money laundering, identity theft, sexual harassment, theft of trade secrets, cyberterrorism, and cyberstalking.

Computer investigations, like other forensic investigations, require specialized knowledge to acquire, preserve, analyze, and interpret the evidence. Incriminating evidence may be found in e-mail and logs of Internet activity on a single computer or may reside on many computers that cannot be physically located. Complicating computer investigations are criminals' attempts to avoid detection by deleting electronic files or formatting hard drives to hide the evidence, but even in such cases, trained computer forensic examiners can almost always find electronic evidence of crimes as well as evidence of the efforts made to hide or delete incriminating material.

In some ways, computer forensic examiners must take even greater care than investigators of traditional crime scenes because of the extremely fragile and easily altered nature of electronic evidence.

Because electronic evidence has become increasingly crucial to many civil and criminal cases, the field of computer forensics has gained national recognition. In the United States, the FBI has established fourteen state-of-the-art Regional Computer Forensics Laboratories (RCFLs). In these labs, computer forensics techniques are increasingly applied to the investigation of a variety of crimes, not just those involving computers, as Internet and mobile phone technologies become a pervasive part of everyday life and criminal activity.

The U.S. Secret Service has established a national computer forensics lab in Alabama with partial funding by the Department of Homeland Security's National Cyber Security Division. The facility serves as a national

## The FBI and Cybercrime

*The Federal Bureau of Investigation's stated fourfold "cyber mission" is as follows:*

First and foremost, to stop those behind the most serious computer intrusions and the spread of malicious code; second, to identify and thwart online sexual predators who use the Internet to meet and exploit children and to produce, possess, or share child pornography; third, to counteract operations that target U.S. intellectual property, endangering our national security and competitiveness; and fourth, to dismantle national and transnational organized criminal enterprises engaging in Internet fraud.

cybercrimes training center for prosecutors and judges as well as law-enforcement investigators.

### Preserving Electronic Evidence

Computers can be the instruments used to commit crimes as well as the targets of crimes. These crimes leave electronic evidence, but that evidence is rarely readily apparent. To obtain and protect potential legal evidence for use in criminal prosecutions, investigators must search computers, computer networks, and data storage devices using generally accepted computer forensics methods and tools. Experts use established investigative and analysis techniques to uncover information and system data, including damaged, deleted, hidden, or encrypted files. They seize and collect digital evidence at crime scenes, conduct impartial examination of the computer evidence, and then testify as required.

In matters of evidence, it is mandatory that law-enforcement personnel observe strict procedures regarding chain of custody, and all items must be preserved for independent analysis. The successful prosecution of computer criminals depends on the presentation of evidence that shows the connections between the suspects and the crimes. All records concerning the illegal intrusions or incidents of interest must be preserved; nothing should be deleted, tampered with, or altered.

To ensure the preservation of electronic evidence, an investigator needs to be prepared with a forensic kit that includes the following: tools such as screwdrivers, pliers, and scissors; duct tape; watertight and static-resistant plastic bags to store collected evidence; labels to use in marking items such as cables, connections, and evidence bags; bootable media such as DOS start-up diskettes, bootable CDs, and bootable USB drives; power, USB, printer, and FireWire cables; logbook to record the investigator's actions; and external USB hard drive to transfer large amounts of data or images.

## Steps in the Forensic Examination

When the evidence arrives at the computer forensic lab, the investigator must document the time and date and complete the appropriate chain-of-custody forms. The evidence must be stored in a secure area, where access to it is limited and controlled.

The acquisition phase of a computer investigation can take place either on-site or in the forensic lab. In either case, steps must be taken to ensure the integrity of the evidence. The preferred method is to conduct this phase in the trusted environment of the laboratory whenever circumstances permit. The acquisition of electronic evidence is a crucial step in the investigation because this is where the potential for alteration of the original evidence is greatest. It is vitally important that the investigator follow standard procedures and document all actions in order to ensure the integrity of the evidence beyond a reasonable doubt.

At the start of the acquisition process, the investigator must document the computer hardware and software that will be used to conduct the acquisition and analysis. After this documentation is complete, the next step is to disassemble the suspect computer. The main purpose of this is to allow the investigator access to the storage device on the suspect computer. The investigator must have access to the storage device to get data off the label of the device and to identify all storage devices, both internal and external, that are part of the computer.

The acquisition of evidence then proceeds with the copying of the suspect computer's hard drive; this process is called imaging or mirroring. The acquired forensic image must be verified to be an exact copy of the original. Specialized computer forensics software, such as EnCase or Forensic Toolkit (FTK), is typically used to create and verify the image. After a forensic image has been created, the investigator makes a duplicate to have a working copy of the image to analyze, so that if one image is destroyed or damaged or becomes corrupted, another copy is available without having to involve the original evidence.

The next phase is examination of the forensic image. Although computer forensic examiners should always follow certain basic procedures and start the examination phase in particular areas, an experienced examiner will also try to understand how the suspect thinks and works and then use that information to steer the examination method. For example, if the suspect is a novice computer user, the examination will usually cover only the basics. In contrast, examining the machine of an expert user who can hide or manipulate data forces the examiner to look for stealth activities when searching for evidence. Usually, this work is done with an image of the suspect's drive, and a separate hard drive is used to save evidence and tools for the case.

In the extraction phase, the examiner extracts data files for further analysis. It is during this step of the investigation that the data are searched for proof of crimes. The files are searched using key words, names, dates, and other file properties. One challenge faced by computer forensic examiners is data hiding—that is, the files to be examined may be password protected, encrypted, disguised, compressed, deleted, or corrupted. To crack a password, an examiner needs password-cracking software for the specific data file type. The difficulty of cracking a password is usually in direct correlation to the sophistication of the computer user.

One form of data hiding is the disguising of files by changing their file extensions. This is easily detected by most forensic software packages that do an analysis of file headers and compare them to established file extensions. Passwords on files usually yield clues in and of themselves, in that some passwords are very

## Prosecutor Offices and Types of Computer Crime

This chart shows the percentages of all U.S. prosecutor offices that reported prosecuting computer-related crimes in 2001. The left column for each category shows the percentage of all offices that prosecuted related cases; the right column shows the percentage for offices serving populations of at least one million people.

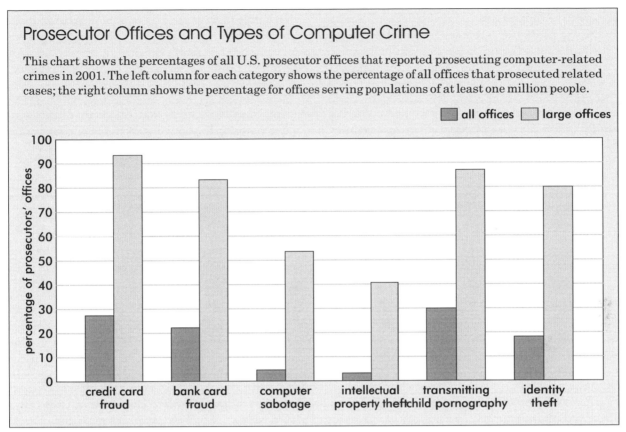

Source: U.S. Bureau of Justice Statistics.

personal in nature and connect users to particular files. Another reason passwords are evidentiary in nature is that they help to prove that suspects intended to hide the contents of their files.

For file compression, forensic examiners use utilities that simply let the software reverse the compression process and specify where the uncompressed versions are to be saved. Dealing with encrypted files is much more difficult, as the encryption of a file itself may be so strong it can literally take years to decrypt.

Another method of data hiding is steganography, in which data are hidden within another file, such as a picture or music file. The technologies used in steganography vary, but the basic premise is that a small portion of an existing file is replaced by an embedded or hidden file. If a suspect has used "stego," it is very hard for an investigator to find the hidden file unless "before-and-after" versions of the file in which it is hidden are available. If the user has kept the original file on the computer's storage device and embedded data in a copy, the investigator can literally compare the two files bit by bit to determine whether they are different. The investigator must then find out which stego program was used to embed the file, because only the software used can realistically reverse the process.

In the final step of a computer forensic examination, the examiner completes the necessary documentation and writes a report of the processing, analysis, and interpretation of the evidence. Most organizations have standard sets of forms that forensic examiners must use in documenting their cases; these forms also provide examiners with guidelines to follow.

### Tracking Criminals in Internet Relay Chat

Investigators sometimes track criminals through their use of Internet chat rooms.

259

Pedophiles and other criminals often meet in such chat rooms to find victims, advertise, learn new skills, or teach others. They may also discuss their personal lives, allowing law-enforcement personnel to learn more about the social cultures of these criminals. System logs can enable investigators to track down criminals because such logs hold evidence that crimes have been committed and where the intrusions occurred. These logs cannot identify intruders, however—that is, they cannot indicate who was physically using given keyboards at any particular times. In Internet Relay Chat (IRC), however, individuals can be identified.

Hackers often do not connect to IRC directly. By using a variety of servers or hosts, hackers can subvert bans or trick others into thinking they are other people. Usually, hackers seek to hide their real IP addresses so that no one can find them and monitor their activities. They do so by using bounce programs (such as BNC and WinGate), which read from one port and write to another.

These programs allow users to make a connection, connect to a destination, and then relay anything from the original connection to the destination. Hackers who have access to such programs can "bounce" through proxy servers to hide their tracks. Even if a complete audit trail shows that an intruder came from a specific account on a specific ISP, the only evidence will be billing information for the account, which does not prove identity.

*Linda Volonino*

## Further Reading

Casey, Eoghan. *Digital Evidence and Computer Crime: Forensic Science, Computers, and the Internet.* 2d ed. New York: Elsevier, 2003. Explains how computers and networks function, how they can be involved in crimes, and how they can be used as sources of evidence. Includes a CD-ROM that provides valuable hands-on training.

_____, ed. *Handbook of Computer Crime Investigation: Forensic Tools and Technology.* San Diego, Calif.: Academic Press, 2002. Collection of fourteen chapters directed toward law-enforcement personnel and forensic examiners. Numerous case studies make this a good reference manual for both new and experienced investigators. Describes how to search hard drives for remnants of illicit images, illegal software, and harassing e-mails.

Kipper, Gregory. *Wireless Crime and Forensic Investigation.* New York: Auerbach, 2007. Presents an overview of the various types of wireless crimes and the computer forensic investigation techniques used with wireless devices and wireless networks. Explores a wide range of wireless technologies, including short text messaging and war driving.

Thomas, Douglas, and Brian D. Loader, eds. *Cybercrime: Law Enforcement, Security, and Surveillance in the Information Age.* New York: Routledge, 2000. Collection of articles covers topics such as criminality on the electronic frontier, hackers, cyberpunks, and international attitudes toward hackers. Points out mistakes that law-enforcement personnel and prosecutors sometimes make during the investigation of computer crimes.

U.S. Department of Justice. Criminal Division. *Federal Guidelines for Searching and Seizing Computers and Obtaining Electronic Evidence in Criminal Investigations.* Washington, D.C.: Government Printing Office, 2002. Explains the guidelines developed by the Justice Department's Computer Crime and Intellectual Property Section in conjunction with an informal group of federal agencies known as the Computer Search and Seizure Working Group.

Volonino, Linda, Reynaldo Anzaldua, and Jana Godwin. *Computer Forensics: Principles and Practice.* Upper Saddle River, N.J.: Prentice Hall, 2007. Explains the use of investigative tools and procedures to maximize the effectiveness of evidence gathering. Also covers the legal foundations for handling electronic evidence, how to keep evidence in pristine condition so it will be admissible in a legal action, and how to investigate large-scale attacks such as identity theft, fraud, extortion, and malware infections.

**See also:** Computer forensics; Computer Fraud and Abuse Act of 1984; Computer hacking; Computer viruses and worms; Cryptology and number theory; Cyberstalking; Identity theft; Internet tracking and tracing; Steganography.

# Computer forensics

**Definition:** Forensic specialty that applies science to the acquisition and analysis of electronic data from computers, other digital devices, and the Internet to assist in civil and criminal investigations.

**Significance:** Every use of a computer or other digital device is recorded, leaving a digital trail of evidence. Because computer crimes as well as physical crimes—and the criminals who commit them—often leave trails of electronic evidence, computer forensics has come to play an increasingly prominent role in law enforcement, crime investigations, civil cases, and homeland security.

Since 1991, when the World Wide Web was developed, rapid growth has been seen in personal, professional, and criminal uses of the Internet—through e-mail, instant messaging, online chat rooms, social networking Web sites, Web logs, and more—and of networked computers and cellular devices. Computers and digital communication devices create and store huge amounts of details in their memory or log files. When computer files are saved, sent, or downloaded, the computer's operating system and other software automatically record and store this information. The records and files stored on computers and other digital devices can be used as evidence to support or defend against allegations of wrongdoing.

Rarely are users aware that their activities have left multiple trails of evidence, and many may not even attempt to purge those trails regardless of how incriminating they are. Even technology-savvy users who want their activities to go undetected may not be able to delete or disguise all their trails of evidence completely. Often it is impossible to delete all traces of electronic evidence. The work of computer forensic investigators involves finding, analyzing, and preserving relevant digital files or data for use as electronic evidence.

The three primary types of evidence presented in legal proceedings are the testimony of witnesses, physical evidence, and electronic evidence. The newest of these is electronic evidence. Common types of electronic evidence are the contents of e-mail and instant messages and chat-room conversations, records of Web sites visited, downloaded and uploaded files, word-processing documents, spreadsheets, digital pictures, Global Positioning System (GPS) records, and data from personal digital assistants (PDAs). Investigations of computer crimes, identity theft, computer hacking and viruses, electronic espionage, and cyberterrorism require computer forensic technical and investigative skills and tools because of the digital or electronic nature of the evidence.

The thorough investigation and unbiased analysis of electronic evidence requires specialized computer forensics tools used by experts who understand both computer technologies and legal procedures. It may seem that because electronic evidence falls into the category of hearsay evidence, which is secondhand evidence, it would not be admissible in court, but electronic evidence is one of the exceptions to the hearsay rule. It is considered reliable provided that it is handled properly.

## Principles of Computer Forensics

A computer forensics investigation uses science and technology to acquire and examine electronic data in order to develop and test theories that can be entered into a court of law to answer questions about events that have occurred. Generally accepted computer forensics principles have been established to ensure that the chain of custody of the evidence can be verified later in court or other legal proceedings. Like physical evidence, electronic evidence can be easily contaminated if investigators ignore the forensic science principle of "do no harm." The crime scene, which is the state of the computer, must be preserved to protect the integrity of the evidence; simply turning on a computer and searching through the files can alter those files and the computer's records.

Forensic investigators are aware that they will need to defend their findings. Their electronic evidence-processing methods, tools, and techniques may be challenged rigorously by the opposing side in a court case. Documentation is important so that investigators can refresh their memories about the steps taken and duplicate the results of processing if necessary. Investigators must thus follow rigorous processes and procedures in the acquisition, authentication, analysis, and interpretation of electronic evidence.

The first step in any computer forensics investigation is acquisition of the evidence through the careful collection and preservation of the original files on a hard drive (or other storage device); this is accomplished through the creation of an exact bit-stream duplicate copy of the entire hard drive using computer forensics software, such as Forensic Toolkit (FTK) or EnCase, that is recognized by the courts as acceptable for verifying evidence. This duplicate, which is referred to as the mirror image or drive image, is used for the analysis; the original evidence is used only in extreme situations. Making a mirror image of a hard drive is simple in theory, but the accuracy of the image must meet evidence standards. To guarantee accuracy, imaging programs rely on mathematical cyclic redundancy check (CRC) computations to validate that the copies made are exactly the same as the originals. CRC validation processes compare the bit stream of the original source data with the bit stream of the acquired data.

The second step in the computer forensics investigation is authentication of the mirror image, or verification that the copy is identical to the original or source. Evidence verification depends not only on the use of the proper software and hardware tools but also on the equipment, environment, and documentation of the steps taken during evidence processing. At a minimum, preservation of the chain of custody for electronic evidence requires proving that no information was added, deleted, or altered in the copying process or during analysis, that a complete mirror image copy was made and verified, that a reliable copying process was used, and that all data that should have been copied were copied. This is accomplished when the mirror image is "fingerprinted" using an encryption

technique called hashing. Hashing ensures the integrity of the file because it makes any modification of the data detectable.

The third and often most extensive step in the investigation is the technical analysis and evaluation of the evidence, which must be done is a manner that is fair and impartial to the person or persons being investigated. Investigators evaluate what could have happened as well as what could not have happened. The key to effective electronic evidence searches is careful preparation. Poor preparation during the early stages of an investigation can lead to failures in prosecution, as information can be ignored, destroyed, or compromised. Experienced computer forensics examiners are skilled in formulating search strategies that are likely to find relevant revealing data. Analyses are more productive when examiners have some sense of what they are seeking before they begin their searches. For example, if the focus is on documents, the investigators need to know names, key words, or parts of words that are likely to be found within those documents. If the issue is trade secrets, it is helpful for the examiners to know which search terms are uniquely associated with the proprietary data. If the focus is child pornography, Web site addresses uniquely associated with prohibited content are valuable.

The final steps are the interpretation and reporting of the results. Examiners' conclusions must be accurate, complete, and usable in legal proceedings. Explaining the findings of computer forensic investigations in court can be difficult, especially when the evidence must be presented to persons with little technical knowledge. The value of the evidence ultimately depends on the way it is presented and defended in court. Because of the complexity of many of the tools involved in computer forensics, investigators must be trained and certified in their use. General training and certifications are also available for computer forensics investigators.

## Regional Computer Forensics Labs

In 1999, the Federal Bureau of Investigation (FBI) launched an innovative pilot program in San Diego, California. The Regional Computer

Forensics Laboratory (RCFL) program was designed to help state, local, and other federal law enforcement gather electronic evidence from computers, PDAs, cell phones, digital cameras, and other digital devices. The FBI undertook the project because computer forensics was one of the fastest-growing disciplines within law enforcement, and the RCFL program quickly became a dynamic tool for fighting crime and terrorism. By 2007, the RCFL program had evolved into a network of cutting-edge electronic evidence labs created to meet a rapidly increasing need. The RFCLs have supported high-profile investigations such as the Enron case, the bribery case against former California congressman Randy "Duke" Cunningham, the public corruption case against former Illinois governor George Ryan, and the dissolution of an international child pornography ring.

Each RCFL is a full-service forensics laboratory and training center devoted to the examination of electronic evidence in support of criminal investigations, including terrorism, child pornography, crimes of violence, the theft or destruction of intellectual property, Internet crimes, and fraud. In 2006, the RCFLs, which are staffed by trained computer analysts from the FBI and more than one hundred other agencies, collectively analyzed almost sixty thousand media items, including CDs, cell phones, hard drives, and PDAs. During 2006, requests for assistance on computer crimes, which included child pornography and other violent acts against children, were the most frequent kinds of requests in eleven of fourteen RCFLs, followed by violent crimes, major thefts, and white-collar crimes.

*Linda Volonino*

### Further Reading

Carrier, Brian. *File System Forensic Analysis.* Boston: Addison-Wesley, 2005. Good reference source for anyone who wants to understand file systems; aimed at professionals who need to be able to testify about how file system analysis is performed.

Kipper, Gregory. *Wireless Crime and Forensic Investigation.* New York: Auerbach, 2007. Presents an overview of the various types of wireless crimes and the computer forensic investigation techniques used with wireless devices and wireless networks.

Sheetz, Michael. *Computer Forensics: An Essential Guide for Accountants, Lawyers, and Managers.* Hoboken, N.J.: John Wiley & Sons, 2007. Provides a useful introduction to the essentials of preserving evidence on a computer, understanding how computer crime occurs, and what to do when it is found and suspected.

Steel, Chad. *Windows Forensics: The Field Guide for Corporate Computer Investigations.* Hoboken, N.J.: John Wiley & Sons, 2006. Presents a primer on how Windows file systems work and how to perform forensic analysis on these systems.

Volonino, Linda, Reynaldo Anzaldua, and Jana Godwin. *Computer Forensics: Principles and*

## Rule 34 of the Federal Rules of Civil Procedure

In 1970, Rule 34 of the Federal Rules of Civil Procedure was amended to address changing technology and communication methods. The amended Rule 34 made electronically stored information subject to subpoena and discovery. Therefore, any communication or file storage device is subject to computer forensic searches to identify, examine, and preserve potential electronic evidence—the electronic equivalent of a "smoking gun."

This rule has had far-reaching implications for electronic records and communications—gateways to evidence of a person's or organization's activities and conduct. Every computer-based activity—whether it is using the Internet for money laundering or identity theft or sending e-mail containing incriminating or threatening messages—leaves an electronic trace that computer forensics may recover. Thus a good probability exists that, deleted or not, electronic mail, histories of Web site visits, drafts and revisions of documents, spreadsheets, and other materials can be retrieved. Computer forensics is playing a growing and major role in legal cases, as new legislation is passed to combat cybercrimes, traditional crimes, and terrorism.

*Practice*. Upper Saddle River, N.J.: Prentice Hall, 2007. Comprehensive work addresses how investigators use forensically sound methodologies and software to acquire admissible electronic evidence. Includes discussion of computer and e-mail forensics, cell phone forensics, and PDA and BlackBerry forensics.

**See also:** Chain of custody; Computer crimes; Computer hacking; Computer viruses and worms; Crime scene documentation; Crime scene investigation; Cyberstalking; Evidence processing; Forensic accounting; Internet tracking and tracing.

# Computer Fraud and Abuse Act of 1984

**Date:** Enacted on October 12, 1984, and amended in 1986, 1996, and 2001

**The Law:** First comprehensive federal legislation in the United States designed to address concerns about the growth of computer fraud and other computer-related crimes.

**Significance:** The enactment of the Computer Fraud and Abuse Act of 1984 generated computer-specific criminal laws and sentencing guidelines for computer criminals.

Prior to the passage of the Counterfeit Access Device and Computer Fraud and Abuse Act of 1984 (commonly referred to as the Computer Fraud and Abuse Act, or CFAA), computer crimes in the United States were prosecuted under a number of statutes generally dealing with interstate communications, wire fraud, and attacks against government property. Little legislation had been passed to deal specifically with computer crimes. Federal statutes addressed crimes against federal institutions, interstate crimes, and acts against the country's security, such as terrorism. Because of the nature of computer networks, hackers were often prosecuted under interstate commerce and federal telecom-

munications laws originally written to address telephone fraud.

## Content

Technological advances during the mid-1980's brought computers into mainstream American homes as well as into high schools, colleges, and businesses. The rapid growth of interconnectivity of computers by telephone lines and modems and the storage of vast numbers of confidential documents on computers compelled the passage of legislation to protect computer users. Existing laws were no longer sufficient to handle the kinds of theft and trespass that were possible using the new technology.

Originally limited in scope to interstate crime and instances involving government computers or those of financial institutions, the purpose of the 1984 Computer Fraud and Abuse Act was to protect classified, financial, and credit information that was maintained on federal government computers. The act made it a crime to knowingly access a federal-interest computer without authorization to obtain certain defense, foreign relations, or financial information or atomic secrets. A federal-interest computer was defined as a computer used by a financial institution, a computer used by the U.S. government, or one of two or more computers used in committing the offense, not all of which were located in the same state. The act also made it a criminal offense to use a computer to commit fraud, to "trespass" on a computer, and to traffic in unauthorized computer passwords.

## Amendments

The Computer Fraud and Abuse Act of 1986 was designed to strengthen, expand, and clarify the intentionally narrow 1984 act. It safeguarded sensitive data harbored by government agencies and related organizations, nuclear systems, financial institutions, and medical records. The 1986 act forbade interference with any federal-interest computer system or any system that crossed state lines. It also prohibited the unauthorized access of any computer system containing classified government information. It specified three categories of classified information: information belonging to a financial institution, credit card issuer, or consumer reporting agency; information from a department or agency of the United States; and information from any computer deemed "protected" or used exclusively by a financial institution, by the U.S. government, or in interstate or foreign commerce or communication.

The 1986 act aimed to safeguard the integrity of computer systems with specific prohibitions against computer vandalism, including transmission of a virus or similar code intended to cause damage to a computer or system, unauthorized access that caused damage recklessly, or unauthorized access of a computer without malicious intent. The law established punishments of prison sentences up to twenty years and fines up to $250,000 for the perpetration of knowing and reckless damage to any computer system. Establishing criminal intent at time of trial, however, can prove difficult.

As computing evolved, the CFAA was further amended in 1996 by the National Information Infrastructure Protection Act, which broadened the law's scope to include conduct committed by or through the use of the Internet, World Wide Web, or other computer networks. It also removed the wording "federal-interest computer" and replaced it with "protected computer." In so doing, Congress broadened the scope of the act's protection from federal computers to include all computers involved in interstate and foreign commerce.

The Patriot Act of 2001 amended the CFAA again, raising the maximum penalties for some violations to ten years for a first offense and twenty years for a second offense, ensuring that violators who cause damage generally can be punished, and enhancing punishments for violations involving any damage to government computers involved in criminal justice or the military, including damage to foreign computers involved in interstate commerce. In addition, the 2001 amendments expanded the act's definition of "loss" to include the time spent by authorities in investigating and responding to damage assessment and restitution.

In its decision in the 2003 case *Theofel v. Farey Jones*, the U.S. Court of Appeals for the Ninth Circuit referred to the Computer Fraud and Abuse Act, holding that disclosure by the plaintiff's Internet service provider of e-mail messages pursuant to the defendant's invalid and overly broad subpoena did not constitute an "authorized" disclosure. This decision has potentially serious implications for law-enforcement authorities because of the limitations it places on their ability to obtain information from Internet service providers without having to obtain search warrants.

*Marcia J. Weiss*

### Further Reading

Cantos, Lisa, Chad Chambers, Lorin Fine, and Randi Singer. "Internet Security Legislation Introduced in the Senate." *Journal of Proprietary Rights* 12 (May, 2000): 15-16. Provides a concise summary of the Computer Fraud and Abuse Act.

Conley, John M., and Robert M. Bryan. "A Survey of Computer Crime Legislation in the United States." *Information and Communications Technology Law* 8 (March, 1999): 35-58. Presents information on the various laws passed by local, state, and federal governments to attempt to address the issue of computer crime.

Montana, John C. "Viruses and the Law: Why the Law Is Ineffective." *Information Management Journal* 34 (October, 2000): 57-60. Addresses the difficulty of creating laws that can have any impact on the global problem of computer crime.

Toren, Peter J. *Intellectual Property and Computer Crimes*. New York: Law Journal Press, 2003. Treatise intended for attorneys and computer security professionals includes useful references to sources of information on intellectual property issues.

**See also:** Computer crimes; Computer hacking; Computer viruses and worms; Cyberstalking; Forensic accounting; Legal competency.

# Computer hacking

**Definition:** Intrusions, unauthorized access, or attempts to circumvent or bypass the security mechanisms of a computer, computer network, computer program, or information system. Unauthorized access includes approaching, trespassing within, communicating with, storing data in, retrieving data from, or otherwise intercepting and changing computer resources without authorized consent.

**Significance:** The financial damage, destruction, and disruption caused by computer hackers worldwide have been tremendous. The incidence and severity of computer hacking have severely worsened since the 1980's, when hackers' primary aims were to steal bandwidth or gain fame in the hacker community. Since 2001, computer hacking has expanded into a global form of white-collar crime motivated by profit, with hackers engaging in data theft, identity theft, computer hijacking, sabotage, extortion, and money laundering for personal financial gain or to fund illegal activities.

The term "hacking" has various meanings, but it is commonly used to refer to forms of intrusion into a computer, computer database, or computer network without authority or in excess of authority. Hackers are criminals who exploit vulnerabilities in computers, information systems, e-mail systems, and digital devices. Hackers routinely break into computer networks through the Internet by "spoofing" the identities of computers that the networks expect to be present.

Hackers may be thieves, corporate spies, or disgruntled individuals; they may work for organized crime organizations or for nations or political groups. Hackers motivated by personal grievances who attack individuals they know or their own companies are the easiest to track down. In contrast, the investigation of hacking and Web-based illegal activities used to finance terrorism is complex, requiring the cooperation of national intelligence agencies. Common to all computer hacking investigations is the use of computer and network forensic tools and techniques to follow digital trails back to the computers used for hacking, to determine the identities of the hackers, or to learn how and why hackers' attacks were successful.

Computer hacking is one type of computer crime that might violate several federal laws in the United States as well as laws in many individual U.S. states. The federal laws under which hacking might be prosecuted include the Computer Fraud and Abuse Act of 1984, the Electronic Communications Privacy Act of 1986, and, depending on whether copies of materials have been made, the Copyright Act.

## Electronic Evidence Left by Hackers

Although hackers vary in their intentions, all tend to use similar techniques, all of which require expertise in computers and computer networks; those who investigate hacking must have this expertise as well. The first step in hacking is usually to gain access to a networked computer and install an unauthorized hacker program, such as a Trojan horse or backdoor. All computer networks create logs that record the exact times of all attempts to log in, the IP (Internet protocol) addresses of the source computers, the commands that were used, and the programs that were installed. Those logs are valuable sources of information in the investigation of hack attacks unless the hackers covered their tracks by deleting entries from log files. Investigators can examine a computer's registry for stored information on installed software.

Not all hacking involves great technical skill. A hacker can sometimes gain access to a corporate system by calling an employee and pretending to be a coworker who needs help logging in. Because hackers can gain access through authorized accounts, investigators must consider the possibility that a person whose account was used to hack was not the hacker.

## Tracing Hackers' Locations

Software programs such as Netstat are available that enable investigators to trace hackers' IP addresses to geographic locations. Hackers often use computers owned by other parties, however, such as those in public libraries or in public Internet cafés. This complicates investigations because such hackers must be prosecuted using evidence they leave on other people's computers. The longer hackers are allowed to compromise particular computers or networks, the more evidence can be collected against them to build solid cases. It is important that law-enforcement investigators are aware of this fact, but in some cases it may be necessary to shut down networks immediately to protect them.

In addition to needing an IP address, investigators need to identify the Internet service provider (ISP) from which an attack originated. Software is available that can reveal this information.

Hackers may try to hide their locations and identities by using software that routes Internet communications through untraceable IP addresses. Determining the IP address of the computer used to launch an attack is an important first step in discovering a hacker's identity. Most often, the IP address will be traceable back to a particular ISP. ISPs usually own "blocks" of IP addresses, in which only the last few digits differ, through which their customers connect to the Internet. These IP addresses are either statically or dynamically assigned, depending on the configuration of the ISP. An IP address of a static cable modem user constitutes a constant, traceable "fingerprint" of both the ISP provider and the specific user's computer terminal.

*Linda Volonino*

## Further Reading

Casey, Eoghan. *Digital Evidence and Computer Crime: Forensic Science, Computers, and the Internet*. 2d ed. New York: Elsevier, 2003. Explains how computers and networks function, how they can be involved in crimes, and how they can be used as sources of evidence.

Kipper, Gregory. *Wireless Crime and Forensic Investigation*. New York: Auerbach, 2007. Presents an overview of the various types of wireless crimes and the computer forensic investigation techniques used with wireless devices and wireless networks.

Thomas, Douglas, and Brian D. Loader, eds. *Cybercrime: Law Enforcement, Security, and Surveillance in the Information Age*. New York: Routledge, 2000. Collection of articles covers topics such as criminality on the electronic frontier, hackers, cyberpunks, and international attitudes toward hackers. Points out mistakes that law-enforcement personnel and prosecutors sometimes make during the investigation of computer crimes.

Thomas, Timothy L. "Al Qaeda and the Internet: The Danger of 'Cyberplanning.'" *Parameters: U.S. Army War College Quarterly* 33 (Spring, 2003): 112-119. Discusses how the Internet is used to support and fund terrorism.

U.S. Department of Justice. Criminal Division. *Federal Guidelines for Searching and Seizing Computers and Obtaining Electronic Evidence in Criminal Investigations*. Washington, D.C.: Government Printing Office, 2002. Explains the guidelines developed by the Justice Department's Computer Crime and Intellectual Property Section in conjunction with an informal group of federal agencies known as the Computer Search and Seizure Working Group.

Volonino, Linda, Reynaldo Anzaldua, and Jana Godwin. *Computer Forensics: Principles and Practice*. Upper Saddle River, N.J.: Prentice Hall, 2007. Explains the use of investigative tools and procedures to maximize the effectiveness of evidence gathering. Chapter 10 discusses how investigators track down hackers and conduct large-scale investigations.

**See also:** Computer crimes; Computer forensics; Computer Fraud and Abuse Act of 1984; Cyberstalking; Steganography.

## Computer viruses and worms

**Definition:** Malicious computer programs, also known as malware, that use embedded instructions to carry out destructive behavior on computers, computer networks, and digital devices.

**Significance:** Computer viruses and worms have the potential to disrupt computer networks and thus to cause great damage to a nation's economy. The U.S. Department of Justice has devoted significant resources to investigating and prosecuting persons who release viruses or worms on the Internet. In addition, government agencies investigate connections between malware and organized crime, identity theft, and terrorism.

Given the capacity of computer viruses and worms to spread to millions of computers within minutes and cause billions of dollars in damage, the distribution of malware is a criminal act. In the United States, causing damage to a computer connected to the Internet is a federal crime that carries substantial penalties for those convicted. The principal U.S. law-enforcement weapon against malware is the Computer Fraud and Abuse Act of 1984.

Many dangerous computer viruses have been spread through e-mail attachments and files downloaded from Web sites, and a rise has been seen in the numbers of professional virus writers—that is, people who are paid to infect computers with malware. Tracking down and catching virus authors is extremely difficult. The investigative methods used in this work include analyzing virus code for clues about the authors; searching online bulletin boards, where virus authors may boast of their accomplishments; and reviewing network log files for originating IP (Internet protocol) addresses of viruses. Even when law-enforcement agencies make concerted efforts in applying these techniques, it is still near impossible to track down virus and worm authors.

Some malware authors have been apprehended, however. When the Melissa virus overwhelmed commercial, government, and military computer systems in 1999, the Federal Bureau of Investigation (FBI) launched the largest Internet manhunt ever. Investigators succeeded in tracking down the virus creator by following several evidence trails. They identified David L. Smith of Aberdeen, New Jersey, as the suspect by analyzing the virus and the e-mail account used to send it, by searching America Online (AOL) log files that showed whose phone line had been used to send the virus, and by searching online bulletin boards intended for people interested in learning how to write viruses. Smith tried to hide the electronic evidence related to Melissa by deleting files from his computer and then disposing of it. The FBI found the computer, however, and used computer forensics techniques to recover incriminating evidence. Smith was caught within two weeks. He was the first person prosecuted for spreading a computer virus. In August, 2005, Turkish and Moroccan hackers released an Internet worm, named Zotob, to steal credit card numbers and other financial information from infected computers. Zotob crashed innumerable computer systems worldwide. Investigators gathered data, including IP addresses, e-mail addresses, names linked to those addresses, hacker nicknames, and other clues uncovered in the computer code. Less than eight days after the malicious code hit the Internet, two suspects were arrested. Computer forensic experts on the FBI's Cyber Action Team (CAT) verified that the code found on seized computers matched what was released into cyberspace.

*Linda Volonino*

**Further Reading**

Dwight, Ken. *Bug-Free Computing: Stop Viruses, Squash Worms, and Smash Trojan Horses.* Houston: TeleProcessors, 2006.

Erbschloe, Michael. *Trojans, Worms, and Spyware: A Computer Security Professional's Guide to Malicious Code.* Boston: Butterworth-Heinemann, 2005.

**See also:** Computer crimes; Computer forensics; Computer hacking; Cryptology and number theory; Steganography.

## Confocal microscopy

**Definition:** Optical imaging technique often used when a high degree of contrast or reconstruction of a three-dimensional image is desired.

**Significance:** Confocal microscopy has rapidly gained popularity in forensic science as a method of choice for imaging evidence samples because confocal microscopes produce images of a quality superior to what can be achieved with conventional fluorescence microscopes.

Forensic scientists can use various microscopic methods to examine samples obtained from accident or crime scenes. The choice of technique is determined in part by the size of the target. Confocal microscopy utilizes point illumination and a pinhole in an optically conjugate plane to eliminate light flare, producing high-quality images.

Three types of confocal microscopes are available: confocal laser scanning microscopes (CLSMs), spinning-disk (Nipkow disk) confocal microscopes, and programmable array microscopes (PAMs). Modern instruments are highly evolved compared with the earliest versions, but the principles of confocal imaging established by Marvin Minsky in 1957 are shared by all confocal microscopes. The method of image formation in confocal microscopes is fundamentally different from that of wide-field microscopes, which light entire specimens. Confocal microscopes produce in-focus images of thick specimens through a process called optical sectioning using focused beams of light. Through the use of digital image-processing technology, serial (consecutive) images can be reassembled to construct three-dimensional representations of the sample or structures being studied.

Prior to imaging with confocal microscopy,

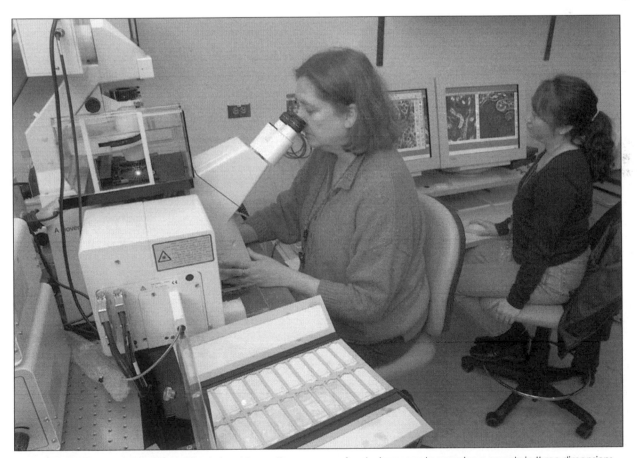

A scientist with the Centers for Disease Control and Prevention uses a confocal microscope to examine a sample in three dimensions. *(Centers for Disease Control and Prevention)*

specimens are usually fixed and stained. The preparatory protocols (that is, cutting, fixing, and staining of specimens) are largely derived from those used in conventional microscopy. During the staining stage, specific regions of specimens (such as specific organelles) can be labeled with antibodies conjugated with fluorescent probes. By examining the relative distribution of epitopes of interest, investigators can ascertain many details about a sample, including the type of specimen, pathological condition, and phase in the cell cycle.

Live-cell imaging and time-lapse imaging can be achieved with confocal microscopy, and inert and nonbiological specimens can also be examined using this technique. Forensic scientists can use confocal microscopes to examine evidence samples that are not easily visualized with conventional microscopes, such as the marks on bullets and cartridge cases as well as gunshot residue that is expelled when a firearm is discharged.

Another application of confocal microscopes in forensic science is in the analysis of paper documents. Specifically, confocal microscopy can enable an analyst to determine the sequence of two crossing strokes in different colors or different types of inks. Because confocal microscopes are able to capture serial images in various depths, with computer reconstruction imaging techniques, scientists can identify the sequence in which marks were made on a given document.

*Rena Christina Tabata*

## Further Reading

Matsumoto, Brian, ed. *Cell Biological Applications of Confocal Microscopy*. 2d ed. San Diego, Calif.: Academic Press, 2002.

Paddock, Stephen W., ed. *Confocal Microscopy Methods and Protocols*. Totowa, N.J.: Humana Press, 1999.

Pawley, James B., ed. *Handbook of Biological Confocal Microscopy*. 3d ed. New York: Springer, 2006.

**See also:** Analytical instrumentation; Fibers and filaments; Imaging; Micro-Fourier transform infrared spectrometry; Microscopes; Microspectrophotometry; Paper; Polarized light microscopy; Quantitative and qualitative analysis of chemicals; Scanning electron microscopy.

## Control samples

**Definition:** Samples of known substances used to ensure that laboratory analyses produce reliable results.

**Significance:** Quality control is an important part of eliminating inaccuracy in laboratory results. Control samples ensure that laboratory results are reliable and can be duplicated in other laboratories following the same quality-control standards.

Control samples (also called controls, known samples, or knowns) provide a level of quality control that can verify laboratory test results. When a control sample is not used, it is possible for a laboratory result to be a false positive (a result that indicates something is true when, in fact, it is false) or a false negative (a result that indicates something is false when, in fact, it is true).

Forensic laboratories may use a variety of control samples to ensure accurate results. For example, they may use known combustibles to verify that particular combustibles are present in arson cases and known drug samples to verify that particular drugs are present in drug cases. Known DNA (deoxyribonucleic acid) samples are used to compare with unknown DNA samples (for example, in the comparison of a suspect's DNA with DNA found at a crime scene).

In many cases, forensic laboratories acquire the known samples they use as controls from reliable outside sources. For example, the Forensic Science Service in England, an internationally recognized leader in applied forensic technology, is a widely respected source of reliable control samples for fibers and paints. Crime labs around the world use control samples from such sources to ensure that they are meeting the quality standards necessary for their results to be accepted in courts of law.

## Strategies for Obtaining DNA Samples Legally

DNA samples collected in the course of criminal investigations are of limited value unless they can be matched with control samples taken from known individuals. Four basic strategies provide law enforcement with legal means of collecting DNA samples from suspects:

- **Noncompulsory compliance:** Asking suspects to provide samples voluntarily by permitting their blood to be drawn or, more commonly, by submitting to the swabbing of the insides of their cheeks.
- **Court orders:** Obtaining court orders by showing reasonable cause to compel suspects to submit DNA samples.
- **Statutory law:** Taking advantage of the fact that certain defined groups, such as convicted offenders or arrestees, are required by law to submit samples for inclusion in state DNA databases.
- **Abandonment:** Collecting items containing suspects' DNA, such as cigarette butts and gum, that suspects have clearly intended to discard and abandon.

*and Investigative Techniques.* 2d ed. Boca Raton, Fla.: CRC Press, 2005.

**See also:** Blood residue and bloodstains; DNA extraction from hair, bodily fluids, and tissues; Drug confirmation tests; Ethics of DNA analysis; Evidence processing; Fire debris; Forensic Science Service; Mitochondrial DNA analysis and typing; National DNA Index System; Quality control of evidence; Trace and transfer evidence.

---

Another type of control sample is a blank, or a control sample that is known to contain nothing. In this type of control, the sample is known to not contain the substance for which an investigator is testing. For example, if a known blank and a substance suspected of being an illegal drug are tested and both tests produce positive results, indicating the presence of the drug, something is wrong with the quality control in the laboratory. It is possible that the equipment is contaminated by previous drug testing and needs to be sterilized, that there is some problem with the questioned sample, or that the control sample has been contaminated in some way.

*Marianne M. Madsen*

### Further Reading

Evans, Colin. *The Casebook of Forensic Detection: How Science Solved One Hundred of the World's Most Baffling Crimes.* Updated ed. New York: Berkley Books, 2007.

Fisher, Barry A. J. *Techniques of Crime Scene Investigation.* 7th ed. Boca Raton, Fla.: CRC Press, 2004.

Genge, N. E. *The Forensic Casebook: The Science of Crime Scene Investigation.* New York: Ballantine, 2002.

James, Stuart H., and Jon J. Nordby, eds. *Forensic Science: An Introduction to Scientific*

---

## Controlled Substances Act of 1970

**Date:** Enacted on October 27, 1970

**The Law:** Legislation that established rules and regulations for the federal control of drugs in the United States in terms of drug classifications and punishments for violations of the legislation's provisions.

**Significance:** Law-enforcement agencies in the United States are frequently concerned with crimes related to trafficking in drugs that are classified as illegal under the Controlled Substances Act.

Part of the Comprehensive Drug Abuse Prevention and Control Act of 1970, the Controlled Substances Act replaced the Harrison Narcotic Drug Act of 1914 by creating five schedules, or classifications, of controlled substances. Drugs fall into different schedules based on three main factors: their potential for abuse, whether or not (or to what extent) they have medical uses, and their potential to lead to psychological or physical dependence. Schedule I drugs, which include lysergic acid diethylamide (LSD) and marijuana, are defined as drugs with the highest potential for abuse and dependence, without any accepted medical use in the United States;

271

these drugs are believed to be unsafe to administer and may not be prescribed. Schedule II drugs, which include amphetamines and morphine, are classified as drugs with high abuse potential, some accepted medical use, and potential to lead to significant psychological or physical dependence.

Schedule III drugs have less potential for abuse than Schedule I or II drugs, have some accepted medical uses, and present moderate to low potential for physical dependence or high potential for psychological dependence. Schedule III and IV drugs are available only by prescription with limitations (only five refills within six months). Schedule IV drugs, which include benzodiazapines, are defined as drugs that have a lower potential for abuse compared with Schedule III drugs. They also have some accepted medical uses and may lead to limited physical or psychological dependence. Schedule V drugs are sometimes available without a prescription and can include medications with small amounts of codeine. Drugs in the Schedule V classification are considered to have the lowest potential for abuse compared with those in all the other schedules, and they have accepted medical uses. These drugs may lead to limited physical or psychological dependence, but the likelihood of dependence is lower than with drugs in the other schedules.

The processes laid out in the act for changing the classification of a drug from one schedule to another or adding a newly developed drug to a schedule are complex, but ultimately the Department of Justice and the Department of Health and Human Services determine the schedules into which drugs are classified. A number of interested parties may petition for changes in drug classifications, including the Drug Enforcement Administration, the Department of Health and Human Services, medical associations, public interest groups, drug manufacturers, state or local government agencies, and individual citizens. The Drug Enforcement Administration investigates all such petitions.

The Controlled Substances Act also requires that any individual or agency authorized by the Drug Enforcement Administration to handle controlled substances must be registered, must securely store the controlled substances, and

must keep accurate inventories and records of all transactions involving those substances.

*Sheryl L. Van Horne*

**Further Reading**

Califano, Joseph A., Jr. *High Society: How Substance Abuse Ravages America and What to Do About It*. New York: PublicAffairs, 2007.
Smith, Frederick P., ed. *Handbook of Forensic Drug Analysis*. Burlington, Mass.: Elsevier Academic Press, 2005.

**See also:** Amphetamines; Anabolic Steroid Control Act of 2004; Barbiturates; Drug classification; Drug Enforcement Administration, U.S.; Harrison Narcotic Drug Act of 1914; Illicit substances; Narcotics; Opioids; Psychotropic drugs; Stimulants.

## Copier analysis. *See* Fax machine, copier, and printer analysis

## Coroners

**Definition:** Presiding officers of special courts, medical officers, or officers of the law responsible for investigating deaths, particularly those that have taken place under unusual circumstances.

**Significance:** The work of coroners ensures that wrongful deaths are noted as such and are investigated, so that the interests of both government and the families of the deceased are served.

The office of coroner seems to have been established in Western culture after the Norman invasion of England in 1066. The term "coroner" is derived from the Latin word *corona*, which means crown, because the original coroners were servants of the crown appointed at the local level to protect the financial interests of the monarch. Although coroners' duties overlapped with the emerging duties of sheriffs, eventually coroners focused primarily on protecting the crown's financial interests, particularly in matters of the property of deceased persons that might be claimed by the crown. Coroners are thus part of the common-law tradition and appear in most of the nations colonized by England, including Australia and the United States. Elsewhere in the world, functions similar to those of coroners are often performed by medical practitioners.

Coroners may be either elected or appointed, depending on jurisdiction (a jurisdiction is usually a county). As the investigator of cause of death, the coroner generally has power to subpoena testimony concerning given deaths and to conduct inquests (reviews of the facts of deaths by panels of jurors). Coroners are not judicial officers; rather, they are considered to be part of the executive branch of government.

## Qualifications

The qualifications required of coroners vary across jurisdictions. In many jurisdictions coroners must have medical degrees, but this is not always a requirement. A general trend has been seen in recent years toward increasing demand for professionalism in the office of coroner. Some U.S. jurisdictions have replaced the office of coroner with that of medical examiner, which differs from coroner in several ways. For example, coroners are generally placed in office through countywide elections (usually serving terms of four years), whereas medical examiners are typically appointed by the chairs of county boards or by county executives. Most jurisdictions with medical examiners require that these officials be qualified medical doctors licensed to practice in the states in which they serve and that they be certified as licensed pathologists in anatomic and forensic pathology.

After coroners or medical examiners are installed in office, they are usually required to attend specialized training programs. In Illinois, for example, new coroners must apply for admittance to the coroners' training program run by the Illinois Law Enforcement Training Standards Board and must then complete the program within six months. In addition, all coroners are required to send their deputy coroners to the same training program.

## Responsibilities

The responsibilities of coroners include, but are not limited to, responding or dispatching deputy coroners to death scenes, collection of toxicological samples and their analysis, making death notifications to next of kin, and coordination and facilitation of organ donation. Coroners also determine the necessity for autopsy in individual deaths, facilitate the autopsy process, coordinate transport of deceased persons from death scenes, conduct death investigations when necessary, schedule and conduct inquests, summon juries for inquests, and issue temporary and permanent death certificates. Coroners are responsible for establishing the autopsy protocols used in their jurisdictions—that is, they determine what must be identified in autopsies and in the toxicology reports that list foreign substances found in the bodies of deceased persons.

Coroners in many jurisdictions are responsible for facilitating the burial of indigent persons, issuing cremation permits, maintaining records of all deaths reported, maintaining permanent records of all inquested cases, and maintaining vital statistics related to all cases reported. Coroners also generally take charge of the personal property of deceased persons until the property can be released. In addition to these duties, coroners are expected to be generally prepared for all possible disaster situations, during which they may need to hire and supervise "disaster deputy coroners."

In some states, coroners have duties beyond those related to death investigations. In Illinois, for example, coroners have the same powers as county sheriffs with regard to conservation of the peace; in the absence of a jurisdiction's sheriff, the coroner is empowered to act as sheriff. In Louisiana, coroners assist in determining the nature and extent of mental illness in living people. Coroners and medical examiners are called upon to investigate many different types of deaths, including those resulting from criminal violence, suicide, and accident. Coroners become involved when persons who were apparently in good condition die suddenly, when deaths are unattended by practicing licensed physicians, and when deaths take place under suspicious or unusual circumstances. Coroners often investigate cases of death attributable to criminal abortion, poisoning, adverse reaction to drugs or alcohol, disease constituting a threat to public health, or injury or toxic agent resulting from employment. They also investigate deaths that have taken place during medical diagnostic or therapeutic procedures and deaths that have occurred to those confined in penal institutions or in police custody. In addition, coroners are generally involved when dead bodies are transported into medicolegal jurisdictions without proper medical certification and whenever any human body is to be cremated, dissected, or buried at sea.

*David R. Struckhoff*

### Further Reading

Gerber, Samuel M., and Richard Saferstein, eds. *More Chemistry and Crime: From Marsh Arsenic Test to DNA Profile.* Washington, D.C.: American Chemical Society, 1997. Collection of chapters covers the history of forensic science as well as developments in the field through the 1990's.

Hendrix, Robert C. *Investigation of Violent and Sudden Death: A Manual for Medical Examiners.* Springfield, Ill.: Charles C Thomas, 1972. Classic work in the field describes the duties of coroners.

National Medicolegal Review Panel. *Death Investigation: A Guide for the Scene Investigator.* Washington, D.C.: U.S. Department of Justice, 1999. Brief work provides guidelines for coroners and medical examiners working at crime scenes.

Spitz, Werner U., ed. *Spitz and Fisher's Medicolegal Investigation of Death: Guidelines for the Application of Pathology to Crime Investigation.* 4th ed. Springfield, Ill.: Charles C Thomas, 2006. Indispensable volume for those conducting forensic investigations and forensic pathology. Includes comprehensive sections on specific cases along with their pathological findings.

Timmermans, Stefan. *Postmortem: How Medical Examiners Explain Suspicious Deaths.* Chicago: University of Chicago Press, 2006. Outstanding work on forensic pathology explains the autopsy process and gives case study examples.

**See also:** Autopsies; DNA typing; Drug confirmation tests; Exhumation; Forensic pathology; Forensic toxicology; Homicide; Medicine; Oral autopsy; Poisons and antidotes; Psychological autopsy; Quantitative and qualitative analysis of chemicals.

## Counterfeit-detection pens

**Definition:** Devices that use a chemical reaction to detect some types of counterfeit money.

**Significance:** Counterfeit-detection pens allow users with no significant training to check paper money for genuineness quickly and cheaply. These tools offer an effective way of combating counterfeiting that is done using computers, copiers, and printers instead of high-technology counterfeiting equipment.

The growing use and availability of technologically advanced devices for reproducing images on paper since the 1990's has created a new breed of counterfeiters, many of whom are amateurs. According to the U.S. Secret Service, the federal agency responsible for fighting attempts to counterfeit American currency, in 1995 less than 1 percent of the money that was confiscated as counterfeit in the United States was created using devices such as commonly available copiers and printers. By the year 2000, however, nearly half of all counterfeited U.S. bills that were confiscated had been created using such relatively simple methods, and it is believed that number has continued to increase. This is probably due in part to the increased use of these methods of attempted counterfeiting, especially by novice counterfeiters, and also because these methods are the most readily detectable. This large increase in the use of widely available technology such as color copiers and laser printers in counterfeiting meant that new methods of detection and prevention were needed.

The paper on which real currency is printed contains cotton and other fibers and does not contain significant amounts of starch. The types of paper used for photocopying and computer printing, in contrast, contain large amounts of starch. The chemical element iodine reacts in a predictable way when combined with starch, and this reaction was the basis for the pens that were developed to help detect counterfeit bills. The first such pen received a patent from the U.S. Patent Office on November 5, 1991. The user of a counterfeit-detection pen swipes the point of the pen across the surface of a piece of paper currency. Instead of ink, the pen contains a solution of iodine that will react with starch, turning dark brown or black. When such a pen is swiped on a bill that was counterfeited using copier or printer paper, an easily recognizable dark mark appears. If the bill has no starch present, the mark made by the iodine solution remains clear or turns a light amber color. Some counterfeit detection pens have colored dyes added to the iodine solution, so that users can easily tell which bills they have already verified. The color usually fades after a day or so, so that no permanent marks are left on the bills.

Counterfeit-detection pens are important tools in the ongoing battle against counterfeiting. They are inexpensive; usually less than five dollars each, and cashiers and other users need no significant training to be able to use them effectively. They are not, however, generally useful for detecting bills made by relatively sophisticated counterfeiting operations, which are more likely to use paper that is somewhat similar to that used in the printing of legitimate currency. The lack of a significant amount of starch in such bills makes them unlikely to be detected with the iodine solution used in counterfeit detection pens.

*Helen Colby*

### Further Reading

Fraudulent Image Solutions. *Counterfeit Detection Manual.* Fraudulent Image Solutions, 2007. A sophisticated handbook of counterfeit detection methods.

Mossman, Philip. *From Crime to Punishment: Counterfeit and Debased Currencies in Colonial and Pre-Federal North America.* New York: American Numismatic Society, 2013. An interesting historical look at how counterfeiting played a role in early America.

Powell, James. *Faking It!: A History of Counterfeiting in Canada.* Renfrew, Ontario: General Store Publishing House, 2013. A lively history of counterfeiting and the people who tried to cheat the system.

Williams, Marcela M. *Handicapping Currency Design: Counterfeit Deterrence and Visual Accessibility in the United States and Abroad.* St. Louis, MO: Federal Reserve Bank of St. Louis, 2007.

**See also:** Counterfeiting; Fax machine, copier, and printer analysis; Forgery; Identity theft; Paper; Questioned document analysis; Secret Service, U.S.

## Counterfeiting

**Definition:** Creation of false currency or other items that are intended to be used, sold, or passed off as original or real.

**Significance:** Counterfeiting, both of currency and of objects such as clothing, accessories, antiques, and pharmaceuticals, costs consumers, governments, and businesses hundreds of millions of dollars annually. Counterfeiters range from amateurs trying their luck to international rings of professional criminals organized solely for the purpose of manufacturing and selling counterfeit merchandise.

The counterfeiting of coins, currency, and artifacts for profit has been a problem for as long as such items have existed. Counterfeiting operations cost honest individuals and businesses hundreds of millions of dollars every year, and governments spend millions more in attempts to prevent and detect counterfeiting and on enforcement of laws against the practice. Methods for detecting counterfeiting and for gathering evidence to use in the prosecution of counterfeiters are constantly evolving as counterfeiters find new ways around them.

## History of Counterfeiting

The first currency ever produced is believed to have originated around 600 B.C.E. in Lydia, a Greek province located in what is today known as Turkey. The first attempts at counterfeiting soon followed. Ancient coins were generally made of precious metals, such as gold, silver, and copper, and were minted by local rulers or national governments. The process of making the coins usually involved heating small pieces of metal and then stamping them with likenesses of rulers, animals, or objects with inscriptions. Because precious metals were valued by weight, each coin was supposed to weigh a certain amount, corresponding with the prescribed amount of metal. The first attempts to alter or counterfeit coins were often made by individuals who removed small amounts of metal from the edges of legitimate coins and then melted the removed bits of metal together to make more coins. Some counterfeiters melted legitimate coins, mixed in other, less valuable, metals, and stamped the mixtures onto the new coins that were no longer pure.

The introduction of paper currency presented new opportunities for counterfeiters as well as new challenges for the groups charged with protecting the integrity of the currency. In the early United States, paper currency was not issued by the federal government; rather, more than sixteen hundred different banks printed their own currency. Each of these banks used a different design for each different denomination of bill, resulting in a total of more than seven thousand designs of bills that were valid currency. It is not hard to imagine how difficult it must have been to determine real bills from counterfeit ones, as people were constantly presented with bills that looked different from any other bills they had encountered before. During the Revolutionary War, the British capitalized on this situation by counterfeiting American currency at a very high rate.

The problem of widespread counterfeiting that was encouraged by varying bill designs was a concern of many early American government leaders, but it was not until 1862 that the U.S. government adopted a national currency and took over responsibility for printing that currency. Counterfeiting was reduced by this action, but it did not stop, and in 1865 the U.S. Secret Service was created to protect American currency and to investigate and combat counterfeiting.

Although the designs used in modern U.S. currency are much more complex than those used in the mid-nineteenth century, counterfeiting is still a significant problem. The Department of the Treasury is constantly seeking new ways to prevent and detect counterfeiting; frequent changes to the designs of bills are part of the department's efforts to make counterfeiting more difficult. The invention and widespread availability of computerized scanning devices and laser printers has allowed increasing numbers of amateur counterfeiters to experiment cheaply with producing false bills. The counterfeiting of items other than currency, such as clothing, accessories, antiques, and medicines, has also emerged as a widespread problem.

## Counterfeiting Currency

At one time, the counterfeiting of American currency was a labor-, time-, and equipment- intensive process. Many counterfeiters used hand-carved metal printing plates, special presses, and carefully created dyes to imitate the printing on legitimate bills. Although the end of the twentieth century saw a surge in counterfeiters' use of materials and technologies available to many people in their homes, the counterfeiting of U.S. currency remains a difficult process, as many complicated security measures have been introduced into modern bills.

Counterfeiters often use high-quality scanners with very high resolutions to create pictures of the bills they want to counterfeit. Such high-resolution images contain many of the features of the original bills, even many of the features intended to prevent counterfeiting. Such bills usually do not look exactly right, but many people do not examine the bills they receive very closely, especially in crowded, busy shopping areas or in dark places such as bars or nightclubs.

## Detection of Counterfeit Currency

Some types of counterfeiting can be detected

## Security Features in U.S. Currency

*The U.S. Department of the Treasury's Bureau of Engraving and Printing provides the following description of the anticounterfeiting security features added to several U.S. currency denominations since 2003.*

There are two distinct security features on the $5, $10, $20 and $50 bills the public can use to check the authenticity of their bills. Hold the bill up to the light and check for:

- **Watermark:** Each redesigned bill includes a watermark, which is a faint image within the paper itself. There are now two watermarks on the redesigned $5 bill. A large number "5" watermark is located to the right of the portrait, replacing the watermark portrait of President Lincoln found on the older design $5 bill. Its location is highlighted by a blank window incorporated into the background design. A second watermark—a column of three smaller "5"s—has been added to the new $5 bill design and is positioned to the left of the portrait. The watermarks for the $10, $20 and $50 bills are images of portraits located to the right of the larger portrait found on each denomination. On the $20

bill, the watermark is similar to the large portrait of President Jackson; on the $50 bill, there is a watermark portrait of President Grant; and on the $10 bill, there is a watermark portrait of Treasury Secretary Hamilton.

- **Security thread:** Each redesigned bill includes an embedded security thread in the paper, which is a plastic strip that runs vertically through each bill. If you look closely, you can see the letters "USA" followed by the number "5" printed in an alternating pattern along the thread on the new $5 bill, "USA TEN" printed on the $10 bill thread, "USA TWENTY" on the $20 bill thread, and "USA 50" on the $50 bill thread. The security thread is visible from both sides of the bill.

The higher-denomination $10, $20 and $50 bills have a third easy-to-check security feature:

- **Color-shifting ink:** Look at the number in the lower right-hand corner on the front of the new $10, $20 and $50 bills, depicting each bill's denomination. The color-shifting ink changes from copper to green when you tilt the bill up and down.

through the visual and tactile examination of the currency in question. Counterfeit bills created using printers and photocopiers do not feel like real bills, and close visual inspection of such bills often reveals lines that run together and images that appear to be slightly off in color. An important first line of defense against counterfeiting is proper training in recognizing the signs of counterfeit bills; bank tellers, cashiers, clerks, and anyone else who frequently accepts money in exchange for goods, services, or credit should receive such training. Many counterfeiting operations, especially those being run by relative amateurs, have been stopped after their bills were detected by just such individuals.

Not every clerk or cashier is likely to receive thorough training in spotting counterfeit bills, however, and during busy times with many cus-

tomers making transactions, it is often not reasonable for businesses to expect employees to inspect closely all bills that pass through their hands. For these reasons, devices have been developed that can make counterfeit detection easier and more efficient. Counterfeit-detection pens offer a fast, easy, and inexpensive way for persons with little or no training to check the authenticity of currency. Such pens contain iodine, which reacts with starch; when the iodine comes into contact with a counterfeit bill made on a printer or photocopier; the mark turns a dark color because of the starch in the paper. On genuine bills, these pens' marks do not change color because the paper in the bills does not contain significant amounts of starch. Ultraviolet counterfeit-detection machines are also fast and effective. Cashiers or tellers quickly view bills under the devices' ultraviolet lights to ensure that the bills contain the security threads found in genuine U.S. currency.

Over time, the U.S. Treasury has added many complex features to paper currency to help prevent counterfeiting. Among these is the use of special types of ink. For example, the denomination is printed in the lower left-hand corner of the front of each bill in a special optically variable ink, which appears to be different colors when the bill is viewed from different angles. This aspect of genuine bills is extremely difficult to reproduce. Another special ink used in the printing of genuine bills is magnetic ink, which can be detected by the bill-accepting devices in vending machines. Such machines will automatically reject bills on which they cannot detect the presence of such ink.

Counterfeit bills are almost always detected eventually. Some are detected very quickly by cashiers or tellers who notice telltale signs, such as bills that feel wrong or multiple bills with the same serial number. Others are not detected until long after the individuals who originally passed them are gone. Many businesses, including banks, scan bills regularly using a variety of devices available to detect counterfeits. The U.S. Treasury Department also regularly scans bills that come back to it, using machines that are extremely complex, with more than thirty separate sensors to help evaluate all aspects of a bill.

Cases of possible counterfeiting are investigated by the U.S. Secret Service. Although it is permissible to make copies of American currency for novelty purposes, the copies must differ from real currency in one or more of these ways: printed in black-and-white ink, 50 percent larger than real bills, or 25 percent smaller than real bills. Anything else can be considered counterfeiting, and the Secret Service has a strict zero-tolerance policy for counterfeiters. Counterfeiting is a felony offense in the United States, punishable by up to fifteen years in prison, a fine, or both. Bleaching and reprinting real currency with larger denominations is also considered counterfeiting and is punishable in the same way.

## Other Types of Counterfeiting

Noncurrency counterfeiting is also a crime of increasing concern in the United States and throughout the world. In general, in such counterfeiting an imitation of something of high monetary value—produced using lower quality, inferior materials and workmanship—is sold or passed off as the high-value item. In some cases, the aspects of the imitated items that give them value are their age or their historical significance rather than their strict monetary value.

One of the most common types of counterfeiting that involves noncurrency items is the counterfeiting of clothing and accessories. Brand-name merchandise is often expensive, and many consumers are happy to find low prices on what they believe to be brand-name goods. Designer and brand-name goods are often made of high-quality fabrics, metals, or plastics and bear trademarked names and logos. Such clothing and accessories are often relatively costly to produce, with the

---

## If You Receive a Counterfeit

*The U.S. Secret Service provides these instructions for anyone who receives a counterfeit U.S. bill.*

- Do not return it to the passer.
- Delay the passer if possible.
- Observe the passer's description, as well as that of any companions, and the license plate numbers of any vehicles used.
- Contact your local police department or United States Secret Service field office. These numbers can be found on the inside front page of your local telephone directory.
- Write your initials and the date in the white border areas of the suspect note.
- Limit the handling of the note. Carefully place it in a protective covering, such as an envelope.
- Surrender the note or coin only to a properly identified police officer or a U.S. Secret Service special agent.Gathering Forensic Evidence

cost including the value of the designs themselves.

The counterfeiters of designer and brandname clothing and accessories often have complex operations, often of a very large scale; they frequently operate outside the United States, where manufacturing and copyright regulations are not stringently enforced. They create very similar products out of inferior-quality components and infringe on trademarks and copyrights by using brand names and logos without permission. They then sell the products to consumers, leading the consumers to believe that the items are genuine. In many cases, counterfeiters attach fake labels and tags to their products to increase their plausibility. Some of these items are easily understood by most consumers to be fakes, such as the "Rolex" watches often sold on urban streets. Others, however, are much harder to identify, and even wary consumers might purchase counterfeit goods occasionally without ever realizing it.

In addition to clothing and accessories, toys, auto parts, and even edible goods such as baby formula have been known to be counterfeited. When goods such as these are counterfeited, they are not produced under the supervision of any regulatory body, so consumers who purchase and use these products are at serious risk of getting inferior, and even possibly dangerous, goods.

The rising prices of prescription drugs in the United States, in conjunction with the fact that large numbers of Americans have no health insurance or inadequate insurance, have led to what is probably the most dangerous of the many kinds of counterfeiting operations: the counterfeiting of medications. This is a problem that presents many different dangers to unaware consumers. Pharmaceutical companies spend millions of dollars developing new drugs and putting them through the extensive testing required before they can be approved for sale by the U.S. Food and Drug Administration. Although this process contributes to the high cost of drugs, it also allows consumers access to many lifesaving medications that have been tested for safety and effectiveness.

Counterfeit drugs, in contrast, may be manufactured under unsanitary conditions, as the factories that produce them are not regulated. Some counterfeit drugs are not even produced in factories at all; rather, they are made in home "laboratories" or warehouses. These products may not contain the ingredients that make the genuine drugs they imitate effective (the active ingredients), or they may contain the wrong amount. In some cases, unsanitary manufacturing conditions or the substitution of ingredients may lead to serious side effects and even death. Counterfeit drugs are often sold over the Internet, although they may also be sold in other locations as well. To protect themselves against the dangers of counterfeit drugs, consumers should always have prescriptions filled at state-licensed pharmacies and should be aware of what the medicines they receive should look like.

## Further Reading

Bhardwaj, Brij. Black Money: Created Through Smuggling and Counterfeiting to Fund Terrorism. New Delhi: Har-Anand Publications, 2013. A look at how counterfeit currency is created and used by terrorist groups to fund their illegal activities.

Craciun, Magdalena. *Material Culture and Authenticity: Fake Branded Fashion in Europe.* New York: Bloomsbury, 2014. An overview of issues of counterfeit fashion good and accessories, how they impact the global fashion trade, and what can be done to stop it.

Freeman, Michael, ed. *Law and Global Health: Current Legal Issues.* Oxford, UK: Oxford University Press, 2014. A look at a variety of global health issues including prescription medication counterfeiting.

Mossman, Philip. *From Crime to Punishment: Counterfeit and Debased Currencies in Colonial and Pre-Federal North America.* New York: American Numismatic Society, 2013. An interesting historical look at how counterfeiting played a role in early America.

Powell, James. *Faking It!: A History of Counterfeiting in Canada.* Renfrew, Ontario: General Store Publishing House, 2013. A lively history of counterfeiting and the people who tried to cheat the system.

**See also:** Art forgery; Counterfeit-detection

pens; Fax machine, copier, and printer analysis; Forgery; Identity theft; Microscopes; Paper; Photograph alteration detection; Questioned document analysis; Secret Service, U.S.

## Courts and forensic evidence

**Significance:** One of the most important reasons law enforcement investigators gather evidence is to prove guilt in a court of law. The techniques used by forensic scientists must be acceptable to courts in order for the evidence obtained through those techniques to be admissible. Forensic scientists must thus be familiar with the types of evidence and the techniques used to gather and examine evidence that are most likely to be admissible in court.

Any evidence that has been gained through the application of scientific means can be considered forensic evidence. However, not all forensic evidence is considered legitimate; in the United States, federal, state, and military courts have had varied histories in regard to different types of forensic evidence. Many types of forensic techniques have not always been accepted, and the legitimacy of many continues to be debated.

Before evidence gathered through the use of a particular forensic technique can be considered admissible in a court of law, the technique must first be proven reliable. Most often, forensic techniques become accepted through common law, which is the practice of following prior decisions made in court. A judge must vet any new forensic technique; usually, this means that an attorney presents the technique in court and argues that the evidence produced using the technique should be admitted in a case.

For example, one of the first courts in the United States to accept the use of DNA (deoxyribonucleic acid) evidence was the Circuit Court in Orange County, Florida. In 1987, Assistant State Attorney Tim Berry successfully argued that the DNA from semen found on a murder victim matched DNA from a blood sample taken from the defendant, Tommy Lee Andrews, and

that DNA comparison was a reliable method of establishing identity. To support his argument, Berry presented testimony by David Houseman, a research biologist from the Massachusetts Institute of Technology, and Michael Baird, a scientist at the laboratory where the samples were analyzed. Berry also compared the use of DNA matching to fingerprint identification, an already commonly accepted forensic method. In 1989, in the case of *People v. Castro*, the use of DNA for identification was seriously challenged in the New York Supreme Court. Over twelve weeks of testimony and arguments, the cases for and against DNA evidence were presented. In the end, the court found that the scientific community accepts DNA evidence and that DNA comparison is an accepted forensic technique. Since then, cases that use DNA evidence usually cite the case of *People v. Castro* to establish the admissibility of DNA evidence.

### Admissibility of New Forensic Techniques

Before judges will accept evidence produced by new types of techniques, the evidence must first pass several tests. The first of these is the traditional relevance test. To pass this test, evidence must bring some fact to light and must not tend to confuse jurors more often than it enlightens them. Beyond that test, differences exist between the federal admissibility standard and the standard used by many state courts, the *Frye* standard, established in the case of *Frye v. United States* in 1923. The *Frye* standard's "general acceptance" test requires merely that the techniques used to obtain or produce evidence must be generally accepted by the scientific community.

Federal courts, in contrast, as well as many state courts, now follow a standard established by the U.S. Supreme Court case of *Daubert v. Merrell Dow Pharmaceuticals* in 1993. The so-called *Daubert* standard has multiple parts: for evidence to be admissible, the technique used to obtain or produce it must be tested and peer-reviewed, the technique's margin of error must be known and controlled, and the technique must be accepted within a relevant scientific community. The determination of whether these tests have been met is the responsibility of the trial judge. Since the *Daubert* decision, a great deal of debate has taken place concerning the role of judges as the "gatekeepers" of evidence. Many experts have lauded the decision as a way to keep pseudoscience out of the courtroom, whereas others have argued that *Daubert* gives judges too much individual discretion over what constitutes acceptable expert testimony.

Unlike fingerprint identification and DNA identification, other forensic techniques have not been accepted by U.S. courts. In 1999, a Washington appeals court had to address an unusual new identification technique used by investigators in the case of *State of Washington v. Kunze*. An intruder who had killed two people in a house before robbing the house of most of its valuables had left a full impression of one of his ears on a wall in a hallway at the crime scene. An investigator from the Washington State Crime Laboratory was able to lift the ear print from the wall using a technique normally used for fingerprints. This print was compared with ear prints taken from the suspect, David Wayne Kunze, and a criminologist from the laboratory, Michael Grubb, concluded that the print from the wall was a likely match to the suspect. During pretrial hearings, however, Grubb admitted that he had never worked with ear prints for identification before and that he had not seen any studies about how often a particular ear shape might occur in the general population. Even though several other identification experts were called in, the prosecution could not establish that ear-print identification was generally accepted by the scientific community (the court in Washington followed the *Frye* test, not the *Daubert* test), and the court refused to accept ear-print identification as a legitimate forensic technique.

There are types of forensic evidence that were accepted by U.S. courts for years and have later been found to be unreliable. In 1879, a French criminologist named Alphonse Bertillon invented a system of identifying individuals based on a series of physical measurements of various body parts. It was believed for many years that each individual had specific body part measurements, and that no two people shared the exact same set of Bertillon measurements. In an age before photography was common, police and judges used these measure-ments to determine identification of criminals. This system was in use until 1903, when a man named Will West was sentenced to prison, only to have it discovered that another man with the same name and the exact same Bertillon mea-surements was already being held in that same prison. This provided sudden, convincing evi-dence that the Bertillon system was flawed. It also, provided positive evidence for the useful-ness of the fingerprint method of identification, as it was discovered that the two men did have clearly differentiable fingerprints.

Not all discredited forensic techniques are in the distant past. One forensic technique that has been discredited, comparative bulletlead analysis (CBLA), was long practiced by the Fed-eral Bureau of Investigation (FBI) and had been accepted by U.S. courts since the 1960s. The technique involves comparing the composition of the metal in a bullet that was used in a crime with the composition of the metal in other bul-lets to establish the origins of the crime scene bullet. The technique is based on the idea that if the composition of two bullets is the same, then the bullets must have been made by the same manufacturer on the same day, using the same batch of material. This technique was used to produce the key evidence in a 1986 case against a man in North Carolina named Lee Wayne Hunt. He was convicted of two counts of murder and had been in prison for more than twenty years. However, in a 2004 report on a study re-quested by the FBI, the National Research Council of the National Academy of Sciences stated that CBLA is unreliable and can produce misleading results. Because of this, many peo-ple have suggested that cases like the one against Hunt should be reviewed. On Septem-ber 1, 2005, the FBI issued a statement an-nouncing that it would no longer conduct bulletlead analysis. With that statement a fo-rensic technique that had been popular for more than four decades was no longer deemed an ac-ceptable investigatory methodology.

Even forensic techniques that have come to be thoroughly accepted have not always been viewed as so reliable. In 1873, in the case of *Tome v. Parkersburg Railroad Company*, the court rejected photographic evidence because it said that photographs produced only "secondary impressions of the original" and that they were susceptible to changes in lighting. Only one year later, in the case of *Udderzook v. Commonwealth*, the Supreme Court of Pennsylvania found that photographs taken by an insurance company should be admitted as evidence. These photographs were used to prove that a body found in the woods was that of a particular man whom the insurance company had photographed when he took out his policy. The court wrote, "The [photographic] process has become one in general use, so common that we cannot refuse to take judicial cognizance of it as a proper means of producing correct likeness." Since that day, attorneys have cited the case of *Udderzook v. Commonwealth* when presenting photographic evidence in court.

### Federal, State, and Military Standards

Case law, also known as common law, is not the only source of determination for admissibility of evidence in court. In 1934, the U.S. Congress passed the Rules Enabling Act, which gave the U.S. Supreme Court the power to prescribe rules of practice and procedure and rules of evidence for the federal courts. Following this mandate, in 1965 Chief Justice Earl Warren appointed an advisory committee to write a comprehensive federal code of evidence. Over a ten-year period the committee debated, researched, drafted, heard public commentary, rewrote, and finally issued its code, the Federal Rules of Evidence (FRE). This code was debated in both houses of Congress and signed into law on January 2, 1975. The advisory committee was then disbanded and the rules were left unreviewed until 1992, when the Evidence Advisory Committee was re-created to oversee revisions to the FRE. Since that time, the committee has made few substantive changes to the code. The FRE

is the codification of decades of precedence, and it is the core of admissibility standards in federal courts.

The FRE applies to all federal courts throughout the United States, but cases tried in state courts are subject to the states' own individual standards of evidence. For the most part, states have followed the federal standards, but some, such as California, have entirely separate sets of rules. Even in states that follow the federal standards, some important differences exist. For example, some states (including Connecticut, Massachusetts, and Texas) follow the federal *Daubert* test, whereas others (including California, Florida, and New York) continue to apply the *Frye* test; still others (such as Delaware, Oregon, and Vermont) follow their own standards regarding the admissibility of forensic evidence. It is important for forensic scientists to understand the evidence standards that apply to their particular states.

In September of 1980, the U.S. military established its own separate rules of evidence to apply to courts-martial and other military courts. Although these rules were designed to

## Gathering Forensic Evidence

Not all forensic evidence that is of a type generally accepted by courts is accepted by the courts in every instance. In addition to a wide variety of rules and common law governing the types of evidence that may be admitted, there are also a variety of rules governing the way in which such evidence can be collected. Evidence that is collected illegally, for example, after a police search for which an appropriate warrant was not issued, is not admissible.

In *Silverthorne Lumber Co. v. United States,* the judge created an exclusionary rule, an extension of which is sometimes referred to as the "fruit of the poisonous tree" rule. This rule disallows any evidence that is gathered using information that was illegally obtained. For example, if during an illegal wiretap a suspect was overheard giving the location of stolen goods, and using this information a warrant was obtained to search the area the suspect mentioned, even if the stolen goods are found, that evidence will not be admissible in court, because the initial wiretap that lead to their finding was illegal. The initial wiretap is the poisonous tree, and all the fruit it bares is thus also tainted. This type of issue can seriously affect the outcome of a trial, and forensic experts must always be extremely careful to obtain evidence through appropriate and legal methods.

follow the FRE closely, there are some noteworthy differences. One such difference stems from the 2005 Detainee Treatment Act, which says that military judges must, for statements made after the act was passed, determine whether the statements were obtained through cruel, inhuman, or degrading treatment before the statements can be considered as evidence. Some significant differences also exist between the FRE and military rules regarding hearsay, because witnesses in military trials are likely to be foreign nationals who are not amenable to the process.

The American legal system has had a difficult relationship with new forensic techniques because of the important role that forensic evidence can play. A case can turn on a single piece of evidence, such as the composition of the metal in a bullet, and the justice system must be careful in the decisions it makes about allowing particular evidence-gathering practices and the admissibility of specific kinds of expert testimony. If a process is not carefully vetted and established, then injustices are likely to occur.

*Robert Bockstiegel*

### Further Reading

Cox, Steven, William McCamey, & Gene Scaramella. *Introduction to Policing.* Thousand Oaks, CA: SAGE Publications, 2014. A guide to criminal investigations that covers investigatory techniques and how evidence is used in court.

Heard, Brian. *Forensic Ballistics in Court: Interpretation and Presentation of Firearms Evidence.* Malden, MA: Blackwell-Wiley, 2013. An in-depth guide to all types of firearm evidence.

Marquez-Grant, Nicholas & Julie Roberts, eds. *Forensic Ecology Handbook: From Crime Scene to Court.* Hoboken, NJ: John Wiley & Sons, 2012. A comprehensive overview of all aspects of forensic ecology.

Nesca, Marc & Thomas Dalby. *Forensic Interviewing in Criminal Court Matters: A Guide for Clinicians.* Springfield, IL: Charles C. Thomas, 2013. A handbook aimed at clinicians that discusses a wide variety of issues and techniques in forensic interviewing.

Oriola, Sallavaci. *The Impact of Scientific Evidence on the Criminal Trial: The Case of DNA Evidence.* New York: Routledge, 2014. A fascinating look at how DNA evidence changed the nature of criminal trials

**See also:** ALI standard; *Daubert v. Merrell Dow Pharmaceuticals*; Direct versus circumstantial evidence; Drug and alcohol evidence rules; Evidence processing; Expert witnesses; Eyewitness testimony; Federal Rules of Evidence; *Frye v. United States*; *Holland v. United States*; Legal competency; *Miranda v. Arizona*; *People v. Lee*; Quality control of evidence; *Tarasoff* rule; Trial consultants.

# Crack cocaine

**Definition:** Form of cocaine that transforms into rocklike chips during its creation and is believed to produce a more intense high than powder cocaine.

**Significance:** Crack cocaine emerged during the early 1980's, and a seeming epidemic of use of the drug led to an intense media frenzy in the United States. Powder cocaine had been in use in the United States for many years, but crack cocaine quickly became the more popular of the two because of its cheap price and intense high. The hysteria surrounding the drug was in part a reaction to the amount of systemic violence created by crack cocaine dealers establishing territories within the black market.

Crack cocaine remains one of the most problematic drugs in the United States because of its impacts on users and their communities. Significant resources are spent on attempts to decrease the supply of crack cocaine within the United States through law-enforcement efforts, to decrease demand for the drug through education and prevention programs, and to decrease the number of those addicted to it through drug treatment. Cocaine is listed as a Schedule II drug under the Controlled Substances Act of 1970, meaning that it has a high potential for abuse, is used medically with restrictions, and can lead to severe physical and psychological dependence.

## Production of Crack

Crack cocaine is a pure form of cocaine that is manufactured by a simpler method than that used to create freebase cocaine. In making freebase cocaine, which was popular in the 1970's, powder cocaine is dissolved in water with ammonia and ether added; a solid cocaine base is then separated from the solution and used for smoking. Freebase cocaine was overshadowed by crack during the 1980's.

Unlike other forms of cocaine, crack does not include hydrochloride salt. In the manufacture of crack, cocaine is mixed with water and baking soda; this mixture is then heated, and when it cools, cocaine "rocks" are formed. The rocks can be smoked in pipes, heated and then inhaled, or even injected. One reason for crack cocaine's popularity is that, unlike powder cocaine, it can be produced in small quantities; thus users at all income levels can buy the drug.

## Effects of the Drug

Most crack users typically place the drug in a glass pipe with a steel wool filter and heat the pipe from below. When smoked, crack cocaine passes into a user's bloodstream much faster than cocaine that is snorted. The drug is then transported to the brain, where it interferes with a neurotransmitter, or chemical messenger, called dopamine. Dopamine sends signals of pleasure from neuron to neuron during pleasant activities. It does so by attaching to the synapse of the neuron, sending a message, and then being reabsorbed back into the neuron. Crack cocaine disrupts this process and slows the absorption of dopamine, creating longer-lasting feelings of pleasure. Crack is thus considered to be a stimulant drug because it causes dopamine to build up and send exaggerated feelings of exhilaration. Users generally begin to feel the effects of crack cocaine in fifteen seconds, compared with fifteen to twenty minutes for cocaine that is snorted. Cocaine is a highly addictive drug, and there seems to be a higher correlation between addiction and cocaine in its crack form as opposed to its powder form. Researchers

have not been able to rule out extraneous factors that may affect this correlation, however, such as the income levels of the users of crack cocaine. In other words, it has not been determined conclusively whether crack cocaine is more highly addictive than powder cocaine or whether its users, who are generally poor, may be more susceptible to drug addiction than users of other forms of cocaine.

The use of crack cocaine is associated with many of the same physical problems found in users of powder cocaine: constricted blood vessels, increased blood pressure, and risk of heart attack and stroke. Crack cocaine users may also experience extreme respiratory problems, including lung trauma and coughing. Crack use can also affect the digestive tract, causing users to lose their appetites or to feel nauseated. In large amounts, crack can make users feel restless, anxious, or even paranoid.

Unlike heroin addiction, for which treatment with methadone maintenance is available, addiction to crack cocaine has no proven effective medical treatment, although a number of medications have begun to be investigated for this purpose. Other treatment strategies are used to counteract crack addiction, including cognitive therapy, psychotherapy, and twelve-step programs.

*Brion Sever and Ryan Kelly*

## Further Reading

Brownstein, Henry. *The Rise and Fall of a Violent Crime Wave: Crack Cocaine and the Social Construction of a Crime Problem*. Guilderland, N.Y.: Harrow & Heston, 1996. Examines the crack cocaine crime wave of the 1980's as well as the responses of the mass media and governments. Discusses the crime problem posed by crack cocaine as a social construction and analyzes the reasons behind the phenomenon.

Cooper, Edith. *The Emergence of Crack Cocaine Abuse*. New York: Novinka Books, 2002. Discusses the evolution of crack cocaine, its emergence in the black market during the early 1980's, and the factors that led to the drug epidemic that surrounded crack cocaine during the mid- to late 1980's. Also reviews the process by which crack cocaine is made and the effects the drug has on users' health.

Smith, Frederick P., ed. *Handbook of Forensic Drug Analysis.* Burlington, Mass.: Elsevier Academic Press, 2005. Focuses on methods used to detect drugs in the human body. Presents analyses of a number of drugs, including cocaine, and discusses their chemical properties and the ways they are identified in tests.

Washton, Arnold. *Cocaine Addiction: Treatment, Recovery, and Relapse Prevention.* New York: W. W. Norton, 1991. Focuses on some of the causes of crack addiction, including the psychological state of the cocaine addict. Discusses the various stages of addiction as well as addiction treatment.

**See also:** Amphetamines; Antianxiety agents; Drug abuse and dependence; Drug classification; Drug confirmation tests; Drug Enforcement Administration, U.S.; Drug paraphernalia; Harrison Narcotic Drug Act of 1914; Illicit substances; Psychotropic drugs; Stimulants.

## Crime laboratories

**Definition:** Public and private facilities at which forensic specialists analyze materials collected from crime scenes for purposes of identification and interpretation.

**Significance:** Since the founding of the first such facility in France in 1910, crime laboratories have employed a scientific approach to dealing with evidence collected by crime scene investigators. The work conducted by crime labs provides invaluable assistance to criminal investigators and legal professionals around the world.

Forensic scientists, also known as criminalists, apply scientific methods to the analysis, identification, and interpretation of evidence gathered at crime scenes. They conduct much of their work at crime laboratories, facilities that are specially equipped with the technological and other tools they need to carry out the careful examination of evidence.

### Sherlock Holmes and Early Crime Laboratories

A direct connection can be drawn between the detective novels of Sir Arthur Conan Doyle and the establishment of the first crime laboratory. Renowned for the creation of the fictional detective Sherlock Holmes, Doyle was well trained in science. He was a practicing physician with a strongly held conviction that scientific method can be applied logically and effectively to solving crimes. In 1887, Doyle introduced the world to Sherlock Holmes and his sidekick, Dr. Watson. He continued to write about them for the next thirty-five years.

Among Doyle's most ardent fans was Edmond Locard, a Frenchman who devoured the Sherlock Holmes stories. Convinced of the efficacy of applying scientific method to solving crimes, Locard established the world's first forensic crime laboratory, the Institute of Criminalistics for the Rhone Prefecture of the University of Lyon in France. This early laboratory occupied modest quarters in the Lyon courthouse. Locard, whose laboratory equipment consisted of a microscope and a spectroscope, gained credibility by using scientific means to solve a puzzle surrounding the counterfeiting of coins in the Lyon area. Obtaining some clothes belonging to a suspect, he extracted from them samples of dirt in which he found traces of metal that matched the metal in the counterfeit coins. This discovery caused the suspect to confess and gave people confidence in Locard's methods.

The first crime laboratory in the United States was established in Los Angeles by August Vollmer in 1923. It was not until 1932 that the Federal Bureau of Investigation (FBI), under the leadership of J. Edgar Hoover, established its first crime laboratory. From modest beginnings, equipped with only a microscope and minimal ultraviolet light equipment, the FBI Laboratory grew to become the most extensive and sophisticated crime laboratory in the world.

### Discovering and Preserving Evidence

One of the most important elements in gathering evidence from the scene of a crime or accident is the preservation of that evidence so that it is not contaminated following its discovery. For each piece of evidence, a record (referred to as the chain of custody) is kept of every single person who deals with the evidence from the time it is discovered to the day the evidence is used in court or in some other official venue.

Evidence must be gathered by people trained in forensic science techniques. Before evidence samples are collected for transportation to a crime laboratory, investigators examine the evidence as they find it at the crime or accident scene, which the police preserve as nearly as they can, making it inaccessible to unauthorized or untrained people. In the early stages of an investigation, the scene is photographed from a variety of angles and careful measurements are taken; a forensic artist also sketches the scene.

Among the kinds of evidence that criminalists gather are fingerprints. Surfaces that may hold prints are carefully dusted with a powder that creates strong contrasts in the ridges and valleys of such prints. Fingerprints that are uncovered in this way are first photographed and then are lifted from the surface with a sterile adhesive tape and transferred to a fingerprint card. Visible prints, such as those found on surfaces in blood or grease, are photographed and transferred to fingerprint cards.

Criminalists also collect tire-track and footprint evidence, measuring and photographing such impressions and often making plaster casts of them to preserve them for analysis. Trace evidence—substances such as hairs, fibers, and fragments of glass or paint—is collected with vacuum cleaners specially designed for this purpose. Items such as knives, shell casings, and instruments that may have been used as weapons are carefully collected so that any fingerprints or traces of blood, hair, or flesh on them are preserved. Each piece of evidence collected is properly packaged and carefully labeled before it is transported to the laboratory for analysis.

## Laboratory Equipment and Techniques

Crime laboratories are equipped with a variety of specialized microscopes that are used to examine closely the materials found at crime scenes. Stereoscopic binocular microscopes are essential for the examination of trace elements detected at the scenes of crimes and are also used to examine and classify handwriting and text created by typewriters and computer printers.

Polarizing microscopes enable forensic scientists to examine and identify minerals, narcotics, and other elements by enlarging their crystal forms. Essential to those engaged in ballistic examinations, comparison microscopes enable forensic scientists to compare the markings on shells and casings found at crime scenes with other samples, possibly linking them to particular weapons.

Using spectrophotometry, investigators can uncover light and heat rays that the human eye cannot see. The spectrophotometer shows the patterns of such rays, and by examining these patterns criminalists can detect alterations on documents, such as erasures, that may indicate fraud or forgery. The gas chromatograph, a sophisticated instrument that identifies the constituent components of substances and measures each component, is used to identify many different unknown substances. It is also the instrument that forensic scientists employ to determine the blood alcohol levels of persons suspected of driving under the influence.

The analysis of DNA (deoxyribonucleic acid) evidence has become an increasingly important part of the work of crime laboratories. By comparing DNA profiles derived from the DNA extracted from biological materials—such as blood, semen, saliva, and hair—found at crime scenes with the DNA profiles of known persons, forensic scientists can identify victims, link suspects to crimes, and exclude innocent persons from suspicion.

## Training of Crime Lab Personnel

Nearly all law-enforcement officers receive some training in identifying and handling the evidence with which they come into contact at crime scenes. Because of the growing level of sophistication of the work done in crime laboratories, many colleges and universities in the United States have established special programs designed to train forensic scientists.

Generally, one requirement for employment in a crime laboratory in the United States is an undergraduate degree in chemistry or in some aspect of criminology. The undergraduate preparation of forensic scientists usually includes extensive course work in a variety of chemistry subdisciplines as well as courses in anatomy, physics, biology, geology, and psychology.

Some major American universities offer training in forensic science that leads to a master of science degree; some offer doctorates in criminalistics or forensic science. Many institutions of higher learning provide short training courses in forensic science for law-enforcement personnel and for practicing attorneys; these are helpful for persons within the criminal justice system who lack the typical undergraduate background in forensics or who seek to update their training.

Most forensic scientists in the United States work for local, state, or federal public agencies, although some are private consultants for businesses, industry groups, or other private organizations. The American Academy of Forensic Sciences encourages training and research in the field. Its quarterly publication, the *Journal of Forensic Sciences*, informs readers about current research in all branches of the forensic sciences. The American Society of Crime Laboratory Directors, a professional society open to past and current laboratory directors and forensic science educators, was established in 1974 to grant accreditation to crime laboratories that voluntarily invite examiners to evaluate their programs.

*R. Baird Shuman*

## Media Perceptions Versus Real-Life Caseloads

As crime labs have become increasingly important in the investigation of crime, they have faced a growing number of challenges. One of these is overwhelming caseloads and limited personnel and budgets. In 2002, for example, the fifty largest crime labs in the United States received more than 1.2 million requests for services. Although these labs had 4,300 full-time employees, they had a backlog of 270,000 requests by the end of that year. As a result of such backlogs, and contrary to what is often depicted in popular television shows such as *CSI: Crime Scene Investigation*, real-life law-enforcement agencies must often wait more than a month to obtain the results of scientific analyses. This situation contributes to slowing down the criminal justice system's response to crimes. The delays allow some guilty people to escape justice, and suspects who are in fact innocent are detained for longer periods than they would be if forensic analyses could be performed more quickly.

*Phyllis B. Gerstenfeld*

### Further Reading

Baden, Michael, and Marion Roach. *Dead Reckoning: The New Science of Catching Killers*. New York: Simon & Schuster, 2001. Provides detailed information on how law-enforcement agencies track down criminals through the use of modern forensic techniques. Shows how Sherlock Holmes stories led to the founding of the first crime laboratory in 1910.

Bass, Bill, and Jon Jefferson. *Death's Acre: Inside the Legendary Forensic Lab the Body Farm Where the Dead Do Tell Tales*. New York: G. P. Putnam's Sons, 2003. Presents a fascinating account of the University of Tennessee's Body Farm, the facility that Bass established to study the process of decomposition of the human body.

Bell, Suzanne. *Encyclopedia of Forensic Science*. New York: Facts On File, 2004. Provides a brief and incisive account of the development of crime laboratories in France, the United States, and other countries.

Campbell, Andrea. *Forensic Science: Evidence, Clues, and Investigation*. Philadelphia: Chelsea House, 2000. Overview of the forensic sciences intended for young adult readers includes information about the genesis and importance of crime laboratories.

Conklin, Barbara Gardner, Robert Gardner, and Dennis Shortelle. *Encyclopedia of Forensic Science: A Compendium of Detective Fact and Fiction*. Westport, Conn.: Oryx Press, 2002. Includes an overall account of crime laboratories and also deals separately with the FBI Laboratory.

Innes, Brian. *Bodies of Evidence*. Pleasantville,

N.Y.: Reader's Digest Association, 2000. Presents extensive forensic case studies and devotes a section to the establishment of crime labs in England.

James, Stuart H., and Jon J. Nordby, eds. *Forensic Science: An Introduction to Scientific and Investigative Techniques*. 2d ed. Boca Raton, Fla.: CRC Press, 2005. Section III contains eleven chapters that focus on the functions of crime laboratories.

**See also:** American Academy of Forensic Sciences; American Society of Crime Laboratory Directors; Analytical instrumentation; CODIS; Control samples; Environmental Measurements Laboratory; European Network of Forensic Science Institutes; Federal Bureau of Investigation Forensic Science Research and Training Center; Federal Bureau of Investigation Laboratory; Forensic Science Service; National Crime Information Center; Quality control of evidence; University of Tennessee Anthropological Research Facility.

## Crime scene cleaning

**Definition:** Professional cleaning and decontamination of a crime scene, including disposing of biologically or chemically hazardous materials and restoring the site to habitable condition.

**Significance:** Crime scene cleaners restore a site after forensic investigators have documented the event, collected evidence, and released the scene. Sometimes, in the course of complete restoration of a crime scene, professional cleaners uncover forensic evidence previously overlooked by investigators.

Police and forensic investigators officially release a crime scene after it has been documented and all victims and evidence have been physically removed. Such a scene, particularly if it was the site of a violent crime or drug-related activity, may then be uninhabitable and unusable until it has been cleaned by specialists. The owners of crime scene locations may hire professional cleaning services to avoid the psychological and emotional impact of cleaning these sites themselves. In addition, crime scenes often pose a hazard of contamination by blood-borne pathogens, microscopic organisms that can cause disease, including hepatitis B, hepatitis C, and human immunodeficiency virus (HIV). In the United States, federal law prohibits employers from exposing workers to blood-borne pathogens unless they have been trained to handle blood; thus commercial enterprises, landlords, and business owners usually hire specialists rather than have their janitorial staff restore crime scenes where blood has been spilled.

Crime scene cleaning is sometimes referred to as biohazard remediation, bioremediation, crime and trauma scene decontamination, or biorecovery. Crime scene cleaners are also called biorecovery technicians or trauma scene practitioners. Technicians in the United States can be trained and certified by occupational groups according to standards set by the U.S. Occupational Safety and Health Administration (OSHA).

Crime scene cleaning involves complete disinfection of floors, walls, ceilings, plumbing, and furniture, where possible, and safe disposition of irretrievably damaged furniture and personal items. Potentially infectious substances—such as bone fragments, blood and other bodily fluids, human tissue, and insects—are isolated, packaged, and disposed of in accordance with state and federal regulations for handling biohazardous material. Chemicals left behind by emergency medical personnel or investigators are completely removed.

Biohazard technicians also clean areas where suicides have occurred or where bodies have decomposed over time, accident scenes, and places damaged by animal waste or remains, mold, water or fire, odors, and chemicals left behind by illegal drug manufacturing (typically the poisonous substances used to make methamphetamine). Some are prepared to respond to bioterrorism, decontaminating areas where disease-bearing bacteria have been deployed.

Beyond surface cleaning, professional crime scene cleaners search for bodily fluids and other materials hidden under floors, in plumbing, and underneath or behind installed furnishings. They may therefore find evidence relevant to an investigation that was not immediately apparent to police or forensic investigators. Crime scene cleaners should be trained to identify and report such findings; otherwise, their thorough cleaning and remediation of a scene will completely destroy any evidence left behind.

*Maureen Puffer-Rothenberg*

### Further Reading

Cooperman, Stephanie. *Biohazard Technicians: Life on a Trauma Scene Cleanup Crew*. New York: Rosen, 2004.

Jacobs, Andrew. "Cleaning Needed, in the Worst Way." *The New York Times*, November 22, 2005, pp. B1-B6.

Reavill, Gil. *Aftermath, Inc.: Cleaning up After CSI Goes Home*. New York: Gotham Books, 2007.

**See also:** Bacterial biology; Blood agents; Blood residue and bloodstains; Chemical Biological Incident Response Force, U.S.; Crime scene protective gear; Decomposition of bodies; Decontamination methods; Illicit substances; Pathogen transmission.

## Crime scene documentation

**Definition:** All documents, notes, sketches, and photographs generated in the processing and recording of a crime scene.

**Significance:** The very act of processing a crime scene alters the scene. The purpose of crime scene documentation is to create as accurate a record as possible of all information about the scene that may be relevant to the investigation. This documentation subsequently provides the only permanent record of the scene and is the only way of conveying information about the scene to investigators, scientists, lawyers, and the court.

Any type of environment or location has the po-

tential to become a crime scene. Crimes can occur in urban, suburban, or rural areas, indoors or outdoors, in commercial or residential buildings, in public or private areas, in sparse, clean, tidy locations or hideously filthy and cluttered locations. Each crime scene, and each crime event, is in some way unique, and, correspondingly, each scene has unique aspects that are relevant to the investigation.

One of the primary purposes of the crime scene examination is to produce accurate and comprehensive records of everything at the crime scene that has the potential to be relevant to the current criminal investigation and any subsequent prosecution. The information in the records must be sufficient to support any expert interpretations, conclusions, or opinions.

At the early stages of an investigation, the information available to the scene examiner may be very limited. It may be that the only thing known is that a body is in an alley. It is often difficult, sometimes impossible, to predict how an investigation will progress and develop over time. Some item, fact, or detail that does not appear to be particularly significant during the scene examination may turn out to be crucial. Because poor documentation of a crime scene can greatly affect the investigation's progress and outcome and, ultimately, any trial that may eventuate, crime scene examinations and their resulting documentation have become increasingly comprehensive.

### Background Scene Information

The first law-enforcement officer to arrive at a crime scene may be one of the few individuals to see the scene in a pristine condition. The observations of that first officer often direct the actions or the focus of any investigators subsequently involved with examination of the scene. For example, the first officer on the scene could observe a trail of shoe prints leading away from the scene on grass wet with early-morning dew, whereas scene examiners attending later in the day would not be able to see those prints. If such observations are not documented appropriately and conveyed to the scene examiners, important aspects of the scene exam may be missed.

From the moment a crime scene is made secure, it is important that investigators are able to demonstrate that control of any items within the scene has been maintained. Scene logs are used to record information regarding who has had access to the scene and therefore access to items within it. The chain of custody of scene items begins at the scene and is recorded in exhibit registers, or evidence logs.

## Types of Documentation

Crime scene documentation can encompass a huge range of documents or records. In principle, records should be kept of all observations made and any actions taken by all persons involved in securing and processing the crime scene. This includes any handwritten notes and notes transcribed from audio recordings, any photographs taken, and any sketches made by investigators. Depending on the case circumstances, it may also include any notebook entries, or daily job sheets, from the first attending law-enforcement officers or paramedics, scene guard logs, and records from others who have had some contact or involvement with the scene that was peripheral to the actual scene examination.

Photography is a significant part of recording the crime scene, and comprehensive photographing of the scene prior to and during the scene examination is essential. The use of video recording of scenes can also be of value.

Where it was once considered sufficient for crime scene examiners to make notes regarding their observations and the various things they found at a crime scene, it has become increasingly common for examiners to make notes also regarding things they do not find. That is, absences of some kinds of items are often recorded, particularly where those absences allow conclusions to be drawn about actions or events that could subsequently be claimed or suggested.

## End Users

In many cases, criminal trials take place months, or even years, after the crimes occurred. It is not realistic to expect anyone to remember accurately the minute details of a crime scene that he or she processed long ago when presenting evidence in court. Consequently, crime scene examiners are allowed the use their notes to aid their recall when they appear as witnesses. In fact, such notes are often deemed more accurate than an individual's recall if significant time has passed.

For many years, investigators' notes were precisely that—their own notes. Gradually, however, it has become accepted that crime scene notes are made to be reviewed, or scrutinized, by others.

In many crime laboratories, peer review of notes is a standard quality-assurance practice. Correspondingly, it is expected that notes should be clear and comprehensive enough not only to support any findings, interpretations, and conclusions but also to allow other suitably qualified colleagues to reach those same findings, interpretations, and conclusions independently. Defense analysts may also request copies of scene notes for review. They rely solely on the information, or lack thereof, contained in the scene documentation.

Reviews of older unsolved crimes, or "cold cases," are becoming increasingly commonplace. These case reviews, many of which are driven by advances in technology, have revealed that gradual alterations and improvements have occurred over time in the practices of crime scene documentation.

As is true of many things, some of the practices deemed acceptable as recently as ten years ago have come to be seen as lacking by more current standards. Crime scene examiners can make an effort to "future-proof" their scene examination notes by documenting every scene as thoroughly as possible.

*R. K. Morgan-Smith*

## Further Reading

Elliot, Douglas. "Crime Scene Examination." In *Expert Evidence: Law, Practice, Procedure, and Advocacy*, edited by Ian Freckelton and Hugh Selby. 3d ed. Pyrmont, N.S.W.: Lawbook, 2005. Covers broad aspects of crime scene examination, including scene processing and recording.

O'Hara, Charles E., and Gregory L. O'Hara. *Fundamentals of Criminal Investigation*. 7th ed. Springfield, Ill.: Charles C Thomas, 2003. Detailed work devotes significant discussion to the processes of crime scene documentation.

Saferstein, Richard. *Criminalistics: An Intro-*

*duction to Forensic Science.* 9th ed. Upper Saddle River, N.J.: Pearson Prentice Hall, 2007. Good general text covers a broad range of topics, including crime scene examination and documentation.

Walton, Richard H. *Cold Case Homicides: Practical Investigative Techniques.* Boca Raton, Fla.: CRC Press, 2006. Comprehensive volume on cold-case investigation includes discussion of the use of original crime scene documentation when old, unsolved cases are examined.

**See also:** Chain of custody; Crime scene investigation; Crime scene measurement; Crime scene reconstruction and staging; Crime scene sketching and diagramming; Evidence processing; Forensic photography; Quality control of evidence.

---

# Crime scene investigation

**Definition:** Process of recognizing, preserving, collecting, analyzing, and reconstructing evidence located at a crime scene

**Significance:** By using proven principles and procedures to ensure that all physical evidence at a crime scene is discovered and analyzed, crime scene investigators help to clarify exactly what happened there. The information they gather can link possible suspects to the scene or eliminate them from suspicion.

"Crime scene investigation" is an umbrella term often used to refer to a range of methods and techniques applied during a criminal investigation. Focused on the discovery, recovery, and processing of evidence, crime scene investigation applies reasoned principles in the pursuit of truth. From the moment a crime is discovered until the final appeal in court, the methods and techniques employed during crime scene investigation are under scrutiny.

Modern crime scene investigators combine the logic of fictional detective Sherlock Holmes with advanced scientific techniques in identifying and processing evidence. The basic crime scene procedures used by forensic scientists focus on physical evidence recognition, documentation, collection, packaging, preservation, and analysis. A systematic approach to the investigative task reduces the likelihood of error and improves the investigators' chances of attaining the ultimate goal of justice.

## Crime Scene Classification

Crime scenes are traditionally classified based on location, complexity, and relation to the crime in question. The first step in classifying a crime scene is to define the outer boundaries of the physical location. These boundaries establish the geographic limits within which the initial crime will be investigated; this area is known as the primary scene.

The nature of some crimes may involve more than one physical scene, and these are often identified as the secondary, tertiary, and subsequent scenes. For example, in a murder case the death may occur in one location and the body of the victim may be found in another. The primary scene is where the killing took place; the secondary scene is the location where the body was discovered. Both scenes may reveal relevant evidence, and the processing of both constitutes an important part of the criminal investigation.

Crime scenes are also classified as macroscopic or microscopic. A macroscopic crime scene is one that can be viewed and analyzed with the naked eye. Such a scene also includes the potential for several levels of the investigation. Each macroscopic scene is a part of the larger crime. For instance, the scene of a robbery at a convenience store may involve the doorway where the culprit entered, the cash register from which money was stolen, and the back room of the store where the offender placed the clerk before leaving. Each of these scenes is a part of the larger crime scene, but each also constitutes an individual scene for processing. The methods and techniques employed by crime scene investigators depend on both the larger scene and the individual portions within it.

A microscopic crime scene is one in which trace evidence, residues, and similar evidence may be found. Microscopic scenes are often parts of larger macroscopic scenes and therefore require individual processing as well. In processing these scenes, investigators usually require the aid of mechanical or other tools for examination and analysis. A microscopic scene may also be a secondary or higher-level scene that is independent of the primary macroscopic scene. An example is hair or fiber samples from a victim that may be found in a suspect's car. Such samples create a secondary scene that requires microscopic examination. Other examples of microscopic scenes include the clothing of a murder victim, the tire tread left by a getaway car, and the genetic material used in DNA (deoxyribonucleic acid) identification.

A third method of classifying crime scenes is based on the type of crime committed, as different kinds of evidence may be found at the scenes of homicides, robberies, sexual assaults, and other crimes. The methods for processing crime scenes are often determined by the types of crimes and the expected evidence. For example, the scene of a sexual assault is likely to involve evidence very different from the evidence found at the scene of a robbery.

The type of criminal behavior associated with particular crimes may also be used in classifying crime scenes. This is especially important when investigators are attempting to establish the perpetrator's modus operandi, or method of operation (MO), and to recognize potential "signatures" of the perpetrator. The MO used by the perpetrator of a particular crime can often help to define potential suspects, and forensic investigators can help identify and analyze elements of the crime scene that point to the perpetrator's MO.

## Crime Scene Objectives

Each crime scene requires a specific systematic investigative approach that is adapted to the needs of that particular crime or scene. The objectives of any crime scene investigation are to identify, preserve, collect, and interpret each piece of evidence. In processing a scene and analyzing evidence, crime scene investigators typically follow a pattern aimed at meeting specific objectives.

The first objective is to determine the essential facts of the case as they relate to the establishment of a crime and its corpus delicti (Latin for "body of the crime"—commonly defined as the substantive nature of the crime). The corpus delicti makes up the essence of a crime, including the legal elements and proof arising from evidence. By first defining the essential facts, investigators can best determine the types of evidence likely to be found and the appropriate processes for recovery of that evidence.

The second objective of the crime scene investigator is to determine the perpetrator's MO. Each crime type requires that the perpetrator perform specific actions to achieve the criminal goal, but perpetrators use many different means for achieving their goals. Individual perpetrators may have specific methods they tend to use in carrying out given crimes. By establishing the MO, investigators can help to define the type of evidence as well as its application to the criminal conduct.

The third objective of the crime scene investigator is to identify witnesses and secure sufficient statements from them. This task includes verifying witness statements, corroborating the statements with other evidence, and, in some instances, disproving the statements as related to physical evidence. The identification of witnesses often helps define other processes and objectives for the crime scene investigation.

The next objective is the identification of suspects. Often a culmination of the earlier objectives, the identification of suspects brings together physical evidence, witness statements, and evidentiary conclusions and allows the investigators to move to their final objective: reconstruction of the crime and the potential evidence related to it. Crime scene investigation focuses on the how and why of the criminal act. In crime scene reconstruction, investigators put together the pieces of evidence, including witness statements, to create a picture of the crime in question.

## Methods of Crime Scene Investigation

Crime scene investigation often involves two distinct processes. The first, known as linear progression, focuses on the systematic identification of evidence. Often performed by technicians, this process follows specific guidelines and patterns for identification and management of evidence. In this process, proper procedure is crucial to guarantee the high quality of the evidence and thus support an effective investigation.

Linear progression focuses first on a system of recognition. Initial steps in this part of the crime scene investigation include scene survey and documentation. The investigators describe the crime scene in narrative reports that are often supplemented by diagrams, sketches, photographs, and related material.

The next step in linear progression is identification, which may include comparison and testing. In this step, the investigators identify potential evidence to separate it from irrelevant items found at the crime scene and to help in the collection, preservation, and processing of the evidence. For example, fingerprints discovered in the initial phase of identification of evidence may be lifted at the scene and later identified through a logical system of comparison. The testing of evidence may include chemical, biological, physical, and other methods.

Together, the collection and preservation of evidence constitute an important step in linear progression. Specific collection and preservation methods must be used for particular evidence types, so that the evidence is best protected for later use. In some instances, evidence may be collected and preserved for archival purposes, whereas in others it may be secured for later analysis. Investigators must follow a specific set of procedures for processing each type of evidence.

The final step of linear progression is known as individualization. This involves the evaluation of evidence and interpretation of the findings as related to the crime. For example, although many fingerprints may be found at a

---

## A Crime Scene Example

Officers respond to a homicide call at a residence and discover the body of a young woman in the bedroom. After securing the scene, they set up the crime scene log, which controls all people having the right of access to the crime scene. The preliminary survey requires written notes, sketches, and identification of fragile evidence. Officers identify footprints outside the bedroom window. They alert investigators and crime scene specialists to the locations of fragile evidence.

Officers establish a pathway for medical personnel; this pathway prevents destruction of physical evidence. If emergency medical responders request assistance from the pathologist, the pathway allows such follow-up investigators opportunities to locate obvious physical evidence—for example, a weapon, blood, and footprints. The initial point-to-point search turns up additional evidence to be photographed.

Special attention to points of entry and exits assists in identifying the offender's travel pattern. Officers locate broken glass near a damaged window and notice a bloody fingerprint below the putty line. This is a strong indicator that the offender pulled the broken glass from the window frame.

The corpse represents a secondary crime scene. The autopsy examination provides essential information on the manner of death, which in this case is determined to be homicide (as opposed to the other four possible findings: natural, accidental, suicide, or undetermined). The autopsy report links trace evidence from the victim to the scene and the offender.

---

given crime scene, only select prints will be usable for helping to determine the suspect. The individualization of each set of prints allows investigators to identify persons on the scene, which in turn helps to build a better understanding of the crime itself.

The second process in crime scene investigation is known as nonlinear progression. This process focuses on patterns of recognition and reasonable inference. Also known as a dynamic process, in this step investigators search for patterns and links between evidence and the elements of the crime. This step focuses on critical scene analysis and specified definition techniques. During this process, which is less systematic than linear progression, investigators use inferences and logic to draw connections that lead to reasonable conclusions.

## Processing the Crime Scene

The first step in processing a crime scene is to secure it. This begins when the first responding officer arrives at the scene. Initial concerns are for the safety of any victims, witnesses, and others who may be on the scene, but as soon as the responding officer is sure that no persons are in danger, the focus turns to the protection of potential evidence. In many instances, responding officers work to address these two concerns simultaneously. Securing the crime scene allows investigators to control the potential for loss or destruction of evidence. It also provides an opportunity for investigators to begin the chain of custody—that is, the documentation of the location of all the evidence recovered during the investigation and its eventual use in the courts.

In large police departments, and especially on major crime scenes, the tasks associated with crime scene investigation may be assigned to different individuals. In some instances a lead investigator takes a proactive and supervisory role, controlling and monitoring all activities at the crime scene. In other agencies, a crime scene supervisor takes that role; in still others, various crime scene duties are assumed by individual units. Small crime scenes and relatively low-level crimes may involve limited numbers of investigators. For example, a classic case of burglary may initially involve only the responding officer, who then has the duty to evaluate the scene and make recommendations concerning additional investigative needs. A crime scene technician may be called to the scene to process physical evidence, but in smaller departments this task may actually fall on the responding officer.

## Forensic Science and Crime Scene Investigation

The tools, methods, and techniques used in modern crime scene investigation have made tremendous advances in the past fifty years. The role of forensic science in law-enforcement investigations has increased steadily as methods have improved. Scientific testing that was once prohibitively expensive is now readily available, and new technologies have increasingly improved the accuracy of the findings of criminal investigations. These advances have come at some cost, however. For instance, jurors in general may have high expectations regarding what investigators can do at crime scenes, in part because of the fictional portrayals of forensic investigators that have become common on television and in films. This means that investigators must be particularly careful to follow standard operating procedures as well as the accepted techniques related to individual kinds of crimes.

Crime scene investigation has also changed dramatically because of changes in the investigative approach taken by many law-enforcement agencies. The trend toward community-oriented policing, among other developments, has led to more accommodating approaches to interagency investigation. The nature of criminal activity, especially when similar crimes take place across multiple jurisdictions, demands that agencies cooperate with each other in the investigation process.

The foundations of science change slowly, but the application of scientific methods to criminal investigations has changed very quickly. Forensic science has seen great improvements in technologies that enable the identification of trace or microscopic evidence, and crime scene investigators in the field have increasing access to devices that were once reserved for the laboratory.

*Carl Franklin*

## Further Reading

Adams, Thomas F., Alan G. Caddell, and Jeffrey L. Krutsinger. *Crime Scene Investigation.* 2d ed. Upper Saddle River, N.J.: Prentice Hall, 2004. Handbook for law-enforcement professionals focuses on excellence in the conduct of crime scene procedures.

Bennett, Wayne W., and Kären M. Hess. *Criminal Investigation.* 8th ed. Belmont, Calif.: Wadsworth/Thomson Learning, 2007. Provides in-depth discussion of forensic techniques and procedures.

Fisher, Barry A. J. *Techniques of Crime Scene Investigation.* 7th ed. Boca Raton, Fla.: CRC Press, 2004. Provides a broad overview of many areas of forensics, including the specific methods used by investigators at crime scenes.

Gilbert, James N. *Criminal Investigation*. 6th ed. Upper Saddle River, N.J.: Pearson Prentice Hall, 2004. Comprehensive text includes discussion of the procedures forensic scientists follow at crime scenes.

Ogle, Robert R., Jr. *Crime Scene Investigation and Reconstruction*. 2d ed. Upper Saddle River, N.J.: Prentice Hall, 2007. Well-organized text covers all aspects of the work of forensic scientists during criminal investigations.

**See also:** Chain of custody; Crime laboratories; Crime scene cleaning; Crime scene documentation; Crime scene measurement; Crime scene protective gear; Crime scene reconstruction and staging; Crime scene screening tests; Crime scene search patterns; Crime scene sketching and diagramming; Criminalistics; *CSI: Crime Scene Investigation*; Evidence processing; First responders; Forensic photography; Quality control of evidence.

## Crime scene measurement

**Definition:** Precise recording of the exact locations of all elements of a crime scene, including all items found there and all evidence collected.

**Significance:** The accurate recording of all measurements of a crime scene, particularly the locations of the various items found there, enables investigators to reproduce the scene at a later date, so that they can examine each item in relationship to the others and to the overall scene.

After a crime scene has been identified and the evidence found there has been located, numbered, tagged, and photographed, the scene must be measured in detail. This procedure allows investigators to reproduce the scene later, with all items of evidence and other important items depicted. This reproduction, made to scale, may take the form of a detailed sketch; it may be used for investigative purposes, for courtroom presentation, or both. A three-dimensional reproduction of the crime scene may also be made to assist jurors in visualizing the scene as it was found. Photographs are helpful, but they are limited because they are two-dimensional and do not indicate the exact locations of all the items present and the relationships among the items.

When a crime scene is measured, it is critical that each item be measured from a fixed point, so that it can be repositioned in its exact location at a later date. It would not be helpful, for example, to position an item found in the street by measuring its position in relation to a car parked next to the curb, because the car will be moved at some point. The position of an item in the street should be measured from something that will not move, such as a piece of curb or a point on a building. For a crime scene in a house, a measurement could be made from a specific point on a given wall.

Using the example of a crime scene in the street, a measurement could be made from curb prolongations (usually employed in traffic accident investigations) or other fixed objects, such as buildings or power poles. For example, at the scene of a shooting in which investigators find an expended twelve-gauge shotgun shell in the street, a triangulation method of positioning the shell could be used. The notes on such a measurement might read as follows:

Evidence item 1: One 12-gauge shotgun shell, Remington Express, 3″ mag, red, expended. Found in the center of First Street, south of Los Osos Blvd. Shell was 22′ southeast of ConEd Power Pole #3216, located on the southwest corner of First St. and Los Osos Blvd. and 29′8″ southwest of the northwest corner of Bean's Café located at 1608 First St., Big City.

The items noted can be cross-referenced with crime scene photographs.

Using the example of a gun found on the floor of a room, the measurements could be made from the walls of the room:

Evidence item 6: Gun, S&W blue steel revolver, 4″ barrel, Mod 28, serial number unknown. Found 6′3″ south of the north wall of bedroom number 3 and 18″ from the west wall of said bedroom.

In this example, two right angles are employed to fix the exact position of the gun on the floor of the bedroom; this is frequently referred to as the rectangle method.

In crime scene measurement, the most critical issue is precision. All measurements must be exact, so that the crime scene can later be reproduced accurately, with all items placed where they were found. Many law-enforcement agencies have begun to employ computer programs designed to assist in this endeavor.

*Lawrence C. Trostle*

### Further Reading

Gilbert, James N. *Criminal Investigation.* 6th ed. Upper Saddle River, N.J.: Pearson Prentice Hall, 2004.

O'Hara, Charles E., and Gregory L. O'Hara. *Fundamentals of Criminal Investigation.* 7th ed. Springfield, Ill.: Charles C Thomas, 2003.

Weston, Paul B., and Charles A. Lushbaugh. *Criminal Investigation: Basic Perspectives.* 9th ed. Upper Saddle River, N.J.: Prentice Hall, 2003.

**See also:** Accident investigation and reconstruction; Crime laboratories; Crime scene documentation; Crime scene investigation; Crime scene reconstruction and staging; Crime scene search patterns; Crime scene sketching and diagramming; Forensic photography.

## Crime scene protective gear

**Definition:** Clothing worn by forensic scientists at crime scenes to minimize their direct contact with materials at the scenes.

**Significance:** It is important that forensic scientists, as well as other professionals who attend crime scenes, take precautions to prevent the inadvertent transfer of potential evidence between them and the scenes. These precautions include the wearing of protective gear, which serves both to protect crime scenes from contamination and to protect forensic scientists from coming into direct contact with possibly dangerous substances.

The examination of a crime scene is essentially like the examination of any exhibit in a forensic laboratory, in that a main function of the crime scene examiner is to collect evidence from the scene, just as a laboratory scientist collects evidence from an exhibit. Both types of investigators should wear protective clothing during their respective examinations.

The wearing of protective gear at a crime scene serves three primary purposes. First, it minimizes the chances that a forensic scientist will leave trace evidence at the scene or on samples collected, which could result in contamination of the evidence and thus affect the interpretation of any results. Second, it minimizes that chances that a scientist will carry trace evidence from the scene to the laboratory or to other collected samples relating to the case being investigated or to other cases. Third, it helps protect the scientist from any biological, physical, or chemical hazards at the scene, which may or may not be directly related to the case being investigated.

### Protecting the Scene

Simply wearing protective clothing is not enough. Forensic scientists must follow established procedures that specify the kinds of protective gear they must wear, when they must wear it, and when they must change it. They must also follow appropriate crime scene management procedures.

Protocols for the use of protective gear need to consider all the types of evidence that forensic scientists can leave at a scene or collect from a scene. Scientists may shed hairs from their heads or facial hairs. They could shed fibers from their clothing. They could leave fingerprints on any items they touch. In walking through the scene, they could leave shoe prints.

Increasingly, forensic scientists have come to realize that DNA (deoxyribonucleic acid) should be regarded as a form of trace evidence, especially given the steadily increasing sensitivity of DNA analysis. A bloodstain or semen stain is not a fixed deposit of potential DNA evidence. Rather, just as fibers can be shed from an item of clothing, DNA-containing cells can be shed from a biological stain onto other items or stains. Scientists who attend crime scenes need to be aware of this potential for contamination and must dress accordingly.

Scientists also need to be aware that they may shed DNA from themselves to crime scenes and thus contaminate items. By touching an item, a person can transfer skin cells that could give a DNA profile. Coughing, sneezing, or breathing on objects may also transfer cells. The analysis of this sort of DNA sample, often called trace DNA, is an important part of the work of forensic scientists.

### Essential Gear

A minimum standard of protective gear for a forensic scientist generally involves gloves, appropriate footwear, and something that covers the scientist's clothing, such as overalls or a lab coat. Many crime laboratories are moving to the use of disposable overalls, eliminating the need to have overalls laundered. Disposable overalls make it easy for scientists to change their protective outerwear if it becomes stained or contaminated during crime scene examination, or when they must collect evidence from several areas of a crime scene that need to be kept separate or from multiple scenes associated with the same incident. In addition, because such overalls are disposed of according to protocols established for biohazardous waste, their use minimizes potential contamination from the scene to the laboratory.

Gloves are an essential part of crime scene examiners' gear because no matter how well-intentioned examiners are, they might accidentally touch important surfaces. Generally, disposable gloves made from vinyl or latex are worn. Some scientists wear two pairs of gloves at a time (a practice called double-gloving), especially when the samples collected are likely to be subjected to particularly sensitive DNA analysis techniques.

Forensic scientists have two options for foot-

wear at crime scenes. Some prefer to keep dedicated pairs of scene boots or shoes, which they clean between scenes with 70 percent ethanol or a surface disinfectant such as TriGene. The other option is the use of disposable overshoes. Both approaches minimize the inadvertent transfer of trace or biological evidence from examiners to crime scenes.

Head coverings and face masks provide an extra level of protection at crime scenes. Forensic scientists may cover their heads with the hoods attached to most disposable overalls or with separate disposable caps. If trace DNA analysis is considered as a possible technique in a case, head coverings and masks should be regarded as essential. Low levels of DNA from persons examining the scene could contaminate these sample types if precautions are not taken, and such contamination could render the DNA results difficult or impossible to interpret. Some scientists consider head coverings and face masks to be essential for all scene examinations, whereas others prefer to address the level of protective gear needed based on individual case circumstances, which may change during their examinations.

### Health and Safety Issues

At many crime scenes, forensic scientists can expect to encounter biological fluids. The standard protective gear discussed above should help scientists to avoid possible infection, but some may wish to consider additional precautions if particularly heavy dried or wet blood is present.

Some scene types present particular physical and chemical hazards. For example, examiners collecting evidence at clandestine drug laboratories may encounter volatile chemicals, and they may need to protect themselves with body coverings and breathing apparatuses suitable for such exposure. Because they must often must move through unstable debris, arson investigators protect themselves with heavy footwear and hard hats or helmets.

In testing substances at crime scenes, scientists may need to use reagents that can present health hazards. For example, the reactive dyes used in presumptive testing for blood and semen can be carcinogenic. Also, crime scene examination techniques involving the use of luminol and leuco crystal violet (for the enhancement of bloodstains and bloodied shoe prints or other impressions) require the spraying of scenes with chemicals. In such cases, some kind of breathing apparatus may be needed, particularly if the area being examined is enclosed or not well ventilated.

*Douglas Elliot*

## Further Reading

Elliot, Douglas. "Crime Scene Examination." In *Expert Evidence: Law, Practice, Procedure, and Advocacy*, edited by Ian Freckelton and Hugh Selby. 3d ed. Pyrmont, N.S.W.: Lawbook, 2005. Takes a multijuridictional point of view in discussing all aspects of crime scene examination.

Fisher, Barry A. J. *Techniques of Crime Scene Investigation*. 7th ed. Boca Raton, Fla.: CRC Press, 2004. Provides a broad overview of many areas of the forensic sciences. Includes discussion of the health and safety issues related to crime scene examination.

Geberth, Vernon J. *Practical Homicide Investigation: Tactics, Procedures, and Forensic Techniques*. 4th ed. Boca Raton, Fla.: CRC Press, 2006. Text used in many U.S. police academies includes discussion of the protective gear required for those involved in the collection and handling of evidence.

Houck, Max M., and Jay A. Siegel. *Fundamentals of Forensic Science*. Burlington, Mass.: Elsevier Academic Press, 2006. Good general textbook devotes a thorough section to the safety aspects of the work done by crime scene investigators.

**See also:** Blood residue and bloodstains; Chemical Biological Incident Response Force, U.S.; Crime scene cleaning; Crime scene investigation; Cross-contamination of evidence; Decontamination methods; DNA extraction from hair, bodily fluids, and tissues; Food supply protection; Footprints and shoe prints; Trace and transfer evidence.

# Crime scene reconstruction and staging

**Definitions:** Crime scene reconstruction is an investigatory technique in which evidence is gathered, organized, and analyzed to re-create the precise sequence of events that occurred during the course of a crime. Crime scene staging is a stratagem sometimes used by criminal offenders in which a crime scene is rearranged or fabricated to disguise the true nature of the offense and suggest other causes or perpetrators of the crime.

**Significance:** Crime scene reconstruction is the process of piecing together the evidence in a criminal case to determine what, when, where, and how criminal actions occurred. This process is fundamental to the successful apprehension and conviction of criminals. Without painstaking examination of the crime scene, investigators can easily overlook crucial evidence; if the evidence is not then assembled to tell a coherent story of what happened, the perpetrator of the crime might never be apprehended or convicted. Law-enforcement investigators must also be alert to the possibility that the perpetrator has manipulated elements of the crime scene to mislead them. Crime scene reconstruction and staging are related in that both help answer important questions that can lead to the apprehension of perpetrators.

Criminal investigation is a systematic factfinding endeavor that involves numerous professionals with special expertise and training. Law-enforcement officers arrive at the scene in response to a report that a crime has been committed. Their job is to preserve and protect the crime scene. Criminalists collect physical evidence at the crime scene and deliver that evidence to the laboratory. Crime scene investigators or detectives scour the scene for evidence, ask witnesses questions, and track leads concerning possible suspects. Laboratory scientists analyze and test physical evidence from the scene. In homicide cases, forensic pathologists perform autopsies to ascertain the manner and cause of death. The work of all of these professionals lays the groundwork for crime scene reconstruction.

Criminal investigations must adhere to a deliberate process. Physical evidence is carefully collected, handled, transported, and preserved for the purpose of solving a crime and bringing the offender to justice. Failure to protect the integrity of the evidence can render it inadmissible in court. Notwithstanding its importance, physical evidence, by itself, might not be enough to close a criminal case. Discrete bits of evidence must be properly collated and placed in a context to be useful in the arrest, prosecution, and conviction of offenders.

## Reconstructing Crime Scenes

Crime scenes are locations where illegal acts have been committed and physical evidence is found. Crime scenes can be categorized as primary, secondary, or tertiary. For example, an offender may kidnap a victim from her home (a primary crime scene) and transport her by car (a secondary crime scene) to another location (a tertiary crime scene), where the offender murders her. The place where the offender disposes of the victim's body is yet another tertiary crime scene. Crime scenes thus include any indoor or outdoor locations that afford opportunities for the recovery of direct physical evidence of crimes. Connecting the activities and establishing the nature and sequence of events within and among those scenes is the essence of crime scene reconstruction.

Crime scene reconstruction is a methodology that is used to re-create the events of a crime, including the course of actions that unfolded immediately before, during, and after the incident. Forensic scientists reconstruct a crime scene by examining and interpreting physical evidence as well as the physical layout of the location. Reconstruction begins with the gathering of data from the scene; in the case of homicide, these may include data on blood spatter, gunshot residue, bullet trajectories, and objects from which DNA (deoxyribonucleic acid) evidence can be collected. In a homicide case, the positioning

and condition of the victim's body can also yield valuable details about the specific unfolding and timing of the criminal act.

A thorough reconstruction includes photographs from the crime scene, results of laboratory analyses of physical evidence, and autopsy findings. Measurements and sketches of the scene are also carefully done and integrated to form a logical and evidence-based re-creation of the criminal act. Information from the crime scene is synthesized so that investigators can make educated guesses about what happened during the crime, where it happened, when it happened, and how it happened. Witness statements are compared with the physical evidence to determine whether the hypothesized sequence of actions is refuted or supported by witness recollections.

During the crime scene reconstruction process, investigators typically walk through the crime scene while attempting to apply the mind-set of an offender. They formulate realistic scenarios that might match the actual events of the crime. Investigators must be able to interpret the crime scene from every visual perspective in order to discover, interpret, and collate pertinent facts. One primary focus of investigation involves the determination of the offender's modus operandi, or method of operation, which consists of the actions that an offender employs to complete the crime (choice of target, method of entry, use of weapon, means to control the victim, and so on).

## Crime Scene Staging

The possibility that a crime scene has been staged is another important consideration in crime scene reconstruction and analysis. Staging is a deliberate attempt to thwart or confuse crime scene investigators by rearranging the crime scene. In one type of staging, the offender modifies the elements of the crime scene to make the offense appear as a suicide or an accident. Crime scene investigators must be careful in accepting evidence at face value. For example, a man found in his apartment with a fatal bullet wound in his head and gun in his right hand might not be a suicide victim. Detailed investigation may lead to the conclusion that the case is, in fact, a homicide, as evidenced by the angle of the exit wound, the gunshot residue on the victim's hand, the nature of the wound, the distance of the shell casings from the gun and the body, and the type of gun used in the crime. Crime investigators must be skeptical and methodical in their efforts to explore all possible aspects of a crime scene in order to differentiate between the actual events of the crime and any likely staging of the scene.

In another type of staging, serial killers position physical evidence and victims' bodies to humiliate, punish, and degrade victims and taunt the police. Some serial killers compulsively leave psychological markers, known as signatures, at their crime scenes. These can include posing the victims' bodies or concealing or inserting objects in the victims' bodies after death. A serial killer's signature is unnecessary for the completion of the crime but critical to the killer's psychological and sexual gratification.

*Arthur J. Lurigio and Justyna Lenik*

### Further Reading

Clemens, Daryl W. "Introduction to Crime Scene Reconstruction." *MAFS Newsletter* 27 (April, 1998). Discusses the differences between crime scene reconstruction and criminal profiling. Also describes different types of reconstruction techniques, the steps in the reconstruction process, and how criminal profiling and crime scene reconstruction complement each other in helping investigators understand how and why crimes are committed.

Gardner, Ross M. *Practical Crime Scene Processing and Investigation.* Boca Raton, Fla.: CRC Press, 2005. Thoroughly illustrates and explains the importance of each step in a criminal investigation. Outstanding chapter titled "The Role of Crime Scene Analysis and Reconstruction" explicates the methodology of crime scene investigation and enumerates the steps in event analysis. Includes vivid photographs and sketches from crime scenes to illustrate the various stages of the reconstruction process.

Geberth, Vernon J. "The Homicide Crime Scene." In *Practical Homicide Investigation: Tactics, Procedures, and Forensic Techniques.* 4th ed. Boca Raton, Fla.: CRC Press, 2006. Describes the different types of crime scene staging and presents examples of actual crimes in which the scenes were staged in a section headed "The Staged Crime Scene." Written by a former commander for the Bronx Homicide Division of the New York City Police Department.

Gibson, Dirk. *Clues from Killers: Serial Murder and Crime Scene Messages.* Westport, Conn.: Praeger, 2004. Presents the details of the crimes committed by some of history's most notorious serial killers, including the Unabomber, Jack the Ripper, and the BTK Killer, and analyzes the messages and other forms of communication each of the perpetrators used. Opens with an excellent introduction that discusses the nature of serial killers' signatures and how these idiosyncratic and often cryptic expressions vary depending on what the killers are trying to accomplish.

Ogle, Robert R., Jr. *Crime Scene Investigation and Reconstruction.* 2d ed. Upper Saddle River, N.J.: Prentice Hall, 2007. Provides a good overview of all procedures used in crime scene investigation and discusses the steps taken and the kinds of physical evidence used in reconstructing the events that took place at a given scene.

**See also:** Accident investigation and reconstruction; Bomb damage assessment; Crime scene documentation; Crime scene investigation; Crime scene measurement; Crime scene sketching and diagramming; Criminal personality profiling; Criminalistics; DNA analysis; DNA fingerprinting; Forensic anthropology; Forensic photography; Forensic sculpture; Structural analysis.

## Crime scene screening tests

**Definition:** Color tests that provide rapid information regarding the presence or absence of given classes of drugs or compounds.

**Significance:** At crime scenes, forensic scientists need to provide information to law-enforcement personnel on any possible illicit drugs or other compounds that may be present. They must also make decisions on the most appropriate samples to be collected. The use of crime scene screening tests, generally in the form of chemical reagents that show positive results with distinct color changes, can assist in these decision-making processes by providing initial indications of what questioned substances or compounds may or may not be.

Although crime scene screening tests, commonly known as spot tests, can be used to identify a wide range of compounds, forensic scientists most commonly use these tests at crime scenes related to the use and manufacture of illicit drugs. Spot tests are used to exclude or potentially identify given classes of drugs or compounds as being present in samples. Spot testing may be used to determine whether a large single package seized by police, such as a bulk powder, is homogeneous or to determine whether numerous packages or other items seized at a single scene are all the same. At crime scenes, spot tests can provide forensic scientists with information as to whether particular items should be sampled or whether they should be taken whole to the laboratory for further analysis.

### Properties of a Spot Test

The ideal spot test would be specific for a given drug or compound, would be sensitive (so that only a small amount of sample need be subjected to analysis), and would provide an unambiguous result, allowing no misinterpretation. In the interests of efficiency and safety, the test reagents would be cheap and harmless, and the test itself would be quick and easy to carry out.

In reality, most spot tests sacrifice specificity in favor of fulfilling the other desired criteria; they do not individu-ally identify specific drugs or compounds, but rather given classes. For example, Marquis reagent turns a positive purple color with an opiate alkaloid, whether it be morphine, diacetylmorphine, or one of the many other compounds in the same class.

As most spot tests are relatively sensitive, a negative result provides a good indication of the absence of the class of drug or compound that would normally provide a positive result. A positive result may develop with a compound outside the class of compound being screened for; such a result is commonly referred to as a false positive. Other compounds present in the sample may prevent an unambiguous identification of a drug. Sugars are often used as diluting agents in powered drug samples, and these can turn brown when combined with sulfuric acid (present in Marquis reagent). This brown color may obscure any color change resulting from a drug present in the sample, such as an amphetamine, which would produce a positive orange color. Spot tests require no sophisticated equipment and can easily be carried out away from the laboratory at crime scenes. A forensic scientist generally carries out a spot test by adding the test reagent to a small amount of the sample material in a small glass tube or on the well of a

## Spot Tests at Clandestine Drug Laboratories

The use of spot tests at clandestine laboratories manufacturing drugs can help forensic scientists to determine whether powdered materials found there are final products or precursors, in which case the whole items will need to be seized, or less important compounds that need only be sampled. Spot tests may also be used to determine the presence of other chemicals at such crime scenes. For example, the identities of common acids found at clandestine drug laboratories may be tentatively distinguished through the use of spot tests employing a silver nitrate solution. Hypophosphorous acid, commonly used in the manufacture of methamphetamine, will produce a black precipitate, although further testing is required to distinguish it from phosphorous acid. Hydrochloric acid will produce a white precipitate, and sulfuric acid will produce no reaction. Forensic scientists need to combine the results of spot tests with other observations to determine the nature of the acids at drug lab crime scenes, and, in all cases, further testing is required to confirm the identities of the acids.

spotting tile.

Spot tests tend to be destructive, but each test requires only a small amount of the sample material, leaving the bulk of the sample for further testing if required. The reagents are not necessarily harmless; they often contain strong acids or chemicals with undesirable properties. They are required only in small amounts, however, and can be safely transported to scenes in suitable containers.

## Quality Control

The age of spot test reagents and the conditions under which they have been stored may affect the colors produced during use. Forensic scientists need to run positive and negative controls with spot test reagents on a regular basis to ensure that they are working correctly.

Little training or expertise is required in the use of spot tests, and such tests may be readily carried out by nonscientific staff, such as police or customs officers. Because it is unlikely that a positive control will be able to be carried out at every scene where a sample is tested, persons using spot tests should carry out their own positive and negative controls with the test reagents to ensure that they are familiar with the color changes expected. In addition, tests should be carried out on compounds known to produce "false positive" results. This will prevent misinterpretation of results owing to subjectivity when describing colors.

*Anne Coxon*

## Further Reading

Camilleri, Andrew M., and David Caldicott. "Underground Pill Testing, Down Under." *Forensic Science International* 151 (2005): 53-58. Evaluates the use of spot tests for identification of the drugs contained in so-called party pills.

Cole, Michael D. *The Analysis of Controlled Substances.* New York: John Wiley & Sons, 2003. Describes the major classes of drugs of abuse in a clear manner and addresses the use of spot testing, thin-layer chromatography, and instrumental analysis.

Horswell, John, ed. *The Practice of Crime Scene Investigation.* Boca Raton, Fla.: CRC Press, 2004. Collection of essays covering all aspects of scene investigations includes a chapter on drug operations that provides a good explanation of the use of spot tests and discusses how their use coincides with other important forensic aspects of such investigations.

Moffat, Anthony C., M. David Osselton, and Brian Widdop, eds. *Clarke's Analysis of Drugs and Poisons.* 3d ed. 2 vols. Chicago: Pharmaceutical Press, 2004. Comprehensive work provides data and describes methods relating to the detection, identification, and quantification of drugs and poisons.

O'Neal, Carol L., Dennis J. Crouch, and Alim A. Fatah. "Validation of Twelve Chemical Spot Tests for the Detection of Drugs of Abuse." *Forensic Science International* 109 (2000): 189-201. Presents the results of research that assessed the specificity and sensitivity of twelve spot tests commonly used in drug analysis.

United Nations. *Rapid Testing Methods of Drugs of Abuse.* New York: Author, 1995. Manual intended for forensic laboratories and law-enforcement personnel provides technical detail but is easy to read and includes clear information relating to the practical use of spot tests for drugs.

**See also:** Acid-base indicators; Crime scene investigation; Crime scene measurement; Drug classification; Evidence processing; Illicit substances; Meth labs; Presumptive tests for blood.

# Crime scene search patterns

**Definition:** Geometric template method used to search for evidence at a crime scene.

**Significance:** The orderly approach of utilizing a geometric pattern in the search for and gathering of evidence at a crime scene maximizes discovery efforts and minimizes the disturbance of evidence prior to discovery.

Law enforcement investigators organize their searches of crime scenes to maximize the likelihood of finding evidence and to minimize the likelihood that they will fail to discover existing evidence. The discovery process itself should not cause undue disturbance of the scene, as this could cause evidence to be damaged or overlooked.

To organize their searches, investigators choose from various geometric templates that can be imposed on the scenes to be searched. Four commonly used templates are the spiral, the strip, the wheel, and the zone patterns. Evidence discovery points at a crime scene can be diagrammed at corresponding points on a paper or digital record that serves as a blueprint of the crime scene.

A spiral search emanates from a center point and travels in widening curves from that point like a coiled snake. The search path may begin from either end of the spiral. For example, a bloody knife found on the street would most likely generate a spiral search path starting at the location of the knife (center of the spiral) and working outward. A crime scene with a victim inside a room having a single entry would probably generate a spiral search that starts from the entry (outer end of the spiral) and works inward, toward the center.

A strip (or linear) pattern divides a crime scene into long, narrow sections. Investigators may begin an evidence search at either end of the strip. This sort of search is often used across large land areas to look for evidence such as the presence of a person in that vicinity. In a typical strip pattern search, searchers walk shoulder to shoulder or separated by an equal distance in a line that moves simultaneously across an area.

The wheel pattern has a center point from which spokes radiate outward to connect to a circle enclosing the search area. Sections of the wheel pattern are shaped like slices of a pie. Using a wheel pattern, multiple searchers can simultaneously investigate sections from the outer perimeter toward the center without crossing or disturbing possible evidence in other sections. A wheel pattern search may be used when time for searching is limited, such as when adverse weather conditions make it likely that the crime scene will soon be disturbed.

The zone (or grid) pattern uses perpendicular lines that form square search areas (quad-

rants); each quadrant can be further divided into smaller quadrants pertinent to the search. Crime scene investigators who need to search buildings often do so by dividing each floor into zones. Zoned investigations may quickly rule out particular zones that are not pertinent to the crime, thereby freeing investigators to concentrate on the zones that do contain evidence.

*Taylor Shaw*

## Further Reading

Genge, N. E. *The Forensic Casebook: The Science of Crime Scene Investigation.* New York: Ballantine, 2008. Presents examples of evidence gathering from actual cases to illustrate the work involved in forensics.

James, Stuart H. , Jon J. Nordby , Suzanne Bel, eds. *Forensic Science: An Introduction to Scientific and Investigative Techniques.* Boca Raton, FL: CRC Press, 2014. Presents the law as it relates to forensic science, using input from experts who examine pertinent case studies.

Miller, Marilyn T. *Crime Scene Investigation Laboratory Manual.* San Diego, CA: Academic Press, 2014. Provides explanatory data and exercises for teaching techniques of securing and documenting a crime scene, of preserving evidence, and of visualizing and reconstructing crime scene events.

**See also:** Blood residue and bloodstains; Buried body locating; Crime scene documentation; Crime scene investigation; Crime scene measurement; Crime scene sketching and diagramming; Disturbed evidence; Evidence processing; Forensic archaeology; Locard's exchange principle; Metal detectors; Physical evidence.

# Crime scene sketching and diagramming

**Definition:** Creation of representative depictions of locations and appearances of important and relevant features and objects found at crime scenes.

**Significance:** In creating sketches and diagrams of crime scenes, examiners extract from the abundance of background visual information at such scenes only those features that are relevant and portray them in visual form. Such sketches are complementary to the scene notes and photographs that also document crime scenes.

Crime scenes are often very cluttered, jumbled, and confusing. Crime scene photographs can contain vast amounts of visual information, much of which may not relate to the particular incident being investigated. By making a sketch or diagram, a crime scene examiner can create a document that visually highlights only those aspects of the scene that are considered to be relevant to the crime. Like all crime scene documentation, sketches can be made to aid the recollection of the investigators who make them, but ultimately they serve to convey information to other investigators, attorneys, and courts.

An annotated sketch or diagram, with appropriate measurements marked, can provide a format for focusing the attention on one aspect, or a small number of aspects, of the crime scene that may be particularly relevant. For example, a single sketch of a light switch showing the general appearance and location of a bloodstain and indicating where a sample of the stain was taken from provides a clear, easily understood visual representation of one aspect of the scene examination. Another, more typical, example would be a sketch of the floor plan of a room indicating the location of a body relative to items of furniture and other significant objects, such as the murder weapon.

Rather than attempting to include a lot of information in a single sketch, which can lead to confusion, a crime scene examiner may create multiple sketches of the same area of interest. One such sketch might indicate the location of a body and other physical items relative to each other, a second might depict the locations of bloodstains, and a third might show the locations of shoe prints. This kind of separation of layers of information allows viewers of the sketches to comprehend the individual points of interest more easily.

Most crime scene sketches are not intended to be perfectly accurate scale re-creations of the scenes. Rather, they are nearly always companions to detailed scene photographs. Sketches are valuable because they are simple to create and can readily convey specific information. Increasingly, however, crime scene examiners are making use of modern surveying equipment and associated computer software to create accurate visual depictions of crime scenes and the locations of items within them.

*R. K. Morgan-Smith*

## Further Reading

Elliot, Douglas. "Crime Scene Examination." In *Expert Evidence: Law, Practice, Procedure, and Advocacy*, edited by Ian Freckelton and Hugh Selby. 3d ed. Pyrmont, N.S.W.: Lawbook, 2005.

Horswell, John, ed. *The Practice of Crime Scene Investigation*. Boca Raton, Fla.: CRC Press, 2004.

Saferstein, Richard. *Criminalistics: An Introduction to Forensic Science*. 9th ed. Upper Saddle River, N.J.: Pearson Prentice Hall, 2007.

**See also:** Composite drawing; Crime scene documentation; Crime scene investigation; Crime scene measurement; Crime scene reconstruction and staging; Crime scene search patterns; Evidence processing.

## Criminal personality profiling

**Definition:** Investigatory technique in which a detailed composite description of an unknown perpetrator is constructed on the basis of crime scene evidence.

**Significance:** By providing police officers with descriptive information about what type of individual probably committed an offense, including demographic and psychological characteristics, profiling narrows the range of likely offenders and helps investigators concentrate their limited resources and time in search of suspects.

Criminal personality profiling is based on the notion that serial offenders engage in similar patterns of behavior and that each serial offender leaves a unique trail of evidence with each crime. Profilers believe that the actions of serial offenders are deeply motivated, however bizarre, random, or senseless those actions might appear to untrained observers. The criminal activities in which these offenders engage are windows into their hidden desires, tendencies, and psychological traits. Conversely, these offenders' thoughts as well as their emotional and sexual needs drive their criminal behaviors.

## Serial Criminals

Profiling is most often employed in cases of serial homicides or rapes. These crimes, which tend to receive widespread media coverage, often involve female victims with common physical characteristics. The general profile of serial murderers, which matches the actual characteristics of most of the persons apprehended for such crimes, is as follows: They are white men with average or above-average intelligence, in their mid-twenties to mid-thirties, who have an interest in criminal law and police work. Serial killers also tend to be interpersonally adept; they are typically friendly, charming, and engaging, which explains their success at attracting and luring victims to horrific deaths. Other types of serial criminals have also been the subjects of criminal personality profiling, including arsonists, bank robbers, kidnappers, and child molesters.

Profilers assume that perpetrators leave telltale signs of their psychopathology at their crime scenes (in the case of serial murderers, the locations where they kill, torture, and mutilate their victims) and in the areas where they conceal their victims' bodies—so-called dump sites. Profilers examine these clues to characterize an unknown suspect (that is, an individual who is likely to have committed the crime given the evidence at the scene). However, they rarely provide police investigators with the specific identity of an actual perpetrator.

## Major Profiling Tasks

The three primary tasks of a criminal person-ality profiler are to generate details about an unknown perpetrator's personality and socio-demographic characteristics, to predict the items that are likely to be discovered in a suspected offender's possession, and to recommend various interrogation strategies for suspects in custody. In accomplishing the first of these tasks, the profiler provides police investigators with leads that narrow the pool of unknown suspects with respect to age, race, ethnicity, employment, education, and marital status. Profiling unfolds a biographical sketch of an at-large killer or rapist as the number of that person's crimes increases and more information becomes available to the profiler. Profiling can also give investigators insights into where a perpetrator might live relative to the locations of the crimes.

The most important aspect of the profiler's first task is to arrive at an educated guess about a likely offender on the basis of police and autopsy reports as well as the consistent elements found at different crime scenes, such as how the victims were killed (for example, stabbing, bludgeoning, strangling, suffocating) and how the bodies were positioned or displayed (for example, naked, partially clothed, posed). Based on these data, the profiler can help police officers to focus their attention on a certain type of suspect. The profiler can also provide police with information on where the offender is likely to live as well as when and where the offender is likely to strike again.

The defining aspects of a criminal's behaviors are the individual's modus operandi (MO) and signature. The modus operandi consists of the steps the offender follows and the techniques and tools the offender uses when engaging in criminal activities. An offender's MO can evolve. In other words, an individual's criminal skills are honed and practices are modified with experience. As criminals become more seasoned, their MOs becomes more effective and efficient; they also become less likely to leave clues that will lead to their capture. An example of an MO is that of the serial rapist who uses burglary tools to pry open the bedroom windows of women sleeping in basement apartments. He wears gloves and thus never leaves fingerprints, and he enters and exits the apartment through the same window.

This serial rapist might also display a signature—an action taken not to accomplish the crime but to satisfy the perpetrator's distinctive and perverse psychological needs. For example, the bedroom rapist might force his victims to assume degrading poses while he photographs them following the act of sexual violence. Signatures are unique to specific offenders because they emerge from the offenders' idiosyncrasies and personal tendencies. MOs can be replicated by other offenders, but signatures cannot. Offenders who appropriate the MOs of fellow criminals are committing so-called copycat crimes. Signatures are often tied to the pathological sexual satisfaction that serial killers obtain from their offenses.

The second profiling task occurs after a prime suspect or person of interest has been identified. Knowledge about the alleged offender's belongings can reinforce other evidence that ties that person to the crimes. For example, some serial killers collect crime scene souvenirs, newspaper clippings, photographs, fetish items, pornography, or other materials that help them remember, relive, and re-create their crimes, providing them with prolonged sexual or other types of gratification. The items taken from crime scenes for these purposes are sometimes referred to as "trophies." Jeffrey Dahmer, for example, showcased the macerated skulls and bones of his victims in his apartment and consumed pieces of his victims' flesh to re-create the pleasure he received from sexually violating their corpses.

The third profiling task follows the arrest of the suspect. Based on inferences about the suspect's personality traits and psychological disturbances, the profiler guides the police in the selection of interrogation techniques that will best elicit incriminating information from the suspected offender. Different strategies must be implemented with consideration of each suspect's personality and psychological disorders. For example, with some offenders, unrelenting and aggressive questioning is most productive, whereas with others, a more relaxed and conversational tone is most likely to elicit confession. Still other serial offenders respond best in interrogation situations in which they perceive

themselves, rather than the police investigators, as being in full control.

## Pioneers in Profiling

Cesare Lombroso (1836-1909) was among the first criminal profilers. He and many of his contemporaries believed that criminals, unlike noncriminals, could be identified by physical characteristics such as bushy eyebrows or a receding chin. Early profilers also noted criminals' tendency to wear shabby clothes and to be tattooed. Dr. James Brussel, a New York-based psychiatrist and the first renowned profiler in the United States, was influenced by these theories in his work with the New York Police Department. From the late 1950's to the early 1970's, Brussel helped investigators track suspects in cases of serial bombing, arson, and murder. His most famous criminal personality profile, of the "Mad Bomber," was uncanny in its accuracy.

From 1940 to 1956, New York City was terrorized by a series of bombs planted randomly in crowded public places, such as busy streets, stores, and movie theaters. These actions were attributed to the ever-mysterious, paranoid, and elusive character the city's newspapers called the "Mad Bomber." Over the years, the bombs became deadlier, and the Mad Bomber's letters to the police and the news media, signed "F.P." for "Fair Play," became increasingly hostile and grandiloquent.

Despite the diligent efforts of seasoned police officers and investigators, no viable clues brought authorities any closer to identifying a suspect and ending the terror. Frustrated with traditional police measures to catch the Mad Bomber, Inspector Howard Finney of the New York City Crime Lab suggested a radical approach. After one of the Mad Bomber's devices injured six patrons in a movie theater on December 2, 1956, Finney summoned Brussel and posed basic questions that the police had failed to answer in their work on the case: "What kind of demented person would hurt innocent people in such a horrific manner?" "What is motivating the Mad Bomber?" "Who is he and what is the best way to catch him?" With his impressive background as assistant commissioner of mental hygiene for the state of New York and head of the U.S. Army's Neuropsychiatry Unit during the Korean War as well as his training as a psychoanalyst, Brussel was dubbed by the press the "Sherlock Holmes of the couch."

Brussel pored over the police records of the bombings and developed the following criminal personality profile. The bomber was a man—historically, most bombers had been male. His letters suggested that he was a former employee of Consolidated Edison, the city's electric power company, and that he harbored a deep-seated grudge against the company for real or imagined injuries. The bomber was paranoid and believed that the electric company and the public were "out to get him." Brussel surmised that the bomber was approximately fifty years old because paranoid ideation peaks at the age of thirty-five and the bombings had been occurring for sixteen years. He also surmised from the bomber's carefully crafted letters and explosive devices that the bomber was a deliberate person who dressed fastidiously and was highly sensitive to criticism.

Brussel concluded from his analysis of the Mad Bomber's letters that the bomber was from Eastern Europe (a part of the world where bombs were weapons of choice) and self-educated. The postmarks on the letters suggested to Brussel that the bomber lived in Connecticut and commuted to New York City for the purpose of planting his bombs. Brussel guessed that the unknown suspect was unmarried and that he lived with his brothers or sisters; he further conjectured that the bomber had been unable to form mature relationships with women because he suffered from an "Oedipus complex."

Brussel told the detectives that they should publicize his criminal personality profile of the Mad Bomber in order to antagonize the perpetrator and force him out into the open. He also instructed them to search the records of Consolidated Edison carefully for disgruntled former employees. Brussel's strategy worked. Soon after his profile was published in the newspapers, the Mad Bomber revealed his motive in a letter to the press: He had been injured on the job and believed the company was cheating him out of his worker's compensation payments. This revelation confirmed the bomber's identity and led to his capture.

The Mad Bomber was George Metesky. He lived in Connecticut with his two sisters. He was middle-aged, Slavic, and very well groomed. Before the detectives went to Metesky's home to place him under arrest, Brussel told them to expect Metesky to be wearing a double-breasted suit, buttoned. When the police took him into custody, he was indeed wearing a double-breasted suit—carefully buttoned. Metesky was found insane by the courts and was committed to the Matteawan Hospital for the Criminally Insane. In 1973, he was released and returned to his family home in Connecticut. In 1994, he died there quietly, and in obscurity, at the age of ninety.

Brussel attempted to systematize and standardize his profiling techniques, working with two agents of the Federal Bureau of Investigation (FBI), Howard Teten and Patrick J. Mullany. In the 1970's, they created a seminal course in applied criminology that helped to spawn the FBI's Behavioral Science Unit, later renamed the Behavioral Analysis Unit, which is now a part of the National Center for the Analysis of Violent Crime in Quantico, Virginia.

## Types of Serial Criminals

Expert criminal personality profilers trained by the FBI have created several typologies or groupings of serial murderers. One scheme for categorizing these offenders focuses on their mobility. Geographically stable serial killers (examples include Ed Gein, Wayne Williams, and John Wayne Gacy) live in the same areas where they hunt for, kill, and bury their victims. Geographically transient serial killers (examples include Ted Bundy and Henry Lee Lucas), in contrast, move from place to place in search of victims and bury the bodies in areas that are distant from the killing sites.

These killers travel to confuse law-enforcement authorities, and they are much less vulnerable to capture than geographically stable serial killers. Another categorization scheme differentiates among four types: visionary serial killers, who have serious mental illnesses and select victims by listening to auditory command hallucinations; mission serial killers, who are driven to murder certain types of people; hedonistic serial killers, who murder for

## Profiling Serial and Mass Murderers

*Given that every serial and mass murderer is unique, it can be dangerous to generalize about "typical" offenders. Nevertheless, multiple-murder offenders have many characteristics in common.*

| Trait | Patterns |
| --- | --- |
| Gender | Most offenders are male. Female serial killers occur, but they are much less common than male killers. Female mass murderers are extremely rare. |
| Race | Most offenders are white, but there are exceptions to this rule. For example, Wayne Williams, the Atlanta child killer of 1979-1981, was African American. |
| Age | Serial killers usually begin killing when they are in their twenties. Mass murderers are typically ten to twenty years older than that when they begin killing. |
| Intelligence | Serial killers are typically intelligent but often have experienced severe failures in their careers and personal lives. Mass murderers are often unemployed, sometimes losing their jobs only shortly before they begin killing. |
| Personal histories | Serial killers often display patterns of sociopathic behavior and may have histories of deviant sexual or violent behavior, including animal abuse. Mass murderers usually do not display such patterns. |
| Fantasy lives | Serial killers often fantasize about their crimes. |
| Alcohol and drugs | Serial killers sometimes use drugs or alcohol before or while committing their crimes. Mass murderers rarely do so. |
| Childhoods | Serial killers often have had miserable childhoods and have suffered physical or mental abuse. They may also have histories of serious head trauma and neurological disorders. |
| Military | Mass murderers often have served in the military. |

sexual gratification; and power/control serial killers, who achieve sexual pleasure from dominating and controlling their victims.

One of the most widely known criminal profiling methods was developed by FBI agents John Douglas and Robert K. Ressler; their system categorizes serial killers on the basis of whether their crime scenes are organized or disorganized. Organized offenders are likely to be average or above average in intelligence, engaged in skilled occupations, married or living with partners, and interested in the media's coverage of their crimes. In contrast, disorganized offenders are likely to be below average in intelligence, socially awkward, living alone, and uninterested in the media's coverage of their crimes.

### Caveats and Ethical Issues

Criminal personality profiling is more an art than a science. Profilers use a few general approaches that can be readily adapted to fit specific types of crimes, but no tried-and-true profiling techniques have been developed that work in every case. Instead, the formulas that profilers use are based largely on the particular circumstances of each case and the evidence at hand; these yield educated guesses derived from knowledge, practical experience, and clinical acumen.

Despite the fact that profiling has often been glamorized or sensationalized in novels, films, and television programs, it is only one component in a wide range of strategies used by law-enforcement agencies to apprehend serial offenders. Profiling is an adjunctive tool that supplements and complements the investigatory activities of experienced law-enforcement officers. Profilers are consultants to the police; they are generally summoned after officers have failed in their attempts to identify or question suspects. Profilers must be careful not to oversell their capabilities.

Many experienced homicide investigators regard criminal personality profiling with skepticism and disdain. The field is without a sound scientific basis and relies on weak standards of proof, although psychologists have begun to conduct more research on the validity of profiling techniques. The field of profiling is also lacking in professional standards and minimal educational requirements, and no credentialing bodies exist to govern and oversee the conduct of practitioners.

Profilers have an ethical obligation to be unbiased and impartial in their collection and interpretation of evidence, to restrict their opinions to the specific facts of the case, to present their qualifications honestly and openly, and never to use a profile to assert the guilt or innocence of any suspect.

*Arthur J. Lurigio*

## Further Reading

Brussel, James. *Casebook of a Crime Psychiatrist*. New York: Bernard Geis, 1968. Classic volume presents case studies drawn directly from Brussel's files. A must-read for profiling enthusiasts.

Hickey, Eric. *Serial Murderers and Their Victims*. Belmont, Calif.: Wadsworth, 2002. Offers an extensive account of serial murder that is grounded in social science research. Examines the lives of four hundred serial murderers and attempts to explain their behaviors from biological, psychological, and sociological perspectives.

Holmes, Ronald, and Stephen Holmes. *Profiling Violent Crime: An Investigative Tool*. Thousand Oaks, Calif.: Sage, 1996. Solid introductory text on profiling presents the principles and techniques that investigators employ in developing the profiles of violent criminals.

Petherick, Wayne. *Serial Crime: Theoretical and Practical Issues in Behavioral Profiling*. Burlington, Mass.: Academic Press, 2006.

Text designed for advanced students is divided into two sections, one on behavioral profiling—including its theoretical foundations and history as well as discussion of media depictions—and one on specific serial crimes, including arson, murder, rape, and stalking.

Turvey, Brent E. *Criminal Profiling: An Introduction to Behavioral Evidence Analysis*. San Diego, Calif.: Academic Press, 2002. A definitive source of information on deductive profiling methods. Describes crime scene reconstruction techniques as well as procedures for the collection and analysis of evidence.

**See also:** Bite-mark analysis; Crime scene investigation; Criminology; *Diagnostic and Statistical Manual of Mental Disorders*; Federal Bureau of Investigation Forensic Science Research and Training Center; Forensic psychiatry; Forensic psychology; Geographic profiling; Minnesota Multiphasic Personality Inventory; Police psychology; Psychopathic personality disorder; Questioned document analysis; *Silence of the Lambs, The*; Unabomber case.

# Criminalistics

**Definition:** Use of scientific principles in the evaluation of physical evidence to detect, analyze, and solve crimes.

**Significance:** Criminalists work in various professional settings, but they have a common goal: To use the evidence from crime scenes to tell the stories of what happened there in order to link offenders with crime victims and scenes. Criminalists analyze and interpret various forms of physical evidence and then disseminate their findings in reports that can be used by law-enforcement officers, lawyers, judges, and juries.

The term "criminalistics" is often used interchangeably with "forensic science," and criminalistics may be broadly interpreted as the science of policing or the profession of forensic science. A narrower definition of criminalistics, however, focuses on the use of scientific principles in the evaluation of physical evidence of crimes. Science has an important role to play in the criminal justice system, and this role continues to develop and change as technology advances and improves the techniques available for investigating crimes. Criminalistics is a broad field that incorporates the use of the scientific method in the processing of evidence and the investigation of crimes.

The practitioners of criminalistics, known as criminalists, work in many different settings and in a variety of professions. Some work in crime labs as medical professionals, dentists (forensic odontologists), chemists, toxicologists, biologists, geneticists, physicists, geologists, or anthropologists, whereas others work as researchers in university settings. Generally, criminalists have some specialized training in science as it is applied to the recognition, collection, analysis, and preservation of physical evidence from crime scenes. Criminalists may also be found in courtrooms as expert witnesses, providing testimony to help juries understand the science behind particular findings concerning evidence.

## Work of Criminalists and Criminologists

The discipline of criminalistics is often confused with the discipline of criminology, but the two differ in several ways. Although both criminalists and criminologists seek to understand the patterns and truth behind criminal activities, they use different approaches and ultimately have different goals. Criminalists seek to examine evidence in order to detect class and individual characteristics. The ultimate goal of a criminalist is to link three things: a victim, a crime scene, and an offender. The physical evidence that may be found at a crime scene may be invisible to the naked eye, such as fingerprints; it may be minute trace evidence, such as fibers from the clothing or the environment of the offender; or it may be as obvious as a body and a pool of blood. The job of the criminalist is to uncover the story that the evidence has to tell.

The investigative tasks in which criminalists are involved are widely varied. For example, a criminalist in a crime lab may examine the chemistry of inks in a threatening letter to identify the types of materials used in an effort to determine the origin of the letter. Another criminalist may apply techniques of forensic chemistry to understand the use of drugs in a homicide investigation. Yet another may examine fragments of a broken taillight from a hit-and-run accident, with the goal of identifying class characteristics that can be used to identify the type of vehicle from which the taillight came. In such a case, the criminalist's next job may be to look for individual characteristics in the evidence that could link it to a specific vehicle.

Criminologists are also interested in understanding why and how crime occurs, but they do not usually examine and evaluate the physical evidence left at crime scenes to try to link crimes to specific persons or specific groups. Rather, criminologists examine psychological and sociological causes of crime, such as mental illness, low cognitive abilities, certain personality traits, socioeconomic disadvantage, poor neighborhood conditions, and dysfunctional families. Criminologists often try to understand why crime occurs and attempt to predict who is at risk to engage in criminal endeavors by finding patterns in offending. They use various methods to achieve these ends, including survey research methods and statistical analyses.

Criminalists ask questions, examine patterns, and analyze evidence to answer legal questions. In other words, the starting point for the criminalist is to translate legal questions into scientific research questions. The goal is to use the evidence to formulate hypotheses and test the research questions. The evidence and the questions vary depending on the crime scene, but the goal remains the same: to disseminate the findings in reports that can be used by law-enforcement officers, lawyers, judges, and juries.

*Stephanie K. Ellis*

## Further Reading

Barnett, Peter D. *Ethics in Forensic Science: Professional Standards for the Practice of Criminalistics.* Boca Raton, Fla.: CRC Press, 2001. Examines various ethical scenarios in light of the codes of ethics of the most prominent professional organizations for criminalists in the United States.

Eckert, William G., ed. *Introduction to Forensic Sciences*. 2d ed. Boca Raton, Fla.: CRC Press, 1997. Textbook intended for students considering careers in the forensic sciences includes discussion of all aspects of criminalistics.

Fisher, Barry A. J. *Techniques of Crime Scene Investigation*. 7th ed. Boca Raton, Fla.: CRC Press, 2004. Comprehensive work provides an overview of the uses of the forensic sciences, particularly in criminal investigations.

Gaensslen, R. E., Howard A. Harris, and Henry C. Lee. *Introduction to Forensic Science and Criminalistics*. New York: McGraw-Hill, 2008. Covers the types of forensic science techniques used in crime laboratories as well as those employed by private examiners in civil cases. Discusses various crime scene procedures and analyses.

Girard, James E. *Criminalistics: Forensic Science and Crime*. Sudbury, Mass.: Jones & Bartlett, 2008. Examines the procedures that criminalists undertake at crime scenes and in laboratories. Explains scientific concepts clearly for readers with no background in chemistry or biology.

Inman, Keith, and Norah Rudin. *Principles and Practice of Criminalistics: The Profession of Forensic Science*. Boca Raton, Fla.: CRC Press, 2001. Addresses the interpretation of various kinds of evidence, with a focus on best practices in the forensic science profession.

Saferstein, Richard. *Criminalistics: An Introduction to Forensic Science*. 9th ed. Upper Saddle River, N.J.: Pearson Prentice Hall, 2007. Comprehensive introductory textbook provides in-depth discussion of the activities carried out by criminalists.

**See also:** American Academy of Forensic Sciences; Crime laboratories; Crime scene investigation; Criminology; Forensic anthropology; Forensic entomology; Forensic geoscience; Forensic nursing; Forensic odontology; Forensic pathology; Forensic photography; Forensic toxicology; Living forensics; Locard's exchange principle; Medicine.

# Criminology

**Definition:** Scientific study of crime and criminal behavior.

**Significance:** Criminologists examine how people interact with the criminal justice system. They also study crime victims to understand why offenders target them and what risk factors increase the likelihood of victimization. The research that criminologists conduct into the causes of crime and social deviance assists with the classification and treatment of offenders as well as the identification of forensic evidence in relation to crime.

More than two hundred years ago, two utilitarian philosophers, Cesare Beccaria (1738-1794) and Jeremy Bentham (1748-1832), studied human behavior. They asserted that human beings conduct cost-benefit analyses regarding their future behavior and then act out of greed and personal need. The theory now known as classical criminology is based on these premises: Potential criminal offenders have the free will to choose to act, and in making their decisions they compare risks to possible gains.

Although this theory lost popularity to newer theories over time, it has seen a resurgence in recent decades. Routine activities theory, for example, is a perspective in criminology that attempts to use deterrence theory to explain crime (and the treatment of criminal behavior). According to routine activities theory, in order for a crime to occur, three elements must be in place at the same time: someone who is motivated to commit that crime, a target worthy of victimizing, and the lack of a capable person to protect that target.

A potential criminal is less likely to victimize someone who has no money or material goods, or to victimize a person who is walking with a group of other people. Such circumstances should deter someone from committing a crime because they decrease the offender's chances of financial gain and increase the offender's chances of being caught, hurt, or identified. To design successful punishments based on deterrence theory, however, criminologists would need to prove that all criminals are rational human beings, that they think about the consequences of their actions, and that they actually believe they could be caught.

## Challenges to Classical Criminology

Several criticisms have been directed toward classical criminology and deterrence theory. First, many offenders commit crimes under conditions that make it likely for them to be caught (that is, witnesses or victims can identify them). Second, most offenders know the risks involved (arrest, jail time, loss of the respect of friends and family) when they commit crimes. Further, some criminals do know the difference between right and wrong, but they nevertheless cannot stop themselves from committing crimes; mental illness or very low IQ, for example, might prevent some from understanding the consequences of certain behaviors.

Given the shortcomings of classical criminology and deterrence theory, some criminologists have suggested other explanations for criminality. For example, some theorists believe that the behavior of offenders is not something that can be controlled. Instead, factors beyond these individuals explain why they would commit crimes under less-than-ideal circumstances. These theories are part of the positivist school of criminology.

## Positivist Criminology and Other Theories

In the nineteenth century, Cesare Lombroso (1836-1909), known as the father of positivist criminology, developed a theory of criminal behavior related to his medical research. As a doctor, he had noted similar physical characteristics among delinquents. He asserted that criminals exhibited apelike physical traits and that they were biologically and physiologically similar to the primitive ancestors of humans. Some criminologists and other theorists postulated that psychological problems (such as personality disorders) caused criminal behavior. Sigmund Freud (1856-1939), the founder of psychoanalysis, believed that human behavior was controlled by unconscious processes.

Criminologists have also examined how environmental factors play a role in predicting criminality. Sociological explanations of crime focus on social structure, culture, poverty rates, racial disparities, and neighborhood instability in relation to criminal behavior. They also examine community changes, the strength and weakness of social controls, and the role of the family, school, peers, and religion in explaining behavior. All of these theories blame criminality on factors outside of offenders' control.

Criminologists have developed many competing theories that attempt to explain why crime happens and what the relationships are among offenders, victims, and the criminal justice system. Each theory has merit, yet a single explanation is insufficient, in part because each criminal is unique—an individual with a particular past and a person who may or may not have a conscience. Just as experts continue to debate the role of nature versus nurture in shaping human behavior, arguments continue between classical and positivist theorists in criminology. At the same time, some criminologists are attempting to develop integrated theories that combine some of the characteristics of both to explain criminal behavior.

*Gina M. Robertiello*

## Further Reading

Belknap, J. (2015). Activist Criminology: Criminologists' Responsibility to Advocate for Social and Legal Justice. *Criminology* 53 (1) 1-22. Author stresses the responsibility of criminologists to advocate for social and legal justice, especially in the three important areas of research, teaching and service.

Cohen, Albert K. *Delinquent Boys: The Culture of the Gang.* New York: Free Press, 1955. Early study explains class differences in expectations of boys and asserts that lower-class boys have less ability to defer gratification than do middle-class boys.

Cohen, Lawrence E., and Marcus Felson. "Social Change and Crime Rate Trends: A Routine Activity Approach." *American Sociological Review* 44 (1979): 588-608. Explains how people's everyday behaviors can increase their likelihood of becoming crime victims.

Cohn, E.G., D.P. Farrington, A. Iratzoqui. *Most-Cited Scholars in Criminology and Criminal Justice, 1986-2010.* New York: Springer Briefs in Criminology, 2014. Authors examine the scholarly influence of different scholars in the field of Criminology and Criminal Justice over the last 25 years, noting that the prestige associated with certain theories does vary over time.

Cullen, Francis T., and Robert Agnew, eds. *Criminological Theory: Past to Present—Essential Readings.* 3d ed. Los Angeles, CA: Roxbury, 2006. Collection of writings brings together past theories on crime and criminology and reports of more recent research in this field.

Merton, Robert K. "Social Structure and Anomie." *American Sociological Review* 3 (1938): 672-682. Classic article on strain theory as an explanation of criminal behavior provides a sociological viewpoint. Asserts that criminal offenders develop adaptations to the strain of their lack of opportunity to reach universal norms.

Rock, P.E. (2014). The Public Faces of Public Criminology. C*riminology and Criminal Justice* 14 (4) 412-433. Author examines the recent calls for a "public criminology" noting that the term is really not defined well, though it is not new. Author also explains what would need to occur for its popularity to re-emerge.

Shaw, Clifford R., and Henry D. McKay. *Juvenile Delinquency and Urban Areas: A Study of Rates of Delinquency in Relation to Differential Characteristics of Local Communities in American Cities.* Rev. ed. Chicago, IL: University of Chicago Press, 1969. Addresses the ecology of crime, specifically focusing on the geographic locations of cities' central business districts in relation to where crime occurs.

Vito, Gennaro F., Jeffrey R. Maahs, and Ronald M. Holmes. *Criminology: Theory, Research, and Policy.* 2d ed. Sudbury, MA: Jones & Bartlett, 2007. Comprehensive text discusses the criminological theories of the past as well as modern theories and reviews the research conducted on these theories.

Winslow, Robert W., and Sheldon X. Zhang. *Criminology: A Global Perspective.* Upper Saddle River, NJ: Pearson Prentice Hall, 2008. Provides in-depth information on the field of criminology across the United States and internationally.

**See also:** Criminal personality profiling; Criminalistics; Drug abuse and dependence; Federal Bureau of Investigation; Forensic psychiatry; Forensic psychology; Geographic profiling; Insanity defense; Irresistible impulse rule; Mens rea; Police psychology; Psychopathic personality disorder; Racial profiling; Victimology.

## Croatian and Bosnian war victim identification

**Definition:** Identification effort of genocide victims recovered from mass graves in Bosnia-Herzegovina and Croatia.

**Significance:** The deaths of thousands of individuals in the Former Yugoslavia during the 1990s presented a daunting victim identification effort for forensic scientists. Positive identification of victims is hindered by a number of factors, including the lack of antemortem dental and medical records of missing persons and comparative DNA samples from living relatives.

The Balkan Wars in the Former Yugoslavia (1991-1995) resulted in the disappearance of an estimated 40,000 individuals in Bosnia-Herzegovina and Croatia alone. Many individuals were executed in acts of genocide and buried in mass graves throughout the countryside. Since 1996, forensic scientists have had the task of locating these clandestine gravesites and identifying the victims.

Thousands of individuals have been excavated from mass graves and their remains have been examined for the purpose of identification and for determining the cause and manner of death. Investigators, pathologists, anthropologists, archaeologists, odontologists, radiologists, DNA experts, and database technicians work collaboratively in the identification process.

## Identification

A number of agencies have played a role in the identification effort of genocide victims from Bosnia-Herzegovina and Croatia, including Physicians for Human Rights (PHR), the United Nations International Criminal Tribunal for the Former Yugoslavia (UN-ICTY), the Bosnia State Commission on Missing Persons, and the International Commission on Missing Persons (ICMP). Much of the initial efforts of the UN-ICTY involved the documentation of genocide, including the use of forensic evidence from mass graves for the prosecution of war criminals. However, efforts over the last decade have largely focused on the identification and repatriation of remains to living relatives.

A number of factors have hindered identification efforts of the missing from Bosnia-Herzegovina and Croatia. In wealthier nations, antemortem medical and dental records or fingerprints are common methods used for positive identification of remains.

However, these records are often nonexistent or are difficult to locate in the Former Yugoslavia. The unidentified population is also relatively homogenous—the majority of the victims are young to middle-aged adult males. Methods for estimating age-at-death and stature from skeletal remains are often based on standards developed from other populations, a limiting factor in anthropological assessments. Soon after the war ended, clothing and personal effects (e.g., identification cards) were heavily relied on for making identifications. It has become increasingly apparent that these criteria are too unreliable, since clothing and personal effects associated with remains may not actually belong to the deceased.

Finally, many mass graves were re-excavated by the perpetrators who attempted to hide the remains in secondary graves. This resulted in large-scale commingling of individuals and also the separation of intact bodies into multiple body parts.

### International Commission on Missing Persons

In 1996, the ICMP was established to develop an antemortem database of missing persons that could be compared against postmortem records of unidentified remains. This effort involves a close working relationship with families of the missing, and since 1999 has included the widespread collection of DNA samples from living relatives. Unfortunately, nuclear DNA is often degraded in decomposed remains from mass graves. However, recent advancements now permit the use of mitochondrial DNA (mtDNA) for identification, which is more abundant in the cell and less susceptible to degradation. This type of DNA is inherited along the maternal line so samples taken from unidentified remains can only be matched to relatives who share the same maternal mtDNA as the victim. DNA analysis has been essential in the identification of the victims from the Srebrenica massacre that took place in July of 1995, resulting in the deaths of approximately 8,000 Bosnian Muslim men.

The ICMP considers DNA testing the gold standard for positive identification and places less emphasis on presumptive methods of identification. The DNA program resulted in the identifications of approximately 1,200 individuals in 2002 alone, more than a ten-fold increase compared with all previous years combined. As of July, 2014, the ICMP has positively identified over 22,000 individuals from the Former Yugoslavia through DNA. New developments in DNA technology continue to provide the best path to identification in the former Yugoslavia, where traditional methods have had limited success. However, archaeologists, anthropologists, and pathologists will continue to serve a pivotal role in the meticulous excavation of remains recovered from mass graves, in the sorting of commingled remains from primary and secondary gravesites, and in the assessment of the circumstances surrounding death.

*Eric J. Bartelink*

## Further Reading

Ball, Howard. *Working in the Killing Fields: Forensic Science in Bosnia.* Lincoln, NE: University of Nebraska Press. 2015. A book that outlines the history of the forensic identification effort of Bosnian genocide victims, as well as the roles and contributions of forensic scientists.

Haimes, Erica, and Victor Toom. *Hidden in Full Sight: Kinship, Science and the Law in the Aftermath of the Srebrenica Genocide. New Genetics and Society* 33. No. 3 (2014): 277-294. An article focused on the concept of kinship in DNA analysis as it pertains to the forensic identification of Bosnia genocide victims from the Srebrenica massacre.

Haglund, William D. "Recent Mass Graves, An Introduction". *In Advances in Forensic Taphonomy: Method, Theory, and Archaeological Perspectives.* Haglund, William D. and Marcella H. Sorg, ed. Boca Raton, FL: CRC Press, Inc., 2002: 243-261. A comprehensive overview for professionals that addresses mass graves, forensic identification, and war crimes investigations with an emphasis on the Former Yugoslavia.

Komar, Debra. "Lessons from Srebrenica: The Contributions and Limitations of Physical Anthropology in Identifying Victims of War Crimes". *Journal of Forensic Sciences* 48, no. 4 (July, 2003): 1-4. An illuminating discussion of prospects and challenges of the use of anthropological methods in the identification of victims from Srebrenica, Bosnia.

Skinner, Mark F., and Jon Sterenberg. "Turf Wars: Authority and Responsibility for the Investigation of Mass Graves." *Forensic Science International* 151 (2005): 221-232. Discusses the ethics, professionalism, and responsibility of forensic scientists in relation to human rights investigations. Also addresses the challenges faced by forensic teams composed of individuals from a wide variety of backgrounds.

**See also:** Buried body locating; DNA interpreting mass graves; Ethics of forensic science; Expert witnesses; Forensic anthropology; Forensic archaeology; Genocide investigation; Mitochondrial DNA analysis and typing; Skeletal analysis; Taphonomy; War crimes trials.

# Cross-contamination of evidence

**Definition:** Failure to preserve the purity or exclusivity of physical evidence related to a crime scene through the introduction of transferred materials from other sections of the crime scene, various related crime scenes, or other sources.

**Significance:** Crime scenes yield evidence that can link suspects, victims, and the actions of persons present when the crimes occurred. Collecting and preserving evidential materials without cross-contamination is crucial, as incorrect conclusions may be drawn from contaminated evidence.

Forensic investigation of a crime scene relies on Locard's exchange principle, which states that when two objects come in contact, they exchange trace evidence. Therefore, a crime scene contains evidence that may place a suspect at the scene, and analysis of that evidence may reveal the associations between perpetrator and crime that are necessary for a prosecutor to obtain a conviction in a court of law. Evidence may also refute theories that link a suspect to a crime and thus may exonerate the innocent.

The methods used in the collection and preservation of evidence are intended to ensure that the preserved materials did originate from the crime scene, that the materials are pertinent to the crime, and that the materials can be analyzed in a comparable state to the way they were found at the scene. The failure to protect an evidence sample from the transfer of other material onto or into it results in cross-contamination of evidence. Evidence may become cross-contaminated at the crime scene during collection and packaging of evidential materials, during transportation to laboratories or other facilities, during storage, or while it is undergoing analysis. At the crime scene, cross-contamination of evidence is most likely to occur when the actions of first responders and others move materials such as hairs, fibers, and fluids around the scene. Evidence may also be compromised by cross-contamination when investigators do not use crime scene protective gear or use such gear improperly, resulting in leaving their own fingerprints, hair, and fluids at the scene. Also, when investigators leave the crime scene to search related areas (such as a suspect's car), evidence may be transferred from one scene to the other, resulting in cross-contamination.

Materials other than the evidential materials gathered at the crime scene may cause cross-contamination if the evidence samples are not properly packaged and safeguarded during transportation to labs or other locations. In addition, evidence must be stored properly and protected while it is being analyzed or tested so that cross-contamination may be prevented.

*Taylor Shaw*

## Further Reading

Genge, N. E. *The Forensic Casebook: The Science of Crime Scene Investigation.* New York: Ballantine, 2008. Presents examples of evidence gathering from actual cases to illustrate the work involved in forensics.

James, Stuart H., Jon J. Nordby, Suzanne Bell, eds. *Forensic Science: An Introduction to Scientific and Investigative Techniques.* Boca Raton, FL: CRC Press, 2014. Presents the law as it relates to forensic science, using input from experts who examine pertinent case studies.

Miller, Marilyn T. *Crime Scene Investigation Laboratory Manual.* San Diego, CA: Academic Press, 2014. Provides explanatory data and exercises for teaching techniques of securing and documenting a crime scene, of preserving evidence, and of visualizing and reconstructing crime scene events.

**See also:** Accident investigation and reconstruction; Crime scene investigation; Crime scene protective gear; Disturbed evidence; DNA extraction from hair, bodily fluids, and tissues; Evidence processing; First responders; Locard's exchange principle; Physical evidence; Quality control of evidence; Trace and transfer evidence.

# Cryptology and number theory

**Definitions:** Cryptology is the scientific study of the hiding, disguising, or encryption of messages. Number theory is the branch of mathematics that is concerned with the properties of the positive integers.

**Significance:** Computer security experts use public-key cryptography to ensure the confidentiality of electronically transmitted messages through encryption and the integrity of messages with digital signatures. Cryptology is an important part of investigations regarding attempts by computer hackers to decrypt messages or modify digital signatures. Hackers sometimes use public-key encryption to hide attacks, such as Trojan horses, and forensic analysis techniques have been developed to detect such attempts.

Cryptology encompasses both cryptography, the hiding of messages, and cryptanalysis, the revealing of hidden messages. Number theory is involved in cryptography in many ways, but its most important use is in public-key encryption.

A number of computationally intensive algorithms exist in number theory, one of which is factoring the product of two large prime numbers. In 1978, Ron Rivest, Adi Shamir, and Leonard Adleman published a public-key encryption algorithm named RSA (from the initials of the inventors' last names) that uses the difficulty of factoring large numbers to protect the value of a private key. RSA has been used to encrypt electronic files to ensure their confidentiality and to create digital signatures for e-mail to ensure its integrity.

When computer hackers want to see encrypted files, they often devise attacks to steal the receivers' private keys, which will allow them to decrypt the files. When such attacks occur, forensic experts can use tools designed to detect the attacks; similar tools are available to defend against such attacks. Hackers recognize that digital signatures can be used to guarantee the integrity of e-mail. They often intercept e-mail messages, modify the contents, and then attach invalid signatures. The hackers then have to ensure that the receivers use fake public keys to check the signatures. One way hackers could do this would be by replacing certificate authorities' public keys in the recipients' e-mails. Antivirus software can protect against this kind of attack by performing its usual checks of e-mail.

## Encryption and Number Theory

Encryption is the process of using a key to transform a readable plaintext message into an unreadable ciphertext message. Decryption reverses encryption to recover the plaintext message. When the encryption and decryption key are the same, the encryption is described as algorithm-symmetric. Although symmetric algorithms are complex, they do not use much number theory.

Public-key encryption algorithms, which are often based on number theory, use different keys for encryption and decryption. The most famous public-key encryption algorithm, RSA, selects two large prime numbers (a prime number is divisible only by one and by itself) and forms a modulus, $n$, as their product. The modulus $n$ is too large to be factored. The ciphertext message, $C$, is created by raising the integer value of the plaintext message, $M$, to the power $e$ modulo $n$, and the plaintext message is recovered from $C$ by raising $C$ to the power $d$ modulo $n$. The public key is the pair $(e, n)$ and the private key is the pair $(d, n)$.

RSA is widely used for encrypting files and signing messages. It has proven to be very resistant to brute-force attacks on the private keys. A major part of the RSA scheme involves creation of the private keys and the safe distribution of the corresponding public keys. Usually, the private key is safely transmitted to its owner by a trusted public-key infrastructure (PKI) vendor who then uses digital certificates, which contain the owner's public key and are signed by the PKI vendor, to distribute the public key.

## Computer Hacking and Encryption

In 1976, Whitfield Diffie and Martin Hellman developed an algorithm that allowed two people to create a shared symmetric key. The al-

### Early Cryptographers

Julius Caesar is generally recognized as the earliest military leader to utilize ciphers to encrypt and decode messages. His ciphering system became the basis for many more advanced ciphers in later centuries. Eventually, mechanical devices were invented to make encryption and decryption faster and easier. In the late eighteenth century, Thomas Jefferson invented a drumlike device that was used to encode and decode messages. During World War II, the Enigma machine, a brilliant conception of the German military, was used to add complexity to codes. Enigma's scheme was eventually broken, first by Polish mathematicians suspicious of the intentions of Germany's Nazi rulers. The Polish then shared their knowledge with the French and British. None of these early pioneers in cryptology could have envisioned the impacts that computers would have on the necessity for systems of covert communication to be used not only in wars and by spies but also by average people in daily life.

*Heidi V. Schumacher*

gorithm is similar to the RSA public-key algorithm and makes considerable use of modular exponential arithmetic. To create the shared symmetric key, each person involved uses a secret number that never leaves his or her computer but generates the shared secret key as the result of several data exchanges. If a hacker knows that a purchaser and an online store are generating a symmetric key with the Diffie-Hillman key exchange, the hacker could drop a Trojan horse into the purchaser's computer, capture the secret information, and then masquerade as the purchaser to buy items for personal gain. In investigating such an attack, a forensic expert could log into the purchaser's computer and check to see if the Trojan horse is still there; if it is, it might provide information on the location of the hacker.

Hackers can gain access to other people's computers in a number of ways, not the least of which is through Web browsers. When they gain access, they often try to leave files that contain worms, Trojan horses, or viruses. Given these threats, computers have become increasingly well equipped with antivirus software that is designed to protect users from such attacks.

One of the most important techniques used by antivirus software is to check all files and quarantine any files that look suspicious. A clever trick used by modern hackers is to encrypt attack files with private RSA keys so that the files are not detected by antivirus software. This allows the hackers to return later, decrypt the files, and carry out their intended attacks. Web browser helper objects are especially susceptible to this kind of delayed attack. Increasingly sophisticated forensic software has been developed to catch multilevel attacks of this type.

*George M. Whitson III*

### Further Reading

Hellman, Martin. "An Overview of Public Key Cryptography." *IEEE Communications Magazine*, May, 2002, 42-49. Very good survey article provides basic information. Written by one of the founders of the field of public key encryption.

Mandia, Kevin, Chris Prosise, and Matt Pepe. *Incident Response and Computer Forensics.* 2d ed. Emeryville, Calif.: McGraw-Hill/Osborne, 2003. Includes several chapters on incident response to cryptology attacks.

Shieneier, Bruce. "Inside Risks: The Uses and Abuses of Biometrics." *Communications of the ACM* 42 (November, 1999): 136. Brief but informative article describes methods of defeating encryption by subversion.

Shinder, Debra Littlejohn. *Scene of the Cybercrime: Computer Forensics Handbook.* Rockland, Mass.: Syngress, 2002. Bridges the gap between the computer professionals who provide the technology for cybercrime investigations and the law-enforcement professionals who investigate the crimes.

Vacca, John R. *Computer Forensics: Computer Crime Scene Investigation.* 2d ed. Hingham, Mass.: Charles River Media, 2005. Provides a good introduction to computer forensics. Devotes several chapters to cryptology forensics.

Yan, Song Y. *Cryptanalytic Attacks on RSA.* New York: Springer, 2008. Covers most of the known cryptanalytic attacks and defenses of the RSA cryptographic system. Also provides a good introduction to the use of number theory in the RSA encryption algorithm.

**See also:** Computer crimes; Computer forensics; Computer hacking; Computer viruses and worms; Crime scene search patterns; Electronic voice alteration; Internet tracking and tracing; Steganography.

## CSI: Crime Scene Investigation

**Date:** First aired on October 6, 2000

**Identification:** Popular television series involving a team of crime scene investigators who solve unusual crimes through the collection of physical evidence and analysis of this evidence using technologically advanced forensic procedures.

**Significance:** The original *CSI: Crime Scene Investigation* television series and its two spin-offs (*CSI: Miami* and *CSI: NY*) are very popular both within and outside the United States. Some criminal justice authorities and legal scholars have voiced concern that exposure to these shows has generated unrealistic expectations in the general public about the collection and forensic analysis of crime-related evidence. This phenomenon is commonly referred to as the "*CSI* effect." Although the existence of such an effect has not been confirmed by systematic research, anecdotal evidence of the *CSI* effect has been widely shared among legal authorities, and concerns regarding the television programs' negative impact continue to be a topic for discussion and debate.

*CSI: Crime Scene Investigation* is a television crime drama that depicts how a team of criminal investigators solve crimes by gathering and examining forensic evidence using technically advanced methods and tools. Created by Anthony E. Zuiker, the original *CSI* debuted in 2000 and soon became one of the most-watched crime dramas on television. The show's popularity can be attributed to its fresh and modern portrayal of criminal investigation. What made *CSI* different from traditional police shows of the past was its story lines, which focus more on the "how" of crime than on the "who." The popularity of *CSI* eventually led to two spin-off series, *CSI: Miami* began airing in 2002 and *CSI: NY* in 2004. Both of these programs follow the same premise: a team of crime scene investigators solve crimes through the collection and examination of forensic evidence. By 2007, the original *CSI* was being aired in two hundred countries and was watched by an estimated two billion viewers. In addition to the two spin-off television series, *CSI* spawned comic books, novels, and computer games.

## Examples of Forensic Evidence

*CSI* episodes depict many different types of physical evidence that can be collected at crime scenes as well as the various tools and procedures that can be used to analyze such evidence. The types of physical evidence that can be collected from crime scenes vary greatly and depend heavily on location and type of crime. For example, the physical evidence available for collection at the scene of a robbery is quite different from that available at a murder scene. Physical evidence might include marks on a victim's body, such as abrasions or bite marks. Fingerprints on a door or a window frame also constitute physical evidence, as does blood left behind by a likely perpetrator. Trace evidence is a type of physical evidence that can be collected and forensically examined; this kind of evidence is commonly depicted in *CSI* episodes. Trace evidence is found when a small amount of material has transferred from either one location or person to another location or person. Examples of trace evidence include gunshot residue and fibers from clothing or carpeting.

Just as many types of physical evidence can be found at crime scenes, forensic scientists use many different tools and procedures to examine and test physical evidence. The tools of crime scene investigators may range from the brushes used to apply powder to fingerprint areas to the

zNose, an "electronic nose" that has the ability to detect and identify different types of gases and vapors. Crime scene investigators use a number of different tools to collect blood samples, fiber samples, tire impressions, shoe impressions, and bite marks. These and many other types of tools allow for the identification and collection of potentially important samples of physical evidence. By collecting and testing samples from crime scenes, forensic scientists help to piece together the events that took place there, which can lead to the identification of the perpetrators.

## The Impact of *CSI*

In the television world, crime scene investigators have a variety of responsibilities in addition to the collection and analysis of the physical evidence found at crime scenes. On *CSI* they also interview witnesses, victims, and suspects. If the forensic evidence reveals an individual's guilt, the crime scene investigators are involved in tracking down, confronting, and arresting the perpetrator. These dramatic embellishments of the role of crime scene investigators and their use of forensic evidence have generated a great deal of concern and debate among legal authorities.

This concern is directed at the possibility that *CSI* and similar shows have created unrealistic expectations among viewers and the general public regarding how forensic evidence is used in the criminal justice system, and these expectations may have repercussions in the courts. For example, when *CSI* viewers serve on juries, they may expect all types of forensic evidence, specifically DNA evidence, to be presented during trial, and they may expect this evidence to be conclusive in revealing the guilt or innocence of defendants. This potential problem is popularly referred to as the *CSI* effect.

Although this topic has received a great deal of attention, the existence of the *CSI* effect has yet to be confirmed. Despite many anecdotal reports from prosecuting attorneys and other legal authorities, no systematic empirical research has proven that the *CSI* effect has had any real impact on legal proceedings. In another way, however, *CSI* and similar television programs have had a clear impact: After they began to air, forensic science programs across the United States experienced noticeable increases in applications.

*Erin J. Farley*

**Further Reading**

Cather, Karin H. "The *CSI* Effect: Fake TV and Its Impact on Jurors in Criminal Cases." *The Prosecutor* (National District Attorneys Association), March/April, 2004, 9-15. Presents interviews with attorneys to show support for the seriousness of the concept of the *CSI* effect.

Genge, N. E. *The Forensic Casebook: The Science of Crime Scene Investigation.* New York: Ballantine, 2002. Good source for an overall description of different kinds of crime scene investigators and their job responsibilities.

Marrinan, Corinne, and Steve Parker. *Ultimate "CSI: Crime Scene Investigation."* New York: Dorling Kindersley, 2006. Discussion of *CSI* focuses on how forensic evidence and techniques have been used on the program.

Podlas, Kimberlianne. "'The *CSI* Effect': Exposing the Media Myth." *Fordham Intellectual Property, Media, and Entertainment Law Journal* 16 (Winter, 2006): 429-465. Presents findings of a research study that call into question the existence of the *CSI* effect.

Ramsland, Katherine. *The "C.S.I." Effect.* New York: Berkley Books, 2006. Not a critical discussion of the so-called *CSI* effect but rather a discussion of how various types of forensic evidence are used in real criminal investigations, with a focus on demystifying forensic processes and technologies. Features examples from the *CSI* program throughout.

_____. *The Forensic Science of "C.S.I."* New York: Berkley Books, 2001. Uses the television show to discuss how various types of forensic evidence are employed in real-world cases. Attempts to demystify the process of forensic investigation.

Tyler, Tom R. "Viewing *CSI* and the Threshold of Guilt: Managing Truth and Justice in Reality and Fiction." *Yale Law Journal* 115, no. 5 (2006): 1050-1085. Offers a relatively complex discussion of the *CSI* effect, with a review of prior research findings that support or refute the existence of the effect.

**See also:** Celebrity cases; *Cold Case*; Composite drawing; Crime laboratories; Crime scene documentation; Crime scene investigation; Crime scene measurement; Crime scene reconstruction and staging; *Forensic Files*; Journalism; Literature and forensic science; Misconceptions fostered by media.

## Cyanoacrylate fuming. *See* Superglue fuming

## Cybercrime. *See* Computer crimes

## Cyberstalking

**Definition:** Electronic communication in which perpetrators repeatedly contact victims with the intent of abusing, exploiting, annoying, threatening, slandering, terrifying, or embarrassing them.

**Significance:** Cyberstalkers use the anonymity allowed by electronic communications technologies to disguise their true identities while they harass and threaten their victims. Depending on its severity, cyberstalking can be a misdemeanor or a crime punishable by jail time. Investigating cyberstalking is difficult for several reasons, not least of which is the lack of physical evidence in many cases. To find and prosecute cyberstalkers and authenticate the electronic evidence in these cases, law-enforcement personnel must typically use computer forensics investigative methods.

Rather than engaging in physical confrontation, cyberstalkers take advantage of the impersonal, nonconfrontational, and anonymous nature of the Internet and e-mail to harass or threaten their victims. This makes it difficult for authorities to measure the full extent of the crime of cyberstalking. Perpetrators can use various Internet-based technologies from any location; they may live next door to their victims or on the other side of the world.

In cases where cyberstalkers know their victims, the most common motive is revenge. Cyberstalking frequently occurs in workplace settings, perpetrated by employees who are angry with management or fellow workers. Pedophiles also sometime engage in cyberstalking, using social network Web sites, such as MySpace, to find potential victims. Law-enforcement investigations of cyberstalking may be valuable to defend against child sexual exploitation and other physical crimes, as many cyberstalking attacks have the potential to escalate to violent criminal acts. Some law-enforcement agencies are able to respond aggressively to cases of cyberstalking by following trails of digital evidence and seizing computers of suspects, but others lack the expertise and resources to pursue such cases.

## Legal Defenses Against Cyberstalking

The incidence of cyberstalking has increased over the years as growing numbers of people around the world have gained access to the Internet. In response to this trend, nations have enacted increasingly strict legislation to deal with cyberstalking. The first antistalking legislation in the United States went into effect in 1990. Since 1999, federal and state jurisdictions have amended existing general antistalking and antiharassment statutes to include instances of cyberstalking or have enacted new statues to protect victims of cyberstalking.

By mid-2007, forty-five U.S. states had laws against cyberstalking. The federal antistalking law prohibits anonymous Internet communications "with intent to annoy, abuse, threaten or harass." Laws to combat cyberstalking include federal statute 18 U.S.C. 875(c), which makes it a federal crime, "punishable by up to five years in prison and a fine of up to $250,000, to transmit any communication in interstate or foreign commerce containing a threat to injure the person or another." Because most states have also enacted their own specific legislation, investigators as well as victims of cyberstalking in the

United States may face complicated sets of laws offering varying definitions, protections, and penalties. A growing number of law-enforcement agencies have recognized the serious nature and extent of cyberstalking and have responded by providing training in computer forensic techniques and software. In large cities, such as New York and Los Angeles, police departments and district attorneys' offices have developed specialized units to investigate cyberstalking cases. The Federal Bureau of Investigation (FBI) has established Computer Crime Squads throughout the country; these units investigate all kinds of computer crime, including cyberstalking.

## Nature of Cyberstalking

Cyberstalking is similar to traditional forms of stalking in several ways. Many stalkers, both online and off, are motivated by a desire to control their victims, and both kinds of stalkers engage in behaviors aimed at gaining control. Online forums such as chat rooms, blogs, and social network sites make it easy for cyberstalkers to trick third parties into harassing or threatening the cyberstalkers' intended victims. To carry out such ruses, cyberstalkers post inflammatory or salacious messages in online forums while impersonating their victims, causing viewers of the messages to send unwelcome or threatening messages to the victims. Cyberstalkers with knowledge of their victims' screen names may use software that advises them when their victims are online; the stalkers then send their victims lewd or threatening instant messages.Cyberstalking is different from other types of stalking in that it may not involve any physical contact at all. As with other types of stalking, the majority of perpetrators are men and the majority of victims are women, although cases of women cyberstalking men and same-sex cyberstalking have been reported.

## Tracking Down Cyberstalkers

In cyberstalking cases, computers and the Internet are the weapons. Experienced cyberstalkers often use anonymous remailers, which can make it impossible for investigators to determine the true sources of e-mail and instant messages, Internet Relay Chat (IRC), or other

## Contentious Legislation Versus Legal Recourse

In the United States, laws concerning cyberstalking have generated controversy because many civil libertarians maintain that prohibiting anonymous communication that merely annoys others is a restraint on free speech online. They assert that the right of free speech extends to the Internet and even includes anonymous free speech. In contrast, many of the victims of cyberstalking have argued that legislation is necessary to provide victims of this behavior with legal recourse.

electronic communication. Anonymity gives cyberstalkers an advantage over investigators. Anonymous services on the Internet allow individuals to create free Web-based e-mail accounts, and most Internet service providers (ISPs) provide their services without authenticating or confirming users' identities. The investigation of cyberstalking thus requires the use of sophisticated computer and e-mail forensics methods to trace cyberstalkers' activities through their phone records. Investigators usually need subpoenas to obtain such records, whether from telephone companies or ISPs.

After investigators have identified suspects in cyberstalking cases, or the addresses of suspects' computers, they generally obtain search warrants that allow them to seize the computers, any electronic storage equipment, and digital devices. Because of the fragile nature of such equipment, these are usually transported to computer forensics labs, where experts make copies of the electronic evidence to investigate further.

Law-enforcement officers are sometimes frustrated by jurisdictional limitations in cyberstalking cases, as when they find that stalkers are located in other cities or states, making further investigation difficult or impossible. Officers who travel to other legal jurisdictions to continue their investigations may have trouble obtaining assistance from other agencies. It is likely that such limitations on law enforcement will diminish in the future, as cybercrimes, including cyberstalking, become increasingly widespread.

Statutes that require a showing of a "credible threat" may hinder prosecution in some cyberstalking cases. Cyberstalkers often do not threaten their victims overtly or in person, although they engage in conduct that would cause reasonable persons to fear violence. In the context of cyberstalking, the legal requirement of the existence of a credible threat is especially problematic because cyberstalkers may in fact be located far away from their victims (although their victims do not know that), and so the threats they pose might not be considered credible.

### Preserving Evidence

Connecting suspects to the crime of cyberstalking is a challenge without some evidence in addition to the electronic evidence, such as a former romantic or work-related link between the stalker and victim. With or without such other evidence, the key to successful prosecution in cyberstalking cases is the preservation of the full electronic trail of evidence.

Tracking down cyberstalkers and convicting them depends a great deal on the cooperation of the victims. Victims of cyberstalking should save all communications from their harassers as evidence; these should not be altered or edited in any way. Victims should also keep logs of the times and dates of their Internet activity and when they received communications from the stalkers. The requirements for the preservation of electronic evidence for legal purposes differ from the requirements for other types of evidence. The admissibility of electronic evidence in court depends on the existence of a reliable record of chain of custody for that evidence. Investigators must be able to demonstrate that they have not added to or otherwise altered the data or communications presented as evidence. They can help to satisfy this requirement by write protecting and virus checking all the media used. Investigators must be able to demonstrate to the court that what is purported to be a complete forensics copy of a suspect's hard drive or storage medium is indeed such a copy.

*Linda Volonino*

## Further Reading

Bocij, Paul. *Cyberstalking: Harassment in the Internet Age and How to Protect Your Family*. Westport, Conn.: Praeger, 2004. Discusses how Internet and communication technologies are used to harass and what individuals can do to prevent technological harassment.

D'Ovidio, Robert, and James Doyle. "A Study on Cyberstalking: Understanding Investigative Hurdles." *FBI Law Enforcement Bulletin* 72 (March, 2003): 10-17. Bulletin for law-enforcement personnel focuses on the challenges of tracking the digital trails of cyberstalkers.

Proctor, Mike. *How to Stop a Stalker*. Amherst, N.Y.: Prometheus Books, 2003. Provides information on various types of stalkers and their methods of stalking and discusses the courses of action people can take when they are being stalked. Presents many examples taken from actual cases.

Smith, Russell G., Peter Grabosky, and Gregor Urbas. *Cyber Criminals on Trial*. New York: Cambridge University Press, 2004. Discusses the results of an international study of the ways in which cybercriminals are handled by different nations' judicial systems.

Willard, Nancy E. *Cyberbullying and Cyberthreats: Responding to the Challenge of Online Social Aggression, Threats, and Distress*. 2d ed. Champaign, Ill.: Research Press. 2007. Discusses cyberstalking and other cyberbullying against students and offers advice regarding how victims can prevent and respond to those threats.

**See also:** Computer crimes; Computer forensics; Computer Fraud and Abuse Act of 1984; Computer hacking; Electronic voice alteration; Internet tracking and tracing; Rape.

# D

## Daubert v. Merrell Dow Pharmaceuticals

**Date:** Ruling issued on June 28, 1993
**Court:** U.S. Supreme Court
**Significance:** In *Daubert v. Merrell Dow Pharmaceuticals*, the U.S. Supreme Court held that under the Federal Rules of Evidence, a judge is required to make an independent reliability and relevance determination before allowing expert testimony to be admissible.

*Daubert v. Merrell Dow Pharmaceuticals* was a suit brought by two minor children who were born with serious birth defects, which they alleged were the result of their mothers' ingestion during pregnancy of Benedectin, a prescription antinausea drug marketed by Merrell Dow Pharmaceuticals. A U.S. district court granted summary judgment in favor of Merrell Dow because a great deal of scientific evidence demonstrated that Benedectin did not cause birth defects and because the scientific evidence offered by the plaintiffs was found to be inadmissible, as the evidence lacked general acceptance in the scientific community. The court of appeals agreed, stating that expert opinion is inadmissible unless the scientific technique on which the opinion is based is generally accepted by the relevant scientific community.

The U.S. Supreme Court disagreed and remanded the case for a new determination of the admissibility of the scientific evidence in question.

The Court explained that the Federal Rules of Evidence (FRE) govern the admissibility of evidence in federal court, thus the rule stated in *Frye v. United States* (1923) requiring general acceptance of a scientific technique is no longer an absolute requirement and has been superseded by Federal Rule of Evidence 702.

Under the governing rule of FRE 702, judges should examine the reliability and relevance of proffered expert scientific evidence in determining the admissibility of that evidence.

## Specific Requirements of *Daubert* and FRE 702

To determine the reliability of scientific evidence, judges should assess whether the methodology is scientifically valid and whether the methodology offers scientific knowledge that will assist the trier of fact (the jury in a jury trial, the judge in a bench trial) in determining the outcome of the case. Specifically, the four factors that judges should consider are whether the methodology and scientific evidence being offered can be and has been tested for validity, whether the scientific theory or technique has been peer-reviewed and published, what the known or potential rate of error is of the technique and the existence and maintenance of standards that control the technique's operation and use, and whether the methodology is generally accepted by the relevant scientific community.

In using the consideration of these four factors as a guide for evaluating scientific evidence, trial judges have great latitude in determining the reliability of evidence. The Supreme Court thus concluded in *Daubert v. Merrell Dow* that general acceptance of scientific evidence is no longer a precondition of admissibility under the Federal Rules of Evidence, but that factor may still have some bearing. In *Kumho Tire Company v. Carmichael* (1999), the Supreme Court later extended the requirements of *Daubert* in a loosened form to all experts, regardless of whether or not the experts are testifying as to scientific evidence.

## Applications of the *Daubert* Standard

Because forensic scientific evidence is often presented in the courtroom through the use of expert testimony, the *Daubert* standard greatly affects the admissibility of such evidence. For example, evidence that was previously rejected under *Frye* as not being generally accepted has been reexamined by courts to see if the evidence does embody good science. Polygraph results were viewed as inadmissible under *Frye*, but under *Daubert*, this form of evidence is no longer subject to a per se ban. Although polygraph evidence is still rarely admitted, judges at least give its admissibility minimal consideration.

In some cases, courts have reevaluated the validity and applicability of evidence that many would previously have accepted automatically as being valid under *Frye*. For instance, court decisions allowing handwriting comparisons and fingerprint identification date back to before the 1920's, but no empirical studies were conducted on the validity of handwriting comparisons or fingerprint identification because empirical scientific foundations for these methods were not required under *Frye*.

Some commentators have questioned the

## From the Court's Decision in *Daubert v. Merrell Dow*

Respondent expresses apprehension that abandonment of "general acceptance" as the exclusive requirement for admission will result in a "free-for-all" in which befuddled juries are confounded by absurd and irrational pseudo-scientific assertions. In this regard, respondent seems to us to be overly pessimistic about the capabilities of the jury and of the adversary system generally. Vigorous cross-examination, presentation of contrary evidence, and careful instruction on the burden of proof are the traditional and appropriate means of attacking shaky but admissible evidence. . . . Additionally, in the event the trial court concludes that the scintilla of evidence presented supporting a position is insufficient to allow a reasonable juror to conclude that the position more likely than not is true, the court remains free to direct a judgment, . . . and likewise to grant summary judgment. . . . These conventional devices, rather than wholesale exclusion under an uncompromising "general acceptance" test, are the appropriate safeguards where the basis of scientific testimony meets the standards of Rule 702.

tacit acceptance by courts of forensic fingerprint identification evidence because they believe that such evidence is not as reliable as previously assumed, as indicated by erroneous convictions and inconsistencies in protocols. It is extremely difficult to make accurate comparisons of poor-quality latent fingerprints left at a crime scene with rolled fingerprints taken directly from a defendant, and such comparisons often require fingerprint analysts to make subjective assessments. The scientific bases underlying fingerprint identification have yet to be tested fully under *Daubert*, but this form of evidence may one day be found to be unreliable and inadmissible. No appellate court has held that such evidence is definitively inadmissible, but in 2003 the U.S. Court of Appeals for the Fourth Circuit, in *United States v. Crisp*, became the first appellate court to hold that expert testimony on handwriting comparisons and fingerprint identification is admissible under *Daubert*.

The *Daubert* decision thus created a gatekeeper role for judges, who became responsible for assessing the reliability of the opinions of expert witnesses. This new role might result in previously accepted expert testimony being found inadmissible at the same time modern techniques of forensic science may have greater opportunities to alter the outcomes of cases as they are deemed admissible by more courts.

*Vivian Bodey*

## Further Reading

Benedict, Nathan. "Fingerprints and the *Daubert* Standard for Admission of Scientific Evidence: Why Fingerprints Fails and a Proposed Remedy." *Arizona Law Review* 46 (Fall, 2004): 519-549. Explores the history behind the *Daubert* standard and its possible application to fingerprint identification evidence.

Judicial Gatekeeping Project, ed. *The Judge's Role as Gatekeeper: Responsibilities and Power.* Cambridge, Mass.: Berkman Center for Internet and Society, Harvard Law School, 1999. Collection of essays, written for a general audience, provides detailed discussion of *Daubert* and the case's ramifications.

Klein, Daniel A. "Reliability of Scientific Technique and Its Acceptance Within Scientific Community as Affecting Admissibility, at Federal Trial, of Expert Testimony as to Result of Test or Study Based on Such Technique: Modern Cases." In *American Law Reports, Federal.* St. Paul, Minn.: Thomson/West, 2007. Offers analysis of court cases dealing with the admissibility of expert testimony involving a wide range of scientific and technical areas and techniques.

National Research Council. *The Polygraph and Lie Detection.* Washington, D.C.: National Academies Press, 2003. Provides interesting discussion of the polygraph and concludes that use of the polygraph for legal purposes is not likely to increase.

Rothstein, Paul F., Myrna S. Raeder, and David Crump. *Evidence.* St. Paul, Minn.: Thomson/West, 2003. Presents a broad discussion of the Federal Rules of Evidence as well as a detailed description of the history and current analysis of the admissibility of expert testimony and scientific evidence.

**See also:** Cognitive interview techniques; Courts and forensic evidence; DNA fingerprinting; Drug and alcohol evidence rules; Ethics; Expert witnesses; Federal Rules of Evidence; *Frye v. United States*; Polygraph analysis; Pseudoscience in forensic practice; Toxic torts.

---

## Decomposition of bodies

**Definition:** Process by which cadavers become skeletons through the destruction of the body's soft tissue.

**Significance:** Understanding the processes that take place during decomposition of a human body can help investigators determine a number of important pieces of information, including approximate time of death and whether the body was moved after death.

Sometimes, the decomposition of remains can contribute to the determination of cause and manner of death. Investigators need to remember that because of the number of variables involved in decomposition, it is rare to find two instances that share identical processes.

Decomposition begins at the moment of death, when all of the internal functions that work together to maintain the body's homeostasis cease. At this stage, decomposition manifests as the result of two processes: autolysis, which is the breaking down of tissues by the body's own internal chemicals and enzymes; and putrefaction, which is the breaking down of tissues by bacteria. These processes release gases that are the chief source of the distinctive odor of dead bodies. A great many factors affect the progression of decomposition, accelerating, hampering, or otherwise changing the process; these factors vary from body to body .

Knowledge of the decomposition process can help investigators and forensic pathologists to estimate time of death and to determine whether the body has been moved. Although often on popular television shows and in movies, characters portraying forensic experts make impressive specific statements about time of death, estimating using intervals of thirty or sixty minutes, in reality, forensic investigators are grateful if the time of death can be narrowed to a twelve-hour window. In contrast, analyis of decomposition manifestations makes the determination that a body has been moved more clear-cut. The fact that a body has been repositioned provides investigators with a very important piece of information—someone was on the scene before their arrival.

### Initial Body Changes

Immediately upon the discovery of a body, investigators look for four initial body changes. All of these changes begin at the moment of death; thus the presence or absence of manifestations of these changes can be used in the determination of an estimate of time of death. The four all have Latin names ending in *mortis*, the Latin word for death: pallor (paleness, fading) mortis, algor (cold or cooling) mortis, rigor (stiffening) mortis, and livor (black and blue mark, bruise) mortis.

Pallor mortis is the paleness that is associated with death; it results from the fact that the blood is no longer at the skin's surface because circulation has ceased. Full paleness happens in the first three hours after death. It is difficult to quantify the progression of this process, however, so this change generally is of little value in determining the time of death.

Algor mortis is the cooling of the body's temperature following death as it falls from the static 98.6 degrees to the ambient temperature. A body's temperature—usually measured using a rectal thermometer—provides some information that is useful in estimating the time of death, but bodies do not all cool at a consistent rate, so a somewhat complex equation must be used. Many factors can influence the rate of a body's cooling, including the presence of excessive humidity, lack of humidity, and the body's position near a heat source (such as a radiator), so any estimation has a wide margin of error.

Rigor mortis is the stiffening of the body's muscles after death. The muscles become so stiff that they are nearly impossible to move or manipulate. If the entire body is moved from its position at death while rigor mortis is fully established, the body's limbs will maintain their original pose, appearing to defy gravity. The cause of rigor mortis is a chemical reaction in which water reacts with the body's adenosine triphosphate (commonly referred to as ATP) and converts it to another compound. ATP is the chemical energy source required for movement in living tissue.

Rigor mortis follows what is typically referred to as the "rule of twelves." It normally takes the first twelve hours after death for rigor mortis to set fully and the body to become completely rigid. The body stays in full rigor for the next twelve hours (twelve to twenty-four hours after death), and then rigor begins to release during the third twelve hours (twenty-four to thirty-six hours after death). After thirty-six hours, the rigor mortis is fully released and the body is once again limp. Knowing what stage of rigor mortis a body is in can help in the determination of time of death, but many factors—such as ambient temperature, antemortem physical condition, and humidity—can vary the rigor schedule by hours.

A body's stage of rigor mortis can be very helpful in the determination of whether the body has been moved. If a body's limbs appear to be defying gravity or the body is in a position that does not make sense given the circumstances (leaning against a wall instead of crumpled on the floor, for example), investigators can conclude with certainty that the body was moved several hours after death. Livor mortis occurs when the blood, no longer in circulation, passes through the capillaries to settle in the gravity-dependent areas of the body. The blood stains the skin a dark red color in those areas. Lividity, as this process is also called, begins within the first hour of death and continues until full staining occurs at approximately twelve hours after death. An estimation of time of death can be made based on how deeply the skin is stained, but such an estimation is not specific and cannot be made until after full lividity is reached.

If the body is moved before full lividity is reached, the blood will shift and settle in the new gravity-dependent areas of the body. Partial staining may have already occurred in the original position, meaning the body has dual lividity. The only way dual lividity can occur is if the body is moved after death and prior to full livor mortis. Another sure indication that a body was moved after death is that it has reached full livor mortis, but the staining is not in the gravity-dependent areas of the body. In other words, if a body has full lividity of the chest but is found found lying on the back, the body must have been flipped over after full lividity was reached while the body was facedown.

## Autolysis and Putrefaction

Autolysis is the destruction of a cell after its death by the action of its own enzymes, which break down its structural molecules. Human cells have an organelle known as the lysosome, which is a membrane containing up to forty digestive enzymes that are made by the endoplasmic reticulum and Golgi apparatus (sometimes called the Golgi complex). The lysosomes are responsible for digesting nucleic acids, polysaccharides, fats, and proteins within the cell. They are active in recycling the cell's organic material and in the intracellular digestion of macromolecules. At the point of a person's death, the digestive enzymes are released from the lysosomes' membranes and begin destroying the cell. Putrefaction usually begins concurrent with autolysis in the first stages of decomposition. Putrefaction is the breaking down of flesh and tissue caused by bacteria, which creates the strong, unpleasant odor associated with decomposition. The stages of putrefaction vary, as do the times within each stage, depending on environmental conditions. Some of the factors that influence the speed of putrefaction include the atmospheric temperature and humidity level, the movement of air, the state of hydration of the tissues and the nutritional state of the body before death, the age of the deceased, and the cause of death. Low temperatures, which inhibit the growth of bacteria, retard the process considerably.

One of the earliest signs of putrefaction in human decomposition is the discoloration of the lower abdominal wall near the right hip bone because of the proximity of the cecum and large intestine to the skin's surface there. Human bodies house many bacteria that assist in the digestion process. After death, as intestinal bacteria begin the putrefaction process, the lower-right abdomen turns a greenish to black color. The gases produced by the bacteria are also responsible for swelling of the face and neck. This swelling may cause the eyes and tongue to protrude and may make visual identification of the decedent difficult. Other effects produced by the gases include a marked increase in the volume of the abdomen, which is under tension, and of the scrotum and penis, which may become larger than normal.

The intestinal bacteria begin colonizing the entire body, utilizing the venous system as pathways. The discoloration of the abdomen eventually spreads as the bacteria migrate, changing the veins and arteries of the rest of the abdomen, the thighs, the chest, and the shoulders to the same green and black. The discolored venous system makes visible lines across the body; this is referred to as marbling.

A few days to a week after death, as the bacteria continue to devour tissue, the skin begins to blister in the sloping regions of the body. Eventually the blisters, which contain a thick reddish liquid, erupt, making the epidermis (the outer layer of skin) fragile. Ultimately, the epidermis becomes so delicate that it tears easily

and may come off in large areas, leaving the red dermis below visible. This phenomenon is referred to as skin slippage. At times, the epidermis of an entire hand may detach, creating a glove of skin. If the skin of the fingertips detaches, identification of the body through fingerprints may be difficult, but as long as the fingertip skin is still available, fingerprints may be retrievable; forensic scientists have had success in placing such skin over their own latex-gloved fingers to retrieve the fingerprints.

As the body enters the second week following death, the increased pressure on the abdomen produced by putrefactive gases leads to the ejection of feces and urine. This pressure also leads to the expulsion of liquids from other body orifices, particularly from the mouth and nostrils. Because this liquid is often bloody, its presence sometimes leads to a misdiagnosis of injury. At this stage, the orifices as well as the organs may take on a foamy appearance as the gases mix with liquids internally.

In the following weeks, the skin begins to darken to black, making identification even more difficult. The face becomes even more bloated and blackens as well, so that racial characteristics may be masked. The cadaver continues to bloat with internal gases, giving the impression that the deceased was a very heavy individual.

Internal decomposition of the organs tends to occur at a slower pace than that of the rest of the body. The capsules of the kidney, spleen, and liver resist putrefaction more than do other tissues, but eventually they become sacs containing a thick reddish liquid. These sacs will ultimately burst. The viscera and soft tissues disintegrate, whereas organs such as the uterus, heart, and prostate last longer, as do tendon tissues and ligaments attached to the bones. These different rates of decay of the organs may be proportional to the amounts of muscular and conjunctive tissue they contain.

### Saponification

Decomposition tends to be slower in water than in air because of the usually lower temperature of water, which retards bacterial growth. Water also protects the body from insects and predatory animals, with certain birds and fish as notable exceptions. A body typically floats head down, because the head does not develop gas formation as easily as the abdomen; this causes fluids to gravitate to the head. Putrefaction of a body that has been decomposing in water is thus more visible on the face and front of the neck, making visual identification particularly difficult. Identification is further hampered by saponification, which is a chemical process in which water converts the body's fatty acids into a different compound called adipocere. A grayish-white or tan spongy substance that adheres to the body, adipocere can act as a preservative, counteracting the effects of decomposition.

Saponification requires at least partial immersion of the body in an aquatic environment with warm temperatures. It normally presents as peeling, blanched skin. Adipocere has been found on bodies in bathtubs, ponds, lakes, and oceans. It has also been discovered on bodies inside caskets, on bodies found in caves, and on remains wrapped in plastic.

## Mummification

Mummification is the process of drying out the tissues of a body. It is characterized by dryness and brittle, torn skin, especially on the protruding areas of the body, which is generally brown in color. It is possible for slight adipocere to form in mummified bodies, as the hydration needed to create the fats contributes to the drying of the body. Mummification is found in dry, ventilated environments and generally in warm places where bodies lose fluids through evaporation. Mummification is often found in desert environments, but it can also occur in dry, closed spaces, such as attics and closets. Dehydration before death may contribute to the process of mummification.

Mummified bodies are often found in a state of preservation, so that it is usually much easier to investigate the identities of the deceased than it is in cases of saponification. Performing autopsies on mummified remains is very difficult because the skin is extremely brittle and disintegrates easily. A variety of methods have been developed to rehydrate mummified bodies for better autopsy results. This rehydration is often referred to as tissue building.

## Skeletonization

Skeletonization, or the removal of all soft tissue from the bone, is generally considered the last stage of decomposition. Skeletonization may be complete, meaning the entire body has no flesh, or partial, with areas of the body in different stages of decomposition.

Under normal conditions, skeletonization occurs only after a considerable amount of time has passed. An unembalmed adult body buried six feet deep in ordinary soil without a coffin normally takes ten to twelve years to decompose fully to a skeleton, given a temperate climate. Immerse the body in water, and skeletonization occurs approximately four times faster; expose it to air, and it occurs eight times faster. The intervention of predatory insects or animals can greatly speed up this timetable, however.

## Insect and Predator Activity

Predatory insects and animals can accelerate decomposition by eating the flesh of a cadaver, separating the body into parts, or using the body as a repository for their eggs. The involvement of insect predators in particular can be beneficial to investigators in that it can help in the determination of an estimate of time of death. Insects are the first organisms to arrive on a body after death. They colonize the remains in a predictable sequence, as each stage of decomposition, from fresh body to skeletonization, is attractive to a different group of insects.

When remains are found weeks or months after death, the examination of insect evidence is often the only method available that can help investigators to determine an approximate time of death. Forensic entomologists study what insects are present in and on the body and pinpoint the development stages of those insects. They also take note of the species that are not present. Every group of insects that has inhabited the body will have left evidence of having been there, even the groups that have moved on as the body progressed through successive decomposition stages. Blowflies, which can detect death from great distances, are the first to colonize a body.

*Russell S. Strasser*

## Further Reading

Catanese, Gerard, and Tamara Bloom. "Recovery of a Mummified Pregnant Woman from a Fifty-five-Gallon Drum More Than Thirty Years After Her Death." *American Journal of Forensic Medicine and Pathology* 23, no. 3 (2002): 245-247. Interesting article on mummification discusses the case of a twenty-eight-year-old woman whose mummified remains were found in steel drum in a crawl space under a house.

DiMaio, Vincent J., and Dominick DiMaio. *Forensic Pathology.* 2d ed. Boca Raton, Fla.: CRC Press, 2001. One of the best reference sources available in the field of forensic pathology. Includes a very informative section on human decomposition.

Mann, Robert, William Bass, and Lee Meadows. "Time Since Death and Decomposition of the Human Body: Variables and Observations in Case and Experimental Field Studies." *Journal of Forensic Sciences* 35, no. 1 (1990): 103-111. Excellent comprehensive study of the decomposition of a body includes discussion of determination of time of death.

O'Brien, Tyler G., and Amy C. Kuehner. "Waxing Grave About Adipocere: Soft Tissue Change in an Aquatic Context." *Journal of Forensic Sciences* 52, no. 2 (2007): 294-301. Presents the results of a study of the saponification process on submerged bodies. Excellent source for further information on this phenomenon.

Rodriguez, William, and William Bass. "Decomposition of Buried Bodies and Methods That May Aid in Their Location." *Journal of Forensic Sciences* 30, no. 3 (1985): 836-852. Interesting article coauthored by one of the foremost forensic anthropologists in the United States; Rodriguez has conducted extensive research on the decomposition of human bodies.

Spennemann, Dirk H. R., and Bernd Franke. "Decomposition of Buried Human Bodies and Associated Death Scene Materials on Coral Atolls in the Tropical Pacific." *Journal of Forensic Sciences* 40, no. 3 (1995): 356-367. Informative, penetrating study of decomposition focuses on the effects of tropical conditions.

Spitz, Werner U., ed. *Spitz and Fisher's Medicolegal Investigation of Death: Guidelines for the Application of Pathology to Crime Investigation.* 4th ed. Springfield, Ill.: Charles C Thomas, 2006. Indispensable volume for those conducting forensic investigations and forensic pathology. Includes comprehensive sections on specific cases along with their pathological findings.

**See also:** Adipocere; Algor mortis; Autopsies; Bacteria; Body farms; Coffin birth; Forensic anthropology; Forensic archaeology; Forensic entomology; Livor mortis; Mummification; Rigor mortis; Taphonomy; University of Tennessee Anthropological Research Facility.

## Decontamination methods

**Definition:** Chemical and physical methods of eradicating, inactivating, or cleaning potentially dangerous biological, chemi- cal, or radiological agents that are present on persons or objects, including surfaces and building structures..

**Significance:** Exposure to certain kinds of biological, chemical, and radiological agents can be detrimental to human beings. Forensic scientists as well as members of the general public may find themselves in situations where they may be exposed to such agents, thus decontamination procedures need to be in place. Such procedures in- clude removal of contaminants, preven- tion of infectious transmission from biological hazards, reduction of contaminant levels to ensure protection from harm, and provision of decontaminated objects or surfaces that are safe for use, handling, storage, or disposal.

Exposure to various hazardous agents can take place in the home, in the workplace, or in other environments. For example, workers in health care institutions and in laboratories of many kinds (forensic, clinical and research) are often exposed to bloodborne pathogens and other potentially infectious materials. Individuals who work in manufacturing industries are also often exposed to potentially toxic chemicals specific to their work environments. In addition to such everyday exposure, public concern has risen regarding the prospect of the use of chemical and biological agents as weapons. A radiological (nuclear) agent was last used as a weapon in World War II, but such agents are also present in nuclear power plants, in some weapons manufacturing plants, and in small quantities in forensic, clinical, and research laboratories when particular experiments require them. Forensic scientists may be exposed to biological, chemical, or radiological agents in the course of their work.

Because of the dangers of exposure to hazardous agents, the issue of decontamination is increasingly important. Decontamination methods include two broad categories: chemical and physical. Specific cleaning and decontamina- tion procedures apply to different situations. For example, different methods of cleaning and decontamination would be used for a crime scene, for an operating room in a hospital, for a patient examination room in an outpatient clinic, for a blood bank, for a research laboratory, and for a facility exposed to a biological or chemical war agent, such as the anthrax-laden letters that contaminated the Hart Senate Office Building and the associated U.S. Postal Service mail-handling and -sorting centers in the fall of 2001. Moreover, specific protocols are in place in the United States for decontaminating civilians as opposed to military personnel in military set- tings, where quick and efficient strategies need to be employed. The choice of decontamination methods depends also on the severity and con- sequences of the exposure and on the nature of the item that will be decontaminated, including the material of which it is made.

## General Methods

The U.S. Occupational Safety and Health Administration (OSHA) recommends several general measures of decontamination. Hand decontamination by completely washing hands with soap and water, rinsing, and drying with a clean towel or air-drying can help prevent transmission of disease. This method is useful in many different settings, including food-related industries, health care institutions, and forensic laboratories.

Clothing, tools, and appropriate equipment should be washed completely using soap and clean water. A solution of chlorine bleach (sodium hypochlorite) and water (one-fourth cup of bleach per gallon of water) should be used to wipe down surfaces; gloves, eye protection, and appropriate clothing should be worn by those using bleach solutions for decontamination..

## Chemical Methods

Chemical disinfectants that are often used in medical, surgical, and research facilities include alcohols (isopropyl and ethyl alcohol, usually 70 percent solutions, are used to inactivate biological hazards, including adenoviruses, murine retroviruses, and human immunodefi- ciency virus, or HIV); halogen-containing compounds such as iodophors (iodine combined with an organic substance); oxidizing chlorine solu- tions such as bleach (a 10 percent chlorine solu- tion made fresh daily is recommended); phenolic compounds such as chlorhexidine; strong bases such as calcium, sodium, and potassium hydroxides; mild acids such as vinegar; surface- active compounds such as soaps and detergents (quaternary ammonium compounds commonly known as quats); and aldehyde compounds such as glutaraldehyde and formaldehyde.

The necessary length of exposure to these chemical decontaminating agents depends on the level of disinfection required (low, medium, or high) as well as the limitations of each situation (for example, the nature of the item being disinfected is a factor, whether it is a sample ccontaining bloodborne pathogens or other potentially infectious materials, the surface of a laboratory workbench, or a soft surface such as a carpeted area). One type of chemical decontamination used in forensic science involves dichloromethane. Forensic investigators often obtain samples of DNA (deoxyribonucleic acid) from hair, teeth, body fluids, and fingernails. Hair is usually decontaminated with dichloromethane for two minutes before extraction of DNA. In addition to the chemical decontamination, most of these objects are placed in specially designed biohazard bags or containers for disposal; these are then sterilized using an autoclave, a device that employs heat, steam, and pressure to destroy biological pathogens.

Chemical disinfectants that may be used for decontamination of building structures in cases of toxic industrial events or biological or chemical attacks include three broad categories: liquid-based topical agents (such as bleach and aqueous chlorine dioxide), foams and gels (such as the L-Gel System and a decontamination foam created by Sandia National Laboratories), and gaseous and vapor technologies, or fumigants (such as chlorine dioxide gas, vapor-phase hydrogen peroxide, and paraformaldehyde).

The L-Gel System is an innovative decontam- inant of biological hazards as well as of chemical and biological warfare agents, such as the spores of Bacillus anthracis, the bacterium that causes anthrax. L-Gel, which was developed at the Lawrence Livermore National Laboratory in California, is based on a Du Pont Corporation product called Oxone, a commercial oxidizer that uses potassium peroxymonosulfate as its active ingredient. L-Gel incorporates Oxone so- lution and a silica gelling agent, which allows it to cling to walls, ceilings, and other surfaces.

The decontamination foam developed at the Sandia National Laboratories in New Mexico, known as Sandia foam, uses aqueous-based hydrogen peroxide as its active ingredient. Sandia foam can also eradicate bacterial spores through its surfactant and oxidizer properties.

Radioactive material contaminants, especially from water-cooled nuclear reactors, are decontaminated with chemical reagents. For example, alkaline permanganate is used for pretreatment, citrate-oxalate solution for treatment, acidified hydrogen peroxide solution for posttreatment, and demineralized water for rinsing in between steps

Radioactive contamination from spills that occur in laboratories is usually minor and easily contained. Exposed personnel are decontaminated using the protocols in place for such events. Chemical decontamination methods include using soaps or detergents with chelating compounds and special decontaminants for ra-

dioactivity, such as Decon90, Count-Off, and Radiacwash. For personnel decontamination, hydrogen peroxide, potassium permanganate, and sodium metabisulfite can be used for decontamination of exposed skin, provided there are no wounds and the skin does not become inflamed or irritated. If radioactive material is ingested, vomiting is induced and copious amounts of water are given to dilute the radioactivity. Most institutions where radioactive materials are present have environmental health and safety officers and radiation safety officers who are responsible for reporting radioactive contamination incidents and for more extensive decontamination per institutional protocols.

Most of the decontamination technologies developed in the United States for use in case of biological, chemical, and radiological attacks have been developed for military purposes, but these technologies and their potential uses have been expanded to include civilian purposes since the events of fall, 2001, when the United States experienced terrorism on a scale that it had never before seen.

**Physical Methods**

Physical methods of decontamination range from simply scrubbing off microbes with an antimicrobial chemical agent to more sophisticated methods, such as the use of ultraviolet (UV) light, ionizing radiation, microwave irradiation, absorbents, filtration, dry heat, and moist heat (steam). UV light is often used to cause mutation experimentally; its main application as a decontaminant is in laboratories that use hazardous microbes and in irradiation of air near important surgical sites. Ionizing radiation includes electron beams, X rays, cathode rays, and gamma rays; these have greater energy than UV light. Ionizing radiation is often used in industrial processes such as the sterilization of disposable medical and surgical supplies. Microwave irradiation has been used to sterilize items such as sponges and scrub pads.

Absorbents are natural materials, such as fuller's earth, that can take up liquid contaminants or impurities. An absorbent used by the military is M291, a dried resin used for rapid decontamination of the skin. Filtration is a method of sterilizing large volumes of liquid to remove contaminants by passing the liquid through one or more filters. Dry-heat sterilizers are often used to disinfect instruments that can withstand high temperatures. Moist heat (steam) is used in autoclaves to sterilize equipment, liquids, and other objects. Some bacteria that form spores (such as those that belong to the genera Bacillus and Clostridium), however, cannot be completely eradicated by autoclaving because the spores can survive extremely high pressures and temperatures.

*Miriam E. Schwartz and Charlene F. Barroga*

## Further Reading

The American National Red Cross. Preventing the Spread of Bloodborne Pathogens Fact Sheet. Washington, DC: Bloodborne Pathogens Training, 2011. Informational publication that highlights prevention

Boss, Martha J., and Dennis W. Day, eds. *Biological Risk Engineering Handbook: Infection Control and Decontamination*. Boca Raton, FL: CRC Press, 2003. Provides extensive coverage of biological contaminants in relation to industrial hygiene, including methods for measuring, controlling, and containing human exposure.

Environmental Protection Agency. *Compilation of Available Data on Building Decontamination Alternatives*. Washington, D.C.: Environmental Protection Agency, 2005. Presents information on the technologies that could be used for decontam- inating buildings in the event of chemical or biological attacks in the United States.

Johansson, I., and P. Somasundaran, eds. *Handbook for Cleaning/Decontamination of Surfaces*. 2 vols. New York: Elsevier, 2007. Comprehensive reference resource includes up-to-date discussion of the physicochemical features of the cleaning process, different materials used for decontamination, effects of cleaning on the environment, and other related matters.

The Joint Commission. Improving Patient and Worker Safety: Opportunities for Synergy, Collaboration and Innovation. Oakbrook Terrace, IL: The Joint Commission, November 2012. An authoritative guide to increase awareness on the potential synergies between patient and worker health and safety activities

Kohli, Rajiv and L. Mital Kashmiri L., eds. Developments in Surface Contamination and Cleaning: Cleaning Techniques. Waltham, MA: Elsevier, Inc., 2015. A critical analysis of surface contaminants and mechanisms for their removal.

O'Neal, Jon T. *The Bloodborne Pathogens Standard: A Pragmatic Approach*. New York: Van Nostrand Reinhold, 1996. Provides practical information to help employers interpret and implement the OSHA standard and discusses what to do if exposure to pathogens occurs.

Occupational Safety and Health Administration (OSHA). OSHA's Bloodborne Pathogens Standard Fact Sheet. Washington, D.C.: Government Printing Office, 2011. One of OSHA publications and educational materials that highlight OSHA programs, policies or standards.

Raber, E., et al. *Universal Oxidation for CBW Decontamination: L-Gel System Development and Deployment*. Springfield, VA: National Technical Information Service, 2000. Presents a comprehensive discussion of the L-Gel System, which is used for decontamination of chemical and biological agents.

Ryan, Kenneth J., and C. George Ray. *Sherris Medical Microbiology: An Introduction to Infectious Diseases*. New York: McGraw-Hill Medical, 2003. Textbook on microorganisms includes discussion of the spread and control of infections.

U.S. Department of Homeland Security and U.S. Department of Health and Human Services. Patient Decontamination in a Mass Chemical Exposure Incident: National Planning Guidance for Communities. Scotts Valley, CA: On-Demand Publishing, LLC, doing business as CreateSpace Independent Publishing Platform, 2015. Discusses decontamination of patients exposed to chemical warfare agents or toxic industrial chemicals or materials.

Walker, Jimmy, d. Decontamination in Hospitals and Healthcare (Woodhead Publishing Series in Biomaterials). Cambridge, UK:

Woodhead Publishing, 2013. Describes the significance of decontamination in healthcare facilities and discusses decontamination practices in hospitals, including sterilization of surgical instruments.

**See also:** Air and water purity; Anthrax; Anthrax letter attacks; Biohazard bags; Biological terrorism; Biotoxins; Brockovich-PG&E case; Chemical agents; Chemical Biological Incident Response Force, U.S.; Chemical terrorism; Chemical warfare; Crime scene cleaning; Crime scene protective gear; forensic toxicology Radiation damage to tissues; U.S. Army Medical Research Institute of Infectious Diseases.

## Defensive wounds

**Definition:** Injuries received by victims as the result of trying to defend themselves during physical attacks.

**Significance:** Defensive wounds can provide key pieces of evidence during investigations of criminal acts. Because they are inflicted on victims while the crimes are being committed, they can reveal a great deal about the crimes themselves.

Defensive wounds often occur during crimes of violence, such as homicides, rapes, and other assaults. Most such wounds are found on victims' forearms and palms of hands, but they can also be found on other parts, such as the lower legs and feet of victims who attempt to kick their attackers. Defensive wounds are typically inflicted by knives or other sharp instruments or result from blunt force trauma from objects such as baseball bats and hammers. Less commonly, defensive wounds are inflicted by firearms.

Defensive wounds can reveal where perpetrators were in relation to their victims, what types of weapons they used, and the amount of force they used. Such wounds can also be important in reconstructing the time lines of crime scenes, and they may produce other kinds of evidence. For example, blood from wounds may leave smears or spatters. When victims scratch their attackers—as they often do in physical struggles—traces of the attackers' skin cells can almost always be found under the victims' fingernails. These traces can be scraped, and the DNA (deoxyribonucleic acid) they contain can be analyzed. At the same time, considerable amounts of trace and transfer evidence can be transferred between victims and their attackers.

A popular misconception about defensive wounds is that if they are not found on victims' bodies, the victims must not have chosen to fight back or were compliant. This is often untrue, especially in cases of sexual assault. An absence of defensive injuries may indicate several possible sequences of events. For example, victims may fight back without sustaining any injuries. More frequently, however, victims simply cannot fight back, usually because they are quickly overpowered or are incapacitated during the attacks. Victims may be asleep or rendered unconscious through the use of drugs or alcohol during their attacks. Victims might also be caught unaware by their attackers and thus not have time to fight back. When the body of a victim has many fresh wounds, none of which seems to be defensive in nature, it may mean that the victim was already dead or unconscious when the wounds were inflicted. The victim may also have been restrained to prevent defensive movements.

*Ayn Embar-Seddon and Allan D. Pass*

### Further Reading

Hopping, Lorraine Jean. *The Body as Evidence.* Milwaukee: Gareth Stevens, 2007.

Houck, Max M. *Forensic Science: Modern Methods of Solving Crime.* Westport, Conn.: Praeger, 2007.

_____, ed. *Mute Witnesses: Trace Evidence Analysis.* San Diego, Calif.: Academic Press, 2001.

**See also:** Antemortem injuries; Bite-mark analysis; Blood residue and bloodstains; Blood spatter analysis; Blood volume testing; Blunt force trauma; DNA extraction from hair, bodily fluids, and tissues; Gunshot wounds; Hesitation wounds and suicide; Homicide; Knife wounds;

Puncture wounds; Rape; Strangulation; Trace and transfer evidence.

## Deoxyribonucleic acid. *See* DNA

## Diagnostic and Statistical Manual of Mental Disorders

**Date:** Predecessor published 1844; First published under the present name 1952; Fifth edition published 2013

**Identification:** The fifth edition of the *Diagnostic and Statistical Manual of Mental Disorders,* commonly called the DSM-5, provides an authoritative scheme used to classify psychological disorders.

**Significance:** The DSM-5, published by the *American Psychiatric Association,* provides detailed information about mental disorders, including information about diagnostic features, associated features supporting diagnosis, prevalence, development and course, risk and prognostic factors, functional consequences, differential diagnosis, and co-morbidity. For many disorders, the DSM-5 also includes information on culture- and gender-related diagnostic issues, suicide risk, and specifiers such as "with poor insight."

In the United States, mental health professionals use the DSM-5 in research and treatment; insurance companies use the DSM-5 to make decisions about what treatments to cover; and, courts and attorneys use the DSM-5 when assessing the forensic consequences of mental disorders. Forensic applications include determining competency to stand trial and making involuntary civil commitment decisions, which typically hinge on imminent harm to self or others. The DSM-5 is comprehensive, listing twenty-two categories of disorders, many of which have multiple subcategories. For example, disorders might include mental retardation, schizophrenia, or anxiety disorder; subcategories of anxiety disorders include separation anxiety disorder, selective mutism, specific phobia, social anxiety disorder, panic disorder, agoraphobia, generalized anxiety disorder, substance/medication-induced anxiety disorder, and other anxiety disorders. The DSM-5 was developed in coordination with the tenth and eleventh editions of the *World Health Organization's International Classification of Diseases* (ICD-10 and ICD-11), which covers both medical and psychological disorders. The DSM-5 is the most widely used classification system for mental disorders in the United States, other parts of the world use the ICD-9, 10, or 11.

## Structure

The DSM-5 has three sections. First, a brief introduction gives background on how the DSM-5 evolved from previous versions, stressing the fact that it is a living document that will continue to evolve. Second, the actual diagnostic codes are organized based on developmental and lifespan considerations so that it begins with problems that manifest early in life, followed by those most common to adolescence and young adulthood, ending with those most relevant to adulthood and later life. Third, emerging measures and models gives comprehensive symptom measures, cultural interviews, and conditions for further study such as internet gaming disorder.

The DSM-5 disorders include neurodevelopmental disorders (i.e., mental retardation, autism, and attention-deficit/hyperactivity), schizophrenia, mood disorders including bipolar, depression, and anxiety, obsessive-compulsive disorders, trauma and stress-related disorders (i.e., post-traumatic stress disorder), dissociative disorders, somatic symptom disorders, feeding/eating disorders (i.e., anorexia and bulimia), elimination disorders, sleep-wake disorders, sexual dysfunctions, gender dysphoria, disruptive or impulse-control disorders, substance-related and addictive disorders, neurocognitive disorders (i.e., delirium), personality disorders (i.e., antisocial or borderline), paraphilic disorders, other mental disorders, medication-induced disorders, and a general other category.

## Strengths and Weaknesses

Two issues with any kind of diagnostic system are reliability (that is, different people agree on the diagnosis) and validity (that is, the diagnosis is accurate). The people who developed the DSM-5 conducted extensive reviews of research to pinpoint which categories in past versions of the DSM had been too vague. They next developed some new diagnostic criteria and categories and conducted field trials at 11 different medical-academic sites. In the field trials, many professionals and researchers used the new criteria in their work. Work groups considered feedback from the field trials as well as from web-site postings designed to facilitate public and professional input. Much but not all of the time, the same clients or kinds of clients received the same diagnoses. Thus, although not totally reliable or valid, the most recently published version of the DSM-5 represents the best information currently available about diagnosis. The DSM-5 is designed to be primarily descriptive, so it avoids suggesting underlying causes for a person's behavior. Instead, it paints a picture of the behavior itself. Also, it provides precise information so that researchers can explore causes of a problem, and two persons diagnosing the same person will arrive at the same diagnosis. This emphasis on behavior could be considered a strength or a weakness of the DSM-5's approach.

A potential problem with the DSM-5 is that it compartmentalizes people into inflexible, all-or-nothing categories rather than considering the degree to which individuals display disordered behavior. Co-morbidity is common, and the DSM-5 does not necessarily capture the widespread sharing of symptoms and risk factors that occurs across many disorders. In addition, some mental health professionals have expressed concern that labelling someone as "abnormal" imparts a dehumanizing, lifelong stigma. Further, a particular diagnosis might cause professionals who deal with that person to concentrate on the diagnosed problem to the neglect of other problems. Despite such drawbacks, which are inherent in any labeling system, the DSM-5 offers a logical way to organize the major types of mental disturbance.

*Lillian M. Range*

## Further Reading

American Psychiatric Association. *Desk Reference to the Diagnostic Criteria from DSM5*. Washington, D. C.: Guilford, 2014. Abridged version of the DSM-5 is designed to be more portable and easier to use than the full 947-page edition. Includes the DSM-5 classification chart, a differential diagnosis decision tree, and a list of the appendixes that appear in the unabridged edition.

Durand, V. Mark, and David H. Barlow. *Essentials of Abnormal Psychology*. 7th ed. Belmont, CA: Wadsworth, 2013. Uses an integrated approach that considers biological, environmental, social and cultural causes of different disorders. Presents thorough descriptions of the different diagnostic groups and includes real case profiles of individuals who have specific disorders.

Morrison, James. *DSM-5® Made Easy: The Clinician's Guide to Diagnosis*. New York: Guilford, 2014. Includes more than 130 detailed case vignettes illustrating typical patients, with down-to-earth discussions that demonstrate how to arrive at a diagnosis and rule out other likely possibilities. Conveys the idea that diagnosis is not about labeling but about organizing a person's experience so that one can understand psychiatric problems and design appropriate treatment.

Reichenberg, Lourie W. *DSM-5 Essentials: The Savvy Clinician's Guide to the Changes in Criteria*. Hoboken, NJ: Wiley, 2013. Presents a comprehensive overview of the changes from DSM-4 to DSM-5. For example, covers the division of anxiety disorders into separate chapters for anxiety/panic disorders, trauma-related disorders and obsessive-compulsive disorders. Explains questionnaires that provide a quick assessment of symptoms that may impact diagnosis, treatment or prognosis. Includes a list of free assessments available for download at the APA website.

Zimmerman, Mark. *Interview Guide for Evaluation of DSM-V Disorders and the Mental Status Evaluation*., East Greenwich, RI: Psych Products Press, 2013. Lightweight but highly usable tool designed to be carried around and used as needed. Contains complete diagnostic information structured in the form of easily usable questions, as well as "how-to" information, an overview of mental status examinations, and a good short guide to taking psychiatric histories.

**See also:** Borderline personality disorder; Competency evaluation and assessment instruments; Drug abuse and dependence; Forensic psychiatry; Guilty but mentally ill plea; Hallucinogens; Minnesota Multiphasic Personality Inventory; Psychopathic personality disorder; Victimology.

## Dial tone decoder

**Definition:** Device that deciphers all numbers dialed from a particular telephone and sends the information to an external recorder.

**Significance:** During criminal and foreign intelligence investigations, information about what telephone numbers have been called from specific telephones can be important for establishing connections among individuals.

When a number key is pressed on a touch-tone telephone, two tones are generated. Each vertical column on the keypad generates a high-frequency tone, and each horizontal row produces a low-frequency tone. When the high- and low-frequency tones of any key are mixed, they produce a tone of unique frequency associated with that specific keypad number. A dial tone recorder deciphers these unique frequencies on an outgoing telephone line and uses the information to route the call to the correct receiving telephone.

When a dial tone decoder is connected to an external device, information about the number called can be recorded, so that a third party can tell what number has been dialed. This is called a pen register tap. The telephone conversation is not accessible to the third party, only the number called. A modern pen register tap usually sends the information to a computer with an infrared port (an infrared data association, or IRDA) that can communicate wirelessly with the dial tone decoder in the same way a remote control turns on a television. The presence of a pen register tap on a telephone line is difficult to detect.

Historically, wiretap laws in the United States were designed to protect the content of telephone conversations. Initiating a telephone wiretap required a court order and a high level of proof that the wiretap was essential to an investigation. Because pen register taps (or the reverse, trap and trace taps, which decipher the numbers of the telephones that originate incoming calls) do not allow access to the contents of calls, it has historically been much easier for investigators to obtain court orders for these types of taps. The Patriot Act, which was passed following the 2001 terrorist attacks on the Pentagon and the World Trade Center in New York City, made it even easier for law-enforcement agencies to place pen register taps. All the act requires is that the requesting agency certify that information likely to be obtained from the tap is relevant to an investigation.

In the twenty-first century, telecommunication companies routinely record originating and receiving telephone numbers of all calls for billing purposes, so pen register taps are not as useful as they once were. Law-enforcement agencies can get the same information by obtaining court orders that require telecommunication companies to release the calling information for particular individuals or telephones.

*Martiscia Davidson*

### Further Reading

Diffie, Whitfield, and Susan Landau. *Privacy on the Line: The Politics of Wiretapping and Encryption.* Cambridge, Mass.: MIT Press, 2007.

Olejniczak, Stephen P. *Telecom for Dummies.* Indianapolis, Ind.: Wiley, 2006.

**See also:** Computer crimes; Crime laboratories; Electronic voice alteration; Internet tracking and tracing; Telephone tap detector.

# Direct versus circumstantial evidence

**Definition:** Evidence that links directly to material facts is direct evidence; evidence that requires inferences to link it to material facts is circumstantial evidence.

**Significance:** Most forensic evidence collected from crime scenes is circumstantial evidence in its relationship to the material issue of whether suspects are guilty of the crimes charged, although such evidence may be direct evidence of lesser material facts of the crimes.

Direct and circumstantial evidence of a series of material facts related to a crime builds the case and leads to an outcome of guilt or innocence. In obtaining evidence, forensic scientists rely on Locard's exchange principle, which states that every contact of an individual with another person, place, or object results in an exchange of materials. The work of forensic science applies scientific disciplines to the law and encompasses the discovery, gathering, investigation, preservation, examination, comparison, documentation, and quality control of materials found at the scenes of crimes. The work of forensic science enables investigators to use the physical evidence or the absence of particular physical evidence at crime scenes to develop associations that prove or disprove material facts as those facts relate to the crimes.

Direct evidence is evidence that links directly to material issues in a case; it may take the form of witness testimony, video or audio recordings of the events that took place, or confession of the suspect. Fingerprints also may be direct evidence of material facts. The fact finder (judge or jury) does not have to infer anything from this evidence, as the evidence is considered to speak for itself. For example, a witness testifies that he saw the suspect strike the victim. The eyewitness testimony relates directly to the material fact that the suspect struck the victim. A video surveillance tape showing that the suspect struck the victim would also be direct evidence relating to the material issue of the suspect's guilt or innocence.

Direct evidence may link directly to a lesser material fact but not directly to the material issue of guilt or innocence. For example, a fingerprint found at a crime scene is direct evidence that a particular person was at the crime scene at some point in time. However, it is not direct evidence that the person was at the crime scene at the time the crime was committed or that the person committed the crime. The fingerprint evidence does not directly prove guilt or innocence. A photograph taken by a passenger on a passing tourist bus that shows a suspect entering a bank that was robbed may be direct evidence that the suspect was at the crime scene, but the same evidence would be circumstantial evidence that the suspect robbed the bank.

Circumstantial evidence does not establish proof in a direct sense. It requires the drawing of inferences between the evidence and a material issue before a conclusion is reached. For example, the material issue may be that the suspect struck the victim with a baseball bat. A date-stamped credit card receipt for the purchase of a baseball bat may be direct evidence that the suspect bought the bat, but it is indirect, or circumstantial, evidence that the suspect struck the victim with the bat. The receipt directly proves one fact (the purchase), but it does not directly prove the other fact (the suspect struck the victim with a baseball bat). With circumstantial evidence, the fact finder must infer any number of things to link the suspect to the material issue of guilt or innocence. The majority of forensic evidence found at crime scenes is circumstantial evidence as it relates to the material issue of suspect guilt or innocence because inferences must be made to link the evidence to guilt or innocence.

Direct and circumstantial evidence may also be found at secondary scenes of crimes—other locations where evidence connected to crimes are discovered. For example, a piece of jewelry found on a body in a shallow grave may contain a fingerprint that can be direct evidence that a suspect handled the jewelry of the deceased, but it is circumstantial evidence that the suspect had involvement with the victim's death. A fiber from a victim's clothing found in the home of a suspect may be direct evidence that the suspect had contact with the victim's clothing, but it would be circumstantial evidence that the suspect killed the victim. In each of these examples, one must infer other actions from the indirect evidence to reach a conclusion of guilt or innocence.

Courts in the United States make no distinction between direct and circumstantial evidence in terms of importance toward proving guilt or innocence. In most of the fifty states, evidence in court cases falls under the guidelines of the Federal Rules of Evidence, which specify all instances in which evidence is relevant (pertaining to the case at hand), probative (likely to aid a fact finder in determining truth), and admissible (obtained under proper legal sanctions) to establish the facts of a case. Relevance is important in terms of whether or not a piece of evidence will be seen or heard by the court and in terms of how the evidence relates to the material issues of the case, but a determination of whether evidence is direct or circumstantial is not pertinent to the determination that the evidence is relevant and admissible at trial.

Direct evidence and circumstantial evidence hold equal weight in a court of law. Likewise, from a forensics point of view, evidence is evidence. Each piece of evidence serves to build the associations that prove or disprove material facts related to a crime.

### Further Reading

Best, Arthur. *Evidence: Examples and Explanations.* 9th ed. New York: Aspen, 2014. Uses the Federal Rules of Evidence to organize examples and explanations of types of evidence, relevance requirements, and exclusionary rules.

Genge, N. E. *The Forensic Casebook: The Science of Crime Scene Investigation.* New York: Ballantine, 2008. Presents examples of evidence gathering from actual cases to illustrate the work involved in forensics.

Giannelli, Paul C. *Understanding Evidence.* 4th ed. Albany, NY: LexisNexis/ Mathew Bender, 2013. Provides an informative summary of the basic concepts of evidence law.

James, Stuart H. , Jon J. Nordby , Suzanne Bell, eds. *Forensic Science: An Introduction to Scientific and Investigative Techniques.* Boca

## Case Example: Direct and Circumstantial Evidence

If valuable assets have been stolen from a company safe that was opened without the use of force at a time when no company employees had any business on the premises, evidence for the crime would fall into two categories. Direct evidence might include fingerprints on the safe, trace evidence inside the safe, a video surveillance camera tape showing the thief opening the safe, an eyewitness sighting of the thief entering or leaving the premises, or discovery of the stolen assets in someone's possession.

If such evidence is not available, investigators may turn their attention more closely to circumstantial evidence. Suspicion might then fall on a company employee who knows the combination to the safe, who shortly after the robbery quit his job and left the area, and who cannot account for his whereabouts at the time of the theft. None of these facts would directly link the employee to the crime, but in combination such circumstantial evidence could be used to build a case against him. One must infer other actions from the indirect evidence to reach a conclusion of guilt or innocence.

Raton, FL: CRC Press, 2014. Presents the law as it relates to forensic science, using input from experts who examine pertinent case studies.

Miller, Marilyn T. *Crime Scene Investigation Laboratory Manual.* San Diego, CA: Academic Press, 2014. Provides explanatory data and exercises for teaching techniques of securing and documenting a crime scene, of preserving evidence, and of visualizing and reconstructing crime scene events.

National Forensic Science Technology Center in cooperation with the National Institute of Justice for the Office of Justice Programs. Crime Scene Investigation Guide. Washington, DC: United States Department of Justice, 2013. Provides a systematic approach for the preservation and documentation of evidence that law enforcement personnel may employ during the initial stages of a crime scene investigation.

**See also:** Accident investigation and reconstruction; Class versus individual evidence; Courts and forensic evidence; Crime scene documentation; Crime scene investigation; Criminal personality profiling; Evidence processing; Eyewitness testimony; Federal Rules of Evidence; Locard's exchange principle; Physical evidence; Quality control of evidence.

---

## Disturbed evidence

**Definition:** Materials that have been altered, moved, or destroyed at the scene of a crime after the crime has occurred.

**Significance:** An undisturbed crime scene yields the most reliable physical evidence to support the investigative process. When evidence is disturbed, the truth of what happened at the crime scene may be compromised or impossible to determine and may be impossible to prove in a court of law.

The objective of crime scene investigation is to gather evidence that supports or refutes theories surrounding the crime. Toward this end, investigators carefully choose and employ procedures that will maximize the likelihood of the discovery of pertinent evidence and minimize actions that could disturb that evidence. Taking into account Locard's exchange principle (which states that every contact of an individual with another person, place, or object results in an exchange of materials), it is implausible that all evidence at a crime scene will remain undisturbed throughout the duration of the investigation.

Although investigators may make every effort to maintain evidence in an undisturbed state, it is not unusual for evidence to be disturbed in many different ways. Frequently, evidence is disturbed in the period between discovering the crime and securing the scene, when numerous individuals may be present. Evidence such as blood trails, footprints, fingerprints, and pertinent biological fluids may be smeared or inadvertently erased by first responders. Materials not pertinent to the crime, such as fibers from blankets, may be introduced to the scene. Moving a living person or a dead body from the scene without taking precautionary steps to preserve surrounding evidence may result in disturbed evidence.

Evidence may be disturbed when individuals at the scene move objects, break objects, spill liquids, wipe up spills, remove clothing, cover victims, or otherwise introduce materials onto the scene that are not pertinent to the crime. Natural occurrences can also disturb evidence, such as when a crime victim dies in an outdoor setting and is exposed to weather conditions that alter or wash away materials. Evidence may also be disturbed by inappropriate or careless investigative techniques, such as when a technician pours casting material into a depression on a surface before checking the surface for fingerprints.

Investigators minimize or prevent the disturbance of evidence by securing the crime scene, by choosing an appropriate crime scene search pattern, and by following an effective sequence of evidence collection. Securing the crime scene entails controlling who is allowed onto the crime scene, designating the entrance and exit paths for responders administering to any victims, and establishing the search methods that will be used. An appropriate crime scene search pattern guides a methodical search that maximizes evidence discovery efforts while minimizing disturbance of the scene. In an effective sequence of evidence collection, pertinent materials are gathered before other investigative actions are taken that could disturb those materials.

Through these actions and methods, investigators attempt to ensure that crime scene evidence is not disturbed. When these methods are followed and evidence is nevertheless somehow disturbed, investigators make note of any reasonable explanation for the disturbance so that it does not jeopardize the utilization of pertinent evidence in a court of law.

*Taylor Shaw*

**Further Reading**

Genge, N. E. *The Forensic Casebook: The Sci-*

*ence of Crime Scene Investigation.* New York: Ballantine, 2008. Presents examples of evidence gathering from actual cases to illustrate the work involved in forensics.

James, Stuart H. , Jon J. Nordby , Suzanne Bell, eds. *Forensic Science: An Introduction to Scientific and Investigative Techniques.* Boca Raton, FL: CRC Press 2014. Presents the law as it relates to forensic science, using input from experts who examine pertinent case studies.

Miller, Marilyn T. *Crime Scene Investigation Laboratory Manual.* San Diego, CA: Academic Press, 2014. Provides explanatory data and exercises for teaching techniques of securing and documenting a crime scene, of preserving evidence, and of visualizing and reconstructing crime scene events.

**See also:** Blood residue and bloodstains; Casting; Chain of custody; Crime scene investigation; Crime scene search patterns; Cross-contamination of evidence; Evidence processing; Fingerprints; First responders Footprints and shoe prints; Homicide; Locard's exchange principle; Physical evidence; Quality control of evidence.

## DNA analysis

**Definition:** DNA analysis is the process whereby genetic material is extracted from biological specimens and prepared for DNA typing. DNA analysis includes the isolation and purification of DNA, quantification and amplification of the regions of interest. These processes dictate the quantity and quality of the data that is to be used for DNA typing.

**Significance:** Deposition of biological specimens at a crime scene provide investigators the opportunity to collect these samples and perform a series of set procedures in aims of enabling links between suspects and evidence or exclude associations of innocent individuals with a given criminal scenario. The applied workflow consists of three general steps: extraction, quantification and amplification of the sample all of which are critical for the successful attainment of a DNA fingerprint useful for comparison.

Deoxyribonucleic acid (DNA) is the blueprint of life. It is contained in every living organism and in every cell of the human body except mature red blood cells. This genetic material can be utilized to aid in criminal investigations as well as to assist with the identification of victims of mass disasters like the 9/11 terrorist attacks, resolve paternity cases or help establish links between missing persons and alleged relatives. It can also be used to establish the provenance of certain plants or microorganism strains such as marijuana or *B. anthracis* (anthrax) in cases in which it is deemed necessary.

The first step in the analysis process is DNA extraction. This can be performed manually or using automated protocols and can be based on liquid-liquid or solid phase separation procedures. In short, chemicals or mechanical force are used on the sample to lyse the cellular membrane and release its contents, including the genetic material. The DNA is then bound to a membrane or to magnetic beads and washed repeatedly to eliminate any excess cellular debris and purify the molecule of interest. After the washes, the DNA is dislodged from the membrane or magnetic beads by dissolution in water or other polar compound. The success of the outcome of this step is dependent on the type of sample, the quantity available for collection, and the conditions in which the sample was found. It is expected, for example, that a biological sample exposed to the elements will yield a lower amount of DNA than one that was well preserved. In addition, the presence of inhibitory substances (tannic and humic acids, melanin, heme) or the suspected presence of mixed samples can also play a role in the outcome of this procedure. Analysts should either further purify or carefully separate, when possible, the fractions that comprise the mixture.

Quantification is the method used to determine how much genetic material was recovered during the extraction procedure. There are several methods available to quantify the DNA –

spectrophotometry, fluorometry and agarose gels but these can lack sensitivity and specificity to human DNA. The most accurate procedure available to-date to quantify human DNA is real time polymerase chain reaction (qPCR).

During this procedure, primers and a fluorescently labeled molecular probe are added to the sample along with other reagents that enable polymerase chain reaction (PCR). The primers and probe will bind to a specific region within the DNA once they find their complementary sequence within the sample. As the reaction continues and the DNA strands get copied, the fluorescence will be detected and transferred to a computer where it will be converted to a numerical value. This value will be used by analysts to establish the dilution factor to attain a concentration suitable for the PCR amplification procedure. The quantification process can also be used as a quality assurance metric to predict the level of inhibition present in a sample. This information is attained by monitoring the amplification efficiency of an internal positive control and it provides the analyst with an idea of what to expect during the subsequent DNA PCR amplification.

The final step in DNA analysis is the amplification of target regions of the genetic material in the sample. This process exponentially copies the fragments of DNA that are of interest to analysts. The sample is mixed with fluorescently labeled primers that will define the areas to be copied and with an enzyme capable of extending those primers. The mixture is then subjected to alternating cycles of repeated heating and cooling all of which provide the optimal conditions for the fragments of interest to be replicated in vitro. All the fragments generated will have a fluorescent tag corresponding to their particular primer and this fluorescence is detected and measured during the process of DNA typing.

Recent advances in DNA technology provide the ability to obtain genetically relevant information in a short amount of time by combining all the DNA analysis steps using instruments that enable the production of DNA profiles in a short amount of time with no sample manipulation or analyst intervention. This new technology, known as Rapid DNA is useful to obtain quick leads in those cases in which time plays a substantial role in the outcome. Briefly, a swab containing the sample of interest is loaded onto a chip that contains all the necessary reagents to conduct the DNA analysis process. Once the sample is loaded, the chip is inserted into the instrument and directed through the press of a button to start the analysis process. The results are automatically generated and displayed at the end of the run.

*Lilliana I. Moreno*

## Further Reading

Butler, John M. *Fundamentals of Forensic DNA Typing.* Burlington, MA. Elsevier Academic Press, 2009. In simple terminology, provides the framework of forensic DNA analysis. Includes information on historic and novel techniques and detailed descriptions of each step in the process.

Hummel, Susanne. *Ancient DNA Typing: Methods, Strategies and Applications.* Berlin: Springer, 2003 edition. Details the identification and processing techniques for DNA analysis of old and degraded biological samples. Describes enhanced methodologies and troubleshooting approaches as they relate to compromised exemplars.

Shewale, Jaiprakash G. and Ray H. Liu. *Forensic DNA Analysis: Current Practices and Emerging Technologies.* Boca Raton, FL: CRC Press, 2014. Delineates the most up-to-date technologies associated with biological sample processing; including next generation kits and deep sequencing approaches.

Weising, Kurt, H. Nybom, M. Pfenninger, K. Wolff and G. Kahl. *DNA Fingerprinting in Plants: Principles, Methods and Applications.* 2d ed. Boca Raton, FL: CRC Press, 2005. Provides case studies, protocols and technology advancements for the DNA typing of plant material.

**See also:** CODIS; DNA extraction from hair, bodily fluids, and tissues; DNA fingerprinting; DNA isolation methods; DNA profiling; DNA sequencing; DNA typing; Ethics of DNA analysis; Federal Bureau of Investigation DNA Analysis Units; Mitochondrial DNA analysis and typing; National DNA Index System; Polymerase chain reaction; Postconviction DNA analysis; Y chromosome analysis.

# DNA banks for endangered animals

**Definition:** Facilities that preserve genetic materials from and information about endangered animal species.

**Significance:** Building on the advances being made in DNA-related technologies in forensic science and the knowledge being accumulated in the related field of wildlife forensics, some organizations have undertaken to collect and store the genetic materials of endangered animal species in the hope that someday technological advancements will enable scientists to use these materials to restore the species.

Organizations that are concerned with the loss of animal species to extinction have established banks to preserve the DNA (deoxyribonucleic acid) of endangered animals. In addition to collecting and storing biological samples from endangered species (sperm, embryos, and body tissues), preserving them in liquid nitrogen at nearly −400 degrees Fahrenheit, these organizations store information on the species' natural habitats and maintain databases to keep track of the materials that have been collected. Organizations devoted to preserving animal DNA have been established in the United States, Great Britain, China, India, and Australia; among the most widely known animal DNA banks are those maintained by the Frozen Ark Project in England and the Frozen Zoo Project in San Diego, California.

Several factors have come together to fuel the animal DNA bank movement, including advances in DNA technology and growing environmental activism. The banking of animal DNA is a conscience-driven effort by people who also want to increase awareness of the threats posed to existing species by human advancement. Estimates of potential extinctions in the twenty-first century are ominous, with some researchers asserting that the world is in the midst of a mass extinction period. Many species considered to be endangered or threatened in the early twenty-first century may someday benefit from DNA banks, including the California condor, the Florida panther, the polar bear, the killer whale, the black rhino, the panda, and the yellow seahorse.

Critics of the organizations that maintain DNA banks for endangered animals have asserted that these organizations may inadvertently create an underground market for the animals they mean to protect; the stored genetic materials could potentially have high monetary value. Moreover, many scientists believe that species extinction is a natural part of the planet's life cycle, one that humans should not tamper with, at least until they have had much more time to observe the interactions between species and Earth's environment. The animal DNA banks, however, enjoy widespread support among scientists, if only for the value they provide as historical databases.

*Brion Sever*

**Further Reading**

McGavin, George. *Endangered: Wildlife on the Brink of Extinction.* Richmond Hill, Ont.: Firefly Books, 2006.

Stone, Richard. *Mammoth: The Resurrection of an Ice Age Giant.* New York: Basic Books, 2002.

**See also:** Animal evidence; DNA extraction from hair, bodily fluids, and tissues; DNA isolation methods; DNA typing; Forensic botany; Polymerase chain reaction; Wildlife forensics

# DNA database controversies

**Definition:** Debates on social, ethical, and legal issues that surround the existence of databases containing the individual DNA profiles of large numbers of persons.

**Significance:** DNA databases constitute extremely important tools for law enforce ment. However, the existence of such repositories raises social, ethical, and legal issues, particularly concerning privacy rights, confidentiality, and fair trials. Because of the potential for misuse of the information stored in DNA databases, issues of public safety need to be balanced with the protection of civil liberties.

Each person has a unique deoxyribonucleic acid (DNA) profile that may be used to identify that individual. DNA samples, however, may also be used for other purposes; a person's DNA may reveal susceptibility to certain diseases, a predisposition to certain behaviors, familial relationships, as well as race and ethnicity. DNA evidence is considered the "gold standard" of forensics in law enforcement today. The establishment of DNA databases has helped law-enforcement agencies greatly in identifying suspects, but many observers have expressed concerns regarding the potential for misuse of the information stored in these databases or in the original DNA samples kept in storage at forensic laboratories.

## Under-regulated DNA Databases

In 1994, Congress authorized the FBI to set up a database program known as the Combined DNA Index System (CODIS). The data are stored in the National DNA Index System (NDIS), a part of CODIS. The human genome contains several regions that do not encode genes ("non-coding sequences" often referred to as "junk DNA"). These regions contain multiple short tandem repeats (STR) where the number of repeat copies varies from person to person. Thirteen regions of STR DNA were selected to provide a unique DNA profile such that the probability of a "random match" is greater than one in more than 100 trillion. Generally, data from all 13 DNA loci must be submitted to be included in NDIS. Included profiles are made up of convicted offenders, arrestees, crime scene DNA, unidentified human remains, and missing persons and relatives of missing persons. The profile of anyone who is not charged with a crime, found innocent, or has a conviction overturned must be removed. However, oversight of this requirement is poor. CODIS does not retain

the actual DNA sample, but the laboratory submitting a DNA profile may retain the sample for later retesting.

These DNA samples may be corrupted over time and may not be tightly secured. In contract to CODIS, many state (SODIS) and local (LODIS) databases have requirements far less stringent. These includes the retention of all profiles regardless of convictions or not, samples from victims of crimes, use of less than the 13 CODIS loci, use of DNA samples that may be corrupted, degraded, or contain mixed crime scene DNA from several persons. Furthermore, access to these databases may granted to persons or organization other than law enforcement. An extreme case is the State of Utah database that allows insurance companies, psychologists, and other third parties access. Many SODIS and LODIS databases often do not provide adequate privacy protection.

## Does DNA Sampling Violate Constitutional Rights?

The courts have ruled that the taking and use of DNA samples does not violate the 5th Amendment concerning self-incrimination. Such samples are not considered "testimonies" per se, and, therefore, do not violate 5th Amendment rights. Similarly, they do not violate the 8th Amendment right against cruel and unusual punishment. While the 4th Amendment does not give an *expressed* right of privacy, it does give a reasonable *expectation* of privacy, as it requires a warrant for any searches. Anyone who has watched a crime show has observed a scene where someone being questioned is given a cup of coffee or a soft drink. The interrogator then takes the item for DNA analysis.

DNA is constantly being sloughed off as flakes of skin, hair, saliva, sweat, and even on a fingerprint. Does this constitute unreasonable search and seizure and a violation of the 4th Amendment? Although the Supreme Court has not ruled on this issue, the 9th Circuit Court of Appeals in 2010 has ruled that such DNA is considered "abandoned" and may be taken and used. In addition, anyone reasonably suspected of a crime may be compelled to give a DNA sample. The 1st Circuit Court of Appeals in 2010 has also ruled that once the DNA profile is in the database, the information may be kept and used for subsequent investigations such as familial searching (see below). The 4th Amendment does not protect the information per se, but protects against how the information was acquired.

## DNA Dragnets and Fourth Amendment Issues

After serious crimes have been committed, law-enforcement agencies sometimes conduct so-called "DNA dragnets" to attempt to identify suspects; that is, they obtain DNA samples from all persons in selected groups of individuals to compare with DNA found at the crime scenes. In these cases, the people involved are generally pressured to "volunteer" DNA samples or the samples are taken without due process. In one case, all men in Truro, Massachusetts (a town with a population of approximately eighteen hundred), were requested to volunteer a DNA sample after a murder. In Baton Rouge, Louisiana, samples were collected from about twelve hundred men during a hunt for a serial killer. Collection of DNA samples without probable cause (a reasonable belief that the individuals have some involvement with the crime) constitutes an "unreasonable search". collect DNA samples from suspected illegal immigrants, and those profiles are entered into CODIS.

## Familial Issues

People who are related by blood have similar, but not identical, DNA profiles. Given this fact, law enforcement agencies sometimes search DNA databases for less-than-perfect matches to their suspects' DNA profiles. This is known as "familial searching" or "database trawling". By finding first-degree relatives, the police may identify suspects. Such searches have been criticized as violating the privacy rights of the parties involved. However, familial searches have been upheld by the courts.

One of the most publicized examples is that of Los Angeles serial killer Lonnie David Franklin, Jr. called "The Grim Sleeper". He was dubbed this name because he committed several murders in 1985-1988 but then not again for 14 years until 2002. In 2010, a familial search produced a "hit" after his recently con-

victed son's profile had been entered into the database. Familial searching has also been criticized as racially discriminatory. For instance, because African Americans are disproportionately represented in CODIS, they are approximately four times more likely than Caucasians to be "findable" through familial searching. In addition to the use of DNA databases by law-enforcement agencies, the storage of DNA profiles in repositories raises many other issues, particularly in the areas of privacy and confidentiality. Information on adoption and sperm and egg donation, for example, can be very sensitive, with many parties wishing to remain anonymous. Such anonymity is threatened by the placement of DNA profiles in searchable databases.

## Universal Databases and Discrimination

By 2015, more than a dozen countries including Iceland, Sweden, United Kingdom, Estonia, Austria, Netherlands, Canada, Japan, Singapore, Switzerland, Portugal, and Poland had established or were establishing population-based DNA databases. These were to be resources for the study of genealogy and gene-disease relationships. In some nations, initiatives have been undertaken to include DNA profiles of all newborns in these databases. The storage of this information may be useful to scientists and doctors who seek to understand the genetic components of disease, but it raises issues of privacy and confidentiality. Of particular importance is the question of who has the right to access the data and to what end.

---

## Fourth Amendment to the U.S. Constitution

The right of the people to be secure in their persons, houses, papers, and effects, against unreasonable searches and seizures, shall not be violated, and no Warrants shall issue, but upon probable cause, supported by Oath or affirmation, and particularly describing the place to be searched, and the persons or things to be seized.

In the United States, the courts have yet to decide whether such DNA database information falls under the security and privacy provisions of the Health Insurance Portability and Accountability Act (HIPAA) of 1996. It has been argued that universal DNA databases and disease gene databases have great potential for abuse. One issue is a person's *right not to know* if he or she is at risk for a disease. More than 4000 disease-associated genes have already been identified. In addition to government databases, hundreds of private DNA databases are being established. They will be less likely to protect individuals' anonymity. Moreover, as critics have pointed out, the availability of information on individuals' genetic characteristics has the potential to lead to discrimination by insurance carriers, employers, educational institutions, and government agencies. Other abuses bring to mind eugenics programs in the United States earlier in the 20th century and the Nazi atrocities during World War-II.

## Retention of DNA samples

A DNA profile only identifies the individual, but the DNA sample from which the profile was created contains all of that person's genetic information. Most U.S. states do not have laws that require the destruction of DNA samples after DNA profiling is complete.

Moreover, hospitals, clinics, and doctors' offices store tissue samples taken for biopsies or retained for research from which DNA may be extracted and analyzed. No set policy exists among forensic laboratories regarding destruction of DNA samples, and many preserve such samples in case additional testing is deemed necessary or the results of previous tests need to be confirmed. It has been argued that governmental agencies have not adequately regulated the retention and future potential uses of such DNA samples.

*Ralph R. Meyer*

## Further Reading

Greeley, Henry T. "The Uneasy Ethical and Legal Underpinnings of Large-Scale Genomic Biobanks." *Annual Review of Genomics and Human Genetics* 7 (2007): 343-364. Discussion of private databases and associate ethical issues.

Kitchen, Adrienne N., "Genetic Privacy and Latent Crime Scene DNA of Non-Suspects: How the Law Can Protect an Individual's Right to Genetic Privacy While Respecting the Government's Important Interest in Combatting Crime." *The Criminal Law Bulletin* 52 (2015): in press. Good discussion of rights of non-suspects.

Luther, Lori, and Trudo Lemmens, "Human Genetic Data Banks: From Consent to Commercialization – an Overview of Current Concerns and Conundrums" *Encyclopedia of Life Support Systems, Biotechnology* XII, 2012.

Mercer, Stephen, and Jessica Gabel. "Shadow Dwellers: The Underregulated World of State and Local DNA Databases." *New York University Survey of American Law* 69 (2014): 639-698. A good discussion of problems with state and local databases.

Primorac, Dragan and Moses Schanfield, ed. *Forensic DNA Applications, An Interdisciplinary Perspective.* Boca Raton: CRC Press, 2014. Excellent 23 review chapters in this book covering all aspects of DNA forensics.

**See also:** Argentine disappeared children; CODIS; DNA analysis; DNA fingerprinting; DNA typing; Ethics of DNA analysis; Federal Bureau of Investigation DNA Analysis Units; Jefferson paternity dispute; National DNA Index System; Paternity testing; Short tandem repeat analysis.

---

# DNA extraction from hair, bodily fluids, and tissues

**Definition:** Techniques used to obtain DNA from different kinds of biological materials so that the DNA can be analyzed.

**Significance:** DNA comparison has become a critical tool for identifying victims and suspects in a variety of crimes, and biological evidence such as hairs, bodily fluids, and tissues can provide the DNA needed for comparisons.

When biological materials that have been found at crime scenes—such as hairs, bodily fluids, and tissues—are submitted for deoxyribonucleic acid (DNA) analysis, the samples must first undergo DNA extraction procedures. The most common methods for extracting DNA from such materials are organic extraction, Chelex extraction, extraction using preservation paper, and extraction using silica-based columns. An organic extraction uses detergent and proteinase to break open (lyse) cells, followed by introduction of an organic solvent to separate proteins and other cellular debris from the DNA. Chelex extraction is a quick and easy procedure, but the purity of the DNA extracted is low. Chelex binds metal ions that could otherwise lead to poor DNA typing results, but little other purification is done.

Preservation papers provide another quick method for extracting DNA. Bodily fluids are applied directly to the paper, where the cells are immediately lysed. Once the sample is dried, a small portion can be punched out, washed briefly, and then moved directly to DNA amplification. Silica-based columns bind DNA following cell lysis, allowing cellular debris to be washed through. The DNA is then eluted in relatively pure form.

## Hair

Given their ubiquity, hairs are often found at crime scenes. Hairs with roots attached are excellent sources of DNA, whereas hairs without roots contain little or no nuclear DNA for short tandem repeat testing. Shed hairs, which are most often found at crime scenes, generally do not have intact roots and thus require mitochondrial DNA testing. Hair roots are processed like other tissues, as described above. A shed hair is first cleaned to remove any exogenous DNA; an enzymatic detergent such as Terg-A-Zyme is often used for this purpose. The keratin (protein) of the hair is broken down with proteinase, detergent, and dithiothreitol, releasing any trapped DNA. Prior to this, the hair may be ground or homogenized, which further helps to free DNA.

An alternative method for extracting DNA from hair is alkaline extraction. The hair is washed and then is exposed to a strong basic solution (such as sodium hydroxide), which destroys the protein without harming the DNA. The solution is neutralized and filtered, leaving the DNA ready for analysis.

## Bodily Fluids

The bodily fluids most commonly processed in crime laboratories (generally in dried form) are semen and blood; these are followed in frequency by saliva and urine. Other fluids, including vaginal secretions and perspiration, are also sources of DNA. In blood, the abundant red blood cells do not have nuclei and therefore do not contain DNA. In contrast, white blood cells, which make up less than 1 percent of cells present in blood, harbor a full DNA component. This means that blood is a valuable source of DNA, although not an ideal one.

Semen, which contains huge numbers of spermatozoa, each containing its complement of DNA, is considered one of the richest sources of genetic material. Owing to the strength of sperm cell walls, isolation of DNA from semen requires treatment similar to that of hair shafts. In cases of a mixture (e.g., sperm and vaginal epithelial cells are comingled) the relative strength of spermatozoa cell walls allows for an alternative technique known as differential extraction, where an initial "gentle" digestion ruptures the epithelial cells, the sperm are pelleted through centrifugation, the solution containing DNA from the vaginal cells is removed and purified, and the pelleted sperm are subjected to a harsher digestion as described for hair. The resultant sperm ('male') and non-sperm ('female') fractions are highly enriched for a single source of DNA.

The other bodily fluids contain DNA somewhat by chance, in that epithelial cells are shed into them, such as from the mouth (saliva) or urinary tract (urine). DNA from these sources can be isolated using any of the procedures noted above.

## Skin, Bone, and Other Tissues

Shed epithelial cells (e.g., skin) are a viable source of DNA and can potentially be collected from any item that has come into contact with skin, such as clothing, backpacks, or handled items. In general, cells are collected by swabbing or excising a portion of the contacted area followed by an organic or silica based extraction. Reference DNA samples are usually obtained by swabbing the inside of an individual's cheek (i.e., buccal swab) due to the ease of the procedure and of the plentiful DNA found within epithelial cells. It should be noted that the level at which skin cells shed varies among individuals, substrates, and factors like weather and hygiene, thus two pieces of evidence that seem similar often produce differing levels of DNA typing success.

Skeletal remains are frequently included in forensic investigations, in general owing to their relative longevity. Fresh skeletal material is a rich source of DNA, but the longer bones are in contact with the environment, the more degraded the DNA becomes. Likewise, components of skeletal tissue such as collagen and minerals like carbonated calcium phosphate (i.e., hydroxyapatite), as well as environmental substrates like humic substances found in soil that leach into bone, can inhibit PCR amplification of the DNA. Furthermore there is substantial variation in recoverable DNA from skeletal material based on the type of bone (compact verses spongy), which bone is sampled (e.g., femur verses rib), what region of the bone is sampled (middle verses end), and its environment (buried, submerged, etc.). The bone is cleaned and then ground or drilled to create a powder, from which DNA is extracted as described above. Often bone is demineralized using high concentrations of chelating agents such as EDTA (ethylenediaminetetraacetic acid) or EGTA (ethylene glycol tetraacetic acid), dissolving the hydroxyapatite component of bone into solution prior to or in conjunction with tissue digestion.

Other tissues are also potential sources of DNA. Generally, tissues that do not harbor degradative enzymes (as does the digestive tract, for instance) are favored. Small pieces of tissue may be homogenized to disrupt cells prior to DNA extraction using any of the procedures described above.

*David R. Foran and Timothy C. Antinick*

## Further Reading

Butler, John M. *Forensic DNA typing : Biology,* *Technology, and Genetics of STR Markers.* 2d ed. Amsterdam: Elsevier Academic Press, 2005. A detailed overview of forensic DNA methodologies.

Davis, C.D., J.L. King, B. Budowle, A.J. Eisenberg, and M.A. Turnbough. "Extraction platform evaluations: A comparison of Automate Express™, EZ1®, Advanced XL, and Maxwell® 16 Bench-top DNA extraction systems." *Legal Medicine* 14 (2012): 36–39. Comparison of several automated platforms for DNA extraction.

Deedrick, D.W. "Hairs, Fibers, Crime, and Evidence – Part 1: Hair Evidence." *Forensic Science Communication* 2, no. 3 (2000). http://www.fbi.gov/hq/lab/fsc/backissu/july2000/deedric1.html. An overview of hairs used as forensic evidence.

Graffy, E.A. and D.R. Foran. "A Simplified Method for Mitochondrial DNA Extraction from Head Hair Shafts." Journal of Forensic Science 50, no. 5 (Sept, 2005):1–4. Introduction of the alkaline method for DNA extraction from head hairs.

Edson, S.M., J.P. Ross, M.D. Coble, T.J. Parsons, and S.M. Barritt. "Naming the Dead—Confronting the Realities of Rapid Identification of Degraded Skeletal Remains." *Forensic Science Review* 16 (2004):63–90. Detailed account of handling, processing, and recovering DNA from skeletal remains used by the Armed Forces DNA Identification Laboratory (AFDIL).

Walsh, P.S., D.A. Metzger, and R. Higuch. "Chelex® 100 as a Medium for Simple Extraction of DNA for PCR-Based Typing from Forensic Material." *BioTechniques* 10 (1991):506–513. The first detailed application of the Chelex technique for DNA isolation.

**See also:** Blood residue and stains; Cross contamination of evidence; DNA isolation methods; Mitochondrial DNA analysis and typing; PCR (Polymerase chain reaction); Rape Kit; Saliva; Semen and sperm; Skeletal analysis; STR analysis (short tandem repeat).

# DNA fingerprinting

**Definition:** Laboratory procedure for analyzing patterns of sequence variation in DNA samples for the purpose of identifying evidence in forensic investigations.

**Significance:** The development of DNA fingerprinting represents one of the major breakthroughs in forensic science. Using techniques from molecular biology and increasingly detailed databases, investigators are able to examine the DNA contained within biological evidence obtained from crime scenes and compare their findings with known samples, resulting in a high degree of probability that particular pieces of evidence can be associated with individual suspects or victims.

In 1985, the English geneticist Alec Jeffreys proposed that newly discovered repetitive sequences in DNA (deoxyribonucleic acid) could be used as a form of genetic fingerprint to identify individuals. DNA fingerprinting represents a combination of both molecular biology and population genetics in that in this process, pieces of DNA are examined for the presence of specific markers and the findings are compared against known samples in a database to establish the prevalence of those markers in the general population.

## Types of Genetic Markers

The human genome comprises more than 3.2 billion nucleotides, the letters that are responsible for coding for the proteins that make up and carry out bodily functions. The sequences of the human genome that code for these proteins are called genes. Humans are believed to have approximately twenty-five thousand genes. Between these genes are vast stretches of DNA that do not code for proteins. Within these areas are repetitive sequences called variable number of tandem repeats, or VNTRs. One class of VNTRs is made up of the minisatellites, sequences of up to one hundred nucleotides that may be repeated in tandem up to one thousand times. In addition to the minisatellites, microsatellites have been identified. These are also known as short tandem repeats (STRs) or simple sequence repeats (SSRs). Microsatellites are sequences of two to seven nucleotides that may be repeated hundreds of times. An example is the CA repeat (CACACACA) that occurs on average every thirty-thousand base pairs in the human genome.

Every human being has two copies of genetic information in each cell. This represents the genetic information contributed by each of the individual's parents. Each STR thus exists in two copies. Often, the number of repeats within a specific STR differs in the parents. These differences are called alleles. In a population, a given STR may be polymorphic, meaning that many different forms (or alleles) of the STR exist in the population. For each allele used in forensic analysis, population geneticists have determined the percentage of the population at large that contains that given allele. This information forms the basis of DNA fingerprinting.

## Analysis of DNA Fingerprints

When DNA fingerprinting was initially developed, analysts examined DNA patterns using a procedure called the Southern blot. In a Southern blot, DNA is extracted from cells and then cut with a special enzyme called a restriction endonuclease. Restriction endonucleases recognize specific sequences of nucleotides in the DNA. When the sequence has been identified, the enzyme makes a cut in the DNA, generating short fragments that may be separated by size through gel electrophoresis. A radioactive probe is then used to identify specific fragments that contain sequences of nucleotides of interest. Initially, analysts accomplished this task by using minisatellites and restriction fragment length polymorphisms (RFLPs). When exposed to photographic film, the radioactive probes revealed patterns in the DNA that could be used to identify evidence.

Soon after DNA fingerprinting began, the entire process was greatly simplified by the invention of the polymerase chain reaction (PCR). Instead of cutting the DNA with restriction enzymes, the analyst copies specific sections of the genome, in this case the area containing the microsatellite repeats, millions of times. The amplified sections are then separated by gel electrophoresis, stained, and photographed. Because the fragments are much smaller than those generated during a Southern blot, the results may be ready in just a few hours of time. As with a Southern blot, the length of the fragment is determined by the number of repeats. The larger the number of repeats in the amplified section of DNA, the slower its movement during gel electrophoresis. This allows the analyst to discriminate among STRs that differ in the numbers of repeats within the amplified sequence.

In the United States, thirteen STRs have been identified for use during forensic and criminal investigations. Most investigative laboratories also include an additional test for amelogenin, a gene associated with dental pulp, which allows an investigator to determine whether a sample comes from a male or a female subject. For each of the STRs, researchers have determined the prevalence of that allele in the general population. Although the allele for one STR may be shared by a large percentage of the population, the power of discrimination becomes much greater as the number of STRs being analyzed is increased. For example, when three STRs (A, B, and C) are used, the probability of a certain combination ($A_1$, $B_3$, $C_2$) is equal to the product of the frequency of that allele in the population ($A \times B \times C$). As the number of STRs increases, the chances that two individuals will share the same identical pattern decrease.

When coupled with additional evidence found at a crime scene, DNA fingerprinting can be a powerful tool for proving the guilt or innocence of a suspect. DNA fingerprinting is also used to identify human remains that have degraded over time or that have been badly damaged by exposure to chemicals or fire.

*Michael Windelspecht*

### Further Reading

Butler, John M. *Forensic DNA Typing: Biology, Technology, and Genetics of STR Markers*. 2d ed. Burlington, Mass.: Elsevier Academic Press, 2005. Provides a detailed examination of DNA fingerprinting analysis using STR markers. Intended for readers with background in the sciences.

Jeffreys, A. J., V. Wilson, and S. L. Thein. "Individual-Specific 'Fingerprints' of Human DNA." *Nature* 316 (1985): 76-79. Landmark paper that introduced the concept of DNA fingerprinting as a method of identification.

Kobilinsky, Lawrence F., Louis Levine, and Henrietta Margolis-Nunno. *Forensic DNA Analysis*. New York: Chelsea House, 2007. Presents a comprehensive introduction to the use of STRs in DNA fingerprinting. Includes discussion of future directions, including mitochondrial and Y chromosome analyses.

Rudin, Norah, and Keith Inman. *An Introduction to Forensic DNA Analysis*. 2d ed. Boca Raton, Fla.: CRC Press, 2002. Provides a good introduction to the use of biological evidence in forensics as well as the history and application of DNA fingerprinting in forensic investigations.

**See also:** CODIS; DNA analysis; DNA database controversies; DNA isolation methods; DNA profiling; DNA typing; Electrophoresis; Ethics of DNA analysis; Mitochondrial DNA analysis and typing; National DNA Index System; Polymerase chain reaction; Postconviction DNA analysis; Restriction fragment length polymorphisms; September 11, 2001, victim identification; Short tandem repeat analysis.

# DNA isolation methods

**Definition:** Techniques used to obtain DNA from biological materials.

**Significance:** DNA obtained from forensic samples can be used to link suspects to crime scenes, associate suspects and victims, identify the remains of missing individuals, or determine parentage. Numerous techniques are available for isolating DNA from cellular material; choosing the most appropriate helps to ensure that a DNA profile will be successfully obtained.

The isolation of DNA (deoxyribonucleic acid) from biological material can be relatively straightforward, but forensic scientists must consider several factors before commencing. The first of these is the subsequent DNA analysis, including whether the DNA can be single-stranded, as for polymerase chain reaction (PCR) analyses, or must remain double-stranded, as for some types of DNA sequencing methodologies.

The source of the sample (e.g. blood, semen, hair, or bone) will also influence isolation choices because some samples must be processed in advance (e.g., a hair shaft or skeletal material may need to be ground). Other considerations include the required level of DNA cleanliness, maximizing yield, minimizing processing steps, the number of samples, the presence of mixtures, and potential PCR inhibitors (such as iron from blood or humic acid from soil).

Commonly used strategies for DNA isolation in forensic laboratories include organic extraction, differential extraction, Chelex, preservative papers, DNA isolation kits, and robotics. All of these involve breaking open cells (lysis) to release DNA, purification to remove unwanted material, and harvesting the DNA for analysis.

Once an extraction method is chosen, the analyst must take steps to prevent contamination. Proper training of laboratory personnel is imperative; disposable gloves and protective clothing should be worn, and equipment must be cleaned regularly. A reagent blank control, containing no cellular material but undergoing the same extraction process, should be included to ensure that reagents are not contaminated.

## Organic Extraction

Organic extractions are widely used in forensic laboratories owing to their general applicability and purity of the resultant DNA. Following cell lysis (with a proteinase and detergent), undesired cellular components (e.g. fats and proteins) are solubilized into an organic solvent such as phenol or chloroform. A centrifugation-based column step can also be performed for further purification.

DNA from organic extractions is relatively clean, can be used for any type of subsequent analysis, and is amenable to any tissue type. Disadvantages include lengthy time expenditure, exposure to hazardous chemicals, and the

fact that some undesired water-soluble components may remain.

## Differential Extraction

An expanded organic method is the differential extraction, which is used on samples from sexual assaults, particularly vaginal swabs, which can contain epithelial cells from the victim and sperm from the perpetrator. Differential extractions take advantage of the dissimilar nature of sperm acrysomal caps and epithelial cell walls. The sample is first placed in a mild lysis buffer that releases epithelial cell DNA while sperm remain intact. The sperm are pelleted by centrifugation, and the liquid containing epithelial DNA (the nonsperm fraction) is removed and purified. The sperm are then lysed under stronger conditions, and this sperm fraction is purified. Differential extraction allows DNA enrichment of each fraction by upward of 90 percent, helping to clarify mixture results.

## Chelex Extraction

DNA preparation using Chelex (iminodiacetic acid bound to polystyrene beads) has two positive attributes: it is fast and it is easy. The entire procedure is carried out in a single tube and is generally performed on blood and saliva, although other tissues may be considered. The major objective of a Chelex extraction is to bind (chelate) unwanted metals that can inhibit PCR, notably polyvalent cations such as iron and calcium. The sample is boiled, and upon centrifugation the beads are forced to the bottom of the tube, leaving the single stranded DNA in solution ready for analysis. Because minimal purification steps are involved the DNA is not pristine, hence it may not amplify or store well.

## Preservative Papers

One of the simplest methods for extracting DNA is through the use of special papers chemically treated to lyse cells and denature proteins on contact, thus removing any biological hazard from the sample. A liquid sample such as blood or saliva is applied to the paper and dried, then stored at room temperature or used immediately. A small punch of the stained paper is collected, washed, and subjected directly to PCR. Extended sample stability is the major advantage of preservative papers; disadvantages include possible difficulty in manipulating the papers, the fact that this method produces no DNA quantification, and that the paper can be overloaded, resulting in sample degradation.

## Commercial DNA Isolation Kits

Many companies have developed commercial kits for DNA purification. Recently these kits have become more tailored to the specific sample type being tested, such as blood, solid tissue, or soil. The process tends to be quick (as little as thirty minutes) and easy to conduct, but relatively expensive. Kits allow for a large number of samples to be processed simultaneously, and manufacturers provide necessary solutions as well as other materials, such as tubes and columns. Generally, cells are lysed and the DNA is bound to immobilized silica using a high salt solution. The silica is washed with alcohol, and the DNA is released via a low salt solution. The DNA isolated tends to be pure, but sample digestion is short, and therefore yield may be sacrificed. There may also be problems with overloading the silica when high quality samples are processed, thus losing DNA, or retrieving all of the DNA when processing low quality samples.

## Automation

The use of robotics for DNA preparation allows the processing of large numbers of samples in short amounts of time, while eliminating the human factor. Automated DNA isolation is most desirable for high-quality material such as database samples; evidentiary materials are less often processed in this manner. The DNA isolation procedures are similar to those detailed above (particularly those for kits), with reagent transfer being automated. The robots involved are expensive, as are the proprietary reagents required, but the savings in technician time can be substantial.

*David R. Foran and Kaitlyn J. Germain*

## Further Reading

Belgrader, P., et al. "Automated DNA Purification and Amplification from Blood-Stained Cards Using a Robotic Workstation." *Bio-Techniques* 19 (September, 1995): 426-432. Discusses the automated isolation of DNA from paper matrices

Brevnov, M.G., et al. "Developmental Validation of the PrepFiler™ Forensic DNA Extraction Kit for Extraction of Genomic DNA from Biological Samples" *Journal of Forensic Sciences* 54 (2009): 599-607. Evaluates the use of an extraction kit for multiple sample types.

Butler, John M. *Forensic DNA Typing: Biology, Technology, and Genetics of STR Markers*. 2d ed. Burlington, MA: Elsevier Academic Press, 2005. Provides a detailed overview of the basic biology of DNA and forensic DNA methodologies.

Greenspoon, S. A., et al. "Application of the BioMek 2000 Laboratory Automation Workstation and the DNA IQ System to the Extraction of Forensic Casework Samples." *Journal of Forensic Sciences* 49 (2004): 29-39. Reports on the automated isolation of DNA through the use of a commercial kit.

Nagy, M., et al. "Optimization and Validation of a Fully Automated Silica-Coated Magnetic Beads Purification Technology in Forensics." *Forensic Science International* 152, no. 1 (2005): 13-22. Describes the automated isolation of DNA using silica.

Walsh, P. S., D. A. Metzger, and R. Higuchi. "Chelex 100 as a Medium for Simple Extraction of DNA for PCR-Based Typing from Forensic Material." *BioTechniques* 10 (April, 1991): 506-513. Reports on the first detailed application of the Chelex technique for DNA isolation.

**See also:** Blood residue and bloodstains; Cross-contamination of evidence; DNA analysis; DNA extraction from hair, bodily fluids, and tissues; Mitochondrial DNA analysis and typing; National DNA Index System; Polymerase chain reaction; Rape kit; Saliva; Semen and sperm; Short tandem repeat analysis.

DNA postconviction analysis. *See* Postconviction DNA analysis

# DNA profiling

**Definition:** The process by which a qualified analyst, using statistical methods, imparts significance to previously generated DNA data. During this process, the probability of encountering a different, un-related individual in the general population who shares the same genetic fingerprint as that developed from the evidentiary material is calculated and reported.

**Significance:** DNA typing data provides little help in a criminal proceeding when presented with no statistical interpretation or significance. The frequency of occurrence of the combination of alleles generated for a given sample can be established by comparison to data generated from population databases for which the occurrence of each individual allele for every loci examined has been previously estimated. A random match probability or likelihood ratio can then be determined and shared as part of the DNA analysis report.

The power of DNA resides greatly on the fact that, contrary to other types of evidence, the likelihood of occurrence of a particular genetic fingerprint can be included with the report. Various statistical approaches exist and they will vary depending on the type of scenario being investigated. For example, establishing the probability of paternity requires the use of statistical methods that are different from those used to compare a DNA profile generated from evidence to one from a person of interest in the case.

During the DNA analysis and typing process, information corresponding to several individual targets within the sample is generated. The amount of information attained and number of targets successfully typed will vary from sample-to-sample depending on the initial conditions of the exemplar. For exclusionary purposes, the observation of at least one difference in the genetic information obtained is sufficient and no statistical analyses are required. Nevertheless, the observation of no differences between the data generated from two different sources (e.g. evidence and suspect) requires statistical calculations to impart weight to the results. As a rule of thumb, the greater the information obtained the more powerful the significance of the results.

Individuals are made up of genes inherited from their parents. Half of the genetic makeup of one person originates from the mother and the other half from the father. Therefore, for each gene any given individual has two copies (or alleles). These alleles come in various forms and an individual can have, by chance, two copies of the same form of that allele or two different forms of that allele. For example, a person can have two copies of the allele for red hair or one copy of the allele for red hair and one copy of the allele for blonde hair. Because the inheritance of one allele has no effect on the inheritance of the other the events are said to be independent. This independence of inheritance allows analysts to multiply the frequency of occurrence of individual alleles to establish the overall frequency of occurrence of a given DNA fingerprint.

To enable the calculation of genetic frequencies, databases have been generated by DNA typing hundreds of individuals to obtain an estimate of the frequency of occurrence of the alleles for each of the markers targeted during DNA analysis. To do this, analysts tally the number of observations obtained for alleles X, Y and Z for each individual genetic marker and divide the number of observations by the number of individuals used to generate the database. This is done individually for different ethnic groups in an effort to obtain a general sense of the differences between populations. The Federal Bureau of Investigation (FBI), National Institute of Standards and Technology (NIST) and other groups have generated allelic frequency databases that are available to analysts for use in their calculations. These databases, although generated from different individuals and by different agencies offer no significant differences in the overall results, therefore the results obtained should have no substantial impact on the case regardless of which is used.

In a case, individual DNA target fragment frequencies are calculated using the Hardy-Weinberg formula which assumes that the probability of two independent events that occur simultaneously is the product of the probability of each event occurring separately.

The Hardy-Weinberg principle uses the following formula $p^2 + 2pq + q^2$, where p and q represent the various forms of a particular gene. If an individual inherits two copies of the same form of a gene the frequency that particular DNA target fragment is calculated using $p^2$ or $q^2$. If an individual is heterozygous – has different copies of that gene, then the formula to calculate the frequency for that particular DNA fragment is 2pq. Once the analyst obtains the individual frequencies for each of the markers, these are multiplied to determine how common or rare the overall results are. The larger (rarer) the result, the more likely that the generated profile originated from the suspected individual.

Since databases offer frequency information for several population groups and the ethnicity of the suspect cannot be assumed; analysts calculate the overall results for each of the populations for which information is available and usually report the most conservative result in order to favor the defendant and reduce biases that could compromise the investigation.

It should be noted that the calculations used to establish the likelihood of paternity are different than those described as they assume a fifty percent chance that the alleged parent is related to the individual donating the sample. In addition, some modifications in the calculations and precautions should be taken when working with degraded and/or inhibited samples as some of the information might have been lost.

The presence of a mixed DNA exemplar usually requires more advanced statistical calculations or probabilistic approaches that take into consideration the sharing or loss of certain alleles and the various combinations in which alleles could have been inherited for each of the markers.

*Lilliana I. Moreno*

## Further Reading

Adam, Craig. *Essential Mathematics and Statistics for Forensic Science.* Hoboken, NJ: Wiley and Sons, 2010. Equips the reader with the basic math skills necessary for the interpretation of forensic DNA analysis data. Provides a variety of examples and practice exercises to facilitate learning.

Balding, David J. *Weight-of-Evidence for Forensic DNA Profiles.* West Sussex, England. Wiley and Sons, 2005. Describes the importance of DNA data statistical calculations as they relate to the assessment of evidentiary material. Uses simple language and examples to illustrate the concepts presented.

Butler, John M. *Advanced Topics in Forensic DNA Typing: Interpretation.* San Diego, CA: Elsevier Academic Press, 2015. Includes information on the various statistical approaches that can be used to interpret and report DNA typing results. It also contains all the necessary allelic frequencies to perform the calculations.

Kam Fung, Wing and Yue-Qing Hu. *Statistical DNA Forensics: Theory, Methods and Computation.* West Sussex, UK: Wiley and Sons, 2008. Offers computational solutions to the complex process of statistical forensic DNA data interpretation.

**See also:** CODIS; DNA analysis; DNA database controversies; DNA fingerprinting; DNA typing; Federal Bureau of Investigation DNA Analysis Units; Interpol; Paternity testing; Postconviction DNA analysis; Restriction fragment length polymorphisms.

## DNA recognition instruments

**Definition:** Instruments used by crime scene investigators to detect the presence of biological materials from which DNA may be isolated for analysis.

**Significance:** The use of biological evidence, specifically DNA, to prove the guilt or innocence of suspects is an important component in modern criminal investigations. By using DNA recognition instruments at crime scenes to identify the presence of materials from which DNA evidence may be isolated—such as hair, saliva, or semen from suspects or victims—investigators increase the efficiency of evidence gathering.

The detection of DNA (deoxyribonucleic acid) at a crime scene begins with the identification and isolation of biological evidence such as blood, semen, saliva, or hair. Historically, such evidence has been found through physical searches of crime scenes, but the search process has been expedited by the development of specialized light sources and chemical tests.

Most commonly, the detection of biological samples has been aided by the use of ultraviolet (UV) light sources. UV lights belong to a class of instruments known as alternate light source (ALS) instruments. Unlike light sources that emit wavelengths of light across a broad spectrum, ALS lights use filters or special bulbs to emit a much narrower range of wavelengths. For example, UV lights emit wavelengths in the 400-200 nanometer range. The most common UV light is called a "black light," which emits wavelengths in the 400-320 nanometer range, also known as UVA. These wavelengths are invisible to the human eye but may cause certain chemicals, mainly proteins, to fluoresce. UV lights are useful in the detection of blood, semen, and saliva. Other ALS instruments include copper and argon lasers and modified arc lamps. The use of lasers in DNA detection is becoming increasingly popular because lasers do not damage DNA strands and can emit very specific wavelengths of light.

ALS instruments can indicate fluorescing molecules, but upon finding such samples, investigators must confirm the presence of specific forms of biological evidence by using certain chemicals to perform presumptive tests. These are usually colometric tests, meaning that the reagents used in the tests change colors when exposed to specific compounds. For example, the presumptive test for semen is specific for acid phosphatase, an enzyme that is more abundant in semen than in other body fluids. The presumptive tests for blood use human-specific antibodies that allow investigators to distinguish between human blood sources and the blood of other animals.

In addition to light sources and chemical tests, several commercially produced detection kits are available to forensic investigators. Among these are kits that can detect the proteins present in semen and kits that can detect the presence of DNA. Kits are also available that can disregard female DNA and indicate the presence of male DNA only, making them especially useful in rape and sexual assault cases.

*Michael Windelspecht*

## Further Reading

Butler, John M. *Forensic DNA Typing: Biology, Technology, and Genetics of STR Markers.* 2d ed. Burlington, Mass.: Elsevier Academic Press, 2005

James, Stuart H., and Jon J. Nordby, eds. *Forensic Science: An Introduction to Scientific and Investigative Techniques.* 2d ed. Boca Raton, Fla.: CRC Press, 2005.

**See also:** Blood residue and bloodstains; Crime scene investigation; DNA extraction from hair, bodily fluids, and tissues; National DNA Index System; National Institute of Justice; Presumptive tests for blood; Semen and sperm.

# DNA sequencing

**Definition:** Analytical process used to determine the order of the DNA nucleotides (adenine, cytosine, guanine and thymine) in a given genome/sample.

**Significance:** Samples obtained from criminal settings are often degraded due to prolonged exposure to the elements (sun, water, air) and other harsh environments. In addition, the samples at times present themselves in quantities insufficient for the more common nuclear DNA typing. In an effort to recover information from these types of exemplars, analysts often recur to sequencing. Current sequencing methods target mitochondrial DNA which is present in many copies within a given cell thus providing a greater opportunity in the recovery of genetic material.

The sequencing process is performed by copying a particular region of the genome of interest using unlabeled forward and reverse primers and the polymerase chain reaction amplification method. The targeted regions usually span between 300 and 1000 base pairs. Once amplified, the product is cleaned to remove unincorporated nucleotides and primers prior to being quantified. Depending on the length of the fragment targeted, the sample is diluted to a particular concentration and the sequencing template is amplified with a single primer (forward or re-

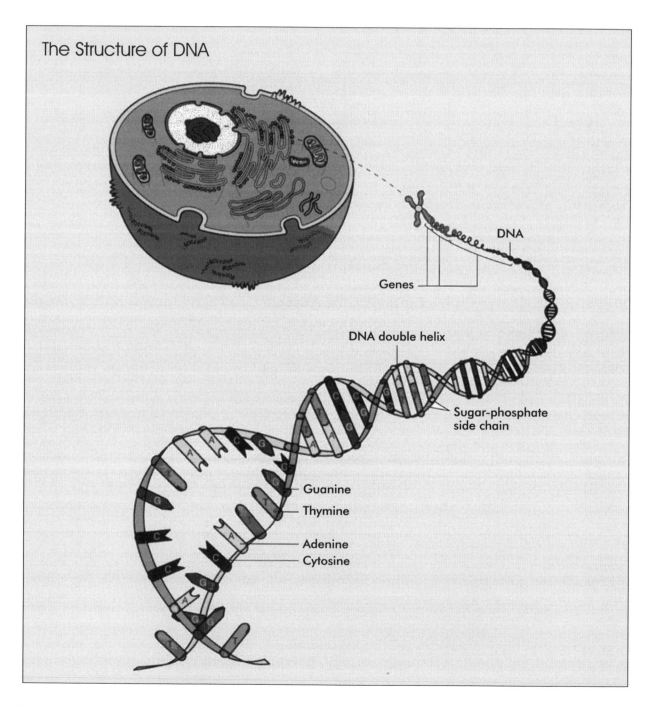

The Structure of DNA

DNA

Genes

DNA double helix

Sugar-phosphate side chain

Guanine

Thymine

Adenine

Cytosine

verse) and fluorescently labeled dideoxyribonucleotides (ddNTPs). The fluorescent tags in each of the ddNTPs are of different colors. As the amplification reaction proceeds, these ddNTPs are incorporated at random in the newly synthesized DNA and in doing so halt the DNA elongation process. The resulting product is then cleaned to remove any unincorporated nucleotides, diluted in formamide and 'read' using a genetic analyzer.

After completion of the sequencing process the sample is electrokinetically injected into a thin capillary filled with polymer capable of providing one base pair resolution. A voltage is applied to aid the migration of the sample through the capillary. As the sample travels through the capillary, the wavelengths emitted by the fluorescently tagged nucleotides are captured and recorded by a camera. The collection data is decrypted by specialized computer software and made available to the analyst for further interpretation.

Although DNA sequencing can aid in cases in which no nuclear DNA is recoverable, the power of discrimination of the results is limited due to the pattern of inheritance of the mitochondria. In addition, the current Sanger sequencing process is cumbersome and long in comparison to other established DNA analysis techniques. Nevertheless, in recent years new sequencing technologies have been developed that allow analysts to process more challenging samples and obtain a wealth of information with very small amounts of genetic material. These new, massively parallel sequencing methodologies allow sequencing of millions of strands of DNA at the same time and have the potential to increase the discriminatory power of the DNA data and improve the cost and speed of the sequencing process by yielding information not only corresponding to the mitochondrial DNA but also data corresponding to single nucleotide polymorphisms, autosomal and gender specific short tandem repeats.

This new process is characterized by the amplification of the fragment(s) of interest in each sample and subsequent incorporation of barcodes and adapters to these target fragments. The samples are then cleaned and pooled together into one sample library. The pooled sample library is loaded onto a flow cell where the various fragments become attached to the surface and amplified to form clusters. The sequencing process encompasses the addition of sequencing reagents and sequential addition of single nucleotides. If the added nucleotide is complementary to the template strand, it will become incorporated and a fluorescent signal or change in hydrogen ion concentration will be detected by the system and recorded. Unincorporated nucleotides are removed before adding additional sequencing reagents and a new nucleotide. The process is repeated for a predetermined number of cycles to complete the sequencing reaction. Specialized software is used to deconvolute the samples into the original individual specimens based on the barcode tag attached to them at the beginning of the process. The sequences of the individual samples are then made available to the analyst for interpretation.

*Lilliana I. Moreno*

## Further Reading

Butler, JM. *Advanced Topics in Forensic DNA typing: methodology*. Boston, MA: Elsevier, 2011. Provides the reader with information on the most cutting-edge technologies available for biological sample processing.

Mardis, ER. Generation DNA Next sequencing methods. *Annu Rev Genomics Hum Genet* (2008), 9:387-402. This article contains useful general information on the newest approaches and platforms for DNA sample sequencing.

Shendure, J., RD Mitra, C. Varma and GM Church. Advanced sequencing technologies: Methods and goals. *Nature Reviews Genetics* (2004), 5:335-344. Provides a broad overview of the advances in the field of DNA sequencing – from its inception to the newest technologies available and their applications.

## DNA typing

**Definition:** Process by which amplified DNA fragments of interest are separated and detected in order to yield a DNA profile useful for interpretation and comparison to known exemplars or for upload into the Combined DNA Index System (CODIS) to be searched against other unknown DNA profiles.

**Significance:** The ultimate goal of the processing of biological samples is to obtain information that can help convict or exonerate an individual from any given crime. The information gleaned from the DNA typing result can be a very powerful tool as it can exclude, include or generate sufficient information to undoubtedly identify potential suspects as sources of a given sample.

The genetic material of each individual is 99% identical to that of other individuals. Nevertheless, in forensics we exploit the differences in the remaining 1% to obtain clues pertaining to the source of a particular sample in hopes of aiding legal investigations. Differences in the genetic material can present themselves as short fragments of repetitive sequences (short tandem repeats, STRs) or as differences in a single nucleotide in a given location within the genome (single nucleotide polymorphisms, SNPs). Because the number of repeats in any given STR location within the genome can vary greatly in comparison to the variation in SNPs which is often one of two options (C/G or A/T); analysts usually target STRs as the primary source of information for legal investigations as it offers the greatest potential for discrimination between individuals.

Until recently, analysts could concomitantly target and amplify a maximum of sixteen variable STR locations within the genome of which only thirteen were required to enable the sample to be uploaded into the offender National DNA Database.

Currently, up to twenty four STR locations can be amplified at once to generate a genetic picture of an individual and soon the requirement for upload into the database will be increased to twenty specific target regions. This expansion of the number of markers offers a substantial increase the power of discrimination of DNA technology.

During the process of DNA amplification, fluorescently tagged primers are added to the reaction to direct the polymerase enzyme to extend the primer and generate copies of the fragments of interest. Because half of the genetic material is inherited from the mother and the other half from the father, each individual is expected to have two copies of each targeted DNA fragment. Nevertheless, because the mother and father each has a distinct genetic fingerprint, a different number of sequence repetitions within each particular target fragment is not unexpected. For example for target A, mom could have donated 8 repeats of the sequence whereas dad could have donated 10. That would make the individual an 8,10 at that particular location. At times, the mother and father could have by chance donated the same number of repeats for a given sequence making the individual a 9,9, for example.

The number of repeats inherited from the parents is determined for each target location and the compilation or genetic fingerprint is used for comparison purposes. Some individuals might share the same number of repeats for one or more locations within the genome but a difference in just one of these target regions indicates that the sample did not originate from the same person.

Various DNA typing techniques exist and can be used depending on the sample available and the needs for a particular investigation. An analyst can choose to perform mitochondrial DNA (mtDNA) typing in a missing person case to establish relatedness of the missing individual to a particular family, single nucleotide polymorphisms (SNP) to generate investigative leads by providing ancestry information about the sample, short tandem repeats (STRs) if trying to link evidence to a particular suspect or Y-chromosome typing in cases in which sexual assault is suspected. Forensic DNA typing can also target regions of interest in microbial, plant or animal genomes using the same principles described. These types of evidentiary material are at times available and can provide important information in the resolution of crimes.Although several methods are available for the visualization of DNA typing products, capillary electrophoresis is the one most commonly used as it provides good resolution, high-throughput and automation capabilities.

These instruments separate the fragments of DNA generated based on size and charge and are coupled to cameras that will detect the various wavelengths emitted by the different fluorescent tags applied to the primers during the process of amplification and convert the signal to an output that can be interpreted by a DNA analyst through a process known as DNA profiling.

*Lilliana I. Moreno*

## Further Reading

Butler, JM. *Fundamentals of Forensic DNA typing.* Burlington, MA/Elsevier Academic Press, 2009. In simple terminology, it provides the framework of forensic DNA analysis and typing. It includes information on historic and novel techniques and detailed descriptions of each step in the process.

Garcia, CD and KY Chumbimuni-Torres. *Capillary Electrophoresis and Microchip Capillary Electrophoresis: Principles, Applications and Limitations.* Hoboken,NJ:Wiley and Sons, 2013. Provides current information on the fundamentals of electrophoretic separations and their various applications. The most recent advances in this technology are also discussed.

Miller Coyle, H. *Nonhuman DNA typing: Theory and casework applications.* Boca Raton, FL: CRC Press, 2008. Introduces the field of non-human DNA typing and offers case ex-amples to describe the importance of these types of evidentiary materials in criminal investigations.

**See also:** Bacterial biology; DNA analysis; DNA extraction from hair, bodily fluids, and tissues; DNA fingerprinting; DNA profiling; DNA sequencing; Electrophoresis; Mitochondrial DNA analysis and typing; Paternity testing; Postconviction DNA analysis; Restriction fragment length polymorphisms; Semen and sperm; Short tandem repeat analysis; Y chromosome analysis.

---

# Document examination

**Definition:** Application of analytical techniques to questions of the authenticity or origins of materials that bear marks, signs, or symbols that have meaning or convey messages.

**Significance:** An important component of forensic science is the investigation of questioned documents, which may be anything from written death threats to ransom notes to suicide notes to adulterated wills. The analysis of documents can help to connect suspects to such crimes as kidnapping, bank robbery, and forgery.

In the forensic science field of document examination, anything that bears marks, signs, or symbols that have meaning or convey messages is considered to be a document. Document examiners establish the authenticity or inauthenticity of contested materials, detect alterations in documents, and trace documents to their places of origin. Among the tasks performed by document examiners are handwriting comparisons, comparisons of type styles, ink analyses, and comparisons of documents created using typewriters, fax machines, and computer printers.

## Handwriting Identification

Handwriting analysis is conducted in many types of investigations, including cases of fraud, homicide, suicide, drug trafficking, sexual offenses, threats, extortion, blackmail, arson, and robbery. No two individuals have the same handwriting style; each person's handwriting displays unique features that distinguish it from the writing of all other persons. Among the features of handwriting that differ from person to person are the use of margins; the spacing, crowding, alignment, and slope of letters; the pressure applied to the writing instrument; and the speed with which the writing is done. In addition, document analysts look at related matters such as spelling, punctuation, phraseology, and grammar.

Handwriting analysts compare the handwriting on questioned documents with the handwriting of any identified suspects using authenticated handwriting samples (writing exemplars) obtained from those individuals. Ideally, writing exemplars are produced in a manner that makes them as close as possible to the questioned documents under examination; that is, the size and type of paper and the kind of writing instrument used should be the same, and the same text should be written. The text to be written is dictated to the suspect, and no instructions are given concerning the spelling, punctuation, or arrangement of the requested writing sample.

The writing of several pages of dictation yields exemplars that best represent a suspect's subconscious style and characteristics. As the amount of writing that a suspect is asked to produce increases, it becomes more difficult for the suspect to conceal his or her own writing style and to imitate the writing style of another. The suspect is also required to provide writing samples from both the right and left hands. In addition, when possible, the analyst compares the requested exemplars and the questioned document against writing examples from the suspect that were produced before that person was officially contacted by law enforcement. Such examples might include business records, personal correspondence, and canceled checks.

### Indented Writing

Forensic document examiners are sometimes able to connect suspects to crimes by examining the indentations left on sheets of paper when other sheets that rested above them have been written on, such as on notepads. For example, a bank robbery note may be connected to a writing pad recovered from a suspect's residence.

The clarity of such impressions is influenced by the amount of pressure that was used by the writer and the thickness of the paper. If the indentations are deep (from heavy pen pressure, for instance), they may be visible to the naked eye. If the indentations are too shallow to be seen clearly, the analyst may enhance them by using the Electrostatic Detection Apparatus (ESDA). This instrument uses a vacuum to seal a thin plastic film over the sheet of paper with the suspected indentations. The plastic film is then given an electrostatic charge, and black toner is applied to it. The toner adheres to any indentations in the paper, making them clearly visible. A sticky transparent plastic film is then placed over the indentation patterns on the paper to preserve them for examination and possible presentation as evidence.

### Detection of Alterations

Document examiners sometimes are called upon to detect whether documents have been modified through erasure, addition, or the blotting out of information. One of the most common ways in which documents are altered is through erasure of parts of the writing or type. Whenever a part of a document is erased (whether through use of a rubber eraser, a piece of sandpaper, or a razor blade, for instance), the surface fibers of the paper are disturbed. Microscopic examination of a document can thus reveal whether areas of it have been erased.

Some alterations to documents involve the overwriting or blotting out of segments of text. To uncover text that has been overwritten, a document examiner may employ the Video Spectral Comparator (VSC), an instrument that uses infrared illumination. Different kinds of inks have distinct chemical compositions that reflect light differently, and the VSC highlights such variations in light reflectivity. Differences in the inks that appear on a document are a strong indication that the document has been altered. The VSC is also sometimes able to uncover text that has been overwritten or blotted out because the light reflection of the ink of the text that has been covered up may be discernible under that of the ink that was used to cover it up. If precisely the same ink used in the original document was used to overwrite or blot out text, however, recovery of the original text may not be possible.

## Identification of Typewriters

Typewriters have been used in the production of many kinds of questioned documents, from travel papers to wills to terrorist manifestos. In the forensic examination of typed documents, analysts are often concerned with identifying the documents' sources by determining the makes and models of the typewriters used and when the typed documents were produced. They might also need to determine whether particular series of documents (such as several bomb threats) were prepared on the same typewriter.

Knowledge of distinguishing features among typewriters allows investigators to identify the kind of typewriter used to produce a given document. In many cases, analysts can match a document up with an individual typewriter. Some of the distinguishing characteristics among typewriters that make such identification possible include the typeface that was produced, whether the type was produced by a manual or electric typewriter, whether the typewriter used fabric or carbon ribbon, and whether the type was imprinted with a type bar or with daisy wheel or ball printing elements.

The style of typeface that appears in a typed questioned document is useful for tracking down the make and model of the typewriter, as the typeface styles produced by different makes and models of typewriters are limited. Document examiners can compare the typefaces in questioned documents with typefaces in available databases to identify the makes and models of the typewriters that produce them.

A document analyst may connect an individ-

---

### Certification of Forensic Document Examiners

Forensic document examiners receive their specialized training on the job from experienced examiners; no colleges or universities in the United States offer degree programs or majors in forensic document examination. The American Board of Forensic Document Examiners (ABFDE), founded in 1977, is the only certifying board for the profession that is sponsored by the American Society of Questioned Document Examiners, the Canadian Society of Forensic Sciences, the Southeastern Association of Forensic Document Examiners, and the Southwestern Association of Forensic Document Examiners and is recognized by the American Academy of Forensic Sciences. The ABFDE's minimum requirements for certification as a forensic document examiner are a bachelor's degree, completion of a full-time training program (a two-year apprenticeship) in a recognized document laboratory, and full-time practice of forensic document examination.

---

ual typewriter to a document by examining the impressions left on the typewriter ribbon to find the portion of the ribbon on which particular text was typed. In addition, unique features (that is, tool marks) are imparted on documents by the typewriters that produce them, because every typewriter has moving parts that experience random damage and general wear. Such unique features can be used to connect documents to particular typewriters.

## Identification of Computer Printers, Photocopiers, and Fax Machines

In cases that involve documents produced by computer printers, photocopiers, or fax machines, analysts may be asked to identify the makes and models of the machines used or to compare questioned documents with samples printed from suspected machines. In conducting such an analysis, an examiner usually produces ten samples from each suspect machine to obtain a sufficient representation of the machine's characteristics. The examiner then undertakes a side-by-side microscopic comparison of the questioned document and the printed exemplars, focusing on such details as character shapes, the type of toner used, and the method by which the toner was applied to each document.

Different computer printers (including inkjet, laser, thermal, and dot-matrix printers)

## The FBI's Questioned Document Databases

The Federal Bureau of Investigation's Questioned Documents Unit maintains several electronic databases that can be extremely helpful to document examiners: the Anonymous Letter File, the Bank Robbery Note File, the National Fraudulent Check File, and the Watermark File. By comparing questioned documents with the images of ransom notes, extortion letters, and other anonymous communications stored in these files, examiners can establish associations between different cases. The FBI reports that these databases have been particularly effective in helping law-enforcement authorities to solve crimes committed across state lines.

have characteristic ways of printing documents. Investigators also look for any tool marks on documents that have been made by the belts, pinchers, rollers, and gears that move the paper through a machine.

Many laser printers are designed to mark documents so that documents may be traced back to them. A document analyst may identify the source of a photocopied document by noting defects that are reproduced on copies from the glass platen, lens, or drum of a particular machine. The source of a document produced by a fax machine may be identified by the document's header, known as the transmitting terminal identifier (TTI). The TTI, which appears at the top of each fax page, identifies the machine that sent the document. Law-enforcement investigators have access to a database of TTI fonts and the corresponding fax machines that use them.

*Daniel Pontzer*

### Further Reading

Bennett, Wayne W., and Kären M. Hess. *Criminal Investigation.* 8th ed. Belmont, Calif.: Wadsworth/Thomson Learning, 2007. Introductory text discusses the elements of effective criminal investigations and the equipment, technology, and procedures used by forensic scientists.

Gaensslen, R. E., Howard A. Harris, and Henry C. Lee. *Introduction to Forensic Science and Criminalistics.* New York: McGraw-Hill, 2008. General introduction to forensic sci-

ence includes discussion of the types of document examination work done in crime labs for criminal cases and by private examiners for civil cases.

Kelly, Jan Seaman, and Brian S. Lindblom, eds. *Scientific Examination of Questioned Documents.* 2d ed. Boca Raton, Fla.: CRC Press, 2006. Collection of essays by experts in the field provides comprehensive coverage of the history and techniques of document examination.

Morris, Ron N. *Forensic Handwriting Identification: Fundamental Concepts and Principles.* New York: Academic Press, 2000. Illustrated text addresses the major principles of handwriting analysis, including information on how various physiological conditions can affect writing. Useful for both students and practitioners.

Saferstein, Richard. *Criminalistics: An Introduction to Forensic Science.* 9th ed. Upper Saddle River, N.J.: Pearson Prentice Hall, 2007. Comprehensive introductory textbook covers all aspects of forensic science, including the methods and technologies used in document examination.

**See also:** Check alteration and washing; Fax machine, copier, and printer analysis; Forensic accounting; Forensic linguistics and stylistics; Forgery; Handwriting analysis; Hitler diaries hoax; Hughes will hoax; Oblique lighting analysis; Paper; Questioned document analysis; Secret Service, U.S.; Steganography; Typewriter analysis; Writing instrument analysis.

## Dosimetry

**Definition:** Calculation of radiation exposure (quantity or dose of ionizing radiation—such as X rays or gamma rays—absorbed by matter in tissue) over a given period of time.

**Significance:** A high degree of concern surrounds the illicit acquisition and dissemination of radioactive materials by criminals and terrorist organizations. Forensic scientists apply dosimetry in investigating such crimes through geological and archeological dating, retrospective dosimetry, and personnel dosimetry.

Using dosimetry, investigators can determine how much radiation exposure a given sample has received, the sample's origination point, who has come in contact with the material, and whether or not the sample poses a potential hazard.

A radiation dosimeter is a device that measures cumulative (total) radiation exposure. Dosimeters differ from Geiger counters, which are also radiation detectors but give only moment-to-moment readings of radiation levels. Radiation doses are reported in grays (Gy) for matter and sieverts (Sv) for biological tissue. The non-SI (International System of Units) unit for radiation is rads, and that for dose equivalent is rems (1 Gy = 100 rads and 1 Sv = 100 rems). Mineral specimens produce radioactivity ranging from 0.5 to 200 millirems per hour measured at approximately one-half inch from the specimen.

The governments of most nations have established guidelines for permissible occupational radiation dose levels. Typically, the whole-body dose limit for routine exposures is 5 rems per year. This limit is based on the total amount of internal and external exposure. Specific limits have also been set for individual organs that must be met in addition to the whole-body dose limit: For the extremities the limit is typically 50 rems per year; for skin and other organs, 50 rems per year; and for the lens of the eye, 15 rems per year.

A personal radiation dosimeter is a small electronic device that resembles a pen; it is often worn clipped to clothing to measure an individual's radiation exposure. By using a magnifying and illumination lens, the wearer can read the exposure level directly by looking into the dosimeter. This is considered to be the most effective method of determining personal radia-

tion exposure, as the biological damage caused by radiation is cumulative.

The film badge dosimeter is an inexpensive alternative to the electronic dosimeter. It is a plastic badge containing a piece of photographic film. The badge is worn on the individual's clothing, and the film is gradually exposed with the wearer's radiation exposure. The film is periodically removed from the badge and developed, and through analysis of the developed film's optical density, the cumulative dosage measurement can be determined.

*Rena Christina Tabata*

**Further Reading**

Ehmann, William D., and Diane E. Vance. *Radiochemistry and Nuclear Methods of Analysis.* New York: John Wiley & Sons, 1991.

Moody, Kenton James, Ian D. Hutcheon, and Patrick M. Grant. *Nuclear Forensic Analysis.* Boca Raton, Fla.: CRC Press, 2005.

Stabin, Michael G. *Radiation Protection and Dosimetry: An Introduction to Health Physics.* New York: Springer, 2007.

**See also:** Chemical terrorism; Crime scene investigation; Crime scene protective gear; Decontamination methods; Environmental Measurements Laboratory; Isotopic analysis; Radiation damage to tissues.

## Driving injuries

**Definition:** Injuries caused by air pressure or projectiles driven from an explosion.

**Significance:** By examining the driving injuries caused by an explosion, forensic scientists can help determine where and how the explosion occurred and whether the explosion was caused by low-order or high-order explosives.

The most common injuries that result from an explosion are injuries caused when the force of the blast drives air pressure or objects, such as pieces of glass, into the body. By determining the type of object that caused such an injury, the material making up the object, the angle at which the object hit the body, and the force with which it entered or hit the body, investigators can help determine where the bomb or other explosive device was placed when it detonated and where and how it was manufactured.

## Types of Explosions

Driving injuries can occur with any type of blast or explosion, either natural or human-made. Such injuries are often seen following industrial explosions, such as mining accidents or chemical explosions, and as the result of motor vehicle accidents. Terrorist attacks involving explosions, such as car or suicide bombings, can also result in driving injuries, as can the explosions associated with warfare. Driving injuries may also occur as the result of hurricanes, tornadoes, or fireworks explosions.

Human-made explosions are particularly damaging to the body because most are specifically designed to project objects into the surrounding area, with the goal of causing bodily harm. For example, military ordnance is designed to shatter into shrapnel to cause body damage, and bombs are often filled with metal objects such as nails or glass that are flung out into the surrounding area. Explosions that occur in enclosed places—such as a mine shaft, a building, or a bus—cause higher rates of driving injuries, and more serious injuries and deaths, than do explosions that occur in open areas.

## Types of Driving Injuries

The types of driving injuries are generally classified as primary, secondary, tertiary, and miscellaneous, or quaternary. Primary driving injuries are caused by air pressure emitted, or driven, from the explosion. Because they involve air pressure, they are usually limited to those areas of the body containing air or fluid, such as the lungs, eardrums, eyes, and stomach or intestinal tract, which can rupture from the force. These injuries occur with high-order explosives and may include abdominal hemorrhage or perforation, concussion, eye rupture, pulmonary rupture ("blast lung"), and tympanic (eardrum) rupture.

Secondary driving injuries are caused by pro-jectiles or other objects, such as glass or shrapnel, being driven into the body by the force of the explosion. These injuries occur with either high- or low-order explosives and may include blunt trauma injuries (skin is not broken but significant surface and underlying damage is present) and penetrating injuries (an object actually penetrates the skin and enters the body, often in the eye).

Tertiary driving injuries occur when the force of the blast is so strong that the body actually becomes a projectile. The body may be slammed into a standing object or even into other bodies. These injuries occur with high-order explosives and may include amputation, brain injuries (closed or open), and fractures.

The category of injuries termed miscellaneous or quaternary driving injuries encompasses all types of injuries not contained in the first three categories. These may include brain injuries (closed or open), breathing injuries (such as asthma from dust or smoke or lung damage from toxic fumes), burns (from fires caused by the explosion), complications from preexisting conditions (such as heart problems), and crushing injuries (caused by the collapse of buildings or other structures).

## Specific Driving Injuries

Certain abdominal, brain, ear, eye, and lung injuries form a pattern specific to driving injuries from a high-order explosion. Abdominal injuries from such an explosion may not be noticeable at first because they occur with no open wounds, but abdominal organs may suffer injuries such as bowel perforation, testicular rupture, abdominal hemorrhage, and organ lacerations. A high-order explosion can also cause concussion even without a direct blow to the head, and rupture of the eardrum may occur with no blow to the ear or head itself.

About 10 percent of survivors of high-order explosions have eye injuries, some of which are significant. These injuries are usually perforations from objects driven into the eye from the force of the blast and are noticeable at the time, but some may not appear or be noticed until days or weeks after the explosion.

"Blast lung" is the most common injury that causes death if an injured person survives the initial explosion. It occurs when air is forced into the lungs, exploding lung tissues and causing bleeding. It produces a very distinctive "butterfly" pattern on a chest X-ray. Symptoms of blast lung are usually obvious immediately after the explosion, but occasionally they do not show up for a few days after the injury.

*Marianne M. Madsen*

## Further Reading

Bolz, Frank, Jr., Kenneth J. Dudonis, and David P. Schulz. *The Counterterrorism Handbook: Tactics, Procedures, and Techniques.* 3d ed. Boca Raton, Fla.: CRC Press, 2005. Explains procedures to be followed in the event of a terrorist bombing attack, including procedures for handling victims of driving injuries.

Crippen, James B. *Improvised Explosive Devices (IED): A Comprehensive Guide.* Boca Raton, Fla.: CRC Press, 2008. Examines the mechanics of IEDs and how they cause driving injuries.

Ellis, John W. *Police Analysis and Planning for Homicide Bombings: Prevention, Defense, and Response.* Springfield, Ill.: Charles C Thomas, 2007. Discusses how law-enforcement agencies respond to homicide bombings, including the handling of driving injuries.

Hattwig, Martin, and Henrikus Steen, eds. *Handbook of Explosion Prevention and Protection.* Weinheim, Germany: Wiley-VCH, 2004. Discusses how people can protect themselves and others from driving injuries caused by explosions.

James, Stuart H., and Jon J. Nordby, eds. *Forensic Science: An Introduction to Scientific and Investigative Techniques.* 2d ed. Boca Raton, Fla.: CRC Press, 2005. Comprehensive introductory textbook includes a chapter on the investigation of explosions.

**See also:** Antemortem injuries; Blast seat; Blunt force trauma; Bomb damage assessment; Bombings; Bureau of Alcohol, Tobacco, Firearms and Explosives; Improvised explosive devices; Oklahoma City bombing; World Trade Center bombing.

# Drowning

**Definition:** Death caused by a lack of oxygen that may have resulted from the presence of water in the lungs or from the closure of the upper airway, leading to cardiopulmonary arrest.

**Significance:** Unexpected deaths require forensic investigation to determine cause and manner of death. In drowning cases, cause of death is not always obvious, so it is important that forensic examiners be familiar with the types of evidence that may point to drowning.

The majority of drowning deaths are accidental. Nearly half of drowning victims are small children who were unsupervised and unable to swim. Among adults, accidental drowning is often associated with the consumption of large amounts of alcohol. With intoxication, judgment becomes impaired and risky behavior becomes more likely. Many of these drowning deaths are preventable. Close supervision of children around water and swimming lessons early in childhood can decrease the likelihood of accidental drownings. Adult deaths from drowning can be reduced through the limitation of alcohol use during water activities and requirement of appropriate use of life-preservation devices.

Suicide is the second-most-common cause of death by drowning. Such suicides may be mistaken for accidental deaths. Murder of adults by drowning is rare; murder of children by this method is also rare, but may be less rare than murder of adults.

In drowning cases the cause of death is not always obvious. This is particularly true when the deceased person has been found submerged in water, whether in a bathtub or in an ocean. In such circumstances, it may be assumed that the cause of death is drowning, but this may or may not be correct. Initially, the only known information is that the person was found in water; it is not known whether the person may have been dead prior to entering the water.

No tests are available that can prove or disprove drowning as the cause of death. Most drowning victims have water in their lungs, but a small percentage experience "dry" drowning, which occurs when the airway closes before water can enter the lungs. Water found in the lungs on autopsy, moreover, proves only that the person was in water at some point. Foamy fluids, vomit, mud, or plant material may be found in the mouth of a body pulled from water, but such evidence does not prove cause or manner of death.

When a body found in water is removed from the water, it may or may not exhibit signs of trauma initially. Neck or head injuries may have occurred if diving was involved, but these may not be apparent until an autopsy is performed. The body may have small injuries as a result of coming into contact with objects in the water. Animals may have fed on the body if it remained submerged in water for a prolonged time. The eyes may appear bloodshot from asphyxiation, which may indicate death by drowning. The presence of injuries or bloodshot eyes, however, does not prove death by drowning.

*Amy Webb Bull*

**Further Reading**

Brenner, John. *Forensic Science: An Illustrated Dictionary.* Boca Raton, Fla.: CRC Press, 2003.

Dix, Jay, Michael Graham, and Randy Hanzlick. *Asphyxia and Drowning: An Atlas.* Boca Raton, Fla.: CRC Press, 2000.

James, Stuart H., and Jon J. Nordby, eds. *Forensic Science: An Introduction to Scientific and Investigative Techniques.* 2d ed. Boca Raton, Fla.: CRC Press, 2005.

Shkrum, Michael J., and David A. Ramsay. *Forensic Pathology of Trauma: Common Problems for the Pathologist.* Totowa, N.J.: Humana Press, 2007.

**See also:** Asphyxiation; Buried body locating; First responders; Hypothermia; Petechial hemorrhage; Suffocation; Toxicological analysis.

# Drug abuse and dependence

**Definition:** Chronic but treatable brain diseases involving compulsive drug-seeking and drug-using behaviors that persist despite immediate or potentially harmful consequences for the drug-abusing individuals, their families, and their communities.

**Significance:** Drug abuse and drug dependence are major threats to public health and safety, costing billions of dollars annually in health care and criminal justice system expenditures in addition to losses related to work productivity and unemployment. Addictive behavior is one of the most pervasive and intransigent mental health problems in the world, affecting millions of people annually.

Drugs are psychoactive substances that affect moods and behaviors by altering brain chemistry and function. Drugs of abuse include medically prescribed (barbiturates and pain relievers), legal (cigarettes and nicotine), and illegal (marijuana and heroin) substances. Some drugs, such as alcohol, have been used since ancient times, whereas others, such as methamphetamine and so-called designer drugs, are relatively new. People consume drugs to feel good (some drugs result in feelings of euphoria, confidence, and relaxation), to keep from feeling bad (some drugs combat feelings of anxiety, depression, and hopelessness), to accelerate performance (some drugs heighten alertness and enhance physical strength and prowess in athletic competition), and to experience altered sensory perceptions (some drugs cause users to see or hear unusual or unreal phenomena).

Drugs of abuse can be placed into five major classes according to their effects. The first class consists of stimulants, which increase alertness and decrease fatigue. Examples of stimulant drugs are amphetamines, Benzedrine, caffeine, Dexedrine, ephedrine, and nicotine. The second class consists of depressants, which reduce tension, alleviate nervousness, and induce sedation. Examples of sedative drugs are barbiturates (such as Nembutal, Seconal, Tunial, and

Veronal), Valium, and Xanax. The third class consists of hallucinogens, which change sensory perceptions. Examples of hallucinogens are cannabis (marijuana), lysergic acid diethylamide (LSD), mescaline, phencyclidine (PCP), and psilocybin. The fourth class consists of opiates, which induce sleep, euphoria, and relaxation and also relieve pain and anxiety. Examples of opiates are codeine, heroin, opium, OxyContin, Percodan, and morphine. The fifth class consists of performance enhancers, which increase athletic strength and speed and stimulate skeletal muscle growth and recovery. Examples of performance enhancers are anabolic steroids such as Anadrol, Depo-Testosterone, Dianabol, and Winstrol.

Individual drug abusers typically prefer some classes of drugs over others and prefer some particular drugs within given classes. When they have difficulty obtaining their preferred drugs, they often substitute others in the same classes that produce similar effects. Psychoactive drugs in the same class can be compared based on their potency and efficacy. "Potency" refers to the amount a user must ingest to experience a certain effect, whereas "efficacy" refers to whether a drug can produce an effect regardless of dosage. Both the strength and the potency of substances can determine abusers' drugs of choice as well as the drugs' potential for abuse and dependence.

## The Addictive Process

Drug use can escalate to abuse or dependence problems, which are also called substance-use disorders. The progression to uncontrolled use depends on several risk factors. For example, biological factors play a role in addiction—that is, genetics can predispose an individual to addictive behavior. Such a predisposition is shared among close biological relatives. Scientists estimate that genes account for nearly half of a person's vulnerability to a substance-use disorder.

Age of first use and psychiatric history are also important elements in risk for problems with drug use. Younger users are more likely to become addicted because developing adolescent brains are more susceptible to drugs' ability to change brain chemistry and function. Persons with mental illness are also more likely to abuse

or become dependent on drugs. In addition, exposure to parents' or peers' use of drugs can increase the risk of addiction. The mode of drug ingestion can also increase the potential for drug abuse and dependence. A drug that is inhaled or injected intravenously is more addictive than a drug that is ingested orally. The former reaches the brain faster and produces more intense highs and lows. Drug-seeking behavior intensifies in response to the cycle of peaks and valleys that the user experiences.

Psychoactive drugs are thought to become addictive through their activation of the brain's mesocorticolimbic dopamine pathway, which extends from the brain's ventral tegmental area to the nucleus accumbens to the frontal cortex. Drugs of abuse stimulate this pleasure circuit by increasing the amount of dopamine in the brain two- to tenfold; this is extremely rewarding to users and compels them to repeat the experience. Drugs of abuse either mimic the effects of dopamine on neurotransmitters or block the reabsorption of dopamine to activate neurons. Eventually, the brain shuts down its own capacity to produce dopamine, causing the user to ingest the drug merely to stave off feelings of listlessness, depression, and other withdrawal symptoms. Drugs of abuse also affect the brain's frontal regions, impairing judgment and leading addicts to pursue drugs compulsively, even as the rewards of use steadily diminish. Relapse (return to drug use following a period of abstinence) is thus common among persons with substance-use disorders; it can be triggered by stress, mood changes, and drug-related cues that remind the abuser of the substance.

## Substance-Use Disorders

Substance-abuse and -dependence disorders are diagnosed according to the criteria specified in the American Psychiatric Association's *Diagnostic and Statistical Manual of Mental Disorders*. A substance-abuse disorder is diagnosed when drug use in the past twelve months leads to significant distress and impairment in functioning and meets at least one of the following diagnostic criteria: failure to fulfill obligations at work, school, or home; recurring use of substances in dangerous situations (such as driving while intoxicated); recurring substance-use-related criminal justice involvement; and continued substance use that leads to interpersonal conflicts.

A drug-dependence disorder, which is more serious than a drug-abuse disorder, is diagnosed when drug use in the past twelve months has reached the level of abuse and meets at least three of seven criteria that include tolerance (increasing amounts of the drug must be taken to achieve desired effects), physical withdrawal (symptoms that accompany the cessation of drug use, such as tremors, chills, drug craving, restlessness, bone and muscle pain, sweating, and vomiting), and persistent failure to reduce drug consumption.

### Prevalence of Substance-Use Disorders

The annual National Survey on Drug Use and Health assesses the prevalence of substance-use disorders in the United States in the preceding twelve months. In 2005, the findings of this survey indicated that an estimated 22 million persons aged twelve and older were classified with a substance-abuse or -dependence problem (9 percent of the U.S. population). Among these individuals, more than 3 million were classified with abuse of or dependence on both alcohol and illicit drugs, more than 3.5 million abused or were dependent on illicit drugs but not alcohol, and more than 15 million abused or were dependent on alcohol but not illicit drugs.

*Arthur J. Lurigio*

### Further Reading

Abadinsky, Howard. *Drug Use and Abuse: A Comprehensive Introduction.* 6th ed. Belmont, Calif.: Thomson/Wadsworth, 2008. Covers all aspects of drug and alcohol abuse, including the history of drugs and their pharmacological effects. Also discusses the impacts of drug abuse on society.

Hoffman, John, and Susan Froemke, eds. *Addiction: Why Can't They Just Stop?* New York: Rodale, 2007. Companion volume to a television series of the same name presents detailed descriptions of the effects of drugs on the brain, drug treatment methods, and recovery. Features many engaging case studies and sidebars.

Karch, Steven B., ed. *Drug Abuse Handbook.* 2d ed. Boca Raton, Fla.: CRC Press, 2007. Provides a compendium of authoritative information on various aspects of drug abuse. Contributing authors include medical, legal, and treatment professionals.

National Institute on Drug Abuse. *Drugs, Brains, and Behavior.* Washington, D.C.: National Institutes of Health, 2007. Brief, highly readable document explains the science of addiction in nontechnical terms.

Substance Abuse and Mental Health Services Administration. *Results of the 2005 National Survey on Drug Use and Health: National Findings.* Washington, D.C.: Author, 2006. Presents the findings of an annual survey on drug use conducted by the U.S. Department of Health and Human Services with a sample of the general population of the United States aged twelve years old and older. Includes information on national estimates of rates of use, numbers of users, and other measures related to illicit drugs, alcohol, and tobacco products.

**See also:** Amphetamines; Antianxiety agents; Barbiturates; Club drugs; Crack cocaine; Drug classification; Drug paraphernalia; Forensic odontology; Hallucinogens; Harrison Narcotic Drug Act of 1914; Illicit substances; Inhalant abuse; Narcotics; Opioids; Psychotropic drugs.

## Drug and alcohol evidence rules

**Definition:** Proper procedures for collecting and handling evidence to ensure its acceptance by a court in criminal proceedings related to the use or possession of drugs or alcohol.

**Significance:** To be sure that the drug and alcohol evidence collected and analyzed during an investigation is accepted in court, first responders, investigators, and laboratory technicians must handle and document the evidence in ways that meet the requirements for admissible evidence.

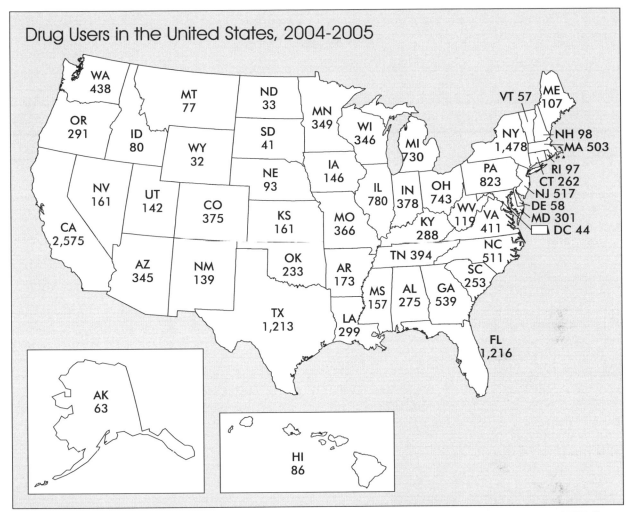

Drug Users in the United States, 2004-2005

WA 438
MT 77
ND 33
MN 349
WI 346
MI 730
VT 57
ME 107
OR 291
ID 80
WY 32
SD 41
IA 146
NY 1,478
NH 98
MA 503
NV 161
UT 142
CO 375
NE 93
IL 780
IN 378
OH 743
PA 823
RI 97
CT 262
NJ 517
DE 58
MD 301
DC 44
CA 2,575
KS 161
MO 366
KY 288
WV 119
VA 411
NC 511
AZ 345
NM 139
OK 233
AR 173
TN 394
SC 253
TX 1,213
MS 157
AL 275
GA 539
LA 299
FL 1,216
AK 63
HI 86

*Source:* U.S. Substance Abuse and Mental Health Services Administration, *National Survey on Drug Use and Health, 2004 and 2005*. Figures represent the estimated numbers (in thousands) of persons over the age of twelve who used any illicit drug at least once within the month preceding the moment of the study. "Illicit drugs" included marijuana, cocaine, heroin, hallucinogens, inhalants, and psychotherapeutics used for nonmedical reasons.

Statutory rules of evidence are laws that help determine what evidence will be accepted by the court. They are designed to produce a fair, orderly, and efficient legal process that results in the determination of the truth. For example, statutory laws prevent the court from accepting hearsay evidence or evidence that may have been tampered with or altered. In 1975, the U.S. Congress established the Federal Rules of Evidence. In addition to federal evidence laws, each U.S. state has its own set of statutes concerning the admissibility of evidence.

**Alcohol Evidence**

Alcohol is relevant evidence primarily in cases of underage consumption of alcohol and driving under the influence (DUI) of alcohol. The amount of alcohol a person has consumed can be determined through the use of machines that measure breath alcohol (such as the Breathalyzer), urine testing, or blood testing. In cases of alcohol consumption by underage persons, testing must prove only the presence of alcohol in the body, because any amount of alcohol consumption by an underage individual is a violation of the law. In those of legal drinking age, the evidence must show that the amount of alcohol in the bloodstream is above the legal limit.

The most common reason for a police officer to make a suspected DUI stop is observation of a pattern of driving consistent with the driver's being under the influence of alcohol. If the officer then observes behavior consistent with DUI or smells alcohol, the driver may be asked to perform a field sobriety test. This involves actions such as touching the nose, walking on a road line, or reciting the alphabet. Based on the results of the field sobriety test, the individual may be asked to take a preliminary alcohol screening (PAS) test, commonly called a Breathalyzer test. The PAS gives a rough estimate of the amount of alcohol in the bloodstream. If the individual is arrested for DUI, he or she must provide a blood or urine sample. Each jurisdiction establishes a standard procedure for the collection of these samples.

Urine and blood samples are analyzed by the toxicology section of the crime laboratory. Although procedures vary from state to state, the statutory laws of evidence require that each sample be labeled with the time, place, and person from which it came; that it be handled in a way that will not allow it to be tampered with or altered; and that a chain of custody (a written record of who had possession of the sample at all times, how it was stored, and what tests were done on it) is established and maintained.

## Drug Evidence

Controlled substances can take the form of liquids, capsules, tablets, powders, plant material, or irregular masses. Unlike alcohol evidence, where testing is done to measure the quantity of alcohol in the blood, drug testing usually requires only identification of the type of drug in the evidence sample. The job of the toxicology laboratory is to use an array of standard chemical tests to identify the drug. Just as with other physical evidence, a chain of custody must be established for the evidence to be accepted in court.

Each jurisdiction establishes its own procedure for handling different types of drugs. If a large quantity of a drug is seized, only a small sample is taken, following an established sam-

pling protocol, and sent for analysis. When a person is suspected of being under the influence of drugs, the laboratory determines what drug or its metabolites (breakdown products) are present in the individual's blood or urine. The quantity of illicit drug consumed is usually irrelevant. A standard six-drug panel screens for benzodiazepines, cocaine, marijuana, methamphetamine, opiates, and phencyclidine (PCP). The laboratory techniques used in drug analysis include gas chromatography, mass spectrometry, and immunoassay.

Investigators can request screening for drugs outside those detected by the six-drug panel. Prescription and so-called designer drugs may be difficult to identify, and extensive testing may be required to establish their presence. When a prescription drug is found in the blood, the quantity of drug is also measured and compared with the therapeutic medicinal dose. So long as the chain of custody is maintained, cross-contamination and tampering are prevented, and good records are kept of the tests performed, blood and urine samples generally meet the requirements for statutory submission of physical evidence.

*Martiscia Davidson*

## Further Reading

Best, Arthur. *Evidence: Examples and Explanations.* 8th ed. New York: Aspen, 2012. Provides useful examples that illustrate the rules of evidence. Intended primarily for law students.

Bocchino, Anthony. *A Practical Guide to Federal Evidence: Objections, Responses, Rules, and Practice Commentary.* 11th ed. Boulder, CO : National Institute for Trial Advocacy, 2015. Updated rules and interpretations for handling evidence.

Federal Rules of Evidence 2015. Grand Rapids, MI: Michigan Legal Publishing, 2015.

Saferstein, Richard. *Criminalistics: An Introduction to Forensic Science.* 11th ed. Upper Saddle River, NJ: Pearson/Prentice Hall, 2014. A basic introduction to evidence collection and chain of evidence requirements.

Young, Tina J. and P. J. Ortmeier. *Crime Scene Investigation: The Forensic Technician's Field Manual.* Upper Saddle River, NJ:

Pearson/Prentice Hall, 2011. An introduction to collecting and preserving evidence in the field.

**See also:** Alcohol-related offenses; Breathalyzer; Chain of custody; Courts and forensic evidence; Crime laboratories; Cross contamination of evidence; *Daubert v. Merrell Dow Pharmaceuticals*; Drug confirmation tests; Drug paraphernalia; Forensic toxicology; Illicit substances; Sobriety

---

## Drug classification

**Definition:** System of categorizing types of drugs according to their properties, therapeutic effects, or other features.

**Significance:** Drugs can be classified in many different ways, but the system of drug classification to which forensic scientists refer most often is that created by the Controlled Substances Act of 1970. Law-enforcement agencies are often concerned with criminal activities related to drugs classified as controlled substances under this act.

Drugs may be divided into categories based on a number of different factors. Medical practitioners, for instance, most commonly use a system of drug classification based on therapeutic effects; for example, drugs that alleviate headaches are classified with other substances that have the same effect. Alternatively, drugs can be classified based on their pharmacodynamic effects—that is, the ways in which they interact with the human biological system. This way of classifying drugs is most commonly used by researchers who study drugs and their effects. Drugs can also be classified based on the risks they pose for abuse and dependence. Using such a system, many researchers who study addiction place alcohol and nicotine in the same category as other commonly abused substances, such as heroin and cocaine. The system of drug classification used most often in the forensic sciences is the system created by the Controlled Substances Act of 1970, which attempts to weigh the potential medical benefits of drugs against the risks the drugs pose for abuse, physical dependence, and psychological dependence.

### Five Drug Schedules

The Controlled Substances Act created five schedules, or classifications, of drugs. The U.S. Department of Justice and the U.S. Department of Health and Human Services, which includes the Food and Drug Administration, are responsible for deciding which drugs should be included on the rather exhaustive list of substances that are regulated by the federal government. The list of substances includes drugs, minerals, organic materials, and the precursors to pharmacodynamic substances.

Schedule I drugs are those deemed to have a high potential for abuse and dependence while at the same time having no currently accepted medical uses in the United States. Drugs in this schedule are not available to the general population, no prescriptions can be written for these drugs, and only limited research has been conducted to examine their effects. Examples of Schedule I drugs are cannabis, heroin, ecstasy, and peyote.

Schedule II drugs are also considered to have high potential for abuse and dependence, but these drugs are considered to have some legitimate medical use. These drugs are legally available to the general population by prescription only, and the distribution of these drugs is subject to considerable regulation. Among the drugs included in Schedule II are morphine, oxycodone, methadone, opium, and phencyclidine (PCP). Drugs that meet the criteria to be classified under Schedule III are thought to have lower risk for abuse than those regulated under Schedules I and II, have acceptable medical uses, and are considered to pose only moderate risk of dependence. These drugs are also available legally only by prescription, but the regulation of their distribution is less strenuous than that for Schedule II drugs. Drugs in Schedule III include anabolic steroids, hydrocodone, ketamine, and LSA (also known as d-lysergic acid amide or d-lysergamide), a precursor to and chemical relative of LSD (lysergic acid diethylamide).

The drugs included in Schedule IV are thought to have low risk for abuse, have medically acceptable uses in the United States, and have relatively low potential to create physical or psychological dependence. These drugs are available legally only by prescription and are regulated similarly to those in Schedule III. Schedule IV drugs include alprazolam (brand name Xanax), diazepam (Valium), dextropropoxyphene (Darvocet), and phenobarbital.

Drugs that are classified in Schedule V are thought to have a low risk for abuse, have medically accepted uses, and are considered to have limited risk for dependence. These drugs are legally distributed for medical purposes only by prescription. Some commonly used medications that are included in Schedule V are cough suppressants that have small amounts of codeine, antidiarrheal medications with small amounts of opium, and pregabalin (brand name Lyrica), a medication used to treat seizures and pain.

### Criticisms of the U.S. Drug Classification System

The drug classification system created by the Controlled Substances Act has been the source of ongoing controversy, in large part because of the process by which drugs are assigned to each of the different schedules. Many observers have asserted that the process is political rather than based in science. Medical practitioners and researchers have argued, for example, that some of the drugs listed in Schedule I have legitimate medical uses, such as cannabis for cancer patients, and that these drugs are included in Schedule I only because changing their classification would be politically unpopular. Many have advocated for the reclassification of some substances so that additional research can be done to assess the drugs' medical value empirically.

Critics of the five-schedule classification system have also suggested that substances such as alcohol and nicotine, which are addictive and have no medical use, should be included in the list of controlled substances. In addition, some have noted inconsistency in the classification of drugs, pointing out that many drugs with similar pharmacological properties are classified into different drug schedules. For example, heroin, morphine, opium, and methadone all have similar chemical properties but they are listed in different schedules.

Some scholars have argued that the classification of drugs within the five-schedule system has been motivated by fear and xenophobic beliefs rather than science. Researchers have drawn connections between the passage of legislation banning the availability of certain drugs and the migration patterns of historically disenfranchised groups in the United States as well as stereotypes regarding their drug use. One specific example is the banning of peyote, which has long been a part of some Native American religious ceremonies.

*Jennifer L. Christian*

### Further Reading

Earleywine, Mitch, ed. *Mind-Altering Drugs: The Science of Subjective Experience.* New York: Oxford University Press, 2005. Collection of essays by leading researchers focuses on the subjective experiences of drug users and how these are related to drug abuse.

Gahlinger, Paul M. *Illegal Drugs: A Complete Guide to Their History, Chemistry, Use, and Abuse.* New York: Plume, 2004. Wide-ranging work includes discussion of drug classifications.

Perrine, Daniel M. *The Chemistry of Mind-Altering Drugs: History, Pharmacology, and Cultural Context.* Washington, D.C.: American Chemical Society, 1996. Provides information on the pharmacological effects of psychoactive substances and highlights the cultural contexts in which illicit drugs are used.

Smith, Frederick P., ed. *Handbook of Forensic Drug Analysis.* Burlington, Mass.: Elsevier Academic Press, 2005. Comprehensive text covers all aspects of forensic drug analysis.

**See also:** Amphetamines; Antipsychotics; Club drugs; Controlled Substances Act of 1970; Crack cocaine; Drug abuse and dependence; Drug Enforcement Administration, U.S.; Hallucinogens; Illicit substances; Narcotics; Opioids; Psychotropic drugs; Stimulants.

# Drug confirmation tests

**Dateline:** Drug confirmation testing began on a national level in the 1980s under the Reagan administration  with guidelines published by the Substance Abuse and Mental Health Services Administration (SAMHSA). An earlier instance of drug and alcohol confirmation testing was seen in the Mississippi Code of 1972. Drug confirmation tests are updated on a regular basis. The most up-to-date tests and guidelines are regularly published by the Mayo Clinic.

**Definition:** According to the Substance Abuse and Mental Health Services Administration, drug confirmation tests involve the application of a second analytical procedure to verify the presence of a specific drug or drug metabolite identified in an initial drug test. According to SAMHSA guidelines, this test conducted on the initial sample must be completely independent of the initial test, and use a completely different technique. According to guidelines, all confirmation tests must be of equal or greater sensitivity than the original test was. The guidelines currently in use are regularly updated by the Mayo Clinic medical laboratories.

**Significance:** With the advent of mandatory drug testing for purposes of employment, participation in sports or other activities, it became apparent that there were many false positives. These false positives indicated that drugs were found in the bodily substances (blood, urine, sweat, saliva, or hair) of individuals who were actually drug free. Drug confirmation tests are done in order to verify or disallow the findings of the original drug test. This is done in order to try to ensure that an individual is not wrongfully dismissed from a job or denied participation in an event.

When drug testing is done, it can be done on a wide variety of different bodily substances (as indicated above), using a variety of different tests. The initial test is known as a drug-screening test, while follow-up tests to verify or disprove the original finding are known as drug confirmation tests

## Federal Guidelines

The Substance Abuse and Mental Health Services Administration established the most recent guidelines on drug testing in September of 1994. For all initial screening and confirmation tests, a chain of custody must be established and followed in obtaining the specimen. Handling and transportation of all specimens is only through authorized individuals in accordance with the chain of custody. Care must be taken to ensure that there is no dilution of the sample (by the addition of water or any other substance).

If the result of an initial screening test is negative, no further testing needs to be done. If any specimen yields positive results on an initial screen, a confirmatory retest of that specimen will be done. According to the federal guidelines, these confirmation tests should always be done using gas chromatography or mass spectrometry. Standard cut-off values (confirmatory test levels) exist on these tests for marijuana, opiates, cocaine, morphine, codeine, phencyclidine (PCP), amphetamines, and methamphetamines. Any sample that has a test level above the standard cutoff is reported as positive. If a drug confirmation test result is negative, in spite of a positive initial screening, then no further testing is done, and the test is reported as negative. If the drug confirmation test is positive for a specific substance, then that is considered a confirmed positive result for that specific drug, and again no further testing is done.

## Substances Commonly Used in Drug Testing

Various bodily substances can be analyzed for the presence of drugs or their breakdown products (metabolites). While blood analysis does yield valid and reliable results, it is rarely done because of the invasive nature of blood testing. Urine drug testing (urine toxicology screens) has probably been the most commonly used drug screening technique, whether for initial or confirmation screening. Using a urine sample to analyze for drugs or metabolites requires that one be sure of the source of the urine (no substitutions) as well as its purity. Saliva-based drug screens are becoming more widely used; they are easily done, can be done in the presence of a witness (thus confirming no substitution), can not be altered, and yield valid and reliable results similar to those obtained by drug testing. Drugs and their metabolites will be detected in saliva immediately after drug use and for up to three days following use. Sweat drug screens involve the use of patches that are applied to the skin (usually on the chest) for ten to fourteen days. Sweat tests are rarely done because of issues with security and problems in detecting certain drugs. Hair testing has been commonly used to detect drug use, since it is reasonably accurate and reflects drug use for a period of at least three months prior to testing. Recently there have been some questions about false positives on hair tests because of different hair structure in different ethnic groups. No matter what the source of the test, confirmation tests are run any time there is a positive result.

## Effectiveness of Testing Methods

All drug testing is done in a laboratory setting. All samples brought into the laboratory are subjected to initial testing, known as the screening test. These initial tests are normally done by immunoassay, and are less sensitive and less expensive than later tests. As a result, they are more likely to produce more false positive results. Any sample that tests positive initially is then subjected to confirmation testing. As indicated above, confirmation tests are typically done using mass spectrometry or gas chromatography.

These confirmation tests are much more accurate than immunoassays, so that prior false positives typically appear negative on these confirmation tests. Laboratory error, antibiotic use, the use of nonprescription drugs like ibuprofen and nasal decongestants, or eating of poppy seeds are some of the causes of false positives.

Even when false positive initial results are shown to be incorrect using more precise confirmation tests, an individual's record may still remain tarnished by the initial findings. More

credence needs to be placed on results of drug confirmation tests.

*Robin Kamienny Montvilo*

## Further Reading

Jenkins, A, J. & B.A. Goldberger..*On-site Drug Testing.* Totowa, NJ: Humana Press, 2002. Point of-care or on-site drug testing moved drug testing out of the hospitals and into the workplace or sports arenas. With the advent of testing in public situations, the types of testing done to confirm drug usage, the guidelines used, and the chain of custody used had to be clearly identified as they are in this book.

Mayo Clinic Medical Laboratories. *Drug Testing: An Overview of Mayo Clinic Tests Designed For Detecting Drug Abuse.* Rochester, M: Mayo Clinic, 2015. This volume presents an overview of currently used drugs of abuse. It details how testing is done to confirm the presence of these drugs, as well as the thresholds that are used to indicate the presence of each individual drug.

Mrozek, J. . *Drug Screen Manual: The Tests, the Technology, the Risks, the Reality.* Boulder, C: Paladin Press, 1998. This book was one of the early manuals in the field of drug abuse. It covers the early means of confirmation drug testing as well as the risks involved.

NCAA Drug-Testing Program. *Report All Medicines: Don't Play With Your Eligibility.* Indianapolis, IN: NCAA Publishing, 2014. ists all substances banned by the NCAA and outlines testing guidelines for these drugs. It also includes an in-depth description of the laboratory procedures and chain of custody required for confirmation testing.

**See also:** Amphetamines; Barbiturates; Presumptive tests for blood; Club drugs; Crack cocaine; Hallucinogens; Illicit drugs; Mandatory drug testing; Narcotics; Opiates; Performing-enhancing drugs; Stimulants.

## Drug Enforcement Administration, U.S.

**Date:** Established in July 1973 by an executive order.

**Identification:** Federal agency established to coordinate all U.S. laws and regulations regulating illicit drug use and trafficking in this country. This agency was established in response to a huge increase in illegal drug use in the U.S. during the early part of the twentieth century.

**Significance:** The Drug Enforcement Agency (DEA) was established by the Nixon administration for the purpose of providing a unified center for federal drug control. The problem of drug use in the United States was a recognized concern since at least 1915 when the Internal Revenue Service was charged with drug control. In the 58 years that followed, various federal agencies were involved in enforcing laws dealing with drug possession/use. Increased drug trafficking and drug use made it essential that federal drug control should be housed in one agency, thus leading to the development of the Drug Enforcement Agency. This agency is charged with preventing, deterring, and investigating the illegal growing, manufacture, or distribution of controlled substances in, or destined for, the United States.

When the DEA was established in 1973, it was formed from the merging of two organizations that were involved in drug control. The Bureau of Narcotics and Dangerous Drugs joined with the Office of Drug Abuse Law Enforcement to form the Drug Enforcement Agency. This new agency provided a centralized means of responding to the increased concerns of drug trafficking in this country.

As a subsidiary of the United States Department of Justice, this law enforcement agency was charged with ensuring that the Controlled Substances Act of 1970 was enforced. This act was designed to limit access to and control use of drugs of abuse within the United States and internationally.

### Mission of the DEA

The Drug Enforcement Agency is charged with enforcing the laws of the United States, which deal with the regulation of controlled substances in this country or any "competent jurisdiction." It is under their jurisdiction to prosecute any organization/individuals who are growing, manufacturing, or distributing any controlled substances intended for illegal use within the United States. The Drug Enforcement Agency is also involved in the organization of and support of programs designed to lessen the availability and illegal use of controlled substances within this country. Additionally the Drug Enforcement Agency works in conjunction with governments of foreign countries to reduce the import/availability of drugs of abuse by developing/supporting programs dealing with crop eradication and/or substitution. Along these lines, the Drug Enforcement Agency works in conjunction with the United Nations, Interpol, and any other international organizations that manage drug control programs to reduce illicit drug use throughout the world. The DEA is also responsible for seizing any assets that result from illegal drug use and putting them to appropriate use to help in the war against drugs.

### Organization of the DEA

The head of the Drug Enforcement Agency is known as the Administrator of Drug Enforcement. This individual is appointed to the post by the President of the United States, and confirmed by the Senate of the United States. The individual in this post reports directly to the Office of the Attorney General of the United States. The Administrator oversees a large number of executives and other employees, but only the Administrator and the Deputy Drug Enforcement Agency Administrator are direct appointments of the President of the United States. There are over thirty major offices that are under the auspices of the Drug Enforcement Agency. All individuals employed by the Drug Enforcement Agency are considered career employees of the United States government.

## Registration of Controlled Substances

The Drug Enforcement Agency has established a system which mandates the registration of medical professionals, researchers, and manufacturers with access to any Schedule I drug. Schedule I drugs are those that have not yet been approved for medical use, do have a large potential medical value, but also have a large potential for abuse. The Drug Enforcement Agency also mandates the registration of medical professionals to allow them to prescribe Schedule II drugs. Schedule II drugs are those that do have known medical use, but great potential for abuse and dependence. Medical professionals are issued DEA numbers that allow for tracking of controlled substances.

## Diversion Control System

It has been found that many legally prescribed drugs are often used for purposes other than that for which they were prescribed. This "diversion" of legitimate drugs for illegal purposes has been relatively widespread, and is now under the control of the Drug Enforcement Agency. All medical professionals who prescribe, dispense, or administer prescription drugs must be registered with the Drug Enforcement Agency, and must comply with regulatory requirements set forth by the DEA. This helps to prevent the diversion of drugs for illegal purposes.

## Effectiveness of the
### Drug Enforcement Agency

The programs of the Drug Enforcement Agency lack the means to carry out quality independent evaluations of the programs' impact on reducing drug availability. Thus, the effectiveness of the programs of the Drug Enforcement Agency is in question.

While the Drug Enforcement Agency managed to seize over 1.4 billion dollars in drug related assets and over 420 million dollars worth of drugs in 2005, this was negligible compared to the 64 billion dollars of illegal drugs sold in the United States in a given year. Based on this figure, from the White House Office of Drug Control Policy, it would appear that the Drug Enforcement Agency has been relatively ineffective in controlling drug trafficking. The de-mand for illegal drugs in this country continues, and the ability to obtain them also continues. Most studies actually indicate that the price of cocaine on the streets had dropped over recent years, making the drugs more accessible to the general public. Data in dicate that the Drug Enforcement Agency has focused its energy on programs that allow for the interception of heroin and cocaine across federal borders.

While this has proved to be an important function of the Drug Enforcement Agency, and one that is cost-effective, it does not touch upon the drugs that are most widespread in terms of use. It is felt by most in the field of drug control, that the Drug Enforcement Agency should focus more attention on the use and sale of marijuana, and on the use of prescription drugs used recreationally. While there is much work left for the Drug Enforcement Agency to accomplish, it is clear that the programs of the DEA are having an impact in this country. They have published a National Drug Threat Assessment Summary that presents an overview of the type of illegal drugs that are now widely used in the United States. They have also created a series of publications for parents and adolescents to make them aware of problems associated with illegal substance use and guidelines for avoiding such use. The DEA has developed new program goals and measures, along with a strategic plan to help determine how successful these programs are in reducing the availability of drugs in the U.S.

*Robin Kamienny Montvilo*

## Further Reading

Gray, M. . *Drug Crazy: How We Got into this Mess and How We Can Get Out of it.* New York: Routledge, 2000. A full description of the use of drugs in the U.S., and of means to control their use.

Lyman, M.D. . *Practical Drug Enforcement.* 3rd ed. Boca Raton, FL: CRC Press, 2006. This book describes the methods that are used by the DEA and other law enforcement agencies to control drug trafficking and drug use in the United States. It includes a comparison of different methods that are used in different jurisdictions.

Neubauer, D.W. . *America's Courts and the*

## DEA's Forensic Laboratories

*The U.S. Drug Enforcement Administration provides this description of the work of the DEA's laboratories:*

Scientific support to DEA Special Agents and other law enforcement personnel is one of the critical functions provided by DEA forensic chemists. This encompasses a wide variety of duties and forensic disciplines, including: Analyses of controlled substances and related substances and processing chemicals; crime scene investigation; latent fingerprint identification and photographic development; analysis and evaluation of digital (computer) evidence; development, monitoring, and processing of hazardous waste cleanups and disposals; and expert witness testimony.

In addition, DEA laboratories derive strategic intelligence through in-depth analysis of seized drugs. This includes: The identification of occluded (trapped) solvents in cocaine, heroin, methamphetamine, and methylenedioxymethamphetamine (Ecstasy); the examination of logos and tablet characteristics of Ecstasy and related "Club Drug" tablets; and the determination of the geographical and/or synthetic origins of cocaine, heroin, and methamphetamine. These "Signature Programs" help DEA monitor the trafficking patterns of drugs entering the United States. The analysis of Domestic Monitor Program samples provides price/purity information for heroin sold at the retail level.

Since their inception, DEA laboratories have applied the latest technologies to support criminal investigations. Beginning in the 1970's, DEA laboratories were at the forefront of forensic science by applying gas chromatography/mass spectroscopy (GC/MS), nuclear magnetic resonance (NMR) spectroscopy, and high performance liquid chromatography (HPLC) to forensic drug analysis. The novel use of state-of-the-art instruments continued into the 1990's as DEA's laboratories kept pace with developments in scientific instrumentation and computer technologies. Today, DEA laboratories are working with innovative technologies that will enable the laboratory system to remain at the forefront of forensic drug science.

*Criminal Justice System*. Berkely, CA: Wadsworth, 2004. This text deals with the American system of criminal justice including a review of how drug traffickers are dealt with.

Robbins, David. *Heavy Traffic: Thirty Years of Headlines and Major Ops from the Case Files of the DEA*. New York: Chamberlain Bros., 2005. Uses news stories and DEA case files to describe the agency's work on some particularly important cases.

Sells, D.H. Jr & D.H. Sells. *Security in the Health Care Environment*. Sudbury, MA.: Jones and Bartlett Publishers, 2000. This book describes mechanisms that should be used to provide a safe and effective health care environment utilizing best practices within the setting while following laws set forth by and enforced by the federal government.

U. S. Drug Enforcement Agency. *A History of the Drug Enforcement Agency from 1978 to 2003*. Washington, D.C.: Government Publications, 2003. This short book published on the thirtieth anniversary of the DEA reviews the role of the agency in drug control in the U.S.

U. S. Drug Enforcement Agency. *Growing Up Drug-free: A Parent's Guide to Prevention*. Washington, D.C.: U.S. Justice Department, 2012. This 55 page booklet for parents teaches them about the types of illegal drugs typically used by adolescents and what they can do to prevent their children from using these drugs.

U. S. Drug Enforcement Agency (2013). 2013 *National drug threat assessment summary*. Washington, D.C.: U.S. Justice Department. This publication presents an overview of the types of drugs that are currently a threat to public welfare in the U.S. These drugs range from prescription drugs being used inappropriately through cocaine, heroine, marijuana, and the newer designer drugs.

**See also:** Anabolic Steroid Control Act of 2004;
Bureau of Alcohol, Tobacco, Firearms and Explosives; Canine substance detection; Chain of
custody; Drug classification; Drug paraphernalia; Federal Bureau of Investigation; Federal
Rules of Evidence; Harrison Narcotic Drug Act
of 1914; Mandatory drug testing; Narcotics.

## Drug paraphernalia

**Definition:** Products that have been created,
modified, or adapted from their intended
uses for the purposes of making, using, or
concealing illegal drugs.

**Significance:** Law-enforcement agencies devote significant resources to the investigation of crimes related to drug abuse and
drug trafficking. Forensic scientists are often involved in examining items collected
from crime scenes to determine whether
they have come into contact with illicit
drugs and, if so, the exact nature of those
drugs.

In the United States, the classification of particular items as drug paraphernalia may depend
on the answers to three questions: Does national or local advertising address how the
items are employed in the production, concealment, transportation, or use of illegal drugs?
Are the items sold in a manner that implies that
they are to be used in relation to illegal drugs?
Can expert testimony establish that the items
are employed in the production, concealment,
transportation, or use of illegal drugs?

Whereas some items are specifically designed for the production, concealment, transportation, or use of illegal drugs, many items
that can be classified as drug paraphernalia
have other legitimate uses as well. For instance,
aluminum foil is used to package drugs and to
fashion temporary pipes for smoking marijuana
or crack cocaine. Eyedrops are used to clear the
redness from bloodshot eyes (a common side effect of drug use). Eyedroppers may be used to
deliver LSD or to insert injection drugs into syringes. Small mirrors, razor blades, and credit

cards are often used to cut up powder cocaine,
and rolled-up dollar bills may be used to snort
the drug. Sensitive electronic and mail scales
are used to weigh drugs for sale. Ropes, belts,
and pieces of rubber tubing are used as tourniquets to help veins pop so that drugs may be administered intravenously.

Some items of drug paraphernalia are sold
under disclaimers that purport that they are to
be used for smoking tobacco. Pipes, water or ice
bongs, hookahs, and rolling papers are sold in
various tobacco product shops (so-called head
shops) with the unwritten implication that they
are to be used to smoke marijuana.

### Marijuana Paraphernalia

The most widely produced and used illegal
drug in the United States is cannabis, more
commonly known as marijuana. Marijuana typically consists of green or brown dried flowers
and leaves, but the color and texture may vary
greatly depending on the strain, batch, and
freshness of the product. Marijuana produces
psychoactive and disorienting physiological effects such as decreased motor coordination, dizziness, sleepiness, and increased appetite.

Marijuana is usually smoked, whether in the
form of a cigarette (known as a joint) or a hollowed-out cigar (blunt) or in some kind of pipe,
such as a water or ice bong. It is also sometimes
ingested in foods, such as brownies. Cannabis
resin is also collected, dried, and compressed into
black balls or sheets to produce hashish. Users
of hashish break off pieces of these balls and
place them in pipes or bongs to smoke the drug.

The following are examples of items of paraphernalia associated with cannabis:

- Plastic sandwich bags and similar small
  containers (used to store and transport
  the drug)
- Sensitive electronic and mail scales (used to
  weigh the drug to set prices for sale)
- Tobacco rolling papers (used to roll
  marijuana cigarettes)
- Razor blades (used to slit cigars and remove
  the tobacco so that it may be replaced
  with marijuana)
- Incense and air deodorizers (used to
  disguise the odor of marijuana smoke)

- Fabric softener sheets (used in making "blow tubes" from empty toilet paper rolls to absorb the odor of exhaled marijuana smoke)
- Pipes and bongs (used for smoking the drug)
- Roach clips (items used to hold the ends of marijuana cigarettes so that they may be smoked in their entirety, such as alligator clips, tweezers, and medical hemostats)

## Cocaine and Crack Cocaine Paraphernalia

Cocaine is a highly addictive white powder processed from the coca plant. It stimulates the central nervous system and acts as an appetite suppressant. When taken in small amounts, cocaine typically makes the user feel euphoric, energetic, talkative, and mentally alert. Powder cocaine is usually consumed through inhalation through the nose, or snorting.

Crack cocaine is made from processing cocaine with baking soda and water. The addition of baking soda forms the drug into a solid that may be vaporized and inhaled. (The name "crack" is derived from the crackling sound made when the drug is vaporized.) Inhalation of crack cocaine vapors provides users with a more intense, but short-lived, high than would be achieved from snorting it. On average, crack is made up of about 40 percent cocaine. The amount of cocaine in a batch of crack, as well as the other substances present, depends on the manufacturer. On the street, crack is sold as little white to tan pellets or "rocks." A user places a rock in a pipe fitted with a fine mesh screen, heats the rock with a flame, which causes it to vaporize, and then inhales the fumes.

The following are examples of items of paraphernalia associated with cocaine and crack:

- Small mirrors or glassy surfaces, razor blades or credit cards, and rolled-up dollar bills or short plastic straws (used to cut up and snort cocaine)
- Glossy, nonporous magazine paper folds or aluminum foil that will not absorb powder (used to conceal the drug)
- Strainers (used to break up cocaine and to mix up crack)

- Small spoons (used to snort cocaine)
- Pipes with fine mesh screens (used to smoke crack)
- Cigarette lighters (used to vaporize crack so that it may be inhaled)

## Inhalant Paraphernalia

Most inhalant abuse involves everyday household products. Among the products commonly used by inhalant abusers are ink correction fluids, marking pens, nail polish removers, butane, gasoline, glues and adhesives, paint and paint thinners, and aerosol sprays of many kinds, including cooking sprays, hair sprays, disinfectants, furniture polishes, oven cleaners, and deodorants. Some users spray the contents of aerosol sprays into plastic bags and then inhale the vapors produced. With substances such as propane and butane, users generally inhale the gases directly or from saturated rags. The effects of solvent intoxication vary widely, depending on the amounts and types of solvents or gases inhaled.

## Paraphernalia Intended to Fool Drug Tests

A variety of products are marketed in head shops and on the Internet that claim to help drug users pass drug tests. Various drinks, pills, powders, and teas are advertised as being able to speed up the body's ability to metabolize and thus wash out or disguise the presence of drugs. Some Web sites sell "clean" urine and urine powder or agents that a person can supposedly add to his or her own urine to produce a clean sample. Certain shampoos are advertised as being able to negate evidence of drug use in hair follicle testing. Whether any of these products works or not depends on the type of drug tested for, the level of drugs in the body, the amount of time since last use, the type of test being performed, and the method used to fool the test.

*Daniel Pontzer*

## Further Reading

Abadinsky, Howard. *Drug Use and Abuse: A Comprehensive Introduction.* 6th ed. Belmont, Calif.: Thomson/Wadsworth, 2008. Provides an interdisciplinary survey of the impacts of drugs on American society, including the pharmacological effects of drugs on the body, implications of U.S. drug policy, and the criminal justice system's response to the drug problem.

Hicks, John. *Drug Addiction: "No Way I'm an Addict."* Brookfield, Conn.: Millbrook Press, 1997. Discusses drug-abuse treatment strategies, with particular focus on amphetamine addiction.

Karch, Steven B., ed. *Drug Abuse Handbook.* 2d ed. Boca Raton, Fla.: CRC Press, 2007. Compendium of authoritative information on various aspects of drug abuse includes contributions by medical, legal, and treatment professionals.

LeVert, Suzanne. *Drugs: Facts About Cocaine.* Tarrytown, N.J.: Marshall Cavendish, 2006. Discusses cocaine use and abuse in detail. Features personal stories of addiction and treatment.

Menhard, Francha Roffé. *Drugs: Facts About Amphetamines.* Tarrytown, N.J.: Marshall Cavendish, 2006. Provides information on the characteristics, legal status, history, abuse, and treatment of addiction to amphetamines and methamphetamine.

Walker, Samuel. *Sense and Nonsense About Crime and Drugs: A Policy Guide.* 6th ed. Belmont, Calif.: Thomson/Wadsworth, 2006. Challenges many common misconceptions and myths about crime control and drug policies in the United States, with the aim of stimulating critical thinking.

**See also:** Amphetamines; Barbiturates; Club drugs; Crack cocaine; Crime scene screening tests; Drug abuse and dependence; Drug and alcohol evidence rules; Drug classification; Drug Enforcement Administration, U.S.; Inhalant abuse; Mandatory drug testing; Narcotics; Opioids; Psychotropic drugs.

*DSM-IV-TR. See Diagnostic and Statistical Manual of Mental Disorders*

Duty to warn. See *Tarasoff* rule